1992
Medical and Health Annual

Encyclopædia Britannica, Inc.

CHICAGO

AUCKLAND•GENEVA•LONDON•MADRID•MANILA•PARIS•ROME•SEOUL•SYDNEY•TOKYO•TORONTO

1992 Medical and Health Annual

Editor	Ellen Bernstein
Senior Editor	Linda Tomchuck
Contributing Editors	Charles Cegielski, Barbara Whitney
Editorial Adviser	Drummond Rennie, M.D. Professor of Medicine Institute for Health Policy Studies University of California, San Francisco; Deputy Editor (West), *The Journal of the American Medical Association*
Creative Director	Cynthia Peterson
Operations Manager	Marsha Mackenzie
Senior Picture Editor	Holly Harrington
Picture Editors	Harriett Hiland, Cathy Melloan
Art Production Supervisor	Richard A. Roiniotis
Illustrators/Layout Artists	Kay Diffley, John L. Draves, John J. Mahoney, Stephanie Motz
Art Staff	Patricia A. Henle, Margaret Liebezeit, Diana M. Pitstick
Manager, Copy Department	Anita Wolff
Copy Supervisor	Barbara Whitney
Copy Staff	Ellen Finkelstein, David Gottlieb, Lawrence D. Kowalski, John Mathews, Julian Ronning
Manager, Production Control	Mary C. Srodon
Production Control Staff	Marilyn L. Barton, Stephanie A. Green, Lee Anne Wiggins
Manager, Composition/Page Makeup	Melvin Stagner
Supervisor, Composition/Page Makeup	Michael Born, Jr.
Composition/Page Makeup Staff	Eram A. Ahmad, Griselda Cháidez, Duangnetra Debhavalya, Carol A. Gaines, Vertreasa Hunt, John Krom, Jr., Thomas J. Mulligan, Arnell Reed, Gwen E. Rosenberg, Yu-chu Wang, Danette Wetterer
Director, Management Information Systems	Michelle J. Brandhorst
Management Information Systems Staff	Steven Bosco, Ronald Pihlgren, Philip Rehmer, Vincent Star
Manager, Index Department	Carmen-Maria Hetrea
Index Supervisor	Mary L. Reynolds
Index Staff	Bernard J. Jablonski, Steven M. Monti
Librarian	Terry Miller
Associate Librarian	Shantha Uddin
Curator/Geography	David W. Foster
Assistant Librarian	Robert M. Lewis
Yearbook Secretarial Staff	Dorothy Hagen, Kay Johnson

Editorial Administration

Robert McHenry, General Editor
Robert F. Rauch, Director of Yearbooks
Karen M. Barch, Vice President, Editorial Development
Elizabeth P. O'Connor, Director, Editorial Financial Planning

Encyclopædia Britannica, Inc.
Robert P. Gwinn, Chairman of the Board
Peter B. Norton, President

Foreword

The first two feature articles in this volume chronicle a remarkable public health undertaking: the eradication of a terrible disease from the face of the Earth. The disease is dracunculiasis (or guinea worm disease), which until recently afflicted some 10 million people annually, mainly in Africa and Asia.

Readers may be surprised to find that the author of the first of these articles is Jimmy Carter. Why is a former U.S. president writing about the eradication of a disease—moreover, one that most of the *Annual's* readers probably have never heard of? Not long ago, like most Westerners, President Carter knew nothing about guinea worm disease; then, on a trip to Africa in 1988, he and Rosalynn Carter witnessed the devastating effects of the parasite on villagers in Ghana. They were shocked by what they saw: children and adults with worms coming out of their ankles, knees, legs, arms, and other parts of their bodies. One woman, the Carters vividly recall, had an abscess the size of a fist on her breast, where a guinea worm was about to emerge.

Since leaving the White House in 1981, Carter has been actively working to reduce the toll of human suffering throughout the world. The Carter Center in Atlanta, Georgia, is home to Global 2000 Inc., a project that grew out of the former president's desire to help people in the less developed world break the cycle of poverty and misery created by hunger and disease. Carter became impassioned about eradicating guinea worm when he learned that an infection that causes such unspeakable suffering as he saw in Ghana is eminently preventable. If people do not drink water that contains the guinea worm larvae, they will not become infected. Of course, there are dozens of diseases afflicting people in less developed countries, but Carter saw that something tangible and immediate could be done about this one. Beginning on page 6 is the former president's eloquent account of why he has personally committed himself to seeing dracunculiasis banished from the globe in this decade.

Following Carter's article, public health specialists Donald and Ernestine Hopkins report on the guinea worm eradication campaign initiated by Global 2000 and now well under way in Pakistan, India, and 14 endemic countries in Africa. Donald Hopkins, who has had extensive experience in conquering epidemic diseases in the less developed world, is leading that effort. If the goal is met—and there is every indication that it will be—dracunculiasis will become only the second major infectious disease to be officially conquered on a global scale.

The first disease to be successfully eradicated was smallpox, in 1977. That achievement was hailed as "a public health miracle." It also set the stage for the conquest of other diseases; the international mobilization of resources, the cooperation among countries, and the subjugation of national interests to a common goal offered hope that equally ambitious enterprises would be possible in the future. Donald Hopkins, who was active in the smallpox campaign and is the author of the book *Princes and Peasants: Smallpox in History,* saw that just as smallpox affected the very fabric of societies, so too does dracunculiasis, and it was he who first suggested that guinea worm disease was, in fact, eradicable.

Although rarely fatal, guinea worm disease leaves its victims so incapacitated that they cannot live productive lives; thus, it takes a toll not just on individuals but on communities and on entire nations attempting to emerge from underdevelopment. Now, with the introduction of very basic preventive measures, that situation is changing as, village by village, endemic countries rid themselves of the affliction that has oppressed them for so long.

When the Hopkinses submitted their article in February 1991, they wrote, "So much is happening so fast that we shall continue to send you updates." During the ensuing months they wrote and called frequently to report progress: heads of state in endemic African countries joining the battle against guinea worm; major new donations from business, governments, and charitable organizations; dramatic reductions in cases in specific African villages; and the declaration that Pakistan was on the verge of becoming guinea worm free. The excitement generated by these developments was duly conveyed to this editor and the *Annual's* staff, as it will be to readers. The Hopkinses' account of this medical milestone begins on page 10.

The enthusiasm for conquering a loathsome parasite was immediate when Carter and Hopkins approached E.I. du Pont de Nemours & Co. of Delaware to see if the petroleum products manufacturer could develop a filter that would rid drinking water of guinea worm larvae. Du Pont accepted the challenge, joined forces with the Precision Fabrics Group of North Carolina, and produced a specially woven, ultrafine reusable nylon filter with a sole purpose: preventing people on another continent from contracting guinea worm disease. The companies not only produced but also donated several million such filters for use in every African country where dracunculiasis is endemic. This example demonstrates the important role that wealthy nations can play in alleviating the suffering of people in parts of the world that are less well off. Said the president and chief executive officer of Precision Fabrics Group, "Don Hopkins and President Carter gave our people a sense of the difference between simply laying a brick to build a walk and building a cathedral. This is a unique opportunity for us to help people lead a better life."

On his desk, Hopkins has a 2½-foot-long guinea worm preserved in a jar of formaldehyde. About his "pet" parasite (named Henrietta) he says, "I'm looking forward to the day when she will be the last of her kind left in the world."

⋀ ⋀ ⋀

Of course, guinea worm eradication is just one of the topics covered in the lavishly illustrated "feature" articles in this volume. These articles span a very broad range and, we hope, reflect many of the challenges and achievements in medicine and health. The 1992 *Annual* also contains the 175-page "World of Medicine," a review of recent developments in selected medical specialties as well as 11 particularly newsworthy Special Reports. Finally, 14 practical and instructive articles constitute the "Health Information Update," with subjects ranging from how to take medicine wisely to the role of meat in the "prudent" diet to the advantages and disadvantages of being an only child to Graves' disease.

The editors and art staff have attempted to prepare an *Annual* that is timely, stimulating, and attractive and that will help readers keep pace with the rapidly evolving advances in medicine today. We hope we have succeeded.

Ellen Bernstein

—Editor

Contents

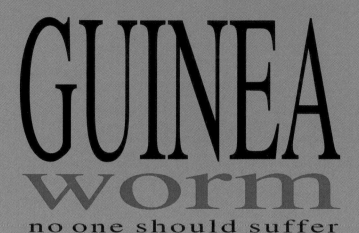

GUINEA
worm
no one should suffer

by Jimmy Carter

Once you've seen a small child with a two-foot-long live guinea worm protruding from her body, right through a large sore between her toes, you never forget it. I first saw the devastating effects of guinea worm disease in two villages near Accra, Ghana, in March 1988. In fact, Rosalynn and I saw more than 200 victims, including people with worms coming out of their ankles, knees, groins, legs, arms, breasts, and other parts of their bodies. When I revisited those villages in 1989, only four residents in one of the villages still had guinea worm. Health education, combined with the use of cloth filters, the chemical Abate, and the addition of three borehole wells, had nearly eliminated the disease.

Impact of an affliction

I first learned about guinea worm disease in 1986. I was shocked to find that this debilitating illness, which afflicts nearly five million people each year, could be easily prevented. In that same year the World Health Organization chose guinea worm as the next disease to be eradicated from the face of the Earth—by 1995. It is my hope that by then this horrible disease will be only a painful memory for the people of the villages in Ghana and others like them across Africa and in parts of Asia.

A reporter in Africa once asked me, "Why in the world are you involved in a program to eliminate guinea worm?" The answer is easy. There is no reason people should suffer from an affliction that is so easy to prevent. The disease not only is physically debilitating but has great economic consequences as well. As a farmer, I understand the impact of having a third or more of the people in a community unable to work during planting

Jimmy Carter, the 39th president of the United States, is the founder of the Atlanta, Georgia-based Carter Center, a nonprofit organization that works to resolve conflict, promote democracy, preserve human rights, improve health, and fight hunger around the world.

Denchira, near Accra, Ghana, is one of two villages that Jimmy and Rosalynn Carter visited in March 1988 (previous page). At that time the Carters saw more than 200 cases of guinea worm disease in a total population of about 500. When they visited again a year and a half later (above), guinea worm had all but been eliminated (there were fewer than half a dozen cases). The former president sampled the safe drinking water that Denchira residents now have—thanks to the installation of borehole wells, the use of cloth filters and a larvicide, and intensive health education.
(Overleaf, above, and opposite page)
Photographs, The Carter Center

or harvesting times. And guinea worm strikes at the heart of a society in other ways, by preventing children from going to school and keeping mothers from caring for their children.

Working with governments and their leaders

During a visit to Pakistan in 1986, I persuaded Gen. Mohammad Zia-ul-Haq, who was then president, to let the Carter Center work with his public health leaders to eradicate guinea worm. General Zia did not know about guinea worm, but his prime minister came from a village that had suffered from the disease. We quickly launched an eradication program that came to serve as a model for programs in other countries. Since that time, the Carter Center, in Atlanta, Georgia, through its Global 2000 project, has mounted guinea worm eradication campaigns in three African countries and has assisted with efforts in many more. Owing in large part to the dedication of Donald Hopkins, who has been directing the Global 2000 guinea worm eradication efforts since 1987, these projects are working; we are proving that it is possible to stop this disease.

The only other Asian country that still has the disease is India, and an eradication program has been under way there since 1980. Now we are increasing our efforts in Africa.

As chairman of the Global 2000 project, I feel a personal obligation to help carry out the fight against this cruel disease. In the summer of 1990, I accepted an invitation to speak about the importance of eradicating guinea worm to heads of state and government at the annual meeting of the Organization of African Unity in Addis Ababa, Ethiopia. While there, I also met with the foreign ministers of seven endemic francophone West African countries, where the incidence of guinea worm is very high, to urge them to support their ministers of health in eradicating the disease. When meeting with heads of government and other high-level leaders in countries where guinea worm is still prevalent, I try to enlist their support in eradication efforts; once they see that this is a popular and relatively easy thing they can do for their people, they are usually quite willing to help.

Combined efforts

In 1988 Flight Lieutenant Jerry Rawlings, the head of government in Ghana, visited 21 villages in the northern region of his country to personally show people how to filter their water to prevent the disease. And when a plane carrying an unusual fabric landed in Ghana in September 1990, millions of Africans took another major step toward freeing themselves from guinea worm. The fabric, which was woven into 1.4 million reusable nylon filters, was the first shipment from E.I. du Pont de Nemours & Co. and Precision Fabrics Group. Together, these two companies have agreed to donate more than eight million filters through the Carter Center over the next five years.

Help has also come from many other sources. In early 1990 the American Cyanamid Co. donated more than $2 million worth of Abate larvicide, which destroys the guinea worm larvae in water supplies yet leaves water safe for drinking. Many international agencies are working hand in hand with the Carter Center and with each other to rid Africa of this disease. These combined efforts will be instrumental in ending the unnecessary suffering of millions of people.

Spreading the message

There is yet another vital link in the guinea worm eradication chain, and that is education. When villagers, often illiterate, are taught the causes and prevention of this disease, they learn the rudiments of more basic primary health care at the same time. Also, the nation's health specialists evolve better knowledge of their people's needs and are stimulated in their efforts by involvement in a successful project.

Because this is an obscure disease that afflicts people in poor rural areas, it has not received much attention in the national or international news media. I hope that in the future the media will pay more attention to the plight of those who are afflicted by this disease and to the exciting story of its eradication. The press is a very powerful weapon. My visits to endemic countries generate considerable local coverage and help inspire public support for eradication programs. Through our visits, Rosalynn and I hope to spread a message of hope and encouragement to the people of Africa and to those who suffer needlessly from hunger and disease all over the world.

A project for the world community

Because of the progress that has been made thus far, there is little doubt that, working together, we can rid the world of guinea worm by the end of 1995. But the world community must choose to do so, and the United States must do its part. We are a compassionate nation with a long history of helping others. Thomas Jefferson actively supported efforts to disseminate smallpox vaccine in the United States when he was president, and in 1965 Pres. Lyndon Baines Johnson committed our government, through the Agency for International Development and the Centers for Disease Control, to helping 20 countries of West and Central Africa eradicate smallpox. Pres. Franklin Delano Roosevelt contributed immeasurably to the battle against polio through personal example, his support for the National Foundation for Infantile Paralysis, and his establishment of the Georgia Warm Springs Foundation.

The world is full of difficult problems that we cannot yet solve. This is one we can solve, and we can do it quickly if we set our minds to it. Helping a village free itself of guinea worm has far-reaching consequences. Children can go back to school, and farmers can return to their fields. Most important, when people are healthy, they are more self-reliant and better able to improve their own lives. The eradication of guinea worm disease will be a gift whose full value is impossible to measure.

The Carters met a young guinea worm victim in July 1989 in the village of Idiori, in Ogun state, Nigeria. A guinea worm is emerging from the boy's right ankle. Children and adults suffer horribly as the worms emerge—a slow and excruciatingly painful process. Unfortunately, modern medicine has no treatment to offer those who are infected. It was seeing sufferers like this child that convinced the Carters of the importance of preventive measures. Through the Global 2000 project, the Carter Center has mounted guinea worm eradication programs in Nigeria, Ghana, and Uganda—efforts that have already yielded great benefits to the people.

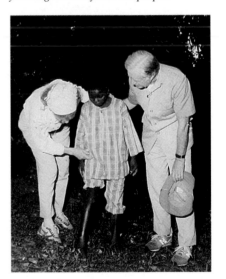

GUINEA WORM
THE END IN SIGHT

by Donald R. Hopkins, M.D., M.P.H., and
Ernestine M. Hopkins, M.A., M.P.H.

Along with smallpox and perhaps polio, guinea worm disease (dracunculiasis) is not expected to survive the 20th century. An eradication campaign that began in 1980 aims to end guinea worm's centuries-long affliction of humankind by 1995. The achievement will be an especially meaningful tribute to advances in international public health, as some scholars believe that the very symbol of medicine itself, the caduceus—the staff of Asclepius, entwined with a serpent—depicts the ancient practice of treating guinea worm disease by winding the parasite around a small stick as it emerges from the skin of its human victim.

Dracunculiasis is presently limited to fewer than five million victims in India, Pakistan, and 17 African countries; it was formerly much more widespread in Asia and Africa and in parts of the Americas. Over 100 million persons, however, are still at risk of contracting the disease in those remaining affected countries.

Ancient scourge

The earliest evidence of dracunculiasis is found in ancient Egypt, where an account of how to properly extract the worm is included in the Ebers Papyrus, one of the oldest known collections of medical texts, dating from about 1550 BC: "The process of winding the worm around a stick . . . is appropriately described by the same verb used for drawing out thread during a similar type of spinning." The Bible (Numbers 21:6) describes the "fiery serpents" that attacked Moses' followers in the 12th or 13th century BC, during their prolonged encampment on the shore of the Red Sea near modern-day Aqaba. Alfred J. Bollett, clinical professor of medicine at Yale University School of Medicine, has provided highly persuasive evidence that the biblical "fiery serpents" were indeed guinea worms. Physical confirmation that dracunculiasis existed in about 1000 BC in ancient Egypt came in the 1980s when a calcified guinea worm was found in the mummy of a 13-year-old girl. Significantly, both lower legs had been amputated from this New Kingdom girl shortly before her death, perhaps in an unsuccessful attempt to combat a gangrenous complication of her guinea worm infection. Guinea worm is apparently even mentioned in a myth about the Egyptian sun god, Ra, who was plagued by a worm that attacked his ankle.

Donald R. Hopkins, M.D., M.P.H., is Senior Consultant to Global 2000, the Carter Center, Atlanta, Georgia, and has directed its guinea worm eradication campaign since 1987.
Ernestine M. Hopkins, M.A., M.P.H., has assisted in public health projects in Africa, Asia, and Latin America. In June 1991 she received her Master of Public Health degree from the University of Illinois at Chicago School of Public Health.

(Overleaf) Photograph, Daniel Heuclin

Medical historians have speculated that the "fiery serpents" that afflicted Moses' followers in the 12th or 13th century BC may well have been guinea worms. Dracunculiasis, or guinea worm disease, was once endemic in the Middle East, particularly along the shore of the Red Sea—the site of Moses' prolonged encampment. Whether historically accurate or not, "fiery serpent" is indeed an appropriate description of the guinea worm. The female parasite grows within its victim's body to a length of up to 90 centimeters (3 feet), then migrates, usually to a lower limb, where it secretes a toxin that causes a painful, burning blister. The worm then begins to emerge at a rate of a few centimeters a day—a slow, excruciating process that can take several weeks or more.

Several Greco-Roman writers, including Plutarch (AD 50–117) and Galen (AD 129–c. 199), mention the disease. Leonides, a Byzantine surgeon, is said to have referred to its occurrence in India and Ethiopia in the 2nd century AD. Galen, who admittedly saw no cases himself in his practice in Rome, first named the condition "dracontiasis," although he thought it was due to a protruding nerve. It was also during this period, when enlightened people realized the importance of not breaking the worm while extracting it, that the familiar extraction process may have served as a model for the symbolic healing staff of Asclepius, the son of Apollo and father of Hygieia, the goddess of health. Although the animal coiled about Asclepius' staff is often taken to be a snake, there appears to be no reason to wrap a snake around a stick—certainly no reason related to a treatment, as is the case with guinea worm. The confusion may be perpetuated by the modern scientific name of the genus of the worm, *Dracunculus,* which means "little snake." (Ironically, among the many species of *Dracunculus* are a few that infect snakes.)

Arabic-speaking medieval physicians were also very familiar with the infection. Rhazes (*c.* 865–923/32), the Persian-born physician in chief of the hospital at Baghdad, concluded that the swellings on the bodies of affected persons were due to a parasite. Avicenna (980–1037), who was a native of Bukhara, left the first detailed clinical description of the disease, which he called "Medina sickness" (*Vena Medina*) because it was so common in the holy Islamic city of Medina. In his influential *Canon of Medicine,* Avicenna also noted that the disease was found in Egypt. Furthermore, he wrote, "Should the worm be ruptured, much pain and trouble ensue, and even if rupture does not take place, the condition is tiresome enough."

European physicians and explorers began to take note of the infection in the 16th century, when the French surgeon Ambroise Paré thought, like Galen, that the worm was a damaged nerve. Amato (João Rodriguez de

Castell Branco; 1511–68), a Portuguese physician, saw persons suffering from guinea worm infection at Salonika (now Thessaloniki, Greece) and reported that it was also known in India and Egypt. A Dutch navigator, Jan Linschoten, confirmed the disease's occurrence at Ormusz, on the Persian Gulf in present-day Iran, in 1584.

Supposedly, it was a European from Basel, Switzerland, who first called the disease "guinea worm," in 1611, after he saw it among Africans along the West African Guinea coast (modern Nigeria). It was reported from the area of the Elmina fortress on the coast of modern Ghana again in 1623 and 1625, and the Scottish explorer Mungo Park mentions it in his account of his travels in the inland area of modern Mali (1795–97).

Perhaps the most telling testimony to the disease's long existence in West Africa, however, is the fact that it is mentioned in the Dahomeyan legend explaining the kingdom's origin. A Dahomeyan prince named Homenuvo, son of king Tegbesu, could not flee when his village was attacked because he was crippled by guinea worm. He was captured by spirits. Through this captured prince, whom they cured of guinea worm and released, the spirits taught the Dahomeyans about the gods of the Sky, Earth, and Thunder and instructed them how to perform the ceremonies in worship of their ancestors and how to bury the dead.

Another Scottish explorer, James Bruce, contracted guinea worm himself during his travels in search of the source of the Nile (1768–73). A century later an expedition of Englishmen suffered from the same disease in the course of their invasion of Ethiopia. The Egyptian conquest of the Sudanese kingdom of Sennar (1820–21) is said to have led to a resurgence of dracunculiasis in Egypt, especially among Nubians enlisted subsequently into the Egyptian Army. It was also reported in Ceylon in 1805 and again in the years 1845–50.

Modern understanding of the infection, apart from the ancient admonition against breaking the worm while removing it, began with G.H. Velschius of Vienna, who published a thorough account of dracunculiasis, *Exercitatio de Vena Medinensis,* in 1674. Velschius' treatise included illustrations of Persian physicians removing the worm by wrapping it around any of several specially designed instruments. Around this time there is said to have been a consensus finally that the infection was caused by a parasite—*i.e.*, a worm—and not by a protruding nerve or vein. The famous Swedish botanist Carolus Linnaeus gave the worm its modern scientific name, *Dracunculus medinensis,* in 1758. In the 19th century the scientific designations *Filaria medinensis* and *Gordius medinensis* came into use. Colloquially, the parasite has also been called "Medina worm" or "dragon worm."

Ten years after Linnaeus first called the worm *Dracunculus medinensis,* the British naval surgeon James Lind, after traveling in Africa, published his suspicion that the disease was transmitted by drinking water. During his travels in the years 1795–97, Park had found that inland peoples of the savannah near the Niger River "allege that the people who drink from wells are more subject to it than those who drink from streams." Indeed, as early as 1650, when Msgr. de la Motte Lambert, the bishop of Beirut, came upon many infected persons in the Persian town of Lar, he reported

In 1674 G.H. Velschius of Vienna published a comprehensive treatise on the parasitic disease dracunculiasis. His text included the illustration below, which shows Persian physicians (in the foreground and background) wrapping a guinea worm around a small, slender instrument as it slowly emerges from its victim. This ancient practice of carefully winding the worm about a stick had been recognized for centuries as the proper method of extraction. If the emerging worm is broken—a dreaded circumstance—the remaining part of the worm retracts into the skin wound, where larvae and toxins are spilled into the victim's tissues, causing inflammation, pain, and often serious secondary infection.

13

the local wisdom that "the way to avoid this worm is to drink only wine, or if water is used, only such as has been carefully filtered through linen."

These rudiments of understanding about transmission of guinea worm disease were sporadic, however, and not generally accepted. Many observers mistakenly believed that the worm invaded people through the skin of their lower limbs, where the adult worms were usually seen when emerging. Scientific proof that the spectacular worm arose from drinking water contaminated by a type of water flea came only in 1871, when a young Russian scientist, Aleksey Fedchenko, published the results of his studies conducted two years earlier in Turkestan. He thus provided the first demonstration of an invertebrate host of a medically important disease of humans. His countrymen later used this knowledge to eliminate dracunculiasis from the southern reaches of the Soviet Union in the 1920s and '30s.

A dreadful disease

In January 1988 Peter Schantz, an epidemiologist from the Centers for Disease Control (CDC) in Atlanta, Georgia, visited the village of Budo Ayan Moro in Kwara state, Nigeria. His report following that visit described several of guinea worm's young victims.

We met Wahab Mahmoud, who is a twelve year old boy who had 21 worms emerging this year. The only way he could get around was by cane. He was a very bright boy and had been nominated as the "head boy" at [his] school, which means he is a special assistant to the teacher; this is a reflection of his academic achievement and good discipline. He has been unable to attend school, however, since the worms first started emerging in December.

We saw a pregnant fifteen year old girl with a worm emerging from her breast. In fact, three worms emerged from her breast. She had been treated by a local practitioner by a local custom of inserting a hot iron into the lesion caused by the emerging worm.

Unsafe drinking water is a major cause of sickness in the less developed world. Of the many waterborne diseases, none is as painful—or as preventable—as guinea worm disease. (Above) A West African woman draws water from a pond that harbors the Cyclops, *a tiny water flea that contains embryonic guinea worm parasites.*

Guinea worm infection starts when people drink the water from such infested stagnant water. In India (right) step wells that provide drinking water for entire communities are the most common sites of transmission of guinea worm. When people with emerging worms step into the water— often the only way to quell the pain of a burning blister—larvae from their wounds are released into the water. The pernicious cycle is perpetuated as others then consume the contaminated well water.

Life cycle of the guinea worm

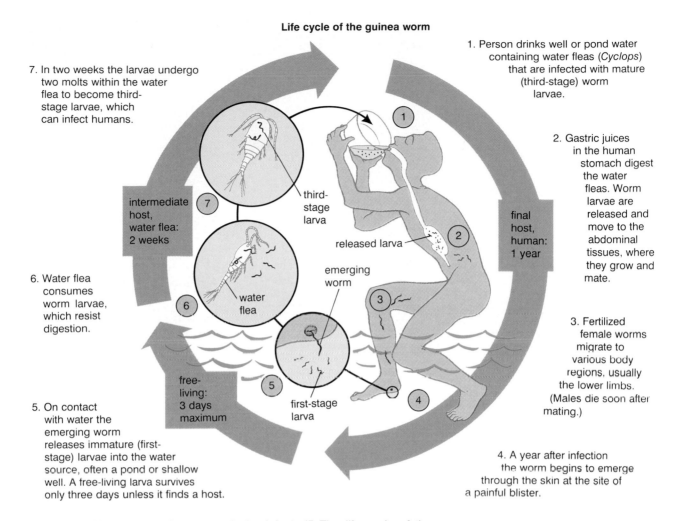

7. In two weeks the larvae undergo two molts within the water flea to become third-stage larvae, which can infect humans.

intermediate host, water flea: 2 weeks

6. Water flea consumes worm larvae, which resist digestion.

5. On contact with water the emerging worm releases immature (first-stage) larvae into the water source, often a pond or shallow well. A free-living larva survives only three days unless it finds a host.

third-stage larva

released larva

emerging worm

water flea

free-living: 3 days maximum

first-stage larva

1. Person drinks well or pond water containing water fleas (*Cyclops*) that are infected with mature (third-stage) worm larvae.

2. Gastric juices in the human stomach digest the water fleas. Worm larvae are released and move to the abdominal tissues, where they grow and mate.

final host, human: 1 year

3. Fertilized female worms migrate to various body regions, usually the lower limbs. (Males die soon after mating.)

4. A year after infection the worm begins to emerge through the skin at the site of a painful blister.

How did these youngsters come to be infected? The life cycle of the guinea worm is relatively simple: people are infected when they drink from a stagnant water source (pond or step well) that harbors the *Cyclops,* a tiny crustacean, or water flea (copepod), containing the embryonic parasite. The copepods are killed by digestive juices in the person's stomach, thus releasing the larvae of the worm, which penetrate the stomach or intestine and migrate into the tissues of the abdomen. In a few months the worms mate; then the male worms die. The female migrates, usually to the victim's lower leg, where it emerges as a slender 60–90-centimeter (2–3-foot)-long adult worm about 12 months after the infected water fleas were swallowed. (The worms sometimes migrate to and emerge from other body parts, such as the breast, scalp, tongue, scrotum, or uterus.) When a person with an emerging worm enters a body of water, the female worm releases hundreds of thousands of larvae into the water, where they may be eaten by copepods to begin the cycle again.

The water fleas may be barely seen as tiny moving flecks if a glass of water containing them is held up to the light. The immature larval form of the parasite itself is invisible to the naked eye. People who are infected experience no symptoms until the adult female worm is ready to emerge.

15

Typically, those who are infected by guinea worm are incapacitated for a month or more. The more unlucky victims develop secondary infections that can lead to abscesses, arthritis, and other complications and in some cases may cause permanent disability. In the village of Kati, Togo, a mother, who is very sick from guinea worm infection (right), suffers from extreme lethargy and is unable to care for her playful child. The man below is not only in great pain from his infection but severely crippled as well. Dracunculiasis rarely causes death, but the toll on communities can be staggering; adults cannot work, and children cannot go to school.

The worm secretes a toxin that causes a painful, burning blister to appear on the skin (hence, "fiery serpent"). When the victim attempts to quell the "fire" by immersing the affected body part in cool water, a common practice of villagers in areas where the infection is endemic, the blister ruptures, relieving the pain and releasing the larvae, after which the long worm slowly begins to emerge. An ulcer often forms around the emerging worm at the base of the blister. The thin, cream-colored worm usually takes weeks to emerge completely; only a few centimeters are freed from the tissues each day as the worm releases declining numbers of larvae each time it is immersed in water. All the female worms emerge from the body within a year; those that do not are either absorbed by the body or become calcified in body tissues—usually a benign situation.

The pain associated with the blister at the site of the worm's emergence is often only the beginning of the victim's troubles. Over half of the sites of the worms' emergence become infected secondarily with various bacteria, causing abscesses, sepsis, arthritis, and other common complications. If the emerging worm is broken, the remainder of the worm retracts into the wound, where larvae and other substances that are spilled into the tissues from the ruptured worm cause a severe inflammation—a dreaded phenomenon that has been recognized for centuries. Especially unlucky patients may contract tetanus from contaminated wounds, which can then become fatal. Most victims experience only one worm, but some may suffer up to a dozen or more worms emerging simultaneously.

Because of the associated pain, half or more of the victims may be temporarily incapacitated for periods averaging as much as one to three months. A small number of victims are permanently crippled by scarring from the secondary infections. No matter how often they are infected, people do not become immune, so many suffer year after year.

16

The social and economic havoc wrought by dracunculiasis is compounded by the high prevalence rates in some communities (up to 50% or more in some African villages); by the disease's seasonal occurrence, often coinciding with the harvest or planting, periods of high demand for agricultural labor; and by the fact that productive adults—especially laborers such as farmers, who need to drink large volumes of water—are affected more often than others. School absenteeism may exceed 60% during the "guinea worm season," either because children themselves are afflicted or because they must replace another stricken family member on the family's farm. In recent years, in a fertile rice-growing area in southeastern Nigeria, the rice farmers alone in a heavily affected population of 1.6 million persons were losing an estimated $20 million per year in potential profits because so many of them were affected by guinea worm during the harvest season. In this way, dracunculiasis effectively crushes the key building blocks of poor rural societies—health, education, and agriculture—as year after year the disease cripples communities attempting to emerge from their status of underdevelopment.

Modern medicine offers no cure or vaccine for dracunculiasis. Palliative drugs (such as aspirin for pain and antiseptic ointments and liquid dressings for inflamed blisters) can help relieve the pain and minimize secondary infections, but once persons are infected, they can scarcely do better than await the worm's emergence and begin winding it carefully around a small stick. If the adult worm is detected beneath the skin before it raises the blister to begin emerging, a physician or other medical practitioner can slip it out readily via a small surgical incision. Most worms remain deep in the tissues, however, and once the body's response is manifest in a blister, inflammation around the body of the worm creates resistance to pulling the worm out easily.

Fortunately, dracunculiasis can be completely prevented in three different ways: (1) by providing safe sources of water such as borehole wells, where the underground water cannot be contaminated by copepods or guinea worm larvae; (2) by teaching villagers to filter their drinking water through a fine cloth or to boil it (less common because most cannot afford the cost of sufficient fuel)—and not to contaminate the source of drinking water in the first place by entering it when they have emerging guinea worms; and (3) by treating contaminated pond water with a chemical, temephos (Abate), which kills *Cyclops* and infective larvae but leaves the water safe for human and animal consumption. These three interventions are similar to those employed over 60 years ago by the Soviets to eliminate dracunculiasis from southern areas of the U.S.S.R.

Early eradication efforts

In the early 20th century, dracunculiasis was prevalent in the Indian subcontinent, southern parts of the Soviet Union (Turkestan), Iran, coastal Saudi Arabia and Yemen, several North African and other Middle Eastern countries, and sub-Saharan Africa as far south as present-day Tanzania and Botswana. Some cases still occurred in northeastern Brazil, Guiana, and islands of the West Indies as a result of infections imported during the

A Pakistani man is treated for a secondary infection of guinea worm disease. Modern medicine offers no cure or vaccine for guinea worm, and people who are infected do not become immune.

The Carter Center

17

Actively combating guinea worm

1986

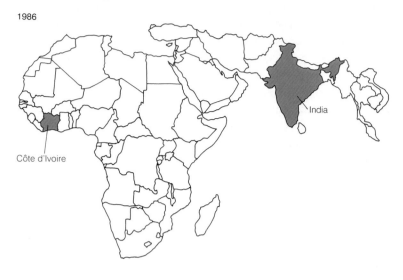

1991

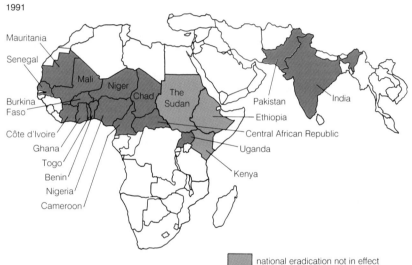

national eradication not in effect

Several characteristics of dracunculiasis make it an ideal target for eradication. India and Pakistan launched highly successful guinea worm eradication efforts in the early and mid-1980s, respectively; by the early 1990s both countries had nearly eliminated the disease. By 1991 all but three endemic countries in Africa (Ethiopia, The Sudan, and Kenya) were actively combating guinea worm and were formally committed to achieving eradication by 1995.

slave trade. In 1947 the parasitologist Norman R. Stoll estimated that there were about 47 million cases of dracunculiasis worldwide.

The Soviet Union began its campaign to eradicate dracunculiasis in 1926, when guinea worm still affected an estimated 10,000 persons in Bukhara and surrounding areas. Using health education, installation of safe water supplies, controlled expulsion of larvae, topical treatment of victims' wounds, and disinfection or destruction of contaminated water sources, by 1933 officials had eliminated the disease from the U.S.S.R.

A similar eradication effort led to the reported demise of the disease in Iran in the 1970s. Elsewhere, notably in the Americas, North Africa, and other parts of the Middle East, dracunculiasis quietly disappeared, apparently as an indirect consequence of improvements in drinking water supplies. In the early 1970s, however, there existed at least one small area in Saudi Arabia and adjacent Yemen where the disease was still prevalent.

18

An ideally eradicable disease

By 1980 guinea worm disease was limited to India, Pakistan, and about 19 African countries, although at that time it was thought that the disease still existed in a few others as well. In the late 1970s and early 1980s, the World Health Organization (WHO) estimated that guinea worm disease affected about 10 million persons each year. Just before WHO inaugurated the International Drinking Water Supply and Sanitation Decade in December 1980, one of these authors, Donald R. Hopkins, then assistant director for international health at the CDC, pointed out that the aim to provide safe drinking water for all peoples of the world by December 1990 afforded an unprecedented opportunity to eradicate dracunculiasis—the only infectious disease that is transmitted by drinking water alone. Consequently, in April 1981 the steering committee for the Water and Sanitation Decade issued a statement supporting dracunculiasis eradication as a subgoal. In 1986 the World Health Assembly adopted its first resolution formally targeting dracunculiasis as the second major infectious disease to be eradicated—after smallpox—but set no target date. By 1988 African ministers of health, meeting under the auspices of WHO, resolved to eradicate guinea worm from Africa by 1995. Finally, in May 1991 the 44th World Assembly adopted a resolution that calls for the global eradication of dracunculiasis by the end of 1995.

A number of characteristics of dracunculiasis enable it to be singled out for eradication. First, the disease is easy to diagnose. Second, there is no animal reservoir from which the infection could reenter the human population once it has been eliminated. (Many species of *Dracunculus* infect wild animals, including animals in North America, but those parasites do not infect humans, and *D. medinensis* does not naturally infect animals.) Third, the infection has a self-limited duration of one year in humans if they are not reinfected. Fourth, naturally occurring seasonal declines in incidence and the one-year-long incubation period can be exploited to increase the efficiency of control measures. Fifth, though it does not usually kill its human victims, guinea worm is nonetheless a common, important cause of misery in affected areas; thus, political support for a cost-effective eradication effort is feasible. Finally, there are the three previously mentioned effective and practical ways to completely prevent the infection, even though it cannot be treated or cured.

Slaying the fiery serpent

The strategy of guinea worm eradication programs is simple: identify the affected villages and then help the inhabitants prevent the infection. The first step is for each affected country to conduct a nationwide, village-by-village search to identify all endemic areas and the numbers of cases occurring annually. Such a baseline survey is needed for planning, monitoring, and evaluating the eradication program. It is also useful for increasing awareness of the disease and creating political support for efforts to eliminate it. In the national search for cases, health workers and other volunteers are sent to each village in the country. If the residents say that there has been no guinea worm infection in their village in the past year, the workers pro-

Education is among the most important strategies in the conquest of guinea worm. People must be made aware of the disease and taught to change their daily habits. Many endemic villages suffer year after year largely because the people do not know how the infection is transmitted. On March 20, 1991, Nigeria held its second annual National Guineaworm Eradication Day. On the same day, the Nigerian Postal Service Department issued three guinea worm commemorative postage stamps. The postmaster general expressed his "sincere hope" that the stamps would "carry the message [of eradication] to all nooks and corners of Nigeria." The stamp below was designed by Nigerian artist G.N. Osuji.

Nigerian Philatelic Service

19

ceed to the next village. Where villagers say that there have been persons infected in the past year, the workers conduct a house-to-house search to count the number of guinea worm victims during a given period.

The value of thorough national searches to discover the true extent of dracunculiasis was graphically demonstrated in Ghana and Nigeria, each of which conducted such searches within a few months during 1988–89 (Nigeria) and 1989–90 (Ghana). Previously Ghana and Nigeria had relied on passive reporting from rural health centers, and both countries reported only about 4,000 cases of guinea worm annually to WHO in the early 1980s. Underreporting of cases was common because incapacitated guinea worm sufferers in remote areas have no incentive to travel for treatment to distant health centers, where cases could be recorded, since most of them know that modern medicine offers no cure for the disease. Thus, when they conducted their first national searches, Ghana found nearly 180,000 cases and Nigeria discovered more than 650,000. These shockingly high figures helped increase the national concern and, indeed, the governmental willingness to cooperate in eradication programs in both countries.

Once the geographic extent and magnitude of the problem are known and most of the affected villages have been identified, the next step is to begin interventions in those villages as quickly as possible. The fastest method will usually be education of villagers—promoting the use of cloth strainers to filter out water fleas and infective larvae from drinking water. At the same time, wherever possible, priority should be given to introducing new sources of safe drinking water, such as borehole wells. In selected villages, chemical control of the larvae-containing copepods with Abate is utilized as an additional intervention. Although theoretically it is possible to stop transmission of the disease in only one year, generally two to four years of active intervention are needed to eliminate the disease totally in affected communities.

In the early 1980s one of the first examples of a successful approach to community education and participation in construction of safe drinking water sources occurred in Kati, a village of about 3,000 persons in Togo. Nearly a third of Kati's population (928 persons) had guinea worm disease in 1981. With the assistance of two nongovernmental organizations that trained volunteers from the village itself, residents were educated in 1982 and 1983 about the cause and prevention of guinea worm. The villagers then raised funds for several borehole wells, which were constructed and fitted with hand pumps in 1984 and 1985. These efforts resulted in dramatic declines in the incidence of guinea worm disease: 263 cases in 1983, 7 cases in 1985, and 5 cases in 1987. There have been no reported cases since 1987.

The successful Kati eradication effort has been repeated in many other African villages. One that occurred well before a global eradication plan was inaugurated was in a town of 30,000 persons in Nigeria in the 1960s. Before piped water was introduced, 60% of the population were afflicted by guinea worm annually; with the new water source, the incidence plummeted to zero within two years.

The early 1980s saw the incidence of guinea worm reduced to zero in three villages in Burkina Faso, from previous rates of 54, 37, and 24%. This was achieved within only two transmission seasons simply by educating villagers to filter their drinking water. A United Nations Children's Fund (UNICEF)-assisted rural water supply project in Nigeria reduced the average prevalence of dracunculiasis in 20 villages from 59.6% in the 1983–84 transmission season to 11.3% three years later, with rates in three of the villages falling to zero (from 62, 52.7, and 44.8%). The apparent disappearance of guinea worm disease in the 1980s from the country that shares its name—the Republic of Guinea—is attributed to an extensive rural water supply program begun in the 1960s.

Progress in Asia

In the early 1990s the two remaining endemic countries where the most progress has been made nationally are India and Pakistan. India enumerated over 44,000 cases in its first national search for cases in 1983. The total number of cases detected in 1990 was about 5,000. The rigorous Indian guinea worm eradication program, supported mainly by the Indian government with assistance from UNICEF, the Swedish International Development Agency, and WHO, is presently emphasizing both provision of safe drinking water supplies to known endemic villages and chemical treatment of contaminated water sources with Abate. Guinea worm was eliminated from one of the seven originally endemic states of India, Tamil Nadu, in 1984. Tamil Nadu had started its own statewide control measures over a decade before the Indian national program began. One of the remaining six endemic states, Gujarat, had only a handful of cases in 1989, all of which were imported from other nearby endemic states.

Pakistan began its eradication program in 1987. A national search conducted that year detected fewer than 500 affected villages, with an estimated 2,400 cases. The program then selected and trained at least one person from each of the affected villages to initiate control measures. Interventions emphasized prompt detection and topical treatment of victims'

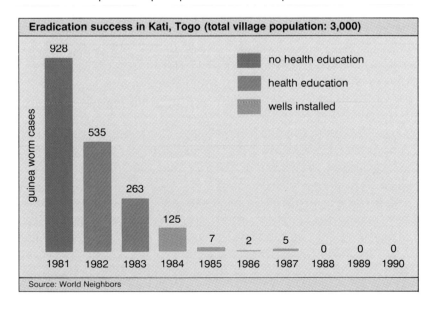

Eradication success in Kati, Togo (total village population: 3,000)

guinea worm cases

- no health education
- health education
- wells installed

| 1981 | 1982 | 1983 | 1984 | 1985 | 1986 | 1987 | 1988 | 1989 | 1990 |
| 928 | 535 | 263 | 125 | 7 | 2 | 5 | 0 | 0 | 0 |

Source: World Neighbors

The West African village of Kati, Togo, demonstrated in a matter of a few years how health education and the provision of a safe water supply can effectively break the cycle of guinea worm infection and end the misery it causes.

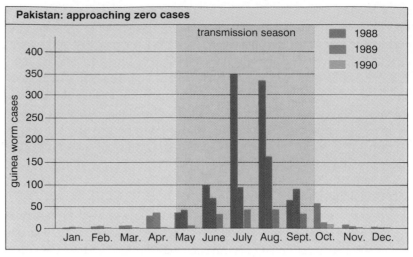

Pakistan: approaching zero cases

transmission season

■ 1988
■ 1989
■ 1990

guinea worm cases

Jan. Feb. Mar. Apr. May June July Aug. Sept. Oct. Nov. Dec.

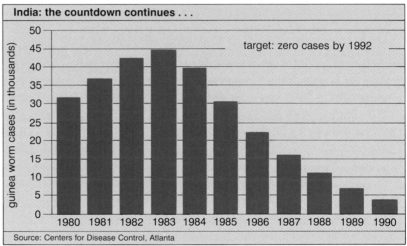

India: the countdown continues . . .

target: zero cases by 1992

guinea worm cases (in thousands)

1980 1981 1982 1983 1984 1985 1986 1987 1988 1989 1990

Source: Centers for Disease Control, Atlanta

By the early 1990s complete elimination of guinea worm was in sight in both Pakistan and India, the two remaining endemic countries in Asia.

wounds, the use of cloth filters for water in all households, treatment of local drinking water sources with Abate, and monthly reporting of cases from each endemic village. In 1990 only 160 cases were found in the entire country of Pakistan, and stringent control measures were rapidly instituted for each of those. The country was expected to be completely free of guinea worm in 1991.

Africa: the final battleground

As India and Pakistan are both on the verge of eliminating guinea worm, the main area of concern now is Africa, where all of the remaining endemic countries (except The Sudan) are formally committed to eradicating dracunculiasis by the end of 1995.

Having conducted national searches in 1989 or before, Cameroon, Ghana, and Nigeria are ahead of their neighbors, and all three countries were mounting intensive interventions against the disease nationwide early in 1991. Preliminary indications were that Ghana and Nigeria had already reduced the incidence of dracunculiasis by more than 30% during the previous two years. At the same time, at least 12 of the 17 endemic African countries had begun guinea worm eradication programs, and over half of them had conducted or begun nationwide searches. Burkina Faso found over 40,000 cases of guinea worm in its first national search late in 1990— a time when powerful allies were engaged in supporting the struggle against dracunculiasis in Africa. (Early in the campaign, resources were far less available.)

Despite the endorsement of dracunculiasis eradication as an official subgoal at the beginning of the Water and Sanitation Decade, actual support for eradication activities, especially in Africa, was very slow in coming (apart from continued leadership by CDC epidemiologists). In June 1982 in Washington, D.C., the U.S. National Research Council convened a workshop focusing on opportunities for the control of dracunculiasis, with funding provided by the U.S. Agency for International Development (USAID). This was the first international meeting devoted to the disease, and it provided a firm scientific basis for further action. Still, the various international assistance agencies stuck to their own priorities, which did not include dracunculiasis eradication. An early exception was the UNICEF mission in Nigeria: in 1983, largely because of the presence of guinea worm disease, UNICEF began installing borehole wells in selected areas of the country; two years later UNICEF provided vital support for Nigeria's first national conference on dracunculiasis. Also in 1983, both WHO and UNICEF, along with epidemiologists from the CDC, helped initiate guinea worm eradication investigations in Benin, Côte d'Ivoire, Togo, and Uganda.

After the 1986 World Health Assembly adopted the first resolution calling for guinea worm eradication, the first African regional dracunculiasis conference was convened in July of that year in Niamey, Niger, with considerable support from the Carnegie Corporation of New York. In November 1986 Global 2000, a charitable project of the Carter Center, based in Atlanta, Georgia, agreed to provide major assistance to Pakistan in eradicating

A watershed in support for guinea worm eradication came at an international donors conference, held in Lagos, Nigeria, in July 1989. Approximately $10 million was pledged in cash and gifts-in-kind from sources as diverse as the Peace Corps, the Japanese government, UNICEF, and the American Cyanamid Co. The conference's key sponsor was Global 2000, whose chairman, former U.S. president Jimmy Carter, and senior consultant, Donald R. Hopkins, are pictured above. At left, in August 1989, Jimmy and Rosalynn Carter inspect a borehole well in the Ghanaian village of Elevanyo; the well and pump, a pipe-borne source of safe drinking water, were installed as a result of the former president's earlier visit to the village in March 1988.

Filtering drinking water is one of three basic ways of preventing guinea worm disease. (Right) In June 1988 Ghana's head of state, Flight Lieutenant Jerry Rawlings (second from left), visited 21 villages in the northern region of his country to show people how to filter their water properly. (Below) A Nigerian woman pours water through a nylon filter to catch the guinea worm larvae that cause the disease. The filters were developed and donated by E.I. du Pont de Nemours & Co. in partnership with Precision Fabrics Group; the companies pledged to provide over eight million filters to meet the needs of the entire guinea worm eradication campaign through its target date of 1995.

E.I. du Pont de Nemours & Co.

guinea worm disease from all endemic parts of that country. Prior to that pledge of support, former U.S. president Jimmy Carter had gone to Pakistan to meet with and enlist the support of the country's president, Gen. Mohammad Zia-ul-Haq. Over the next several years, Global 2000 made formal commitments to work with the Ministries of Health of Ghana (in December 1987), Nigeria (in June 1988), and Uganda (in March 1991) in initiating national guinea worm eradication programs. In all three of the African countries, the assistance pledged by the Carter Center included the assignment of one experienced public health adviser and the provision of a small operating budget so that local public health personnel could conduct national searches for cases, plan the national eradication programs, and mobilize necessary resources. Nigeria's Anambra state had already secured over $5 million in support from the Japanese government for water supply projects in the state's endemic villages, and Japan soon began a similarly targeted rural water supply project in Ghana.

Carter helped draw more attention to the problem in Africa when he and his wife, Rosalynn, attended Africa's second regional conference on dracunculiasis in Accra, Ghana, in March 1988. The Carters also visited Ghanaian villages where guinea worm disease was still rampant, and they witnessed firsthand the terrible suffering of afflicted children and adults. Their appearance among Ghanaian guinea worm victims and their stopover in Lagos, Nigeria, for the official signing of Global 2000's agreement with Nigerian authorities gained wide local and national press coverage.

Dollars against disease

A year later, on the last day of July 1989, the real watershed in international support for the initiative to eradicate dracunculiasis came when approximately $10 million in new support was announced at an international

24

donors conference in Lagos called "Target 1995: Eradication of Guinea Worm." The conference was organized by Global 2000, and Carter, the project's chairman, gave the keynote address. Official cosponsors were the United Nations Development Program (UNDP)—whose regional director for Africa, Pierre-Claver Damiba, chaired the meeting—and UNICEF.

UNICEF headquarters in New York began to take an active role after the organization's executive director, James Grant, witnessed the ravages of guinea worm during a visit to a village in Ghana in March 1989. In his poignant opening address, Damiba described to a rapt audience the suffering he endured as a young boy growing up in Upper Volta (now Burkina Faso), when he was infected by guinea worm. Another emotional highlight of the meeting was the showing of a film made during a June 1988 tour of 21 endemic villages in Ghana, when the nation's head of state, Flight Lieutenant Jerry Rawlings, provided personal instruction to villagers on the proper technique for filtering their drinking water.

The true commitment to eradication was marked by pledges. The two UN agencies and Global 2000 each pledged over $1 million in cash support, while the CDC pledged $1 million (in kind). Gen. Ibrahim B. Babangida, Nigeria's head of state, announced on behalf of the government $1 million in new support for his country's eradication program. The Peace Corps, in association with USAID, announced that volunteers would be trained to help villagers in local guinea worm eradication efforts in all endemic African countries where the Corps was active. Less than a week after the donors conference, the USAID mission to Ghana announced a grant of over $2 million to that country's Ministry of Health for its eradication program. Later that year Japan worked out an $8 million agreement to help Nigeria's Niger state place borehole wells in villages affected by guinea worm, and in 1990 the Japanese government further agreed to provide $1 million in motor vehicles for Nigerians to implement their eradication strategy. The

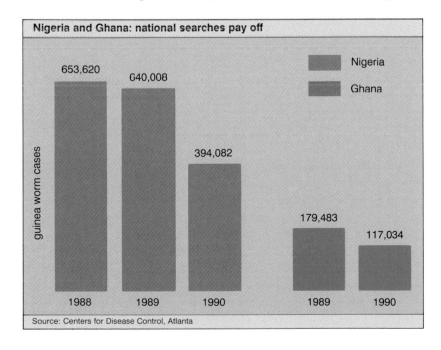

Nigeria and Ghana discovered shockingly high rates of guinea worm infection when they conducted their first national searches, beginning in 1988 and 1989, respectively. Thanks to the rapid introduction of intervention programs in affected villages, by early 1991 both countries were able to announce dramatic reductions in the number of guinea worm cases.

In March 1991 the Nigerian government stepped up its "war on guinea-worm," directing local governments throughout the country to allocate 10% of their health budgets for eradication. Vice Pres. Augustus Aikhomu emphasized that if the disease was phased out completely at the grassroots level, the whole nation would be free from the menace that for such a long time has stricken so many of its citizens and prevented socioeconomic gains. Just one of the dividends of eradication will be that the Nigerian people finally will be able to lead lives that are more socially and economically productive.

New NIGERIAN

No. 7,764   THURSDAY, MARCH 21, 1991   ₦1.50

RAMADAN 6, 1411 A.H.

TOTAL WAR ON GUINEA-WORM

A villager in Aga Laav, Benue state, Nigeria, helps spread the word: "Stop guinea worm disease!"

Rubina Imtiaz, M.D., Centers for Disease Control, Atlanta

latter donation was especially welcome and timely; during the first national search for cases in Nigeria in 1988–89, Nigerian health workers and volunteers had depended on haphazard means of transportation—borrowed or rented trucks and cars, motorbikes, bicycles, taxis, and personal vehicles—and some had walked long distances in order to reach villages all over the country.

In 1990 major pledges to the dracunculiasis eradication campaign came from U.S. businesses. In March the American Cyanamid Co., the world's only manufacturer of Abate, announced that it would donate through the Carter Center enough larvicide to eradicate guinea worm in all the affected African countries up to 1995—the target date for full conquest of the disease. UNICEF subsequently agreed to ship the donated Abate to Africa. Then in October, E.I. du Pont de Nemours & Co., in partnership with Precision Fabrics Group, donated over a million nylon filters and promised to supply another several million filters for water-filtration purposes throughout the eradication effort.

There is now committed and substantial support from many sources as efforts are under way in all of the affected countries in Africa to eradicate the "fiery serpent" by 1995. While additional strategic assistance and financial support are needed, the encouraging response on an international scale bodes well for Africa—and the world—to be guinea worm free before the end of the century.

The road to 1995

In February 1990 WHO took the first step in the process toward official certification of successful eradication of guinea worm disease. At a meeting of experts at its headquarters in Geneva, criteria were established for certifying the elimination of dracunculiasis in the many countries of Africa, Asia, and Latin America where the disease has been known to occur in the 20th century. In countries where guinea worm was still present during the 1980s, national authorities will have to show that their country has looked for but found no indigenous cases of the disease for at least three years. Recently endemic, geographically contiguous countries will only be considered for certification together, when the full requirements have been met in each of the countries. Pakistan has already requested WHO's assistance in preparations for certifying its eradication of guinea worm.

Civil wars in northeastern Africa are the most serious remaining obstacle to eradication of dracunculiasis, but at worst even they can only delay, not prevent, its achievement. The Smallpox Eradication Program succeeded only 10 months after its target date despite civil wars in Nigeria, Pakistan, and The Sudan. The apathy of some national and international officials and misunderstanding of guinea worm disease by villagers still must be overcome in some areas, but that, too, is only a matter of a little more time.

In October 1989 Global 2000 campaign leaders visited the village of Nkwanta in Wenchi district of Ghana's Brong Ahafo region, which was experiencing for the first time a notable decline from previous years in the number of cases of guinea worm disease because the Roman Catholic Church had recently built a well there. Among the victims in Nkwanta was a young man, 19 years old, whose story was particularly poignant. He had been afflicted with guinea worm several times before and had recovered completely; that year he was recovering from what would likely be his last episode of guinea worm ever, for the disease was close to being eliminated in his village. Unfortunately, however, this time the parasite had emerged from a blister near his right knee, causing severe scarring at the site. The result was that his right leg was permanently flexed at the knee, and he would be crippled for life. For this victim, tragically, eradication came too late.

By December 1995 there should be no more such tragedies. Future generations in Africa and Asia will not know what they are missing. Medicine's very symbol, the staff of Asclepius, will have a new significance.

The eradication of guinea worm disease will give new significance to the very symbol of medicine. Some scholars believe that the "serpent" entwined about the symbolic healing staff of Asclepius, the Greco-Roman god of medicine, in fact depicts the mode of treating guinea worm. The caduceus is also the logo chosen by the World Health Organization (WHO) to stand for its global commitment to the highest level of health care for all people. In the late 1980s WHO selected guinea worm disease as the second major infectious disease—after smallpox—for eradication from the face of the Earth. WHO believes that all people deserve health services that will enable them to lead socially and economically productive lives. With that dedication, the organization has played a leading role in the conquest of guinea worm thus far. In early 1990, confident that the target date of 1995 for the disease's complete elimination could be met, WHO took the first step in the official eradication certification process. Pakistan was expected to be the first country declared guinea worm free.

Photographs, (left) National Library of Medicine, Bethesda, Maryland; (right) World Health Organization

Just Relax!

By Daniel Goleman, Ph.D.

February 17–21, 1991

Third International Congress on Stress. Five Star Grand Excelsior Hotel, Montreux, Switzerland. Overlooking Lake Geneva and the Swiss and French Alps. Category 1 credit offered. Registration strictly limited. Information: Director of Communications, American Institute of Stress, 124 Park Avenue, Yonkers, NY 10703; 800-24-RELAX, in New York, 914-963-1200, Fax: 914-965-6267

—notice in *Annals of Internal Medicine,* Dec. 15, 1990

In the late 20th century, stress has become a fact of life. "Stressors," the events that make people feel stressed, range from minor hassles (traffic jams, oversleeping, lost keys) to major changes (birth of a baby, loss of a job) to "stress overload" (multiple situations that are beyond an individual's control) to situations of helplessness (when there is "no way out").

The causes of stress may differ, but its presence in one form or another crosses the boundaries of class, age, gender, race, and religion. The need to alleviate the pressures of modern life is a pervasive one; physicians hold international congresses to become more informed about both the causes of and remedies for stress, while people from all walks of life quest for ways to relax.

"The world is too much with us"

The emergence of stress as a central concern of the present era is a result of the intense economic, political, social, and personal demands that permeate people's lives. Traditional ways of living—*e.g.,* family and gender roles—are rapidly becoming outmoded. More and more families need two wage earners for economic survival, and child care has become a major dilemma. Many middle-aged people find themselves faced with caring for elderly parents and battling a health care system in which costs are sky-rocketing and quality is diminishing.

Many recent studies have focused on the unique stresses of women, who have the burden of juggling careers and family responsibilities; must cope with the physical and emotional effects of menstruation, pregnancy, childbirth, and menopause; and experience the stress of worrying about rape. Furthermore, women often hold jobs that are low in autonomy and control—a situation that is associated with a high level of stress. Recently,

Daniel Goleman, Ph.D., is a contributing writer on behavioral science for the New York Times.

(Opposite page) A trader on the floor of the Chicago Mercantile Exchange gets his first look at the board on Black Monday, Oct. 19, 1987.

Photograph, Anne Cusack/Chicago Tribune

David Woo—Stock Boston

therapists have also been seeing more effects of stress in men than ever before. As more women are working outside the home, more demands are being made on men to share in child care and housework. Children today have unique stresses as well. They are adversely affected by divorce, chronic marital conflict, and unstable family life. They have concerns about their abilities and physical appearance and anxiety about school. Many child development specialists lament that children today are "cheated out of childhood"; they are forced to grow up too soon.

On the world front, there are ominous large-scale threats, such as rampant pollution and global warming. Dwelling on these realities of contemporary existence causes stress.

The toll of stress

Stress is the response of the body to mental and physical demands. Stress can result in physical arousal, emotional distress, and mental agitation. People under stress respond variously; they become anxious, depressed, confused, and unable to concentrate, or they may experience heart-pounding exhilaration and excitement. The psychological effects of stress can be measured through questionnaires and psychological tests, but the reliability of these methods is not as great as that for measuring physiological aspects of stress.

For the body, stress begins as an adaptive response to the pressures of life. The body increases its level of physiological arousal in response to increased environmental demands. The late Canadian physiologist Hans Selye, who was the world's ranking expert on stress and its effects, proposed that as demands increase, the body mobilizes a "general arousal response." This adaptive reaction involves an intricate interplay between the hypothalamus area of the brain, the pituitary gland, and the adrenal glands, which prepares the body to handle an emergency.

The general arousal response causes the hypothalamus to release chemical messengers that signal the pituitary gland to release adreno-

Robert E. Daemmrich—Tony Stone Worldwide

Liane Enkelis—Stock Boston

corticotropic hormone (ACTH) into the bloodstream. ACTH then activates the adrenal glands to produce adrenaline and norepinephrine. These natural chemicals speed up the metabolism of the body, increasing blood pressure, breathing and heart rates, muscle tension, and blood flow. This quickened metabolism is sometimes called the "fight or flight" reaction. This reaction occurs when an animal or human attempts to escape from danger or protect itself—to fight or flee—or when a person is faced with a psychologically demanding situation.

This physiological state can be beneficial—what Selye called the "spice of life." For example, feeling distressed enough over the possibility of failure mobilizes students to study hard for a big exam. This kind of "positive" stress, however, is short term; once the challenge has been met, the body naturally relaxes. But as demands multiply or intensify, people feel less able to control or cope with them. They become overwhelmed, and what was initially an adaptive response often becomes a harmful one. For example, a woman may generate the arousal reaction as she leaves work early without finishing a project, hurries to pick up her children so that they will not be late for their weekly piano lessons, and then rushes home to prepare the family's dinner. Or, after staying up all night with their three-day-old daughter, a young couple may feel overcome with love for her at the same time they feel overwhelmed by new financial and emotional responsibilities and the physical strain of going without sleep.

Unfortunately, chronic elicitation of the general arousal response can take its toll on the body in major ways. For example, continued intense stress can result in hypertension, not merely brief elevation of blood pressure but chronic high blood pressure. Hypertension is dangerous because it increases the rate of hardening of the arteries, the condition called atherosclerosis. Hypertension and atherosclerosis are two primary causes of heart attacks and strokes. Additional ills commonly associated with stress include ulcers and other digestive ailments, headaches, backaches, rheumatoid arthritis, insomnia, obesity, alcohol and drug abuse, accidental

(Opposite page) Stress crosses boundaries of age, gender, and ethnicity. Women who have families and full-time careers must be eminently resourceful just to meet the everyday demands of their lives. Traditionally, men were the family breadwinners and could relax after a hard day's work. But now, as more wives and mothers are employed outside the home, husbands and fathers are increasingly sharing in domestic tasks—and so, too, experiencing the pressures of unrelenting demands on them. The toll of stress on children today is considerable. Psychologists recently ranked the top 20 stressors of third-through ninth-graders in the United States, Australia, Japan, the Philippines, Egypt, and Canada. Among them were: losing a parent, being held back in school, having parents who fight, receiving a poor report card, being ridiculed in class, being picked last for a team, having a scary dream, and adjusting to a new sibling.

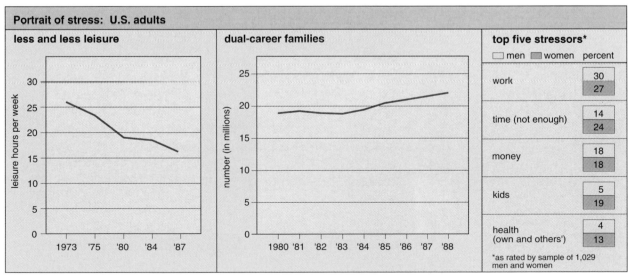

Portrait of stress: U.S. adults

less and less leisure — leisure hours per week (Left) Louis Harris Associates and Philip Morris Companies, Inc.

dual-career families — number (in millions) (center) Bureau of Labor Statistics

top five stressors*

	men	women
work	30	27
time (not enough)	14	24
money	18	18
kids	5	19
health (own and others')	4	13

*as rated by sample of 1,029 men and women

(right) Bruskin Associates

injuries, and certain skin diseases. Research has also shown that the response to stress, in excess, may lead to decreased efficiency of the immune system (the body's line of defense against disease), which can increase an individual's vulnerability to infections and, possibly, cancer.

The physiology of relaxation

Relaxation is the antidote for the physiological and psychological effects of stress. The general arousal response and the fight-or-flight reaction are produced by the sympathetic nervous system, which, along with the parasympathetic nervous system, makes up the autonomic nervous system. The autonomic nervous system has connections to the midbrain and controls the body's smooth muscles and glands. The natural counterpart to the sympathetic nervous system is the parasympathetic nervous system, which is designed to conserve the body's energy. It is this system that, when activated, decreases heart rate, respiration, blood pressure, muscle tension, and metabolism. Herbert Benson, professor of medicine at Harvard

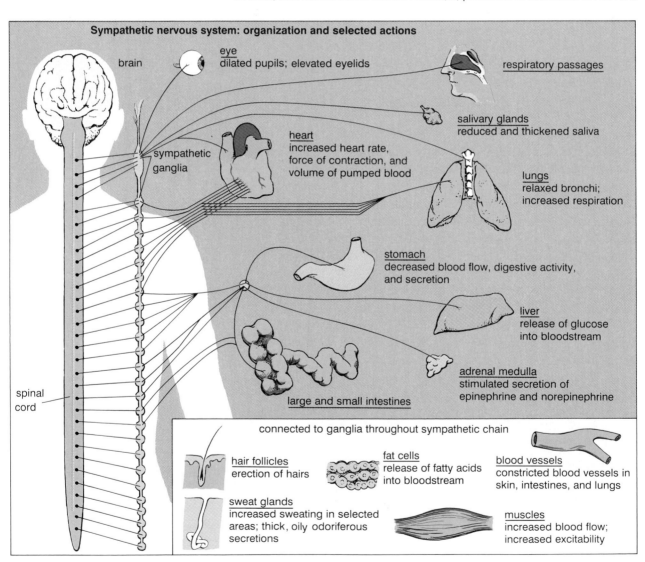

Sympathetic nervous system: organization and selected actions

brain

eye
dilated pupils; elevated eyelids

respiratory passages

salivary glands
reduced and thickened saliva

sympathetic ganglia

heart
increased heart rate, force of contraction, and volume of pumped blood

lungs
relaxed bronchi; increased respiration

stomach
decreased blood flow, digestive activity, and secretion

liver
release of glucose into bloodstream

adrenal medulla
stimulated secretion of epinephrine and norepinephrine

large and small intestines

spinal cord

connected to ganglia throughout sympathetic chain

hair follicles
erection of hairs

fat cells
release of fatty acids into bloodstream

blood vessels
constricted blood vessels in skin, intestines, and lungs

sweat glands
increased sweating in selected areas; thick, oily odoriferous secretions

muscles
increased blood flow; increased excitability

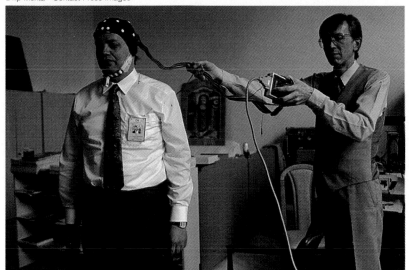
Dilip Mehta—Contact Press Images

The physiological changes that occur with relaxation can be dramatic. They can also be measured. At left, a research scientist monitors a meditator's brain waves. During meditation a high degree of alpha activity in the brain is observed: alpha waves increase in frequency and intensity as muscle tension is reduced, blood pressure and heart rate are lowered, and a state of deep physical relaxation is attained.

Medical School and chief of the section of behavioral medicine at New England Deaconess Hospital, Boston, has called this reaction the "relaxation response." The response restores balance to the body by counteracting the excessive arousal and energy expenditure of the sympathetic nervous system's response.

The physiological changes that occur in the relaxation response can be measured. A cardiac monitor can measure heart rate; an electromyograph can measure muscle tension; a galvanic skin response meter can measure the electrical conductivity of the skin (increased sweating leads to greater conductivity). Finally, the synchronicity of the nervous system can be measured by an electroencephalogram (EEG). Neural synchrony is characterized by low-frequency, high-voltage brain activity and is produced by the coordinated activity of many millions of neurons (nerve cells).

One physiological indicator of relaxation that has been given a good deal of attention is alpha activity in the brain. Alpha and beta states are two basic patterns of brain activity that are apparent when people are awake. Alpha activity is observed when a person is resting quietly—is not excited or engaged in rigorous activity—and most often when the eyes are closed. The presence of alpha activity, along with reduced muscle tension and lowered heart rate and blood pressure, indicates a relaxed state. Alpha activity is replaced by beta activity when a person becomes aroused—*e.g.,* when faced with solving a problem.

The mind-body connection

Neal E. Miller was one of the first scientists to conduct research on whether physiological components of relaxation could be controlled by psychological processes. In the late 1960s Miller demonstrated that the autonomic nervous system could be voluntarily controlled. In his laboratory at Rockefeller University, New York City, Miller trained rats that were completely paralyzed by the drug curare to vary their pulses, blood pressure, and intestinal contractions in order to obtain a reward. In Miller's experiments,

33

A patient undergoes biofeedback testing, which records information about continuously changing physiological processes—cardiovascular activity, temperature, brain waves, and muscle tension. Although such activity of the autonomic nervous system was once thought to be beyond an individual's control, it has been demonstrated that biofeedback training enables people to effectively alter their responses to stress and thereby relieve or eliminate many stress-related ailments—high blood pressure, migraine headaches, tics, ulcers, and low back pain, to name a few.

particular changes in the autonomic nervous system were monitored and reinforced. His findings in rats had implications for humans. He speculated that by becoming aware of the body's involuntary physical processes, such as heart rate or muscle tension, humans might be able to control those functions. He showed that this was possible with the process he called biofeedback.

Benson and his colleagues built on Miller's work and demonstrated that biofeedback could result in the control of blood pressure. They found that subjects who generated relaxing thoughts—a cognitive event—produced a physiological change—reduced blood pressure. This made it clear that relaxation is both a mental and a physical process.

Biofeedback has become a popular form of therapy for many stress-related ailments. Its practice involves the use of external sensors attached to the body to record information about a continuously changing physiological process (*e.g.*, perspiration, muscle tension). Information is then displayed to the patient in an intensified form (*e.g.*, blinking lights or audible tones). The machinery thus acts as a facilitator of a "dialogue" between one's conscious mind and one's physiology.

Beginning in the late 1960s, research by Benson and his colleagues revealed that the practice of meditation produced dramatic physiological results. During meditation, for example, oxygen consumption declined between 10 and 20%, a decrease greater than that experienced after seven hours of sleep. Alpha waves increased in intensity and frequency, and fatty acid levels in the blood—an indication of a state of anxiety—decreased significantly. Benson's work demonstrated that meditation produced the same degree of control of the autonomic nervous system as was generated by biofeedback. Moreover, meditation offered the advantage of not requiring the expensive equipment or specialized training needed for the practice of biofeedback.

The newest explorations of the mind-body connection are in the emerging field of psychoneuroimmunology, an area concerned with the interaction between the central nervous system and the immune system. One

34

of the pioneers of this work is psychologist Robert Ader at the University of Rochester, New York. Research has focused on examining the relationship between psychological stress and immunologic disturbance. For example, a study conducted in the 1970s by Australian researchers found that bereaved spouses had lower immune responses, as determined by lower lymphocyte (white blood cell) counts, up to two months following their spouses' deaths. In the late 1980s other research found that immunologic components that stimulate certain T lymphocytes ("natural killer cells") were consistently less active following exposure to stress-inducing agents. Janice Kiecolt-Glaser and colleagues at Ohio State University studied the effect of stress on the immune function of 75 medical students. The students' T cells were less active on the day they took an important exam. Their saliva also contained fewer antibodies on that day than it had a month earlier, when the academic pressure was not as great.

Recent investigations have also focused on "immunoenhancement"— *i.e.,* improving the responsiveness of the immune system. In a study in the early 1980s, hypnotized subjects were told that their white blood cells were "sharks," which would attack the "germs" in their bodies. Following this hypnotic suggestion, some actually increased their number of lymphocytes. Kiecolt-Glaser found that relaxation and guided imagery techniques produced an increase in natural killer cells in the immune systems of geriatric patients. Studies at the University of California School of Medicine at San Francisco found that relaxation training could delay the progression of AIDS in seropositive males.

Kenneth Pelletier and his colleagues at the University of California at San Francisco have proposed studying the effects on immunologic functioning of specific visualization techniques as practiced by experienced meditators in the Nyingmapa tradition of Tibetan Buddhism. If the hypothesized relationship between the meditation practice and immunologic functioning is supported, the researchers plan to instruct untrained volunteers to use such techniques. The ultimate goal is to determine whether the progression and outcome of immunologic and autoimmunologic diseases can be changed when patients meditate and relax regularly.

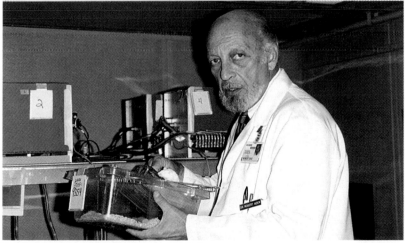

Robert Ader, M.D., University of Rochester Medical Center

Psychologist Robert Ader is one of the leaders in the field of psychoneuroimmunology, which is uncovering a chemical basis for mind-body interactions. Ader and colleagues at the University of Rochester, New York, began their studies in the early 1980s, examining the effects of stress on the immunologic functioning of laboratory rats. Many important insights have been gained into the ways that the central nervous system influences immunity. A number of investigators have shown that stress reduces the body's natural antibodies, diminishing resistance to disease. One application of this research that is now being widely explored is immunoenhancement— employing relaxation methods to boost immunity—i.e., to increase the number of infection-fighting white blood cells.

Maharishi Mahesh Yogi (a name that signifies Great Seer, Destroyer of Ignorance) meditates in the tranquillity of his ashram in The Netherlands. The retreat in the Dutch countryside is one of the newest enclaves established for followers of Transcendental Meditation (TM). The Maharishi introduced TM to the world in the 1960s; today it has an estimated three million devotees, many celebrities among them. Those who practice TM claim it is a simple way to achieve inner peace; scientific studies have shown that 20 minutes of meditation once or twice a day can lower blood pressure, heart rate, and oxygen consumption and is a dependable means of attaining a physiological state of deep relaxation.

These investigations in psychoneuroimmunology are promising. They indicate that relaxation techniques—including meditation, hypnosis, progressive relaxation, and guided imagery—can have a positive effect on immunologic function. Considerably more research in this area is needed, however, before firm conclusions can be drawn.

The art and the science of relaxing

There are now a number of techniques commonly used to induce a state of relaxation—techniques that have been scientifically studied and found to be effective. Usually these methods are best learned from experienced instructors.

Transcendental Meditation (TM) is a simple yogic technique developed by Maharishi Mahesh Yogi. It first gained popularity in the West in the 1960s when celebrities such as the Beatles were attracted to it. A person practicing TM receives a secret "mantra" from his or her instructor. The mantra is a sacred word, sound, or phrase that, when repeated, has a calming effect on the person. The individual sits quietly and repeats the mantra for 20 minutes once or twice a day. While repeating the mantra, the TM practitioner maintains a passive focus and lets go of cares and preoccupying thoughts. Widespread research has confirmed that, if practiced regularly, TM reliably produces a state of relaxation. It has also been found to reduce blood pressure, heart rate, and oxygen consumption.

In *Zen meditation* the practitioner sits upright, with hands held lightly together at the navel; the eyes are open and focused about a meter straight ahead. One form of Zen requires one to be mindful of breathing; the aim is to keep the mind from getting lost in thought. An erect posture is emphasized in order to maximize alertness and stabilize breathing. Zen meditation has been found to increase alpha waves, reduce blood pressure and heart rate, and lower metabolism.

Progressive relaxation training, sometimes called *deep muscle relaxation,* was developed by physiologist Edmund Jacobson at the University of Chicago in the 1930s. It involves the alternate tensing and relaxing of the major muscles, leaving each muscle group in a relaxed state. Subjects lie back in a comfortable chair or on the floor and are instructed to alternately tense and relax their toes, then their feet, ankles, calves, buttocks, and so on, until all major muscle groups of the body are relaxed. The procedure usually takes from 20 to 40 minutes to produce a state of deep muscle relaxation. Practicing this head-to-toe relaxation exercise results in reduced tension in the largest muscles of the body and lowered metabolism.

Hypnosis is an altered state of consciousness in which a person becomes detached from his or her surroundings and focused on certain psychological realities. Once this special state has been induced, the hypnotist uses it to help the person imagine a sought-after state, such as relaxation, and to transform his or her other thoughts, behavior, or feelings accordingly. Standard hypnotic induction involves repeated suggestions to the subject that he or she is tired, needs a rest, and is feeling more and more relaxed. These suggestions are made until the subject enters a trance. Following the induction, further suggestions are given to produce the behavioral or cognitive effects that are intended—in this case, calmness and relaxation.

One of the cardinal features of the hypnotic state is increased susceptibility to suggestions combined with a vivid state of the imagination. In a hypnotic trance, the person focuses on suggestions without making stressful associations. The trance is described as a state of "resting alertness." Posthypnotic suggestions, which the subject carries over into his or her day-to-day life, may also be given. For example, the hypnotist may suggest that a subject will be relaxed and confident during an upcoming job interview or while performing in a music recital. Hypnosis is effective in treating headaches, chronic pain, hypertension, and a wide variety of other disorders. As a method of achieving relaxation, it has been shown to decrease heart rate, respiration, and metabolism.

Brownie Harris—The Stock Market

Joan Borysenko (second from left) is the director of the Mind/Body Group at Boston's New England Deaconess Hospital. Borysenko uses relaxation and visualization techniques in her work with seriously ill patients, including people with AIDS and cancer, to help them cope with their disease. It is believed that such methods "de-stress" the body and can actually promote physical healing. In the picture she is teaching a group of cancer patients to relax and visualize positive, health-promoting images. The technique, known as guided imagery, has helped many cancer patients tolerate chemotherapy. Some scientists believe that such relaxation methods may even cause tumors to shrink.

Relaxation techniques that elicit physiological changes						
	oxygen consumption	respiratory rate	heart rate	alpha waves	blood pressure	muscle tension
Transcendental Meditation	decreases	decreases	decreases	increases	decreases*	not measured
Zen and yoga	decreases	decreases	decreases	increases	decreases*	not measured
autogenic training	not measured	decreases	decreases	increases	inconclusive	decreases
progressive relaxation	not measured	not measured	not measured	not measured	inconclusive	decreases
hypnosis with deep relaxation	decreases	decreases	decreases	not measured	inconclusive	not measured

*in persons with elevated blood pressure

Herbert Benson, M.D., *The Relaxation Response,* © 1975; used by permission of William Morrow and Company, Inc., Publishers, New York

A technique that may be used as a component of hypnosis or on its own is known as *guided imagery;* it is a visualization method that is sometimes described as a "mental vacation." In it a person imagines that he or she is in peaceful, calm surroundings, such as floating on a cloud or in a pool of warm water. The image is rehearsed until it is vivid. Whatever setting is imagined, the individual should not be a passive observer but an active participant in the vision. Some therapists who use guided imagery to help people relax (or lose weight, stop smoking, or cope with illness) actually have patients draw pictures of what they are trying to visualize.

Autogenic training was developed by physicians Johannes Schultz and Wolfgang Luthe. It involves mental exercises to control the body functions that are activated in the fight-or-flight response (*e.g.,* heartbeat, breathing, blood pressure). The exercises are done while lying down or sitting in a comfortable chair in a quiet room with eyes closed. The practitioner silently repeats phrases such as "my legs feel heavy and warm," while concentrating on *experiencing* that warmth and heaviness. One literally tells the body how to feel. In another exercise the person tries to make his or her heart beat more slowly and steadily; another involves passive concentration on slow, steady, calming breathing. Autogenic training requires time, practice, and commitment, but research indicates that these exercises can reliably produce a state of relaxation characterized by slow heart rate, reduced respiration, and slowed metabolism.

Benson's *relaxation response* technique was developed after years of research at Harvard Medical School. The person sits quietly with eyes closed, breathing naturally and relaxing the body's muscles, while silently saying "one" or some other meaningful sound, word, or prayer with each exhalation. This is repeated for about 20 minutes. The method is most similar to TM. Benson points out that a receptive, "letting-go" attitude is necessary in order for relaxation to occur. For some individuals, using spiritual images and phrases may heighten the effectiveness of the technique. The relaxation response reduces blood pressure, heart rate, and metabolism. It has also been effective in treating migraine headaches, back pain, hypertension, cardiac arrhythmias, and anxiety attacks.

Virtually all of these methods generate feelings of calm and decrease heart rate, respiration, and oxygen consumption. TM, Zen, and the relaxation response appear to be best at reducing blood pressure.

Although the techniques described above are among the "tried and true" ones that have been studied, other approaches to relaxation may achieve similar effects. For those who experience stress mainly physically, progressive relaxation, yoga, aerobic dance, bicycling, swimming, rowing, brisk walking, getting a massage, or soaking in a hot bath are likely to relieve bodily tension. Those who experience stress mainly mentally (*e.g.,* negative or worrisome thoughts) will likely benefit most from the techniques of meditation and autogenic training. These people may also derive benefits and achieve a state of calm from activities that redirect the mind—*e.g.,* reading, doing crossword puzzles, playing chess or cards, knitting, or becoming involved in virtually any absorbing hobby.

Many people choose to "get away from it all" in order to relax. Perhaps the quintessential retreat for relaxing is the spa. Spa is the name of a town in Belgium with a celebrated natural pool whose waters have long been recognized as extremely pure. This name has since been given to other places with a calming atmosphere, and famous spas are located throughout the world. Enthusiasts claim that nothing can match the calming effects of soaking in a hot mineral bath. Many also emphasize diet, exercise, massage, and a full array of relaxation techniques. In the U.S. a spa "industry" has burgeoned in the past decade. Advertisements for spas offer such things as "a new start in life," "hours of blissful quiet," and "serene settings" and "exotic massages, Dead Sea mud baths, Zen meditation—and more." People go to these spas to have a supportive environment for managing stress, losing weight, and improving the quality of their lives.

Le Segretain—Sipa Press

Opulent spas have long been popular retreats for European relaxation seekers. Devotees claim that the thermal waters can alleviate ailments ranging from rheumatism to gynecologic disorders. At left, bathers at the Szechenyi baths in Budapest, Europe's largest thermal pool, escape the pressures of the world. Soaking in the warm, calming water relieves their physical tensions; mental stress is eliminated as they concentrate on the moves in their chess game and forget their everyday cares and worries.

Ultimately, the choice of technique depends on a person's life-style and beliefs. More exotic methods, such as Zen, may not appeal to everyone. The other critical consideration for any method is adherence to the practice. The more one practices the method, the better the effect, and the more deeply relaxed one becomes, the greater the mental and physical benefits.

How relaxation works

People who have practiced a technique of relaxation regularly report that they feel calm, peaceful, and refreshed. And although the techniques differ, the resulting physiological effects of relaxation are the same. It is important to appreciate the relationship between mind and body in order to understand how relaxation methods work.

In stress there is both physiological and psychological tension. In addition to increases in blood pressure, heart rate, muscular tension, and other physical signs of tension, thinking typically becomes agitated, worries increase, and negative expectations develop. Attention becomes selective; thus, the person tends to tune in to events that confirm his or her negative attitudes. Such biased thinking and perception, which are typical when one is anxious, limit effective response. Thus, people fall back on familiar, yet counterproductive, responses. The following example illustrates this destructive process: A man who is threatened with a layoff worries about not being able to provide for his family; he begins to think negatively about himself, feeling confused and uncertain and ultimately fearing that his wife and children will see him as a failure. *Feeling* a failure, he resumes smoking after having quit a year before, and his blood pressure, which had been in the normal range, rises.

40

On a physiological level, such an inefficient mind-set, which in turn promotes ineffective responses, serves to heighten sympathetic nervous system activity. It is this pattern that, if left unchecked, can produce the health problems that are associated with chronic arousal of the sympathetic nervous system. The cycle is worsened by physical troubles. Back pain, arthritic disorders, hypertension, ulcers, and so forth, in and of themselves are likely to cause mental and physical tension. If a person is already stressed—say by family obligations—the symptoms of physical problems become an added source of tension and are often exacerbated.

Regular induction of a state of relaxation, however, interrupts this escalation of symptoms, and significant health benefits result. In one study, for example, regular practitioners of a meditation technique reduced their cholesterol by 35%. Benson and his colleagues found repeatedly that hypertension, arrhythmias, and angina all improved with the regular elicitation of the relaxation response. These scientists also found that relaxation methods helped patients with cancer tolerate chemotherapy better and that people suffering from panic disorder had fewer panic attacks. Other researchers found that stress can trigger episodes of genital herpes simplex virus infection and that relaxation techniques, stress management, and mental imagery reduced outbreaks. Subjects who learned relaxation had about half as many herpes recurrences as those who did not practice relaxation, and the episodes of the former group were less severe. Psychologist Alice Domar, a colleague of Benson at New England Deaconess Hospital, has used the relaxation response in women being treated for infertility. In a two-year period, 130 patients participated in 10 sessions of relaxation training. Although the method is by no means a panacea, and Domar has not published her statistics, some long-term infertile women were able to conceive following relaxation therapy.

Larry Barnes

Employees take time out from their workday to attend a stress-reduction class. Stresscare, a Long Island, New York, company, creates customized relaxation programs to which businesses subscribe. Studies show that job stress takes a huge toll; it is responsible for lowered on-the-job performance, stress-related illness, absenteeism, and worker "burnout"—not to mention skyrocketing health insurance costs and the large sums spent on disability payments. Many employers are now seeing the logic of offering stress-management training for employees—a step that is likely to provide health benefits for workers and be cost-effective as well.

A healthy high

Relaxation is a state that everyone is capable of attaining. Unlike the "high" experienced by many drug users, relaxation is a natural, energy-conserving response of the body. Although relaxing makes one feel good, as many narcotics do, relaxation is not addictive. Addiction by definition involves habituation—the buildup of tolerance for the substance so that there is a craving for more and more of it—and withdrawal symptoms—feelings of intense discomfort when the substance or stimulus is removed. The relaxation experience occurs readily, without the need to practice a technique more and more in order to generate the same degree of calmness. There is no evidence of habituation, nor are there withdrawal symptoms during periods when the relaxation technique is not practiced.

Many people attempt to relax by using antianxiety drugs (tranquilizers)—most often one of the benzodiazepines (*e.g.,* diazepam, chlordiazepoxide, lorazepam). These widely prescribed drugs often are perceived as the "perfect answer" to stress. However, their physiological effects are quite dissimilar to those achieved by relaxation techniques. Benzodiazepines increase fast beta activity and decrease alpha activity in the brain. They decrease the amount of time spent in REM (rapid eye movement) sleep, the active sleep state in which dreaming occurs; when the drug is discontinued there is a withdrawal effect, resulting in increased restlessness, bizarre dreaming, and nocturnal waking. Antianxiety agents produce decreased vigor and increased fatigue and confusion. While the drugs may appear to calm patients, over time they actually increase hostility and aggression.

Finally, benzodiazepines and other antianxiety agents produce tolerance; that is, more of the drug is needed over time in order to produce the same effect. They create dependency, and the symptoms of withdrawal

Zen is a Buddhist practice for achieving enlightenment. The word itself derives from the Sanskrit dhyana, *meaning "meditation." The Zen meditator adopts an erect, seated posture that maximizes alertness while focusing attention on slow, steady, calming breathing and clearing the mind of extraneous thoughts. Herbert Benson, who has been investigating meditative techniques for several decades, points out that a receptive, "letting-go" attitude is required for meditation to be effective. Although religious faith is not necessary for attaining physical and mental benefits, integrating one's beliefs with meditation—e.g., using spiritual images or phrases that are personally meaningful—can heighten the experience and deepen relaxation.*

Linda Bladholm

Michael Kienitz—Picture Group

Not all relaxation methods are equally effective for everyone. Hypnosis is a state of altered consciousness, or resting alertness, brought about by the mechanism of suggestion. In highly susceptible individuals hypnosis can be highly effective for eliciting the relaxation response, which restores balance to mind and body by counteracting excessive activity of the autonomic nervous system. At left, a 10-year-old patient is induced into a state of deep relaxation by her psychiatrist; children are often good candidates for this type of stress-reduction therapy.

from antianxiety drugs are similar to those of withdrawal from alcohol or barbiturates. None of these symptoms is produced by any of the previously described techniques of relaxation.

Can everyone benefit from relaxing?

Benson and many others have found that hypertension patients can lower their blood pressure significantly by practicing a relaxation technique regularly; however, a recent study at the University of Amsterdam found no such benefit. Half of 35 subjects with mild, uncomplicated hypertension used relaxation therapy; they were trained in muscle relaxation, yoga, and stress management and practiced it twice a day. The other half (the controls) were simply told to maintain their life-style but to "sit and relax" twice a day. Those in the intensive-therapy group did not benefit any more than those who had the nonspecific advice.

Jan Passchier, in the department of medical psychology at Erasmus University, Amsterdam, examined the relationship between stress and headaches. He found that when subjects were shown stressful imagery, it increased the tension of muscles in the head. The headaches of migraine patients had shorter duration and intensity following an imagery exercise involving hand warming and relaxation. While vascular migraine headaches improved with an imagery-based relaxation procedure, the tension headache group in Passchier's study did not benefit from relaxation. This latter group received progressive relaxation training and stress-management counseling, and half of the group of 29 tension headache patients had biofeedback training in addition to the other treatments. None of the headache variables was significantly decreased by this treatment.

As the negative findings of Passchier indicate, not all relaxation techniques are equally effective for every person or every condition. By some estimates, 15–20% of the population are not hypnotizable. Some techniques are more effective with specific kinds of problems or with individual

43

patients. Ronald Pekala and Elizabeth Forbes at Thomas Jefferson University, Philadelphia, studied the effects of several stress-management strategies. They found that progressive relaxation was often effective in "low susceptibles" (those who were not responsive to hypnosis). Hypnosis and progressive relaxation were equally effective for "high susceptibles." They also found that deep breathing was an effective, quick, and easy strategy to help many individuals decrease distractive rumination and detach themselves from negative emotions.

The intensity and frequency of sympathetic nervous system arousal are factors that determine whether a person finds it easy or difficult to relax. The more intense or chronic the sympathetic arousal, the more difficult it is to learn to relax. Beliefs, too, can help or hinder the process. Some people unconsciously associate relaxation with passivity and vulnerability. For example, victims of rape, violence, or child abuse sometimes find it difficult to learn to relax. In many cases, this is because they relate being in a state of relaxation to being in the helpless or weak condition that they associate with their victimization. Sometimes these people may require psychotherapy in order to come to terms with the traumatic events in their lives before they can benefit from one or another of the relaxation techniques. For them, the best approach may be to combine a particular relaxation technique, such as repeating a mantra and clearing the mind of distracting thoughts, with a form of physical exercise that involves rhythmic, repetitive movements, such as jogging or swimming.

Spirituality and relaxation

Many of these relaxation techniques, which have been explored over the past 30 years, have roots in the spiritual traditions of the East. Much of the experimental investigation of relaxation has focused on evaluating the medical and psychological benefits of meditation. Scientists have confirmed that practitioners of techniques like Zen, TM, and yoga can produce

In a converted church at the TM retreat in Vlodrop, The Netherlands, advanced practitioners of yoga assume the "all limbs" posture, or shoulder stand. Scientists have studied Eastern yogis and found that they are able to produce remarkable changes in the internal environments of their bodies. Quite unlike the antianxiety drugs (Valium, Librium, Ativan, etc.), yoga produces a "healthy high," generating intense feelings of tranquillity without the potential for addiction or the adverse effects of withdrawal from tranquilizers.

remarkable changes in the internal environments of their bodies. For example, Benson found that Tibetan monks who practiced "heat yoga," involving intricate visualizations, breath control, and other techniques, were able to raise their temperatures dramatically. Traditional meditation practitioners seek relaxation not as an end in itself but as a means of transforming the human experience and realizing an enlightened mind. The physiological effects of relaxation are by-products of a more profound endeavor—the deepening of spiritual awareness.

This is not to say that a specific religious belief is necessary for relaxation techniques to be effective. However, studies have shown that the best results may be achieved when there is a spiritual component. Benson found that belief, or what he calls the "faith factor," is useful for enhancing relaxation. Integrating one's beliefs with a specific relaxation technique leads to a state of inner peace that is personally meaningful.

One such integration is between Buddhist mindfulness meditation and behavioral medicine methods. At the stress clinic of the University of Massachusetts Medical Center, Worcester, physician Jon Kabat-Zinn complements medical treatment for patients who suffer from a full spectrum of disease, including asthma, cancer, and rheumatoid arthritis, with instruction in mindfulness meditation. This form of meditation involves being aware of what one's mind and body are doing moment by moment. It is a process of directly perceiving the natural inner movements of one's being through careful, nonjudgmental self-awareness. One becomes mindful of breathing and other sensations throughout the body and at the same time lets go of distracting thoughts. At his clinic Kabat-Zinn instructs patients to "Ride the waves of your own breathing. Feel your breath move, even if it seems silly or boring." Proponents of mindfulness training believe that learning to pay attention to one's inner being enables people to elicit a state of deep calm whenever stress from the outside world threatens. Kabat-Zinn holds that mindfulness meditation has a unique advantage over other relaxation techniques because it leads to an experience of "wholeness."

The need to find tranquillity amid life's ever mounting pressures is both vital and universal. Although literally "getting away from it all" whenever stress from the outside world threatens is not possible for most people most of the time, everyone can (and should!) learn to relax.

Stress: a fact but not a way of life

When people complain about the effects of stress, they may be told by family, friends, and even physicians to "just relax." Many people, however, find relaxing to be no simple matter. Moreover, the things they do to relax—watching TV, having a cigarette, popping a tranquilizer, or drinking alcohol—do not genuinely relax them and are often bad for their health. Learning an effective relaxation technique can be a path to renewal and good health. People can choose from methods as diverse as Zen meditation, hypnosis, and guided imagery.

The stresses of modern life are not going to vanish; in fact, they are likely to increase. Thus, the quest for ways to relax will take on greater importance. As medical researchers continue to study the harmful effects of stress and discover the remarkable potential of its antidote—relaxation—physicians will be more and more likely to "prescribe" relaxation for their patients. "Take 20 minutes of meditation morning and evening" may be the best prescription yet.

Encounters with Death

by Bruce Greyson, M.D.

> I felt myself lift out of my body. . . .
> I passed rapidly through a tunnel toward a being of light, which I experienced as total love. . . .
> Reviewing my life, I became profoundly aware of the consequences of my actions for others. . . .
> I saw deceased relatives. . . .
> I entered a luminous realm in which caring and compassion were the only values. . . .
> I returned to life and tried to tell my story to others but was met with only disbelief. . . .

Such accounts, formerly regarded as meaningless hallucinations, now are heard frequently by health professionals from a significant number of their patients. Long regarded as unworthy of serious attention, the near-death experience, or NDE, has been the subject of serious study by medical and other researchers in recent years. To some extent, this relatively new and growing professional concern is due to the inescapability of the NDE. The ever increasing sophistication of biomedical technology has allowed patients who otherwise would have died to be resuscitated. The experiences that many of these patients attempt to relate to medical personnel are so real to the patients—and so consistent—that the medical community now finds them difficult to ignore.

The NDE is not a new phenomenon, however. Almost every culture has left records of experiences that are now recognized as NDEs. Plato's *Republic,* written in the 4th century BC, includes the case of Er, a soldier who was killed on the battlefield only to revive on his funeral pyre and recount an elaborate journey of his disembodied soul. The Anglo-Saxon scholar the Venerable Bede includes in his *Ecclesiastical History of the English People,* written in the 8th century, the case of Drythelm, who reportedly died of illness but came back to life to tell of his otherworldly travels. NDEs have been preserved in the folklore or writings of societies as disparate as those of Egypt, India, Tibet, China, Japan, Melanesia, and Native America. While the interpretation of the NDE tends to vary with cultural expectations, the basic phenomena vary little over the centuries and across the globe.

Bruce Greyson, M.D., is Associate Professor of Psychiatry, University of Connecticut School of Medicine, Farmington, and Editor, Journal of Near-Death Studies.

(Overleaf) "The Ascent into the Empyrean," by Hiëronymous Bosch; photograph, Scala/Art Resource

Nature of the experience

What is a near-death experience? While various investigators have emphasized different aspects of the experience, the NDE is generally accepted to be a profound subjective event with transcendental or mystical elements that many people experience on the threshold of death. Once thought to be rare, the NDE is now reported by about one-third of people who come close to death. A Gallup Poll estimated that about 13 million people in the United States—about 5% of the population—have had NDEs.

Given the widespread occurrence of these experiences, a single definition of the NDE must be somewhat arbitrary. Psychiatrist Raymond Moody, author of *Life After Life* (1975), coined the term *near-death experience.* He used it to refer to an ineffable experience occurring on the threshold of death, which may include hearing oneself pronounced dead, having feelings of peace, hearing unusual noises, sensing movement through a dark tunnel, having a sense of being out of the physical body, meeting spiritual beings, meeting a being of light, conducting a life review, crossing a border or point of no return, sensing a return to the physical body, being frustrated in attempts to tell others about the experience, having one's attitudes and values change profoundly, overcoming a fear of death, and independently corroborating knowledge gained while out of the body. Moody emphasized that no two individuals' NDEs are exactly the same and that few near-death experiences contain all these features.

The common features of the NDE can be grouped into four categories. Most near-death experiences tend to be dominated by one or more of these four components.

Cognitive features. The first component includes cognitive elements—features related to changes in thinking, such as the loss of one's sense of time, a speeding up of thoughts, a panoramic life review, and a sense of sudden understanding or revelation. A historical example of an NDE dominated by cognitive elements was recorded by British Rear Adm. Sir Francis Beaufort, who on June 10, 1791, fell off a boat into Portsmouth Harbor:

Near-death experiences are not only ineffably real to those who have had them but remarkably consistent. One of the most commonly reported features is a panoramic life review. Important memories may be relived; crucial stages of one's life may be viewed and experienced all at once; and one may encounter deceased loved ones. Although these profound, subjective events occurring at the time of a close brush with death may resemble vivid dreams or hallucinations, they are now viewed by medical scientists as a distinct and unique phenomenon.

"The Artist's Dream"; photograph, Mary Evans Picture Library

Dante, having passed through the spheres of Heaven, accompanied by his beloved Beatrice, faces the glorious vision of the Empyrean; light, love, and joy have become the only realities. People who have near-death experiences often describe feelings of overwhelming peace and joy, utter well-being, and painlessness. Not uncommonly, they report having a revelatory encounter with a loving being of light.

With the violent but vain attempts to make myself heard I swallowed much water; I was soon exhausted by my struggles, and before any relief reached me sank below the surface—all hope had fled—all exertions ceased—and I *felt* that I was drowning. . . . From the moment that all exertion had ceased—which I imagine was the immediate consequence of complete suffocation—a calm feeling of the most perfect tranquillity superseded the previous tumultuous sensations—it might be called apathy, certainly not resignation, for drowning no longer appeared to be an evil—I no longer thought of being rescued, nor was I in any bodily pain. On the contrary, my sensations were now of rather a pleasurable cast. . . . Though the senses were thus deadened, not so the mind; its activity seemed to be invigorated, in a ratio which defies all description, for thought rose above thought with a rapidity of succession that is not only indescribable, but probably inconceivable by any one who has not himself been in a similar situation. The course of those thoughts I can even now in a great measure trace. . . . Travelling backwards, every past incident of my life seemed to glance across my recollection in retrograde succession; not, however, in mere outline, as here stated, but the picture filled up with every minute

49

Accounts of near-death experiences often include paranormal features—e.g., a convincing sensation of being out of the physical body, the phenomenon of astral projection. Many artists have depicted the human soul departing from the body at death. Illustrated, below right, is the case of a Dutch patient who had an indelible out-of-body experience during surgery. In the patient's words: "I saw myself— my physical self—lying there. I saw a sharply outlined view of the operating table. I myself, freely hovering and looking downward from above, saw my physical body, lying on the operating table. I could see the wound of the operation on the right side of my body, see the doctor with an instrument in his hand, which I cannot more closely describe. All this I observed very clearly. . . . To me the experience will never be forgotten."

and collateral feature. In short, the whole period of my existence seemed to be placed before me in a kind of panoramic review. . . . Indeed, many trifling events which had been long forgotten then crowded into my imagination, and with the character of recent familiarity. . . . The length of time that was occupied by this deluge of ideas, or rather the shortness of time into which they were condensed, I cannot now state with precision.

Emotional features. The second component of the NDE includes affective elements such as feelings of overwhelming peace, painlessness, well-being, joy, and cosmic unity and an encounter with a loving being of light. A celebrated example of an NDE dominated by affective elements was described by Albert von St. Gallen Heim, a Swiss geologist, who lost his footing climbing the Alps in 1871:

As soon as I began to fall I realized that now I was going to be hurled from the crag and I anticipated the impact that would come. With clawing fingers I dug into the snow in an effort to brake myself. My fingertips were bloody but I felt no pain. I heard clearly the blows on my head and back as they hit each corner of the crag. . . . Everything was transfigured as though by a heavenly light and everything was beautiful without grief, without anxiety, and without pain. . . . I felt no conflict or strife; conflict had been transmuted into love. Elevated and harmonious thoughts dominated and united the individual images, and like magnificent music a divine calm swept through my soul. I swept into it painlessly and softly and I saw that now I was falling freely through the air and that under me a snow field lay waiting. . . . Quite certainly it is incomparably more painful in both the feeling of the moment and subsequent recollection to see another person fall than to fall oneself. . . . I have seen others fall several times . . . these memories remain ever dreadful . . . while my own misfortune is registered in memory as a pleasant transfiguration—without pain and without anguish—just as it actually had been experienced.

After his own experience, Heim collected a series of accounts from other mountaineers who had survived falls, which were published in 1892.

Paranormal features. The third component of the NDE consists of what appear to be paranormal or psychic elements, such as hyperacute physical

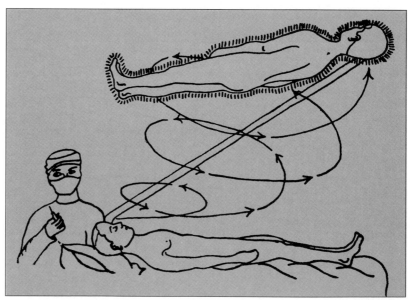

senses, apparent extrasensory perception and precognitive visions, and a sense of being out of the body. A famous example of an NDE dominated by paranormal elements was recorded by Sir Alexander Ogston, professor of surgery at the University of Aberdeen, Scotland, who served as an army surgeon during the Boer War. In 1901 he was hospitalized with typhoid fever in the midst of the war.

I lay, as it seemed, in a constant stupor which excluded the existence of any hopes or fears. Mind and body seemed to be dual, and to some extent separate. I was conscious of the body as an inert tumbled mass near a door; it belonged to me, but it was not *I*. I was conscious that my mental self used regularly to leave the body . . . and wander away from it under grey, sunless, moonless, and starless skies, ever onwards to a distant gleam on the horizon, solitary but not unhappy . . . until something produced a consciousness that the chilly mass, which I then recalled was my body, was being stirred as it lay by the door. I was then drawn rapidly back to it, joined it with disgust, and it became *I,* and was fed, spoken to, and cared for. When it was again left I seemed to wander off as before . . . and though I knew that death was hovering about, having no thought of religion nor dread of the end, and roamed on beneath the murky skies apathetic and contented until something again disturbed the body where it lay, when I was drawn back to it afresh, and entered it with ever-growing repulsion. . . .

In my wanderings there was a strange consciousness that I could see through the walls of the building, though I was aware that they were there, and that everything was transparent to my senses. I saw plainly, for instance, a poor R.A.M.C. surgeon, of whose existence I had not known, and who was in quite another part of the hospital, grow very ill and scream and die; I saw them cover his corpse and carry him softly out on shoeless feet, quietly and surreptitiously, lest we should know that he had died. . . . Afterwards, when I told these happenings to the sisters, they informed me that all this had happened just as I had fancied.

Mystical features. The fourth and final component of the NDE consists of transcendental or mystical elements, such as travel to an apparently unearthly realm and encounters with a mystical being, visible spirits of deceased or religious figures, and a barrier beyond which one cannot return to earthly life. A classic example of an NDE dominated by transcendental elements was recorded by the Swiss founder of analytic psychology, Carl Jung (1875–1961), who suffered a heart attack in 1944:

A short distance away I saw in space a tremendous dark block of stone, like a meteorite. It was about the size of my house, or even bigger. It was floating in space, and I myself was floating in space. I had seen similar stones on the coast of the Gulf of Bengal. They were blocks of tawny granite, and some of them had been hollowed out into temples. My stone was one such gigantic dark block. An entrance led into a small antechamber. To the right of the entrance, a black Hindu sat silently in lotus posture upon a stone bench. He wore a white gown, and I knew that he expected me. Two steps led up to this antechamber, and inside, on the left, was the gate to the temple. Innumerable tiny niches, each with a saucer-like concavity filled with coconut oil and small burning wicks, surrounded the door with a wreath of bright flames. . . .

From below, from the direction of Europe, an image floated up. It was my doctor, Dr. H. . . . As he stood before me, a mute exchange of thought took place between us. Dr. H. had been delegated by the earth to deliver a message to me, to tell me that there was a protest against my going away. I had no right to leave the earth and must return. The moment I heard that, the vision ceased. I was profoundly disappointed, for now . . . I was not to be allowed to enter the temple, to join the

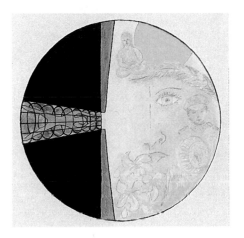

A young woman who survived a dreadful automobile accident—her brakes went out on wet pavement, causing the car to skid into several moving cars before crashing into the side of a large truck—attempted to visually re-create the experience she had on the brink of death. As she explained it, the left of the picture shows her life up until the time of the accident, confined by time and space. At the center of the drawing she reached "an opaque curtain of some kind," which she passed through into a vast, cosmic realm where she experienced unity with everything about her. "Every part of me . . . felt without question a far-reaching and encompassing continuum beyond what I had previously thought of as death. It was as though the force that had moved me toward death and then past it would endlessly continue to carry me, through ever-expanding vistas." It was at that point that her car struck the truck with great impact and she realized that "by some miracle" she was still alive. "As I sat in the midst of the tangled metal, I felt my individual boundaries begin to melt. I started to merge with everything around me."

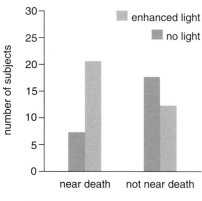

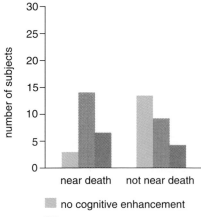

no cognitive enhancement

1–3 functions enhanced

4–7 functions enhanced

J.E. Owens, *et al.*, "Features of 'Near-Death Experience' . . . ," *Lancet*, vol. 336, no. 8724 (Nov. 10, 1990), pp. 1175–77

people in whose company I belonged. . . . Suddenly the terrifying thought came to me that Dr. H. would have to die in my stead. . . . In actual fact I was his last patient. On April 4, 1944—I still remember the exact date—I was allowed to sit up on the edge of my bed for the first time since the beginning of my illness, and on this same day Dr. H. took to his bed and did not leave it again. I heard that he was having intermittent attacks of fever. Soon afterward he died of septicemia.

Recent insights

These kinds of NDE have been reported by individuals who had been pronounced clinically dead but then were resuscitated, by individuals who actually died but were able to describe their experiences in their final moments, and by individuals who, in the course of accidents or illnesses, feared that they were near death. Initial scientific studies suggested that NDEs were not influenced by the manner in which one came close to death—or by the actual closeness to death. More recent research, however, indicates that physiological details of the close brush with death may play a role.

It appears, for example, that NDEs dominated by cognitive features, such as the loss of a sense of time, thought acceleration, and a life review, are far more common when the near-death event is sudden and unexpected than when it may have been anticipated. Furthermore, while all elements of the NDE have been reported by individuals who merely perceive themselves to be near death, certain features—such as an encounter with a brilliant light, enhanced cognitive function, and positive emotions—are significantly more common among individuals whose closeness to death can be corroborated (by medical records).

As a result of this experience, the near-death experiencer, or NDEr, is often permanently transformed in attitudes, beliefs, and values. Typical aftereffects of near-death experiences, reported by many independent researchers, include increases in spirituality, concern for others, and appreciation of life and decreases in fear of death, materialism, and competitiveness. NDErs tend to see themselves as integral parts of a benevolent and purposeful universe in which personal gain, particularly at another's expense, is no longer relevant. These profound changes in attitude and behavior have been corroborated in long-term studies of NDErs, in interviews with those closest to them, and in research comparing NDErs with survivors of close brushes with death who do not recall NDEs.

The past decade has seen an increase in both scientific exploration of NDEs and public awareness of these profound events. The International Association for Near-Death Studies, founded in 1981, sponsors annual professional conferences, publishes a scholarly journal, and promotes local support groups for NDErs and interested others throughout the United States, Canada, the United Kingdom, and several other countries.

Why study NDEs?

Why should scientists be interested in pursuing near-death experiences? If NDEs are regarded only as indications that people do survive bodily death—which most NDErs take them to be—then they may not in fact interest many scientists. As evidence of an afterlife, the NDE with its

unpredictable occurrence and subjective nature offers no advance over other presumed psychic phenomena that have been investigated for the past century. However, though they resemble other mystical experiences, NDEs differ in their pervasive and profound aftereffects, and scientists are gaining unique understanding of many facets of human experience from their study of the phenomenon.

One of the questions medical scientists are posing is: What causes some people to have NDEs when they come close to death, while the majority of people in similar circumstances do not have, or at least later do not remember having, such experiences? Because near-death research is in its infancy, scientists have yet to find variables that can predict who will have an NDE or what kind of NDE a person may have. Retrospective studies of those who have had such an experience have shown them to be psychologically healthy individuals, and neither age, gender, race, religion, nor religiosity seems to predispose them. Some studies have suggested that NDErs as a group tend to be good hypnotic subjects, remember their dreams more often than most people, and are adept at using mental imagery; they describe themselves as "intuitive" rather than "rational" and "feeling" individuals rather than "thinking" ones. It is not yet known, however, whether those traits are the results of having had an NDE or whether people who already have those characteristics are more prone to have NDEs when they come close to death.

Virtually every culture has left records of what are now recognized as near-death experiences. The interpretations of these events tend to vary according to cultural beliefs and practices, but the basic phenomena have far-reaching similarities. The Islamic view of paradise (above) is a place of joy and bliss to which faithful Muslims go according to the will of Allah—a vision that differs little from Judaic and Christian concepts of the life beyond.

53

One of the questions that medical scientists are trying to answer is why some people on the threshold of death have profoundly transfiguring experiences while others do not.

Product of the imagination?

Several hypotheses have been proposed to explain NDEs and their consistent features. A reasonable psychological explanation suggests that they are products of the imagination, constructed from people's personal and cultural expectations, that serve to protect them from facing the threat of death. However, empirical data do not support this theory. Cross-cultural studies do not show the expected variations in content of NDEs, and individuals often report experiences that conflict with their specific religious and personal expectations of the passage to death. Furthermore, people who had never heard of or read about NDEs describe the same kinds of experiences as do people who are familiar with the phenomenon, and the knowledge individuals had about NDEs previously does not seem to influence the details of their own experiences.

Another reason to question the above hypothesis is that children too young to have received substantial cultural and religious conditioning about death report the same kinds of NDEs as do adults. David Herzog, a child psychiatrist at Harvard Medical School and Massachusetts General Hospital, Boston, has published in the medical literature the case of a six-month-old girl who, following a close brush with death, appeared frightened and overwhelmed when encouraged by her siblings to crawl through a tunnel at a local department store. When she later learned to speak and was told of her grandmother's impending death, she spontaneously asked, "Will Grandma have to go through the tunnel at the store to get to see God?"

Several researchers have now published collections of childhood NDEs, including some reported to have occurred before the child had acquired any language skills. In fact, a case was published of an infant who was pronounced dead at birth, strangulated by her own umbilical cord, but who survived and then was haunted for years by recurring dreams of being drawn down a tunnel to a light at the far end. If such reports can be credited, they certainly cannot be attributed to the newborn's expectations of death.

Studies of children show that their NDEs follow the same basic patterns as do those of adults. They may experience a sense of well-being, peace, and painlessness; a separation from the physical body; a sense of being in a tunnel; and encounters with spiritual beings. While NDEs are recounted by a large proportion—in some studies, more than half—of children who survive critical illnesses, they are not recounted by children who suffer serious illnesses that are not potentially fatal. Interestingly, children generally do not report the life review that is common in adults, and they report meeting fewer deceased friends and relatives—two differences that might be expected from their brief experience with life.

Hallucinations?

Since NDErs report seeing and experiencing a reality that others around them cannot see or experience, some researchers have proposed that NDEs are elaborate hallucinations produced either by drugs given to dying patients or by metabolic disturbances or brain malfunctions as a person approaches death. Studies have shown, on the contrary, that dying patients who are given drugs report *fewer* and *briefer* NDEs than do patients who remain drug free. This finding may suggest that drugs, rather than causing NDEs, in fact prevent them from occurring, or it may suggest merely that patients who are drugged tend not to recall their experiences.

Many NDEs have been recounted by individuals who had no metabolic or organic malfunctions that might have caused hallucinations. Furthermore, organic brain malfunctions in general produce clouded thinking, irritability, fear, belligerence, and idiosyncratic visions—quite unlike the exceptionally clear thinking, peacefulness, calmness, and predictable content that typifies the NDE. Finally, patients who have experienced both hallucinations and NDEs generally discount the superficial similarities between the two and describe the "world" of the NDE as being "more real" than the physical realm—the physical realm being "more real" than the world of hallucinations.

Triggered by neurochemicals?

Several neurochemical models have been proposed for the NDE, invoking the role of endorphins (morphinelike proteins produced by the brain under stress) or various neurotransmitters (substances in the brain that transmit nerve impulses), and comparable neuroanatomic models have been suggested, linking the NDE to specific sites in the brain. Presently such models are not testable, but they offer the hope that scientists may someday bridge the gap between mystical experience and physiological events. While correlating the near-death experience with physical structures or chemicals in the brain would not necessarily reveal what *causes* the NDE, it would potentially make new tools and techniques available for investigating the mechanisms and aftereffects of these experiences.

Much yet to learn

The most promising aspects of NDEs for future research involve their role in personal transformation, as this is certainly the most easily measured and arguably the most important feature of the experience. As more is learned about the various kinds of NDE, correlating different types of experiences with their aftereffects may help identify the critical elements of the NDE. For example, preliminary studies suggest that atypical NDEs that are frightening or "hellish" rather than comforting and "heavenly" tend to be associated with greater physiological brain malfunction and with fewer profound aftereffects.

As neuroscientists develop more sophisticated tools for exploring brain chemistry and function, useful probes for identifying how the NDE effects such radical change will become available. Comparison of NDEs with other experiences that appear superficially similar—both mystical events and hallucinatory experiences—may yield insights into the meaning and mechanisms behind the NDE. Some investigators of human consciousness regard the NDE and its aftereffects as an example of psychospiritual evolution, which they see as accelerating in the contemporary world. Regardless of their orientation, however, most near-death researchers see the importance of near-death experiences not in their association with death but in their implications for life.

With continuing advances in medical technology, it is inevitable that more and more people will be snatched from the arms of death. The most promising lessons to be learned from future investigations of near-death experiences are likely to be those about life.

"Reunion of the Soul and the Body," engraving after Blake; photograph, Jean-Loup Charmet, Paris

THREE, FOUR, AND MORE

Multiple Births and Their Consequences

by Frances Price, Ph.D.

Temper tantrums times four are no laughing matter . . . running through the house like a wild pack, upsetting toy boxes, drawers of clothes, cupboards of food at a whim.

The thing I found was we were so busy caring for the triplets, we didn't find the time to enjoy it. The aim in the day was to get them to bed at night.

Around 2500 BC Ruddedet gave birth to the male triplets Userkaf, Sahure, and Kakai, all of whom survived to become pharaohs of the 5th dynasty of ancient Egypt. In 1934 quintuplets were born to Elzire and Oliva Dionne near Callander, Ontario. Inspiring excitement and curiosity around the world, these five identical girls, Émilie, Yvonne, Cécile, Marie, and Annette, were made wards of King George VI of England. However, this did not protect them from becoming a commercial peep show. Even before they reached the age of 10, they had been viewed from behind a one-way screen by some three million people.

To conceive, deliver, nurture, and care for triplets, quadruplets, quintuplets, or more—children of so-called higher order multiple births—is an extraordinary situation for any woman to confront. With only two breasts, two arms, two hands, and two knees, a human mother is not fashioned to breast-feed or knee bounce triplets, quadruplets, quintuplets, or more. Indeed, there are those who find this mismatch deeply disturbing. In the United Kingdom, as the Human Fertilisation and Embryology Bill moved through Parliament before it became law in 1990, one member of the House of Commons referred to "the awful problem of the birth of litters."

Faced with three, four, or more infants of the same pregnancy, how *do* parents cope? The very notion is beyond most people's grasp. Ruddedet was able to summon wet nurses to feed her triplets. And the Dionne quints lived in a seven-bedroom house built for the family by the Canadian government. But parents today do not generally have options of that sort.

When Patti Frustaci gave birth to septuplets in California on May 21, 1985, the image of her husband, Sam, hugging the obstetrician was transmitted around the world. "It's a neat experience. Family life is great," he proclaimed. The Frustaci family's ebullience, however, was not to last.

Frances Price, Ph.D., is Senior Research Associate, Child Care and Development Group, University of Cambridge, England.

(Opposite page) Triplets Jonathan, Nicholas, and Holly Cakebread celebrate their first birthday on the lawn of Bourn Hall, the Cambridge, England, clinic where they were conceived by in vitro fertilization.
Photograph, Nick Kelsh

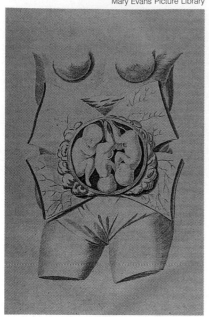

Triplet births have been recorded throughout human history. The drawing above showing a triplet gestation appeared in A Key to Physic, and the Occult Sciences *(1794), by the British physician and astrologer Ebenezer Sibly.*

How common are multiple births?

In humans three, four, five, six, seven, and more babies may be born of the same pregnancy. Sextuplets have sometimes all survived, but septuplets never have. Octuplets were born in Mexico City in 1967; none of the four boys and four girls, who were born prematurely, survived more than 14 hours. A case of nonuplets (nine) is probably the largest recorded multiple birth; an Australian woman gave birth to five boys and four girls in 1971. Two boys were stillborn; the remaining seven infants died within a week.

Pregnancies with more than three fetuses are rare, however. Around the turn of the century, the German statistician D. Hellin suggested a formula (known as Hellin's law) by which the incidence of higher order births in a given population could be calculated: if n is the incidence of twins in a population, n^2 is the incidence of triplets, n^3 is that of quadruplets, and so on. On this basis, for populations such as those in Europe and North America, where one set of twins is born once in about 100 deliveries, the incidence of triplets should be one in 10,000 and that of quadruplets one in one million.

Missing from Hellin's formulations, however, was any distinction between the incidence of different types of twins, triplets, quadruplets, and so forth. These children may arise from two, three, or more separate zygotes (each the product of the fertilization of one egg with one sperm), from a single zygote that divides, or from a combination of the two. The Dionne quintuplets, for example, were shown to be a one-zygote set.

Very little is known about the reasons separation occurs within a single zygote, but separation into two (a monozygotic, or identical, pair) is remarkably constant in all human populations at about 3.5 deliveries per 1,000; this is in contrast to the marked variations around the world in twins, triplets, and larger births that arise from the fertilization of separate eggs (dizygotic, trizygotic, or higher order zygosity, or nonidentical sets). Rates of nonidentical twinning are particularly high in parts of Africa such as Nigeria and particularly low in Japan. There may well be a genetic predisposition to multiple ovulation, which perhaps is modified by environmental factors. Also, the likelihood of a woman's having a nonidentical multiple birth increases both with advancing age, peaking in the late thirties, and with the number of children she has previously borne (parity)—the more children, the higher her chances.

New horizons in human conception

What is of far greater significance in considering the incidence of multiple births, however, is the unpredictable impact of developments in the medical management of infertility since the mid-1960s—in particular, the rapid rise in the number of triplet and higher order births around the world. In England and Wales 183 sets of triplets, 11 sets of quadruplets, and 1 set of quintuplets were born in 1989, compared with 70 sets of triplets and 6 sets of quadruplets in 1982—28.6 multiple sets per 100,000 deliveries in 1989, compared with 12.2 per 100,000 in 1982.

Human reproduction is remarkably inefficient, but despite this, most women who attempt to conceive do so within a year. Usually in a woman's

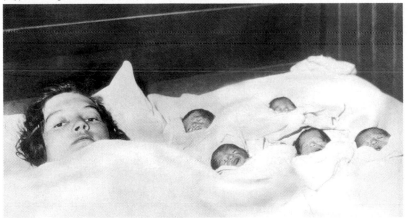

On May 28, 1934, several decades before the introduction of fertility drugs, Elzire Dionne, a simple, religious woman near Callander, Ontario, gave birth to five identical girls, who had developed from a single zygote. Elzire had had six children already—all delivered in the same wooden bed at home. The "miracle" of the quintuplets' birth, as their mother viewed it, brought the Dionnes instant international fame. (Bottom) In 1946, at age 12 (left to right), Annette, Yvonne, Marie, Émilie, and Cécile were quite a handful for father, Oliva Dionne. Émilie died at age 20 during an epileptic seizure, and Marie died at 36 from a blood clot; Annette, Marie, and Cécile are still living in Canada.

monthly ovulatory cycle, a dominant single egg develops in one of her two ovaries. This egg grows in a fluid-filled cyst (a follicle) until it is mature. During ovulation it bursts from the follicle and passes into one of her fallopian tubes. The developing follicle, which is visible on ultrasound scans, goes on to produce hormones that are detectable in the woman's body.

Usually, if conception is to take place, sperm meet the egg in the woman's fallopian tube. If fertilization results, an early embryo is formed, which travels down the fallopian tube to the uterus (womb). If the embryo implants in the wall of the womb, a pregnancy is established. If two eggs are released and fertilized, or if a released, fertilized egg divides, a twin pregnancy results.

Fertility drugs. The recent and dramatic increase in the number of triplets and larger births is to a great extent a consequence of the use of so-called fertility drugs. When ovulation is induced by the use of certain drugs, the likelihood of such a birth is magnified.

Some infertility problems arise as a consequence of a failure to ovulate. The drugs that are in wide clinical use are very likely to stimulate multiple ovulation; more than one ovarian follicle develops and ruptures, and a

59

The ways that triplets and quadruplets can be produced are shown at right. The possibilities for producing quintuplets range from all five being identical, i.e., a one-egg set (as the Dionnes were), to all being fraternal (five eggs), with various combinations of identicals and fraternals in two-egg, three-egg, and four-egg sets in between.

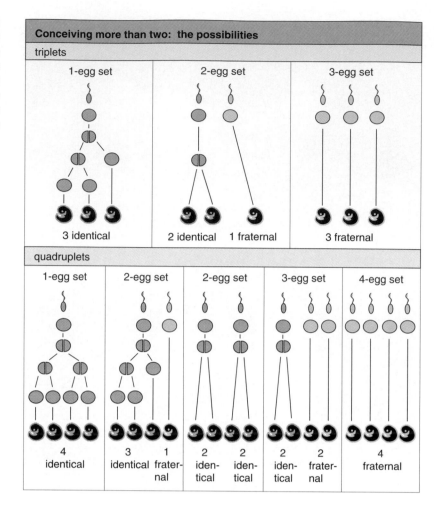

number of eggs are released. If two or more are fertilized, a multiple pregnancy is then possible. In studies published between 1953 and 1976, rates of multiple ovulation after induction of ovulation by gonadotropins (hormones that stimulate the ovaries) were reported as ranging between 18 and 53.3%. One study, published in 1970, reported 78 pregnancies after ovulation induction—47 singleton, 23 twin, 5 triplet, 2 quadruplet, and 1 sextuplet births, giving a multiple-birth rate of 39.7%.

One ovarian stimulant that has been in use for about a quarter of a century is the drug clomiphene citrate (Clomid; Serophene). The manufacturer of Clomid states that the drug is associated with a 6–8% risk of a multiple pregnancy. Other reports have found the risk to be about 10% for twins and less than 1% for triplets or more. Another drug in frequent use is human menopausal gonadotropin, or hMG (Pergonal). This drug is given in conjunction with human chorionic gonadotropin (hCG) and is said to be associated with a 15% risk of having a twin pregnancy and a 5% risk of conceiving three or more fetuses. Refinements in gonadotropin administration—utilizing improved hormone monitoring by rapid assay methods and high-resolution ovarian ultrasound scanning—may have lowered the risk of a multiple pregnancy somewhat, but the difficulty of controlling the number of follicles that develop in response to this and other ovulation-inducing drugs and the consequent risk of such a pregnancy remain.

Several well-publicized "grand multiple" births and deaths have promoted public awareness that the acceptance of certain forms of medical assistance in the quest for a pregnancy may have untoward consequences. Widespread publicity was given to the aforementioned Frustacis and their septuplets in 1985. Following the birth of their first child, conceived after Patti Frustaci had taken a fertility drug, the couple sought medical assistance for a second time. Her septuplet pregnancy followed a course of Pergonal. One septuplet was stillborn, three died within 19 days, and the three survivors—one girl and two boys—were to suffer from impaired vision, hernias, chronic lung damage, and developmental delay; the two boys also had heart damage. Soon after the birth of their seven babies, the parents instigated malpractice litigation on the grounds that the Pergonal dosage was too high and the obstetric monitoring by ultrasonography inadequate. (The suit was settled out of court in July 1990, with the fertility clinic agreeing to pay the Frustacis $450,000 and give the three surviving children monthly payments. The total award could be more than $6 million.)

Two years later, in 1987, Susan Halton gave birth to septuplets in Liverpool, England. No child lived longer than 16 days. A simple headstone in a cemetery in Merseyside, England, records the date of death of each child. The birth and early death, despite intensive neonatal care, of all the Halton septuplets created intense public and professional consternation. Both tragedies served to heighten the professional concern that induction of ovulation is not always monitored adequately.

Multiple egg and embryo transfer. A more recent concern is the rate of multiple pregnancies after doctors have transferred several eggs or embryos in assisted-conception techniques such as *in vitro* fertilization (IVF) and gamete intrafallopian transfer (GIFT). IVF is the method pioneered in England by Robert Edwards and the late Patrick Steptoe, which resulted in the birth of the first "test-tube baby," Louise Joy Brown, on July 25, 1978. Since then, more than 15,000 babies have been born worldwide by the IVF method. In IVF, eggs are removed from a woman's ovaries and mixed with sperm. This is done in a laboratory under special conditions intended to help fertilization take place. Fertilized eggs are allowed to develop into early embryos and are later transferred to the woman's womb in the attempt to establish a pregnancy. In the GIFT method, eggs are removed from the woman's ovaries, just as they are in IVF, but then are placed together with sperm in her fallopian tubes so that fertilization, if it occurs, takes place inside her body.

Many clinics practicing IVF and GIFT have achieved high rates of both egg recovery and fertilization. Although early development of such embryos is satisfactory, the rates of implantation remain low. The vigor of research and the considerable publicity surrounding births following IVF and GIFT belie the low success rate in establishing clinical pregnancies.

New combinations of ovulatory drugs and an ultrasound-guided retrieval procedure that enables better access to ovarian follicles have resulted in the collection of larger numbers of eggs. In the early 1980s fertility special-

ists asserted that pregnancy rates with IVF would be higher if the number of embryos transferred in each procedure were increased. By the mid-1980s pooled reports from IVF centers throughout the world supported such predictions and encouraged the transfer of three, four, five, or six embryos in clinical practice; concern about the marked increase in multiple pregnancies came later. Because a greater-than-expected frequency of identical twins has also been observed after the induction of ovulation with drugs and after IVF, the transfer of three eggs or embryos can result in a quadruplet or perhaps even a higher order pregnancy.

Annual statistics from the U.K. show a clear association between the rise of multiple births after 1985 and the increased use of IVF, GIFT, and associated procedures. Britain's Medical Research Council Working Party on Children Conceived by In Vitro Fertilisation reported that 23% of deliveries following assisted conception resulted in a multiple birth of twins or more, compared with about 1% for natural conceptions.

In Australia and New Zealand in 1988, six or more eggs were collected in almost half of all IVF treatment cycles in which a pregnancy was established. Almost 80% of pregnancies after IVF in that year occurred after the transfer of three or more embryos. Triplet births in the two countries occurred in 3.9, 5.2, and 5.9% of pregnancies after the transfer of three, four, and five embryos, respectively.

In 1986 British neonatal specialists began to voice their concern about the consequences of multiple births. Since 1987, the guidelines established by the Interim Licensing Authority for Human In Vitro Fertilisation and Embryology (ILA) have recommended that no more than three eggs or embryos be transferred in any one cycle unless there are exceptional clinical reasons.

Anxieties about higher order multiple births as an outcome after transfer of four or more embryos were also being voiced by Australian fertility specialists. Consequently, Australia's Reproductive Technology Accreditation Committee recommended late in 1988 that no more than three embryos be transferred in a treatment cycle.

Clinical practice is varied. In the U.K. in 1988, the majority of ILA-licensed clinics reported having restricted the number of embryos transferred to three; however, one large clinic transferred four embryos in over 60% of cases. In 1991 at least two licensed fertility centers in Great Britain were routinely transferring no more than two embryos per cycle when more than two embryos were available. One center reported that it utilizes the woman's natural cycle with the intention of retrieving a single mature egg and subsequently transferring a single embryo without the use of ovulatory drugs. What constitutes "good practice" in the field of infertility medicine turns, to a great extent, on the subjective evaluations of acknowledged clinical risks.

A British study

Little has been known about the coping strategies of parents of triplets, quadruplets, and more or about the extent to which they can elicit support and help from friends, relatives, and outside agencies. In the late 1980s, as the rise in the numbers of multiple births became more marked in national registration data and pediatricians increasingly gave voice to their anxieties about the health consequences for the babies, the British Department of Health saw the need to look into these concerns. A study was undertaken, called the United Kingdom Study of Triplets and Higher Order Births (or simply, the National Study). It was the first investigation in the world to look at the multiple problems encountered by those who care for the children of higher order births.

Three complementary surveys were done. In two of them information was collected from the doctors concerned with 313 sets of triplets and 27 sets of quadruplets, quintuplets, or sextuplets born in the early to mid-1980s. Surveys of obstetricians, pediatricians, other specialists, and family doctors were conducted jointly by the Office of Population Censuses and Surveys in London and the National Perinatal Epidemiology Unit in Oxford.

The rates of twins that result from fertilization of separate eggs (dizygotic, or fraternal, twins) are highly variable among populations. The Yoruba of western Nigeria (opposite page, top) have the world's highest rate of nonidentical twins— accounting for 3% of Yoruban births. Certain populations may have a genetic predisposition to multiple ovulation; it is also speculated that environmental factors may play a part. Recently, scientists have attributed the unusual Yoruban phenomenon to the consumption of yams—a staple in their diet. The vegetable contains a substance that is chemically similar to the female hormone estrogen and may encourage the production of follicle-stimulating hormone, causing the release of more than one egg at a time. In the U.S. there are well over two million sets of twins (identical and fraternal), and an estimated 35,000 new sets are born each year. (Opposite page, bottom left) Twins celebrate their twinship at an annual festival in Twinsburg, Ohio. A formula known as Hellin's law is used to calculate the expected number of multiple births in a population. The number of triplet sets is determined by squaring the number of twin sets ($n =$ twins; $n^2 =$ triplets). (Opposite page, bottom right) The three identical nine-year-old beauties (left to right) are Arlene, Bernice, and Cindy Torres from East Harlem, New York. (Above, left) Pictured on the momentous occasion of their second birthday are the nonidentical Walton girls of Liverpool, England (from left to right): Jenny, Hannah, Lucy, Sarah, Ruth, and Kate, who are believed to be the world's only one-sex sextuplets; the chance of such an occurrence is estimated to be about one in a zillion.

The recent dramatic increase in the number of higher order births in England and Wales is a direct result of advances in the medical management of infertility. Similar high rates are occurring in the U.S., Australia, and many Western European countries where fertility drugs and assisted-conception techniques are widely used. Several well-publicized "grand multiple" births have promoted public awareness that such treatments, which women may undergo in the desperate quest for a pregnancy, can have devastating consequences.

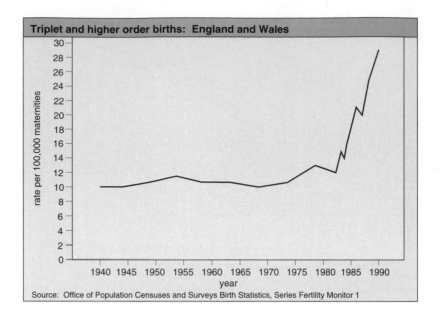

Triplet and higher order births: England and Wales

rate per 100,000 maternities

year

Source: Office of Population Censuses and Surveys Birth Statistics, Series Fertility Monitor 1

The University of Cambridge's Child Care and Development Group sought information from the parents of the "multiples" (the Parents' Study).

Surprise! Some parents did not know until delivery how many babies the mother was carrying. Even with ultrasonography, triplets, quadruplets, and sometimes even quintuplets can come as a complete surprise. One woman who gave birth to quintuplets had been told that her ultrasound scan showed "a lot of arms and legs, two babies or possibly three."

Over half of the women with triplet pregnancies knew that triplets were expected by or during the 16th week of their pregnancy, and over a third

Father Sam Frustaci of Riverside, California, watches as a neonatal nurse tends Baby A (later named Patricia Ann), the firstborn of the septuplets delivered by mother Patti on May 21, 1985. The seven infants, conceived after Patti took the fertility drug Pergonal, were born 12 weeks early; the last was stillborn, and the rest suffered from many complications of prematurity and low birth weight (each weighed less than 0.9 kilogram [2 pounds]). The Frustacis sued the doctor and clinic for use of "excessive and inappropriate dosages" of drugs and for inadequate monitoring of Patti's progress.

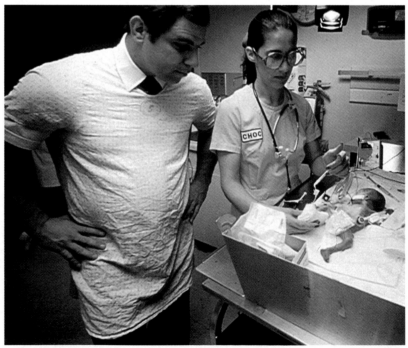

Celebrating their third birthday, Stephen Earl, Patricia Ann, and Richard Charles Frustaci (seated left to right) sample their cake, with older brother Joseph looking on. All three surviving septuplets suffer from developmental delay and assorted impairments and health problems.

had been diagnosed by or during the 12th week. However, nearly one-quarter did not know until beyond the 20th week, and 11 women did not discover that they were carrying three babies until the time of the delivery. Those who had been scanned several times without any hint of more than two babies were shocked to deliver triplets instead of the twins they had been led to expect.

A surprised mother of four gave this account:

I was told throughout my pregnancy that I was expecting triplets. Right up until the previous day to delivery no one mentioned the possibility of more. When I went into hospital (on that day) they took an X-ray—but still couldn't decide, but I gave birth the next morning and therefore settled the argument!

Infant status. The National Study found that triplets and quadruplets are more likely than single babies to be of low birth weight and to be born prematurely, with all the associated neonatal difficulties as well as increased risks of disability and continuing developmental problems. Over half of the quadruplets and just over a quarter of the triplets weighed under 1,500 grams (3.3 pounds) at birth. Births occurred before 32 weeks' gestation (at least one month prematurely) in about half the quadruplet or higher order births and a quarter of the triplets. By contrast, during the same time period only 1% of singletons and fewer than 10% of twins were born before 32 weeks. Furthermore, the National Study surveys indicated that 28% of the triplets and 62% of the quadruplets spent a month or more in neonatal intensive care.

With advances in the past two decades in neonatal medicine, more triplets, quadruplets, and quintuplets now survive. Their mortality rates, however, have not fallen to the same extent as have those for single births. Figures for England and Wales suggest that their risk of stillbirth is about six times that for singletons, and the risk of death in the first year is about 10 times higher.

It is now possible to retrieve large numbers of eggs from a woman's ovarian follicles, and many fertility clinics have made it standard practice to transfer three, four, five, or even six eggs or embryos at once. Assisted-conception techniques that all too frequently result in multiple pregnancies are shown at right.

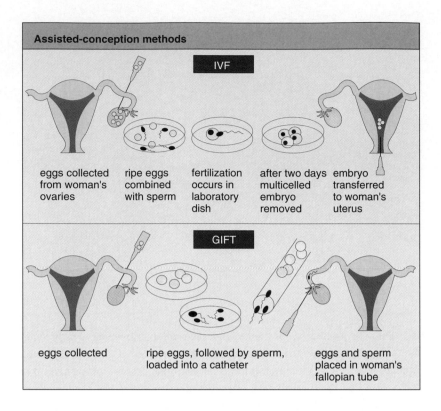

Assisted-conception methods

IVF

eggs collected from woman's ovaries

ripe eggs combined with sperm

fertilization occurs in laboratory dish

after two days multicelled embryo removed

embryo transferred to woman's uterus

GIFT

eggs collected

ripe eggs, followed by sperm, loaded into a catheter

eggs and sperm placed in woman's fallopian tube

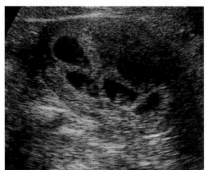

A first-trimester ultrasound scan shows a mother-to-be's four gestational sacs; fetuses are not seen in uppermost and lowermost sacs because they are outside the plane of the ultrasound beam. The pregnancy was the result of a fertility drug. How did the mother feel when she learned she was carrying quadruplets? "Scared."

Courtesy of Rudy Sabbagha, M.D.

Compared with singletons, triplets and higher order birth children have a higher rate of serious congenital malformations. Malformations of the central nervous system and of the cardiovascular system are about twice as common among multiple birth children as among singletons. Complications of prematurity and of uteroplacental insufficiency—a lack of adequate nourishment and space to develop within the womb for all the fetuses—are the main contributors to perinatal morbidity and mortality. These children are at an increased risk for cerebral palsy, particularly spastic diplegia, eye disorders (*e.g.,* crossed eyes), pyloric stenosis (obstruction of the opening of the stomach, causing serious digestive problems and often requiring surgery), and repeated hospital admissions.

A taxing situation in every respect. The National Study showed that multiple birth children are, in all senses, high cost. The average cost for parents to feed and clothe triplets in the first year was £6,000 ($11,350). There were also entirely unexpected cash outlays for nannies, bigger cars, and washing machine replacements. The study did not collect data directly on family income, but some households were definitely crippled by the costs, particularly when their situation was compounded by the husband's unemployment or some other adverse circumstance. Some had their houses repossessed by a mortgage company. Others had to take lower paid jobs or alternative employment because they could not function properly in the jobs that they had before the babies were born.

The difficulties presented by the child-care situation are not only financial but also practical and emotional. The parents soon discover that relationships ordinarily taken for granted and usual priorities are difficult, if not im-

66

possible, to sustain. The very infrequency of three, four, or five babies born of the same delivery creates an exasperating additional burden for the parents. There are no norms or guidelines on appropriate parenting for them to follow; thus, to behave "as normal" may be distressingly inappropriate.

When asked about the experience of caring for triplets, quadruplets, and quintuplets, the parents described the literally endless everyday tasks, the difficulties of getting out and of maintaining relationships beyond the home, and the sheer exhaustion exacerbated by insufficient sleep. They described situations where there was not enough time, space, or authoritative advice—not to mention an adequate number of hands.

Housing problems. At the time of diagnosis, some parents-to-be were living in one- or two-bedroom accommodations or living with their parents or in-laws. The study questionnaire did not directly cover the issue of living space, but multiple birth parents spoke of confined space as an issue of great consequence. Existing space was managed, often with great ingenuity, with furniture and mattresses maneuvered around. The financial costs of home moves and of building additions were substantial and inevitably involved the households' being thrown into turmoil.

The number of bedrooms was just one important issue in the decision to move or to add on to the home. Space and privacy were sometimes sacrificed in an effort to get help from relatives. One woman reported that she and her husband and triplets had moved in with her parents to secure their help with child care. A family with quadruplets reported moving to a smaller house to be near the maternal grandmother, who was a main source of help. Yet this situation was far from ideal:

Confined space is a real problem, particularly bedroom- and playroom-wise. The four sleep in one bedroom, and apart from the obviously cramped arrangements for sleeping (two in a bed) . . . they obviously create discipline problems as they keep each other awake. . . . It's far more exciting to run riot in a bedroom (and acting

AP/Wide World

In February 1990 the seven year old Chikaraishi quintuplets from Chicago (left to right), Jami, Ben, Kristi, Juli, and Kari, helped introduce Tyco Toys' new line of dolls, the "Quints." A vast array of accessories, including diapers, bottles, a rocking horse for five, and a five-room house, can be purchased along with the three-girl, two-boy doll sets. An article in the New York Times *announcing "the birth of Quints" described the dolls as quite like the real thing—"a housekeeping nightmare." Nonetheless, the dolls were reported to be "doing fine," with sales totaling $20 million in the first 10 months.*

together, they have the confidence to do it) than to settle down to sleep. And if there simply is nowhere else to put them to sleep this problem can continue for a long time.

Obstacles to getting around. It was learned that mothers of multiples risk becoming isolated and housebound, particularly in the first two years. Transportation difficulties were an impediment to outings. It was not only those who could not drive or who had no access to a car who became housebound. Some accommodations (in a high-rise flat, for instance) were totally unsuitable; one mother of triplets found that she just could not use the elevator and was therefore marooned day after day in her third-floor flat. The experience of prolonged isolation had many consequences. Mothers spoke of feeling at times that they had lost their sense of control over their own lives. Several spoke in interviews of their loss of identity except as "the mother of the quads" or triplets. Some described how their sense of self-esteem was worn down:

Mother: I mean I wasn't able to go to the dentist, go to the optician, go and have my hair cut. My husband couldn't take time off work for me to do that.
Interviewer: So how did you cope with that?
Mother: I just didn't do it.

Physically transporting the infants was itself a great challenge to the ingenuity of the mothers. In the early months some mothers managed to transport their triplets in one pram. One mother struggled alone with two of her triplets in a twin pram and one in a single pram until the children were eight months old. Frequent complications with unwieldy pushchairs were reported, as was the difficulty of clamping two or more together. Buggies for three were sometimes available, but often they were too wide for sidewalks and shop entrances. Most triplet mothers had used a double and a single pushchair, and most mothers of quads used two double pushchairs. Only two mothers mentioned sometimes using slings for their triplets.

Mexican parents María and Baldemar Chávez thought it was time to give their four-year-old daughter, Valeria, a little brother or sister. They gave her a lot more than that! The parents were expecting twins, but on May 23, 1988, five weeks earlier than expected, María delivered two girls and three boys. The quintuplets were not the result of fertility treatment. To accommodate the suddenly big household, the Chavezes moved to Texas to the larger home of a grandmother; they needed not only more space but more hands. Despite the fact that every new day brought another 35 meals to bottle-serve and 48 diapers to change—not to mention baths to give, temper tantrums to quell, tears to dry, and kisses to distribute—María insisted that she was the happiest of mothers.

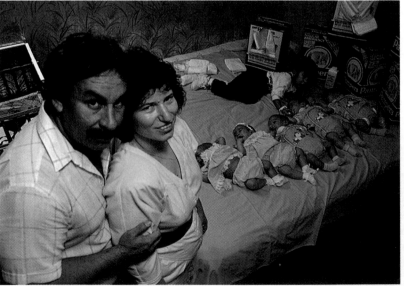

Help wanted. Rarely in such circumstances is it obvious who can be turned to for help, regularly and reliably—that is, to provide enough time at the time it is most needed: at night, at the babies' feeding times, when they are bathed, at their bedtime, and at the times one parent or the other wants to get out of the house or to be released from sole responsibility for the children. Where the responsibility for the children is shared, the dynamics of the relations between carers and the continuity of quality care are of crucial importance for the well-being of all concerned.

Most of the mothers in the Parents' Study had at least one relative on whom they relied for support and practical help in the crucial early months at home with their babies. Few relatives could provide sustained support beyond this time. Relatives were not always able, or willing, to help. More than half of the parents reported that their relatives had difficulty providing assistance because of their age, infirmity, distance, or lack of transportation. In addition, fewer than half of the parents reported that they had one or more friend or neighbor who had provided regular support and practical help during the first year. About a third of the parents had *no* help from relatives, friends, or neighbors in the first year after the birth.

Problems at schooltime. By no means did the problems end when the children went to school. Although most of the children from triplet and higher order births had some experience in a play group or nursery school, many had little experience of separation from each other. Some of them were markedly dependent on each other; at the time of their entry into school, this posed a problem for their teachers, who were unlikely to have experience in dealing with triplets or more. The issue of whether, and at which stage, it is preferable to put the children into separate classes is important but unresolved. Furthermore, a number of the parents expressed the view that the teachers at their children's school did not readily appreciate the situation that they (the parents) confronted—the sheer impact of attending to, caring for, and stimulating three or more youngsters of the same age.

Parents of multiple birth children are unlikely to be any less concerned or active than are parents of singletons in promoting the welfare and optimum development of all their children. But their circumstances are significantly different. There are three, four, or more same-age, language-learning youngsters all clamoring for adult attention. Taking turns is something that has to be developed over the years. The situation is not comparable to one in which there are one adult and one child or one adult and several children of different ages. Not surprisingly, parents reported how stressful it was to attempt to provide each child with individual attention, particularly when one or more of the children had special needs or required sustained extra help.

Impact of caring: parents' health and well-being. The impact on adult health of caring for triplets, quads, or quints is important in its own right. Physical and psychological ill health profoundly complicates parenting and may have long-term consequences for all relationships in the household.

It was evident in written questionnaires that parents glossed over their own health problems. But it became clear in interviews that not only were

The cost for quints	in British pounds
prams, 2 double, 1 single	700
padding for prams (5)	100
babies' bedroom furniture	300
5 cots and mattresses	600
lampshades (2)	20
curtains (2)	30
changing mats (2)	8
potties (2)	12
various toys; e.g., mobiles, teddy bears	60
sterilizers	30
bottles	20
clothes (socks, sleepsuits, etc.)	200
pacifiers	2
decorating of children's rooms	120
carpets for children's rooms	150
highchairs (5)	200
travel to and from hospital while babies were in special care unit	80
bouncing cradles (5)	50
carrying nests (5)	40
duvets (5)	50
sheets for cots (10)	50
pillowcases (10)	10
safety pillows (5)	30
duvet covers (10)	100
cot bumpers (5)	40
plastic sheets (10)	10
baby alarms (2)	40
bottle warmers (5)	50
baby baths (2) plus stands	30
nappy bill for the first two years	3,000
total	£6,132 ($9,934)

British parents of quintuplets born in 1987 drew up a rough list of what was needed for their five babies and estimated their initial cash outlay.

High risk and high cost		
	days in NICU	cost (calculated at $1,000 per day)
singletons	36	36,000
twins	4,168	4,168,000
triplets	20,015	20,015,000
quadruplets	26,300	26,300,000

Source: Louis Keith, M.D., Northwestern University; Emile Papiernik, M.D., University of Paris; and Barbara Luke, Sc.D., Johns Hopkins School of Medicine

Increasingly, clinicians are viewing multiple births as a calamity for all concerned. The recent United Kingdom Study of Triplets and Higher Order Births found that triplets and quadruplets are considerably more likely than single babies to require care in a neonatal intensive care unit (NICU) for a month or more. The need and cost for NICU days per 1,000 live births for singletons, twins, triplets, and quadruplets based on the collective experience of three hospitals (in Chicago; Baltimore, Maryland; and Paris) are shown above. Not surprisingly, many doctors are now urging that all possible steps be taken to ensure that multiple pregnancies are avoided.

ill health and chronic depression underreported in the first year but so were accidental injuries. It was learned that at least two fathers fell down flights of stairs while carrying one or more of their triplets, with resultant injury to all of them. Indeed, injuries to parents such as limb fractures and cuts requiring hospital treatment were not uncommon. The combined efforts of three or four toddlers can be remarkable. They can push down safety gates, trundle heavy furniture in front of fireplaces, and initiate injury-provoking "team" ventures unimaginable to those whose only experience is of singleton children.

In interviews strong adjectives like *terrible* and *dreadful* were used in the accounts of parents' health status. Stress-related disorders, back problems from "lifting them all the time," frequent infections, total exhaustion, and depressive conditions of varying degrees of severity predominated. "Both permanently tired," reported one couple. Another noted, "We were both very run down and seemed to pick up any bug that was around." And one mother summarized her health as follows: "Started with rheumatoid arthritis due to exhaustion. Gastric stomach. Depression (related to stress)."

For many mothers, however, there was no time to deal with their own stress-related problems. It was a case of attempting to control their worries and of struggling on regardless:

You reach a point where you no longer worry. You just think "I cannot worry any more. I'm just going to take things how they come and just muddle through the best I can." Because that's all one can do. You know, you could easily have a nervous breakdown if you started worrying too much.

People were always . . . saying: "Gosh, you are amazing . . . I don't know how you do it." And a lot of people say: "How do you cope?" and I say: "Because I have no choice. Absolutely no choice. You either go under a bus or you cope, one or the other."

Nonetheless, for some, matters did become "too much." Mothers and fathers described, sometimes in harrowing detail, reaching or approaching the breaking point. One consequence of coping with the work and strain of triplets or more was that relationships broke down. Several mothers recounted how in the first few years their relationships with their husbands and with others came under great stress. There was frequent quarreling, and in a few cases a partner left or the marriage broke up. Most partnerships survived, however, and several couples reported that in the joint struggle to cope with their circumstances and to provide the best possible care for the children their relationship had been strengthened, although there was considerable turbulence along the way.

Many unresolved problems. One of the National Study's aims was to gather more information about the problems encountered by parents of triplets and higher order birth children and to suggest how the support given to these families by health authorities, social services departments, and voluntary agencies might be better targeted. More than anything else, the study made it quite clear that having more than two babies at once is not a merry situation. Another aim was to determine how the doctors involved viewed higher order births. The surveys emphasized the frequency and serious nature of the children's medical problems; the high perinatal

70

mortality rates; the strain placed on available neonatal intensive care units; the extraordinary costs for the medical care, food, and clothing for the infants; and the constant struggles and hardships faced by the parents and others involved in the children's care. All this leads to the question: What solutions are there?

Tailoring multiparity: a controversial option

A woman diagnosed as having a multiple pregnancy can continue the pregnancy and confront not only the possible medical complications for herself and the probable prematurity of her babies but also all the ensuing consequences of bringing up so many children born of the same delivery. Alternatively, she can ask to have the pregnancy terminated. In recent years, with advances in ultrasonography and fetal surgery, a third option has become available. This involves a medical intervention in the first trimester to stop the development of some fetuses in the womb in the hope that the outcome for the survivors will be improved. This procedure is known as "selective feticide," "selective birth," or, more recently, "selective reduction."

The usual procedure involves a lethal injection of potassium chloride into the heart of one or more of the fetuses. Although the practice is not widespread, it has been employed in the United States and the United Kingdom for more than a decade following the prenatal diagnosis of a severe abnormality or genetic anomaly in one of a pair of twins. In such cases the abnormal twin is sacrificed, usually some time after the fourth month of pregnancy, with the hope that the surviving twin will flourish.

The use of the procedure on the grounds of number instead of abnormality is more recent. The first published report of selective reduction in a higher order multiple pregnancy was in 1986; a quintuplet gestation in The Netherlands was reduced to a twin gestation, which continued to term, with normal, spontaneous labor, and resulted in the birth of two healthy girls. Other selective reductions have been reported subsequently in the U.K., France, Australia, West Germany, and the U.S.—all justified on the grounds of the number, not the abnormality, of the fetuses. The surviving three

Most people cannot begin to imagine what it is like to care for and support triplets or more. Parents of higher order birth children find that there are no norms or guidelines for them to follow. They describe the literally endless everyday tasks and the sheer exhaustion, inevitably exacerbated by insufficient sleep. Mothers report how hard it is just to get out of the house and how their ingenuity is constantly challenged by simply trying to transport their infants. When they do get out, they find they are a constant spectacle; one mother said that curious onlookers made her feel "a bit of a freak."

Illustration by Kate Charlesworth

fetuses in a selective reduction case reported in West Germany involving 12 fetuses were delivered at 34 weeks' gestation.

The clinical advantages of fetal reduction under various circumstances have been discussed in the medical literature and, to an extent, so have the ethical issues. Inevitably, legal questions regarding abortion have arisen. What is entirely absent is a rigorous study of those who have undergone the procedure. Although the pregnant woman involved may accept the option with relief, later she may experience guilt and bereavement. No one has yet explored the potential psychological and social complications for the mother and the surviving infants.

Nor is there any record of the number of selective reductions undertaken each year in the management of multiple pregnancy. Where legal uncertainties are involved, obstetricians are understandably wary. In some countries it is difficult to find a physician who will undertake the procedure. In the United Kingdom the Human Fertilisation and Embryology Act of 1990 brought selective reduction under the Abortion Act of 1967. At least one British center is currently prepared to offer this operation to women who request it even if they are not already under its care, and a handful have stated that they would be prepared to consider performing the technique on patients who have been in care at their facilities. In France, by comparison, several infertility clinics make selective reduction routinely available to women with triplet or higher order pregnancies.

Fertility medicine: a Pandora's box

There are now increasing numbers of clinicians who regard multiple pregnancies as a disaster for all concerned, besides spelling trouble for hospital neonatal intensive care units. Views differ, however, about good practice in this burgeoning field of fertility medicine. Questions about how many embryos and eggs to transfer in assisted-conception procedures and about selective reduction on the basis of number remain at the forefront of the controversy. Some clinicians regard both these contested zones as matters solely for clinical judgment. Some, however, see the issues as having a social significance that extends beyond the confines of the doctor-patient relationship.

The services available in clinics that treat infertility have posed challenges to accepted notions of motherhood and fatherhood. Some would say that they have opened up a Pandora's box. It is of concern that people seeking the sophisticated infertility services that are now available may be leaping into something for which they are in no way prepared. In fact, for some couples, at least initially, the idea of a multiple pregnancy may even seem attractive after years of infertility. But it is important that prospective parents have the chance to make informed reproductive decisions and to envisage the possible consequences for their lives. And here lies the dilemma. Because the transfer of three or four embryos or eggs in IVF and GIFT is believed to offer the best chance of a pregnancy, it is now regarded as the "normal" practice internationally. This is true even for a fertile woman who has an infertile partner or one who is undergoing IVF as a surrogate mother.

72

The Pisner quintuplets were born to parents Pam and Dan of Olney, Maryland, on June 21, 1983. Pictured before their first birthday, they are: Elliot (nicknamed "Googie"), Ian ("Popeye"), Devin ("Devil"), Michael ("Our Little Spitter-Upper"), and Shira ("Minnie Mouse"). Dan, who was unemployed at the time of the delivery, took on the daytime job of caring for the babies while Pam went back to work. And what a job he had! "You truly can't watch them carefully enough—and you can't focus your attention in five directions. It's nuts." On the surface, at least, Dan kept a sense of humor through the daily ordeals. In his words, "There is no time of day when it's not a zoo. . . . The telephone rings, the baby puts the cord in the applesauce, and I talk into a dirty diaper."

Should there be moves toward international guidelines on egg and embryo transfers? There are now data from at least two of the larger assisted-conception centers in the United Kingdom that demonstrate that pregnancy rates are just as high when the number of embryos transferred is limited to two (when more than two are available). There are also developments in alternatives to drug-stimulated IVF—in particular the close monitoring of the hormonal fluctuations within a woman's natural menstrual cycle and the retrieval of a single mature egg.

The question "Are the risks of high multiparity justified?" is one that many ethicists and social scientists now believe should be pursued beyond the clinical discussions about individual cases. The social context and social consequences of higher order multiple births must be taken into account. In fact, developments in the future may even result in women and men who appear to have risked a triplet or higher order pregnancy being charged with irresponsibility.

Elzire Dionne considered the natural birth of her quintuplets a "miracle"—and so did much of the world. There is no question that for some couples the modern means of achieving pregnancy are a boon, but recent experience of parents who have had to cope with children of multiple pregnancies has made plain the extent and magnitude of the difficulties. Today those who undergo fertility treatment and conceive triplets, quadruplets, quintuplets, or more are likely to be devastated by the news. Moreover, sources of help, in practice, are unlikely to be readily available. Many clinicians are now urging that all possible steps be taken to ensure that the risk of such a pregnancy is avoided.

Depression in Perspective

by Richard M. Glass, M.D.

Why is light given to one that is in misery, and life to the bitter in soul, who long for death, but it does not come, and dig for it more than for hidden treasures; who rejoice exceedingly, and are glad, when they find the grave?

—Job 3:20–22

What I had begun to discover is that, mysteriously and in ways that are totally remote from normal experience, the gray drizzle of horror induced by depression takes on the quality of physical pain. But it is not an immediately identifiable pain, like that of a broken limb. It may be more accurate to say that despair, owing to some evil trick played upon the sick brain by the inhabiting psyche, comes to resemble the diabolical discomfort of being imprisoned in a fiercely overheated room. And because no breeze stirs this caldron, because there is no escape from this smothering confinement, it is entirely natural that the victim begins to think ceaselessly of oblivion.

—William Styron, *Darkness Visible: A Memoir of Madness,* 1990

Separated in time by several millennia, the biblical author of the book of Job and contemporary writer William Styron have attempted to describe the pain of severe depression—a hopeless despair from which death seems the only release. The two accounts illustrate that depression sometimes begins as an understandable reaction to life events; other times it seems inexplicable. Job's depressed mood followed a series of personal tragedies, explained in the Bible as a test of his faith in God. In contrast, Styron's account of his descent into depression details how his condition turned severe during a trip to Paris to accept a prestigious award marking his successful career as a novelist. To further complicate matters, some people have severe depressive illness without being aware of *feeling* depressed.

Depression: three meanings

In order to understand the apparent contradictions, it is important to be clear about the meaning of the term *depression,* which can have three distinct meanings.

Normal mood. In brief periods of sadness, or the "blues," depression is a normal emotion, distinguished from clinical (pathological) varieties of

Richard M. Glass, M.D., *is Clinical Associate Professor of Psychiatry, University of Chicago, and Deputy Editor,* Journal of the American Medical Association.

(Overleaf) "The Disillusioned One" by Ferdinand Hodler, 1892; collection, Los Angeles County Museum of Art, Gift of B. Gerald Cantor

depression by its short duration, low intensity, and minimal effects on the person's functioning. Although brief periods of feeling "down in the dumps" can sometimes occur for no apparent reason, careful exploration usually uncovers a psychologically meaningful loss as the source of the depressed mood. Thus, depression as a normal mood is essentially synonymous with grief—a process of mourning a loss. Grieving seems to be a necessary part of coping with loss, leading eventually to the ability to form substitute psychological attachments that compensate for the loss. Significant losses can include virtually anything of importance to an individual: persons, pets, money, objects, jobs, titles, reputations, ideals.

One of life's most painful experiences is the loss of a beloved family member, especially a spouse or a child. Here, the effects of grief can be pervasive and can even include the symptoms of a clinical depression, such as sleep and appetite disturbance; grief may then be difficult to distinguish from pathological depression. Every culture has practices designed to assist bereaved individuals with the grieving process: designated social supports from family and friends, religious rituals, and temporary relief from responsibilities. The culturally prescribed mourning period also has a time limit, although the specificity of such limits varies among cultures. Determining whether a response to loss has exceeded the cultural limits of time and intensity can be an important factor in deciding whether grief has progressed to clinical depression.

Thus, depressed mood following a significant loss is not only normal but necessary. The absence of grief after such a loss is often followed by subsequent problems—emotional or physical symptoms or a delayed but distorted and prolonged grief reaction triggered by later events. The appropriate intervention under those circumstances is to identify the unresolved grief and its sources (usually some kind of "unfinished business" concerning the loss) and to facilitate normal grieving.

Depression can be a normal emotion— usually synonymous with grief—suffered by people who have lost something of great value to them. (Right) "Hard Times" (c. 1870): an aggrieved couple is forced to mortgage the old homestead.

Culver Pictures

One of life's most painful experiences is the loss of a child. The emotion can be so profound as to be virtually indistinguishable from pathological depression. The grieving process following such a loss is not only normal but necessary, and every culture has designated social supports and rituals to assist the bereaved through their sorrow.

"The Mother's Lament"; photograph, Culver Pictures

A symptom. Depression can also be a symptom. Such a symptom may occur either in the course of some other physical or mental disorder or as a mood that is too severe or persistent to be called normal but has too few associated symptoms to qualify as a full depressive syndrome (described below). Anyone who has had a viral infection (*e.g.,* the flu or a bad cold) is familiar with the accompanying low mood, low energy, and loss of interest in normal events—depressive symptoms.

Depressive symptoms can complicate almost any physical disorder and also occur in the course of other psychiatric disorders. For example, patients with panic disorder frequently experience depression because of the effects that recurrent panic attacks have on their lives. For instance, an individual may restrict daily activities dramatically in order to avoid situations that are likely to produce panicky feelings, becoming reclusive— even housebound—and lonely. The best intervention in such a situation is recognition and treatment of the underlying disorder.

A group of disorders. Third, depression can refer to one of several syndromes (clusters of specific symptoms). Depressive syndromes are classified in the *Diagnostic and Statistical Manual of Mental Disorders,* third edition, revised (*DSM-III-R*), the official diagnostic manual for psychiatric disorders, as "mood disorders." This is a change from the previous designation of "affective disorders," reflecting the technical distinction between *mood,* which describes pervasive, sustained emotions, and *affect,* which refers to shorter-term emotional states (lasting minutes to hours). Four specific depressive disorders are distinguished in *DSM-III-R.*

The extreme of hopelessness: major depressive episodes

A diagnosis of a major depressive episode requires the persistence for at least two weeks of either depressed mood or loss of interest, plus at

77

least four other persistent symptoms (*see* Table 1). Sleep and appetite disturbance are particularly common and can occur as either a decrease (less than normal sleep, loss of appetite with weight loss) or an increase (increased sleeping, overeating with weight gain). Thoughts of death or suicide are the source of the life-threatening nature of clinical depression. About 15% of persons suffering from a major depressive episode kill themselves. This tragic outcome is often preceded by talk about death or suicide or by steps to make final financial arrangements. Such hints from a depressed person should be taken very seriously and should prompt consideration of hospitalization. Hopelessness about recovery is another important indicator of suicide risk and an example of the negative, pessimistic thinking characteristic of depression.

Table 1. Diagnostic criteria for a major depressive episode

A. At least five of the following symptoms have been present during the same two-week period and represent a change from previous functioning; at least one of the symptoms is either (1) depressed mood or (2) loss of interest or pleasure (symptoms that are clearly due to a physical condition, mood-incongruent delusions or hallucinations, incoherence, or marked loosening of associations are not included)

    (1) depressed mood (or irritable mood in children and adolescents) most of the day, nearly every day, as indicated by either subjective account or observation by others
    (2) markedly diminished interest or pleasure in all, or almost all, activities most of the day, nearly every day (as indicated by either subjective account or observation by others of apathy)
    (3) significant weight loss or weight gain when not dieting (*e.g.,* more than 5% of body weight in a month) or decrease or increase in appetite nearly every day (in children, consider failure to make expected weight gains)
    (4) insomnia or hypersomnia nearly every day
    (5) psychomotor agitation or retardation nearly every day (observable by others, not merely subjective feelings of restlessness or being slowed down)
    (6) fatigue or loss of energy nearly every day
    (7) feelings of worthlessness or excessive or inappropriate guilt (which may be delusional) nearly every day (not merely self-reproach or guilt about being sick)
    (8) diminished ability to think or concentrate, or indecisiveness, nearly every day (either by subjective account or as observed by others)
    (9) recurrent thoughts of death (not just fear of dying), recurrent suicidal ideation without a specific plan, or a suicide attempt or a specific plan for committing suicide

B. (1) disturbance not initiated or maintained by an organic factor
    (2) not a normal reaction to the death of a loved one (uncomplicated bereavement)

    Note: morbid preoccupation with worthlessness, suicidal ideation, marked functional impairment or psychomotor retardation, or prolonged duration suggests bereavement complicated by major depression

C. at no time during the disturbance have there been delusions or hallucinations for as long as two weeks in the absence of prominent mood symptoms (*i.e.,* before the mood symptoms developed or after they have remitted)

D. not superimposed on schizophrenia, schizophreniform disorder, delusional disorder, or another type of psychotic disorder

Adapted with permission from the *Diagnostic and Statistical Manual of Mental Disorders,* third edition, revised. Copyright 1987 American Psychiatric Association

An estimated 15% of those who experience a major depressive episode kill themselves. Often the event is preceded by hints of the intended act—talking about death or taking steps to make important final arrangements, financial and otherwise. (Left) The tragic suicide of the young English poet Thomas Chatterton was the subject of a famous painting by the Pre-Raphaelite artist Henry Wallis. Chatterton had an unhappy childhood, much of it spent in solitude. During that time he began to write verse and prose. In his adolescence he was apprenticed to a Bristol attorney but wanted to devote himself to his writing. At one point he used a mock suicide threat ("The Last Will and Testament of Me, Thomas Chatterton of Bristol") to force his employer to release him from his contract. He then set off for London, where he lived abstemiously, attempting to support himself with his writing, but met with little success. Desperate after one of his poems was rejected by a leading magazine, on the night of Aug. 24, 1770, not yet 20 years old, he took arsenic and died alone in his garret.

Although depressed mood is usually a prominent part of a major depressive episode, some patients have every part of the syndrome of clinical depression except for depressed mood. Such patients often consult their family doctor about sleep and appetite disturbance, loss of energy, and other physical symptoms. They do not complain about feeling depressed and may even deny such feelings when questioned. Usually, however, they acknowledge a loss of interest or pleasure in their usual activities. Because of the importance of recognizing a depressive disorder in such patients, depressed mood is not an absolute requirement for the diagnosis.

The length of major depressive episodes is highly variable, but most last considerably longer than the minimum two-week requirement; three to six months is about average without treatment. Though some people have only a single episode, mood disorders typically recur. Over half of those who have an initial episode of major depression will eventually have at least one more episode. The course of recurrences is also variable. Some people have only occasional episodes, separated by years, while others have clusters of episodes. Functioning usually returns completely to normal between episodes, but for an unfortunate minority of patients (estimated at 20–35%), clinical depression becomes chronic, often with profound effects on social and occupational functioning.

So low, so high: bipolar disorder

It seems strange that there would be a connection between the sad mood, low self-esteem, and slowed speech and behavior of depression and the elevated mood, grandiosity, and intensified speech and activity of mania. Yet the occurrence of these polar opposites is the distinguishing characteristic of bipolar disorder. Manic and depressive episodes can occur in any order, not necessarily alternating, sometimes separated by symptom-free intervals lasting several years, sometimes following immediately after an episode of the opposite kind. The occurrence of four or more episodes per year is called "rapid cycling" and has important implications for treat-

79

ment. Almost everyone who has an episode of mania will eventually have an episode of clinical depression; when a patient has experienced one or more manic episodes, the diagnosis of bipolar I disorder is made.

Mania, according to the *DSM-III-R* diagnostic criteria, involves a marked departure from the individual's usual behavior and personality and can include psychotic features—grossly impaired ability to test reality. Delusions, or false beliefs (such as the conviction that one has supernatural powers), and hallucinations, or false perceptions (such as hearing a voice say that one is destined to save the world), are examples of psychotic features. The severity of such symptoms and the impaired judgment that regularly accompanies a manic episode (leading, for example, to spending sprees) can have devastating consequences for patients and their families.

DSM-III-R distinguishes manic episodes from hypomania—describing a less severe form of abnormally elevated mood that does not cause marked impairment. Patients who experience hypomania and major depressive episodes are generally diagnosed as having bipolar II disorder.

In some patients' disorders, there is a regular seasonal pattern to the beginning and end of episodes, a pattern not explained by seasonally related stress (such as "holiday blues"). Such depressions usually start in the fall and either remit or switch to hypomania in the spring. This pattern has been called seasonal affective disorder, or SAD.

Two chronic mood disorders

Two other mood disorders, milder in severity than either major depression or bipolar disorder, follow a chronic course. Both usually have begun by early adulthood and can last from several years to a lifetime.

Dysthymia (previously called depressive neurosis) is defined as a depressed mood persisting for at least two years, accompanied by at least two other depressive symptoms (*e.g.,* sleep or appetite disturbance, low energy) but fewer symptoms than would qualify for a diagnosis of major depression. A person can suffer a superimposed episode of major depression, a situation sometimes called "double depression."

Cyclothymia is a mild, chronic version of bipolar disorder, so defined by the occurrence for at least two years of numerous episodes of hypomania and also numerous periods of depressed mood not meeting the criteria for major depression. Such persons usually have periods of normal mood, but for no more than two months at a time. Persons with cyclothymia can be very productive during hypomanic periods, but that benefit is usually overshadowed by the disruptive effects of the recurrent mood cycles and the pain and impairment of the depressive episodes. Eventually, many persons with cyclothymia develop full-blown bipolar disorder.

An era of melancholy

How common is clinical depression? Medical epidemiology seeks to determine rates of illnesses in populations, as well as significant changes in illness rates over time. Since many persons with a mental disorder do not seek or obtain treatment, counting cases in hospitals or clinics will not yield good estimates of illness rates. For this purpose, it is necessary

The manic and depressive episodes of bipolar disorder can occur in any order. Typically mania is manifested by profound mood elevation and intensified speech and activity; in some instances psychotic features—delusions and hallucinations—are present. The drawing below, commissioned for an early-19th-century atlas of mental disorders by the French psychiatrist Jean-Étienne-Dominique Esquirol (1772–1840), depicts the exaggerated affect, verging on rage, of a manic patient at the Salpêtrière Hospital in Paris. Esquirol was noted for his precise clinical descriptions of psychiatric disorders and his introduction of reforms in the treatment and housing of mental patients.

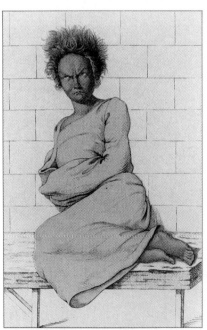

The National Library of Medicine, Bethesda, Maryland

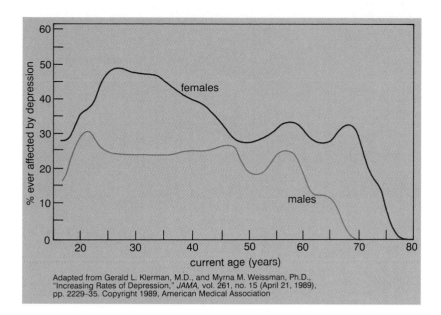

Adapted from Gerald L. Klerman, M.D., and Myrna M. Weissman, Ph.D., "Increasing Rates of Depression," *JAMA,* vol. 261, no. 15 (April 21, 1989), pp. 2229–35. Copyright 1989, American Medical Association

Large-scale epidemiological surveys have shown important temporal trends in depression rates: increasing rates in people born after World War II; a persistent family effect, i.e., those who have a first-degree relative with depression have an increased risk of developing depression themselves; and a gender effect—consistently higher rates in women. (Graph) A study of depression in a sample of more than 2,500 relatives of persons with a major depressive disorder found that lifetime prevalence rates—the percentage of relatives who had had a depressive episode at any time in their lives—were highest in younger groups and in women. Several recent studies have attributed the prevalence of depression in women to social factors, such as the wage gap between the sexes and the level of violence against women.

The Bettmann Archive

to conduct surveys of persons in representative community samples. The development of specific and reliable diagnostic criteria for mental disorders has permitted large-scale population studies that have made it clear that mood disorders constitute a major public health problem.

On the basis of analysis of a number of such surveys in several Western countries (the United States, Canada, Sweden, West Germany, and New Zealand), Gerald Klerman of Cornell University Medical College, New York City, and Myrna Weissman of Columbia University, New York City, have shown that there has been a progressive increase in the prevalence of major depression throughout the 20th century. The increase has occurred particularly since World War II, with those in younger age groups being more likely than those in older age groups to have experienced an episode of major depression. This is true even though older persons have lived longer and therefore have had a longer period of risk.

Such a pattern was also shown in a study sponsored by the National Institute of Mental Health, known as the Epidemiologic Catchment Area (ECA) study. Over 17,000 subjects were interviewed in five locations across the U.S. The investigators found an overall lifetime prevalence for major depression of approximately 5%, but the prevalence rates varied from about 8% for persons aged 25–40 to only about 1.5% for persons aged 65 and over. About 3% of the total sample reported symptoms consistent with major depression in the six months before being interviewed. These figures suggest that well over five million Americans suffer from major depression during any given six-month period.

These studies documenting lower rates of major depression in older persons were based on epidemiological surveys of older people who were healthy and resourceful enough to live in the community. The rates of clinical depression among the elderly in hospitals and nursing homes, however, are notably higher. A recent study directed by psychiatrist Barry Rovner of Johns Hopkins University School of Medicine, Baltimore, Maryland, found

81

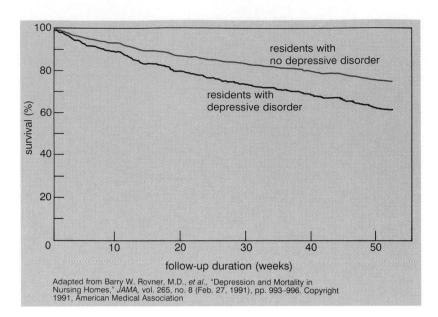

Adapted from Barry W. Rovner, M.D., *et al.*, "Depression and Mortality in Nursing Homes," *JAMA*, vol. 265, no. 8 (Feb. 27, 1991), pp. 993–996. Copyright 1991, American Medical Association

Many studies have documented considerably higher rates of depression in the institutionalized elderly population compared with those for older individuals living in the community. Research psychiatrists from Johns Hopkins University School of Medicine recently found that depression in residents of eight Baltimore, Maryland, nursing homes not only was prevalent but was associated with increased mortality: patients with depressive disorders had a 59% higher risk of dying than did all other residents. The graph shows the probability of survival of this nursing home population over one year.

that 13% of patients admitted to nursing homes in the city of Baltimore had major depression and another 18% had some symptoms of depression.

As additional documentation that Western societies are experiencing an era of melancholy, Klerman and Weissman also found that the age of onset of major depression has decreased (now occurring most frequently in late adolescence and the early adult years) and that rates of depression for all ages increased during the 1960s and 1970s. Similar time trends were not found in comparable epidemiological surveys conducted in South Korea and Puerto Rico or among Mexican-Americans living in the United States—an important difference that could be explained by either genetic or cultural factors (or both).

Clinical depression may begin at any age, including infancy, although the diagnosis can be difficult to make in children. As a result, prevalence rates among children have not been established. Sleep and appetite disturbance, withdrawal from social activities, unexplained physical complaints, and marked changes in behavior can be clues to depression in children, who often do not complain spontaneously about depressed mood.

Another consistent finding in epidemiological surveys is that rates of depression for women are two to three times higher than for men. The ECA survey found a lifetime prevalence for major depression of about 3% for men and 7% for women. Explanations for this difference have focused on either biological (*e.g.,* hormonal) or social status differences between men and women. Typically, men distract themselves from depressed feelings by taking action, while women tend to dwell on the feelings, increasing the chance that they will progress to a clinical depression. It seems likely that, compared with men, women experience persisting limitations in power and control over difficult social circumstances, which result in higher rates of depression. This would fit with the "learned helplessness" model of depression proposed by psychologist Martin Seligman at the University of Pennsylvania. Experiments have shown that when laboratory animals are repeatedly unable to escape a painful or frightening stimulus (*e.g.,* electric shocks), they become listless and helpless—a condition resembling human depression. A woman involved in an abusive marriage, to cite just one example, may experience an analogous situation; her lack of physical and economic power, as well as being bound by social expectations, can create major obstacles to change or "escape." However, as society moves in the direction of gender equality, the male-female differential in depression rates may be diminishing.

The impact of suffering

For anyone who has had a major depression, or who has suffered through an episode with a friend or relative, the impact of the suffering and disability is painfully obvious.

As disabling as arthritis. The resulting impact on functioning, which has long been apparent to depressed persons and their families, has recently been documented in a large survey sponsored by the RAND Corporation, known as the Medical Outcomes Study (*see* Table 2). Data on over 11,000 outpatients in Boston, Chicago, and Los Angeles were obtained through a questionnaire. Those whose responses indicated they had a current depressive disorder (major depression or dysthymia) or a certain number of depressive symptoms (exceeding a cutoff point on the questionnaire) tended to have decreased physical, social, and role-functioning scores. These scores were comparable to or worse than those of patients with any of eight chronic medical conditions.

Mind-body implications. The Baltimore nursing home study found an increased death rate from physical illness in patients with depression. One explanation for this finding is that depression can adversely influence the body's natural disease-fighting mechanisms. Connections of this kind between mind and body have spawned a new field, known as psycho-neuroimmunology. Early findings have shown that depressed patients have high levels of cortisol, a stress-related steroid hormone secreted by the

Table 2. Impact of suffering: depression and chronic medical conditions				
	physical functioning*	social functioning*	free of pain*	bedridden[†]
depression	77.6	81.2	64.5	1.40
hypertension	86.4	94.9	77.5	0.36
diabetes	81.5	89.6	76.3	1.02
coronary artery disease	65.8	83.9	70.8	2.08
angina	71.2	89.8	70.0	0.30
arthritis	80.6	92.1	60.4	0.53
gastrointestinal problem	82.8	88.8	65.1	0.93
lung problem	75.5	88.5	73.0	1.14
back problem	79.0	93.2	66.8	0.76
no chronic condition	88.1	94.6	76.2	0.41

*higher score = better functioning
[†]higher score = poorer functioning

From Kenneth B. Wells, M.D., "The Functioning and Well-Being of Depressed Patients," *JAMA,* vol. 262, no. 7 (Aug. 18, 1989), pp. 914–919. Copyright 1989, American Medical Association

Epidemiological surveys have shown a progressive decline in the age of onset of depression; at the same time, youth suicide rates have increased threefold. In the U.S. depression accounts for more than 5,000 suicide deaths annually in the 15–24-year-old population. Social and cultural factors, including the availability of firearms to young people, contribute to these tragic deaths.

adrenal glands that suppresses responses to inflammation. Some initial studies reported that the number of specialized infection-fighting white blood cells or their functioning was reduced in depressed patients. Other studies reported a connection between depression and the development of cancer, and some case reports suggested that successful treatment of depression improved the chances for curing cancer.

As is so often true, the initial wave of excitement has been dampened by difficulties in replicating the early findings. A blood test for the diagnosis of severe depression (the dexamethasone suppression test—based on the tendency for hypersecretion of cortisol), for example, proved to be too nonspecific for clinical use. Moreover, several carefully controlled studies have found that not all depressed patients have defects in cellular immunity, although there continues to be support for the existence of such abnormalities in older patients. Finally, a depression-cancer link was not found in a large-scale population study. After a careful review of research on the relationship between depression and the immune system, Marvin Stein and colleagues at Mount Sinai School of Medicine, New York City, concluded that "it is premature to consider any therapeutic effects of the treatment of depression on immunocompetence and disease. Nonetheless, the value of psychosocial interventions on the quality of life and mental state of seriously ill persons should not be underestimated."

The most tragic outcome. The most important complication of depression, one intimately connected with the nature of the disorder but preventable through effective treatment, is suicide. In addition to the tragic premature loss of life, suicide leaves a searing legacy for friends and family. Struggling with such painful questions as "Why did this happen?" and "What could I have done to prevent it?" they are the continuing victims of suicide. After it occurs, suicide is an occasion for grief rather than blame. However, before it occurs, identification and treatment of depressive illness are essential aspects of prevention.

Death by suicide of a young person who is just embarking on life seems especially tragic. Since the 1950s there has been a threefold increase in the suicide rate for adolescents. This increase is consistent with the previously noted increase in depressive disorders in young people, although social and cultural factors also play a role. For example, a "contagious" aspect of suicide among young people has been noted—adolescent suicides that occur in clusters. The availability of firearms to teenagers is important, too.

Fortunately, the rate of adolescent suicide appears to have leveled off. The highest suicide rates now occur in white men over age 65. This suggests that although the overall prevalence of depression is low for older persons, when it occurs in this group it tends to be particularly severe.

Possible causes

The causes of depression often involve a complex interaction among genetically determined biological vulnerabilities and psychological and environmental factors. Although depressive disorders tend to aggregate in families, it is clear that their genetics do not follow classic Mendelian inheritance patterns, in which either 25 or 50% of children born into affected families can expect to inherit the disorder. In the language of genetics, there is "incomplete penetrance" (not all persons who have genetic susceptibility manifest the disease) with "environmental cofactors" (life experiences that tend to lead to the illness in susceptible persons). Furthermore, there are "phenocopies" (occurrences of the disorder in the absence of evidence for genetic susceptibility). Thus, mood disorders appear to have a continuum of causation. At one end, persons with very high genetic vulnerability can have an episode of illness with minimal or no apparent environmental precipitants. At the other end, a mood disorder can occur after severe psychosocial stress in an individual with no apparent genetic susceptibility.

While the environmental factors usually involve some kind of psychosocial stress—especially losses—biological stressors can also precipitate mood disorders in vulnerable persons. Such stressors include physical illnesses and certain drugs. For example, reserpine, a medication used to treat high blood pressure, has been shown to cause depression in vulnerable individuals.

There are several factors that may moderate the effects of psychosocial stress. Social supports (such as cultural or religious mourning rituals) are one such factor. Another is so-called cognitive style—an individual's characteristic ways of perceiving and evaluating environmental events. Does one perceive a glass of water as half empty, as half full, or as a 16-ounce glass containing 8 ounces of water? Some cognitive theorists postulate that persons who tend to evaluate events negatively are at increased risk for depression. Stereotypical negative thinking, which is characteristic of full-blown depression, serves as the basic target of cognitive therapy (described below).

The biological bases of mood disorders continue to be active topics of research. For example, considerable excitement was generated by the publication in 1987 of a paper reporting that bipolar disorder in a large Old Order Amish family was linked to two marker genes on chromo-

Erik Neuhaus—Stock, Boston

In 1987 researchers reported that they had analyzed the DNA of cells from blood samples of 81 members of an Old Order Amish family and found certain variations on two specific marker genes on chromosome 11 in those who had bipolar disorder. The large and close-knit Pennsylvania family was selected for study because it had an unusually high prevalence of bipolar disorder and had kept extensive genealogical records. The finding was hailed by the scientific community as a major advance in the understanding of the complex mood disorder; it was hoped that the discovery might lead to better methods of diagnosis and treatment. Two years later, however, the same group of researchers reported new evidence that cast doubt on the likelihood of there being a responsible faulty gene. The more recent discovery did not change the fact that there can be an inherited predisposition to depressive disorders, and the search for genetically determined biological bases of mood disorders remains an active one.

neurotransmission occurs

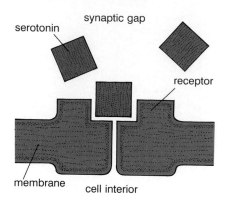

neurotransmission prevented

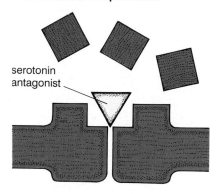

The precise mechanisms in the brain that may trigger depression remain to be determined. Recent research has pointed to a role for serotonin activity in mood disorders, including depression. Serotonin is one of numerous natural chemical substances, called neurotransmitters, that serve to carry signals from one nerve cell (neuron) to neighboring target neurons. Investigators are focusing in particular on serotonin receptors, the sites of the neurotransmitter's action. (Top) Released from a firing neuron, serotonin crosses the tiny gap between that cell and adjacent cells and attaches to specialized molecular receptors on the target cell surfaces. The binding of serotonin to its receptors starts a chain of reactions that ends in activation of the target cells and transmission of the signal. (Above) Substances that inhibit serotonin activity and appear consequently to exacerbate depression include serotonin antagonists, which bind to serotonin receptors, blocking serotonin from transmitting its signal.

some 11, even though neither of these genes was itself implicated in the disease and the finding was not replicated in other affected families. In 1989, however, the same research group reported that two people in the original Amish pedigree had developed bipolar disorder in the absence of the genetic markers and that an additional branch of the family did not show the linkage.

Though it was disappointing that the earlier finding did not provide a biological key to bipolar disorder, the later developments illustrate the self-correcting process of good science. Moreover, this particular reversal has no bearing on the more general issue of genetic predispositions to mood disorders. Genetic factors have been strongly supported by many family studies, twin studies, and adoption studies showing an increased risk for mood disorders in the biological offspring of parents with mood disorders, even when they are raised by adoptive parents without mood disorders.

The exact mechanisms, both genetic and biochemical, of biological factors in mood disorders remain to be determined. Potential candidates include derangements of the brain's neurotransmitter systems that are known to influence mood and behavior—involving the neurotransmitters norepinephrine and serotonin in particular. Special attention is being focused on the receptors (specialized recognition sites in the membranes of neurons) that are the sites of neurotransmitter action. Research in this area has been hampered by the difficulty of directly studying the living brain, as well as the limitations of measurements performed on blood, urine, or even cerebrospinal fluid. Recently developed techniques of brain imaging, which allow at least limited direct observation of various brain functions, hold considerable promise of increasing present understanding of the biology of mood disorders.

Lifting the dark cloud

Successful treatment begins with a careful evaluation to rule out physical disorders that cause depression-like symptoms. These include thyroid and adrenal disorders, neurological disorders, cancer (especially carcinoma of the pancreas), and chronic infections. Such disorders can usually be ruled out on the basis of a careful medical history and physical examination. However, one common condition, hypothyroidism (insufficient thyroid hormone), can cause depression and decreased energy in the absence of overt physical signs; therefore, a sensitive screening test to determine the level of thyroid-stimulating hormone is done. Hypothyroidism, if present, is readily treatable with thyroid hormone.

The diagnosis of mood disorders depends on a knowledgeable interviewer obtaining a careful history of symptoms. One particularly vexing diagnostic problem is the occurrence of severe, disabling fatigue persisting for over six months, usually following a viral infection. Systematic evaluations of patients with this problem—now termed chronic fatigue syndrome (CFS)—indicate that a majority of them meet diagnostic criteria for depressive disorders, but it remains unclear whether this syndrome is a variant of mood disorder triggered by an infection or whether it is a still-unidentified organic illness that produces depressive symptoms. In any case, patients with CFS should have thorough evaluations by both a psychiatrist and an internal medicine specialist. Treatment with antidepressant medications is often at least partially beneficial for this difficult clinical problem.

For purposes of description, treatments for mood disorders are divided into biological and psychosocial categories. However, combinations of both kinds of treatments (*e.g.,* antidepressant medication plus psychotherapy) have been shown to be optimal for many patients.

Antidepressants

Since the introduction of imipramine in the 1960s, many additional antidepressant drugs have been developed, extensively tested, and marketed in the United States as effective treatments for clinical depression. The drugs can be divided into three categories (*see* Table 3): (1) tricyclic antidepressants, which share a similar chemical structure and have similar effects (although side effects from the various drugs can differ considerably), (2) monoamine oxidase inhibitor drugs (MAOIs), and (3) several more recently marketed drugs that do not fall into either of the first two classes.

All of the antidepressant drugs share one important characteristic—they require at least several weeks of continuous daily administration before they can achieve therapeutic results. Thus, unlike many other drugs, the patient will experience no beneficial effects from taking single doses of these medications. Their side effects, however, usually begin with the initial doses and, in fact, are often most severe when a patient begins taking a new medication, gradually moderating over time. The result is a difficult period, lasting several weeks, when a depressed patient may have uncomfortable side effects before experiencing any relief. It is important, therefore, that patients and their families be aware of this time lag and avoid becoming discouraged or making premature conclusions about the efficacy of a particular drug.

All of the marketed antidepressant drugs have been shown to be effective in clinical trials, usually for about 70% of the patients who have received them. The choice of drug rests heavily on what has and has not worked for the patient in the past and on the side effects that are most likely to be tolerated by the individual patient. Some patients can take high doses of a particular drug and experience no side effects, whereas others have severe side effects from the lowest doses of the same drug, owing, in part, to individual variability in rates of metabolism of the drugs. Consequently, the optimal dose of the drug—the dose that is high enough to lift the depression but low enough to avoid severe side effects—must be individually determined for each patient, a process requiring considerable cooperation between patient and doctor. For three of the commonly used tricyclics (desipramine, imipramine, and nortriptyline), therapeutic blood-level ranges have been established. Therefore, intermittent measuring of the level of the drug in the blood can help determine the optimal dosage. Owing to their increased sensitivity to side effects, elderly patients usually require lower doses than younger patients.

The most common side effects of the tricyclic antidepressants are listed in Table 4. Some people do not experience these effects, or the effects

Scans made by means of a diagnostic imaging technique called SPECT (single-photon-emission computed tomography) reveal reduced blood flow in the brain of a sufferer of chronic fatigue syndrome (bottom) when compared with blood flow in a normal person (below). Although many chronic fatigue patients exhibit depression, it is not yet clear whether the condition is a kind of mood disorder or an organic illness whose symptoms include depression. It is hoped that new imaging methods like SPECT, which makes use of short-lived radioactive tracer compounds to observe various brain functions, will help distinguish among various causes of depression and offer insights into the biology of mood disorders.

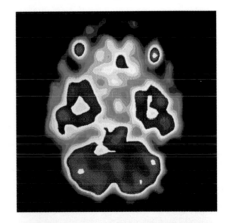

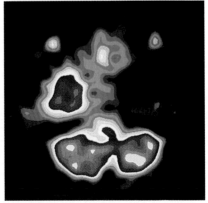

Photographs, Ishmael Mena, M.D., Harbor U.C.L.A. Imaging Center

are mild and decrease with time. For most patients who find relief from the painful and disabling effects of clinical depression, some annoying side effects are a tolerable trade-off. Since the tricyclics are long-acting drugs, they can be taken conveniently in a single daily dose, often at bedtime, when their initial central nervous system effect of sedation can aid sleep.

There is some evidence that patients with "atypical" depressive symptoms (oversleeping, increased eating with weight gain, a "leaden" feeling of fatigue, and oversensitivity to social rejection) tend to respond best to MAOIs. These drugs may also be used for patients who have not responded well to or have had severe side effects from other antidepressants. The common side effects of MAOIs are similar to those of tricyclics,

---

Table 3. Antidepressant medications (generic and trade names)

tricyclics	monoamine oxidase inhibitors
amitriptyline (Elavil, Endep)	isocarboxazid (Marplan)
desipramine (Norpramin, Pertofrane)	phenelzine (Nardil)
doxepin (Adapin, Sinequan)	tranylcypromine (Parnate)
imipramine (SK-Pramine, Tofranil)	
nortriptyline (Pamelor)	others
protriptyline (Vivactil)	
trimipramine (Surmontil)	amoxapine (Asendin)
	bupropion (Wellbutrin)
	fluoxetine (Prozac)
	maprotiline (Ludiomil)
	trazodone (Desyrel)

Table 4. Common side effects of tricyclic antidepressants

anticholinergic effects	central nervous system effects
(reactions caused by the blocking of the neurotransmitter acetylcholine)	sedation
	"spacey" feelings
	jitteriness
dryness of mouth and nose	
constipation	allergic effects
difficulty starting urination	
blurred vision	skin rashes
autonomic nervous system effects	other effects
dizziness on standing up	weight gain
increased sweating	impotence
hand tremor	inhibited orgasm

Table 5. Food and drug restrictions for patients taking MAOIs

drugs that must be avoided	foods that must be avoided
other MAOI drugs	aged cheeses
epinephrine, norepinephrine, pseudoephedrine, phenylpropanolamine	concentrated yeast extracts (e.g., Marmite)
sympathomimetics, including amphetamines, cocaine, diet pills	sauerkraut
local anesthetics containing vasoconstrictors	fava or broad bean pods
L-dopa, methyldopa	all spoiled foods
cold remedies (e.g., Contac, Nyquil)	other precautions
meperidine (Demerol)	if medication appears to cause headaches, it should be discontinued and blood pressure should be checked
fluoxetine (Prozac)	the above-listed foods and drugs should not be taken for two weeks following discontinuation of an MAOI drug

although they are less likely to cause anticholinergic effects (*e.g.,* mouth dryness, constipation, blurred vision) and more likely to cause the autonomic nervous system effect of dizziness. The MAOIs can also cause insomnia and weight gain. The biggest risk, however, results from their blockage of monoamine oxidase enzymes throughout the body, retarding the metabolism of certain drugs or foodstuffs that are normally metabolized quickly. This can cause a marked increase in blood pressure, with a risk of stroke or even death. It is therefore essential for anyone taking an MAOI to avoid those drugs or foods that can cause an adverse interaction (*see* Table 5). Some of the drugs that cause problems are over-the-counter cold preparations; it is wise for patients on MAOI antidepressants to consult their physician before taking *any* other drug. The foods that can cause problems are those containing large amounts of tyramine, a substance that can raise blood pressure if it is not metabolized normally.

The two most recently marketed antidepressant drugs, bupropion and fluoxetine, have side effect profiles that are very different from both the tricyclic antidepressants and MAOIs. Although there are individual exceptions, most patients on either of these new drugs do not experience prominent anticholinergic effects, sedation, dizziness, or weight gain. Nausea, tremor, and nervousness can occur but are usually mild and transient.

Because of its low rate of side effects and ease of use (for most patients carefully calibrated adjustments of dosage are not required), fluoxetine (Prozac) became the most widely prescribed antidepressant drug soon after it was first marketed in the U.S. in 1987. It then received bad publicity after a report in the February 1990 issue of the *American Journal of Psychiatry* noted that six patients taking fluoxetine had developed severe suicidal impulses. Several patients alleging the same effect have sued the manufacturer for damages, and some persons accused of violent crimes have used the fact that they were taking fluoxetine for depression as a defense in their trials (*see* Table 6).

A possible connection between fluoxetine and suicidal thoughts or impulses is difficult to establish. First, depression itself can be a source of suicidal thoughts and intentions. Second, patients tend to be at increased risk of suicide during the early phase of improvement in depression—a time when patients may initially become more active and capable of making decisions but before their depressed mood is completely relieved. Thus, any treatment that activates a depressed patient could potentially be associated with an increase in suicidal thoughts or actions. Finally, in controlled clinical trials comparing fluoxetine with a placebo (blank pills) or another antidepressant, there has been no evidence of an increase in suicidal thoughts in patients receiving fluoxetine.

Patients who respond well to an antidepressant should continue the medication for at least several months after symptoms of depression have abated. The question of whether to continue the drug substantially beyond that time should then be carefully considered by the doctor and patient. A recent study from the University of Pittsburgh, Pennsylvania, demonstrated that continuation of the full dosage of imipramine after recovery from an episode of major depression could prevent recurrence.

Table 6. Prozac: controversy over side effects
commonly observed effects (listed by manufacturer)
nervous system complaints: anxiety, nervousness, insomnia
drowsiness and fatigue or asthenia (loss of strength)
tremor
sweating
gastrointestinal complaints: anorexia, nausea, diarrhea
dizziness or light-headedness
severe effects (alleged in lawsuits)
suicidal tendencies, ideas, and obsessions
attempted and actual suicide
self-mutilation
violent behavior
homicidal thoughts, behavior, and actual homicide

For the most part, there is no evidence that taking antidepressants over a prolonged period produces adverse effects. One exception, however, is amoxapine (Asendin), which has a mild dopamine-blocking effect similar to the stronger effect produced by the antipsychotic drugs that are used to treat schizophrenia. As a result of that effect, a few cases of a persistent abnormal muscle movement disorder known as tardive dyskinesia have developed in patients taking amoxapine. Therefore, this particular antidepressant generally should not be used over a long term.

Drug treatment for bipolar disorder involves a number of special issues that are beyond the scope of this article. In brief, the introduction of lithium treatment in the 1950s was a major advance, both for the treatment of acute manic episodes and for the prevention of recurrences of either mania or depression. Lithium is a naturally occurring element that alters sodium transport in cells. Its precise mode of action in relieving bipolar symptoms, however, has not been clearly established. Patients with bipolar disorder may require treatment with one of the antidepressants described above plus lithium during a depressive episode but usually should not be maintained on an antidepressant, which could lead to more frequent episodes of mania or to rapid cycling. For patients who do not respond well to lithium, several alternative drugs, including the anticonvulsant drug carbamazepine (Tegretol), may be effective.

Psychotherapies: two that work

Good communication and an understanding relationship are important aspects of all treatments. Psychotherapies attempt to go further by using particular kinds of communications and interactions as treatments. In the past, evaluation of psychotherapies was hampered by the prominence of ideologies—competing beliefs about the value of various kinds of psycho-

"Listen, everybody feels a little depressed around this time of year!"

Psychiatrist Aaron T. Beck, pictured at left, developed cognitive therapy in the mid-1970s as a treatment for depression. The approach is based on the theory that distorted and irrational thinking processes (cognitions) lead to negative views of the self and self-defeating patterns of behavior. The therapy is designed to help the patient recognize and monitor faulty cognitions and find alternative, positive ways of thinking and acting. Patients may be given "homework" assignments that facilitate adaptive thinking. Cognitive therapy has shown the most promising results in those who are mildly to moderately depressed.

therapy. Over the last 15 years, the field has moved in the direction of careful, empirical evaluations, and there is now a substantial body of evidence regarding the efficacy of several types of psychotherapy.

The question of whether to utilize psychotherapy, and what kind, is also a matter of judgment to be arrived at after an appropriate evaluation. In general, the greater the role of life events, interpersonal problems, or psychological conflicts, the stronger are the indications for psychotherapy. Major factors to consider are the qualifications and skill of the therapist and the "fit" of therapist and patient. Two types of psychotherapy have been developed specifically for depression.

Cognitive therapy. The first of these is cognitive therapy, a method that is based on an appreciation of the powerful influence of thoughts and appraisals on moods and behavior. This was well summarized by the 2nd-century Roman stoic philosopher Epictetus: "Men are disturbed not by things, but by the views which they take of things." Aaron T. Beck, a psychiatrist at the University of Pennsylvania who has been centrally involved in the development of cognitive therapy, has identified three elements characteristic of the cognitions of depressed persons: (1) the cognitive triad, (2) logical errors, and (3) silent assumptions.

The so-called cognitive triad refers to pessimistic, negative views about oneself, the world, and the future. (For example, "I'm no good." "My life is a failure." "Things will never get better.") Logical errors serve to maintain negative appraisals because they prevent appraisals from being influenced by objective facts and alternative interpretations. Examples of such errors include selective attention (emphasizing certain details while ignoring others) and arbitrary inference (drawing conclusions not necessarily warranted by data or logic). Silent assumptions (sometimes called "schemas") are beliefs that have a pervasive influence on the individual, even though such patterns of thinking may not be conscious ones and are rarely made explicit: "If something goes wrong, it's my fault." "If everybody doesn't like me, I can't be happy." "Without him (or her) in my life, I'm worthless."

Cognitive therapy involves a thorough and detailed examination of such thought processes. The therapy is designed to help the patient recognize the faulty and negative thought patterns, then apply objectivity and logic in evaluating them, and finally substitute more accurate and adaptive appraisals. Homework assignments are used between therapy sessions to help the patient identify and respond to negative cognitions in daily experience. For example, keeping a log of the emotions and thoughts associated with particular events can help the patient identify the negative thoughts that mediate between events and feelings.

Interpersonal psychotherapy. The second type of therapy that has been shown to be effective for many patients with clinical depression involves a careful scrutiny of the problems in interpersonal relationships that are associated with a depressive illness. Through discussion of the patient's relationships, patient and therapist identify one of the following interpersonal problem areas commonly associated with depression—abnormal grief, interpersonal role disputes, role transitions, or interpersonal deficits. The goals of the therapy are to help the patient understand the interpersonal context of his or her depression and establish more effective ways of coping. These goals are accomplished through an active dialogue, clarifications, facilitation of mourning for losses, and identification and testing of options for more effective interpersonal functioning.

The cognitive and interpersonal approaches are not the only types of psychotherapy effective for depression. Therapists may use similar techniques effectively without labeling them, and depressed patients have also benefited from other forms of behavioral, psychodynamic, and marital and

Seasonal affective disorder, or SAD, is a type of depression that generally comes on in autumn and remits in spring. Because the depression appears to be directly related to the shorter periods of sunlight in the fall and winter months, many SAD patients benefit from bright light therapy. This innovative treatment approach has several advantages: patients usually respond in a matter of days; the treatments can be self-administered at home—the patient sits in front of a special high-intensity fluorescent light box for a few hours a day; and the potential side effects of drugs are avoided.

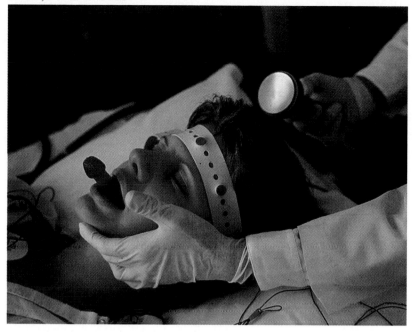

family therapies. Further research is needed to establish relationships between specific approaches and outcomes.

Bright lights

The first report in the psychiatric literature that exposure to bright artificial light was an effective treatment for a patient with recurrent winter depressions appeared in 1982. Since then, there has been considerable scientific research and public interest in this intriguing treatment. Several studies have found that very bright artificial light—*i.e.,* 5 to 10 times brighter than ordinary indoor lighting can be effective in relieving recurrent winter depressions. The treatment usually administered uses fluorescent light that provides at least 2,500 lux for at least two hours per day; some studies suggest that morning exposure may be more effective than evening exposure. It is necessary that the patient's eyes be open but not staring continuously at the lights. Advantages of bright light therapy are that a response often occurs within a few days and the potential side effects of drugs can be avoided. Sometimes, however, the addition of an antidepressant drug is necessary to obtain a full response.

ECT: dramatically effective

Electroconvulsive therapy (ECT), by far the most misunderstood and controversial treatment in psychiatry, has been clearly established as an effective and safe treatment for severe depression. For patients who do not respond to antidepressant drugs, and for patients whose severe symptoms have become life-threatening owing to malnutrition or extreme suicide risk, ECT can be lifesaving. A number of comparative studies have shown that ECT generally produces a higher response rate (up to 90%) and a faster response than antidepressant drugs.

Although not a cure, electroconvulsive therapy (ECT) often produces dramatic remissions in hospitalized patients with severe depression. After patients have been sedated with general anesthesia and a muscle relaxant, electrodes send small charges of electricity through select portions of the brain. The modern approach is highly refined; the risks of pain or injury have been nearly eliminated, and the administration of brief pulses to one side of the brain minimizes confusion and memory loss. The treatments are usually given at a rate of three per week over a period of two to four weeks. (Below) The depiction of ECT in the 1975 motion picture One Flew over the Cuckoo's Nest *was unfortunate. Actor Jack Nicholson (who won an Oscar for his performance as an unruly psychiatric ward patient) was given shock treatments as punishment. ECT, which is neither painful nor brutal, is not given, as the movie implied, to subdue disruptive patients but to release the severely depressed from the depths of their despair.*

In 1987 the U.S. National Institute of Mental Health launched a multimillion-dollar public health campaign known as Depression/Awareness, Recognition, and Treatment. The initiative's aim is to bring depression—a common and treatable illness—out of the shadows.

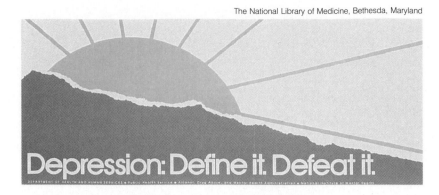

Depression: Define it. Defeat it.

DEPARTMENT OF HEALTH AND HUMAN SERVICES ● Public Health Service ● Alcohol, Drug Abuse, and Mental Health Administration ● National Institute of Mental Health

The continuing controversy about ECT appears to be based on its inaccurate portrayal in fictional accounts as a treatment that is brutal and painful, as in the novels *The Snake Pit* (1946) and *One Flew over the Cuckoo's Nest* (1962)—both of which were later made into motion pictures. There have also been concerns about possible brain damage and memory impairment from ECT. Animal studies, however, show that structural neuronal changes require electric current doses that are far in excess of those that are used in ECT treatments. Seizure activity produced by the current must also be greater than that occurring in patients. Systematic studies of patients who have received ECT show that there can be persisting loss of memory for events during and up to several months before a series of ECT treatments but that memory for events before and after that period, as well as the capacity to learn new material, returns to normal. Modern techniques of anesthesia (the patient is unconscious when the electric current is delivered) have almost eliminated risks of pain or injury, and use of unilateral brief pulse treatments can minimize confusion and memory loss.

A series of 5 to 10 ECT treatments, commonly given at a rate of 3 per week, usually results in remission of depression, a benefit that is often dramatic for patients who have been severely ill. Most patients then require maintenance therapy on one or another of the antidepressant medications to prevent a relapse.

Beginning in 1985, the year he turned 60, the novelist William Styron sank into a depression that was like a "howling tempest in the brain," a "smothering confinement," a "cauldron" that no breeze could stir. During his illness Styron was chagrined to find that ignorance and misconceptions about clinical depression were widespread. He wrote the book Darkness Visible: A Memoir of Madness *because he wanted others to realize that no matter how terrible their suffering or deep their despair, with good treatment people do get well again.*

M.C. Wallo

Hospitalization: sometimes literally lifesaving

Although many depressed patients can be treated on an outpatient basis, severe illness—particularly in the presence of high suicide risk or complicating medical problems—requires hospitalization. This allows for more intensive diagnostic and treatment efforts, as well as continuous monitoring in a safe environment. Hospitalization is usually required for ECT, and patients at high risk for severe drug side effects (e.g., those with heart disease) can be treated for depression more safely in a hospital.

The quality of treatment that is available in many private and university hospitals today is high. These psychiatric hospital units attempt to make the entire ward milieu, including contacts with staff members and a daily schedule of activities, part of the treatment program. Styron described his hospital experience as the main catalyst for his recovery from depression. However, for patients without insurance, treatment in public hospitals and clinics can be woefully inadequate, as many state and local governments have cut back on mental health services. Moreover, many private insurance programs in the U.S. have recently attempted to cut costs by decreasing mental health benefits, a process that puts even more of a burden on public facilities.

It has already been noted that more Americans suffer from depression than ever before. Yet most of them receive no treatment. The irony that fewer citizens have access to the high-quality care that has evolved from scientific and clinical progress is one that society must now address.

In particularly severe cases of depression, hospitalization can save lives. The setting offers a safe environment that allows for intensive treatment. High-quality care is available at many private and university hospitals. Chicago's Rush-Presbyterian-St. Luke's Medical Center (above) has been in the forefront of treatment for mental illness for several decades, building on an inherited tradition (Benjamin Rush, after whom the institution was named, was the "father of American psychiatry"). In 1991 the hospital established the Rush Institute for Mental Well-Being; the cornerstone of the institute will be the Depression Treatment and Research Center, with a commitment to providing the best treatments medicine can offer and to continuing the search for better ones for the most common of all mental illnesses.

95

Stalking an Outbreak

EPIDEMIOLOGY IN ACTION

by Michael B. Gregg, M.D.

In the past few decades the world has witnessed some extraordinarily exciting and important detective work on the part of epidemiological investigators: exciting, as the facts were unraveled day by day; important, because the findings provided a scientific basis for far-reaching disease control and prevention. In April 1955 a nationwide vaccination program against poliomyelitis (infantile paralysis) was begun, using the highly effective killed-virus vaccine developed by Jonas Salk. Within 12 days doctors began reporting cases of paralytic polio in children who had been vaccinated. Intensive field investigation of each case was begun immediately. After two days of state-by-state inquiry, federal epidemiologists were able to show that one of the companies producing the vaccine had made a "lot" that was contaminated with live virus. The defective product was recalled, and a major polio epidemic was aborted.

Beginning in 1958, hospitals around the U.S. began to report mysterious outbreaks of staphylococcal infections; in the early 1960s New Jersey and Mississippi noted numerous cases of shellfish-associated viral hepatitis; and in 1971 a nationwide epidemic of salmonellosis was traced to disease-carrying pet turtles. These are but a few examples of recent instances in which epidemiological investigations resulted directly in the instituting of measures to control and prevent disease—in these cases, rigorous surveillance of hospital-acquired infections, pollution control in shellfish beds, and a ban on the sale of some kinds of turtles.

Investigators from the U.S. Centers for Disease Control (CDC) continue daily to be dispatched to all parts of the country—as well as to any other nation that requests its help. In the summer of 1990 the CDC received a report of a young Florida woman infected with the AIDS (acquired immune deficiency syndrome) virus who had been treated by a dentist who subsequently died of the disease. Laboratory tests confirmed that the strain of virus infecting these two individuals was related. A follow-up investigation, which included reviews of the medical records of all of the dentist's patients and interviews with everyone who worked in his office, identified four more persons who had apparently been infected by him in the course of routine treatment. This incident prompted the agency to reassess the risk of AIDS

Michael B. Gregg, M.D., is an independent consultant in epidemiology. Formerly he was Director of Epidemiology, Centers for Disease Control (CDC), Atlanta, Georgia, and, for 21 years, Editor of the CDC's Morbidity and Mortality Weekly Report.

(Opposite page) A British cartoon entitled "Death's Dispensary" is a bitter indictment of sanitation standards in mid-19th-century London. It was the physician John Snow who first recognized that polluted drinking water was a source of cholera outbreaks in poor districts of the city. Because of this discovery, he came to be known as the "father of epidemiology."
Photograph, The Granger Collection

transmission during invasive medical and dental procedures and ultimately to issue new guidelines for health care workers.

The disease detectives

The job may be tracking an outbreak of vomiting and diarrhea among passengers aboard a Caribbean cruise ship, or it may be studying the incidence of Alzheimer's disease in the population of an entire country. In either case, those who plan and carry out such work—a process that may take days, months, or even years—are *epidemiologists*.

The term *epidemiology* originally referred solely to the study of epidemics—mass outbreaks of infectious disease. In the 1850s John Snow, the English physician known as the "father of epidemiology," began investigating cholera outbreaks in London. After studying a map of the city's water system and plotting the distribution of cases, Snow was able to demonstrate that one particularly hard-hit district was receiving its water from a polluted source. He removed the handle of the neighborhood's communal pump, and the outbreak was contained. Today epidemiology is not limited to discovering the causes of infectious disease but includes solving any mysterious cases of illness affecting any group of people. Still, the practice continues to require the same combination of knowledge, skill, intuition, and initiative that Snow brought to the emerging profession nearly 150 years ago.

The parallel with detective work may be carried further. Like a detective, the epidemiologist examines the scene, collects clues, questions witnesses, catalogs suspects, and, with luck, identifies the culprit. Sometimes this work encompasses all the most adventurous parts of the detective's job: mystery, intrigue, even personal danger (*e.g.,* exposure to a virulent infectious organism). At other times the epidemiologist's job is more akin to that of the desk sergeant: a mountain of paperwork.

Investigating a case: the tasks involved

All epidemiologists perform four basic operations. They count cases of disease (or health events), determine rates, compare these rates, and, finally, draw conclusions or, more accurately, inferences. In contrast to those who practice in an academic setting, field epidemiologists are always "on call." When an acute health problem occurs, field epidemiologists must drop whatever they are doing and go directly to the scene. Often they face a grave situation. New cases are continuing to be discovered; more people are falling ill and some, perhaps, are dying. Yet the source of the disease may be a mystery. Driven by the need to act quickly, objectively, and responsibly, field epidemiologists must possess not only scientific skills but managerial ability and political savvy as well.

The real-life practice of epidemiology in the field actually entails many more tasks, although all are derived from the four basic operations mentioned above. The following will illustrate the range of tasks, or steps, that, taken together, constitute a field investigation by an epidemiological team.

An epidemic—yes or no? When local health officials call for outside help, they usually have good reason to think something out of the ordinary is

Field epidemiologists must be ready to rush to the site of a sudden outbreak at a moment's notice. Once on the scene, they are disease detectives in action—probing, sifting, questioning. (Above) Investigators collect potentially toxic soil samples from a Pennsylvania incinerator suspected of releasing airborne contaminants. (Right) Tracking an outbreak may also entail long hours of paperwork—poring over the masses of data collected in the field.

going on. Nevertheless, establishing the existence of an epidemic is a standard procedure, and usually it is fairly easy. Most local health departments keep reasonably good records of cases reported to them. Sometimes, however, epidemiologists must perform a "quick and dirty"—*i.e.,* somewhat less than purely scientific—survey of clinics, hospitals, schools, or industries to help establish the presence of an epidemic. For example, CDC workers investigating an enormous outbreak of gastroenteritis in Riverside, California, in May 1966 simply picked up the phone and made calls to eight or nine local family physicians. What they learned in this manner was enough to confirm the existence of an epidemic.

The alert epidemiologist must always be on the lookout for so-called artifacts in reporting—artificial causes of apparently meaningful changes in incidence of disease. An example would be an increase in the diagnosis of a particular disease by a local physician or laboratory because of heightened interest in the disease in question or availability of a new diagnostic technique. On rare occasions epidemics may be reported by health departments hoping to secure outside funds. Following Hurricane Camille in 1969, one state health department believed that the state was experiencing an increase in cases of mosquito-borne encephalitis because large bodies of water remaining from the storm were promoting an increase in the mosquito population. If such were the case, federal disaster-relief funds would be made available to the state. However, a careful investigation produced no evidence of an epidemic of hurricane-related encephalitis—and no federal funds were forthcoming.

99

In a heavily wooded area on Nantucket Island, Massachusetts, a scientist uses a cloth snare to collect ticks that carry Lyme disease. The history of this unusual form of infectious arthritis, first identified in 1975, contains all the elements of a classic epidemiological detective tale. It began with a phone call to a state health department official from a worried woman in Lyme, Connecticut. Investigators quickly determined that the many cases clustered in three Connecticut communities represented a genuine "epidemic." But of what? Both the disease and its mode of spread were unknown. A map of the area (opposite page) showing where patients lived helped confirm the researchers' suspicion that the disease was insect-borne and that deer played a part in the transmission process. Another chapter was concluded when they discovered that the characteristic "bull's eye" rash (opposite page, right), an early sign of the illness in many patients, was the result of a tick bite.

In relatively small geographic areas, determining the existence of an epidemic is usually straightforward. However, when as few as 5 or 10 cases of an unusual disease are reported nationwide, it may be simply a chance occurrence—or it may be the start of a major health problem. In the early 1970s a Virginia hospital reported several cases of individuals who had developed overwhelming bacteremia (bacterial infection of the bloodstream) due to an extremely rare bacterium. A local investigation failed to uncover the source. When the CDC learned of the outbreak, however, its staff made immediate contact with nearly 100 other hospitals throughout the U.S. Many more cases were found, clearly representing a nationwide epidemic. Ultimately, 378 cases of bacteremia were recognized, resulting in 40 deaths; all were due to bottles of intravenous fluids made by a single manufacturer, which were found to be contaminated.

The disease—known or unknown? Once it has been determined that an epidemic is indeed occurring, it is necessary to confirm the diagnosis of the disease. Again, this is usually relatively easy. It is generally accomplished by means of widely accepted clinical criteria and laboratory tests. In outbreaks of infectious diseases, local physicians usually will have confirmed several cases by standard laboratory methods well before the field team arrives. Sometimes, however, when the diagnosis is unclear or simply not known—as was the case for investigators in the late 1970s seeking the cause of the tick-borne arthritic condition now known as Lyme disease— this step of the investigation can present an enormous challenge.

100

Who, where, and how many? Finding cases can be very easy or very difficult, depending on how big the epidemic is and what geographic area is involved. In the counting process the epidemiologist applies a fixed, objective case definition—a list of signs and symptoms that, if present, constitute a verifiable case of the disease. Application of a precise case definition is necessary to ensure that "apples" and "oranges" are not counted together. For example, the case definition of chronic fatigue syndrome requires that patients experience at least 8 of 11 symptoms (such as low-grade fever, muscle aches, sleep disturbance, and neurological problems) over a six-month period. Many people with other vague complaints can be quickly ruled out of an investigation by strict application of the case definition.

But simply counting cases is not enough. Critical to every field investigation is the collection of demographic, clinical, and epidemiological data. The patients' age, sex, race, occupation, and address represent some basic demographic facts nearly always collected by the field team. Cardinal signs and symptoms of the disease in question, including the time of onset of symptoms, and pertinent laboratory findings are essential clinical data. If the cause of the disease is known, usually much epidemiological information is available regarding its source, its mode of spread, and those at risk.

The usual scenario, then, is: a known disease, a known epidemiological profile, and a set of relatively straightforward questions specific to the disease under study. Needless to say, if the disease is obscure or truly not known, the investigation will be much more difficult. The field team will have to figure out from the demographic and clinical data what questions to ask. One notable example of this problem occurred in the celebrated investigation of the Legionnaires' disease epidemic in Philadelphia in 1976. The predominant sign of this then-unknown disease was pneumonia, a fact that strongly suggested an agent that infected people via the respiratory route.

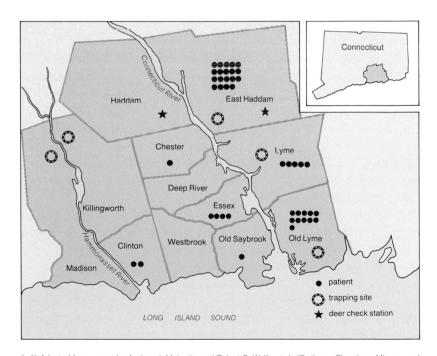

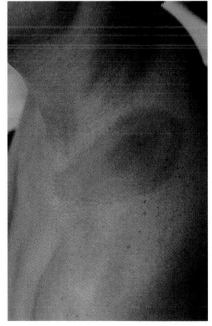

(Left) Adapted from a map by Andrew J. Main, Jr., and Robert C. Wallis *et al.*, "Erythema Chronicum Migrans and Lyme Arthritis: Field Study of Ticks," *American Journal of Epidemiology,* vol. 108, no. 4, (October 1978), pp. 322–327; (right) Michael Weissman, M.D.—Fran Heyl Associates

On Aug. 6, 1976, in Williamstown, Pennsylvania, one of the first victims of the Legionnaires' disease epidemic is carried to his grave by an honor guard of veterans. When a number of apparently healthy middle-aged Pennsylvania men were reported to have died suddenly of a pneumonia-like illness, state health authorities knew they had to act quickly to allay the public's anxiety. The outbreak triggered a massive investigative effort. It quickly became apparent what the victims had in common: all had attended an American Legion convention in Philadelphia during the month of July. (Opposite page, top) In a Chambersberg, Pennsylvania, hospital a CDC epidemiologist questions a sick legionnaire about his symptoms. Even after new cases had stopped occurring, researchers continued to search for the cause of the outbreak, following up those who had been stricken and taking blood samples from healthy individuals who had attended the ill-fated convention (opposite page, right). It was not until January 1977, nearly six months after the first death, that CDC microbiologists discovered the never-before-identified bacterium responsible for the deadly epidemic.

Yet no cases occurred among close family members of sick legionnaires. Given both of these facts, the epidemiologists knew that the disease could not have been transmitted from person to person among attendees at the convention; the only logical conclusion was that those who were ill must have experienced a common exposure to an airborne agent. After careful questioning, epidemiologists were able to show that being in the Belleview Stratford Hotel, where most of the legionnaires stayed, and, specifically, being in the hotel lobby for an hour or more (in fact, breathing the same air) conferred significant risk of developing the disease.

"Picturing" the epidemic. After several days of collecting data, the field investigators are likely to have information on a majority—say 70%—of all the existing cases. Even though not all cases have been found, the community may be pressing for an answer. At this time the team does first-round analysis. The task at this stage is to provide a description of the epidemic: when and where the patients became ill and what characteristics they share. By constructing an epidemic curve, a graph that shows the time of onset of illness for all known cases, epidemiologists can learn a great deal. If both the disease and its incubation period (the time between exposure and onset) are known, such a graph can suggest how the epidemic started and how it spread.

Often, particularly in large, community-wide outbreaks, epidemiologists can learn much about how an infectious agent is transmitted by plotting cases on a map, much as Snow did in the London cholera epidemic. In the above-mentioned 1966 California epidemic of intestinal complaints, some 13,000 people fell ill. A simple map indicated that a vast majority of cases were served by the same city water supply. The distribution of cases led the field team to test the water for bacteria. Indeed, the same strain of salmonella that had produced the outbreak was discovered in the water.

102

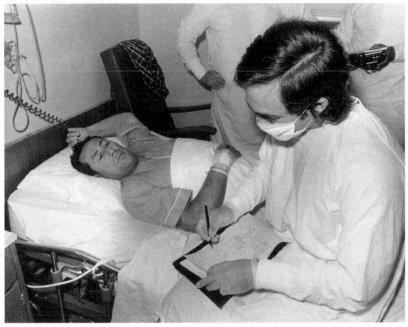

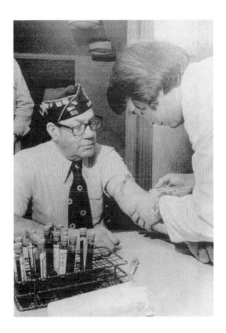

What do victims have in common? The most critical information of all may ultimately come from the detailed case descriptions. Again using the example of Legionnaires' disease, in the summer of 1976 several hospitals in Pennsylvania reported an unusual number of pneumonia deaths in middle-aged men. A unique characteristic of all the victims was that they belonged to the American Legion and had recently attended a convention in Philadelphia. Thus, investigation of what at first appeared to be a coincidence led to the discovery of a previously unidentified infectious agent.

Who is at risk? Once the investigators know the size of the epidemic, when and where people became ill, and what is unique about the victims, they can usually determine with reasonable assurance who else may be at risk. This is relatively easy in epidemics confined to schools, social groups, factories, and medium-sized communities. On the other hand, the investigators sometimes face real obstacles in trying to determine who is most likely to come down with the disease. Such a situation occurs most often with large epidemics in which the many widely scattered victims do not seem to represent a unique cohort (a group of individuals who have a significant trait in common). A classic example occurred in Spain when, in a period of a few months in 1981, thousands of people developed fever, muscle aches, weakness, and difficulty in breathing. Those affected came from all age groups and all parts of the country. Only after exhaustive field surveys and extensive inquiry were epidemiologists able to show that the widespread use of tainted cooking oil had led to an epidemic of the disease now known as toxic-oil syndrome.

Does the scenario make sense? The step that presents probably the greatest challenge is the construction of a meaningful scenario—a full explanation of the epidemic that fits with facts, not fancy. In, say, an epidemic of nausea, vomiting, and diarrhea following a church picnic—

In 1981, when a link was discovered between contaminated cooking oil and a puzzling illness that had caused thousands of persons in Spain to be hospitalized, the government ordered all of the suspect oil impounded. Deciding who was at risk was particularly difficult in this case; the victims came from 14 provinces and represented all age groups. The incidence of disease was high within affected families, but there were was no evidence of contagion in schools, hospitals, and other settings where infectious organisms are likely to spread. The predominance of the disorder among working-class families pointed to an economic or social factor. These considerations led investigators to postulate—rightly—that a toxic substance found in the home environment was probably responsible.

a not-too-uncommon event—one can assume that epidemiologists have (1) established the existence of an epidemic, (2) confirmed the diagnosis, (3) counted cases, and (4) determined the time and place and who was present and, therefore, is at risk. On the basis of this assessment, the epidemiologists feel certain that only attendees at the picnic were at risk, and the signs and symptoms strongly suggest that something they ate made them sick. The team then lists all the foods and beverages that were served and asks those who are ill what they ate and drank. Quite likely, there will be a single food or drink that the majority of them consumed. In fact, ham is found to be such a food. Clearly, then, it would seem that the ham caused the illness, simply because it was eaten by so many of those who became ill. This is a natural but not a scientifically valid conclusion. To determine whether the ham actually caused people to become ill, the team must now question well attendees about what they ate. If eating ham was equally popular among the ill (cases) and the well (controls), the team would have no evidence to support the presumption that eating ham led to the sickness. If, on the other hand, the exposure rates of the two groups were quite different—say 81% of the sick ate ham as opposed to only 14% of those who remained well—this would be strong evidence to support the hypothesis favoring ham, and if other facts were consistent with it, the team's conclusion would be borne out.

The kind of epidemiological study just described is frequently done in the field. It is called a case/control study. While such studies never really prove a cause-and-effect relationship, they can provide overwhelming evidence to support a highly plausible hypothesis.

The end of an epidemic. The control of an ongoing outbreak of disease and the prevention of future outbreaks are the ultimate goal of all field investigations. Instituting sound and sensible means of preventing disease may not be as exciting as sleuthing after a deadly organism, but preventing illness has both immediate and long-term rewards. The Legionnaires' disease epidemic is a classic example of how epidemiologists contribute to medical

104

knowledge and prevent unnecessary suffering. The brilliant work of the field team and those at the CDC who identified the bacterium helped to solve the mystery of earlier undiagnosed outbreaks of the disease. Furthermore, soon after this discovery, subsequent epidemics of Legionnaires' disease were quickly recognized; methods were developed to control disease-causing bacteria in ventilating systems; and an effective treatment for the disease was developed.

"Pontiac fever"

Late on Friday afternoon, July 5, 1968, George Agate, an epidemiologist for the state of Michigan, and Bernard Berman, director of the Oakland county (Michigan) health department, placed a joint telephone call to Alexander Langmuir, chief of the epidemiology branch at the CDC, at the agency's headquarters in Atlanta, Georgia. Within a week some 90 of the 100 employees of the Pontiac health department who worked at the county's Southfield office building had become acutely ill with fever, chills, and muscle aches. In addition, it was reported that 25 people who visited the building during the week had also become sick. Neither Agate nor Berman had any idea what could have caused this explosive outbreak.

A confusing picture. Friday night a team of three medical epidemiologists flew from Atlanta to Pontiac. Working in the Southfield office building throughout the weekend, the CDC team confirmed that no similar illness had been recognized by local physicians or hospitals. Nor had any illness been reported by other county employees in neighboring buildings. Clinically, the illness appeared infectious, yet only scattered cases had been reported in family members of affected workers. Preliminary lab studies offered no clues as to the cause. All but a few patients recovered after a few days and suffered no aftereffects.

Epidemiologically, this outbreak appeared quite unusual. Its explosive nature suggested a single source of exposure over a short time and a very short incubation period. Further, the illness (attack) rate was extraordinarily high—90%—implying a high level of susceptibility and a uniformly high level of exposure to the disease-causing agent—all circumstances that are rare in the case of infectious diseases but quite consistent with exposure to a toxic substance. Yet toxins would have taken effect faster, and it is likely that those exposed would have noticed something unusual in their work environment.

Early in the week of July 8, cases continued to occur, but lab studies yielded no clue as to the cause. Preliminary epidemiological studies concentrating on the employees from the Southfield building revealed the following salient facts: (1) there had been a common social gathering, a potluck dinner on June 28, but 28 of those who were sick had not attended; (2) although there was a snack area in the building where coffee and tea were served, at least 20 of the sick employees had not consumed any coffee or tea at work in the 36 to 48 hours prior to the onset of symptoms; and (3) at least 24 of the sick workers had no history of drinking any building water. Common sense told the team that food and water could not be implicated as the source of an infectious agent.

(Below and opposite page)
Adapted from Thomas H. Glick, M.D., and Michael B. Gregg, M.D., *et al.,* "Pontiac Fever:
An Epidemic of Unknown Etiology . . . ," *American Journal of Epidemiology,* vol. 107, no. 2 (1978), pp. 149–160

After a few days in the field, an epidemiological team usually has collected enough data to begin to put together a picture that will help answer basic questions about the magnitude and duration of the outbreak in question and its possible mode of spread. A key tool in this process is the epidemic curve—a graph that shows the occurrence of all known cases over a given time. In the "Pontiac fever" investigation, the epidemic curve (top) showed an explosive onset, suggesting a simultaneous exposure of health department employees and building visitors to a common source of disease. Where the disease is unknown, as it was in the case of Pontiac fever, a graph depicting the incubation period (bottom)—calculated from the hour of first exposure in the building to the hour of onset of the first symptoms—can provide crucial information about the type of agent involved.

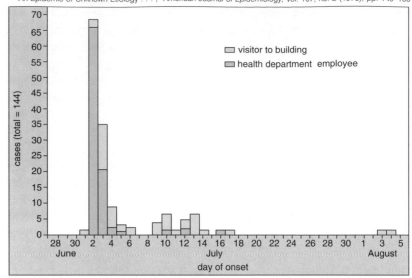

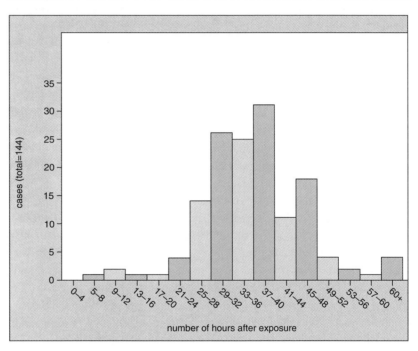

An occupational hazard. Still, the evidence clearly pointed to something that all employees and visitors to the building shared, namely the indoor air, which was cooled by a central air-conditioning system. Moreover, the symptoms of the illness were compatible with, though not highly suggestive of, airborne transmission. Quite suddenly there was further evidence implicating an airborne agent. Within a few hours of each other, on Tuesday night, July 9, all three of the visiting CDC investigators developed chills, fever, and severe muscle pain—classic cases of "Pontiac fever." Calling Atlanta from his motel room the next morning, the team leader requested help in continuing the investigation. Another team arrived the next morning, only to become bedridden 36 hours later with the same symptoms!

106

At this point a relatively clear picture of the epidemiology of Pontiac fever was beginning to emerge. Air was the vehicle for the infectious agent. But how and when did the agent get into the air? Although the numbers were not precise, no person known to have been in the building before June 30 (but not in during the week of July 1) became ill. Exposure to the air of the building did not inevitably produce symptoms within 36 to 48 hours—the members of the first CDC team did not become sick until nearly twice as long after their first exposure.

There was, however, strong evidence indicating that it was not the building air per se but air produced by the air-conditioning system that was the culprit. The system had been shut down over the weekend of June 29 and 30 but was turned on again on Monday morning, July 1. Similarly, during the following weekend, the system was off. The first CDC team became ill some 36 to 40 hours after it was turned on again on Monday, July 8. Although being in the building during the second week of the epidemic was an obvious risk factor, the highest attack rates were among those exposed to building air soon after the air-conditioning system was reactivated—a pattern similar to the one that occurred during the first week of the epidemic.

Consternation and relief. On Monday, July 15, the building was closed to all but essential personnel. Guinea pigs, mice, and fish—animals that might be susceptible to an infectious or toxic agent—were placed throughout the building as "sentinels," and the air was sampled for a variety of toxins. Air-conditioning engineers were consulted. Despite their assurances that there could not possibly be any defect in the system, the CDC team persisted in their theory that it had somehow produced contaminated air. At the team's insistence, the engineers cut a large opening in one of the outflow ducts that provided cool, dry, and theoretically clean air to the building. Much to the consternation of the engineers—but to the great relief of the epidemiologists—the opening revealed a large pool of dirty water. Still, the engineers were at a loss to explain how the dirt and water had entered the system. Within hours, however, the investigative team was able to demonstrate by means of smoke bombs that major defects in the structure of the system had allowed moist air from the cooling tower to enter directly into the building. They also showed that cooling tower water was inadequately treated for purification. These serious defects promoted condensation of water within the outflow ducts and, over time, accumulation of dust, dirt, and microbial growth. Simply turning on the air-conditioning system caused an aerosol of minute particulate matter to be spread throughout the building in a matter of minutes.

Parallel animal, clinical, and environmental studies were not especially rewarding. With the air-conditioning system turned on, the sentinel guinea pigs developed fever and signs of respiratory disease, but the mice and fish remained puzzlingly healthy. Autopsies on the lungs of the guinea pigs, performed back at CDC headquarters, showed evidence of pneumonia, but no causative organism could be isolated. The results of lab tests on human patients revealed nothing. Samples of building air were consistently negative for most known toxic agents. Still, while they did not know pre-

The sudden nature of the "Pontiac fever" outbreak, the high rate of illness among those exposed, and the short incubation period all suggested a high level of susceptibility among the victims and a uniformly high concentration of the disease-causing agent, circumstances that are rare in the case of an infectious agent but quite consistent with exposure to a toxic substance. Still, the epidemiologists were puzzled: when toxic chemicals are present, they usually are noticeable, and none of the victims had noticed anything unusual in the indoor environment. All evidence suggested exposure to something in the building air and, more specifically, in air produced by the air-conditioning system. This suspicion prompted the team to thoroughly examine the ventilation system. They were thus able to prove their theory that the building air was contaminated, to pinpoint the area where the contamination occurred, and to demonstrate that defects in the system had promoted the spread of disease throughout the building.

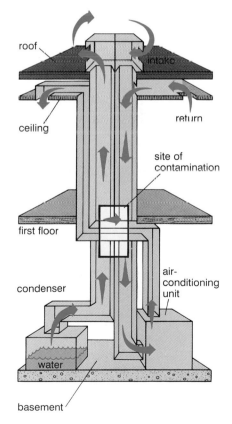

107

cisely what caused the illness, the team had amassed the epidemiological evidence they needed to put together a probable scenario: a defectively constructed and improperly maintained air-conditioning system, harboring some kind of pathogen in the cooling tower, had distributed the agent throughout the building and into the lungs of susceptible individuals.

The Legionnaires' disease connection. All leads pointed to the water in the cooling tower. Several liters were collected and sent to Atlanta for analysis. Extensive experiments performed at the CDC showed that guinea pigs exposed to an aerosol spray of the water consistently developed pneumonia. Still, CDC microbiologists were unable to isolate a causative organism. Disheartened but not defeated, the researchers suspended their experiments; the guinea pig lungs were frozen for posterity or, at least, until there might be reason to reexamine them.

Meanwhile, back in Pontiac, the building remained closed while the entire air-conditioning system was cleansed with disinfectants. (The system was later rebuilt.) No further cases of Pontiac fever were seen among employees or visitors to the building.

It was eight years later, in July 1976, that men who had attended a meeting of the American Legion in Philadelphia mysteriously began to fall ill. Epidemiological evidence there also pointed to an air-conditioning system—that in the Belleview Stratford Hotel. As in Pontiac, no agent could be found in the early stages of the field investigation. However, in January 1977 the CDC announced the isolation of a previously unknown human pathogen from the lungs of a deceased legionnaire. The newly discovered organism was named *Legionella pneumophilia.*

Almost immediately after the announcement, walking down a hallway at CDC headquarters, Charles Sheppard, one of the researchers who isolated *L. pneumophilia,* happened to meet this author, the last remaining CDC medical staffer who had participated in the field investigation in Pontiac. Simultaneously, they said to each other, "Let's test the Pontiac fever blood specimens for antibodies to the Legionnaires' disease bacterium." By the end of the day, the mystery of the Pontiac outbreak had been solved. Thirty-two of 37 blood specimens collected and saved by the field team showed incontrovertible evidence of exposure to *L. pneumophilia.*

One must wonder, however, why—if Pontiac fever was indeed the same as Legionnaires' disease—it was so mild. Why had there been no cases of pneumonia in Pontiac? The answer is: no one knows. Pontiac fever is now considered a forme fruste, or an aberrant, usually abortive ("frustrated") form of Legionnaires' disease, caused perhaps by inhalation of bacterial products or dead bacteria.

How a disease gets its name. What is generally not known—in fact, never published before—is how Pontiac fever got its name. To be sure, the epidemic occurred in the city of Pontiac, but to the CDC field team there was another reason. In the spring and summer of 1968, a series of television commercials was attempting to start an "epidemic" of enthusiasm for a particular General Motors automobile. After an 18-hour day in the field, the CDC investigators, relaxing in front of the TV sets in their motel rooms, saw and heard all America being exhorted to "Get Pontiac fever!"

The Earth Day that made people sick

In a single week in May 1970, more than 200 children and teachers at the Willis Intermediate School in Delaware, Ohio, a town of approximately 15,000, became ill. All had severe respiratory disease with fever, cough and chest pain, headache, and in many cases extreme exhaustion requiring lengthy bed rest. Five persons were hospitalized. Almost immediately, the local health department asked state authorities in Columbus to investigate. On May 12 state officials took specimens from the throats of 18 of those affected and tested the school's water for microbial contamination. No viruses or bacteria were isolated in these tests.

On the trail of "Willis flu." Ten days later John Ackerman, epidemiologist for Ohio, contacted Philip Brachman, then director of the epidemiology program at the CDC. Ackerman requested CDC assistance to continue the investigation of the outbreak—even though no more new cases had been reported. Accordingly, a CDC medical epidemiologist, Alan Brodsky, was dispatched on May 24. Brodsky had no difficulty establishing that an epidemic of respiratory illness—dubbed "Willis flu"—had indeed taken place, centered primarily in the Willis School. The extent of the illness had not yet been assessed, however. Brodsky and a local team interviewed 40 persons who had been sick. To get a better picture of the disease itself, the investigators devised a questionnaire that was given to both students and teachers. Questions included such items as age, sex, race, address, grade attended or taught, homeroom, and class schedule. Subjects were also asked if they had been ill or well in the previous three weeks and whether there had been similar illness in their families. The team also questioned each of the 17 local physicians; contacted all other schools in the town, including Ohio Wesleyan University; and surveyed residents in the neighborhood of the Willis School.

Within a few days a relatively clear picture was emerging. Using a strict case definition that included any two of the three symptoms of fever, chest pain, and headache, along with being sick enough to stay home from school, investigators identified 273 cases among the students. The epidemic curve strongly suggested a common exposure over a relatively short time. School attendance records confirmed this pattern.

By this time important information was coming in from the rest of the community, implicating even more strongly the role of the immediate Willis school environment. Attendance data from other schools for the same time period showed no increase in absenteeism. Likewise, there was no increase in visits to the student health service at the university. However, residents of a fraternity house located only about 15–23 meters (50–75 feet) from Willis School reported having flulike symptoms early in May.

Still unknown was the disease itself and how it was transmitted. The investigative team did learn that one of the sick teachers had visited a specialist in Columbus and was diagnosed with histoplasmosis. This is a disease caused by a fungus that lives in the soil, particularly in the Ohio and Tennessee valleys; its symptoms are similar to those of flu but more severe. Further, histoplasmosis cannot be transmitted from one person to another as flu can but is spread by tiny spores that get into the air and are

109

A posted warning like this one in a Kentucky forest preserve—and the presence of the whitish coating visible on these branches, a sure sign that birds have roosted in the trees—would immediately have alerted the CDC investigators to the true nature of the histoplasmosis outbreak in Delaware, Ohio. In the absence of any such obvious clues, however, they were nearly stumped by the "mystery" illness with which they were confronted.

then inhaled. The fungus lives only in the soil where chickens, birds, and bats congregate. Starlings, grackles, and cowbirds often roost in the same trees years in a row, depositing droppings that promote the growth of the fungus. If the ground is disturbed, aerosols of spores form fairly easily. But if "Willis flu" really was histoplasmosis, the epidemiologists reasoned, the illness would have been more severe. Moreover, they could conceive of no obvious way the children and teachers could have been exposed.

Additional information further focused attention on the Willis School. Although the majority of the town's high school students had not been affected, the disease was reported to have occurred in two groups: members of the cast of the senior class show, *Brigadoon,* and girls who had taken a cosmetology course. During the last two weeks in April, all *Brigadoon* rehearsals and cosmetology classes had been held in the Willis School.

"Stirring up" an epidemic. By now there were also additional data pointing strongly to histoplasmosis. Knowing the incubation period of histoplasmosis and presuming the period of exposure to have been 24 to 48 hours at most (inferred from the epidemic curve), the epidemiologists could extrapolate back in time in order to see if anything unique had happened at the Willis School. Positing an incubation period of 10 to 15 days and using May 7 as the peak of the epidemic, they homed in on possible events during the school week of April 20–24. Careful questioning revealed that there had been no assemblies or class trips that week. However, Wednesday, April 22, was Earth Day, and the students had participated in some special activities. The sixth-grade class had picked up trash in a public park, and seventh and eighth graders had cleaned their lockers. One group of eighth-grade special education students had swept and raked the school's courtyard. Wednesday had been hot and very dry, the teachers remembered. In their enthusiasm, those who had worked in the courtyard raised considerable clouds of dust. The epidemiologists immediately recognized that there had been a clear potential for aerosolization of histoplasmosis spores. But where were the birds—and the droppings—that would account for the presence of the fungus? None had been observed by the epidemiologists.

The school courtyard was a grassy rectangle with bare patches here and there and a few bedraggled fir trees near the center. In one corner an air vent was recessed into the brick wall. By means of large fans, outside air was drawn in through this vent and distributed throughout the school.

Still, there were no birds—or bird droppings. Of course, histoplasmosis epidemics have been known to occur when normal-appearing soil was moved and aerosolized. Perhaps the droppings had been deposited long ago by birds that no longer roosted in the courtyard. The team questioned a teacher of long standing at the school. When asked if she remembered ever having seen flocks of birds in the courtyard, she responded, "Why sometimes we had to cancel classes, the birds were so noisy." What about bird droppings in the courtyard? "Some years in springtime the trees were so white you'd think it was Christmas."

Case closed. The verdict: zealous Earth Day celebrants sweeping the courtyard had stirred up soil containing ample deposits of bird droppings.

The aerosol was drawn into the school's air-handling system, which, in turn, blew spore-laden air into virtually every classroom. At final count more than 380 cases of histoplasmosis were reported in the Delaware outbreak, by far the largest such epidemic on record at that time—all caused by an attempt to clean up the environment!

L-tryptophan: deadly "remedy"

During a two-week period in October 1989, three physicians in New Mexico treated three women for fever and debilitating myalgia (muscle pain). All of the women had extremely high levels of the white blood cells known as eosinophils. Because of the severity of the symptoms, each of the doctors—quite independently—placed a call to the Mayo Clinic in Rochester, Minnesota, to speak with Gerald J. Gleich, an expert on eosinophilias (diseases characterized by high eosinophil counts). The first doctor to call Gleich had thoroughly examined his patient for virtually every known cause of eosinophilia but could find no likely explanation. The only unusual aspect of her history was that she regularly took L-tryptophan (LT), an amino acid sold in drug and health-food stores as an over-the-counter nutritional supplement. LT, which is found naturally in such foods as milk, eggs, red meat, and poultry, was supposedly helpful for a variety of problems, including insomnia, depression, and premenstrual syndrome. It had been taken by thousands with no known adverse effects.

An ominous coincidence. Gleich thought little of the first conversation until the other two doctors from New Mexico called him with almost identical stories: women with massively high eosinophil counts, profound myalgia, and self-prescribed use of LT. This, Gleich thought, was cause for immediate investigation. On October 30 both the New Mexico Health and Environmental Department and the CDC were alerted.

Clinically, at this point, there were three extremely sick women from New Mexico. Epidemiologically, these three cases constituted a cluster:

Gerald J. Gleich (above) of the Mayo Clinic in Rochester, Minnesota, an expert on diseases that affect the white blood cells known as eosinophils, became suspicious when, in a two-week period, he received three reports from New Mexico of women who were sick and had extraordinarily high eosinophil counts. Gleich decided to notify CDC headquarters of this apparent disease cluster. It soon became clear that these three cases represented only the tip of the iceberg. An epidemic had begun, and it was not confined to New Mexico. All those afflicted with the puzzling disorder, which was named eosinophilia-myalgia syndrome (EMS), were discovered to have taken L-tryptophan, a seemingly innocuous product sold in health food stores. In November 1989, within two weeks of Gleich's alert to the CDC, a nationwide surveillance system was established for the reporting of cases of EMS. Using these data, epidemiologists were able to map the geographic incidence of EMS on a state-by-state basis. Updated maps like the one reproduced at left were issued periodically, showing the magnitude and prevalence of the epidemic.

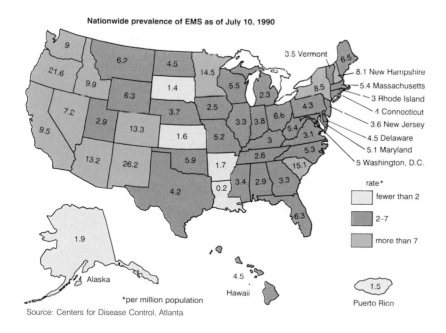

Nationwide prevalence of EMS as of July 10, 1990

3.5 Vermont
8.1 New Hampshire
5.4 Massachusetts
3 Rhode Island
4 Connecticut
3.6 New Jersey
4.5 Delaware
5.1 Maryland
5 Washington, D.C.

rate*
fewer than 2
2–7
more than 7

Alaska
*per million population
Hawaii
Puerto Rico

Source: Centers for Disease Control, Atlanta

a similar disease, occurring over a short time span, in similar patients residing in the same state and all users of a particular substance. Despite an overwhelming impulse to conclude that LT was the culprit and call an immediate statewide alert, the investigators had to first ensure that the apparent association between the disease and the taking of LT was indeed real. Disease clusters are a fairly common phenomenon, and associations between cases of disease and other variables are nothing more than that—associations—unless a cause-and-effect relationship can be established. Yet if LT actually had caused the illness in these three women, how could the epidemiologists reconcile the facts that (1) LT had never produced such a side effect before; (2) thousands of people had been taking LT for years; and (3) cases had been discovered only in New Mexico? On the other hand, three women were already profoundly ill; would it not be logical to assume that others taking LT might also be ill, undiagnosed and unreported?

Searching for victims. On November 7 the *Albuquerque Journal* carried a story about the three cases. Doctors soon began reporting more cases, and the state health department issued a warning that anyone taking LT should stop. On November 9 the first out-of-state cases of LT-associated myalgia and eosinophilia—or EMS (eosinophilia-myalgia syndrome), as the condition was named—were reported. That same day saw the arrival in the state of Food and Drug Administration (FDA) and CDC investigators, and a statewide case/control study was begun. In order to conclusively identify those with the disease, the investigators established the necessary criteria. A case was defined as anyone with (1) an eosinophil count of at least 2,000 per microliter (a normal count is 100–200), (2) incapacitating myalgia, and (3) no clinical evidence of any one of 30 disease conditions already known to cause eosinophilia. After reviewing the hospital records and interviewing possible cases, the epidemiologists identified 11 "true" cases. Twenty-two controls were chosen for comparison. Questionnaires

James W. Mayer, the New Mexico rheumatologist who first linked EMS to L-tryptophan, speaks to a group of Santa Fe women affected by the disease. Many EMS patients are immobilized by joint problems; some suffer from excruciating muscle pain. A number have died. Thanks to the quick work of the CDC epidemiologists, however, a rapid recall of all L-tryptophan products on U.S. store shelves spared untold numbers of potential victims.

Steven Pumphrey

When it was discovered that three members of the First Family—Pres. George Bush, his wife, Barbara, and their springer spaniel, Millie—all had autoimmune disorders, White House physicians became suspicious. Was this a disease cluster or simply a coincidence? A number of possible common sources of exposure—such as the drinking water at the White House, Camp David, or the vice-presidential mansion, their former residence—were proposed, but tests of the water failed to find anything unusual. In investigating a disease outbreak or apparent outbreak, epidemiologists must be careful not to assume that associations between factors are anything more than mere associations. A cause-and-effect relationship has to be demonstrated before any theory of disease causation can be accepted as fact.

administered to both groups asked about a variety of possible exposures that could have produced eosinophilia: foods, drugs, dietary supplements (including LT), and others.

Although the number of cases and controls was small, a highly significant difference in exposure rates emerged. All 11 (100%) of the cases reported a history of prior use of LT, while only 2 of 22 (9%) of the controls had taken LT. Both epidemiologically and statistically this difference in exposure rates strongly implicated LT as a major, if not the only, cause of EMS. The chance of such a difference in rates (100 and 9%) occurring independently was one in 50,000. This was enough evidence for the epidemiologists to assume a cause-and-effect relationship.

On November 13 the New Mexico health department issued an order halting the sale of LT in the state. Two days later the CDC established a nationwide reporting system, and other states began reporting findings nearly identical to those in New Mexico—further incriminating LT. Finally, on November 17 the FDA issued a nationwide recall of all LT-containing food supplements.

Two questions remained: (1) Were all LT products causing EMS, or were only certain batches responsible? (2) Was it LT itself or a contaminant that was the causative agent? These questions led to a yearlong investigation of the manufacture of LT and eventually sent CDC epidemiologists to Japan, where a majority of the LT sold in the U.S. is made. In November 1990 it was discovered that certain lots of LT—produced by a single Japanese manufacturer between October 1988 and June 1989—contained an impurity believed to be the cause of EMS. It was still not known exactly how the contaminant had been created or how it had produced the disease. Researchers speculated that it may have triggered an autoimmune response in susceptible individuals. As of late summer 1991, more than 1,500 cases of the disease had been reported to the CDC; among them were approximately 29 deaths.

MEMORIES
ARE MADE OF THIS...

By Richard M. Restak, M.D.

Plato considered memory similar to a block of wax: "When we wish to remember anything which we have seen or heard . . . we hold the wax up to the perceptions and thoughts and in that material receive the impressions of them."

Another ancient Greek, the poet Simonides of Ceos, invented a method for improving memory. The "method of places" involved an imaginary walk through one's house or town square. At selected locations in the walk, Simonides would conjure up a vivid mental picture to remind him of a point he wished to make in a speech.

As Cicero described Simonides' method: "We ought to set up images of a kind that can adhere longest in the memory. And we shall do so . . . if we set up images that are not many or vague but active." The images should be novel or marvelous since "ordinary things easily slip from the memory while the striking and the novel stay longer in the mind." Once formed, these images are then employed "as a wax writing-tablet and the letters written on it."

A change in the brain

Both Plato and Simonides recognized in their own way that memory involves some form of physical modification of the mind. Centuries later scientists recognized that the alteration takes place in the brain. Proof of this idea began accruing in the 1920s when American neuroscience pioneer Karl Lashley started his search for the "engram," the postulated change in a specific area in the brain that corresponds to the stored memory.

After teaching laboratory rats to wend their way through a maze to a reward box, Lashley started cutting out parts of the animals' cerebral cortex. To his surprise he discovered that the rats continued to find their way through the maze even after large portions of their brains had been removed. By 1950, after decades of trying to find where the brain stores memories, Lashley finally concluded that there is no such thing as a

A 19th-century engraving of central Concord, Massachusetts, illustrates the ancient "method of places" invented by Simonides of Ceos for improving memory. The technique involves imagining that the items on a list to be remembered appear in various locations throughout a mental walk in a familiar place, such as one's town square. For example, to remember a market list one might picture a loaf of bread atop the courthouse on the left, a basket of eggs by the tree in front of the courthouse, a string of sausages around the church steeple, and so on. In his approach to making remembered images last longer, Simonides recognized in his own way that memory involves some form of modification of the mind.

Richard M. Restak, M.D., *a neurologist and author, is Associate Clinical Professor of Neurology, Georgetown University School of Medicine, Washington, D.C. His books include* The Brain *(1984) and* The Mind *(1988).*

(Overleaf) Individual nerve cells, the major functional components of the brain, appear in a microscopic view of tissue from a rat's hippocampus. Courtesy of Christine Gall, M.D.

memory engram. Rather, the rat's knowledge of the maze seemed to be distributed throughout large areas of the brain. In the context of Lashley's experiments, "forgetting" did not happen suddenly with the removal of one key bit of tissue. Instead, it took place gradually, with the rats becoming less proficient as additional brain areas were excised. But this explanation led to another question: Does the diffuse storage of memories imply that no part of the brain is more important than another in the formation of memories?

Scientists had some answers to that question a few years after Lashley offered his conclusions about the engram. In 1953 a 27-year-old epileptic, known forever after as H.M., underwent brain surgery aimed at preventing the spread of seizure discharges, the storms of abnormal electrical activity that originate in local areas of the brain during epileptic seizures. Ordinarily the operation for this condition involved the removal of the medial part of one temporal lobe of the brain and its connections, but in H.M.'s operation the surgeons decided to cut out the medial part of both temporal lobes. The results were catastrophic and tragic.

Although the seizures ceased, H.M. lost the ability to retain the memory of any experience for more than a few moments. Now in his sixties, he remains unable to form memories of everyday occurrences such as what he ate for lunch or the identity of the person who called on the telephone just moments earlier. In short, he cannot store new memories—those since the time of his surgically induced injury—although he retains memories for events that occurred prior to the operation, such as his birth date or where he went to school. As a result of his severe anterograde amnesia, as his affliction is called, H.M. lives in a world of disconnected and fragmented experiences. Nevertheless, he retains normal intelligence and the ability to interact and converse with others as long as he is not required to store new information for later retrieval.

116

In the years since H.M.'s operation, scientists have encountered many other individuals with memory problems resulting from brain disorders. Some have suffered strokes, viral infections, tumors, accidents, or temporary loss of oxygen to the brain. Whatever the cause, memory impairment has resulted from interference with the process whereby that "wax impression" described by Plato is encoded, stored, or retrieved within the brain.

Nevertheless, not all of these people have suffered injury in the same areas. In the case of H.M. the injury involved the amygdala and the hippocampus, two paired structures communicating with the temporal lobes on each side of the brain. In other patients amnesia resulted from damage elsewhere, including an area near the brain's center (the medial diencephalon) and a part of the frontal lobe (the medial frontal cortex), along with an area immediately behind and below (the basal forebrain).

Learning about memory on the basis of brain damage alone is a tricky business. Accidents or diseases resulting in brain injury frequently involve many structures, or they may involve only parts of a single structure. How does one decide which damaged area out of many is the one responsible for the memory loss? In addition, the human brain contains several hundred billion nerve cells, each one making connections with between 1,000 and 10,000 other nerve cells. Deciding which of these circuits is important in memory is a daunting task. Even the brains of the rats taught to run mazes contain a larger number of neurons than any computer can keep track of.

It is thus clearer today than ever before that human memory is not amenable to simple interpretation. That view derives not only from studies of brain-damaged individuals but also from information collected over many years of observing and testing people with normal or superior memories and people with transient memory disturbances. While much of the human memory system remains to be understood, psychologists and neurologists have shown that it has a number of unique features.

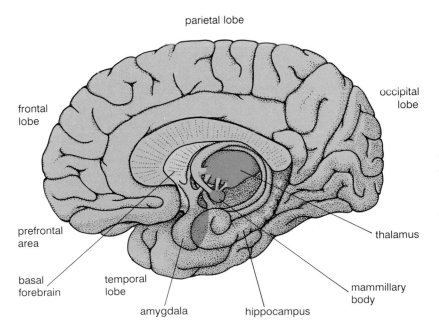

parietal lobe

frontal lobe

prefrontal area

basal forebrain

temporal lobe

amygdala

hippocampus

occipital lobe

thalamus

mammillary body

Regions of the human brain (shown with the left hemisphere removed) known to be important in memory include several deeply buried masses: the amygdala and hippocampus, paired structures that communicate with the overlying temporal lobes on each side of the brain; the paired thalamus and mammillary bodies, which are part of the diencephalon; and the basal forebrain. Other areas of the brain that function in memory are the outer tissue layer, or cortex, of the prefrontal area and the cortex of the medial frontal lobes, those parts of the lobes that face each other across the fissure separating the brain's two hemispheres.

Studies of brain-damaged individuals show that long-term memories are retained differently according to the type of remembered information. Memory for general and specific information, such as the addition tables learned in childhood (top right) or what one did yesterday, is called discursive knowledge; it includes what can be consciously stated or brought to mind in words, symbols, or images. Memory relating to learned skills like dancing (above) is called procedural learning. People suffering from amnesia can acquire and retain such skills even though they may not remember having learned them.

Paul Elledge

Different kinds of memory

Memories can be distinguished in various ways, one of which is by their duration. It is short-term memory that allows a person to hold in temporary storage a telephone number given by the information operator—a number that is usually forgotten the moment the phone begins to ring on the other end. The lifetime of a short-term memory is measured in moments, lasting longer only if one makes a deliberate effort.

"The true art of memory is the art of attention," as English author and critic Samuel Johnson put it. His dictum holds not only for short-term memory but for long-term memory as well. The more a person wants to remember something and the more he or she concentrates on it, the more likely it is that the information will be retrievable at a later time, even decades later. Moreover—and this factor distinguishes human beings from rats and other experimental animals—conscious awareness plays an important, but varying, role in human memory. In most instances people *know* that they know something.

Subdivisions of long-term memory. Most individuals, if asked to recite the names and terms of office of all the U.S. presidents, would have a pretty fair idea before they said "George Washington" whether they were going to come up with all the names and dates. This kind of long-term memory, called discursive (or declarative) knowledge, is seriously impaired in people—like H.M.—having damage somewhere within the system linking the temporal lobes, limbic system (especially the amygdala and hippocampus), and the frontal cortex. There exists, however, another type of remembered information, called procedural (or implicit) learning, that relates to acquired skills like riding a bicycle or playing tennis. Procedural learning remains intact in persons suffering from amnesia. More intriguing, such people may not remember that they possess this knowledge and, in fact, may deny that they can do what is asked. For instance, H.M. can learn how to mirror draw—that is, draw recognizable pictures while guided only by the reflection of his hand in a mirror. And with each attempt his performance improves, proving that his brain remembers even though he has no memory of his previous attempts. This result indicates that even people with amnesia can retain certain kinds of information in parts of the brain inaccessible to language or consciousness.

Yet another way of subdividing long-term memory has to do with general versus specific knowledge. Semantic memory reflects a general knowledge about the world, such as knowing the number of inches in a foot or the months of the year. Episodic memory, in contrast, reflects the storage of specific information, such as what one ate this morning for breakfast or the identity of visitors to one's home over the past few days. Typically, semantic memory is the last to go in a degenerative brain disease like Alzheimer's disease, whereas memory of the episodic variety is usually impaired early in such an illness. In fact, some loss of episodic memory is perfectly normal—few people can recall the exact occasion when, for example, they learned that Paris is the capital of France. Moreover, semantic memory, when it does fail, may break down only within certain limited categories, such as language.

Even within the language sphere (where memory loss is called aphasia), those afflicted may lose access only to limited and highly specific components. For instance, a person may lose the ability to name living things while retaining the ability to recall the names of inanimate objects. Such category-specific semantic deficits are thought to occur because concepts and names are learned and stored through different sensory channels. For example, words for food like *steak* and *bread* may be associated with stored information about taste and smell, while musical terms may be associated with memories concerned with sound. As a result of this specialization within the brain, strokes affecting specific areas may inflict highly selective memory impairments, such as the inability to remember the words to a popular song or to retrieve from memory a mental picture of a friend's facial features.

Transient memory loss. Some of what scientists know about memory comes specifically from studying the memory disturbances that follow head

Specialization of memory ability in the brain extends even to highly specific subcategories of knowledge. For instance, individuals afflicted with aphasia as the result of a stroke may lose access only to certain components of learned language— perhaps the words to a single song—while retaining their basic musical knowledge and vocabulary.

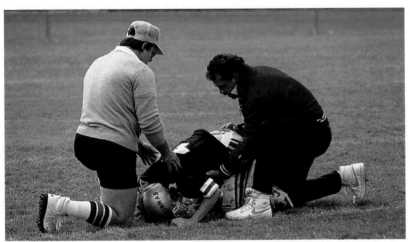

A football player briefly knocked unconscious during a game may soon forget what happened to him in the short period of time just prior to his injury. This phenomenon, a form of retrograde amnesia, suggests that concussion can interfere with the initial coding of a person's preinjury experience into long-term memory. Because the information is never encoded, it cannot later be retrieved.

injuries. If the injury is severe enough to lead to concussion, the memory loss may involve events immediately before (retrograde amnesia) or after (anterograde amnesia) the injury. A football player removed from the game after a brief loss of consciousness following a hard tackle may be able to tell his replacement the signals from the previous play. Twenty minutes later he will have no memory of the 10 minutes prior to his injury. In such cases of trauma-induced amnesia, it is as if the injury interferes with the initial coding of information about an experience into memory. Since the information was never encoded, it cannot subsequently be recalled.

A still mysterious, particularly intriguing form of memory disturbance is called transient global amnesia. The sufferer, almost without exception an elderly but generally healthy person, suddenly loses track of time and place. He or she expresses bewilderment about present location, what is happening in the environment, the identity of companions, and other current information. In contrast to the psychologically induced forms of amnesia called fugue states, which seem to represent attempts to escape undesirable memories, the victim of transient global amnesia does not forget who he or she is. Typically, the condition disappears equally suddenly hours or days later, and the person is restored to normal. Although various theories have been put forth regarding the origin of this uncommon, though not rare, disorder (strokes, epileptic seizures, and variants of migraine, to name a few), a cause is rarely discovered. Whatever its origin, it serves as a reminder that memory may break down in novel ways that, so far, no single theory of memory formation can satisfactorily explain.

From studying people with transient global amnesia and other amnesic disorders, most neuroscientists are now convinced of the existence of multiple memory subsystems wherein immediate, recent, and remote memories are stored in different parts of the brain. This multiplicity also holds true for the processes of registration, retention, and retrieval. Such anatomic distinctions are important to keep in mind when trying to understand a multilayered and complex entity like human memory.

Psychological insights

In addition to studies of the brain, psychological investigations have contributed greatly to the understanding of memory. Simonides' method of places was just the beginning. In the 16th century the Dutch scholar Erasmus claimed, "Though I do not deny that memory can be helped by places and images, yet the best memory is based on three most important things, namely, study, order and care." Along the same lines, Samuel Johnson referred to memory 200 years later as "the purveyor of reason" and argued, "It is indeed the faculty of remembrance which may be said to place us in the class of moral agents." If a person could remember all of the events of his or her life, then meaning and order would naturally follow—or so it has been argued by those who emphasize memory as an integrating force within the personality. According to this view, a superpower memory is the goal, and forgetfulness is the enemy that stands in the way of its attainment. However, too good a memory may bring its own problems—the immersion of its owner in a sea of trivia.

Possibly the most celebrated instance of memory retrieval is that of French novelist Marcel Proust, who used the real-life incident of a childhood memory involuntarily revived by a taste of tea and biscuit—the latter fictionalized as a madeleine—as the starting point for his multivolume Remembrance of Things Past. *In the work, an allegory of his own life, Proust pursues the idea that truth is something stored in one's unconscious memory, using his own prodigious powers of memory to create vivid characters and a vast panorama of French society.*

120

How much is enough? In 1968 Soviet psychologist Aleksandr R. Luria described in his book *The Mind of a Mnemonist* a man with a perfect memory. A 30-year-old journalist when Luria first observed him, S. could remember long series of numbers, words, or letters. Even after 16 years, S. was able to repeat the original sequences without error. Moreover, he could do this in reverse order just as easily. Nor did it make any difference whether the material contained meaningful words or nonsense syllables. Over a period of almost 30 years of testing, Luria came to the conclusion that "the span of his memory had no distinct limits." S. employed an uncommon and yet little understood ability called eidetic imagery (photographic memory), an ability to visualize photographically clear and accurate mental images. Eidetic imagery allowed S. to see and examine later in his "mind's eye" an exact image of the material he wished to remember.

Rather than being an asset, S.'s phenomenal memory worked against him. Since he remembered so much, he found it hard to stick to the point in a conversation. "His remarks would be cluttered with details and irrelevancies; he would become verbose, digress endlessly, and finally have to strain to get back to the subject of the conversation," wrote Luria. Over his lifetime S. achieved little and died an unfulfilled, unhappy man who considered himself a failure.

Marcel Proust, in contrast, enlisted his virtuoso powers of memory to become one of the world's great writers. "I felt suddenly that all external obstacles had been eliminated. . . . And like an airman who hitherto has progressed laboriously along the ground, abruptly 'taking off,' I soared slowly towards the silent heights of memory," he recounted in *Time Regained* (1927), the last volume of *Remembrance of Things Past*.

Do the abilities of people like S. and Proust suggest that the average brain contains within its circuitry memories for all the experiences of a lifetime? And if so, are all the events of one's life at least potentially retrievable? In the 1950s Canadian neurosurgeon Wilder Penfield took an important step toward answering this question.

Penfield discovered that he could elicit memories in patients undergoing neurosurgical procedures by electrically stimulating parts of their temporal lobe and its connections. When Penfield applied the tiny nonpainful current, his patients reported long-forgotten events. In some cases the recollection occurred with such vividness that the patient almost believed that the events were happening again. These "experiential illusions," as Penfield referred to them, support the notion that the brain retains many more previous experiences than a person realizes or could ever hope to retrieve through concerted efforts. Penfield's operating-room experiments did not suggest that *all* experiences are embedded in memory. Instead, many of the patients' reports sound more like composites than memories of specific events.

Memories as personal reconstructions. Memory is also linked with learning and goal-directed processes. "In order to transfer an episode into LTM [long-term memory] we must understand what that episode relates to, with respect to what we already know," stated artificial intelligence expert Roger Schank in *The Connoisseur's Guide to the Mind* (1991). Something is remembered, according to Schank, "so that when it comes up again, we can use that experience to guide future behavior." According to this model, experiences first must be evaluated in terms of one's own interests. "Memory is a knowledge-based affair. . . . Finding things in memory depends upon having been interested in them at the time that they occurred."

A way to elaborate on Schank's point is to consider how a person goes about learning and remembering a law in physics. Hearing about the law in a lecture is helpful but not nearly as effective as seeing a demonstration of the law. Even better is to do something personally that exemplifies the law or to picture something interesting in the mind that relates to the law. But what is the best way to do that?

For the majority of people who are not memory virtuosos, a system based on Simonides' method of places may offer the best chance for improving memory. More modern, though essentially similar, approaches take their inspiration from Swiss psychologist Jean Piaget's directive: "Memory depends on a person's capacity to construct an experience." Memory as a constructive process does away with such analogies as a tape recorder, a file cabinet, or—Sherlock Holmes's favorite—an overcrowded attic, in which information is simply stored away for later examination.

"If we remembered everything we did or saw or said in one evening, our memories would be like an overstuffed chair with no room for any more stuffing," wrote Schank. In order to avoid such an ultimately paralyzing glut

For your Vacation Package, call us at
1-800-ONTARIO (1-800-668-2746).

of information, people actively construct memories and remember their reconstruction rather than the original event. The reconstructions take the form of representations. Those things happening around a person that inter est him or her are likely to be represented and recalled. And since interests vary greatly from one person to another, their memories of even the same event are likely to differ substantially. The things chosen for representation and therefore remembered are the things felt worthy of attention, worthy of thinking about. That is why brute memorization of "boring" material is so difficult. One's boredom and lack of interest preclude going through the necessary processes of representation and construction.

Chunking. Princeton University psychologist George Miller described the principles of reconstructive memory in 1956 in a classic paper, "The Magical Number Seven, Plus or Minus Two." There Miller put into scientific terms an observation dating to the 19th-century Scottish philosopher William Hamilton, who observed that if a handful of marbles are thrown on the floor, "you will find it difficult to view at once more than six, or seven at most, without confusion." As Miller pointed out, however, more items

123

Before the wide availability of books and the modern deluge of mechanical and electronic means for preserving information, important events were passed along in the form of orally transmitted stories, songs, and poems (right). A memory for details was crucial to storytelling, and with each retelling both teller and listener improved their recall of what was significant in their lives and to their community. Today computer diaries, calculators, and memory-dial telephones (below) are said to be freeing the mind from trivia for more meaningful tasks. It is reasonable to ask, however, whether excessive reliance on such devices is encouraging degeneration of the very memory skills needed to retain what one actually wishes to remember.

can be remembered when they are coded, or "chunked." For instance, one can remember long strings of numbers, letters, or words when they are reconstructed into meaningful patterns. The couplet "On old Olympic's towering tops/A Finn and German vied at hops" helps medical students recall the names of the 12 cranial nerves starting with *olfactory* and working down to *hypoglossal.*

Chunking accounts for many inexplicable and seemingly marvelous memory performances. Possibly the most famous example is that of Mozart's memorization of the *Miserere* written more than a century earlier by the Italian composer Gregorio Allegri. In 1770, while in his early teens, Mozart visited the Vatican's Sistine Chapel and heard this choral work performed only twice. He then sat down and wrote out the entire score from memory. Since only three copies (at most) of the score existed and its publication was forbidden by its owner, the Vatican, Mozart had no source for re-creating the score other than his own recall of what he had heard.

Over the years Mozart's performance in memorizing the *Miserere* often has been cited as proof of his genius as a mnemonist, but now that the score is available, his memory feat seems less remarkable. Harmonically

124

the *Miserere* is utterly conventional for the period. Anyone who shared Mozart's familiarity with similar musical forms would not find it a great problem to chunk large parts of the *Miserere* around these standard structures. "Mozart's feat of memory does not involve inexplicable processes which set him apart from other musicians," wrote John Sloboda in *The Musical Mind* (1985). "Rather, it distinguishes him as someone whose superior knowledge and skill allow him to accomplish something rapidly and supremely confidently which most of us can do, albeit less efficiently, and on a smaller scale."

Language as an aid and a limit to memory. Sloboda's claim still seems a bit extravagant, with the possible exception of those possessing finely honed musical talents. There is no doubt, however, about Sloboda's main point that one's memory can be improved by special knowledge, efficient processing, or even the application of special memory techniques (or "tricks" as they are sometimes disparagingly called). Yet few people care enough to learn ways of improving their memories. Perhaps it is because feats of memory are held in far less esteem now than in ages past. Today teachers and students alike disparage brute memorization. Nevertheless, some ambivalence about memory exists as well, since it is also true that among adults few things are more worrisome than the gnawing dread that occasional memory failures may herald the onset of Alzheimer's disease. It seems that all people wish to preserve their memories, but few want to use them. The advent of calculators, personal computers, and electronic diaries further compromises memory capacities. Why bother to remember what can be stored and retrieved in seconds from an electronic memory aid? In the reliance on such memory aids, though, is it possible that memory could suffer an atrophy of disuse?

One way of avoiding such degeneration comes from telling others about experiences that are important. Prior to the invention of the printing press, important events were preserved in the form of orally transmitted stories—epic poems, legends, ballads, and so on. With each retelling, the event was further imprinted on the minds of the listeners and, more important, in the memory of the storyteller. Schank has suggested that people remember significant events in their lives by telling them to others, which, in effect, is a way of telling them to themselves. "If you want to remember something you must tell it to someone. The more you tell it the more you remember it. Our stories *are* our memories."

As with all stories, language sets limits on what can be told and remembered. One can recall "a girl on a red bicycle passing me on the street on my way to work" but not "red-wheels-freckles-moving-large-to-small." People do not remember that way because they do not talk to each other that way. Generally only severely disturbed individuals or incredibly gifted ones are able to extract a coherent image from an incoherent verbal context. To paraphrase philosopher Ludwig Wittgenstein: What one cannot speak about, one must remain silent about.

Communal memory refers to the process of social negotiation that occurs among persons in order to mutually decide "what happened" in a particular situation. A husband and wife, for instance, may negotiate the

Mood, beliefs, imagination, and suggestion all can influence a person's memory of an event. For instance, a witness to a traffic accident (right) may report a nonexistent or erroneous detail if the questioner introduces a subtle unsupported assumption. After being asked "How far from the intersection was the vehicle when the light turned red?" the witness may fail to recall that the vehicle had already entered the intersection when the light changed.

"right" way to remember and report their experiences of the events on a recent vacation. Once this narrative "truth" is worked out, it will become the "official" version of what happened. Since the negotiated version of a past experience is likely to endure within an individual's own mind and other people's minds, it would seem unwise to acquiesce too quickly to that version if it does not sound correct. To this extent, the preservation of one's own memory of events is something worth fighting for.

Effects of mood, suggestion, and other factors. In general, people are better at remembering and telling stories about happy occasions than sad ones, but the opposite holds if they are depressed. Not only do depressed people remember less but what they do remember is tinged with sadness, as past triumphs are recalled as petty and meaningless. With the lifting of the depression, memory improves and past accomplishments are again triumphs. At the other end of the continuum, patients in the manic phase

People who have made hurried visits to the local shopping mall are likely to be familiar with the effects of distraction and inattention on their ability to recall where they parked the car.

of manic-depression possess better than normal memories, though extravagant and expansive ones.

Such transformations of memory occur not only under the influence of mood but also under the influence of judgment, beliefs, and imagination. "Remembering is not the re-excitation of innumerable fixed, lifeless and fragmentary traces. . . . It is built out of the relation of our attitude towards a whole mass of organized past reactions or experience," wrote British memory researcher Frederic Bartlett in his classic *Remembering* (1932).

At all times memory is altered by expectations and suggestions. Hypnotized subjects, for example, may remember things they could not previously recall. In addition, they may remember things that never took place—one of the reasons hypnosis is now outlawed in many courtrooms. Courtroom testimony based on memory can also be "contaminated" by suggestions outside the influence of hypnosis. If a witness to a traffic accident, for example, is asked a question that contains a subtle factual change ("Which car ran the red light?" when the offending car actually ignored a stop sign), the witness may well later recall that the accident had occurred at an intersection governed by a traffic signal rather than a stop sign.

Forgetting and forgetfulness

Not only do people remember with greater or lesser accuracy, they also forget things completely. How much forgetting is normal? When is it a sign of disease?

"Actually, forgetting is a very good thing," according to Schank. "In order to remember an experience some unconscious process in the mind has to decide that experience might somehow be useful to recall later on. Remembering everything actually prevents you from concentrating on what can be learned, allowing the rest to be forgotten."

Whereas forgetting may well be an asset, it is more likely to be branded "forgetfulness" when it frustrates one's plans or becomes the source of embarrassment. The most common causes of forgetfulness are distraction and inattention, which interfere with the initial encoding of the information. And without encoding there can be no storage or later retrieval. Persons who are distracted or overworked frequently seek medical help for memory difficulties stemming from these encoding problems. Improvement in their mental habits or an adjustment in life-style, rather than medications, is often all that is needed to bring about a dramatic improvement in memory. Only when one's memory ability is deficient compared with those of others of the same age, interests, education, and so on should there be cause for concern. For memory loss to be a sign of disease, a falloff from the usual performance should be apparent not only to the person involved but to those around him or her.

With aging—and beginning at around age 30—some degree of forgetfulness is normal. This phenomenon, called age-associated memory impairment (AAMI), is most apparent in tests that have little practical importance in daily life—repeating a series of digits backward, recalling the first in a series of 20 words, or remembering details in a series of pictures. In tests employing real-life, everyday situations, the gap between younger

Milestoning is a group-reminiscence technique that has proved helpful in improving memory in elderly people limited by age-associated memory impairment. Participants discuss and trade recollections about an event or time period that occurred years before their impairment began, while scrapbooks, photos, and other media are enlisted to help retrieve memories long buried.

Photograph, Steve Hansen—Stock, Boston

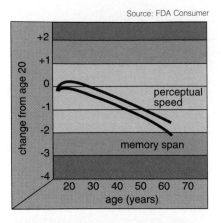

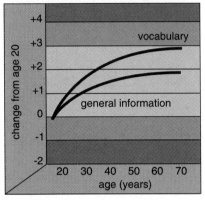

Although speed of information processing and retrieval declines with age, the loss usually has little practical importance in daily life. A healthy elderly person's lifetime accumulation of knowledge and vocabulary—the traditional "wisdom of the aged"—does not diminish and is normally adequate compensation for slower response.

and older individuals narrows. Although elderly subjects learn less rapidly, their rate of forgetting information, once learned, does not differ from that of younger subjects. Their semantic memories, the store of information they have gained over a lifetime, do not decline with age. Easy distractibility and inefficient strategies for handling new incoming information play a large part in the memory problems associated with aging. Finally, older people are often less motivated to do their best on tests that hold little practical importance for them in their daily lives.

A useful approach to improving memory in elderly people who are limited by AAMI involves "milestoning." In one variant, first developed in a psychiatric education and rehabilitation center, elderly people are encouraged to take part in a group reminiscence program involving discussion and recall of some time or event that occurred years before the onset of their memory impairment. In another variant, a group leader selects a year, say 1939, and the residents are encouraged to trade reminiscences of what they can recall from that year. Scrapbooks and magazines are enlisted to jog everybody's memory. Not only do elderly people improve their memories by milestoning but they also feel better and interact better with others.

Nevertheless, in one area—the rapid retrieval of information—the older person, despite any training, is always outclassed by someone younger. The older brain processes information at a slower rate, perhaps owing to slowness of conduction along nerve-cell pathways. Whatever the reason, elderly people do not appear often on "Jeopardy" or other television quiz shows that reward quickness of response and not just accuracy. On the other hand, slower retrieval does not present much of a problem in day-to-day living, since the traditional "wisdom of the aged" has less to do with speed than semantic memory for information gained from life experience. Often this wisdom cannot even be put into words; the older machinist, salesperson, or lawyer just knows by "instinct," *i.e.,* decades of experience, the best course of action to follow in regard to a given task or client.

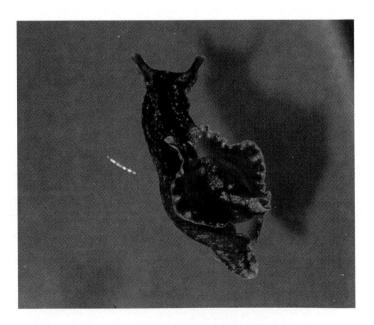

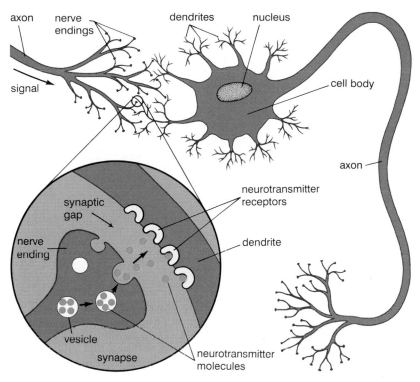

axon · nerve endings · dendrites · nucleus · signal · cell body · axon · neurotransmitter receptors · dendrite · synaptic gap · nerve ending · vesicle · synapse · neurotransmitter molecules

Because of its limited behavior patterns and large, easily identifiable nerve cells, the marine mollusk known as Aplysia *(opposite page, bottom) has become a model for studying the neural mechanisms of memory. Neurobiologists have learned that memory in* Aplysia *depends on biochemical changes involving the synapse, the junction at which one nerve cell passes its signals to another. As illustrated at left, each nerve cell consists of a cell body from which extend branchlike dendrites and a long component called the axon. The axon terminates in a number of nerve endings that make contact at the synapse with the dendrites (and sometimes the cell body) of other nerve cells. Transmission of the nerve signal across the synaptic gap (inset) is chemical in nature; molecules called neurotransmitters are released from vesicles in the nerve endings of the sending nerve cell and diffuse across the gap to act on molecules called receptors on the receiving nerve cells. Changes in levels of various chemicals serve to influence and regulate this process, on both the sending and the receiving sides of the synapse. Studies of the brains of other animals also suggest that the formation of memories is related, at least in part, to modifications in synapses.*

Photograph, opposite page, bottom, courtesy of Eric Kandel, M.D.

Searching for a biological basis

While some researchers have approached remembering and forgetting from their psychological and behavioral aspects, others have continued to pursue the neural foundations of memory. Rather than trying to deal with the billions of nerve cells in the human brain, a number of investigators have concentrated on creatures having less complicated nervous systems.

Memory in a sea slug. One organism that has become a model for neural studies is a species of sea slug called *Aplysia*. This mollusk, which resembles a shell-less snail, displays limited repertoires of behavior, the gill-withdrawal reflex being the most notable. It also possesses small brain-like collections of nerve cells called ganglions packed with large and easily identifiable nerve cells.

Despite the simplicity of this arrangement compared with the human brain, *Aplysia* can establish memories of previous experiences. A gentle prod on a sensitive area, for example, induces the animal to withdraw its gill into a cavity—a defensive reaction against a potential predator. If the same prod is applied again and again with no adverse consequences, however, the sea slug gradually learns to ignore it. In more complicated experiments, *Aplysia* proves capable of associative learning. An electric shock applied to the tail shortly after a gentle tap on the siphon causes the animal to react to the tap as if it were the shock. The "wiring" of the gill reflex responsible for all of this behavior is a model of simplicity; the sensory nerve cell that registers the tap makes direct contact with a motor cell that controls gill withdrawal.

Thanks to research on *Aplysia*, investigators now know that, at least in these humble creatures, memory is dependent on changes brought about

129

(Top) Anita Sirevaag, University of Illinois, (bottom) courtesy of William T. Greenough

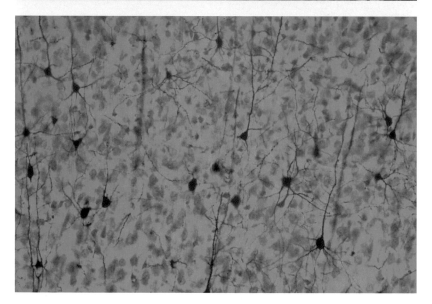

Changes in synapses ascribed to the formation of memories have been detected in rats raised experimentally in contrasting housing conditions. Some rats were reared individually or in pairs in plain laboratory housing—essentially small transparent plastic bins—while others (top) were provided with large cages, about a dozen companions, and a variety of toys that were changed daily. Later examination of the rats' brain tissues showed that in the visual region of the cerebral cortex and in several other cerebral cortical regions, the rats given more opportunity to learn possessed more synapses, a denser capillary network for supplying blood, and more support cells than did the rats raised in less-enriched housing. (Bottom) In a microscopic image of prepared brain tissue from an environmentally stimulated rat, nerve cell bodies and their projecting dendrites appear against a mottled blue background. When compared with corresponding tissue from less stimulated rats, nerve cell bodies from stimulated rats show more extensively branched dendrites, indicating additional synaptic connections with other nerve cells.

at the point where one nerve cell passes its signals to another, a junction called the synapse. These changes involve alterations of the messenger molecules, or neurotransmitters, by which signals are transmitted across the synapse from one nerve cell to another. The evidence is encouraging, although by no means is it certain, that what is being learned about memory in simpler organisms will turn out to be useful in understanding human memory as well.

Long-term potentiation. An important stimulus to understanding the biological underpinnings of memory came decades before studies on *Aplysia* began. As early as 1949 Canadian psychologist Donald Hebb had already proposed that memory depends in some way on the modification of synaptic activity. According to Hebb, the firing patterns of entire arrays of nerve cells become facilitated after repetitive activation. This facilitation occurs at the synapse, the result being that the connection between the

130

communicating nerve cells is strengthened. So far, neuroscientists are in disagreement as to whether this change occurs in the cell that sends the signal or the cell that receives it. In either case, memory depends on the modification of many synapses that, acting together, form a circuit. Once a circuit is established, it becomes that much easier to activate in the future. (At the behavioral level this facilitation is thought to be the basis of habits.) This long-lasting increase in synaptic efficiency and strength is called long-term potentiation. Scientific understanding of how this process works comes from studies of the hippocampus, a brain area long known to be important in memory.

In research carried out in the 1980s by Richard Morris of the University of Edinburgh Medical School, rats were placed in a small pool of murky water. Hidden beneath the surface was a platform that the rats had to find in order to get out of the water. Since the platform could be neither seen nor smelled, during repetitive trials the rats had to depend on spatial clues from the surroundings in order to remember the platform's location. Morris administered the test both to rats whose hippocampus had been experimentally damaged and to normal rats. After several trials the normal rats learned to locate the platform and remember its location from one session to the next. The rats with destructive lesions in their hippocampus could not learn the task; they swam aimlessly until they finally located the platform by chance.

Morris went on to show that the same memory loss can also be brought about chemically. When rats were given a drug that blocks the activity of certain neurotransmitter receptors important to long-term potentiation, the rats lost their ability to remember the location of the platform. According to Morris, the drug worked by interfering at the synapse with the transfer of information into long-term potentiation. Thus, a drug known to block long-term potentiation also blocks learning (and, according to more recent experiments, does so at the same concentration)—a neat demonstration that, at the level of the biochemistry of nerve cells, long-term potentiation is a correlate of memory.

Other studies have detected changes in synapses when memories form. In the mid-1980s William Greenough of the University of Illinois at Urbana-Champaign compared the brains of rats raised in cages filled with toys and other diversions with those of rats living in deprived, less-stimulating environments. He found that rats in the enriched environment grew 20% more synapses in part of their brain than did the deprived rats. It is speculated that the increased number of synapses that formed as a result of greater stimulation and diversity represent memory at the level of intercellular communication.

Biochemical investigations. Contemporary biochemical research is focusing on correlations between chemical mechanisms within the brain and memory processes. These include the role of protein synthesis in memorization, modulation of learning via the use of short chains of amino acids (peptides), and the contributions of the main neurotransmitter systems, especially acetylcholine, the catecholamines (*e.g.,* epinephrine and dopamine), GABA (gamma-aminobutyric acid), and glutamic acid. Although

131

Superman in his later years

one or another of these neurotransmitters may be important in certain kinds of memory, it is unlikely that any one of them is responsible for the overall process of encoding, retention, and retrieval. Nor can memory, once it is biochemically established, be moved from one laboratory animal to another simply by the transfer of brain tissue or chemicals. For a time this feat was thought possible, and many experiments were conducted wherein an animal, after being taught some simple response, would have some portion of its brain transplanted into another animal. Despite initial claims to the contrary, this method does not result in the transfer of the memory of the learned response. Most experts now believe that memory involves many chemicals acting in concert within the individual brain. Further, the chemical codes may differ from one person's brain to the next even in the establishment of similar memories.

Some theories about memory emphasize changes in the nerve cell membrane. These changes may involve special enzymes or alterations in the channels that carry electrically charged atoms or molecules (ions) across the membrane between the cellular interior and the environment outside the cell. For each of these theories, neuroscientists have come up with supporting data, yet not all of the theories can be correct. The challenge is to decide which brain chemicals and which circuits are the most promising candidates and to develop a theory that correlates what is known about the whole brain with what scientists are discovering at the level of cellular brain chemistry and nerve-cell circuitry.

One contribution toward such a synthesis is the work, reported in 1991, of Toshiyuki Sawaguchi and Patricia S. Goldman-Rakic of Yale University School of Medicine. They injected into the brains of rhesus monkeys drugs that counteract the action of the neurotransmitter dopamine at one of three kinds of dopamine receptors present on nerve cells. The site chosen for the drug was the prefrontal cortex, an area established to be important in memory. After the injections the monkeys made many mistakes in learned tasks employing memory. Thus, the researchers concluded, one of the dopamine receptors plays a selective role in memory formation within a specific brain area, the prefrontal cortex. Other neurotransmitters may also play a similar role in the prefrontal cortex or elsewhere.

Whatever the neurotransmitter involved, existing evidence makes it likely that interactions with steroids, a class of compounds that includes the sex hormones and the hormones of the adrenal cortex, are also important. For example, the effects of memory-enhancing drugs can be reversed in animals surgically deprived of their adrenal glands. The same result can be obtained by administration of drugs that chemically oppose the actions of steroids.

Looking for a "memory drug." Treatments for certain kinds of abnormal memory loss, once reliably diagnosed, started with the discovery that chemicals that alter the brain's neurotransmitters can sometimes enhance memory performance. Amphetamines, for instance, lead to an increase at the synapse of the neurotransmitters dopamine and epinephrine. They also increase memory performance in the short run. Unfortunately, as many students from the 1960s onward discovered while cramming for exams under

132

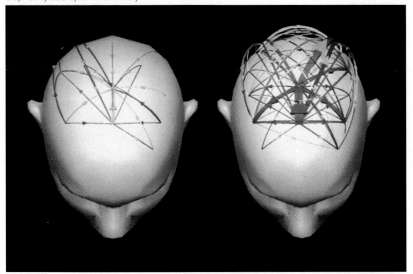

Some of the many questions remaining about human memory are being approached with the aid of recent technological innovations. One example is MANSCAN (mental activity network scanner), a computer-linked combination of electroencephalography, or brain-wave recording, and magnetic resonance imaging (MRI). MANSCAN records electrical activity at 124 points around the skull and correlates it with an MRI image of the head to yield pictures of brain activity as often as every four-thousandths of a second. Many such pictures, viewed sequentially, form an animated video that can trace brain activity as a subject performs a mental task. In the MANSCAN images at left, the neural-activity pattern is seen to be more complex for a mental task that involves immediate (very short-term) memory (near left) than for one that does not (far left). The thickness of the arrows connecting pairs of points is a measure of the similarity of activity between those points, while colors represent the time delay between related peaks of activity.

the influence of amphetamines, the improvement in memory disappears in tandem with the disappearance of the drug from the brain. This "state-dependent" learning is of little use when it comes to retaining and assimilating information for long-term storage. Nevertheless, even this limited achievement of memory enhancement suggested the possibility of treatments for memory disorders based on manipulation of neurotransmitters.

The discovery of diminished levels of acetylcholine in the brains of sufferers of Alzheimer's disease inspired early efforts to treat that disease with foods, such as soybean extract, that contain large amounts of choline, a precursor compound from which the body can make acetylcholine. Other treatments used agents to stimulate the brain to make more dopamine. So far there exists no satisfactory drug capable of permanently helping a failing memory, although biochemical approaches hold great promise. Many major pharmaceutical firms around the world are presently engaged in highly competitive efforts to be the first to discover a successful "memory drug."

Challenges for the future

It is fair to say that human beings have learned more about memory in the past century than in all earlier epochs combined. Despite this impressive advance, it is also true that important challenges remain: How are internal representations encoded within the brain? Is memory retained in the system that learns or elsewhere? Does a memory reside in the connections of a relatively small number of nerve cells, or is it represented by millions of cells organized in several subsystems and spread over wide regions of the brain? What structural and functional changes take place in networks of nerve cells during learning and memory? What are the biochemical and molecular bases for short- and long-term memory, and how do they differ? Fully satisfying answers to these crucial questions remain for future research to find.

AGING:
Don't Take It Sitting Down!

by Peter D. Wood, D.Sc., Ph.D.

Exercise and temperance will preserve something of our youthful vigor, even into old age.   —Cicero (106–43 BC)

In the past half century the practitioners of medical science have produced a glittering array of wonders—snatching the fevered from the jaws of death and protecting the innocent from fearsome diseases. For many developed countries profound reductions in infant mortality and the relative rarity of death from infectious diseases—AIDS notwithstanding—have allowed a very large proportion of men and women to see their 65th birthday and so become, according to a common definition, elderly. In the United States life expectancy in 1900 had not reached 50 years; today this figure has risen above 75 and is approaching 80 for women. Moreover, the number of elderly people is growing at twice the rate of the rest of the population. Thanks to medical research advances and a substantial investment in public health, Americans have been granted an extra 30 years of life—a bonus to be enjoyed in their sixth, seventh, and eighth decades.

Accounting for aging

Usually aging is measured by the calendar—*i.e.,* by one's date of birth. This certainly is convenient for many purposes—deciding when one is eligible for a pension or ineligible to pilot a commercial aircraft, obtaining reduced-price admission to the cinema, and so forth. Another approach would be to subject people to periodic physical and mental examinations and decide, on the basis of their ability to function, what "age" they are. This would be not only costly and revolutionary but undoubtedly controversial, considering that a wrinkled but slim 70-year-old who can jog a mile in 7 minutes would be regarded as "younger" than a smooth-skinned, overweight 30-year-old who cannot cover the same distance in 10 minutes.

The "use it or lose it" theory of aging proposes that if people do not exercise, their anatomic systems will function less well—perhaps not at all. What makes this proposition particularly appealing is its implication that people need not "lose it." The residents of a retirement home in France (right) have lost neither their vigor nor their joie de vivre.

Peter D. Wood, D.Sc., Ph.D., *is Professor of Medicine, Stanford University School of Medicine, and Associate Director, Stanford Center for Research in Disease Prevention, Palo Alto, California.*

(Overleaf) Runners in their sixties and seventies bound over a hurdle in the 10,000-meter cross-country race at the 1989 World Veterans Championships, held in Eugene, Oregon. Every other summer the championships draw thousands of older runners, who thrive on their vitality and defy the assumption that to age is to decline.
Photograph, John Giustina

The very word *elderly* tends to evoke such associations as "gray haired," "retired," "stooped," "frail," "forgetful," "doddering," "decrepit," "spectacles," "rocking chair," "cane," etc. Certainly television ad makers know what sort of actors to employ to promote products intended for the elderly— *e.g.,* denture adhesives and incontinence pads. All of this makes some sense because the incidence of many debilitating conditions does increase steadily with calendar age. In fact, the traditional system of determining age has worked quite well; generally the "calendar old" have been a relatively small group in society, and they have been, well, elderly.

The situation is fast changing, however; the elderly are not a small group anymore. By the turn of the century, 35 million Americans will be 65 or older; and by 2030, 65 million, or one in five, will be elderly by the current definition. And there is little doubt that continuing advances in medicine and surgery will further reduce the impact of many previously debilitating conditions.

Although the aging system based on the calendar may have worked in a general way, it has always been evident that aging proceeds very differently in different individuals. Some men lose hair early, while others keep a full head of hair well into their seventies. About 50% of elderly people have symptomatic arthritis, but 50% do not. About 30% have heart disease, but the majority have good to excellent heart function well into their golden years. All of this suggests that while people have some type of body clock running within them (known as the program theory of aging), it keeps different time for different people. Aging has also been seen as the accumulation of various environmental assaults—sunlight, cosmic radiation, noise, and many others—that progressively damage immunity and other body systems, eventually resulting in death (the error theory). Here, too, it is clear that the mechanism at work functions in ways that are not fully understood, resulting in the large differences in rates of aging among individuals.

136

Yet a third explanation for widely differing aging rates—one that is gaining ground rapidly—is particularly appealing, as it offers some relief from the traditional assaults of the passing years. This is the "use it or lose it" school of thought, which proposes that if people do not exercise their organ systems, and particularly their muscles, those systems will function less well, and perhaps not at all. Many people are learning that by adopting "healthy" life-style habits early in life, they can improve their chances of remaining robust and independent long after they become "elderly." Some, like Walter Bortz II, former president of the American Geriatrics Society and author of *We Live Too Short and Die Too Long,* believe that robust activity throughout life not only improves quality of life in older age but also increases life-span toward a maximum of, perhaps, 115–120 years. It is this third proposition—that regular exercise continued into old age can improve the quality and quantity of life—that is considered here.

Exercise versus death and disease

A number of investigators have followed groups of elite male athletes to determine age at death and cause of death. Generally, such studies have indicated a moderate increase in life expectancy for athletes who participated in endurance sports such as rowing, running, and cross-country skiing compared with life expectancy of nonathletes. This usually reflected a lower death rate from chronic diseases, particularly coronary heart disease. It is very probable, of course, that individuals who are good athletes when they are young are genetically favored and destined to live longer than average. Some athletes continue to exercise regularly after their competitive days are over, but others quit abruptly—after winning the Tour de France or an Olympic medal, for example—and remain sedentary thereafter. For these reasons, studies of elite athletes are not highly relevant to the issue of the health consequences of regular, moderate exercise in middle age and beyond.

Several classic studies have addressed the question of moderate exercise during the working day and in leisure time and its relation to chronic disease. Jeremy Morris at the London School of Hygiene and Tropical Medicine compared deaths from heart disease in drivers and conductors on London's double-decker buses. While the drivers were sedentary, the conductors had a relatively active workday, frequently climbing up to the top deck and down again. Morris found that the conductors suffered fewer heart attack deaths than did the drivers during many years of follow-up. Interestingly, he also noted that the waist size of the drivers' trousers (determined from London Transport's uniform-issue records) was, on average, substantially larger than that of the conductors, suggesting that abdominal obesity, in addition to habitual inactivity, may be a relevant factor in the development of heart disease.

Ralph S. Paffenbarger, Jr., and colleagues at Harvard University School of Public Health and Stanford University School of Medicine conducted a study of some 17,000 Harvard University alumni who were followed for 12 to 16 years. Observing that very few of these men were engaged in occupations that could be described as active (rather, they typically sat

According to the results of a comprehensive study conducted by researchers from the Institute for Aerobics Research, Dallas, Texas, age-adjusted death rates per 10,000 person-years were highest in men and women who were found to be in the "least fit" category (level 1) but dropped dramatically in those who were found to be "moderately fit" (levels 2 and 3). For purposes of the study, a person-year was a year of follow-up observation for one participant. More than 13,300 people were followed for an average of eight years, for a total of nearly 110,500 person-years.

Deaths per 10,000 person-years of follow-up

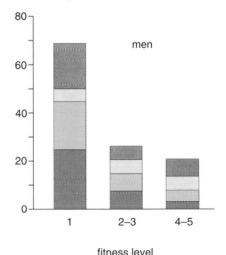

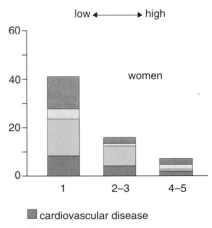

■ cardiovascular disease
▨ cancer
□ accidents/external causes
■ all other causes

Source: Adapted from Steven N. Blair *et al.,* "Physical Fitness and All-Cause Mortality . . . ," *JAMA,* vol. 262, no. 17 (Nov. 3, 1989), pp. 2395–2401. Copyright 1989, American Medical Association

137

Those who keep moving in their advanced years are likely to enjoy fuller, fitter lives than those who take aging sitting down. The study conducted by Steven N. Blair and his coinvestigators showed that even modest amounts of exercise afford substantial health benefits. Moreover, declines in death rates as a result of fitness were most pronounced in older groups—those aged 50 and over.

behind desks), Paffenbarger took careful note of their activities during nonworking time—*e.g.,* blocks walked, flights of stairs climbed, time spent at gardening or in sports play. Fairly consistently, the most sedentary alumni suffered more heart attacks than those who exercised throughout adult life, with the most active having only 50% of the heart attacks seen in the least active men. Continued follow-up suggested that death rates from other chronic diseases, including cancer, were reduced progressively with increasing levels of activity among the alumni groups. Paffenbarger's study also showed that total length of life was modestly increased (by one to more than two years) in those who exercised regularly. The investigators concluded that the evidence from their extended follow-up of Harvard alumni supported the "widespread and longstanding popular belief that adequate physical exercise is necessary to preserve life and its desirable qualities into old age."

In a striking report, Steven N. Blair and colleagues at the Institute for Aerobics Research, Dallas, Texas, recently revealed that physical fitness (measured scientifically, using a treadmill test rather than less reliable verbal or written reports of personal physical activity habits) was strongly related to risk of death from "all causes" in more than 13,000 men and women, who were followed for an average of eight years. The least fit groups had substantially higher death rates from all causes, especially from heart disease and cancer, than the most fit. In fact, the greatest benefit seemed to be derived from moving out of the "least fit" category into the next, the "modestly fit" group. (There were a total of five fitness categories.) Notably, even for those with significant risk factors—*e.g.,* smoking, high blood cholesterol, hypertension—higher levels of fitness proved beneficial to health. The truly exciting implication of Blair's findings is that the benefit threshold is lower than had been previously thought; important health benefits are within virtually everyone's reach. Even a little exercise goes a long way, and activity can be anything from brisk leaf raking to vigorous

(Left) Louise and Fred Wing from Marblehead, Massachusetts, both in their seventies, have excelled as a synchronized swimming duo. In 1983 Fred, who had been a veteran lap swimmer, decided that Louise, who taught synchronized swimming, was having more fun, so he enrolled in her class. With Louise as coach, they began to train and compete together. Over the years, remarkably, their keen sense of timing has not diminished. (Below) aquatic exercise is one of the best overall conditioners. Because the body weight is supported by the buoyant force of water, there is no strain on bones or joints— making it an especially popular form of exercise among seniors. Exercising in water provides an excellent cardiovascular workout as well as toning of the arm, leg, back, and abdominal muscles.

J. Pavlovsky—Sygma

vacuuming to almost any sport (even golf—without the cart). Physical fitness is not necessarily the same as level of habitual activity, but usually the two are closely related.

From head to toe: exercise versus aging

There is a close physiological parallel between traditional aging and chronic sedentariness (at any age). The advancing years typically lead to deteriorations in all the functions that are listed in the table (*see* page 140), producing the stereotypical "old" person: weak, arthritic, osteoporotic, hard of hearing. Exercise clearly opposes the first group of adverse changes. The protective and perhaps restorative potential of exercise in these various areas is a matter of great importance to billions of people who are moving inexorably toward older age. At present, there is little evidence to suggest a clearly beneficial role for exercise in the second group— perhaps because of the very gradual onset of these conditions, perhaps because few controlled studies have been conducted to investigate these aging-affected functions.

The cardiovascular system. The elimination of cardiovascular disease would probably have a major effect on life expectancy from birth, far exceeding that following the elimination of any other disease. A lifetime of regular activity, in particular aerobic sports—such as cycling, brisk walking, swimming, jogging, or cross-country skiing—typically results in a 65-year-old with a relatively big (but not enlarged) heart, supplied by wide, open coronary arteries; a large stroke volume (volume of blood pumped by one beat of the heart); a large cardiac output (volume of blood pumped per minute); a low resting heart rate (an efficient heart needs to beat less quickly at rest); and an average or modestly increased maximal heart rate (heart rate when the body is working at maximum capacity). All of these features of the fit, elderly heart are advantageous for robust good health, and with continued exercise they can be preserved to a considerable

139

extent as the years pass. Older people who have not exercised for many years can also considerably improve cardiac output and resting pulse rate by gradually increasing their exercise level, although they are unlikely to approach the cardiac function of the lifelong exerciser.

Abnormally high pressure within the vascular system (hypertension) is very prevalent in the elderly and is an important risk factor for coronary heart disease and stroke. Fit older people tend to have lower resting blood pressures, and they benefit particularly from lower blood pressures when under physical or emotional stress. Exercise contributes to lower blood pressure in part by facilitating weight control. Several studies suggest that the risk of developing high blood pressure later in life is reduced in those who are physically active. Many studies have shown that adopting an exercise program results in reduced resting and exercise blood pressures in both normotensives (those with blood pressure in the normal range) and hypertensives, especially where weight loss occurs. The extent to which blood pressure is lowered by a combination of exercise and weight loss in many cases is comparable to that obtained by treatment (for life) with potent antihypertensive drugs.

The composition of the blood circulating within the vascular system is affected by exercise level and adiposity. The concentrations of the cholesterol-containing particles, low-density lipoproteins (LDL) and high-density lipoproteins (HDL), are very strongly related to the risk of coronary heart disease in the elderly. Adoption of regular exercise, often accompanied by weight loss, increases levels of HDL-cholesterol ("good" cholesterol), thus substantially reducing the risk of heart attack in later years. Regular exercisers can take comfort in the knowledge that they are exposing their vulnerable coronary arteries, year in and year out, to "friendly blood."

Finally, regular exercise has another, less-often-mentioned cardiovascular advantage; exercisers tend not to smoke. There is evidence that becoming physically active often leads to reduction or abandonment of smoking. The health advantages become strikingly apparent as the exerciser ages and is much less prone to the "tobacco diseases"—emphysema, chronic bronchitis, and lung and mouth cancers, as well as heart disease.

Body composition. A striking and important consequence of regular activity is its salutary effect on body composition. Avoidance of obesity (too much fat—an excess that is measured as a percentage of total body weight) is very important for an enjoyable older age because it improves mobility and self-image, reduces risk of heart disease and certain cancers, and reduces the burden of arthritis. Preservation of as much muscle mass as possible with advancing age helps to retain strength, which in turn allows the older person greatly improved mobility and independence. Many studies have shown that to a considerable degree regular activity offsets the "creeping obesity" that typically accompanies aging; people slowly put on fat as they age because they voluntarily curtail their activities but fail to compensate by eating less. There is some evidence that exercise is particularly helpful in reducing fat in the abdominal region, known as central or abdominal obesity or "apple-shaped" obesity, which medical scientists now know is associated with heart disease and diabetes.

Effects of aging and exercise on the body and its functions	aging	exercise
physical fitness	−	+
stroke volume	−	+
maximal cardiac output	−	+
diastolic blood pressure	−	+
body composition	−	+
muscle mass	−	+
nutritional status	−	+
joint mobility	−	+
bone density	−	+
psychological well-being	−	+
hearing	−	?
eyesight	−	?
taste, smell	−	?
arthritis	−	?
control of urination	−	?
liver and kidney function	−	?
memory	−	?

− (deterioration)   + (improvement)
? (evidence lacking)

140

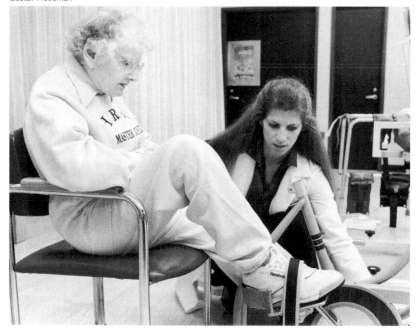

Researcher Maria A. Fiatarone of Tufts University's Human Nutrition Research Center on Aging works with 92-year-old nursing home resident Dorothy Tishler, one of 10 frail nonagenarians who took part in an eight-week program of high-intensity strength training. A pretraining computed tomography scan of the thigh of a participant in the study (below) reveals large amounts of fat (red) under the skin and between muscle fibers; typical of advanced age, the proportion of muscle (yellow) is only 40–50% (compared with the 80–90% that would be seen in a healthy young person). In the posttraining scan of another subject (bottom), an increase in muscle mass of about 10% was seen—a gain associated with measurable improvement in both strength and function.

Loss of muscle protein typically occurs with aging and can be very pronounced in people aged 80 and beyond. Yet in active old people, muscle mass seems to be relatively preserved. In an important recent study by Maria A. Fiatarone, William J. Evans, and colleagues from the U.S. Department of Agriculture Human Nutrition Research Center on Aging at Tufts University in Boston, 10 frail, institutionalized men and women, averaging 90 years of age, took part in an eight-week program of high-intensity resistance training of the leg muscles. Strength increased by 174%; muscle area, measured by a computed tomography (CT) scan, increased by 9%; and mobility substantially improved. Two participants who had previously relied on canes for walking were able to dispense with them after the training program. Strength training has also been shown to reduce the frequency of falls and consequent fractures that are common in older persons owing to muscle decline and weakness in the lower extremities.

Ability to walk, run, swim, or cycle depends partly on the condition of the cardiovascular system but also on the ability of the muscles to use the oxygen and nutrients supplied to them. Training muscles by regular, appropriate use will often dramatically improve the performance of the frail elderly in spite of the presence of multiple chronic diseases; it will also *preserve* the physical abilities of the elderly who are fit.

The "deadly quartet." The grouping of four disorders within the same individual, named the "deadly quartet" by physician Norman M. Kaplan at the University of Texas Southwestern Medical Center, is particularly common—and ominous—in elderly people: obesity (especially in the abdominal region), high blood pressure, blood lipid disturbances (high levels of LDL-cholesterol and triglycerides and low HDL-cholesterol), and insulin resistance (*i.e.,* impaired insulin activity that causes the pancreas to secrete more insulin, leading to high circulating insulin levels). Those afflicted with

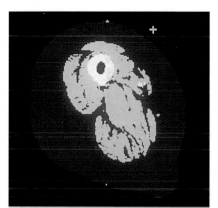

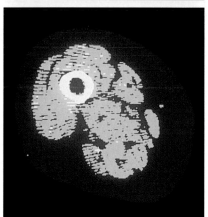

141

It is now quite evident that with proper maintenance the bones and joints can last a lifetime, as Kathleen Goddard Jones (right) can attest. A devoted conservationist and an active member of the Sierra Club, Jones has been hiking California's Nipomo Dunes for more than 30 years, and she has no intention of giving up her passion for exploring the rugged terrain. Studies have shown that years of walking or jogging do not promote osteoarthritis of the knee. Moreover, the gravitational and bone-compressing stimulation of weight-bearing exercise can help stave off osteoporosis (loss of bone mass) and consequent fractures, which take such a huge toll on the elderly—especially on women. Women also need adequate calcium and replacement of estrogen after menopause to protect their bones, but exercise is probably an equally crucial preventive measure.

all four of these common conditions are at greatly increased risk of coronary heart disease, stroke, and non-insulin-dependent diabetes mellitus (type II, or adult-onset diabetes). Of course, one could (and physicians frequently do) treat the hypertension with one or several drugs, the lipid disorder with other drugs, and the diabetes with still others. As Kaplan points out, however, there is one therapy that will improve and often prevent all four conditions—regular exercise.

Bones and joints. Osteoporosis (thinning of the bones) with consequent fractures, especially in women, and arthritis of the joints in both sexes are also particularly common afflictions of the elderly. In women over 50 who have run or jogged regularly for exercise, bone density of the backbone appears to be greater than in sedentary controls. There is also evidence that jogging or a program of brisk, regular walking will partially *reverse* osteoporosis. The gravitational and bone-compressing stimuli of regular aerobic exercise probably combat the progressive loss of bone mass that is so often seen with aging. An adequate supply of dietary calcium and replacement of estrogen around and beyond menopause are also very important preventive measures.

Osteoarthritis is a painful, debilitating, poorly understood disease that afflicts some 16 million Americans, mostly over age 55. The disease results from the degradation of cartilage, which cushions bones; the areas most often affected are hands, feet, hips, and knees. Although the problem may be promoted by rough contact sports played in earlier years, many years of nontraumatic running or walking apparently do not lead to osteoarthritis. It is increasingly clear that joint pain and stiffness, and the increasing debilitation that accompanies them, can be alleviated or prevented with the regular performance of sequences of carefully designed exercises that increase joint mobility.

142

Cancer. This is a collection of diseases with causes that are well understood in some cases (*e.g.,* cigarette smoking in lung cancer) but unclear in others. Older individuals are by far its most frequent victims. People who are active in sports and other regular exercisers who have rejected smoking have a great advantage. Moreover, there is some evidence, which urgently needs further investigation and confirmation, that regular activity is associated with a reduced incidence of breast cancer in women and of colon cancer in men. The study by Blair showed clearly that physically fit men and women develop cancer (all types combined) at a lower rate than their unfit counterparts. On the other hand, there is reason to believe that active older people who exercise regularly outdoors may have increased rates of skin cancer. Therefore, suitable precautions (liberal use of sunscreens, protective clothing, etc.) should be taken.

Depression, anxiety, and self-perception. In an age when life stresses are ubiquitous and anxiety and depression all too common, the Latin adage *mens sana in corpore sano* ("a healthy mind in a healthy body") is particularly relevant. Lessening of anxiety and depression has been reported in numerous studies of both "normal" and mildly to moderately anxious and depressed older individuals who exercised regularly walking, running, doing calisthenics, or participating in other aerobic activities—as compared with nonexercising controls. Moreover, running has been found to be at least as effective as psychotherapy in the treatment of "moderate" depressions.

There is a school of thought holding that the "appropriate" approach to treating depression in the elderly is medication along with activities such as sitting quietly, reading, and playing sedentary games and that the more demanding types of exercise are unsuitable for many older people. Yet investigators have repeatedly commented on the increased sense of well-being and improved self-perception shown by elderly graduates of more vigorous exercise programs. The release of endorphins, or "natural opiates," into the bloodstream occurs with higher intensity exercise and may account for the often-reported euphoria ("runner's high") sometimes experienced during endurance activities. Certainly, in many cases, exercise, with all its other health benefits, would be of greater value to older people than commonly prescribed antidepressant and antianxiety drugs.

The notion that exercise is good medicine is certainly not new to Jack La Lanne. In 1936 he opened America's first known fitness studio in Oakland, California. In 1951, long before there was a fitness boom, he began his daytime television show promoting the benefits of daily systematic exercise; from the start, he advocated strength training for men and women—including seniors. His half-hour, five-day-a-week workouts were immensely popular among his viewers; the syndicated program was carried on 200 stations nationwide and remained on the air for 26 years. Now in his seventies and appearing fitter than most men a third his age, La Lanne, who has been called the "Oral Roberts of sweat" and the "fitness king," is a testament to the rewards of a lifetime of exercise.

Memory and the senses. Failing memory, hearing, vision, taste, and smell are all hallmarks of advancing age. Although there is some evidence that short-term memory, reaction time, and cognitive function (ability to reason and solve problems) are improved by exercise, much research remains to be done in this potentially important area.

Superfit seniors: shattering stereotypes

Years of active living should, if these benefits of exercise are real, result in a fit elderly person. Not so long ago, the summit of Mt. Everest had not been reached, and the four-minute mile had not been run. When indeed those feats were first achieved, it was by the young and superbly athletic. By 1991, however, Everest had been scaled by a number of very hearty senior climbers. In 1983 Americans Dick Bass and Frank Wells conquered the "Seven Summits"—the highest points on each of the continents, including Everest—when both were in their fifties. In 1987, at age 91, Hulda Crooks became the oldest woman to climb Mt. Fuji in Japan.

A glance through the age-group record books for track and field quickly shatters the stereotype and the media-conditioned perception of the elderly. Mavis Lindgren completed her 52nd marathon (42 kilometers [26.1 miles]) in 5 hours 31 minutes at the age of 81; she ran her first race at age 70. And how many cavalierly "fit" young people could imagine competition in the pole vault? Yet Carol Johnston came safely to earth in the 75–79-year-old division in the 1991 U.S. Masters indoor championships after clearing 2.5 meters (8 feet 4 inches).

In 1989 in St. Louis, Missouri, 3,500 athletes aged 55 and up competed in the biennial United States National Senior Olympics (now officially named National Senior Sports Classic), an event begun in 1987 to promote senior citizen fitness and health. The 14 sports ranged from archery to volleyball.

New Zealander Derek Turnbull has been running for over half a century. Although he claims he does not run for medals or records—only for "the pure fun" and the "camaraderie of it"—he continues to break world records for his age group in competitions around the world. What is remarkable about Turnbull is that he has declined very little; in his sixties he comes close to matching some of the best times that he set as a 20-year-old. Turnbull attributes his incredible stamina largely to his daily work on his sheep farm; a typical workday is 15 hours of hard physical labor. Indeed, tossing a 57-kilogram (125-pound) ewe over a fence is no mean feat.

Photographs, Ian Cooper

The oldest male contestant was 91, the oldest female 87, but perhaps the most unusual participant was a 64-year-old Dominican nun from Colorado who completed the five-kilometer race walk in her habit. About 15,000 older athletes qualified to compete in the Sports Classic held in Syracuse, New York, in the summer of 1991. Another competition held every other summer is the World Veterans Championships, which showcases thousands of older runners in both short- and long-distance events; Derek Turnbull, aged 63, a sheep farmer from New Zealand, won six gold medals in the 1989 championships in Eugene, Oregon.

Do the amazingly durable participants in these senior athletic competitions have a built-in genetic advantage? Probably. What proportion of their prowess do they owe to healthy living, training, and determination? Undoubtedly, most of it! While such excellent specimens do not prove that everyone can retain remarkable function and performance into old age, they do demonstrate that it is possible for some, and that probably millions more need not "lose it" as they get on in years.

Running for health, fun, and research

Ruminations of this kind led entrepreneur Ibrohim Clark to found the Fifty-Plus Runners Association, based at Stanford University, in 1980. Currently 2,000 strong, with members from all over the United States and many foreign countries, the association is primarily devoted to the long-range study of the effects of running on health, disability, and longevity. Members participate in scientific research that has been published in medical journals and that contributes to the knowledge of the effects of regular exercise on health. Fifty-Plus members have been eager volunteers in controlled studies, which recently have shown that male and female runners aged 50 and above have a very healthy mental outlook, enjoy greater bone density of the vertebrae than sedentary controls, and do *not* have excessive osteoarthritis of the knee. Women runners in the association recorded higher calorie consumption (and better calcium intakes) than sedentary women yet were much slimmer. The potential negatives of vigorous exercise participation that are currently being investigated are a higher incidence of skin cancers (older exercisers often accumulate a lot of exposure to sunlight) and kidney stones (they also can become somewhat dehydrated in hot weather).

The association holds an annual dinner meeting and race (although it is not primarily a competitive club). In 1991 members were particularly pleased to welcome as guest of honor the 68-year-old Emil Zatopek, perhaps the greatest runner who ever lived; in the 1952 Olympics, the Czechoslovak champion won gold medals in the 5,000-meter, 10,000-meter, and marathon events. The race on the next day saw over 200 men and women aged 50 to 80 cover eight kilometers (five miles) around the Stanford campus during unexpected thundershowers. Splashing through puddles to the finish—to strains of the "Battle Hymn of the Republic"—was an experience participants would not have missed. As one runner, Margaret Mason, wrote in the *Washington Post,* "Speed isn't what mattered. Ours were, I knew, the footprints of the future. Someday that Sunday morning scene of a bunch of old men and women running down the street will not

Paul Spangler, 90, and Sister Marion Irvine, 59, members of the Fifty-Plus Runners Association, run not only for camaraderie, fitness, and fun but also for science. The association's approximately 2,000 members are frequent participants in research on exercise and aging. In the past decade dedicated Fifty-Plusers, along with nonexercising matched controls, have been subjects in long-range studies evaluating the effects of running on bone density, joint preservation, body composition, and mental outlook.

be unusual. We were—and are—role models for the years to come, maybe not for length of life, but certainly for quality."

Proper exercise for seniors

Medically sound activities for people in their advanced years will cover a very wide spectrum of type and intensity; virtually all experts would agree that *some* type of regular activity is likely to be beneficial to *all* older people. Even frail nonagenarians, often institutionalized, can benefit from high-intensity strength training, as Fiatarone, Evans, and colleagues have demonstrated. Other studies have shown that chronically sick older people with arthritis, hypertension, heart disease, lung disease, and diabetes can benefit from moderate-intensity exercise.

For the considerable proportion of older people who have a known disease or are obese, a physician's approval and supervision of an exercise program are essential. Current medication use must also be considered, and sometimes dosages may need to be altered with increased activity levels. Even those in apparently excellent health should keep their physician informed of their exercise habits. Some physicians will carry out tests that can indicate the appropriate type and intensity of exercise that is best for the individual.

Quite unfortunately, many physicians shy away from recommending some sort of exercise to their older patients, perhaps because they are not familiar with the recent evidence of the health advantages of exercise for the elderly (this is not a major topic in the curricula of medical schools). Such reluctance may be partly for fear of untoward results (falls, muscular injuries) with possible malpractice suits, or it may be because of unenlightened beliefs that sedentariness and frailty are "normal" states for seniors and that drugs are the appropriate and expected treatment. Most

It is often assumed that it is too late for people of very advanced age, especially those with impaired mobility and chronic illness, to benefit from exercise. In fact, it has recently been shown that with a program of progressive strength training, even nonambulatory, institutionalized individuals in their 9th and 10th decades of life are able to reverse muscle atrophy and significantly improve their overall physical functioning. Exercise that strengthens upper body muscles and stimulates circulation is routine for wheelchair-bound residents of a Hartford, Connecticut, nursing home. Group bowling is not only a social event for this group but physical therapy.

Unquestionably, exercise influences how people age and what level of function they retain. In addition to having fewer life-threatening and debilitating diseases, those who maintain physical fitness into their later years reap another reward: psychological health. Numerous studies suggest that exercisers are less likely than their unfit counterparts to experience depression, are better able to cope with stress, have less anxiety, are self-confident, and have a manifestly brighter outlook on life.

regrettable of all, many physicians assume that it is "too late" for their 60-, 70-, and 80-year-old patients to benefit from exercise, when, in fact, they are the very patients who could benefit most.

Although increased physical activity promises many benefits—strong bones, efficient and well-toned muscles, ideal body weight, cardiovascular endurance, and mental well-being, to name a few—the dropout rate of older people from exercise programs is high. The elderly person who has been sedentary for decades needs assurance, encouragement, and follow-up. The physician seldom has the time, skills, or enthusiasm for attending to the task of improving fitness in elderly patients. Needed are readily available services—e.g., a network of centers capable of providing appropriate, progressive exercise programs for large numbers of elderly people. Such a system would put "exercise therapy" at the disposal of the busy physician, just as cardiac rehabilitation and physiotherapy services are.

Those sedentary older people who are contemplating starting their own exercise program should check with their medical adviser, consider options and make a suitable choice of an exercise program or type of activity that they are likely to stick with; start very slowly and progress gradually, exercise at an intensity that seems moderate, back off if anything hurts (exercise at all ages should be enjoyable, not painful), and find an exercise companion (mutual support can make all the difference).

Implications beyond the individual

Some 12% of the U.S. gross national product is spent on health care. Yet the last third of most Americans' lives is often beset with illness and failing function to such a degree that younger people frequently fear growing old; they cannot bear to picture themselves at that stage of life. It is still widely

147

assumed that the last 20–30 years of life are a time of declining function, when people no longer have the ability or, perhaps, even the desire to live productively and vigorously. The inability of modern health care systems to get most people to the threshold of maturity in a reasonably robust condition must be considered a very serious failing.

In Tom Stoppard's *Rosencrantz and Guildenstern Are Dead,* Rosencrantz says, "For all the compasses in the world, there's but one direction, and time is its only measure." People have been granted 30 extra years of life but not 30 extra years of youth. Nonetheless, there is a way to make those bonus years productive and enjoyable—and exercise may be its only measure. There is much wisdom to be gained from considering the data that suggest that exercise affords important social, economic, and public health benefits for the huge aging population.

Younger people must realize that, to a considerable degree, they are individually responsible for arriving at age 65 in good shape. Bortz has said, "Aging is a self-fulfilling prophecy. . . . *We* prescribe . . . what we are to become." Doctors, drugs, hospitals, and medical devices have to do with illness. Eating properly, exercising, and refraining from smoking have to do with vitality.

In September 1990 the U.S. Department of Health and Human Services released the report *Healthy People 2000,* which established national health-promotion and disease-prevention goals. The number one "priority area" on a list of 22 was "physical activity and fitness." In practice, however, much remains to be done to motivate people to give regular exercise a prominent place in their lives—especially in an era when the automobile has dramatically reduced the opportunities for people to move about under their own steam. Schools need to reestablish regular periods of exercise of a sensible, enjoyable, and usable sort that will inspire young people to

The surf is still up for 76-year-old Lorrin Harrison. Neither the passing years nor a quintuple coronary bypass operation could keep "Whitey," as he is known by his friends, off a surfboard. Harrison was one of the original southern California "beach boys," who discovered the thrill of riding the waves over half a century ago, long before surfing as a sport became chic or popular.

George Steinmetz/LIFE

The elderly are not a small group anymore, and their numbers will vastly increase as continuing advances in medicine and surgery further reduce the impact of many previously debilitating conditions. The extra years of life people have been granted more often than not can be lived out in vibrant good health by those who devote themselves to remaining active rather than settling into a sedentary old age. Exercise does not preclude all physical decline, but it promises that declines will be less extensive and cause less incapacitation. Perhaps the greatest present challenge is to bring exercise to the "rest home," where the last thing residents need is rest!

remain active throughout life; the present emphasis on competitive team sports does not promote lasting involvement that the majority can benefit from.

In June 1990 Helen Klein ran over 175 kilometers (109 miles) in 24 hours in the Western States race—at age 68. In August 1990 Paul Spangler at 91 won the 5,000-meter race at the Athletic Congress Master Track Meet; Bortz has predicted that Spangler will be the first marathon-running centenarian. Such feats are remarkable, but the benefits can also be considerable from much less; indeed, a large proportion of elderly people could derive substantial health benefits from a brisk half-hour walk every day. A change in society's attitude toward older people's exercising is certainly long over-due. In fact, the provision of suitable exercising areas should be as much on the minds of architects and planners considering the future housing needs of the rapidly aging population as are wheelchair access and bridge rooms. "Exercise is medicine" is a great slogan, borne out by mountains of research. Is it so radical to propose that the costs of exercise programs for older people be reimbursed by health insurance providers, just as drug and doctor bills are?

Perhaps the greatest immediate challenge is to bring exercise to the "rest home." The last thing that institutionalized elderly people need is more *rest!* The idea of "Grandma lifting weights" may seem humorous and incongruous, yet studies show that exercise not only is acceptable but can do wonders for the relative independence and mobility of old people— even 90-year-olds—who all too frequently live lives of sedentary, medicated survival against a backdrop of game shows and soap operas.

149

A Sober Look at
Attitudes Toward Alcohol

by Donald W. Goodwin, M.D.

Many historians credit the victory of the Union Army in the U.S. Civil War to the military genius of Ulysses S. Grant. General Grant had a reputation as a formidable drinker. According to one story, Pres. Abraham Lincoln, on being told of the general's predilection for alcohol, suggested that it might be a good idea to recommend Grant's brand of liquor to the other, less inspired Union commanders.

This is an amusing anecdote to be sure. Yet for the contemporary reader, the story implies a view of drinking that perhaps can best be described as out of step with the times. Imagine Pres. George Bush's response if he had been told that his commander in the Persian Gulf habitually drank too much. This did not happen, of course.

A more instructive example of something that did happen: in 1989 John Tower, a former U.S. senator from Texas, was rejected by the Senate for the post of secretary of defense because of an alleged drinking problem. Tower was only the ninth Cabinet appointee in U.S. history ever to be rejected. While he strenuously denied that he was in the habit of overimbibing, Tower wanted the appointment enough to vow that, if confirmed, he would abstain from alcohol. Commenting on the Tower affair, Sen. Ted Stevens (Dem., Alaska) pointed out that drinking was regarded quite differently among government officials at the end of the 1980s than it had been in the '70s. "All of our [drinking] habits have changed," Stevens remarked to reporters; "haven't yours?"

Only a few short years ago, when half of U.S. adults smoked, nonsmokers tolerated smoke pollution as stoically as coal miners once accepted coal dust: it was unpleasant but inevitable. Today smokers find themselves in a distinct minority. In fact, smoking has become virtually taboo in huge segments of American society, and warning labels on cigarette packs probably had little to do with it. Rather, nonsmokers decided that they did not have to put up with it, and smoking became a social problem.

The recent change in attitude toward drinking has been more sudden and dramatic—although for reasons that will be examined below, it is probably premature to write an obituary for alcohol. U.S. history is replete with examples of Americans' ambivalent attitudes toward alcohol and "about-faces" in both law and social policy regarding drinking.

Donald W. Goodwin, M.D., is Professor and Chairman, Department of Psychiatry, Kansas University School of Medicine, Kansas City, and the author of several books, including Alcohol and the Writer.

(Opposite page) "The Temperance Crusade—Who Will Win?" American cartoon, 1874; photograph, The Granger Collection

A New York state trooper administers a sobriety test to a motorist suspected of driving while intoxicated. Law-enforcement officials around the U.S. have declared an all-out war on drunk driving. The new dedication to this effort is only one of many signs of a dramatic change in society's attitudes toward alcohol. Today, being drunk in public is neither humorous nor chic, and drivers who are "under the influence" are no longer regarded with complacency. The current antialcohol climate owes much to the lobbying efforts of such organizations as Mothers Against Drunk Driving (MADD). (Below) Passing motorists find it hard to ignore the powerful message of a MADD-sponsored billboard.

How can one explain the fact that many Americans today look upon drinking with disfavor? The health fad, the slimness fad, and the greater availability of other intoxicants are no doubt factors. But social changes sometimes occur very rapidly and mysteriously; this appears to be one of them.

Disappearance of the public drunk

The signs of change are nowhere more apparent than in the decline of drinking itself. Except for the Prohibition years, 1919 to 1933, Americans were probably drinking less alcohol in the late 1980s than at any time in their history. Federal tax figures from the year 1830, for example, indicate that per capita consumption was about 26.5 liters (7 gallons), mostly in the form of distilled spirits. In 1987 it was about 9.6 liters (2.54 gallons).

Another indication of changing attitudes is that drunks are no longer considered funny. One need only look at plays, films, cartoons, and other comparable social mirrors to see that there are, for example, no followers in the footsteps of the celebrated comedian W.C. Fields. People still admire Fields's wit, but contemporary performers do not seem inclined to model themselves after a red-nosed inebriate. The character Arthur, as portrayed by Dudley Moore in the 1981 movie of the same name, was a classic funny drunk; in the sequel, however, made seven years later, the producers decided that it was about time Arthur sobered up. When this author informally surveyed cartoons in *The New Yorker* magazine from the early 1970s, one in four showed people drinking alcohol and one in six showed somebody under the influence. Another survey in 1989 turned up only a single drunk. Similarly, 10 years ago the most popular theme of humorous greeting cards—after sex—was drinking. Recently in one large Hallmark store, the author found but a handful of cards with a drinking theme. Sex remained as popular as ever.

Even hard-bitten journalists no longer brag about their capacity for drink. Writing in January 1991 about how the "new sobriety" has affected members of his own profession, *Chicago Tribune* columnist Clarence Page said:

SOMETIMES IT TAKES A FAMILY OF FOUR TO STOP A DRUNK DRIVER.

MADD

- Nei takk, jeg er jo gravid!

"No thanks, I'm pregnant!" says the message on this Norwegian poster warning women of alcohol's dangers to the unborn infant. The development of birth defects in babies born to chronic drinkers was not recognized as a medical syndrome until the early 1970s. Now doctors know that even moderate alcohol intake during pregnancy can cause the physical malformations and mental retardation associated with fetal alcohol syndrome; many advise patients to abstain throughout their nine months of pregnancy.

Poster, National Library of Medicine, Bethesda, Maryland

About two dozen press clubs closed across the nation in the Just-Say-No '80s, all victims of sobriety in the newspaper profession. The victims included the Chicago Press Club, in the two-fisted town of newspeople enshrined as "hoodlumesque half drunken caballeros" in the 1920s play "The Front Page." Some of the clubs reopened, but with reduced hours and only after stocking their bars . . . with cans of fruit and vegetable juice, herbal teas and Perrier water.

If drinking is no longer considered amusing, chic, sophisticated, fashionable, or politically savvy, being drunk in public is viewed as socially irresponsible, and being drunk behind the wheel is downright criminal. The fact is that drunk drivers have always killed people, but only in the past decade or so have forceful measures been taken to get intoxicated drivers off the roads. In the past few years political action groups such as Mothers Against Drunk Driving (MADD) and Students Against Driving Drunk (SADD), backed by a hard-hitting publicity campaign from the Advertising Council, have had a definite impact on tougher laws and increased social opprobrium toward those who drive under the influence. Driver deaths in alcohol-related traffic accidents declined more than 20% between 1980 and 1988. By 1989 every state in the U.S. had raised the legal age for buying alcohol to 21. Any state that did not do so would not have been eligible to receive federal highway funds. Negative attitudes toward drinking almost certainly made it easier for congressional deficit fighters to raise taxes on alcohol in 1990.

153

Even brewers and distillers have got into the business of sponsoring advertising campaigns to encourage moderation, particularly during the holiday season. "Know when to say when" became a tag line for almost every Anheuser Busch commercial in 1990. In December of that year, brewers sponsored programs that offered free taxi rides to all whose indulgence in holiday spirits rendered them unable to drive home safely from a bar or restaurant. The alcohol industry is, of course, acting not only in the public interest but also in self-interest, preferring that people drink less rather than stop drinking altogether.

The change in attitudes toward drinking also shows up in drinking behavior. In *The Last Fine Time* (1991), a book about the life and death of a family-owned tavern on the east side of Buffalo, New York, author Verlyn Klinkenborg reflects on the change in drinking patterns in the saloon since 1947:

> After the war, people drank with a kind of desperation and a sheer capacity that has almost been forgotten. Now the vocation of public drunkenness is beginning to disappear—or, at least, to turn solemn and inward. There is no longer the tolerance there used to be, no longer the sense that a temperance type is a meddler, that a drunk muttering in the narrow streets is expressing a point of view familiar to the men and women passing by.

If the reasons for the intensity and rapidity of the recent reaction against drinking alcohol are obscure, it must be owned that drinking is a behavior that has puzzled philosophers and scientists throughout the ages. Why do people drink? Why do some people drink excessively? Reviewing the research that has attempted to answer these questions is helpful for understanding changes in drinking practices, not only in the U.S. but also in other countries where alcoholism may—or may not—be regarded as a social problem.

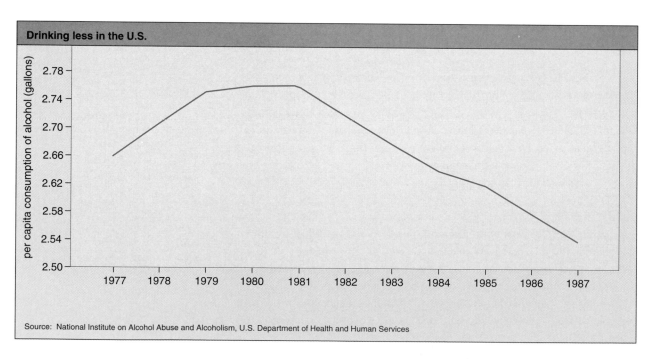

Drinking less in the U.S.

Source: National Institute on Alcohol Abuse and Alcoholism, U.S. Department of Health and Human Services

Animals do not drink

Drinking when not thirsty and making love at all seasons, Madame; that is all there is to distinguish us from the other animals.

—Pierre de Beaumarchais

"The other animals" drink little alcohol, even when given the chance. Scientific attempts to produce an "animal model" of alcoholism began in the 1950s at Rutgers, the State University of New Jersey, at the University of Colorado, and at other academic centers. The experimental animals in these studies were usually mice and rats. What the researchers discovered was that, in a free-choice situation where they could select either alcohol or water, rodents preferred water unless the alcohol was extremely diluted. Even when it was diluted, alcohol was not usually consumed in amounts sufficient to produce intoxication. For this reason attempts to create an animal model were generally a failure until 1983, when T.K. Li, a neuroscientist at Indiana University, found that selective breeding of rodents could produce animals that in many ways drank like human alcoholics; they spontaneously consumed enough alcohol to become intoxicated and seemingly would drink to "feel better" during withdrawal. These animals were found to have low concentrations of serotonin, an important neurotransmitter (a chemical that transmits nerve impulses), in regions of the brain associated with emotion.

If animals when left alone are mostly born teetotalers, why do humans drink and sometimes drink to excess? At one level the answer seems obvious. Berton Roueché, for many years a staff writer for *The New Yorker,* expressed it well when he said that in addition to food, clothing, shelter, and love, the human race has a basic need for occasional release from "the intolerable clutch of reality." "All men," says Roueché, ". . . have known this tyranny of memory and mind, and all have sought, and invariably found, some reliable means of briefly loosening its grip." While

Why do people drink? And why do some drink too much? Some answers have been provided by the study of the physiological effects of alcohol on the brain; to a certain extent, alcohol produces euphoria, which accounts for the heightened conviviality of the cocktail party. For the tipplers in this English alehouse scene, affability and relaxation would seem to be the primary goal of imbibing. But not all those who drink are merely seeking pleasure. Alcohol also bolsters confidence, dissolves inhibitions, and assuages loneliness. For some, as the poster above suggests, dependency makes alcohol a necessity.

Poster, National Library of Medicine, Bethesda, Maryland

155

eloquently expressed, this explanation does not account for variations in drinking behavior—for example, why 70% of Americans drink alcohol while the rest abstain. Nor does it explain why one in 10 drinkers, at some point in life, consumes alcohol in amounts that cause damage to self or others and involve an element of compulsion—what is usually called alcoholism.

Alcohol and the brain

It may be postulated that people drink for one of two reasons (leaving aside drinking that is strictly a social act): (1) they drink to feel pleasure, or (2) they drink to escape pain, the latter being Roueché's explanation. Some would argue that pleasure and release from pain are identical. Urination, according to such a theory, is pleasurable because the urge to urinate is unpleasant; the stronger the urge, the more pleasant its abolishment. Examples can be cited that do not fit this paradigm, however. Is the sexual act pleasurable because it abolishes sexual desire? With orgasm usually comes an abrupt termination of desire, but does this entirely explain orgasmic pleasure? Most people would doubt it. Are chocolate bars, to those who love chocolate, pleasurable only for satisfying hunger? And once they have been eaten, is the desire for chocolate extinguished? "Chocoholics" know better. Likewise, is alcohol enjoyable only when a person is frustrated, insecure, lonely, or miserable? While acknowledging alcohol's power to succor, most drinkers, on reflection, will say alcohol does a great deal more—it makes them feel good even when they are *not* feeling bad.

Studies indicate that alcohol affects the brain in two ways: it has sedative properties, dulling sensation and responsiveness, and it produces euphoria. These effects are related to different structures or chemical systems in the brain. Certain brain centers, for example, regulate sleep. In laboratory experiments scientists have found that stimulating these centers, electrically or chemically, puts animals to sleep, whereas destroying other centers keeps them awake. Another part of the nervous system functions as an activator and is essential in maintaining vigilance and wakefulness. Alcohol affects these areas of the brain selectively, sometimes producing sleep and sedation, other times stimulation.

In the 1950s a new term was introduced by experimental psychologists: the pleasure center. The concept came out of the discovery that cats and rats will press a metal bar repeatedly if the act of pressing delivers a tiny charge of electrical current to certain brain centers. Since there was no better explanation for this seemingly pointless behavior, the observers— mindful of the pointless behavior humans sometimes engage in—concluded that the animals were acting purely for pleasure, and therefore the centers must be "pleasure centers." Recent research indicates that alcohol stimulates these centers.

Thus, scientists do know something about the effects of alcohol on the brain. The reason people talk louder than usual at cocktail parties or are able to forget their worries after a drink or two can be traced in part to known physiological effects of alcohol on the nervous system. Less is known about why a rather small minority drink so heavily that they become alcoholics.

156

Women have traditionally been much less likely than men to become alcoholic. Both cultural factors and hormonal differences have been proposed to account for this gender differential. In most societies, and certainly in the U.S., intoxication has been tolerated to a greater degree in men than in women. This cultural attitude may also account for the observation that a proportionately greater number of women are admitted to alcoholism treatment clinics; social disapproval of female alcoholism is strong and impels women to seek or to be given help.

Why some drink too much

Drunkards beget drunkards.

—Plutarch

Not only is the cause of alcoholism still unknown, there is even disagreement about the definition. This discussion will refer to alcoholism as a compulsion to drink that causes injury to oneself or others. The selection process whereby 10% of drinkers, more or less, become alcoholic is not known. However, there is general agreement about risk factors.

Gender. Male alcoholics outnumber female alcoholics by about five to one. This gender differential apparently has existed throughout history. Cultural factors are usually given credit for the disparity but, on the basis of surveys by this author, more women than men are physiologically intolerant of alcohol. Recent research may shed some light on this observation. In 1990 investigators at the University School of Medicine, Trieste, Italy, and the Alcohol Research and Treatment Center, Veterans Administration Medical Center, Bronx, N.Y., published a report on their findings that women metabolize alcohol differently from men and have higher blood alcohol levels after consuming comparable amounts. This increased vulnerability to the effects of alcohol, like the so-called Oriental flush (discussed below in some detail), may act to reduce the amount women drink and thus protect many women from becoming alcoholic.

Ethnic background. Alcoholism appears to be more prevalent in northern parts of Western Europe than in southern climates. Jewish people have a relatively low rate of alcoholism; the Irish have a high rate. In short, cultural and ethnic differences are associated with different rates of alcoholism. It is difficult to attribute these variations to genetic factors.

157

Vocation. Alcoholism is unevenly distributed among occupational groups. Bartenders and reporters have traditionally had high rates, while ministers and physicians have low rates. As a group, writers are inclined toward alcoholism; Americans who have won the Nobel Prize for Literature have a phenomenally high rate (*see* sidebar, page 160). Of the seven American winners, five—or 71%—were alcoholic: Eugene O'Neill, William Faulkner, Ernest Hemingway, Sinclair Lewis, and John Steinbeck. (The nonalcoholics were Pearl Buck and Saul Bellow.)

Family history. A family history of alcoholism represents the strongest known risk factor. An estimated 20–25% of sons and about 5% of daughters of alcoholics become alcoholic themselves. Estimates of the rate of alcoholism in the general population vary widely, but the rates for relatives of alcoholics are severalfold higher than most population estimates.

All in the family?

Three types of evidence support the possibility that heredity may contribute to alcoholism: family studies, adoption studies, and twin studies. The observation that alcoholism runs in families dates to classical times and is one of the best-documented facts in the field of substance abuse. Not everything that runs in families is inherited, though. Languages, for example, may be said to run in families. For many years it was believed that alcoholism is "learned" in the same way that languages are learned. However, twin and adoption studies tend to challenge this belief.

Studying adoptees is one way scientists attempt to separate the effects of "nature" from those of "nurture." If alcoholism has even a partially genetic basis, one would predict that children of alcoholics adopted in infancy by nonalcoholics would still grow up to have a relatively high rate of alcoholism. In fact, three adoption studies conducted in the 1970s and '80s in three countries—Denmark, Sweden, and the United States—

158

support this theory. The studies concluded that adult children of alcoholics raised by nonalcoholic adoptive parents continue to have a high rate of alcoholism—about as high as that found in children of alcoholics who are raised by their birth parents.

Identical twins share the same genes and presumably have identical susceptibility to genetic illnesses. Fraternal twins, on the other hand, like any other siblings, share a familial susceptibility to genetic illnesses only to the extent that they share the same genes. Five twin studies conducted in four countries—the U.S., Sweden, Finland, and Great Britain—during the past four decades have examined drinking patterns and alcohol dependence. All but one found that identical twins were more often concordant for alcoholism than fraternal twins. That is, when one identical twin was alcoholic, the other twin was alcoholic about 65% of the time; when one fraternal twin was alcoholic, the other twin was alcoholic about 25% of the time. Thus, like those of the adoption studies, most of the data from twin studies are consistent with the presence of genetic factors in alcoholism. The question now is: If the transmission of alcoholism in families is partly inherited, what is the mode of transmission?

The writer Jack London, describing his own drinking, said that there were two forms of alcoholism, a congenital and an acquired form. He believed that he had the acquired form. Indeed, the notion that there are two types of alcoholism—a familial (congenital) and a nonfamilial (acquired) type—dates back many years. The idea was resurrected in the 1980s,

Is alcoholism inherited?

drinking-related problem	sons of alcoholics (%)	controls (%)
hallucinations	6	0
loss of control	35	17
amnesia	53	41
tremor	24	22
morning drinking	29	11
delirium tremens	6	1
rum fits	2	0
social disapproval	6	8
marital trouble	18	9
job trouble	7	3
arrested for drunken driving	7	4
other police trouble	15	8
treated for drinking	9	1
hospitalized for drinking	7	0
drinking pattern		
moderate	51	45
heavy (ever)	22	36
problem drinker (ever)	9	14
alcoholic (ever)	18	5

From Donald W. Goodwin, M.D., *et al.,* "Alcohol Problems in Adoptees Raised Apart from Alcoholic Biological Parents," *Archives of General Psychiatry,* vol. 28 (February 1973), pp. 238–243

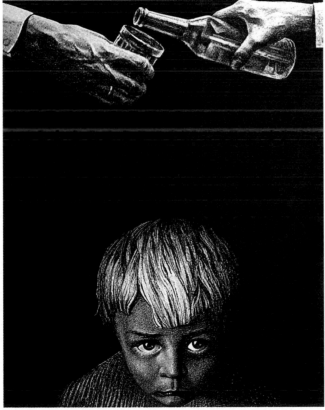

National Library of Medicine, Bethesda, Maryland

Studies of adoptees are one tool scientists use to investigate the relative contributions of "nature" and "nurture" to the development of alcoholism. The table above is from a 1973 study in which the drinking behavior and alcohol-related problems of 55 adopted men who were the biological offspring of alcoholics were compared with those of a matched control group (78 adoptees whose biological parents had no history of alcoholism). The study revealed that significantly more of the sons of alcoholics had drinking problems themselves. Similar investigations focusing on boys raised by alcoholic stepfathers confirm the theory that biological factors are more important than environmental influences. Of course, not all children of alcoholics become alcoholic. Many, however, do suffer from the effects of emotional neglect and domestic violence, as the poster at left, from the U.S.S.R., so poignantly shows.

"During these fits . . . I drank—God only knows how often or how much," wrote Edgar Allan Poe (above) of his periodic binges. Poe came from a family with a history of alcoholism. Ernest Hemingway (below), another U.S. writer with a drinking problem, reportedly said, "I've been drunk 1,547 times in my life but never in the morning." This was not entirely true, according to observers who saw him start the day with a shot of tequila. Do writers drink more than other people? Is vocation a factor, along with gender, ethnic background, and family history? Some authorities think so.

Writers and alcohol

He drank, not as an epicure, but barbarously, with a speed and dispatch altogether American, as if he were performing a homicidal function, as if he had to kill something inside himself, a worm that would not die."

—Charles Baudelaire writing about Edgar Allan Poe

"There's a lot of nourishment in an acre of corn."

—William Faulkner

"Of course you're a rummy . . . but no more than most good writers are."

—Ernest Hemingway to F. Scott Fitzgerald

In the 19th century only one famous U.S. writer had a reputation for drunkenness: Edgar Allan Poe. In the first half of the 20th century, perhaps one-half to two-thirds of well-known U.S. writers were considered alcoholic, including five Nobel laureates. What happened between the second half of the 19th century and the first several decades of the 20th?

Prohibition is one thing that happened. Other Western countries had tried prohibition, but Americans did it with a vengeance. Thus, expatriate American writers of the 1920s beheld a striking contrast in drinking behavior on the two sides of the Atlantic. Frenchmen sipped aperitifs at sidewalk cafes before mass. Back home, it was the era of the speakeasy; drinking was both illegal and sinful—adding greatly to its appeal.

Prohibition, in this author's view, encouraged excessive drinking among U.S. writers by creating so much ambivalence about acceptable standards of drinking that drinking to excess seemed the only solution to the problem. One cannot deny, however, that there was also hypocrisy about drinking—even Bible Belt teetotalers bragged about knowing a bootlegger—which these writers, perhaps more than anyone else, detested.

Alcoholism among Americans, perhaps especially in the case of writers, also may owe something to the American ideal of rugged individualism. Alcoholism, according to historian Gilbert Ostrander, "afflicts people who from early childhood develop a strong sense of being psychologically alone and on their own in the world. This solitary outlook prevents them from gaining emotional release through associations with other people." Writers, Ostrander says, are also loners, and this is one reason they write. "It is a profession which allows the individual to be tremendously convivial all by himself . . . . Writing and drinking are two forms of companionship."

It is a hard theory to prove. Still, whether most alcoholics are loners or not, most creative writers are—or believe they are. In the biographies of celebrated writers, perhaps no theme recurs so frequently as loneliness, shyness, isolation, the sense of being an outsider. The late Belgian-French novelist Georges Simenon, a heavy drinker, declared that he was haunted by the problem of the isolation of individuals and their inability to communicate. This was to him "one of the biggest tragic themes in the world. When I was a young boy I was afraid. . . . I would almost scream because of it. It gave me such a sensation of solitude, or loneliness." This loneliness may be one reason writers write. They can, at least, communicate with their characters. Their sense of isolation may also be one reason they are able to write: distance gives perspective. It may, moreover—if Ostrander is right—be one reason why they drink.

during which numerous studies were conducted comparing alcoholics with a family history of alcoholism and alcoholics without such a history. One consistent finding has emerged: familial alcoholism has an earlier onset than nonfamilial alcoholism. Most studies also find that familial alcoholism is particularly severe and difficult to treat. The evidence suggests that genetic factors influence familial alcoholism.

Some are protected

One factor in the development of alcoholism is definitely inherited: some people are physiologically intolerant of alcohol and thus largely protected from becoming excessive drinkers. After small amounts of alcohol, these people become ill. Adverse reactions to alcohol are most commonly seen in Asians. After ingesting one drink or less, two-thirds or more of Asians develop a reddish skin flush somewhat resembling measles or hives. The so-called Oriental flush is accompanied by nausea and rapid heart beat, plus a marked disinclination to drink more alcohol. Asian infants, given minute amounts of alcohol, also develop this flush.

Unquestionably, this reaction is genetically determined. Among Caucasian men only a few (perhaps 1 or 2%) have a similar reaction. Thus, most Caucasian men are relatively unprotected from becoming alcoholic. To this extent, at least, alcoholism can definitely be said to be influenced by heredity. A larger proportion of Caucasian women appear to be physiologically intolerant—perhaps as many as 50%. Some develop a skin flush; others feel dizzy or develop a headache. Whatever the adverse reaction is, it may also contribute to the lower rate of alcoholism among women.

Brain chemicals: two theories

A genetic tendency toward alcoholism, however, probably involves more than simply the absence of protection provided by genetically determined adverse reactions. In general, two biochemical models have been proposed to explain why some individuals become alcoholic—and why most do not. One model postulates a biochemical deficiency, the other an overproduction of "addictive substances."

According to the deficiency theory, persons with a genetic propensity for alcoholism may be deficient in certain brain chemicals required for optimal well-being. These persons, given alcohol in a suitable cultural milieu, with an absence of countervailing personality traits, may discover that alcohol temporarily corrects the hypothetical deficiency, producing an intense mood change that would not occur in those without the deficiency. This model would suggest that alcohol might have a biphasic effect, first stimulating brain chemical activity and subsequently inhibiting it. There is, in fact, evidence that alcohol has such an effect on serotonin metabolism, which might correspond to the deficiency model. Serotonin is a chemical in the brain, a neurotransmitter, that is partially responsible for the regulation of emotion, drinking behavior, appetite, and aggression. Alcohol appears to increase serotonin activity during acute intoxication; a reduction of serotonin activity to subnormal levels then occurs during the postintoxication period. The "deficient" person would thus have two reasons for drinking.

A complete understanding of the biochemical effects of alcohol may hold the key to the lingering question of why some people become alcoholics while others do not. The diagram at the right (top) illustrates how a normal "social" drinker's response to alcohol might differ from that of one who is an alcoholic. The former experiences gradual and continuous feelings of relaxation; the latter feels momentary but only temporary relief from tension, which, to be sustained, requires increasingly larger quantities of alcohol. One current theory holds that people who are genetically predisposed to becoming alcoholics may be deficient in certain vital neurotransmitters. For them, alcohol might temporarily correct this deficiency but subsequently create an even greater one; the individual who initially drinks to "feel good" must then drink again to keep from feeling bad. The table shows the effects of various blood-alcohol concentrations on two groups of drinkers—alcoholics and people who drink only occasionally. It supports the notion that there is a biochemical difference in the responses of the two groups to alcohol.

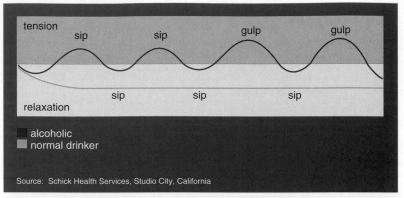

Source: Schick Health Services, Studio City, California

blood-alcohol concentration (g/dL)	effect	
	occasional drinkers	chronic drinkers
0.050 (party level)	congenial euphoria	none observable
0.075	gregariousness, garrulousness	often none
0.100	loss of coordination	minimal
	legal intoxication	
0.125–0.150	loss of inhibition	pleasurable euphoria, loss of coordination beginning
	loss of emotional control	
0.200–0.250	loss of alertness progressing to lethargy	effort required to maintain emotional and motor control
0.300–0.350	stupor or coma	drowsiness, slowing
>0.500	death possible	coma

Adapted from Table 15–1, Benjamin Kissin, M.D., "Alcohol Abuse and Alcohol-Related Illnesses," *Cecil Textbook of Medicine*, J.B. Wyngaarden and L.H. Smith, Jr., M.D., eds.; © 1988 by W.B. Saunders Co., Philadelphia

He or she would first drink to correct the deficiency but would then need to continue drinking to correct an even greater deficiency resulting from the biphasic effect of alcohol on serotonin. Biochemically, this might explain the so-called addictive cycle, in which a person initially drinks to feel good but drinks again later to stop feeling bad.

Three findings may be cited as evidence for this theory. First, as noted above, experimental animals bred to have a high preference for alcohol have lower levels of serotonin in brain centers regulating emotion than do animals bred to have a low preference for alcohol. Second, alcoholics who first begin having symptoms before age 20 and have a family history of alcoholism have lower serotonin activity than do people who become alcoholic after the age of 20 and have no family history. This finding supports the proposal that there are two forms of alcoholism—one characterized by an early onset and a family history of alcoholism and a second (composed perhaps of a more heterogeneous group) in which there is no family history and in which genetic factors are relatively unimportant. Finally, some recently developed pharmacological agents, used in the treatment of depression, increase serotonin activity in the brain. Experimental animals given these drugs drink less, and in three human studies the drugs had the same effect in alcoholics. Fluoxetine (Prozac) is an example of this class of drug. Thus, there is increasing evidence pointing to serotonin as having a critical role in consumption of alcohol and perhaps in the development of alcoholism.

The other theory holds that a genetic propensity to alcoholism involves the overproduction of substances that in some way facilitate addiction. For example, alcohol produces minute amounts of morphinelike compounds in the brain. One study compared assays of the spinal fluid of alcoholics and nonalcoholics after alcohol ingestion; these compounds were present in greater quantities in the spinal fluid of the alcoholics. Other studies show that rats and monkeys drink increased amounts of alcohol when these biochemical substances are injected into their brains. Thus, the possibility exists that a genetic defect resulting in overproduction of morphinelike substances may facilitate alcohol addiction.

Other explanations for genetic vulnerability to alcoholism involve a variety of chemicals, including the neurotransmitters norepinephrine and dopamine; the hormonelike prostaglandins; and the natural pain-killing substances called the endorphins. At the present time none of these theories has as much supporting evidence as the serotonin theory.

Temperance in the U.S.—three waves

To drink is a Christian diversion
Unknown to the Turk and the Persian

—William Congreve

Chemistry cannot explain everything. The Iranians and the Irish, for example, like people of all other nationalities, presumably have the same brain chemistry, but their attitudes toward alcohol and drinking patterns are worlds apart. Traditions and values obviously play a part in shaping attitudes toward alcohol and alcoholism.

This is also readily apparent in the American culture. Today, in the

The Granger Collection

In a cartoon from 1889, Old Man Prohibition is run out of town by broom-brandishing matrons representing those states that did not have prohibition laws. In 1846 Maine became the first U.S. state to pass a so-called dry law; many others followed suit in the years leading up to the Civil War. A renewed enthusiasm for abstinence swept the country toward the end of the 19th century, culminating finally in the passage of the amendment that made Prohibition the law of the land. The waxing and waning of prohibitionist sentiment reflects a characteristic ambivalence about alcohol that has deep roots in American cultural history.

"I cannot tell a lie—I did it with my little hatchet," says temperance advocate Carrie Nation in this 1901 U.S. newspaper cartoon. Alone or accompanied by a band of hymn-singing women, the formidable Nation, nearly 1.8 meters (6 feet) tall and weighing 79 kilograms (175 pounds), would descend upon and dismantle a saloon, smashing every bottle and glass in her path. Her efforts undoubtedly aided in the ratification of the Prohibition Amendment in 1919, during a period of strong antialcohol feeling. Ten years later, however, the pendulum had begun to swing the other way, and the forces of repeal were gaining ground, as illustrated in a 1930 cartoon (below), which depicts the "noble experiment" of Prohibition as a crumbling statue of Uncle Sam. Prohibition did not actually topple for another three years, however.

"The leaning tower shows signs of collapse"

"X-rated" 1990s, one might think that puritanism was long dead in the United States. This is far from true. Puritanism lives, and it imbues many current movements and causes.

The strain of puritanism in American values has produced a curious ambivalence toward drinking. The early puritan divines approved of alcohol and thought it was good for people's health. The celebrated New England minister Increase Mather held this view. On the other hand, his son, Cotton, thought alcohol was dangerous, and it was he who coined the term *demon rum.* This ambivalence in attitude has permeated American culture from early colonial days to the present time.

What of the movement afoot in the U.S. today, the "new sobriety," as it is being called? At least one expert, David F. Musto, a psychiatrist and medical historian at Yale University School of Medicine, believes that the U.S. entered another period of "prohibition" in the 1980s. Musto sees this as the third wave of temperance to sweep over the country in its history. The first began in New England around 1820 and lasted almost until the Civil War. It is probably safe to say that during this time prohibitionists were more numerous than abolitionists. The second temperance movement started in 1920 with the enactment of Prohibition and did not end until the repeal of that "noble experiment" in 1933. The reasons for its downfall were more economic and practical than social and ethical: the federal government, in the depths of the Great Depression, needed the tax revenues it could collect from liquor sales. Banning alcohol had not meant that none was sold, only that none was sold legally. Musto also notes that each era of temperance created a backlash and led in turn to a period of excess.

Certainly there do seem to be cycles in substance abuse, but it is probably too soon to predict how effective the "new sobriety" will be, how long it will last, or when the next reaction against it will begin. Furthermore, the cycles themselves are not as clear-cut as they might at first seem. The Woman's Christian Temperance Union was founded in 1874, for example, between Musto's first two periods of temperance. And the most notorious

164

U.S. temperance advocate, the hatchet-wielding Carrie Nation, did not become an activist until 1890—although her efforts certainly contributed to the ratification of the Prohibition amendment in 1919.

Fine wine and "moonshine" vodka

Drink a glass of wine after your soup, and you steal a ruble from the doctor.

—Russian proverb

There are more old drunkards than old doctors.

—French proverb

Wine is the most healthful and most hygienic of beverages.

—Louis Pasteur

What is happening today in countries other than the U.S.? Are attitudes toward alcohol in flux? The author has recently visited two European countries, both noted for their drinking habits, whose experiences are instructive.

France. The poet Charles Baudelaire had a typical 19th-century Frenchman's view of drinking at home and abroad: alcohol might be a problem elsewhere but not in France. Until recently, the French generally held to this view despite their having the highest rate of cirrhosis of the liver in the world—cirrhosis rates being considered a fairly reliable indicator of how much a population drinks.

E.M. Jellinek, a U.S. biostatistician who was an early proponent of the disease theory of alcoholism, proposed that there were various types of alcoholics, including an American type and a French type. The American alcoholic goes on benders; he cannot stop drinking once started, but he can abstain. The French alcoholic does not go on benders, but he is unable to abstain.

But even in France—a country where alcohol has been as integrated into the society as anyplace one can imagine—there have been changes. The

In a French poster from the 1920s, a woman pleads with her drunken husband to give up the bottle as the couple's children look on in fear. This poster was commissioned by the French Union Against Alcohol as part of a campaign to educate people about the evils of drink. Alcohol in general and wine in particular have always been an integral part of French culture. One can hardly imagine a more comfortable scene of French bourgeois life than Renior's idyllic "Luncheon of the Boating Party" (below), in which half-full wine bottles stand among the remains of a luxuriant meal. The French pride themselves on being able to drink in a civilized manner. The view that drinking may be a problem in other countries but not in France is one that is widely held by the French. Recently, though, the government acknowledged that alcoholism is a serious social ill, and a new campaign against drinking is now under way.

"Luncheon of the Boating Party" by Renoir; photograph, Bridgeman Art Library/Art Resource

French, like the Americans, are drinking less. In the past 30 years, alcohol-related deaths have dropped by nearly 60% and consumption has fallen by one-third. Why? It seems that alcoholism has finally been "discovered." The French government is now spending money on both alcohol research and treatment, although in 1990 there were only two private hospitals in the whole country specifically for the treatment of alcoholism. Also, like the Americans, modern French citizens aspire to be slim and attractive and healthy. Recognition that these goals are incompatible with heavy drinking seems to have seeped into the culture, almost without anyone's noticing.

The Soviet Union. The Soviets, on the other hand, like the Americans, have always been ambivalent about drinking. Throughout their history, temperance movements have abounded—a certain sign of ambivalence. Among the Slavic peoples who make up much of the Soviet Union, however, alcohol dominates the culture to an even greater extent than in vinocultural countries such as France and Italy. A 10th-century Russian prince uttered the memorable words, "Alcohol is the joy of Russia." He, among others, opted for Christianity over Islam at least partly because the Christians did not proscribe the drinking of alcohol.

In the Soviet Union of today, where the need to escape the "intolerable clutch of reality" is great, people are drinking more than ever before. Boris Segal, a Soviet émigré psychiatrist and the ranking authority on Soviet imbibing, wrote in a recent book that alcohol consumption in the Soviet Union in the 1980s was seven times greater than in pre-Revolutionary times. Many Soviets spent one-third of their incomes on alcohol. Problems such as domestic violence were increasing proportionately.

Mikhail Gorbachev's attempt to curb drinking has been a resounding flop. The mid-1980s saw a frenzy of destroyed distilleries, uprooted vineyards, and shut-down breweries. Five years later the deputy chief of police of Moscow spoke out in favor of legalizing "moonshine" to protect civil order. In December 1990 he told the *New York Times:* "The holidays are

A fondness for alcohol is as deeply ingrained in the Slavic peoples as in the residents of the wine-growing regions of western and southern Europe. Despite a massive recent government campaign against alcoholism, the Soviets are apparently drinking more than ever before in this era of political uncertainty and economic collapse. A contemporary antialcohol poster illustrates three Russian sayings. Roughly translated, they read (left to right): "When and where they drink, they fight," "Love of drink destroys the family," and "Better a tea party than a cocktail party." The inscription below the pictures says, "Happy is he who does not drink."

A Soviet cartoon pokes fun at the government's failed attempt to persuade people to stop drinking. Demonstrators (carrying signs that read "Fight drunkenness" and "Support sobriety") confront customers queuing up to buy wine.

coming and if the stores do not get more vodka to sell to the people, the situation might become explosive."

Gorbachev's temperance drive spurred a wave of home brewing, using six-centuries-old peasant recipes for *samogon* ("moonshine" vodka, a clear, distilled liquor usually made from potato mash). In times of desperate need, the Soviets are nothing if not ingenious. For example, the mash-fermenting process usually takes seven days, but Muscovites have found that they can shorten it to four hours by putting the mash in the washing machine on the spin cycle. All this suggests that in the Soviet Union, alcohol is not only a joy but an obsession.

The "new sobriety"

The New Sobriety has displaced the New Morality. Individuals who once were viewed with amusement after they obviously imbibed too much blood of the grape or hops are viewed today with shame, suspicion, pity and condemnation. To do less might make one a "codependent," a word that turns formerly congenial terms like "drinking buddy" on their head.

—Clarence Page

By comparison with the Soviet Union at least, it is refreshing that in the U.S. the old ambivalence about alcohol seems, for the moment, to be disappearing. There is no romance about it anymore. Americans feel they can take it or leave it, and many are choosing to leave it. Like coffee and Diet Pepsi, alcohol is a drink, nothing more. It is certainly nothing to joke about. Drinking, or at least drunkenness, has become a social problem, following U.S. sociologist Seldon Bacon's definition of social problem as "something a minority of people do that the majority think they should not do and is bad for the rest of us."

Is this the end of the story? Or are the reports of the demise of alcohol in the U.S. perhaps exaggerated? Given the deeply ingrained American ambivalence toward drinking, and the history of alternating periods of tolerance and prohibition, the answer can only be "Maybe."

Has the "new sobriety" triumphed in the U.S.? Judging from the proliferation of bottled water and juice drinks, one might say yes. If this is true, however, is another backlash, another period of excess, just around the corner?

LANGUAGE
A Treasury of Anatomic Confusion

John H. Dirckx, M.D.

Tell me where is fancie bred,
Or in the heart or in the head?

—William Shakespeare

A language is a veritable museum, a repository of forgotten conventions and outgrown fancies. In fact, daily speech is so full of dead metaphors and fossilized errors that, without realizing it, one is constantly saying things one does not mean to be taken literally. Referring to Native Americans as Indians, for example, simply perpetuates a 500-year-old mistake. An even older misconception is embodied in the words *sunrise* and *sunset*—everyone is supposed to know nowadays that the apparent motion of the Sun is an illusion created by the rotation of the Earth. A significant part of contemporary English pays lip service to long-abandoned beliefs about anatomy and physiology. Words like *heartbroken, melancholy,* and *frantic* are remnants of past times when much of what was "known" about the human body was based primarily on superstition, supposition, and imagination.

Organs of thought and feeling

Today science can confidently assign perception, cognition, memory, and all other intellectual processes to the brain. The precise mapping of functional areas within the central nervous system, achieved chiefly through studies of persons with severe head injuries and those undergoing surgery for brain tumors or epilepsy, is one of the most valuable advances of modern anatomy. Often a neurosurgeon can determine preoperatively, to within a few millimeters, the site of a tumor simply by observing its effects on brain function. The nerve centers and pathways involved in vision, hearing, tactile sensation, voluntary movement, and speech are as well known to the anatomist as the course of the blood through the circulatory system. This was not always the case, however.

Before the modern scientific era, each culture had its own views as to the anatomic site of thought and feeling. Many peoples, probably the majority, believed the heart rather than the brain to be the center of all mental functions. Others located the mind in other internal organs, such as

John H. Dirckx, M.D., is Medical Director, C.H. Gosiger Memorial Health Center, University of Dayton, Ohio, and author of The Language of Modern Medicine: Its Evolution, Structure, and Dynamics.

Illustration by Stephanie Motz

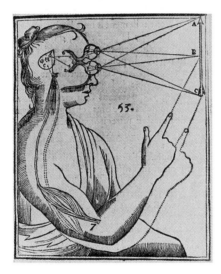

*An engraving from René Descartes's
posthumously published* De l'homme *(c.
1662), considered by many to be the first
modern textbook of physiology, shows the
location of the pineal gland (labeled H),
which the French philosopher-scientist
believed to be the seat of the human soul.
Descartes attributed the motor functions
of the body to the soul's ability to activate
the brain, which in turn generated "animal
spirits" that flowed throughout the trunk
and limbs.*

the liver or the kidneys, or divided it up and assigned judgment or wisdom to one organ, memory to another, and so on.

Because emotions cause obvious changes in muscle tone and, by way of the autonomic nervous system, in the action of other organs and tissues, the emotions themselves were often thought to arise in the structures affected. Racing or hammering pulses seem to point to the heart as the seat of fear or anger, while heaviness in the chest might suggest that grief resides in the diaphragm. Digestive disturbances and abdominal distress (the familiar "gut reaction" to emotional crises) seem to indicate that such diverse feelings as jealousy, depression, and pity spring from the stomach, intestines, liver, or spleen. Among peoples who practiced cannibalism, the belief often prevailed that one could acquire the cunning, valor, or other enviable qualities of a slain enemy by eating the parts of his body where these faculties were thought to reside. In all cultures, beliefs about the physical site of thoughts and emotions exerted profound influences on language, customs, literature, art, medicine, and religion.

The following discussion of such beliefs focuses mainly on the peoples and cultures from which many contemporary Western traditions have evolved—the ancient Hebrews, the Greeks, the Romans, and the western Europeans of the Middle Ages. This survey reveals not only a wide diversity of beliefs but also the extent to which they have penetrated the language, folklore, literature, and even political and religious institutions of English-speaking people.

Linguistic heritage of the Hebrews

The ancient Hebrews were but one of the many peoples who have located all vital functions in the heart. Scarcely a page in the devotional and

An engraving from a 19th-century edition of John Milton's Samson Agonistes *depicts the scene in Judges 16:17 in which Samson, weary of Delilah's questioning about the source of his great strength, finally tells her his secret, which the biblical text describes as "[telling] her all his heart." The confidence that Samson imparted was: "No razor has ever come upon my head, . . . if I am shaven, then my strength will leave me." The ancient Hebrews' belief in the heart as an organ of both emotion and reason, as well as a seat of memory and secret thoughts, is reflected in many passages of the Old Testament.*

prophetic books of the Hebrew Scripture is without some reference to this organ, called, in Hebrew, *lev.* (These references to the heart are not so apparent in English versions of the Old Testament, which often translate *lev* as "life" or "soul" instead of "heart.") The Hebrews could not have failed to observe that injury to the head can cause mental aberrations or unconsciousness, yet there is not a single reference in the Old Testament to the brain as the seat of thoughts or emotions. For the Hebrews, knowledge and cogitation were cardiac functions: "Know therefore this day, and consider it in thine heart, that the Lord he is God in heaven above" (Deuteronomy 4:39). They frequently expressed the notion of thinking as "saying in one's heart"; hence, "The fool hath said in his heart, there is no God" (Psalms 14:1). Memory and, in particular, intimate or secret thoughts were also placed in the heart: "And when Delilah saw that he had told her all his heart . . ." (Judges 16:18).

In several passages in the Old Testament, the Hebrews also associated the kidneys with inmost thoughts. In the King James Version, the Hebrew word *k'lyoth* ("kidneys") is rendered "reins" (from the Latin *ren* via an Old French word): "Examine me, o Lord, and prove me; try my reins and my

171

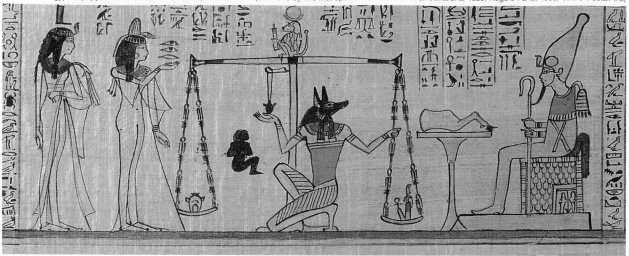

The Hebrews were not the only early people to associate intellect, emotion, and ethical qualities with the heart. An Egyptian funerary papyrus dating from the 21st dynasty (c. 1000 BC) depicts the god Osiris (right) presiding over a "last judgment." In the center of the picture, the jackal-headed god Anubis weighs the heart of the deceased (left side of scale)—the means of determining his moral worth. On the opposite side of the scale are the symbols for truth and justice.

heart" (Psalms 26:2). However, since nearly every use of *kidneys* in this sense in Scripture is accompanied by a reference to the heart, it can probably be concluded that for the ancient Hebrews the word was a metaphor for "something hidden deep within the body" rather than a literal belief that mental functions originate in the kidneys.

In biblical times the whole range of human emotions was thought to reside in the heart: "He will be glad in his heart" (Exodus 4:14); "Having sorrow in my heart daily" (Psalms 13:2); "Though an host should encamp against me, my heart shall not fear" (Psalms 27:3). Moral qualities were assumed to reside there as well: "O continue . . . thy righteousness to the upright in heart" (Psalms 36:10); "The heart is deceitful above all things, and desperately wicked: who can know it?" (Jeremiah 17:9). In other passages bearing on this subject can be found several interesting metaphors. For fortitude and fidelity: "And the Lord thy God will circumcise thine heart" (Deuteronomy 30:6). For stubbornness and cruelty: "But I will harden his heart, that he shall not let the people go" (Exodus 4:21). For treachery and deceit: "With flattering lips and with a double heart do they speak" (Psalms 12:2). For immorality: "The proud have forged a lie against me: . . . their heart is as fat as grease, but I delight in thy law" (Psalms 119:69–70).

Although the Hebrews viewed the heart not only as the seat of mind, will, and emotions but even as the principle of life itself, the vital importance of respiration could hardly escape them. They used the word *nefesh,* derived from a verb meaning "to breathe," as an alternative word for *life* or *soul:* "The Lord shall preserve thee from all evil: he shall preserve thy soul" (Psalms 121:7). The heart can be seen; the breath cannot. This difference seems to reflect the dualism of body and spirit. Thus, *soul* (*nefesh*) is often yoked together with *heart* (*lev*) in many passages where *heart* might have been used alone: "Therefore shall ye lay up these my words in your heart and in your soul" (Deuteronomy 11:18). "And thou shalt love the Lord thy God with all thine heart and with all thy soul, and with all thy might" (Deuteronomy 6:5).

The rich biblical symbolism of blood (Hebrew, *dam*) appears in many

172

passages in which it is virtually synonymous with life. Indeed, the oft-repeated precept forbidding consumption of the blood of an animal along with the flesh is frequently followed by the assertion that "the life [*nefesh*] of all flesh is the blood thereof" (Leviticus 17:14). This should probably be taken as a physiological observation rather than an attempt to place any principle of life in the blood. Similarly, association of the bowels with feelings of passion, as in the Song of Solomon 5:4 (". . . and my bowels were moved for him"), should probably be viewed as descriptions of physical sensations that stop short of placing the origins of such emotions there.

Hearts and minds

The heart-centered physiology and psychology of the ancient Hebrews are relevant to this discussion because their beliefs and customs, and even in some measure their turns of speech, as transmitted in the Old Testament, are among the oldest historical influences discernible in the modern Western world. There is, however, abundant evidence that peoples throughout the world have made this same identification of heart and mind. In languages as divergent as Tibetan and Hopi, the heart is tied to thought and emotion. In the Chinese language, ideographs denoting will or purpose and idea or significance are based on a radical, or character, that not only means "heart" but is plainly derived from a line drawing of the human heart. The identical symbol has been borrowed by the Japanese kanji writing system. An Egyptian papyrus from around 1000 BC contains a picture of the weighing of the heart of a recently deceased person, a method of assessing his moral worth.

Why have so many and such diverse cultures chosen the heart as the seat of intellectual functions, emotions, and moral qualities—the symbol par excellence of the vital force? According to the Swiss psychologist and psychiatrist Carl Gustav Jung (1875–1961), all human beings possess in common a "collective unconscious"—a primitive stock of notions or concepts that are not derived from sensory experience. This collective unconscious supplies images for dreams and delusions, archetypal characters and plots for myths and legends, and universally intelligible symbols for art, religion, and magic. Although this theory would explain why many isolated communities independently adopt the same myths and symbols, it has not won general acceptance among psychologists.

Of course, the heart is not the only vital organ. The brain, liver, lungs, and kidneys are equally indispensable. But among warlike peoples, for whom hand-to-hand combat is a fact of daily life if not a condition of survival, the observation must often be made that penetrating wounds of the heart are the most consistently and rapidly lethal. Even in more peace-loving communities, hunters typically make the same observation from the animals they slay. Inevitably the equation heart = life becomes embedded in the group's cultural matrix and shapes habits of thought and speech. The responses of the heart to strong emotion—the proverbial skipped beat, the sensation of the heart in the mouth, the poignant tug at the (nonexistent) heartstrings—would reinforce the notion that the heart is not only the source of fright, wrath, and grief but also the organ of thought.

The custom of exchanging paper tokens, or cards, expressing affection in observance of St. Valentine's Day is believed to date from the 16th century. "Valentines" from the late 19th (above) and early 20th (top) centuries are a testament to the deeply rooted tradition that holds the heart to be the wellspring of amorous feelings. The many disturbing physical manifestations of infatuation—e.g., the sensation of the heart "standing still" or beating erratically—would seem to validate a connection between that organ and the emotions of romantic love.

173

The mind and the midriff

Since the *Iliad* and the *Odyssey* were the "holy scriptures" of the ancient Greeks, one must turn to the Homeric epics to learn in what parts of the body thought and emotion were believed to reside in early Hellenic culture. Like the classical Hebrew writers, Homer often placed reason, memory, and feelings such as love, anger, and fear in the heart (*kradie,* corresponding to Attic Greek *kardia*). There is, however, an extraordinary degree of anatomic confusion in Homer's language—a confusion that remained a feature of Greek language and thought throughout the classical period.

Like the Hebrews and many other peoples, the Greeks derived nouns meaning "mind" or "soul" from verbs meaning "to breathe" or "to blow," specifically, *pneuma,* from *pneo; psuche,* from *psuo; thumos,* from *thuo;* and *etor* (perhaps), from *aemi*. Although each of these words had its own range of connotations, the ranges tended to overlap broadly. Moreover, all four of these Greek words for "soul" seem, in the works of Homer and later writers, to mean something located in a particular place in the body or rather—and here is the crux of the matter—in a vague, ill-defined place in the body, somewhere about the midriff and apparently encompassing heart, lungs, liver, and sometimes other viscera. Of these four words, Homer most often used *thumos,* but his favorite term for "mind" or "soul" was *phren,* which, interestingly enough, is also the Greek name for the diaphragm, the dome-shaped muscle that separates the thoracic from the abdominal organs.

It is doubtful that the Greeks recognized the role of the diaphragm as the principal respiratory muscle and thus made the chain of association from diaphragm to breath to soul. One cannot even be sure that Homer's contemporaries distinguished clearly between the diaphragm and the pericardium, the membrane that encloses the heart and is continuous with the diaphragm. Indeed, students of language have plausibly connected *phren,* meaning "mind" or "soul," with Latin *ren* and Greek *nephros,* both of which mean "kidney." Nonetheless, amid much confusion about anatomy and physiology, one fact stands out plainly: the Greeks conceived of *phren,* "the diaphragm," as an organ or bodily region in the chest, and they placed *phren,* "the mind," there, making it the seat of reason, wisdom, courage, fear, love, and joy.

Hippocrates' extraordinary prescience

Some centuries after Homer, the Greek physician Alcmaeon of Croton (6th century BC) traced nerves to their origin in the brain and correctly deduced that that organ is the center of sensory experience and the source of muscular activity. Building on Alcmaeon's observations and conclusions, Hippocrates of Cos (460–377 BC) taught that the brain, not the diaphragm, is the seat of both emotions and reason. A somewhat militant tone is evident as Hippocrates announces this doctrine in opposition to the generally received view in the following passage from one of his most remarkable works, his treatise on epilepsy, *On the Sacred Disease:*

It must be clearly understood that both pleasurable and distressing emotions arise exclusively in the brain. Moreover, thought and sensation reside there as well. . . .

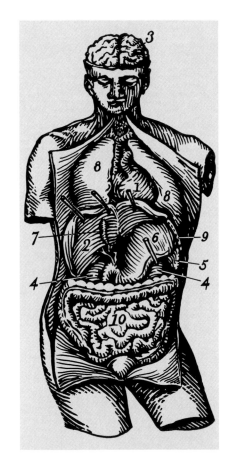

1	heart	6	stomach
2	liver	7	gallbladder
3	brain	8	lungs
4	kidneys	9	diaphragm
5	spleen	10	intestines

174

I assert most emphatically that it is the brain that mediates our responses to sensory experience. The diaphragm [*phren*] owes its name to a popular misconception. A careful assessment of its nature and properties indicates that it has no capacity to know or to reason [*phronein*]. It is true that a momentary contraction of the diaphragm occurs as part of one's reaction to any sudden shock. This I would attribute to its breadth and thinness, its delicacy of structure, and its lack of a hollow interior to absorb forces impinging on it. But since the diaphragm does not receive sensory impressions any more directly than other body structures, the implication that it is an organ of perception, inherent in its name, is erroneous. We might as well expect the auricles of the heart to hear sounds because they are named for their resemblance to ears. As a matter of fact, the heart has been believed by some to be the seat of grief and anxiety, or even of thought. But this also is a mistaken notion, based on the fact that the heart at times constricts much as the diaphragm does—if not, indeed, more violently.

Although he may have persuaded some of his compatriots to change their minds about where their minds were situated, Hippocrates could not single-handedly remodel the Greek language, and he was himself compelled to go on using *phren* as both an anatomic term for "diaphragm" and a word referring to the mind, as in the derivatives *phrenitis* ("madness") and *phrenitikos* ("insane").

The mistakes of Plato and Aristotle

Among those who did not accept Hippocrates' views on the brain as the seat of the mind was the philosopher Plato (428/427–348/347 BC), who clung stubbornly to a visceral psychology. In the *Timaeus* he conceded that the gods had enclosed the immortal soul of man, or the rational soul, in the head, to which they appended the body for support and locomotion. But Plato maintained that within this body the gods had also placed a mortal soul, subject to pleasure, pain, and other emotions. The part of this mortal soul that is endowed with courage, passion, and love of conflict, which he termed the irascible soul, lies above the diaphragm, lodged in and regulated by the heart and lungs. The part that is subject to the desire for food, drink, and other physical gratification, the so-called appetitive soul, resides below the diaphragm in the liver and spleen.

In this anatomic apportionment of the emotions, Plato departed from the common opinion of his time, which traced anger to the liver. The association of anger (*cholos*) with bile (*chole*) may have been a case of folk beliefs influencing etymology, but more likely the similarity of the words reflects some primitive notion that the physical sensations accompanying anger are felt more strongly in the region of the liver. No doubt the bitterness of bile lent metaphoric corroboration. In Greek literature, the liver (*hepar*) sometimes means simply "the vitals." Thus, when a character in Greek tragedy threatens to commit suicide by plunging a dagger into his or her liver, English translators invariably redirect the threat toward the heart.

The Greek philosopher Aristotle (384–322 BC), perhaps the most brilliant anatomist before Galen, blundered badly in his neurophysiology. Although the son of a physician, Aristotle was apparently unacquainted with the writings of Hippocrates. In his treatise *On the Parts of Animals,* he assigned reason and perception to the heart; the brain, he believed, served only as

Hippocrates of Cos, the 5th-century BC Greek physician traditionally regarded as the father of medicine, exerted an enormous influence on the development of Western diagnostics and therapeutics. Whereas most of his contemporaries opined that the mind (phren) resided in the diaphragm—from which misapprehension derive such words as frantic *and* schizophrenic—*Hippocrates firmly believed that emotion, thought, and sensation arose in the brain. To his way of thinking, the fact that the heart or diaphragm might contract violently in response to strong emotion in no way indicated that these anatomic structures had the capacity for knowledge or sentiment.*

175

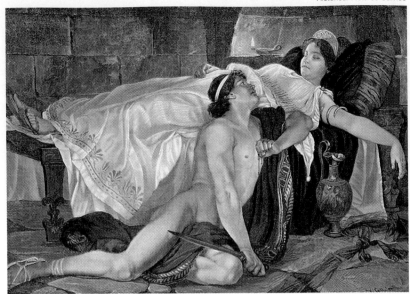

"He straightway leaned with all his weight against his sword, and drove it, half its length, into his side." Thus Sophocles describes the death of Haemon, who killed himself in despair upon discovering the lifeless body of Antigone, his betrothed. In Greek literature it was not uncommon for the word for "liver," hepar, to be used simply to mean "the vitals." However, when a character in Greek tragedy threatens to plunge a dagger into his or her side— presumably the liver—English translators typically redirect the action toward the heart. In the case of this illustration for a modern version of Antigone, *the artist has likewise taken liberties, the youth having thrust his sword not into his side but into his chest.*

a cooling system to moderate the activity of the heart and induce sleep; phlegm, supposedly produced by the brain, acted as a sort of "refrigerant."

One of the words used by the Greeks for "soul," *pneuma,* acquired special importance in the teachings of the Pneumatists, a group of physicians and medical theorists that flourished in the 3rd century BC and afterward. Founded by Erasistratus of Chios (300–250 BC), this school of thinking based all the phenomena of life on breath or spirit—*pneuma*—two variant forms of which were believed to course through the arteries and nerves.

The Romans: imitators and innovators

When Rome conquered Greece in the 2nd century BC and assumed possession of the remains of Alexander's empire, Greek philosophy, science, and medicine were part of the booty. These so aptly filled a void in Roman culture that by the time of Christ, the Hellenic heritage had been completely absorbed and naturalized. Cicero (106–43 BC), Rome's greatest prose writer and most influential popularizer of philosophical doctrines, was merely aping Plato when he wrote, "Brain, heart, lungs, and liver: these are the habitations of life."

Nevertheless, a sense that reason and fortitude as well as affection and other emotions arise in the heart was indigenous to Roman culture, as shown by many traces in the Latin language. Early writers use *cor* ("heart") as a synonym for thought, reflection, or judgment. Its diminutive *corculum,* "little heart," was a term of endearment. The adjective *cordatus* meant "wise" or "prudent," and the verb *recordari,* "to remember." The phrase *cordi habere* ("to have at heart") signified "to value" or "to hold in high esteem."

The Latin name for the diaphragm is *praecordia,* literally "that which lies before the heart." Although this term may at first have referred to the pericardium, by the Augustan era of Latin history (43 BC–AD 18), *praecordia* had been adopted as the Latin equivalent of the Greek *phren* in both

176

anatomic and psychological senses. Horace warned, in one of his satires, that Bacchus, the truth-loving god of wine, unlocks the secret *praecordia* of the dinner guest who imbibes too freely. In the *Aeneid* Virgil speaks of the blood congealing in the *praecordia* of the fear-stricken Arcadians.

The Romans not only followed the Greeks in placing anger in the liver (*jecur*) but also regarded that organ as the seat of erotic passion. A Roman witch, seeking to induce impotence, would thrust a needle into the hepatic region of a wax figurine representing her victim. Horace, cautioning guests against amorous adventures with their host's domestics, said: "Let no maidservant inflame your liver." In the *Satires* he wrote of feeling angry: "The bile burnt my liver"; and in his *Odes* he expressed jealousy: "My flaming liver swells with impetuous bile."

The Romans also viewed the stomach as an organ of emotion. The verb *stomachari* meant "to be peevish or irritable" or "to be annoyed with someone or (less often) something." Similarly, the adjective *stomachosus* meant "angry" or "fretful," and the query *Quid tibi stomacho?* meant "What's bothering you?" One must be cautious, however, in drawing conclusions from such expressions. If a modern writer says that someone makes his blood boil or gives him a pain in the neck, no reader supposes that he means to be taken literally, much less that he believes that the part of his body experiencing anger or annoyance is located in the blood or in the neck. Likewise, when Virgil, in the *Aeneid,* said that suffering "raged in the bones" of Gyas, and Cicero spoke of chronic anxiety "settling into one's veins and marrow," they were simply employing metaphors.

Like the Hebrews and Greeks before them, though, the Romans regarded certain words referring to breathing as more than metaphoric expressions for "life" or "soul." The Latin word *animus* ("mind"), including reason, knowledge, and feelings, plainly developed out of *anima* ("breath, soul, principle of life"), akin to Greek *anemos* ("wind"). Similarly, *spiritus,* from the Latin *spirare* ("to breathe or blow"), meant "character" or "disposition" as well as "breath of life," as in the phrase *spiritum edere*, literally, "to give up one's spirit, to die."

Medieval physiology and diagnostics

After the fall of the Roman Empire, until the Renaissance, intellectual torpor prevailed in Western culture. However, despite its almost total lack of originality and creativity, the medieval mind occasionally spawned innovations, albeit via mistakes in its transmission and interpretation of the remnants of ancient learning to which it clung with superstitious fervor.

In anatomy and physiology the Greek physician Galen (AD 129–199) reigned supreme, his teachings perpetuated by Islamic and, later, Christian scholars. Galen derived his physiology from that of Hippocrates, which was based in turn on the physics of Empedocles (*c.* 490–430 BC). The central doctrine of these systems was that the universe consists of four elements—earth, air, fire, and water—each of which embodies two of four cardinal qualities—hotness, coldness, wetness, and dryness.

The human body, viewed as a microcosm, or universe in miniature, was also believed to be a composite of four elements, or humors—blood,

Illuminations from a medieval manuscript depict the four fundamental personality types (clockwise from top left): melancholic, sanguine, phlegmatic, and choleric. The 2nd-century Greek physician Galen, whose teachings influenced the practice of medicine in Europe in the Middle Ages, elaborated on a system of physiology that he had inherited from his predecessor Hippocrates, which postulated that health depended on the equilibrium of four humors (corresponding to the above): black bile, blood, phlegm, and yellow bile. Galen in his turn classified individuals and assessed their health on the basis of their predominant humor. Galen's diagnostic methods were eventually superseded by more scientific approaches, but the adjectives describing the four distinct temperaments remain very much a part of the language.

phlegm, yellow bile, and black bile. According to Hippocrates and Galen, perfect mental and physical health depended on a balance among the four humors; an excess of any of them resulted in disease. During the Middle Ages, certain temperaments, or complexions, came to be identified with certain of the humors, and their origins placed accordingly. The sanguine, or "bloody," temperament—hot and dry like fire—was characterized by cheerfulness, optimism, and amiability. The phlegmatic—cold and wet like water—was cool, calm, and indifferent. The bilious or choleric—hot and wet like air—was peevish and irascible. The melancholic—cold and dry like earth—was disposed to pensiveness and depression.

The brain, believed to be the source of phlegm, retained its sovereignty as the seat of reason, but emotions and traits of personality were placed elsewhere. Love, kindness, and good cheer belonged to the heart, where the blood was thought to be produced. Anger and jealousy were traced to the liver, responsible for the production of bile (essentially the only accurate notion in the whole system). And depression and sadness arose in the spleen. Because the liver and spleen lie in the upper abdomen beneath the cartilages of the ribs, they were known as *hypochondriacal* (literally "under the cartilage") organs, and persons of querulous, irritable, or gloomy dispositions were said to suffer from hypochondria. This is

178

the origin of the colloquial term *hipped,* meaning "morose" or "dejected," which is often encountered in 18th- and 19th-century novels.

Shakespeare: much ado about brain, liver, and heart

The recovery of classical scientific and medical writings during the Renaissance seemed only to corroborate the details of medieval humoral psychology. Chaucer's writings are full of it, and by the Elizabethan era the system had been fully developed and was deeply ingrained in the popular mind and language. The clergyman and scholar Robert Burton assembled, in *Anatomy of Melancholy* (1621), a fascinating hodgepodge of ancient lore and contemporary foolishness on the subject, seemingly in dead earnest.

Shakespeare was the best illuminator of his contemporaries' beliefs about the seat of the soul. In *Twelfth Night* he wrote of "liver, brain, and heart, these sovereign thrones [of feeling]," and throughout his works are allusions to the doctrine of humors and their effects on personality, mood, and behavior. No one in Shakespeare's day doubted where intelligence resided, and his audiences easily saw the point of remarks such as Falstaff's in *The Merry Wives of Windsor:* "If I be served such another trick, I'll have my brains ta'en out, and butter'd, and give them to a dog." The poet ventured a little beyond his depth, however, when he had the clown Feste say of Sir Toby in *Twelfth Night* that he "has a most weak pia mater," for the pia mater is just one of the membranes covering the brain and has no nervous function.

Even while acknowledging the scientific fact that the brain is the organ of reason and emotion, Shakespeare made much of the sentimental role attributed by folklore to the heart. The two notions were thus entwined in these famous lines of Macbeth:

By the time of Queen Elizabeth I, the doctrine of the four humors had gained popular acceptance. In 1621 the English clergyman-scholar Robert Burton published Anatomy of Melancholy, *a widely read compendium of lore about depression. "If there be a hell upon earth, it is to be found in a melancholy man's heart," Burton wrote. A detail of the title page shows the author (who published the work under the pseudonym Democritus Junior) flanked by four figures: personifications of melancholy associated with love or romantic sentiment, religious melancholy, hypochondria, and insanity. Rich in classical allusion and a treasure trove of curious information, the* Anatomy *also contains some farseeing wisdoms; e.g., that "frequent use of honest sports, companies, and recreations" is a beneficial treatment for depression.*

Sir John Falstaff, "with liver burning hot," makes amorous advances toward Mistress Ford in a scene from William Shakespeare's The Merry Wives of Windsor. *The notion of the liver as the seat of erotic passion derives from the Roman tradition. Shakespearean dramas abound in references to the parts played by various bodily organs in producing thought and feelings.*

Canst thou not minister to a mind diseas'd,
Pluck from the memory a rooted sorrow,
Raze out the written troubles of the brain,
And with some sweet oblivious antidote
Cleanse the stuff'd bosom of that perilous stuff
Which weighs upon the heart?

Shakespeare's references to the heart as the seat of love and other emotions rival those of the Old Testament in their breadth and richness of imagery.

It is his frequent mention of the liver and spleen, however, that strikes the modern reader as the quaintest and perhaps least intelligible. Shakespeare generally chose *choler,* the Elizabethan word for "bile," to convey wrath. When he wrote of the liver, his subject usually was not anger but rather either courage or lust. He subscribed to the popular view that the liver of a valiant man is dark with blood; hence, in *The Merchant of Venice,* Basanio speaks of cowards "who, inward search'd, have livers white as milk." He also bowed to the Roman conviction that erotic passion arises in the liver. Thus, in *The Merry Wives of Windsor,* Pistol tells Ford that Falstaff loves Mistress Ford "with liver burning hot."

180

Says Brutus to Cassius in *Julius Caesar:* "Must I give way and room to your rash choler?. . . Must I stand and crouch under your testy humor? By the gods, you shall digest the venom of your spleen, though it do split you." Most of Shakespeare's references to the spleen are less explicitly anatomic. He used the term for a broad range of concepts, including impetuous irascibility, malice and hatred, and even mirth and silliness.

English as a treacherous tongue

The English language continues to preserve outdated notions about the relationship of body and mind. For thousands of years the pounding heart of a person facing danger was thought to betoken valor. Today this adrenaline-mediated increase in the rate and force of cardiac contractions, part of the normal "fight-or-flight" response, is known to be a sign of fear. Nevertheless, people not only speak of bravery as *courage* (from Late Latin *coraticum,* "function or condition of the heart") but unhesitatingly use such terms as *stout-hearted, fainthearted,* and *disheartened* for traits of character or states of mind that they know perfectly well have nothing to do with the heart.

In expressions such as *good* (or *bad*) *humor, to humor someone, melancholy mood, sanguine expectations, phlegmatic disposition, lily-livered, hypochondriac,* and "that takes a lot of gall," scraps of obsolete medieval humoral psychology and related doctrines still survive. *Melancholia, hypchondriasis,* and *humoral* are words that belong to the technical terminology of medicine. People may refer to bravery as "guts" or, more genteelly, as "intestinal fortitude." *Pluck* means the same thing—the word once referred to the intestines or tripes plucked from a carcass by a butcher.

The ancient identification of breath and life echoes in words such as

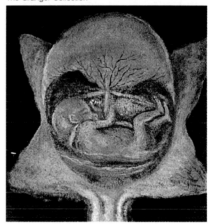

The case of a woman suffering from hysteria, presented by the celebrated 19th-century French neurologist Jean-Martin Charcot to his colleagues at the Salpêtrière Hospital in Paris, is the subject of the famous painting at left. The term hysteria *comes from the Greek word for "uterus" and reflects the notion of earlier generations of physicians that such psychoneurotic manifestations were exclusively a female disorder and related to the functions of the womb.*

psyche, psychology, animal, animation, spirited, dispirited, spiritual, and *expire* (meaning "to die"). *Hysteria* derives from the Greek word for "uterus" because ancient physicians—all of them apparently male—traced to that organ what they considered a uniquely feminine emotional disorder. The odd expression "a man of my own kidney," meaning one of like temperament, dates to Elizabethan times and earlier. *Schizophrenia* contains the old Greek word for "diaphragm," and *frenzy* and *frantic* are simply corruptions of Hippocrates' *phrenitis* and *phrenitikos.*

Even more pervasive are standard expressions, idioms, and catchphrases referring to the heart. An enumeration of those in common use (such as "I know that story by heart" and "I didn't have the heart to tell her") would more than fill this page. The identification of the heart as the physical center of vital bodily processes underlies the use of metaphors such as "the heart of the matter." Remnants of outdated notions about cardiac function survive in the words *hearty, heartless, cordial, accord* (of which the musician's *chord* is a corruption), *concord, discord,* and *record,* in the practice of placing the hand on the heart when taking the Pledge of Allegiance, and in the custom of wearing a wedding ring on the fourth finger, once believed to receive an artery (or, by some accounts, a nerve) directly from the heart.

In modern Western culture the stylized, symmetrical heart shape serves as a universally understood symbol of romantic love. It would be difficult to find a commercially produced Valentine's Day card without one. In comic strips and animated cartoons the heart denotes sexual attraction. On posters and bumper stickers, it proclaims one's predilection (or "love") for a particular city, sport, food, hobby, or breed of pet. Although this well-recognized shape approximates the external configuration of the human heart, it is actually derived from other sources in nature—"heart-shaped" leaves, fruits, nuts, and segments of plants. Probably because of its sim-

The stylized heart shape is a virtually universal symbol for courage and valor, friendship, and romantic love. The motif is also eminently recognizable in expressions of unswerving loyalty to anything from a favorite city to a particular make of car.

U.S. Postal Service

plicity and symmetry, the heart shape is a basic motif in decorative and folk art. It can also be seen in countless everyday objects, from candy and jewelry to swimming pools and beds at honeymoon hotels.

The future of misnomers

It cannot be denied that present-day speech and behavior are full of absurdities that continue to be perpetuated in direct contradiction to established fact. Nonetheless, mixed in with all the nonsense Is a leaven of reason— as in the expressions *addlepated, headstrong, lamebrain, numbskull,* and "I can't get it into (or out of) my head," all references to the brain as the seat of intellect. Such examples serve to emphasize that language and tradition preserve the false along with the true, the superstitious and specious along with the known and proven. It is probably safe to predict that the errors and misconceptions of the past will go on being repeated in speech and influencing the thinking and behavior of generations yet to come. How many *new* inaccuracies and inconsistencies, one might ask, are being built into the language of the future?

Philip Jon Bailey—Stock, Boston

Keeping Up with Medicine

(What Your Doctor Reads)

by Stephen Lock, M.D.

Medical folklore has long portrayed orthopedic surgeons as muscular hunks of little brain who were football or rugby players in college and just barely waded their way through medical school. As practitioners, they allegedly communicate with their colleagues in grunts. Do they, in reality, have more in common with gorillas than their colleagues in other surgical disciplines? This question was given recent attention in the *British Medical Journal* (*BMJ*). In an original research report from the Cleveland (Ohio) Clinic Foundation, three physicians contended, "Critical comparison between orthopaedic and general surgeons is woefully absent in scientific publications, leading to speculation, innuendo, and myth." To investigate the popular myths about the orthopedic surgeon, they undertook a randomized, double-blind study.

From "major hospitals across the United States," they obtained glove sizes of a total of 483 surgeons—217 orthopedic and 266 general surgeons. And "as an adjunct study glove sizes of locally available gorillas were measured." What they found was that the mean glove size for the male orthopedic surgeons was 7.7 and for the female orthopedic surgeons 6.9, compared with figures of 7.4 and 6.4 for the general surgeons. The investigators further reported, "One gorilla in the natural history museum and one from the zoological gardens had a glove size greater than 9.5. (One gorilla was not cooperative and despite many attempts would not allow measurements.)" The team went on to conclude that orthopedic surgeons do have larger hands than general surgeons—probably because they use them more (the "work hypertrophy" theory)—and that they "are slightly closer to gorillas than are general surgeons."

This was not the only paper in that issue of the journal that was concerned with the image of the orthopedic surgeon. D.S. Barrett, a senior registrar at the Royal National Orthopaedic Hospital in Middlesex, England, set out to answer the question "Can Orthopaedic Surgeons Walk on Water?" Barrett reported in detail on his personal investigation: an attempt

Stephen Lock, M.D., was Editor of the British Medical Journal *from 1975 until his retirement in April 1991.*

(Opposite page) Illustration by Skip Williamson

184

From *The Life of Hugh Owen Thomas* by David Le Vay; © 1952 by Churchill Livingstone, London

"Are Orthopaedic Surgeons Really Gorillas?" This was the question posed by three U.S. physicians in an article in the Dec. 22–29, 1990, issue of the British Medical Journal. *Their interest in this question was piqued by the results of a previous study published in the same journal (Dec. 24–31, 1988), which had found that orthopedic surgeons' mean glove size was larger than that of general surgeons (7.6 versus 7.4). Despite that finding, the author of the previous study claimed that the image of orthopedic surgeons as big brutes was undeserved: "These views . . . derive from the early bonesetters,"* who, in the days before modern orthopedics, needed brute strength and big hands to treat fractures and dislocations (as illustrated). *"Perhaps," he speculated, "orthopaedics is still perceived as a macho specialty . . . so that only the largest trainees . . . apply."* The U.S. authors believed the previous study was flawed because it did not consider glove sizes of (1) women surgeons, (2) trainees (residents), or (3) actual gorillas. They, too, found that orthopedic surgeons—male and female—had larger hands than did general surgeons (see table). They were, however, unable to include gorillas' glove sizes in their final data as they had set out to do because not all gorillas were cooperative.

Glove sizes

	male	female
orthopedic surgeons		
staff	7.7	6.9
resident	7.7	6.5
general surgeons		
staff	7.4	6.4
resident	7.4	6.1

Adapted from John S. Fox *et al.,* "Are Orthopaedic Surgeons Really Gorillas?" *British Medical Journal,* vol. 301, no. 6766 (Dec. 22–29, 1990), pp. 1425–26

at barefoot waterskiing. "At the crack of dawn, when the water was at its most calm, the ordeal began. I was duly dragged up and down the lake at unimaginably high speeds until at last I stood on the surface." In sum, Barrett suffered a "hugely swollen scrotum" and "massive muscular breakdown" of the chest, shoulders, and abdomen, all of which caused, in the days that followed, "a tottering, wide based gait inclined forward at 20 degrees during rare periods of ambulation." What did the investigator conclude from his original experiment? "Doctors are often accused of playing God in their dealings with patients," Barrett wrote. "This is one orthopaedic surgeon who will no longer attempt to walk on water."

Also in that *BMJ* issue was a paper entitled "Bell Ringers' Bruises and Broken Bones: Capers and Crises in Campanology," which detailed 79 injuries among 221 ringers. These injuries included rope burns, wrenched fingers, abrasion to the tip of the nose caused by a ringer's thumbnail while he was trying to grasp a flapping rope, and seven deaths (including two suicides). Yet another report, "The Surgeon's Scissor-Jaw Reflex," described the phenomenon of surgeons opening their mouths in time with the opening of their surgical scissors. "We believe that stimulating jaw activity will lead to increased opening and closing of the scissors," which should result in increased surgical productivity, the authors (two army doctors) proposed. Thus, to maximize scissors activity it behooves every member of the surgical team to engage the working surgeon in conversation.

For more than a decade the *BMJ* has devoted its final issue of the year to a special mixture of humor, history, and medical culture. Many of the papers are clever spoofs by physician-contributors that mimic the very content, style, and conclusions of the serious reports appearing in the journal's 50 other issues each year. Other medical journals also lighten their solid blocks of research reports with some entertainment.

Ever since the beginning of World War II, *The Lancet* has had its regular weekly column "In England Now," anonymous pieces—funny, literate, quirky—from peripatetic correspondents who report scenes from the everyday lives of doctors and patients in Britain. These include frequent "Is there a doctor in the house?" episodes. One doctor wrote of a dining experience in a north England country inn—eating roast leg of lamb to strains of Bach's "Sheep May Safely Graze." Then there was the member of the Royal Army Medical Corps who described buying an umbrella.

As I had never possessed such an article, I decided to buy one when next in London. And this I did. It was an immaculate, thin, black pencil. The very epitome of the craftsman's art. I inquired how I should open and rewrap it. The assistant looked at me in horror. "One does not unfurl it, Sir," he said. "Never!" "What will I do when it rains?" I asked. "Quite simple, Sir," he replied. "Hold it out at right angles to the body and shout 'Taxi!' "

On the other side of the Atlantic, the last letter or two in the correspondence column of the *New England Journal of Medicine* (*NEJM*) often describe bizarre injuries and previously unrecognized ailments. Letters to the journal have reported, for instance, sore nipples in joggers, "buffer's belly" (abdominal pain and injury from steadying a large, vibrating floor-buffing machine against the abdomen), and a new cause for tennis elbow—karate. And, in the *Journal of the American Medical Association* (*JAMA*), letters to the editor have described instances of "nine-ball neck" and "glaucoma presenting as hiccups," as well as a case of a man in the Bronx, New York, staggering from a Japanese restaurant and collapsing on the sidewalk after eating green wasabi, a horseradish-like condiment served with his sushi.

Medical communication: serious business

It would be wrong to give the impression that such amusing material is the stuff of medical journals, however. Their major concern, of course, is publishing and commenting on serious primary research reports. Communication is perhaps the most vital part in the whole scientific process and the raison d'être of the medical literature. Journals report the results of medical research, weigh the evidence presented in editorials and the correspondence columns, and then, occasionally, carry campaigns into a broader arena, lobbying for changes that would be of proven benefit for the health of the public at large.

The aim of ensuring that medical advances serve the public is well illustrated by the introduction of anesthesia. Many would argue that safe and effective anesthesia is still the single most important discovery in the history of medicine. Its significance lies not only in alleviating the patient's suffering during surgery but in allowing complex operations on previously inaccessible organs and for previously untreatable diseases.

Ether was first used in surgery in 1842, when the patient James Venable had a neck tumor removed by Crawford Williamson Long in Jefferson, Georgia. However, Long confined his record of the event to his personal ledger, in which he wrote: "James Venable, 1842. Ether and excising tumor, $2.00." The practice was thus kept secret for several years, until the experiment was repeated by 27-year-old William Thomas Green Morton, a dental surgeon, at the Massachusetts General Hospital in Boston, on Oct. 16, 1846. Three months later, in January 1847, the predecessor of the *BMJ*,

Matters such as the size of surgeons' hands and whether orthopedic surgeons can walk on water are considered in the annual Christmas-New Year's issue of the British Medical Journal. *Editor Stephen Lock introduced these end-of-the-year editions—devoted to humor, history, and culture—in 1982, believing that at least once a year readers (and editors!) deserve a bit of a break from the serious research reports that are the journal's regular fare. Lock's primary concern during his 16 years as editor was, of course, publishing valid, scientific work; to ensure the quality of reports appearing in the journal, he emphasized peer review. Lock also had considerable influence beyond his own journal—as a founder of the international group of medical editors (the Vancouver Group) that has set rigorous standards for medical publications throughout the world. He once described the process of medical journal editing as "a balancing act," which was also the title of a book of essays honoring him upon his 1991 retirement. The illustration of Lock—the editor at work—was commissioned for that collection.*

Illustration by Paul Cox

On Oct. 16, 1846, dental surgeon William Morton gave the first successful public demonstration of ether anesthesia before awestruck colleagues at the Massachusetts General Hospital in Boston. The conquest of surgical pain is regarded as one of the single most important advances in medicine. Without medical journals to communicate the discoveries—first of ether, then of chloroform, then of safer and more sophisticated and effective anesthetic agents and methods of administering them—it would not have been possible for surgeons to carry out complex operations with confidence and thereby serve the best interest of patients.

One measure of the importance of a discovery in medicine is how often the published report is subsequently cited in the medical literature. One of the most often cited papers of the past two decades described a "new" cause of diarrheal illness—campylobacter enteritis—discovered in a baby with fever of unknown origin in 1977. Campylobacter organisms (C. jejuni and C. coli) are now known to be among the most common causes of gastrointestinal misery throughout the world—the main routes of transmission being meat, milk, and water.

the *Provincial Medical and Surgical Journal* (*PMSJ*), gave details of several operations in the U.S. in which ether had been used; John Ware of Boston described rendering patients insensible to the pain of surgery by giving them "the strongest sulphuric aether" to inhale. Events followed rapidly, one on another. In February a report from Paris in the *PMSJ* voiced great enthusiasm for the technique of anesthetizing surgical patients with ether, though a month later an editorial in the same journal cautioned against its use and, at the same time, carried the first case report of the death of an anesthetized patient.

At the end of 1847 the *PMSJ* published a description of a new agent, chloroform, only 11 days after it had first been used as an anesthetic by James Young Simpson of the University of Edinburgh Medical School. He claimed that chloroform was cheaper, easier to transport and administer, and pleasanter for the patient to inhale than ether. "Obstetricians may oppose [chloroform]," Simpson wrote, "but I believe our patients themselves will force the use of it upon the profession. I have never had the pleasure of watching over a series of better and more rapid recoveries, nor once witnessed any disagreeable result follow to either mother or child, whilst I have now seen an immense amount of maternal pain and agony saved by its employment."

The seal of respectability was placed on chloroform in 1853 when it was given to Queen Victoria during the birth of her eighth child, following which she had an excellent recovery. All these circumstances, the *PMSJ* commented only two weeks later, would "probably remove much of the lingering professional and popular prejudice against the use of anesthesia in midwifery." Thereafter, the *PMSJ* and then the *BMJ* were to continue this tradition of publishing seminal articles on new uses and methods of administering anesthesia—*e.g.,* Sir William Macewen's report on the use of anesthesia in endotracheal surgery (July 24, 1880), Elmer McKesson on the use of gas ether (Dec. 11, 1926), and Denis Browne on anesthesia for tonsillectomy (Oct. 6, 1928).

188

Medical journals, then, have ensured and continue to ensure that discoveries are translated into action. Without these forums for communication, medical scientists would have found it horrendously difficult to inform their colleagues around the world about their latest clinical and research findings. Indeed, before journals were started, scientists had communicated with one another by letter—a slow and obviously inefficient process.

Not surprisingly, the number of journals has increased steadily since they began to be published over 300 years ago. Several have been published continuously for over a century—*NEJM* (which started publication in 1812), *The Lancet* (started in 1823), the *PMSJ* (1840) succeeded by the *BMJ* (1857), and *JAMA* (1883). The importance of scientific publication was emphasized in the early 19th century by the physicist Michael Faraday: "Work, finish, publish." That statement was echoed over 100 years later by the philosopher of science John Ziman: "The object of science is publication."

Editors make their mark

Each of the major journals has its own distinct voice; the "big four" mentioned above are good examples. A medical journal's character depends partly on the selection of material and partly on its presentation. The pivotal role of the editor in this process should not be underestimated, as was exemplified when a press conference was held early in 1991 to announce the nomination of Jerome P. Kassirer as the successor to Arnold S. Relman, the editor of the prestigious *NEJM* since 1977. *New York Times* medical correspondent Lawrence K. Altman commented on the change at the helm of *NEJM,* noting that in assuming the journal's editorship (on July 1, 1991), Kassirer would become "one of the world's most powerful doctors." Wrote Altman, "By choosing which research papers to publish and which to reject, the editor can help shape medical practice and strongly influence grants for future research projects and for academic promotions. . . . The editor's power to write and select editorials can influence political agendas."

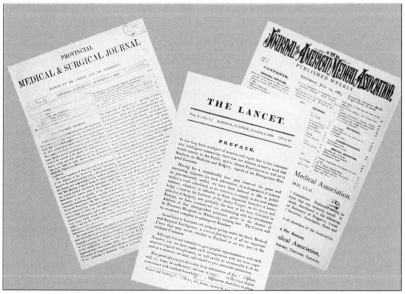

The first scientific journals, which included only occasional articles of medical interest, were published in Great Britain and France starting in 1665. Among the earliest general medical journals, all of which have been published continuously for over a century, were The Lancet *(1823); the* Provincial Medical and Surgical Journal *(1840), the forerunner of the* British Medical Journal; *and the* Journal of the American Medical Association *(1883). Nowadays the contents of these international publications are quickly disseminated to the lay public; virtually every week items from one or another of the major journals make headline news.*

Reproduced by permission of (left) *British Medical Journal* and British Medical Association; (center) *The Lancet* and Williams & Wilkins; (right) JAMA and American Medical Association

During the time that Arnold Relman served as the editor of the prestigious New England Journal of Medicine (1977–91), AIDS emerged as a major threat to public health. The first reports of the new disease—described in four homosexual men—came in 1981. As more and more cases were recorded, Relman saw that the wider social, political, and ethical implications needed to be addressed; the journal became a forum for probing what was to become one of the "most divisive issues of our time." By the time the NAMES Project AIDS quilt (above) was unveiled on the Washington, D.C., mall in October 1987, the epidemic had killed tens of thousands of men, women, and children.

The graphic memorial tribute to AIDS victims—the size of two football fields—traveled to 25 U.S. cities and was viewed by millions.

Relman provides an example of a powerful editor who had strong personal convictions and who was very much a public figure. His case is instructive and worth considering in some detail because it illustrates how the editor, through his journal, helps shape professional thinking and the delivery of health care to the public.

In his term at *NEJM* Relman saw the emergence of AIDS as a major threat to the public health. The first few cases of AIDS were briefly recorded in a weekly report from the Centers for Disease Control, Atlanta, Georgia, in June 1981 but then reported fully in *NEJM* in December of that year. Described were four previously healthy young homosexual men with repeated episodes of infection by *Pneumocystis carinii* (an uncommon microorganism that strikes immunocompromised persons), candidiasis, and perianal ulcerative herpes simplex. "The fact that this illness was first observed in homosexual men is probably not due to coincidence," the authors of the report commented. "It suggests that a sexually transmitted infectious agent or exposure to a common environment has a critical role."

For the next decade not only did the journal continue to carry reports on the most important features of a totally new disease and assessments of treatment methods as they were successively introduced, but Relman solicited expert comment and editorial views on the wider implications of the AIDS epidemic. "Difficult questions of public health policy and private behavior, of politics, economics, and ethics must be faced," Relman was

190

to write in a 1987 journal editorial, "so it was inevitable that AIDS would become one of the dominant and most divisive issues of our time." Relman also made it clear that *NEJM*'s long standing policy of embargo—delaying the release of medical news to the public until official publication of the peer-reviewed paper in the journal—would not apply in the case of AIDS.

During his editorship many other important clinical problems were documented—the life-style-related causes of heart disease, for example—and new and dramatic treatments were first reported (*e.g.,* lung transplantation and gene therapy). But perhaps, most notably, Relman's *NEJM* career was marked by his personal and passionate concern for a particular cause— that of improving the delivery of health care in his own country. During the 1970s and '80s not only were around 15% of U.S. citizens without any health insurance at all, but the costs of care were so out of bounds for the average citizen that an individual who was faced with the need for a major medical procedure, say a liver transplantation, might be financially crippled for life. As Relman was to say in a lecture on human values in 1988, "Uniquely qualified to determine the need for care, as well as monitor its quality, effectiveness, and safety, the medical profession has a special public responsibility. . . . Organized medicine should be in the vanguard of a national movement to ensure adequate, efficient care for all at a price our society can afford to pay." In the Oct. 4, 1990, issue of *NEJM,* Relman wrote, "The difficulties in implementing any type of serious health care reform are daunting, but much less daunting than the prospects for the country if we simply allow present conditions to continue."

In a series of journal editorials, articles published elsewhere, and public lectures, Relman developed his campaign for a fairer health care system. In this he was following the tradition of a long line of great medical editors. Thomas Wakley, the radical and tempestuous founder of *The Lancet,* campaigned for medical reform and against the privileges of the English medical royal colleges. Apart from his main aim of disseminating medical information, Wakley intended in his journal "to make war upon the family intrigues and foolish nepotism that swayed the elections to lucrative posts in the metropolitan hospitals and medical corporations." The name of the journal itself was carefully chosen to imply its function, as Wakley's biographer S.S. Sprigge put it, of incising "the abscess on the medical body politic." Wakley's language was particularly colorful; he described such venerated institutions as the London Society of Apothecaries as "the old hags at Rhubarb Hall" and the Royal College of Physicians as "the castle of indolence." In the 1850s Wakley turned his attention to the British food supply, publishing the names of manufacturers who were selling adulterated foodstuffs. Those revelations led to the passage of a parliamentary act in 1860 aimed at ensuring the safety of food.

Slightly later, a lesser known but equally important figure, Ernest Hart (editor of the *BMJ* from 1866 to 1898), was to achieve as much as any medical editor before or since. He, too, tackled major problems of his day, and his crusades, zealously voiced in his journal, also led to the passage of laws. Among many other things, Hart called attention to London's notorious "fogs" (lethal air pollution); he attacked antivivisectionists; he ardently

A particular cause that New England Journal *editor Arnold Relman made his own was that of improving the delivery of health care in the United States. Relman was alarmed that 15% of the people in his country have no health insurance and that the best medicine is not available to all Americans. The case of young Kina Taylor (below) from New Orleans, Louisiana, is a good example. Kina suffers from chronic asthma. Her mother has no health insurance and earns just over the minimum wage; therefore, she must take Kina to a public hospital in emergencies. Welfare patients and the uninsured throughout the U.S. are routinely routed to public hospitals, many of which are understaffed and poorly equipped. Owing to the high volume of nonpaying patients, the resources of such facilities are rapidly being depleted, forcing many simply to close their doors—a situation that is leaving needy patients with no place to turn.*

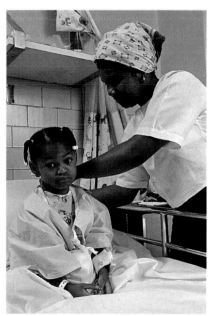

Jackson Hill—Southern Lights

191

In the 1850s Thomas Wakley, editor of The Lancet, *waged a campaign against the widespread practice of adulterating foodstuffs that were then sold to the public. He exposed tradesmen and manufacturers who were the purveyors of tainted, vermin-infested products that caused rampant food-borne illness. The furor generated by the journal's revelations resulted in the establishment of a parliamentary commission and passage of the 1860 Food and Drug Adulteration Act.*

Ernest Hart, editor of the British Medical Journal *from 1866 to 1898, waged many successful public health crusades in the pages of his journal. One hard-fought campaign that he ultimately lost was for the expansion of the Contagious Diseases Act of 1864, which allowed police in British naval ports and garrison towns to detain prostitutes on the suspicion that they were spreading venereal disease. Hart wanted all large towns and seaports to be included. But the act's opponents, who condemned interference with civil liberty and the harsh treatment of women, pressed for and eventually won repeal.*

supported compulsory vaccination against smallpox; and his personal lobbying efforts helped establish a medical service for the armed forces.

Perhaps Hart's greatest distinction was earned from his campaign against the widespread 19th-century practice of baby farming—women raising foundlings for pay. In 1868 Hart placed an advertisement in the *Clerkenwell News,* offering a fee for the adoption of a child—to which he had 333 replies within a week. After visiting many of the homes and meeting women who took in infants, Hart published a series of anonymous articles—which amounted to an in-depth exposé of the baby-farming "industry." While he found that "there are a large class who take charge of infants with really good intentions," he also cited many cases of systematic maltreatment and concealed infanticide; in many of the "homes," children survived less than a year. Public outrage was raised by this series, ultimately resulting in the trial and execution of one Margaret Waters for the murder of two babies and, in 1872, in the passage of the Infant Life Protection Act by Parliament.

The achievements of Wakley and Hart set a pattern that influenced their successors on both sides of the Atlantic. Dawson Williams (*BMJ* editor from 1898 to 1928) exposed quack remedies; Robbie Fox (*The Lancet* editor from 1943 to 1965) persuaded British doctors to accept the introduction of the National Health Service after World War II; and Franz Ingelfinger (editor of *NEJM* from 1967 to 1977) established the "Ingelfinger Rule," which states that the journal will not consider material that has been published already or publicized in advance—maintaining that speed of communication is less crucial than verifying accuracy and ensuring reliability.

Gatekeepers of science

Scientific journals did not begin to be published until 1665—200 years after the invention of printing. The first two journals, the British *Philosophical Transactions* of the Royal Society and the *Journal des Sçavans* (a pub-

lication of the French Academy), were both general journals of science, printing articles of medical interest only intermittently. In its third issue (May 8, 1665) the *Transactions*, for example, contained an account of the death of eight coal miners, and the wife of one of them, from firedamp (a combustible mine gas). It was reported that "some of them adventured to work upon old remains of walls, so near the old wastes. . . . Upon their stepping into the place, where the Air was infected, they fell down, as if they had been shott."

From the beginning both journals insisted on having experts ("referees") check the manuscripts that were submitted to them for the accuracy of the observations and the logical basis of the deductions. Thus, on March 1, 1664, the Council of the Royal Society took a very important step when it instructed editor Henry Oldenburg: "Ordered, that the *Philosophical Transactions,* to be composed by Mr. Oldenburg, be printed the first Monday of every month, if he has sufficient matter for it, and that tract be licensed under the Charter by the Council of the Society, *being first reviewed by some of the members of the same*" [author's emphasis]. This process is now called peer review.

Serious journals do not, of course, publish just anything that is sent to them; no matter how new, exciting, or provocative a research report may be, in most cases it will be evaluated by expert referees before the editors

Whereas the British Medical Journal, *representing the British Medical Association (BMA), vehemently opposed the creation of a National Health Service (NHS) following World War II, its independent counterpart,* The Lancet, *played a key role in persuading British doctors to vote for the proposed new system, despite its shortcomings. On May 28, 1948 (above), after years of dispute, negotiation, and finally compromise, the BMA voted to accept conditional cooperation in the NHS, which was officially launched a month later, on July 5.*

consider its publication. The decision then may be to publish the article unchanged, to publish it after modifications have been made according to the editors' and referees' suggestions, or to reject the article for publication altogether. (Rejection rates are as high as 90% for the top general medical journals such as *NEJM* and *The Lancet*.)

Even once an article is accepted for publication, it is often considerably altered during the process of "subediting." The degree to which such editing is done depends on the journal concerned, but the "big four" general medical journals may have as many as half a dozen scientifically trained subeditors whose main task is not only to check that references and footnotes are correct and that the data in the tables and graphs are accurate but also to ensure that the message is clear and logical.

The journals' refereeing system and editing processes are crucial mechanisms for ensuring quality and also for allowing some work into the public domain and some not. In this way the peer-reviewed medical journal becomes one of the "gatekeepers" of science.

Although peer review is not a gold standard for distinguishing outstanding work from the rest—that is the role of time—it can assess a submitted paper for originality (Has it been published elsewhere?), scientific reliability (Are the data credible? Were the scientific methods sound? Are the analysis and conclusions justified?), and importance (Does the report add to the present understanding of a subject?). Moreover, given that expert referees may be biased or may not be fully knowledgeable, a journal's editor must act as a mediator between the referees (whose function is to advise, not to decide whether to publish a report) and the authors (who are allowed to appeal a decision when this seems justified).

Making an impact

There are also gatekeepers at other stages of biomedical research. Referees evaluate the original idea at the time scientists are seeking funds (*e.g.,* from a governmental agency or charitable foundation) to support their research. In addition, after publication, further refereeing occurs when

"Eureka! A breakthrough! A boon to mankind! But first, an article in the New England Journal of Medicine!*"*

Sidney Harris

To Lancet Subscribers in August of 1941 It Was a Miracle Drug. To Other Journals, It Was Just Moldy Cheese.

Very occasionally advances that are reported in the pages of medical journals represent true breakthroughs. One of these was Ernst Chain and Howard Florey's report in The Lancet *half a century ago that described the growth in a laboratory dish of the mold from which penicillin was extracted and its first use in a patient dying of blood poisoning. "Twenty-four hours after sowing a very delicate fluffy gauze-like growth can be seen with difficulty at the bottom of the vessel (at 24° C). The growth becomes more voluminous during the next day and on the 3rd day . . . throws up dry white mycelium . . . which about 24 hours after it appears begins to turn bluish green." That report effectively launched the antibiotic era.*

the scientific community reads the article, evaluates it, tries to repeat the work, adds to it, or rejects it as not credible or falsely based.

If research results survive all this, then eventually they may become established as scientific facts. The published article is then quoted (or cited) in subsequent scientific articles as well as used as a reference in scientific bibliographies, medical textbooks, and other resources. The Institute for Scientific Information, in Philadelphia, publishes the *Science Citation Index,* which documents what impact a scientific paper has had—how many times and where it has been used as a reference by other authors. The four most cited articles in the *BMJ* between 1945 and 1989, according to the index, were "Effect of Large Doses of Histamine on Gastric Secretion of HCl: An Augmented Histamine Test" in 1953, describing a valuable method for evaluating the secretion of acid by the stomach (820 citations); "Campylobacter Enteritis: A 'New' Disease" in 1977, a description of a now very commonly reported type of food poisoning (808 citations); "A Survey of Childhood Malignancies" in 1958 (577 citations); and "Treatment of Hypertension with Propranolol" in 1969, describing the first beta-blocking drug for lowering blood pressure (546 citations).

However, all this takes a long time, and probably only one-tenth of all medical articles are enshrined in this way with frequent citations; the rest are disproved, superseded, or ignored for some other reason. Moreover, this process of research being acknowledged, then generally accepted, and then built upon applies mainly to the "small" advances in science—what the philosopher Thomas Kuhn calls "normal" science. There is another type of advance—"revolutionary" science, or Kuhn's "paradigm leap"—in which everything goes much faster, and many of the checks and balances do not

195

Florence Nightingale realized that "the connection between health and the dwellings of the population is one of the most important that exists." In the "hard times" of the Victorians (right), some 50,000 Londoners were forced to take shelter anywhere they could. Today (opposite page) homelessness is again an important social problem in England's capital. The consequences of life on the streets can be devastating. Without a roof over their heads, warmth, or adequate food and sanitation, people find it virtually impossible to stay healthy; the homeless easily fall prey to minor illnesses, which go untreated and to which they have no resistance. Skin infections, respiratory diseases—including tuberculosis—and psychiatric problems are common in this population. In 1989–90 a series of reports in the British Medical Journal *examined the contemporary public health impact of inadequate housing throughout Britain, including an exploration of ways that London's medical community could best provide care to its most destitute citizens.*

apply; the facts are too obvious to need proof. Examples of the latter type of advance include the discovery of the bacteria-killing sulfa drugs in the 1930s and of penicillin (reported by Ernst Chain and Howard Florey in *The Lancet* in 1941) and the emergence of an entirely new disease such as AIDS. But most "advances" are rather humdrum (an improved technique for measuring the blood sugar concentration; the discovery of a mutation of a gene in a rare, inherited disease; a possible link between drinking coffee and developing bladder cancer; and so forth), comparable to adding a single brick in the construction of a large edifice.

Baby farming, dirty air, and cigarettes

Even when medical scientists have demonstrated something and accepted it and the discovery has obvious implications for the whole community, it still has to go through the sieves of public opinion—and sometimes through government and the enactment of a law—before the public at large benefits. Then the campaigns waged by medical journals become all important. Over the years, like many other journals, the *BMJ* has run several campaigns, including ones against infanticide and air pollution in the Victorian era and for better housing standards in the present era. Although Florence Nightingale recognized that "the connection between health and the dwellings of the population is one of the most important that exists," housing for many citizens today still does not provide such basic requirements as safety, warmth, sanitation, and privacy. Thus, the *BMJ* ran a series of articles in 1989–90 examining the influences of housing on health in Great Britain. The topics included electromagnetic radiation in homes; indoor air quality; noise, space, and light; homelessness; home accidents; sanitation; housing for persons with AIDS; family life in publicly owned blocks of flats; and special housing needs of the elderly and disabled.

By far the most difficult campaigns follow discoveries that reveal definitive harm to health associated with life-style—when measures to improve health involve changing personal habits, such as wearing seat belts, prac-

ticing "safe sex," or stopping cigarette smoking. One campaign that has concerned medical journals on both sides of the Atlantic is that against cigarette smoking. The suggestion that this particular habit might be dangerous to health was first raised in the 1930s by several physicians. Around that time, physicians were seeing a once rare type of cancer—cancer of the lung—much more frequently. For various reasons they rejected a number of possible causes put forward for this increase—*e.g.,* exposure to diesel fumes—and instead put the blame on cigarette smoking. This theory was supported by the fact that cigarette smoking had not become popular until World War I, when soldiers and munitions workers in particular started to smoke cigarettes instead of pipes. Furthermore, the period of some 20 to 25 years (between 1915 and the late 1930s) was just about the length of time required for other kinds of demonstrated, environmentally caused cancers to develop.

These suggestions remained unexplored for some time owing to the outbreak of World War II. Then in 1950 *JAMA* published the findings of a truly scientific study by Ernest Wynder, a medical student, and Evarts A. Graham, the head of the department of surgery at Washington University School of Medicine, St. Louis, Missouri. They had looked back at the habits of a series of patients with lung cancer. In this "retrospective" study they found that many more patients with lung cancer had smoked, and smoked more heavily, than an equal number of control patients who were hospitalized for operations for conditions unrelated to lung cancer. "Excessive and prolonged use of tobacco, especially cigarettes, seems to be an important factor in the induction of bronchogenic carcinoma," Graham and Wynder concluded. Theirs was not the only study of this kind. Three independent studies had produced such remarkably uniform data that essentially the same conclusions could be deduced from each of them.

Concurrently, another epoch-making study was going on in the United Kingdom. Two medical statisticians, the late Austin Bradford Hill and Richard Doll, matched every lung cancer patient in a hospital sample

197

Covers, reproduced by permission of JAMA and
American Medical Association; cover paintings.
(top) "Skull with Cigarette" by Vincent van Gogh;
(bottom) "Let's Quit Smoking" by Nancy Hild

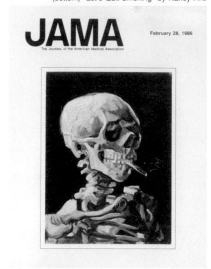

The Dec. 27, 1890, Journal of the
American Medical Association *carried a
report on "The Deadly Cigarette," which
described smoking-related deaths of young
boys, including a 14-year-old whose heart
disease was "superinduced by excessive
use of cigarettes" and a 16-year-old who
"hanged himself because his father refused
to give him money to buy more tobacco."
Over the ensuing century, as the hazards
of tobacco use became known, JAMA
continued to report on them. The covers
above are from special issues devoted
entirely to the subject of smoking.*

against a control of the same age and sex who had been hospitalized for
some other complaint. The results, published in the *BMJ* four years after
Wynder and Graham's paper, were clear-cut; cancer occurred in the patients who smoked cigarettes and was more frequent in those who smoked
more cigarettes than in those who smoked fewer.

Despite these conclusions, there was enormous opposition, not only
from smokers (then in the majority in the U.K.) but from the large, vested
economic interests—tobacco farmers, cigarette manufacturers, tobacco
workers, and the government, which received enough revenue from to-
bacco-product sales to pay for the entire National Health Service.

Nevertheless, the case against cigarettes continued to build. Independent corroboration of Hill and Doll's findings came a few years later from
U.S. Surgeon General Luther Terry, who used the powerful epidemiological
technique the "prospective" study. He surveyed a group of apparently
healthy smokers to see if they developed lung cancer more often than
nonsmokers; they did. Subsequent studies from other countries, reported
in international medical journals, corroborated that finding. The final plank
in the argument was another study by Hill and Doll, again published in the
BMJ—this time of physician smokers and nonsmokers. Many doctors had
stopped smoking as soon as the first journal articles appeared, but some
had not, and comparison of the two populations made it quite obvious that
stopping smoking immediately diminished the risk of lung cancer. "One
of the striking characteristics of British mortality in the last half-century
has been the lack of improvement in the death rate of men in middle
life," Hill and Doll concluded in 1964. "In cigarette smoking may lie one
prominent cause."

The antismoking campaign, waged internationally in the general medical
journals and in specialty journals (especially those on cancer, cardiovascular disease, and pulmonary disease), continues, with frequent reports
encompassing new findings about smoking's toll on health, studies on the
sociodemographic variables, editorials about the politics of cigarette promotion, and articles emphasizing the special role of physicians in helping
their patients quit smoking. In the U.S., *JAMA* devotes an entire issue
every year to the subject of smoking. And Australian medical journals have
been among the most conscientious in consistently campaigning against
the lethal habit. The leading editorial in the *BMJ*'s final issue of the year
1990 (by this author—then the journal's editor) asked the question, "If Preventable, Why Not . . . ?" The message was that the U.K. has "consistently
been among the last countries to adopt effective antismoking policies" and,
as a result of this inaction, its citizens are being sentenced to wasteful,
economically damaging disease and premature death.

Cracks in the edifice?

Although it might seem as if everything is well with medical publications,
in the last few years some disturbing signs have appeared of cracks in
the edifice. The principal problems have been the ever increasing number
of journals, making it difficult for the individual physician to keep up; the
finding that after publication many (perhaps even most) articles are not

198

cited as references even once; the demonstration that, despite peer review, many articles are seriously flawed scientifically; and the realization that journals have become bound up with cases of misconduct in scientific research, including piracy of ideas, plagiarism, and forged results.

Publication "explosion." Ever since serious scientific publishing started, there has been a regular and rapid increase in the number of journals—with new journals appearing at a rate of 6–7% a year, doubling every 10–15 years, and rising 10-fold every 35–50 years. By the end of the 19th century, most developed countries had their own general medical journals; a few major specialty journals had already appeared, but the truly remarkable acceleration in their growth was to be a feature of the 20th century. Nobody is certain precisely how many journals there are today, but most agree on a figure of more than 20,000 biomedical journals out of a total of at least 100,000 scientific ones.

The most recent development in this evolution has been the "super-specialist journal"—one devoted to a single aspect of a specialty (such as *Clinical Gastroenterological Pharmacology*) or a single organ (such as *Pancreas*). Often these journals are begun when a new field of research is not adequately covered by existing publications. The following titles are just a handful of recent additions to the ever growing list: *Immunodeficiency Reviews, Microbial Ecology in Health and Disease, Cytopathology, Quality Assurance in Health Care, Accountability in Research,* the *Journal of Wilderness Medicine, Inhalation Toxicology,* and *Fetal Medicine Review.* Moreover, when a new disease, such as AIDS, suddenly emerges, a new journal is needed to keep up with the high volume of research activity. In the decade from 1981 to 1991, more than 35,000 articles on human immunodeficiency virus (HIV) and AIDS appeared in the medical literature, and no fewer than 18 AIDS journals (including *International Journal of STD and AIDS, AIDS Update, AIDS and Nursery Care,* and *AIDS Law and Litigation Reporter*) were begun.

Is such an explosion "healthy"? The late Derek de Solla Price, professor of the history of science at Yale University, argued strongly that it is. "The people of scholarly knowledge, including that special variety in matters biomedical," he wrote in 1981 in a contribution to the volume *Coping with the Biomedical Literature,* "still read and write for much the same reasons . . . as they did 300 years ago—communication and assessment of results and personal and professional kudos."

One way of looking at the explosion is that new journals are started in line with new subdisciplines, and their number remains in proportion to the number of specialists in the discipline. For example, there have been a constant 17 journals per 1,000 registered health professionals (physicians, dentists, and nurses) in the U.S. over the past 30 years. Probably the general medical journals have survived the increasing specialization of medicine because of their unique ability to inform their physician-readers of developments in disciplines other than their own. On the other hand, many physicians bemoan the fact that it is impossible even to begin to keep up. As David T. Durack, at Duke University Medical Center, Durham, North Carolina, wrote over a decade ago, "Most of us feel weighed down by the

Photographs from David T. Durack, "The Weight of Medical Knowledge," *New England Journal of Medicine,* vol. 298, no. 14 (April 6, 1978), pp. 773–775

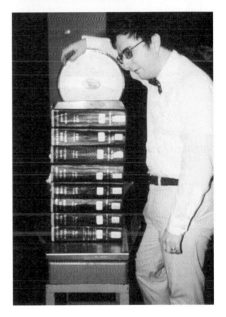

More than a decade ago, David Durack took the matter of the ever growing number of medical journals very seriously. Feeling "weighed down by the heavy and increasing burden of medical reading," he decided to weigh annual volumes of the Index Medicus *from 1879 through 1977 to get an "objective measure of the size of [the] problem." Durack voiced his uneasiness about the years ahead "if the present rate of increase were to continue unabated."*

Perhaps the most troubling development in the world of medical journals today is the "epidemic" of scientifically flawed papers that—despite peer review—have seen their way into publication. Certainly the most publicized case has been that of a paper by Nobel laureate David Baltimore and coauthor Thereza Imanishi-Kari published in the journal Cell *in 1986. A five-year-long investigation found that Imanishi-Kari had fabricated or falsified data in the government-funded research she had conducted in her laboratory at the Massachusetts Institute of Technology. When the full allegations were made public in the spring of 1991, Baltimore requested that the paper be retracted. (Above) In May 1990, at the time a congressional subcommittee was looking into the integrity of her data, Imanishi-Kari consulted her lawyer before a news conference.*

heavy and increasing burden of medical reading." To prove his point, in a now-classic spoof that was published in the *NEJM,* Durack literally weighed annual volumes of the *Index Medicus*—the most complete bibliography of published medical articles—from its first year of publication, 1879, through 1977. The weight of the volumes rose from less than 2 kilograms (4.4 pounds) to over 30 kilograms (66 pounds)—confirming Durack's suspicion that the proliferation of publications was out of hand.

Flaws and fraud. The heightened competition among biomedical scientists for both funds and esteem seems to have been behind several widely publicized cases of misconduct in which papers submitted to journals for publication were scientifically flawed or based on fraudulent research. And, despite peer review, many such papers have been published. Among the best known instances are those of John Darsee, a cardiologist at Emory University School of Medicine, Atlanta, and then at Harvard Medical School, who produced 44 fraudulent articles and 100 fraudulent abstracts—all of them published—and Robert Slutsky, a resident in cardiac radiography at the University of California at San Diego, who at one time was producing an "original" scientific article every 10 days. More recent was the case of Nobel laureate David Baltimore, Thereza Imanishi-Kari, and coauthors, whose paper on transgenic mice, published in the journal *Cell* in 1986, was later deemed seriously scientifically flawed. Revelations that came after years of investigation by the National Institutes of Health (NIH) and the U.S. Congress led to the paper's retraction by Baltimore in March 1991.

Possibly this "epidemic" of fraudulent work is now subsiding—in part owing to the creation of the NIH's Office of Scientific Integrity. In the meantime, at least two important lessons have been learned. First, editorial peer review cannot be relied on to detect fraudulent work; usually the cases, such as Imanishi-Kari's, come to light through colleagues or junior researchers "blowing the whistle." Second, journals should play an important part in setting the record straight by printing prominent retractions of flawed or fraudulent articles.

Although not terminal, these issues have been serious enough for editors to come together for the purpose of studying the problems and making proposals for solving them. In fact, a new term has been coined, *journalology,* to describe the manifold studies that editors are currently undertaking.

Four major editors organizations have been started, three of which (the Council of Biology Editors, the European Association of Science Editors, and the African Association of Science Editors) have members in all the sciences, including medicine. The fourth group (the Vancouver Group, or the International Committee of Medical Journal Editors) is limited to a dozen medical editors of major international journals. Begun in 1978 when editors met in Vancouver, British Columbia, the committee has attempted to agree on a style for citing references that would be accepted by journals around the world, define the editor's role, establish criteria for qualification of authors (*i.e.,* whose names appear on a paper submitted for publication), delineate the role of the correspondence column, ensure that medical journals maintain editorial freedom and integrity, and promote rigorous standards of peer review.

Psychiatry for cats

Clearly, the medical-journal-publishing enterprise takes itself very seriously. Lest it be forgotten, however, journal editors also maintain that readers deserve to be entertained on occasion. So, finally, consider one article that attracted a lot of attention when it appeared in the *BMJ* in December 1989. This was a case report of depressive pseudodementia in a domestic cat—pseudodementia being a condition of extreme apathy that is not caused by actual mental deterioration. "The patient was a female tortoiseshell and white cat of unknown age. . . . She came to the notice of the medical profession after the death of her 89 year old owner. . . . There was clear evidence of self neglect as her fur was matted with filth and complete loss of previous house training skills was apparent. Both ears were infected and discharging." The feline patient was successfully treated with a program of intensive rehabilitation, consisting of regular stroking; encouraging of washing behavior; small, tempting meals; occupational therapy utilizing a catnip mouse and a ball of string; and regular toileting. Moreover, "contact with other cats . . . provided role models and further stimulation." The therapist, a senior registrar in psychiatry, went on to report that her patient's response to treatment was dramatic. "One month after commencing the programme she was alert, sociable, and active."

Despite the subject, the usual editorial practices were not dispensed with. The report was attested by peer review to be original and valid. It was printed with a full photograph of the patient (disguised, of course, for the sake of privacy, with a bar over the eyes). Furthermore, the report had important implications beyond the single case of the cat: "As in elderly humans, social stimulation and encouragement of self care skills were important in restoring normal functioning."

British Medical Journal; photograph, Simon and Sheila Paterson-Brown

A future physician gets a head start on her reading. Not a bad idea, considering that the present "explosion" of medical publications shows no signs of moderating.

"Sleepy Sickness"

Curious Chapter of Medical History

by Macdonald Critchley, M.D.

Macdonald Critchley, M.D., Former President of the World Federation of Neurology and a Commander of the Order of the British Empire, completed his medical residency in the 1920s during the height of the encephalitis lethargica epidemic. He is one of the few physicians who has personal recollections of treating patients in the acute stage of the disease.

(Opposite Page) Photograph, The Granger Collection

In the years from 1917 to 1929, a mysterious disease swept the world, killing large numbers of people and leaving many more in a trancelike state of suspended animation. Until recently, though, when a touching motion picture was made about the lives of some of the survivors—the film *Awakenings,* based on the book of the same name by British-born neurologist Oliver Sacks—this tragic epidemic had been largely forgotten. Undoubtedly it was overshadowed by the influenza pandemic of 1918–19, with a staggering death toll of 15 million; few families were untouched by influenza. Its symptoms were dramatic; death came swiftly, often within three days after the onset of illness. Thus, except in the medical community, the second epidemic, which started almost simultaneously, did not arouse nearly the same degree of concern.

The disease was encephalitis lethargica, popularly known as "sleepy sickness" (not to be confused with sleeping sickness, which is the common name for trypanosomiasis, the tropical disease transmitted by the tsetse fly). It was remarkable, medically at least, in its mysterious origin, the extreme variability of its symptoms, and, in those who survived, its bizarre and long-lasting aftereffects.

This author saw his first case of encephalitis lethargica in 1918 while a medical student at the University of Bristol, England, and observed many more during subsequent appointments at Bristol General Hospital and the Hospital for Sick Children, Great Ormond Street, London. As resident medical officer at the Hospital for Epilepsy and Paralysis in London in 1923, he continued to see such patients, including, for the first time, those with the typical aftereffects of the disease. In December of that year, he began a long career at the National Hospital for Nervous Diseases, London, where he continued to see acute cases of the disease until 1929. Thus, while Sacks and others have observed and attended survivors, some even up to the present day, this author is one of the few living medical practitioners who witnessed the epidemic throughout its acute phase.

The great influenza pandemic of 1918–19—with its death toll of 15 million—dramatically overshadowed the concurrent global epidemic of encephalitis lethargica, or "sleepy sickness"; virtually no family was left untouched by the flu. In the town of Ames, Iowa (above), for example, so many people fell ill that the state university was compelled to turn its gymnasium into a hospital ward. Although encephalitis lethargica also took an enormous toll, today both the epidemic and its victims have largely been forgotten.

Birth of a "new" disease?

About a year before the start of the influenza pandemic, physicians in Europe began to see unusual cases of a serious febrile illness. It varied widely in both character and intensity. In some patients it resembled the influenza-like disease called grippe, but there were no accompanying lung disorders or cardiac complications. The presence of certain curious neurological and psychiatric symptoms indicated, however, that this was something other than influenza.

The first reports of the new illness came in 1917 from Constantin von Economo, professor of psychiatry and neurology at the University of Vienna. It was von Economo who gave it the name encephalitis lethargica. Similar cases were reported in France the same year by neurologist Jean-René Cruchet, who claimed to have seen one patient as early as 1915. Cases also appeared in England in 1917, and by the following year the disease had spread throughout Europe, the Americas, and Asia. The victims included persons of all ages, male and female. While there was a pattern of seasonal variation in incidence—more cases occurred during the winter and early spring—scant evidence of transmissibility or infectivity came to light.

The epidemic reached its peak in 1924, slowly subsiding thereafter; by 1929 it had virtually disappeared. Encephalitis lethargica has been diagnosed and officially reported occasionally since 1930 but, in the absence of verification by autopsy—or, in nonfatal cases, because of the lack of the typical aftereffects of the illness—such a diagnosis must be regarded as unproven. The disease seems, therefore, to have disappeared almost as abruptly and mysteriously as it began.

The cause of encephalitis lethargica remains unknown to this day, but it was—and still is—regarded as a viral disorder. At the time of the epidemic, however, the science of virology was in its infancy, and no causative organism was ever isolated. The onset of the epidemic so close to a pandemic of influenza raised the suspicion that there might have been a causal relationship, but other worldwide influenza outbreaks have occurred without the survivors developing the typical neurological or psychiatric aftereffects of encephalitis lethargica. It should be borne in mind, too, that the epidemic of this strange disease actually preceded the influenza pandemic by at least a year.

British neurologist Samuel Alexander Kinnier Wilson pointed out that while vagueness of description makes it impossible to conclusively identify epidemics that were recorded generations and centuries ago, the encephalitis lethargica of the early 20th century has been linked with a number of earlier episodes. One of these was an epidemic of a condition called *nona* that followed an outbreak of influenza in Italy and southern Europe in the 1890s. Another was *vertige paralysant,* a condition described in 1887 by the Swiss physician Felix Gerlier. In the late 17th century Johan Peter Albrecht of Hildesheim described many typical symptoms of encephalitis lethargica in a report on a young woman suffering from a brain fever. An outbreak of *Schlafkrankheit* (German, literally "sleep disease") in Tübingen around 1712 left many victims with the kind of postencephalitic symptoms seen in those who survived encephalitis lethargica. As Kinnier Wilson also noted, there were isolated English examples of a similar disease in the years immediately prior to 1916, but these, too, are difficult to authenticate. It is quite possible that the worldwide epidemic that occurred in the early

In an attempt to resolve the question of a possible connection between influenza and encephalitis lethargica, Edwin O. Jordan, professor of hygiene and bacteriology at the University of Chicago, compared the incidence and death rates of the two diseases (see tables below). Both occurred in recurrent waves, the numbers of reported cases and deaths increasing during the colder months of the year. But, as the 1924 statistics from England (right) demonstrate, the peak of the flu epidemic anticipated that of encephalitis in some cities—London, for example— while in others, such as Manchester, the reverse was true. Jordan concluded that the epidemiological evidence ruled out "such exact correspondence as would betoken a causal relation."

Reported deaths in New York City

	1920 influenza	1920 encephalitis	1921 influenza	1921 encephalitis	1922 influenza	1922 encephalitis
January	710	...	51	25	96	15
February	2,144	75	39	41	444	11
March	199	57	79	24	141	24
April	64	30	56	19	54	45
May	34	28	39	21	26	20
June	11	13	17	16	9	19
July	5	11	7	15	9	12
August	11	5	7	6	6	19
September	9	6	12	13	4	14
October	13	4	25	7	14	8
November	14	8	27	6	35	3
December	26	12	20	6	30	11
totals	3,240	249	379	199	868	201

Deaths from influenza and cases of epidemic encephalitis, England, 1924

	February 2	9	16	23	March 1	8	15	22	29	April 5	12	19	26
London encephalitis	2	4	0	2	3	1	4	10	20	17	23	33	31
London influenza	122	154	178	148	139	115	89	83	49	45	28	45	21
Bristol encephalitis	0	0	0	1	0	1	1	2	1	4	8	13	8
Bristol influenza	11	19	27	25	14	20	13	13	13	5	4	3	3
Birmingham encephalitis	1	3	0	0	2	2	3	12	6	20	27	29	17
Birmingham influenza	6	6	12	23	25	41	38	36	32	30	21	8	6
Liverpool encephalitis	2	2	0	0	2	0	0	4	15	4	4	3	4
Liverpool influenza	4	8	13	15	21	17	16	8	14	3	5	7	6
Manchester encephalitis	1	9	13	16	22	29	23	18	15	13	10	5	5
Manchester influenza	4	5	3	4	13	22	22	21	44	21	29	19	16
Sheffield encephalitis	0	0	0	0	0	0	4	9	14	19	37	41	26
Sheffield influenza	3	4	5	3	6	7	9	13	14	15	10	12	13

Tables adapted from *Epidemic Influenza* by Edwin O. Jordan; © 1927 American Medical Association

"Towards the end of 1916 the wards of the Vienna Psychiatric Clinic contained quite a number of patients with a strange variety of symptoms . . . [difficult] to fit into any known diagnostic scheme. . . . I noticed particularly in a few of these patients a condition of marked lethargy."
So wrote Constantin von Economo (above), professor of psychiatry and neurology, in the introduction to his 1929 book Encephalitis Lethargica: Its Sequelae and Treatment. *It was von Economo who first reported cases of the baffling illness and he who gave it the name encephalitis lethargica. Two graphs from his book (opposite page) illustrate the seasonal variation in the incidence of the disease (top), with a larger number of cases usually reported in the winter and early spring months, and the distribution of cases by age group (bottom), the greatest number clustered in the third and fourth decades of life.*

British headlines from the 1920s indicate the extent of the "sleepy sickness" epidemic and the horror that was aroused by this now all-but-forgotten disease.

20th century did not represent the development of a truly "new" disease but rather the most dramatic recurrence of one that was already known and documented but little understood.

Flulike but not the flu

The symptoms of encephalitis lethargica were not only diverse, they varied widely in severity from one victim to another. Most patients experienced general malaise, headache, aching limbs, and slight fever, the combination of symptoms resembling influenza. Some cases were so mild that the patient did not take time off work or even retire to bed. The symptoms of the milder cases lasted only a few days.

Over and above the general flulike symptoms were specific features that, when present, clearly refuted the diagnosis of influenza. One of the most prominent of these was unusual sleepiness (somnolence); the patient often, though not always, could be aroused. The other all-important symptom from a diagnostic point of view was double vision (diplopia), sometimes accompanied by various forms of paralysis of the muscles that control the movement of the eyeball. Double vision, in fact, became the key symptom that distinguished this disorder from all other febrile (*i.e.,* characterized by a high fever) illnesses.

At times the onset of symptoms was dramatic. The drowsiness might be profound and even result in coma. The fever sometimes amounted to hyperpyrexia—body temperature of above 41° C (106° F). It was accompanied by delirium, often of the "occupational" type—that is, the affected person unconsciously went through the movements used in his or her work, such as typing, hammering, or sewing. Intense restlessness was also common.

Because the malady was essentially a form of encephalitis—*i.e.,* inflammation of the brain—and because of the attendant somnolence, von Economo's designation encephalitis lethargica seems appropriate. Other terms have been used, among them acute epidemic encephalitis and von Economo's disease (as well as the colloquial "sleepy sickness").

An array of odd symptoms

The acute phase of the illness was often accompanied by many strange signs and symptoms. A doctor could often demonstrate the unusual physical sign of flexibilitas cerea ("waxy flexibility") by taking the patient's arm, lifting it up, and then abruptly releasing it. Instead of falling limply, the arm would remain unsupported in the air in a catatonic-like posture. After a few moments the limb slowly descended to its original resting position.

Obstinate hiccups occurred in a number of cases, but even more common was a diversity of involuntary movements, myoclonic jerks (sudden, shocklike muscular contractions) being most often seen. These might occur anywhere in the body. Sometimes they were violent enough to cause movement of the limbs; sometimes they were restricted to a single muscle. Of grave prognostic import was the development of chorea—wide-ranging involuntary movements of the limbs, accompanied by grimacing—which often heralded a protracted illness or even death. It was not unusual for a child to be admitted to hospital with an initial diagnosis of Sydenham's (rheumatic) chorea, popularly known as Saint Vitus' dance, but the subsequent development of lethargy and, in particular, the all-important symptom of double vision revealed the true nature of the illness.

Another bizarre symptom consisted in spells of rapid breathing (tachypnea), coming on without obvious cause, lasting up to a minute or so, breathing then returning to normal. There was no accompanying cyanosis (bluish discoloration of the face—a sign of oxygen deficiency) and no rise in the heart rate. In one recorded case, the patient's rapid breathing synchronized precisely with myoclonic jerkings of the biceps muscle in the left upper arm.

In acute cases the prognosis was, on the whole, grave but difficult to foretell. Briefly, there were four possible outcomes: (1) death (30–50% of cases); (2) gradual development of steadily progressive neurological and other dysfunctions; (3) apparent recovery from the acute stage for a period of weeks, months, or even years, followed by the gradual appearance of a series of disabilities—the most common of which was a parkinsonian syndrome; and (4) complete recovery—which, of course, would be uncertain until many symptom-free years had elapsed.

Bizarre sequelae in survivors

It was estimated at one time that of those patients who survived the acute phase, half subsequently developed complications. This figure may well be an underestimate, for some authorities suspect that all survivors were afflicted ultimately with aftereffects of the disease.

It was in these late effects, or sequelae, of the disease that encephalitis lethargica was particularly bizarre. Any of the following conditions

Graphs from *Encephalitis Lethargica* by Constantin von Economo, translated by K.O. Newman; © 1931 Oxford University Press

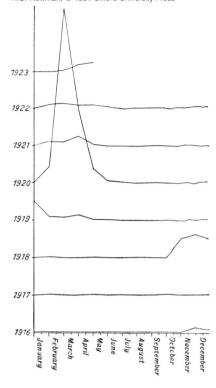

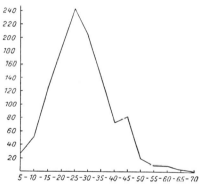

207

A woman with acute "sleepy sickness" lies in a trancelike state from which she cannot be aroused. Her right arm, which has been raised by an examining physician, remains aloft unsupported; after a few moments it would gradually descend to the resting position. This strange physical sign, known as flexibilitas cerea ("waxy flexibility"), was one of many odd manifestations of the acute phase of encephalitis lethargica. The onset of symptoms could be sudden and dramatic. In one case a bride stricken during her wedding ceremony seemed to fall asleep at the altar. Another woman, falling ill shortly before she went into labor, gave birth without seeming to regain consciousness.

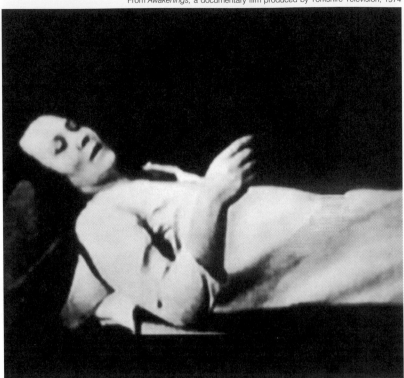

occurred, either alone or in any combination (all are described in detail below): parkinsonism, oculogyric crises, respiratory disorders, involuntary movements, endocrine abnormalities, seizures, sleep disorders, and mental and behavioral disturbances. Often there was no correlation between the severity of the acute attack and the nature and magnitude of the sequelae. Thus, a mild, short-lived acute illness might be followed by a severe, progressive disability.

Parkinsonian aftereffects

In "An Essay on the Shaking Palsy" (1817), English physician James Parkinson vividly described the clinical manifestations of a neurological disorder he had witnessed in several patients:

Involuntary tremulous motion, with lessened muscular power, in parts not in action and even when supported; with a propensity to bend the trunk forwards, and to pass from a walking to a running pace: the senses and intellect being uninjured.

While Parkinson was not the first to describe these symptoms, he was the first to recognize them as constituting a distinct syndrome. Parkinson's disease, sometimes called paralysis agitans (Latin, "shaking palsy"), is a condition of unknown origin that causes one region of the brain to degenerate, resulting in a complex of distinctive movement disorders. It is primarily a disease of older people; onset usually occurs between the ages of 50 and 65. In rare cases it may begin earlier. Generally, however, when a very young person shows signs of parkinsonism, most physicians assume there is some cause other than age-related degeneration. One such cause is brain damage due to encephalitis, a condition termed post-encephalitic parkinsonism.

Despite the rare reporting in the medical literature of cases of Parkinson's disease in young people, it is probably safe to say that in the 1920s few, if any, practicing neurologists had ever seen one. It was, therefore, with great astonishment that physicians suddenly beheld for the first time adolescents and young adults exhibiting the typical manifestations of a syndrome that had hitherto been regarded as an idiopathic affliction (*i.e.,* one of unknown cause) of late middle age. In *Neurology* (1940) Kinnier Wilson wrote that paralysis agitans, once a rarity in juveniles, had become "commonplace." "I have seen it affect a child of seven," he noted.

Parkinsonism was by far the most common complication of encephalitis lethargica. Its development was insidious and might occur during the acute stage, during convalescence, or even after a period of apparent return to health. The general manifestations were typical of idiopathic Parkinson's disease—that is, the gradual adoption of a characteristic bent posture; difficulty of movement (akinesia); an immobile, masklike face with infrequent blinking; slowness of movement (bradykinesia); a distinctive type of muscular rigidity, sometimes called "lead-pipe" rigidity; "pill-rolling" tremor (an involuntary action of the fingers); quiet, rapid mumbling speech; shuffling gait with festination (a progressive increase in pace); and small, cramped handwriting.

Despite similarities between the idiopathic parkinsonism that develops with age and the postencephalitic variety, the clinical pictures were not identical. These differences, although subtle, enabled neurologists to distinguish between the two types. For instance, some ocular signs were more evident in postencephalitic patients. Infrequency of blinking would give way to marked fluttering of the eyelids (blepharoclonus) when patients

A drawing by the celebrated 19th-century French neurologist Jean-Martin Charcot shows an elderly man with the stooped posture and frozen, masklike facial expression characteristic of parkinsonism. The tremors, rigidity, and movement problems typical of Parkinson's disease often plagued victims of encephalitis lethargica and could develop during the acute stage of the illness, during convalescence, or even after a period of recovery and apparent return to health.

Photographs, National Library of Medicine, Bethesda, Maryland

A French caricature, c. 1823, depicts persons suffering from the the neurological disorder known as chorea, a condition that is characterized by involuntary jerking movements of muscle groups in various parts of the body. The development of chorea in a patient with acute encephalitis lethargica often heralded either a protracted illness or a fatal one.

From *Encephalitis Lethargica* by Constantin von Economo, translated by K.O. Newman; © 1931 Oxford University Press

A photograph from Constantin von Economo's book shows a child with postencephalitic parkinsonism. Until the outbreak of the "sleepy sickness" epidemic, parkinsonism in children and adolescents was an extremely rare occurrence. Prior to the 1920s, few if any practicing neurologists had ever seen such a case. Following the encephalitis lethargica epidemic, however, one British neurologist observed that juvenile parkinsonism had become "commonplace."

were told to close their eyes or when the doctor tapped the bridge of the patient's nose. When patients looked from side to side, their eye movements were jerky, and they blinked when their gaze passed the halfway mark (Wilson's blinking sign). Their eyes failed to converge when fixing on a near target and, at the same time, the pupils did not contract when tested for accommodation (focusing on a near object).

The masklike face was often accompanied by a fixed gaping of the mouth or by a broad, mirthless grin. These signs were particularly common in the younger postencephalitics, resembling those seen in the progressive neurological disorder called Wilson's disease.

Difficulty of movement resulted in patients' appearing to be frozen in a statuesque posture from which it was difficult to escape. Nevertheless, some activities were still possible at a time when sufferers could scarcely move or walk, a condition known as paradoxical kinesia. For example, an individual who could neither stroll nor saunter might be able to run, to ride a bicycle, or to dance—even the elaborate Charleston or Black Bottom, popular dances of the 1920s. The upper limbs also shared in this incongruity of movement. Sacks wrote about one patient in an akinetic postencephalitic state who could perform a juggling act, tossing and catching no fewer than seven oranges in rapid succession.

Occasionally a patient would make a deliberate repetitive movement that could not easily be terminated (palipraxia), continuing for an inordinate length of time the action of, for example, hammering a nail, brushing the teeth, or combing the hair. Sometimes the general fixity, or immobility, would give way to abnormal restlessness. This is also present in idiopathic parkinsonism but was probably more conspicuous in postencephalitic patients. For example, while seated, affected persons might cross and uncross their legs over and over again or slowly rise from a chair and then sit down again at once. This is the phenomenon known as akathisia (an inability to sit).

In Parkinson's disease verbal articulation usually is impaired, but in postencephalitic patients an additional anomaly of speech was common; namely, palilalia, in which the last word or phrase just uttered is repeated over and over, becoming more rapid and more indistinct. For example, a patient might say, in an increasingly rapid and hushed fashion, "Thank you; I feel a little bit better today, better today, better today, better today. . . ." One of this author's patients made no fewer than 15 repetitions of the last word he spoke. Palilalia is not diagnostic of a postencephalitic state, however, for it had already been observed in some elderly people with cerebral arteriosclerosis.

While most persons with Parkinson's disease adopt a bowed stance with a fixed flexion, or bending, of the neck and spine, arms, and legs, the converse was seen in some postencephalitic patients. A few cases were reported where the spine was in extension, that is, arched backward in a grotesque fashion. People with Parkinson's disease may display unusual greasiness of the skin, usually of the face, and they are also troubled with excess salivation. These phenomena were even more evident in postencephalitic than in idiopathic cases.

Upturned eyes and compulsive thoughts

All who witnessed them were astonished by the spectacle of oculogyric crises. The patient would suddenly develop a spasm of the muscles that turned the eyes upward, resulting in an involuntary and uncontrollable upward gaze, sometimes toward one side. The head and neck were retracted, causing pain or discomfort in the head and eyes. The episode persisted for about an hour and would then usually be abated by sleep. Oculogyric crises were accompanied by distressing experiences that some patients were reluctant to describe. Uncontrollable thoughts of a sadistic nature were common, and even more usual were compulsive thoughts of a banal kind. One of this author's patients was impelled to count silently the number of words uttered by those around him; another, to think of rhymes or fragments of verse. Smith Ely Jelliffe, a professor of psychiatry at Fordham University, New York City, wrote of a man who had the compulsive thoughts "rape my sister, rape my mother, kill my brother, kill my father" racing through his mind during his attacks.

Oculogyric crises could often be terminated with the anticonvulsant drug phenobarbital, taken to induce sleep. Equally efficacious were amphetamines (stimulants) to rouse the patient. Such attacks might recur at intervals over a period of years and then cease spontaneously, although the parkinsonism grew steadily worse.

Although they were a typical aftereffect of encephalitis lethargica, oculogyric crises had occasionally been reported and described prior the epidemic of 1917–29. Best known among these accounts was that by Albrecht, who wrote:

In the year 1695, a maiden of this place, about 20 years old, daughter of the honest citizen J. F., fell into a continual fever, characterized by acute headache, dryness of the mouth and other symptoms usually noted in the maladies of this kind, of which, in this subject the most notable was an extraordinary propensity to sleep; which in proportion as the headache remitted, became more and more pronounced. In the period of temporary improvement of health, there was plainly noted a distortion of the eyes which propelled the pupil upward toward the upper eyelid, showing the white of the whole lower half of the lower eyeball.

Strange abnormalities of breathing

Sometimes during the acute illness, but more frequently afterward, peculiar respiratory disorders appeared. A progressive state of parkinsonism often coexisted. The respiratory abnormalities affected the rate or rhythm of respiration or produced various respiratory tics.

The first of these usually took the form of spells of tachypnea. These spells would appear for no obvious reason and last for a few seconds without provoking distress or cyanosis. At times the rapid breathing was noisy, like the sound of a dog panting. Each breath was relatively shallow, but when, rarely, the breathing was both rapid and deep (hyperpnea), complications such as hyperventilation tetany (excessively rapid and deep breathing with muscle spasm) and even loss of consciousness might occur. Such tachypneic spells were liable to recur many times a day. Often a conspicuous feature of the acute phase of the disease, they could also appear as a late manifestation.

In a scene from the film Awakenings, *adapted from the 1973 book of the same name by British-born neurologist Oliver Sacks, Dr. Malcolm Sayer (played by Robin Williams), a character loosely based on Sacks himself, administers the drug L-dopa to a woman who has been in a postencephalitic stupor for 40 years. Both the book and the film were based on Sacks's real-life experiences with a group of some 80 survivors of the encephalitis lethargica epidemic, all longtime inmates of the Mount Carmel Hospital in Bexley-on-Hudson, New York. In 1969, following reports of extraordinary success with L-dopa in treating persons with Parkinson's disease, Sacks cautiously but hopefully gave the drug to selected patients at Mount Carmel. The results, at least initially, were spectacular. Sacks later wrote of this experiment that he and other staff members had experienced tremendous excitement "at seeing the 'dead' awaken again . . . at seeing lives which one had thought irremediably blighted suddenly bloom into wonderful renewal, at seeing . . . individuals in all their vitality and richness emerge from the almost cadaveric state where they had been frozen and hidden for decades."*

The opposite phenomenon, that is, intervals of slow breathing (bradypnea), were also observed, but they occurred far less often than tachypnea. In another less common disorder of the respiratory rate, there were intervals when breathing ceased altogether for a few seconds (apnea). The patient was not distressed by these episodes, and sometimes these apneic spells escaped attention.

Episodes of breath holding sometimes occurred in the postacute phase. They could be dramatic to witness. One of the author's patients, a young man of 16 with no signs of parkinsonism, was in the convalescent stage of encephalitis lethargica when he developed daytime restlessness and an obstinate cough. These symptoms, in turn, were replaced on some occasions by periods of breath holding, occurring many times during the day but never in his sleep. Each attack began with deep, labored breaths, steadily increasing in intensity and often accompanied by a barking cough. There was then a stage of apnea that occurred during inhalation. The patient's face rapidly took on a bluish tinge, and the musculature of his chest was fixed in spasm. Then his forearms became flexed and his fists tightly clenched. His neck and upper spine arched, his legs being in full extension. Extravagant gestures followed: he rubbed his chest, clawed the air, and opened and shut his fists. The blue color of the skin deepened, the veins of his forehead became engorged, and his eyeballs bulged. His tongue protruded, but it was never bitten because it was protected by the upper lip. These paroxysms ended with a prolonged exhalation, accompanied by facial distortion in which the mouth opened widely. Sometimes he also screwed up his left eye. The blue facial coloration was then replaced by intense pallor. After a few seconds of expiratory apnea, his breathing returned to normal. This whole cycle lasted only 20–30 seconds. At the height of his attacks, this patient often fell, and occasionally he momentarily lost consciousness.

The author was able to follow up on this case. Three years later the patient's breath-holding spells had long since ceased, and he was still free from any signs of parkinsonism. He had lost weight, and there was weakness of his right arm with evidence of sensory impairment. He remembered the attacks, which he said had taken place "because the Devil told me to hold my breath."

While some patients exhibited respiratory and other tics or mannerisms during the acute illness, these manifestations were much more common afterward. One of the most common was the wide opening of the mouth, as in an exaggerated yawn, which sometimes led to temporary subluxation (partial dislocation) of the jaw joints. Other types of postencephalitic tics included coughing, sniffing, spitting, snorting, and sighing. Yet another was an involuntary protrusion of the tongue. One of this author's patients tried to control this impulse by closing his mouth so tightly upon the protruded tongue that it became swollen to the extent that for days he could not draw it back into his mouth.

Body movements: out of control

Involuntary movements of great diversity appeared both during the acute attack and as a late manifestation of the illness, such as the myoclonic jerkings and chorea mentioned above. The parkinsonian syndrome was often accompanied by the involuntary "pill-rolling" (perhaps better described as cigarette-rolling) action of the fingers.

Unusual spasms of twisting movements were often a feature of the postencephalitic syndrome. The most common was spasmodic torticollis (intermittent spasm of the neck muscles causing jerking of the head to one side). Less often, such movements involved the lower part of the trunk (tortipelvis). One of this author's patients showed an unusual type of localized spasmodic disorder (dystonia) with a slow, uncontrollable abduction

Courtesy of Oliver Sacks, M.D.

This drawing was made by "Sam G.," one of Sacks's patients at Mount Carmel, after he started taking L-dopa. In his youth Sam had been a car buff and a racer but had to give up these pursuits around 1930 because of profound parkinsonism. As Sacks tells the story: "The moment he found himself 'released' by L-DOPA, he started drawing cars. . . . His cars were accurate, authentic, and had an odd charm. When he was not drawing, he was talking, or writing—of 'the old days' in the twenties when he was driving and racing—and this too was full of vividness and immediacy, minute, compelling, living detail." Many of the postencephalitic patients treated by Sacks had equally lively memories and personalities "awakened," which had long been immured by their disease.

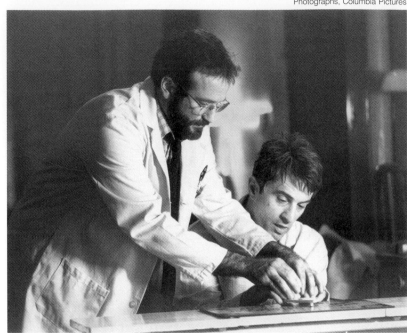

Motion-picture audiences were entranced by Robert De Niro's performance as the patient "Leonard L." in Awakenings. *Early in the film, in the scene at right, Leonard, speechless and unable to move any part of his body except his right hand, uses an alphabet board to spell out words in order to communicate with the fictional Dr. Sayer. The real Leonard L. was, by Sacks's account, a most extraordinary individual. Even with this highly restrictive mode of communication, he and Sacks held "conversations" that were filled with intelligence, humor, and poetic imagery.*

(sideways movement) of the right arm at the shoulder joint. The spasm came to rest only when the arm reached a 90° angle of abduction from the side, the elbow joint fully flexed.

Sleep disorders

The typical lethargy of the acute phase of the illness was sometimes accompanied by nighttime wakefulness, the latter often occurring also as a sequel to encephalitis lethargica, especially in children. A typical case was seen by this author in 1925. The patient was a nine-year-old boy who had contracted acute encephalitis lethargica some 19 months earlier. The youngster's chief symptom was restlessness. He behaved normally during the day, but as the evening drew on, he became noisy, excited, and turbulent, running around the hospital ward and blowing hard through his curled fingers as if playing a musical instrument. Not until the small hours of the morning did he become exhausted and fall asleep. Early in 1926 the patient was transferred to a special institution for postencephalitics. His behavior steadily deteriorated, and his blowing tic persisted for about a year, after which it gradually disappeared. When reexamined by the author in late 1927, he showed no evidence of parkinsonism, but his conduct had become more disruptive and rowdy over the two years.

As a result of the encephalitis lethargica epidemic, there were so many children in England suffering from an inverted sleep rhythm during the 1920s that some of them were segregated in a separate ward of an institution on the outskirts of London run by the Metropolitan Asylum Board. Here the daily routine was reversed, so that night was converted into day.

Narcoleptic-like attacks of irresistible sleep occurring in daytime were also an aftereffect of encephalitis lethargica. Some patients experienced typical episodes of cataplexy (attacks of tonelessness, or muscular flaccid-

214

ity) precipitated by emotion, especially laughter, but these did not occur as often in postencephalitics as they do in those with the idiopathic type of narcolepsy.

Seizures and endocrine abnormalities

Epileptic seizures were reported by various European physicians as appearing after encephalitis lethargica, but epilepsy as a sequel of this illness was rarely seen by British neurologists. Other recurrent convulsive phenomena were recorded, such as seizures in which the individual's limbs went into spasm and the hands and feet adopted the typical attitude of cramp but without the patient's losing consciousness.

Kinnier Wilson described one young neurological patient that he had observed over a period of 10 years. First seen at the age of five, the boy displayed a syndrome of "reflex tonic epilepsy": a trifling jar, a touch, or any emotion was followed by an extension-inversion movement of his left foot, tilting of his head to the left, and arching of his back. His left arm bent at the elbow and was abducted at the shoulder. He remained conscious but did not speak for the duration of the attack—about a minute. When seen again six years later, the boy showed obvious parkinsonism, with muscular weakness and spasticity on the left side of his body. The disability gradually worsened. No history of any preceding illness came to light, but Kinnier Wilson had no doubt that the condition was postencephalitic.

The pediatric neurologist Frank Rudolph Ford of Johns Hopkins Hospital, Baltimore, Maryland, reported the occurrence of extraordinary seizures in a small girl some months after her attack of encephalitis lethargica. Each seizure began with twitching of the right side of her mouth and clenching of one fist while her other hand rubbed her chin and lips. Saliva then gushed from her mouth, tears streamed from her eyes, and there was generalized flushing of the skin. Next came an uncontrollable urge to urinate and defecate, but she did not lose consciousness. These paroxysms occurred every 10–15 minutes, day and night.

Endocrine anomalies, although rare, were also known to follow encephalitis lethargica. In the most common pattern, the patient developed a type of pituitary dysfunction (Fröhlich's syndrome) characterized by obesity, failure to attain mature secondary sexual characteristics, and polyuria (frequent passing of urine) with polydipsia (excessive thirst). In a few reported cases excessive hair growth (hirsutism) and sexual precocity occurred.

Psychiatric disorders

Mental disturbances were common, as both early and late manifestations of the illness, more often in children (particularly males) than in adults. The affected children were not intellectually impaired but showed severe personality disorders marked by flagrant antisocial behavior. Following encephalitis lethargica, young adolescent patients, formerly docile and well behaved, would become aggressive delinquents. Oblivious to exhortation or punishment, they would shamelessly lie, steal, destroy objects, or savagely attack others on impulse; quite often they committed arson. Neurologists spoke of this as an "apache" type of behavior (referring to the Parisian

Oliver Sacks (left) consults with actor Robin Williams during the filming of Awakenings. *Sacks first began working with postencephalitic patients in the mid-1960s, some 30–40 years after most were stricken with "sleepy sickness."*

thugs of the 19th century). In some instances the principal misdemeanor was an uncontrollable, motiveless kind of thieving—compulsively purloining articles that were of no practical use or value to them. This author saw one young patient who habitually stole bicycles. He always chose a bike that was too big for him to ride, but he made no attempt to sell it or profit in any way from the theft.

Acts of sexual aggression were not uncommon in quite young boys. A male patient of Ford's, an 11-year-old, molested young girls, masturbated throughout the day, and crept into the female ward of the hospital at night to get into the beds of adult women. Occasionally patients exhibited aggressive behavior of much greater severity. This author was familiar with two young postencephalitic males who committed apparently motiveless homicides.

In a few older patients, grotesque acts of self-mutilation were reported, such as finger-gnawing, gouging out of their own eyeballs, and self-inflicted burns. When psychotic symptoms of these kinds occurred, there was very little chance of recovery (*i.e.,* return to normal behavior).

Can it happen again?

Sixty years have passed since the last cases of the epidemic of "sleepy sickness" were diagnosed; most of the sufferers have now perished. There are, however, a few aged people with postencephalitic parkinsonism still living, most being cared for in special institutions. The introduction in the 1960s of the drug L-dopa into therapy for neurological conditions played a dramatic part in their lives. Some were aroused from a strange mute immobility, if only for a while. This bizarre, fluctuating state of affairs was vividly described by Sacks in *Awakenings.*

Many questions are still unanswered. The precise number of afflicted individuals throughout the world has never been confidently established. In reports to the League of Nations, six European countries recorded as many as 10,000 cases a year in some years and as few as 2,600 in others in the period from 1920 to 1928. Death rates varied widely. In the U.S. the Matheson Commission, established to study the epidemic in detail, reported that of 7,876 cases surveyed, 50% were fatal. This figure is higher than most other estimates. However, most records indicate that about 35% of patients did not survive.

Whether the epidemic was a unique event in the history of medicine is still a matter of disagreement among medical scientists. Some authorities, including von Economo, have speculated that minor outbreaks of the disease, followed by the typical sequelae, have occurred from time to time over many centuries. Others are skeptical. No new cases of encephalitis lethargica have come to light and been confirmed during the past 50 years. Whether "sleepy sickness" epidemics will ever reappear, no one can foretell. Should such an unfortunate event occur, however, virologists now have sophisticated knowledge and methods for isolating the responsible pathogens. It should, therefore, be possible not only to identify the cause but also to develop effective treatment—and perhaps to eliminate this strange illness for all time.

ENCYCLOPÆDIA BRITANNICA

MEDICAL UPDATE

From the 1991 Printing of *Encyclopædia Britannica*

The purpose of this section is to introduce to *Medical and Health Annual* subscribers selected *Macropædia* articles or portions of articles that have been completely revised or rewritten in the most recent edition of the *Encyclopædia Britannica*. It is intended to update the *Macropædia* coverage of topics concerning medicine or health, and it offers a longer and more comprehensive treatment than can be accomplished by the *Annual*'s yearly review of recent developments in various medical specialties and allied health fields.

The article chosen from the 1991 *Britannica* printing is POISONS AND POISONING. It is the work of distinguished scholars and represents the continuing dedication of *Encyclopædia Britannica* to bringing texts that provide authoritative interpretation and examination of timely issues to the general reader.

Poisons and Poisoning

Although poisons have been the subject of practical lore since ancient times, their systematic study is often considered to have begun during the 16th century, when the German-Swiss physician and alchemist Paracelsus first stressed the chemical nature of poisons. It was Paracelsus who introduced the concept of dose and studied the actions of poisons through experimentation. It was not until the 19th century, however, that the Spaniard Matthieu Orfila, the attending physician to Louis XVIII, correlated the chemistry of a toxin with the biological effects it produces in a poisoned individual. Both concepts continue to be fundamental to an understanding of modern toxicology.

Poisoning involves four elements: the poison, the poisoned organism, the injury to the cells, and the symptoms and signs or death. These four elements represent the cause, subject, effect, and consequence of poisoning. To initiate the poisoning, the organism is exposed to the toxic chemical. When a toxic level of the chemical is accumulated in the cells of the target tissue or organ, the resultant injury to the cells disrupts their normal structure or function. Symptoms and toxic signs then develop, and, if the toxicity is severe enough, death may result.

This article considers humans as the primary subjects of poisoning. It first discusses the actions of poisons on the body and then examines principal types of synthetic and natural poisons.

The article is divided into the following sections:

Nature of a toxic substance

Definition of a poison. A poison is a substance capable of producing adverse effects on an individual under appropriate conditions. The term "substance" is almost always synonymous with "chemical" and includes drugs, vitamins, pesticides, pollutants, and proteins. Even radiation is a toxic substance. Though not usually considered to be a "chemical," most radiations are generated from radioisotopes, which are chemicals. The term "adverse effects" above refers to the injury, such as structural damage to tissues. "Appropriate conditions" refers to the dosage of the substance that is sufficient to cause these adverse effects. The dose concept is important because according to it even a substance as innocuous as water is poisonous if too much is ingested. Whether a drug acts as a therapy or as a poison depends on the dose.

Classification of a poison. Poisons are of such diverse natures that they are classified by origin, physical form, chemical nature, chemical activity, target site, or use.

Classification based on origin. Poisons are of microbial, plant, animal, or synthetic origin. Microbial poisons are produced by microscopic organisms such as bacteria and fungi. Botulinus toxin, for example, is produced by the bacterium *Clostridium botulinum* and is capable of inducing weakness and paralysis when present in underprocessed, nonacidic canned foods or in other foods containing the spores. An example of a plant toxin is the belladonna alkaloid hyoscyamine, which is found in belladonna (*Atropa belladonna*) and jimsonweed (*Datura stramonium*).

Animal toxins

Animal poisons are usually transferred through the bites and stings of venomous terrestrial or marine animals, the former group including poisonous snakes, scorpions, spiders, and ants, and the latter group including sea snakes, stingrays, and jellyfish. Synthetic toxins are responsible for most poisonings. "Synthetic" refers to chemicals manufactured by chemists, such as drugs and pesticides, as well as chemicals purified from natural sources, such as metals from ores and solvents from petroleum. Synthetic toxins include pesticides, household cleaners, cosmetics, pharmaceuticals, and hydrocarbons.

Classification based on physical form. The physical form of a chemical—solid, liquid, gas, vapour, or aerosol—influences the exposure and absorbability.

Because solids are generally not well absorbed into the blood, they must be dissolved in the aqueous liquid lining the intestinal tract if ingested or the respiratory tract if inhaled. Solids dissolve at different rates in fluids, however. For example, compared with lead sulphate granules, granules of lead are practically nontoxic when ingested, because elemental lead is essentially insoluble in water, while lead sulphate is slightly soluble and absorbable. Even different-sized granules of the same chemical can vary in their relative toxicities because of the differences in dissolution rates. For example, arsenic trioxide is more toxic in the form of smaller granules than is the same mass of larger granules because the smaller granules dissolve faster.

A poison in a liquid form can be absorbed by ingestion or by inhalation or through the skin. Poisons that are gases at room temperature (*e.g.*, carbon monoxide) are absorbed mainly by inhalation, as are vapours, which are the gas phase of substances that are liquids at room temperature and atmospheric pressure (*e.g.*, benzene). Because organic liquids are more volatile than inorganic liquids, inhalation of organic vapours is more common. Although vapours are generally absorbed in the lungs, some vapours that are highly soluble in lipids (*e.g.*, furfural) are also absorbed through the skin.

Aerosols

Aerosols are solid or liquid particles small enough to remain suspended in air for a few minutes. Fibres and dust are solid aerosols. Aerosol exposures occur when aerosols are deposited on the skin or inhaled. Aerosol toxicity is usually higher in the lungs than on the skin. An example of a toxic fibre is asbestos, which can cause a rare form of lung cancer (mesothelioma).

Many liquid poisons can exist as liquid aerosols, although highly volatile liquids, such as benzene, seldom exist as aerosols. A moderately volatile liquid poison can exist as both an aerosol and as a vapour. Airborne liquid chemicals of low volatility exist only as aerosols.

Classification based on chemical nature. Poisons can be classified according to whether the chemical is metallic versus nonmetallic, organic versus inorganic, or acidic versus alkaline. Metallic poisons are often eliminated from the body slowly and accumulate to a greater extent than nonmetallic poisons and thus are more likely to cause toxicity during chronic exposure. Organic chemicals are more soluble in lipids and therefore can usually pass through the lipid-rich cell membranes more readily than can inorganic chemicals. As a result, organic chemicals are generally absorbed more extensively than inorganic chemicals. Classification based on acidity is useful because, while both acids and alkalis are corrosive to the eyes, skin, and intestinal tract, alkalis generally penetrate the tissue more deeply than acids and tend to cause more severe tissue damage.

Classification based on chemical activity. Electrophilic (electron-loving) chemicals attack the nucleophilic (nucleus-loving) sites of the cells' macromolecules, such as deoxyribonucleic acid (DNA), producing mutations, cancers, and malformations. Poisons also may be grouped according to their ability to mimic the structure of certain important molecules in the cell. They substitute for the cells' molecules in chemical reactions, disrupting important cellular functions. Methotrexate, for example, disrupts the synthesis of DNA and ribonucleic acid (RNA).

Other classifications. Unlike the classifications described above, there is usually no predictive value in classification by target sites or by uses. Such classifications are done, however, to systematically categorize the numerous known poisons. Target sites include the nervous system, the cardiovascular system, the reproductive system, the immune system, and the lungs, liver, and kidneys. Poisons are classified by such uses as pesticides, household products, pharmaceuticals, organic solvents, drugs of abuse, or industrial chemicals.

TRANSPORT OF CHEMICALS THROUGH A CELL MEMBRANE

In order for a poison to produce toxicity, a sufficient quantity of that chemical must be absorbed into the body. Because the chemical must pass through a number of cell membranes before it can enter the blood, the ability of the chemical to cross these lipid-rich membranes determines whether it will be absorbed, and that ability depends on the chemical's lipid solubility.

Membrane structure

The cell membrane, the most external layer of all animal cells, is composed of two layers of lipid molecules (the lipid bilayer). The lipid molecules each have a hydrophilic (water-loving, or polar) end and a hydrophobic (water-hating, or nonpolar) end. Because they are surrounded by an aqueous environment, lipid molecules of the cell membrane arrange themselves so as to expose their hydrophilic ends and protect their hydrophobic ends. Suspended randomly among the lipid molecules are proteins, some of which extend from the exterior surface of the cell membrane to the interior surface.

A chemical tends to dissolve more readily in a solvent of similar polarity. Nonpolar chemicals are considered lipophilic (lipid-loving), and polar chemicals are hydrophilic (water-loving). Lipid-soluble, nonpolar molecules pass readily through the membrane because they dissolve in the hydrophobic, nonpolar portion of the lipid bilayer. Although permeable to water (a polar molecule), the nonpolar lipid bilayer of cell membranes is impermeable to many other polar molecules, such as charged ions or those that contain many polar side chains. Polar molecules pass through lipid membranes via specific transport systems.

The four types of chemical transport systems through cell membranes are diffusion, facilitated diffusion, active transport, and pinocytosis.

As mentioned above, lipophilic, nonpolar chemicals dissolve in the lipid bilayer. Simultaneously, some of the molecules are leaving the lipid bilayer. The net result is that chemicals cross the membrane until the concentrations of chemical molecules on both sides of the membrane are equal and there is no net flow of molecules across the cell membrane (diffusion). Therefore, chemicals diffuse across the membrane only when a concentration gradient exists across the cell membrane. Diffusion is considered to be passive transport because no external energy is used. Polar molecules, such as water and small water-soluble molecules (*e.g.*, urea, chloride ions, sodium ions, and potassium ions), can diffuse across membranes through the water-filled channels created by membrane proteins. Large polar water-soluble chemicals, such as sugars, however, do not diffuse through the membrane.

Concentration gradient

Certain relatively large water-soluble molecules cross the cell membrane using carriers. Carriers are membrane proteins that complement the structural features of the molecules transported. They bind to the chemicals in order to move them across the cell membrane. Energy is consumed because the transport proceeds against the concentration gradient.

Active transport systems move chemicals essential to cellular functions through the membrane into the cell. Such essential chemicals include calcium ions, amino acids, carbohydrates, and vitamins. Because the structures of poisons usually are not similar to those of chemicals essential to cells, few poisons are absorbed by active transport. Active transport, however, is important in the elimination of organic acids, bases, and foreign compounds by the kidneys and liver.

Molecules of similar structure compete with one another in binding with the carrier molecule. Thus, the transport of one chemical can be inhibited by another chemical of similar structure, a phenomenon called competitive inhibition. The chemical being transported also competes with itself for a carrier molecule, so that only a limited amount of the chemical can be transported by the carrier protein during a specific time.

Transport systems that use carrier molecules but which do not require energy to proceed are called facilitated diffusion. A chemical first binds to the carrier protein in the cell membrane and then diffuses through the membrane. Because no energy is used, facilitated transport into the cell cannot proceed if the concentration of that chemical is greater inside the cell membrane than outside. The involvement of carriers means that the process is also subject to competitive inhibition and saturation.

Large molecules, such as proteins and solid particles, are often transported by means of a process called pinocytosis. The cell membrane engulfs a particle or protein molecule outside the cell and brings it into the cell. Pinocytosis, which is not a particularly efficient transport mode, results in the slow absorption of proteins and particles in the intestine and respiratory tract.

CONDITIONS OF EXPOSURE

Figure 1 summarizes the conditions of exposure to toxicants.

Routes of exposure and absorption of chemicals. *Injection.* Although not a common route of exposure for poisons, injection is the only route in which the entire amount exposed is absorbed regardless of the chemical administered, because the chemical is introduced directly into the body. Chemicals may be injected intravenously (directly into a vein), intramuscularly (into a muscle), subcutaneously (under the skin), and intraperitoneally (within the membrane lining the organs of the abdomen).

Types of injection

Because the blood is the vehicle of chemical distribution in the body, intravenous injection is the most rapid method of introducing a chemical into the body. The almost instantaneous distribution, together with the irreversibility, makes intravenous injection a dangerous method of chemical exposure, with a fair chance of causing drug overdose if improperly administered.

Because there is a relatively large flow of blood to the skeletal muscles, chemicals are absorbed into the blood relatively rapidly after intramuscular injection. The slow absorption of a chemical into the blood after subcutaneous injection is probably due to the low blood flow in the subcutaneous tissues. Intraperitoneal injection is used only in biomedical research. Absorption is relatively rapid

with intraperitoneal injection because of the rich blood supply to the abdomen.

Ingestion. Ingestion is the most common route of exposure to toxic chemicals. Most chemicals diffuse across the cell membrane in the nonionized form, so that the degree to which the chemical is ionized is important in determining whether a chemical is absorbed (see above *Transport of chemicals through a cell membrane*).

Organic acids and bases dissociate into their ionized forms in response to the pH conditions of the environment. Organic acids are in their nonionized form in an acidic environment (such as the stomach), and they thus tend to diffuse across a membrane, whereas organic bases are nonionized and thus diffuse across a membrane in a basic environment (such as in the intestine).

pH influence on ionization

Because the pH and surface areas differ in different segments of the gastrointestinal tract, chemical absorbabilities of these segments also differ. The major sites of absorption of ingested poisons are the stomach and the small intestine, with most of the absorption taking place in the latter. The intestine has a greater blood supply and a much larger surface area. Folds in the mucosa of the small intestine house numerous projections on the luminal surface, which increases the surface area of the 280-centimetre- (110-inch-) long small intestine to up to 2,000,000 square centimetres.

The pH on the mucosal surface of the small intestine is normally about 5.4 (basic). Organic bases tend to be in the nonionized, lipid-soluble form and thus in general are absorbed there. The pH of the stomach contents is in the range of 1 to 2 (acidic), and weak organic acids tend to be in the nonionized, lipid-soluble form. It might be expected that the poisons would be absorbed there, but, because the surface area of the stomach is much smaller than that of the small intestine, often the stomach contents (along with the poisons) are passed to the intestine before the chemicals are absorbed. The acidic environment of the stomach is the main reason for the poor absorption of organic bases by the stomach.

Topical (skin). The skin is composed of three layers of tissues—the epidermis, dermis, and subcutaneous tissues—and is an effective barrier to many substances. The outer skin layer is the epidermis, containing five layers of cells. The stratum corneum, which is the outermost epidermal layer, consists of dead cells and is the major barrier to chemical transfer through the skin. Although nonpolar chemicals cross the skin by diffusion through the stratum corneum, no active transport exists in the dead cells of this layer. The second layer, the dermis, is thicker and is composed of loosely packed connective tissue cells in a watery matrix of collagen and elastin fibres, as well as sweat glands, hair follicles, capillaries, and lymphatic vessels. After crossing the epidermis, chemical molecules are absorbed into the circulatory system via the capillaries. The capillaries drain into venules in the subcutaneous tissue.

Skin structure

The stratum corneum is not very permeable to water-soluble molecules and ions, although lipid-soluble molecules do cross it to a certain extent. The permeability is directly proportional to the lipid solubility of the chemical (*i.e.,* highly lipid-soluble chemicals are readily absorbed) and inversely proportional to the molecular weight of the chemical (*i.e.,* the rate of absorption increases as the molecular weight of the molecule decreases).

The rate of percutaneous absorption also varies with the thickness of the stratum corneum at different sites of the body. The rate of absorption is higher for skin on the forehead, axilla, back, and abdomen than for thicker regions like the plantar surface of the foot and the palm. The condition of the skin also has an effect on permeability. Percutaneous absorption is faster when the skin is moist rather than dry.

Rate of absorption

Solids are not absorbed through the skin because the skin is generally not covered with liquid and because pinocytosis does not operate in dead cells. Liquid chemicals penetrate the skin largely because of their lipid solubility. Gases and certain vapours can be absorbed through the skin also, although to a much lesser extent than via inhalation.

Inhalation. The absorption of inhaled gases and vapours

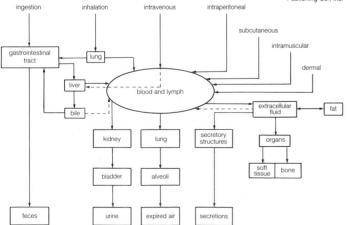

From L.J. Casarett and J. Doull, *Toxicology: The Basic Science of Poisons* (1975); Macmillan Publishing Co., Inc.

Figure 1: Routes of absorption, distribution, and excretion of toxicants in the human body.

differs from that of aerosols and thus will be discussed separately.

Because the same principles govern the absorption of gases and vapours, the word "gases" is used here to represent both gases and vapours. Absorption of inhaled gases takes place mainly in the lungs. Before the gases reach the lung, however, they pass through the nose, where highly water-soluble, or highly reactive, gas molecules are retained by mucosa.

Unlike intestinal and percutaneous absorption of chemicals, respiratory absorption of gases does not depend on the pH of the alveoli, because gas molecules are not ionized. It also does not depend on the lipid solubility of the gas molecules for three reasons. First, the alveolar gas molecules are situated in close proximity to the capillaries. Second, the alveoli form a huge surface for gas absorption. Third, the time it takes for a unit of blood to go through the lungs is more than adequate for gas molecules to diffuse from the alveolar space to the blood.

Gas molecules move into the blood by partitioning, which is a gas-transfer process between two phases, such as between the air and the blood or the blood and the tissues. In partitioning, gas molecules move from a phase of high partial pressure to an adjacent phase of low partial pressure. When an individual first inhales the gas, the partial pressure of the gas is higher in the air than in the blood, driving gas molecules from the alveolar space to the blood. As more gas molecules are driven into the blood, the blood's partial pressure is raised. Eventually the partial pressure gradient between the air and blood dissipates and gas transfer stops; equilibrium is then reached, usually before the blood leaves the lungs.

The blood carries the gas molecules to the rest of the body, where the gas is transferred from the blood to the tissue until equilibrium is reached. The blood picks up more gas molecules in the lungs, and the process continues until the gas in each tissue of the body is in equilibrium with that of the blood entering the tissue. At this time, barring biotransformation, no further net absorption of gas takes place as long as the exposure concentration remains constant. A person can breathe the gas forever and not absorb more, a unique characteristic of gas exposure.

The particle size and water solubility of an aerosol chemical are the important characteristics determining absorption of aerosols. For an aerosol to be absorbed, it must be inhaled and deposited on the respiratory tract. If not deposited, the aerosol particles are exhaled. Aerosols of less than 100 micrometres (0.004 inch) can be inhaled.

The aerosol size also determines the tendency of a particle to be deposited on a certain region of the respiratory tract. The larger aerosols (greater than five micrometres) tend to be deposited in the upper respiratory tract, while the smaller ones (less than five micrometres) have a greater chance of being deposited on deeper sites of the lung. The nose acts as a "scrubber" for larger aerosols and thus protects the lung from injury.

Once deposited, aerosol particles must dissolve in the liquid lining the respiratory tract in order to be absorbed. For most aerosols of poor water solubility, the particles are cleared from the respiratory tract by mechanical or cellular means. In the nasopharyngeal region, mechanical methods of clearance include sneezing and nose blowing for particles deposited on the anterior one-fifth of the nasal cavity. Particles deposited on the remaining portion of the nasal cavity and on the pharynx are removed by tiny hairs, called cilia, on the surface of these two regions, which beat almost continuously to move a covering layer of mucous toward the throat (mucociliary apparatus). Any particles deposited on the mucous are carried along and finally swallowed.

In the tracheobronchial region, mechanical clearance includes coughing and the mucociliary apparatus. The trachea, bronchi, and bronchioles, down to the terminal bronchioles, are covered with mucous and cilia. The mucociliary apparatus moves upward toward the larynx, where the respiratory tract joins the esophagus. The particles are eventually swallowed and may be absorbed by the gastrointestinal tract.

The alveolar region has the slowest rate of particle clearance in the entire respiratory system, unless the particles are water-soluble, in which case they are cleared readily by dissolution. Water-insoluble particles in the respiratory bronchioles and alveoli are removed by cellular means, principally by macrophages—scavenger cells that engulf cellular debris in the body by a process called phagocytosis. Once phagocytosed, macrophages that contain particles are removed by the mucociliary apparatus in the terminal bronchioles. Pinocytosis by the cells lining the alveoli probably move the free particles to the interstitial space, where they either enter the lymphatic capillaries and are carried to the bloodstream, or they undergo a long process of dissolution. It can take years for water-insoluble particles to dissolve, depending on the chemical, which is why water-insoluble particles deposited in the alveolar region tend to remain in the interstitial space for a long time and can cause serious harm.

Frequency of exposure. The second important condition of exposure is frequency: acute (single exposure), subchronic (repeated exposures that in total last for no more than 10 percent of the lifetime of an individual), and chronic (repetitive exposures that last in total longer than 10 percent of the lifetime). The difference between the frequencies of exposure is the length of time a chemical is maintained in a target tissue. A single exposure of a poison at a certain dose may be sufficient to produce a toxic concentration in a target tissue, leading to the development of toxicity. Repetitive exposures at the same dose will then enhance the severity of the injury because of the presence of toxic levels of the chemical in the target tissue. The continuous presence of a toxic amount of poison may impair the ability of the damaged cells to carry out repair and thus prevent any chance of recovery. Consequently, a single dose that produces symptoms and toxic signs can lead to death if repeated over time. Repetitive exposures of some chemicals may also produce a different toxic effect than the acute exposure.

Toxic accumulation is one of the reasons repetitive exposures of a chemical produce toxicity while a single exposure may not. In a hypothetical case, as depicted in Figure 2, a concentration of more than 100 milligrams per gram in a target tissue is required for chemical A to cause toxic injury. If chemical A is administered at a dose that does not produce toxic levels in the tissue and the elimination of the chemical is essentially complete within 24 hours, repetitive exposures at the same dose once a day will not result in toxicity. With chemical A there will be no difference in toxicity between acute and repetitive exposures. Suppose, however, that there is a similar chemical, B, with a slower elimination rate so that chemical B is not completely eliminated from the target tissue within 24 hours. If the exposure to chemical B is carried out at the same dose as chemical A, the concentration of B in the target tissue will not return to zero after 24 hours. Consequently, daily exposures of B will cause the toxin to accumulate, so that the peak target concentration of B increases daily (Figure 2). Eventually, the toxic threshold is reached and injury will develop. Therefore, repetitive exposure can produce toxicity at a dose that does not result in injury if given only once.

Dose of exposure. The amount of chemical to which a person is exposed is extremely important. The chemical acts at a certain site, called the active site, triggering a biological response in a target tissue. Because the biological effect is caused by the presence of the chemical at the active site, the higher the concentration of the chemical at the site, the greater the response. This is the case with all

Types of exposure

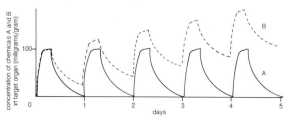

Figure 2: Accumulation of toxicants in the target organ during repetitive exposures.

known poisons, a phenomenon called the dose–response relationship.

The dose–response curve is sigmoid, with the linear portion between approximately 16 percent and 84 percent. To compare the potency of chemicals causing similar responses, the dose that produces a biological response in 50 percent of the subject group is chosen, because it can be calculated with the least chance of error. If the biological response is mortality, the dose that kills 50 percent of the exposed population is known as the lethal dose 50, or LD50. Toxicity ratings for chemicals are based on their LD50s. The toxicity rating indicates the amount of chemical required to produce death, but it should be remembered that all chemicals can kill. Thus, all chemicals are toxic. More important than the toxicity of a chemical is its hazard or risk of usage, a concept that incorporates exposure to dosage. For example, botulinum toxin is not especially hazardous, even though it is supertoxic, because food is well-preserved, keeping the exposure or dose very low. In contrast, ethanol (alcohol) is hazardous even though it is not very toxic, because some people have a tendency to use it to excess.

DISTRIBUTION OF TOXICANTS IN THE BODY

Role of the lymphatics. After a chemical crosses the transport barrier at the portal of entry, it remains in the interstitial spaces, the spaces between cells that are filled with water and loose connective tissue. The absorbed chemical can gain entry into the bloodstream directly via the blood capillaries or indirectly via the lymphatic capillaries.

Lymphatic capillaries are minute vessels located in the interstitial spaces, with one end closed and the other end draining into larger lymphatic vessels. Just like blood capillaries, the walls of the lymphatic capillaries are composed of a thin layer of cells, the endothelial cells. Unlike the blood capillaries, however, the junctions between the endothelial cells of the lymphatic capillaries are much looser, and as a result lymphatic capillaries are much more porous than blood capillaries. Plasma proteins and excess fluid in the interstitial spaces from blood capillaries enter the lymphatic capillaries and eventually flow back to the heart via the lymphatic system. Insoluble aerosols that cross the alveolar wall by pinocytosis may be absorbed into the circulatory system after first entering the porous lymphatic capillaries.

Role of the blood. The chemical is distributed via the blood to the various tissues of the body, where the chemical is transported across blood capillary walls. There are four types of blood capillary walls: tight, continuous, fenestrated, and discontinuous.

Tight capillary walls are characterized by tight junctions between the endothelial cells, which prevent the diffusion of large molecules and impede that of hydrophilic molecules. The capillaries in the brain are typical of this type of capillary and form part of the blood–brain barrier.

In a continuous capillary wall, channels about five nanometres wide exist between endothelial cells, allowing most small molecules to pass through. Capillaries of this type are found in the skeletal and smooth muscles, connective tissue, lungs, and fat. Chemicals given by intramuscular or subcutaneous injection are readily absorbed into the bloodstream, as are deposited aerosols that dissolve in the fluid lining the respiratory system and cross the alveolar wall.

In a fenestrated capillary wall, holes as large as 100 nanometres are found in the endothelial cells. Capillaries in the intestine and glomeruli in the kidney have fenestrated capillary walls, which account for the high permeability of blood capillaries for absorption by the intestine and for filtration of the blood by the kidney.

The discontinuous capillary wall, the most porous of all capillaries, contains large gaps between the cells through which large molecules and even blood cells pass. This type of capillary is found in the reticuloendothelial system (including the liver, spleen, and bone marrow), which assists in the removal of aged blood cells.

The porous nature of capillaries in most tissues or organs means that a chemical in the bloodstream can be distributed almost freely to most tissues, except for organs

with a barrier. The molecules diffuse from the blood to the interstitial spaces of the tissue and finally into the cells by either diffusion or active transport.

Role of tissue blood flow. The rate at which a chemical accumulates in a particular tissue is influenced by the blood flow to that tissue. The well-perfused organs—*i.e.,* organs that receive a rich blood supply relative to organ weight—include major organs like the liver, brain, and kidney. A middle group receives an intermediate blood supply and includes the skeletal muscle and skin. The poorly perfused group includes the fat and bone. As a chemical is distributed to the tissues by the bloodstream, the chemical concentrations in the well-perfused organs rapidly reach a steady state with the blood concentration while the concentrations of the chemical in the poorly perfused tissue lag behind.

Role of protein binding. The plasma contains many proteins, the most abundant being albumin. Some chemicals are known to bind to albumin. Because albumin is too large to cross the blood capillary wall, chemicals that are bound to this plasma protein are confined in the bloodstream and are not readily distributed to the tissues. Chemicals with a high affinity to bind with plasma proteins have lower concentrations in tissues than do chemicals that are not bound to plasma proteins.

Role of distribution barriers. There are barriers in certain organs that limit the distribution of some molecules. The blood–brain barrier consists of tight capillary walls with glial cells wrapped around the capillaries in the brain. Molecules must diffuse through two barriers to get from blood to the nerve cells of the brain. Despite the barrier, water, most lipid-soluble molecules, oxygen, and carbon dioxide can diffuse through it readily. It is slightly permeable to the ions of electrolytes, such as sodium, potassium, and chloride, but is poorly permeable to large molecules, such as proteins and most water-soluble chemicals. The blood–brain barrier is the reason the ions of some highly water-soluble metals, such as mercury and lead, are nontoxic to the brain of an adult. Children, however, are more sensitive to the toxicity of lead because the blood–brain barrier is less well developed in children.

The second distribution barrier is the blood–testis barrier, which limits the passage of large molecules (like proteins and polysaccharides), medium-sized molecules (like galactose), and some water-soluble molecules from blood into the seminiferous tubules of the testis. Water and very small water-soluble molecules, like urea, however, can pass through the barrier. The lumen of the seminiferous tubules is where sperm cells of more advanced stages develop. It is thought that the barrier protects the sperm cells.

The placental barrier between mother and fetus is the "leakiest" barrier and is a very poor block to chemicals. The placenta is composed of several layers of cells acting as a barrier for the diffusion of substances between the maternal and fetal circulatory systems. Lipid-soluble molecules, however, can cross readily, while the transfer of large-molecular-weight molecules is limited.

ELIMINATION OF TOXICANTS

An organism can minimize the potential damage of absorbed toxins by excreting the chemical or by changing the chemical into a different chemical (biotransformation), or by both methods. The body can excrete exogenous chemicals in the urine, bile, sweat, or milk; the lungs can excrete gases such as carbon monoxide.

Urinary excretion, the most common excretory pathway, takes place in the kidney, where the functional units are the glomerulus (a filter) and the renal tubule. The artery entering the glomerulus divides into capillaries, with fenestrated walls encased in the Bowman's capsule. Twenty percent of the blood is filtered through the holes in the capillary walls; molecules smaller than 60,000 molecular weight end up in the filtrate, while red blood cells, large proteins, and chemicals bound to plasma proteins are not filtered.

Chemical exchange can also take place along the renal tubule. As the filtrate flows down the renal tubule, essential molecules, for example, amino acids and glucose, are reabsorbed by active transport in the first portion of the tubule (the proximal tubule). Chemicals in the filtrate are also reabsorbed by active transport if they structurally resemble these essential molecules. Unlike glomerular filtration, the process of tubular resorption of a chemical is not influenced by whether or not the chemical is bound to plasma proteins.

As the fluid flows down the renal tubule, water and some chemicals are reabsorbed from the tubular fluid into the blood by diffusion. The tubular fluid emerges from the kidney and is collected in the urinary bladder. Lipid-soluble chemicals are readily reabsorbed in the renal tubule, and only water-soluble chemicals are excreted in the urine to a significant extent.

The second major excretory route is the bile, which is formed in the liver and flows into the intestinal tract. The liver does not filter chemicals as does the kidney, but the liver does secrete chemicals into bile. Chemicals excreted in the bile are eventually eliminated in the feces.

Biliary excretion of a chemical does not necessarily result in the elimination of the chemical from the body. Bile is dumped into the small intestine; there is a chance that chemicals in the bile may be reabsorbed by the intestine and in turn reenter the liver via the portal vein. This cycling of a chemical, known as the enterohepatic cycle, can continue for a long time, keeping the chemical in the body.

During inhalation exposure, absorption of the gas continues until the partial pressure of the gas in the tissues is equal to that of the inspired gases in the lungs. As soon as the concentration of inspired gases decreases or the exposure terminates, respiratory excretion of the gas occurs. Because the partial pressure of the inspired gas is lower in the lungs than in blood, the blood releases some gas molecules into the alveolar space and these molecules are exhaled. The tissues lose gas molecules to the blood, which carries them to the lungs to be excreted.

The composition of sweat is similar to that of plasma except that sweat does not contain proteins. After secretion, the fluid moves through the sweat duct, where salt and water are reabsorbed. The exact mechanism of sweat secretion is not known. It appears that sweat is a filtrate of plasma that contains electrolytes (such as potassium, sodium, and chloride) and metabolic wastes (like urea and lactic acid). Because sweat resembles a filtrate of plasma, water-soluble chemicals, like some drugs and metal ions, are found in sweat. Sweat is not a major route of excretion of chemicals, however.

Milk is a potential, albeit minor, route of chemical excretion, but more importantly it is a potential means of chemical exposure for breast-fed infants.

Most chemicals enter milk by diffusion. Therefore, only the nonionized, lipid-soluble forms of organic chemicals are found to a significant extent in milk. Chemicals with a molecular weight less than 200 and that are present in plasma not bound to proteins are more likely to be found in milk. Because the lipid content of milk is higher than that of plasma, highly lipid-soluble chemicals can exist in a more concentrated level in milk than in plasma. Therefore, milk can be a significant route of excretion for highly lipid-soluble chemicals in lactating women.

Bio-transformation

Biotransformation, sometimes referred to as metabolism, is the structural modification of a chemical by enzymes in the body. Chemicals are biotransformed in several organs, including the liver, kidneys, lungs, skin, intestines, and placenta, with the liver being the most important. Chemicals absorbed in the gastrointestinal tract must pass through the liver, where they can be biotransformed and thus eliminated before being distributed to other parts of the body. This phenomenon is known as the first-pass effect. As a result, smaller amounts of certain chemicals are distributed throughout the body after oral administration than after other exposure routes, such as intravenous or intramuscular injections. Biotransformation of a chemical primarily facilitates its excretion into urine or bile; however, certain chemicals are biotransformed into more toxic forms and, as a result, biotransformation of chemicals is not always beneficial.

Biotransformation of exogenous chemicals (chemicals that are not naturally found in the body) generally oc-

curs in two phases. In phase I, an exogenous molecule is modified by the addition of a functional group such as a hydroxyl, a carboxyl, or a sulfhydryl. This modification allows phase II, the conjugation, or joining, of the exogenous molecule with an endogenous molecule (one naturally found in the body), to take place. The major end product in most cases is a more water-soluble chemical that is easily excreted.

Phase I reactions can be classified as oxidation, reduction, or hydrolysis. Oxidation is carried out by cytochrome P-450 monooxygenases, mixed-function amine oxidases, and alcohol and aldehyde dehydrogenases. The reactions mediated by cytochrome P-450 monooxygenases can make the chemical less toxic or more toxic. The cytochrome P-450 enzymes can, for example, produce epoxides of some chemicals, which are very reactive and can attack important cellular molecules, such as DNA. The remaining phase I oxidative enzymes act on a narrow range of substrates.

In addition to the oxidation of a chemical, cytochrome P-450 monooxygenases can catalyze the reduction. Another group of enzymes that can carry out reduction is the aldehyde/ketone reductases. Each of the three groups of hydrolytic enzymes (epoxide hydrolases, esterases, and amidases, respectively) creates metabolites with a hydroxyl, carboxyl, or amino functional group.

In phase II reactions an altered exogenous chemical binds with an endogenous molecule, leading to the formation of a final product (the conjugate), which is usually much more water-soluble and easily excreted than the parent chemical. There are four types of parent compounds whose excretion can be enhanced by conjugation: glucuronic acid, glutathione, amino acids, or sulfate. The first two types are the most common phase II reactions.

Conjugation of glucuronic acid with a hydroxyl, carboxyl, amino, or sulfhydryl group leads to the formation of oxygen, nitrogen, or sulfur glucuronides, which are more easily excreted than glucuronic acid because they are more water soluble and because they contain a carboxyl group. Conjugation with glutathione also enhances excretion. Glutathione conjugation yields glutathione conjugates and mercapturic acid derivatives, which are excreted by the liver, kidney, or both.

Two types of conjugations, acetylations and methylation, do not enhance the excretion of the parent chemical. Acetylation and methylation decrease the water solubility of the parent chemical and mask the functional group of the parent chemical, preventing these functional groups from participating in conjugations that increase their excretion. Acetylation acts on chemicals with an amino group and may render them less toxic. Chemicals with an amino, hydroxyl, or sulfhydryl group can be methylated. Methylation is not as important a route of biotransformation for exogenous chemicals as it is for endogenous chemicals.

THERAPEUTIC, TOXIC, AND LETHAL RESPONSES

Because the response to a chemical varies with the dose, any substance can be a poison. Medicine can produce responses that are therapeutic (beneficial) or toxic (adverse), or even lethal. The sigmoid dose–response relationships for the therapeutic and lethal responses typically look like curves A and C, respectively, of Figure 3. If drug X has therapeutic, toxic, and lethal dose–response curves of A, B, and C, respectively, X is a very safe drug, since there is no overlap of the curves. For some medicinal agents, there is overlap of the therapeutic and lethal dose-response curves, so that a dose which causes a therapeutic response in some individuals can kill others. These agents, consequently, are not as safe.

A quantitative measurement of the relative safety of drugs is the therapeutic index, which is the ratio of the dose that elicits a lethal response in 50 percent of treated individuals (LD50) divided by the dose that elicits a therapeutic response in 50 percent of the treated individuals (TD50). For instance, the therapeutic index of drug X is 9,000 milligrams per kilogram divided by 30 milligrams per kilogram and is equal to 300. The larger the therapeutic index, the safer the drug. Diazepam and digoxin are

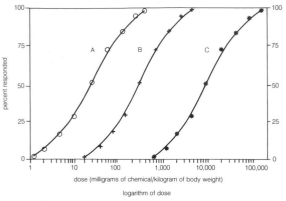

dose (milligrams of chemical/kilogram of body weight)

logarithm of dose

Figure 3: Dose–response curves (see text).

examples of drugs with a large and a small therapeutic index, respectively.

Morphological versus functional toxic responses. Chemicals can elicit various types of toxic responses, which can be classified by the nature of the response, the site of toxic action, the time it takes for the response to develop, and the chance of resolution of the response. The nature of the toxic response can be morphological (structural) or functional or both. In most cases, the chemical produces morphological changes in an organ, which in turn affects the function of the organ. In a small number of cases, the chemical produces functional changes in an organ without changing the structure of the organ.

Inhalation exposures to silica dust at a low concentration for 10 years or more can lead to chronic silicosis, a condition characterized by the formation in the lungs of silicotic nodules, which are egg-shaped lesions composed of layers of fibroblasts (reparative cells) and inflammatory cells surrounding a central silica particle. Such lesions can be considered a morphological toxic response; unless the silica exposure is prolonged, there will be little respiratory impairment because the lungs and certain other organs have a large functional reserve. If the silica exposure is prolonged, however, the silicotic nodules coalesce (complicated silicosis), and the structure of the lungs is altered so drastically that they do not distend easily during inspiration. Oxygen exchange in the alveoli is impaired, causing such functional toxic responses as breathlessness, chest tightness, and coughing with sputum.

Malathion exposure, on the other hand, can lead to functional toxic responses without causing any morphological changes. Malathion does not alter the structure of tissues; rather, it inhibits an enzyme, acetylcholinesterase, which normally degrades acetylcholine, the neurotransmitter of the parasympathetic nervous system. Inhibition of this enzyme leads to an exaggeration of the actions of the parasympathetic nervous system, including sweating, secretion of saliva, adjustment of pupil size, and defecation. The end results are increased perspiration, increased salivation, tearing, blurred vision, abdominal cramping, diarrhea, and if severe enough, death from respiratory depression.

Local versus systemic toxic responses. Toxic responses are also classified according to the site at which the response is produced. The site of toxic response can be local (at the site of first contact or portal of entry of the chemical) or systemic (produced in a tissue other than at the point of contact or portal of entry).

An example of a local toxic effect is the tissue corrosion produced by strong acids (*e.g.*, sulfuric acid) and bases (*e.g.*, sodium hydroxide) in contact with tissues. If the exposure is external, skin burns result; if ingested, the acid or base causes serious local damage to the esophagus and stomach.

An example of a systemic toxicant is methanol, which is absorbed and biotransformed into formic acid. The acid is responsible for metabolic acidosis and optic nerve damage in the retina of the eye, leading to visual impairment, a systemic effect.

Immediate versus delayed toxic responses. Toxic responses may also be classified according to the time it

takes for development of a toxic response. If it takes up to a few days after exposure, the response is considered immediate. There is no universal standard of minimum time for delayed toxic responses, but generally a response that takes more than a few days to develop is considered delayed. The time it takes for a systemic toxicant to act depends on many factors, such as the rates of absorption, biotransformation, distribution, and excretion, as well as the speed of action at the target site.

Reversible versus irreversible toxic responses. Toxic responses differ in their eventual outcomes; the body can recover from some toxic responses, while others are irreversible. Irritation of the upper respiratory tract by inhaled formaldehyde gas, for example, is rapidly reversible in that as soon as the inhalation exposure terminates, the irritation subsides. In contrast, the response produced by silica dust is irreversible because, once the silicotic nodules are formed, they remain in the alveolar region of the lung.

Chemically induced immune responses. The immune system protects the body against foreign substances, especially microbes and viruses. To be antigenic, a substance is usually both relatively large and foreign to the body. Large proteins are often strong antigens. Smaller chemicals can become antigenic by combining with proteins in chemicals called haptens.

The development of immunity toward an antigen is called sensitization. After exposure to an antigen, a combination of cellular and humoral immunity usually develops. Exposure routes that favour slow absorption into the bloodstream, such as percutaneous injection, often primarily elicit cellular immunity, while rapid routes of exposure, such as intravenous injection, favour the development of humoral immunity.

Cellular immunity utilizes phagocytes (such as macrophages, neutrophils, and eosinophils), which engulf antigens, and T-lymphocytes, which are thymus-derived, antigen-specific immune cells containing receptors specific for a special antigen. Cellular immunity is particularly important in defending the body against tumours and infections. Macrophages phagocytize antigens and secrete proteins (monokines) that regulate cells involved in immune responses. One monokine is interleukin-2, which stimulates an increase in the number of T-lymphocytes. The T-lymphocytes then develop surface receptors for specific antigens. Because T-lymphocytes survive for months or years, cellular immunity toward the antigen remains with the individual for a long time. If reexposed to the same antigen, the sensitized T-lymphocytes recognize the antigen and secrete their own proteins (lymphokines), which stimulate phagocytes to destroy the antigen. If an antigen is located on foreign or tumour cells, certain T-lymphocytes are transformed into cytotoxic T-lymphocytes, which destroy the target cells.

Humoral immunity utilizes antibodies, also known as immunoglobulins (Ig), produced by B-lymphocytes. B-lymphocytes are lymphocytes derived from the spleen, tonsils, and other lymphoid tissues. They become plasma cells, which make antibodies. There are five classes of antibodies: IgG, IgM, IgA, IgD, and IgE. IgG, IgM, and IgA are involved in humoral immunity, the function of IgD is not known, and IgE takes part in immediate hypersensitivity (see below).

Humoral immunity involves the inactivation, removal, or destruction of antigens. Antibodies can inactivate viruses by binding to them. With two antigen binding sites per protein unit, an antibody can also precipitate the antigen by cross-linking in a network formed with other antibodies. Because each IgM has five protein units, and thus five potential binding sites, IgM is particularly efficient in precipitating the antigen. After the antigen is precipitated, it can be removed by phagocytes. In addition, antigen binding by IgG or IgM activates a serum protein, called a complement, which can then initiate antigen precipitation, amplifying the inflammatory response. If the antigen is on the surface of certain cells, activated complement can also facilitate the lysis of these cells. IgG or IgM can also link the antigen to phagocytes or to killer cells, resulting in lysis of the cell by an unknown mechanism.

Although the immune system generally protects the body,

Nature of response

Classes of antibodies

Hypersensitivity (allergy)

it can respond in certain ways that are detrimental to some individuals. Allergy, or hypersensitivity, is a condition of increased reactivity of the immune system toward an antigen that leads to adverse effects. Substances that cause allergies are known as allergens.

Confusion is sometimes caused by the terms hypersensitivity, hypersusceptibility, and idiosyncrasy. Hypersensitivity is a reaction to a chemical or substance in certain individuals and has a basis in the immune system. Hypersusceptibility is an increased predisposition of certain individuals to react to a chemical. Because of biological variability among humans, some individuals respond to a chemical at a dose too low to produce a similar effect in others. Idiosyncrasy is a genetically determined hypersusceptibility.

Allergic responses differ from the usual toxic responses in three ways. First, the allergic response does not occur during the first exposure to an allergen, but is evident only after at least one previous exposure. In rare occasions, an allergic response can occur on the first exposure to a chemical if the individual has already developed a hypersensitivity toward a closely related chemical. For example, people allergic to one kind of penicillin are usually allergic to other penicillins as well. Second, allergy is specific to both the allergen and the individual. Unlike in a toxic response, in which everyone exposed develops the response if a sufficient dose is administered, only a small fraction of the exposed population is sensitized by an allergen, regardless of the dose. Third, the amount of a chemical required to elicit an allergic response is usually much less than that required to produce a toxic response.

There are four types of hypersensitivities (allergies): immediate, cytotoxic, immune-complex, and delayed. Each differs from the others in the mechanism of induction and the responses produced. Immediate hypersensitivity is the most common form of allergy. Delayed hypersensitivity is the second most common, whereas cytotoxic and immune-complex hypersensitivities are relatively rare.

Immediate hypersensitivity

Immediate hypersensitivity, also called anaphylaxis, produces IgE in response to an allergen that binds to the surface of mast cells or basophils. When reexposed to the allergen, the antigen-binding end of IgE on mast cells and basophils binds the allergen, triggering a release of anphylactic mediators from these cells. These mediators, such as histamine and serotonin, cause the contraction of certain smooth muscles (e.g., those of the respiratory tract, leading to bronchoconstriction in asthmatic attacks), relaxation of blood vessels (e.g., in the skin, resulting in redness, or in the whole body, causing a fall in blood pressure as in anaphylactic shock), and increased permeability of capillary walls (e.g., in the skin, leading to local edema as seen in urticaria). The unique characteristic of immediate hypersensitivity is its rapid onset, with the response initiated within a few minutes of allergen exposure.

The anaphylactic mediators affect tissues differently. Thus, the allergic response depends on where the immune reaction takes place. In the skin, immediate hypersensitivity can result in skin eruptions or urticaria, characterized by wheals with redness. In the respiratory system, it can produce hay fever or asthma. In the gastrointestinal tract, allergic gastroenteritis, which is an inflammatory condition of the stomach and intestine, may result. Systemic anaphylaxis may involve the entire body, with shock as a key feature of the reaction.

Other hypersensitivities

A second type of hypersensitivity is cytotoxic hypersensitivity, which has a gradual onset. After reexposure to an allergen, the allergen molecules attach to the surfaces of blood cells, forming an antigen new to the body. IgG or IgM binds to the new antigen on the blood cells, lysing blood cells via either complement fixation or antibody-dependent cell cytotoxicity. If the lysed cells are red blood cells, hemolytic anemia results. If platelets (the blood components intrinsic to blood clotting) are lysed, however, the blood clotting mechanism is impaired.

In a third type of allergy, immune-complex hypersensitivity, the allergen-IgG complex precipitates in tissues, resulting in inflammation via complement fixation. Immune-complex hypersensitivity in the kidney results in an inflammatory injury of the glomeruli (glomerulonephri-tis), and in the lung it leads to a pneumonia-like condition known as hypersensitivity pneumonitis.

Delayed hypersensitivity differs from other types in not involving humoral immunity. Upon reexposure to the allergen, sensitized T-lymphocytes release lymphokines, which trigger a series of inflammatory reactions. The inflammation leads to the development of allergic contact dermatitis in the skin and a chronic form of hypersensitivity pneumonitis in the lung. Symptoms of allergic contact dermatitis develop gradually, taking a day or two to reach maximum levels, which is the best way to distinguish allergic contact dermatitis from atopic dermatitis with similar symptoms. In contrast, the chronic form of hypersensitivity pneumonitis develops insidiously and not in a fixed time.

TERATOGENESIS

Teratogenesis is a prenatal toxicity characterized by structural or functional defects in the developing embryo or fetus. It also includes intrauterine growth retardation, death of the embryo or fetus, and transplacental carcinogenesis (in which chemical exposure of the mother initiates cancer development in the embryo or fetus, resulting in cancer in the progeny after birth).

Intrauterine human development has three stages: implantation, postimplantation, and fetal development. The first two stages are the embryonic stages and last through the first eight weeks after conception. The fetal stage begins in the ninth week and continues to birth.

Depending on the developmental stage, chemical exposure in the mother can result in different degrees of toxicity in the embryo or fetus. In the preimplantation period, a toxic chemical can kill some of the cells in the blastocyst, resulting in the death of the embryo. During the postimplantation period, chemical-induced cell death leads to one of two outcomes. If death is confined to those cells undergoing active cell division at the moment, the corresponding organs are affected, resulting in malformation. If the cell death is generalized without significant replication by the remaining cells to sustain life, the embryo dies. During the third, fetal, period, chemical injury can retard growth or, if severe enough, kill the fetus.

Critical periods

The genesis of a particular organ (organogenesis) occurs at a specific time during gestation and is not repeated. Because organogenesis is a tightly programmed sequence of events, each organ system has a critical period during which it is sensitive to chemical injury. Chemical exposure in a critical period is likely to produce malformations of that organ and not others; however, because there is some overlapping of critical periods of organ development and because chemicals frequently remain in the embryo for a period of time, malformations of more than one organ usually occur. Since organogenesis occurs mostly in the embryonic stages, chemical exposure in the first trimester should be minimized, if possible.

Mechanisms

Little is known about mechanisms of teratogenesis. It is thought that some teratogens produce malformations directly by killing the cells in the embryo. Teratogens can also produce malformations indirectly by causing maternal toxicity, resulting in oxygen or nutrient deficiency for the embryo. A few well-known examples are discussed below.

Thalidomide is a drug originally marketed to combat nausea and vomiting in pregnancy. It was discovered in the 1960s in West Germany to cause rare limb defects, among other congenital anomalies. The discoveries about thalidomide triggered legislation requiring teratogenicity testing for drugs.

Chronic alcohol ingestion during pregnancy is the most common cause of congenital problems in mental development. Ingestion of more than 30 millilitres (1 ounce) of ethyl alcohol per day during pregnancy can lead to the development of fetal alcohol syndrome, characterized by intrauterine growth retardation and subsequent learning disabilities, such as distractability, language disorders, and low IQ. Heavier consumption of alcohol, more than 60 millilitres per day, by a pregnant woman can result in malformations of the fetal brain and in spontaneous abortions.

Diethylstilbestrol (DES) is a drug used primarily from the 1940s to the '50s to prevent miscarriage. The drug is an example of a chemical that can produce transplacental carcinogenesis. It was discovered in the early 1970s that exposures to diethylstilbestrol before the ninth week of gestation could lead to the formation of rare vaginal and cervical cancers in female progenies.

CARCINOGENESIS

Carcinogens are chemicals that can produce tumours, abnormal tissue growths caused by a loss of control in cell replication. Most tumours are solid masses (*e.g.,* lung cancer), but some do not occur as tissue swellings (*e.g.,* leukemia).

Tumours may be benign or malignant. Benign tumours are to a certain degree controlled in their growth. As a result, benign tumours maintain some form of cellular organization and grow rather slowly over a period of years. In contrast, cell growth in malignant tumours is almost totally uncontrolled. Cells in malignant tumours grow very rapidly in a disoriented fashion.

Benign tumours are encapsulated by a fibrous layer and so do not invade surrounding tissue. Malignant tumours invade surrounding tissue. Thus, while a benign tumour grows at one site, a malignant tumour sends out cancerous cells via the blood and lymphatic system to distant sites of the body, spreading by a process known as metastasis. The invasion of surrounding tissues by a malignant tumour produces various symptoms.

Human carcinogenesis

Carcinogenesis is a complicated process in which many factors are known to play significant roles. Certain external environmental factors are important. For instance, cigarette smoking is known to cause predisposition to the development of lung cancer. A diet low in fibre content and high in fat is correlated with a high incidence of colorectal cancer. In addition, internal factors, such as hormonal imbalances and immunosuppression, can also increase the chance of developing tumours. Sensitivity to chemical carcinogens is known to be species-dependent. A chemical carcinogen may induce tumours in one animal species but not another, and a species that is sensitive to one carcinogen may be resistant to another. Known human carcinogens include some anticancer drugs, aromatic (containing a benzene ring in its chemical structure) amino and nitro compounds, metals, radionuclides, and miscellaneous chemicals. In humans the respiratory tract is the most common target for chemical carcinogens, followed by the liver and the blood.

Although there have been many theories on the mechanism of chemically induced tumour formation, it is now thought that DNA is the target of most chemical carcinogens. The carcinogens interact with the DNA and interfere with its normal function. Because DNA controls cellular functions, when DNA is damaged, the cell presumably loses control and divides in a chaotic fashion. A clone of the parent cell is generated, and these cells maintain the chaotic replication, which ultimately leads to the formation of a tumour. In general it takes 10 to 20 years for the initial DNA damage in one cell to develop into a recognizable tumour.

Carcinogens that are thought to produce cancer in laboratory animals by altering the DNA are referred to as genotoxic carcinogens. They are either direct-acting or indirect-acting chemicals.

Direct-acting (reactive) genotoxic chemicals can themselves interact with DNA. Indirect-acting genotoxic carcinogens do not bind to DNA until they have been biotransformed in the body to reactive chemicals. Among the indirect-acting carcinogens, polycyclic aromatic hydrocarbons, nitrosamines, and nitrosonornicotine are found in cigarette smoke. Polycyclic aromatic hydrocarbons are also formed in charcoal-broiled meat. Nitrosamines can be formed by the nitrosation of nitrite-cured, protein-rich food, such as nitrite-cured meat and fish, in the intestine.

Chemicals that produce cancer by a mechanism other than by binding to DNA are known as epigenetic carcinogens. The mechanisms by which epigenetic carcinogens produce tumours are not known with certainty, but various theories have been proposed. Cytotoxins are thought to kill cells in the target organ. The cell death increases cell replication by the remaining cells, which somehow results in tumour development, possibly by stimulating the division of cells that have previously had their DNA damaged by a genotoxic carcinogen.

It has been proposed that hormones and chemicals which modify the activities of the endocrine system create a physiological imbalance in organs dependent for their functioning on a particular hormone. With the imbalance, the organ may lose its normal physiological control and tumour growth may occur. This may be the mechanism by which estrogens in postmenopausal women lead to development of uterine cancer and the reason antithyroid agents, such as 3-amniotriazole, produce thyroid tumours.

Chemicals that depress the immune system are thought to produce tumours by impairing cell-mediated immunity, which is important in the normal elimination of tumour cells. The development of tumours involves two main steps: initiation and promotion. Initiation is the creation by genotoxic carcinogens of a cell with abnormal DNA. After initiation, promoters stimulate the replication of these neoplastic cells and facilitate the development of the tumour. Initiators include genotoxic chemicals. Although promoters do not produce tumours directly, they are still considered carcinogens because they can lead to the development of tumours in concert with an initiator. Promoters include large chlorinated hydrocarbon molecules (*e.g.,* DDT, PCBs, TCDD, butylated hydroxy antioxidants, and saccharin) and tetradecanoyl phorbol acetate in croton oil.

Development of tumours

MUTAGENESIS

Mutagenesis is the alteration of genes. Substances able to produce mutations are naturally genotoxic substances. Once a gene is mutated in a cell, the altered gene can be passed on to daughter cells. The body has ways to repair some of these gene alterations so that the genetic damage does not always propagate.

The effect that a mutation has depends on the cell in which the mutation occurs. In the somatic cells of most organs, mutation either has no effect, causes one cell to die, or causes a cell to divide at an uncontrolled rate so that a tumour develops. If the mutation occurs in germ cells (egg and sperms), there may be detectable changes or birth defects, or stillbirth may result.

Types of poison

In regard to poisoning, chemicals can be divided into three broad groups: agricultural and industrial chemicals, drugs and health care products, and biological poisons—*i.e.,* plant and animal sources. These three groups, along with a fourth category, radiation, are discussed below.

AGRICULTURAL AND INDUSTRIAL CHEMICALS

Agricultural chemicals. The majority of agricultural chemicals are pesticides, which include insecticides, herbicides, fungicides, fumigants, and rodenticides.

Insecticides. The four main classes of insecticides are organophosphates, carbamates, chlorinated hydrocarbons, and insecticides derived from plants (botanical). Organophosphate and carbamate insecticides act by inhibiting acetylcholinesterase, the enzyme that degrades acetylcholine (the messenger of the parasympathetic nervous system). As a result, acetylcholine levels remain high, exaggerating the normal functions of the parasympathetic system (Table 1). Effects such as salivation, lacrimation, urination, defecation, twitching of the skeletal muscles, and in severe poisoning, death from respiratory depression occur.

Chlorinated hydrocarbons used as insecticides, such as chlorophenothane (DDT), are larger molecules than the chlorinated hydrocarbons used as organic solvents, such as chloroform. The former stimulate the central nervous system; the latter depress it. The major toxic effect produced by these insecticides is convulsions (Table 1). The use of DDT is banned in many countries because of its environmental effects and because it may cause cancer in humans. DDT is a highly fat-soluble chemical that accumulates in fish, and, when birds eat such fish, the chemical also accumulates in their fat tissues. The DDT in the birds results in fragile eggs, which are prone to

DDT

Table 1: Agricultural Chemicals	
chemicals	toxicity, symptoms, and signs
Insecticides	
Organophosphates (*e.g.*, malathion, parathion)	parasympathetic excess
Carbamates (*e.g.*, carbaryl, carbofuran)	parasympathetic excess
Chlorinated hydrocarbons	
DDT, methoxychlor	CNS stimulation, convulsions, nausea, vomiting
Chlordecone (Kepone)	nausea, vomiting
Insecticides from plants	
Pyrethrins	allergic contact dermatitis, asthma, CNS stimulation
Rotenone	irritation of skin, eyes, and lung; mild CNS stimulation; breast tumours in rats
Herbicides	
Chlorophenoxyacetic acids	
2,4-dichlorophenoxy-acetic acid (2,4-D)	nausea, vomiting, fatigue, diarrhea, muscle ache and twitches, peripheral nerve damage, convulsion, memory loss, colour visual disorder
2,4,5-trichlorophenoxy-acetic acid (2,4,5-T)	irritation to skin, eyes, and nose; teratogenic in animals
Bipyridinium compounds	
Paraquat	lung fibrosis; kidney and liver damage
Diquat	nosebleed, cough, fever, jaundice
Others (*e.g.*, diuron, monuron, atrazine, simazine, chlorpropham, alachlor)	irritation to the skin, nose, and throat
Fungicides	
Pentachlorophenol	quite irritating to eyes, nose, and throat; anorexia; weakness; shortness of breath; chest pain; carcinogenic in animals
Creosote	extremely irritating to skin, eyes, nose, and throat
Ferbam, thiram	moderate irritation to eyes, nose, and throat; mild skin irritation; allergic contact dermatitis
Fumigant nematocides	
1,2-dibromo-3-chloropropane (DBCP)	mildly irritating to skin, eyes, and nose; testicular damage; carcinogenic in animals
Ethylene dibromide	severe irritation to skin, eyes, and throat; headache; anorexia; CNS depression; carcinogenic in animals
Methyl bromide	headache, nausea, vomiting, drowsiness, emotional disturbances, tremors, convulsion, coma, lung irritation, bronchial inflammation
Rodenticides	
Warfarin	internal bleeding
Strychnine	restlessness, increased audio and visual sensitivities, muscular stiffness in face and legs followed by convulsion
Thallium	hair loss; skin eruptions; intestinal bleeding; anorexia; nausea; vomiting; injuries of peripheral nerves, liver, and kidney
Plant growth regulators	
Daminozide (Alar)	carcinogenic in animals

breakage. This will ultimately decrease the population of fish-eating birds.

In general, insecticides derived from plants are low in toxicity. Pyrethrins are widely used insecticides in the home. They have a rapid "knockdown" for insects and have a low potential for producing toxicity in humans. The major toxicity of pyrethrins is allergy. Rotenone is a mild irritant and animal carcinogen (Table 1).

Herbicides. Herbicides are chemicals used to kill plants. Their potential to produce toxicity in humans is rather low. High doses of 2,4-D, however, can produce muscular and neurological symptoms (Table 1). The systemic toxicity of 2,4,5-T is lower than that of 2,4-D, but 2,4,5-T is more irritating.

During the Vietnam War, Agent Orange, a mixture of 2,4-D and 2,4,5-T, was used as a defoliant. The 2,4,5-T used in the Agent Orange was contaminated with tetrachlorodibenzodioxin (TCDD), or dioxin. Although TCDD is extremely toxic to some animals, it is less so to others, but it does cause birth defects and cancer in laboratory animals. The major toxicity of TCDD in humans is in the production of chloracne, a condition characterized by acne that appears between the eyes and the ears. In more severe form, acne may be found on the face, trunk, and buttocks. (Significant adverse health effects in the soldiers exposed to low amounts of TCDD in Vietnam have not been clearly established.) Polychlorinated biphenyls (PCBs) also produce chloracne by damaging the sebaceous glands in skin.

Rodenticides. Warfarin was originally developed as a drug to treat thromboembolism, a disease caused by blood clots, since it inhibits the synthesis of a factor essential for the clotting of blood. The inhibition of blood clotting by warfarin can lead to internal bleeding (Table 1), however. Because of its ability to induce internal bleeding, warfarin is also used as a rodenticide. [marginal note: Warfarin]

Plant growth regulator. Daminozide, also known as Alar, is a plant growth regulator used to improve the appearance and shelf life of apples. Because of its carcinogenicity in animals (Table 1), concerns have been raised that daminozide may produce tumours in children who consume apples. As a result, the use of daminozide has greatly decreased.

Industrial chemicals. The term industrial chemicals is used to refer to chemicals used neither in agriculture nor as drugs. Therefore, it includes chemicals used in industry, as well as chemicals found in or near households. Poisoning with industrial chemicals occurs most often by either percutaneous or inhalation routes.

Depression of the central nervous system is a common effect of most hydrocarbons (Table 2). Examples of common hydrocarbons include gasoline, toluene, and heptanes; n-hexane; and benzene. The hydrocarbons are lipid-soluble and dissolve in the membrane of nerve cells in the brain, perturbing their function. Depression, such as drowsiness, occurs as a result. In addition, many of the hydrocarbons sensitize the heart to fibrillation by epinephrine. The hydrocarbon n-hexane also causes damage to peripheral nerves. Benzene is toxic to organs like the bone marrow that form blood cells and can lead to the production of leukemia.

Most alcohols produce depression of the central nervous system, but some alcohols cause certain unique toxicities. Examples of common alcohols include methanol, ethanol, isopropanol, ethylene glycol, and phenol. Methanol can produce blindness after being metabolized to formic acid, which also leads to acidosis, characterized by an acidic pH in the body (lower than the normal pH of 7.4). Ethanol produces birth defects in both laboratory animals and humans. It also produces fetal alcohol syndrome, a major cause of mental retardation, in children of mothers who drink excessively while pregnant. Ethanol is toxic to the liver in chronic alcoholism and is a major cause of cirrhosis, a condition characterized by hardening of the liver. Phenol differs from other alcohols in causing damage to multiple organs. Finally, ethylene glycol, which is widely used as an antifreeze agent in automobiles, causes renal damage when it is biotransformed to oxalic acid, which crystallizes in the renal tubule (Table 2). [marginal note: Alcohols]

The major toxicity produced by aldehydes, such as formaldehyde, is irritation (Table 2). Formaldehyde can also cause allergic reactions in people who have been sensitized to it. Examples of other common aldehydes include acetaldehyde, glutaraldehyde, and acrolein. The toxicities of ketones and esters are similar to those of aldehydes in causing mainly irritation of the respiratory tract if inhaled and the gastrointestinal tract if ingested. (Table 2).

Aromatic amines and nitro compounds, for example, aniline, toluidine, and nitrobenzene, produce depression of the central nervous system and methemoglobinemia (Table 2). Methemoglobinemia is a condition in which the ferrous ion in hemoglobin, which is responsible for carrying oxygen, is oxidized to the ferric form. Oxidized hemoglobin, called methemoglobin, can still carry oxygen, but it does not readily release oxygen to tissues, so that the body, in effect, has a lack of oxygen. Some aromatic amines and nitro groups are known to cause bladder cancer.

Anhydrides and isocyanates   Because both anhydrides and isocyanates are highly reactive, they are extremely irritating to the upper respiratory tract (Table 2). If the airborne concentration is sufficiently high, the upper respiratory tract cannot remove all of the isocyanate or anhydride molecules, and pulmonary injury (mainly edema) results. Such a situation occurred in Bhopal, India, in the mid-1980s, when methyl isocyanate from a chemical plant was inadvertently released into the air, killing as many as 2,500 people and injuring thousands of others. Because they are chemically reactive, anhydrides and isocyanates also tend to cause hypersensitivity responses, such as asthma and allergic contact dermatitis. Common examples of anhydrides include maleic anhydride and phthalic anhydride; examples of isocyanates include methyl isocyanate and toluene diisocyanate.

Miscellaneous organic chemicals include such compounds as phosgene, carbon disulfide, and the halogenated aromatic compounds. Phosgene gained notoriety when it was used in chemical warfare in World War I. Like anhydrides and isocyanates, phosgene is highly reactive. Instead of reacting with the mucosal linings of the upper respiratory tract, however, it tends to react with the lungs, causing edema. As a result, the lungs' defenses against bacteria are weakened, and pneumonia may occur.

Halogenated aromatic compounds with more than one ring, such as polychlorinated biphenyls (PCBs), polybrominated biphenyls (PBBs), and 2,3,7,8-tetrachlorodibenzodioxin TCDD, can produce a number of toxic effects in laboratory animals, including cancer,

birth defects, liver injury, porphyria, and immunotoxicity (Table 2). The PCBs have been extensively used as a cooling agent in electrical transformers. It appears that humans are more resistant to the toxicity of these compounds than are some species of laboratory animals, and the main toxic effect observed in humans is chloracne, a skin condition similar to juvenile acne.

Examples of metal compounds that are toxic to humans include manganese, lead, cadmium, nickel, and arsenic compounds, beryllium oxide, and the elemental vapours, inorganic salts, and organic compounds of mercury. Chronic manganese exposure can cause damage to the brain, resulting in a condition with symptoms similar to Parkinson's disease, such as slurred speech, masklike face, and muscular rigidity. Mercury can also damage the brain, leading to behavioral changes; however, mercury is also toxic to the peripheral nervous system, causing sensory and motor symptoms. In addition, mercury is toxic to the kidney. Methyl mercury is especially toxic to the developing brain of a fetus.   Metal compounds

Lead is probably the most ubiquitous metal poison. Used for numerous purposes, before World War II it was a major constituent in paint, and it has been used in gasoline. Like mercury, lead is toxic to the nervous system and kidney (Table 2), but its toxicity is age-dependent. In children, the blood–brain barrier is not fully developed, and more lead enters the brain. The extent of damage depends on the exposure; at lower levels of exposure, small decreases in intelligence and behavioral changes may result, whereas high levels result in severe brain damage and death. In adults, lead tends to cause paralysis or weakness, indicative of peripheral nervous system damage.

Table 2: Industrial Chemicals

chemicals	toxicity, symptoms, and signs	chemicals	toxicity, symptoms, and signs
Hydrocarbons Gasoline, toluene, xylene, hexanes, n-hexane, heptanes	CNS depression, headache, nausea, vomiting, irritation of skin and eyes	**Corrosives (acids and alkalies)**	corrosion of skin, mouth, throat, stomach, and intestine on contact; irritation of eyes, nose, and throat if inhaled
Chlorinated hydrocarbons Chloroform, carbon tetrachloride, methylene chloride, and others	CNS depression, sensitization of heart muscle; many cause liver and kidney injuries; some cause liver tumours in animals	**Miscellaneous inorganic compounds** Hydrogen cyanide, potassium cyanide, sodium cyanide	drowsiness, dizziness, headache, rapid breathing, palpitations, weakness, muscle twitches, cyanosis, coma, convulsion
Alcohols Methanol	headache; nausea; vomiting; diarrhea; abdominal pain; restlessness; cold, clammy limbs; shortness of breath; CNS depression; blurred vision; blindness	Hydrogen sulfide, chlorine	irritating to skin, eyes, nose, throat, and lung; chest pain; lung edema; shortness of breath; pneumonia; headache; dizziness; nausea; vomiting
Ethanol	irritation of stomach, CNS depression, fetal alcohol syndrome; brain damage, amnesia, sleep disturbances, heart damage, fatty liver, liver cirrhosis	Sodium fluoride, stannous fluoride	irritations of mouth, stomach and intestine; CNS depression; tooth mottling; increased bone density
Aldehydes Formaldehyde	irritation of eyes, nose, and throat; headache; bronchitis; lung edema; asthma and allergic contact dermatitis; carcinogenic in animals	Bleaches (sodium hypochlorite, calcium hypoclorite)	irritation or corrosion of esophagus, stomach, and intestine; irritation of eyes and skin; acidic condition in the body; rapid breathing; aspiration-induced lung inflammation
Ketones	irritation of eyes, nose, and throat	Silica dust, asbestos fibres	lung fibrosis; shortness of breath; cough; chest pain; cancers of the lung, linings of the lung and abdomen, and intestine (asbestos)
Esters	irritation of eyes, nose, and throat; pulmonary edema	**Air pollutants** Sulfur dioxide	irritation of eyes, nose, throat, and lung; nausea and vomiting; shortness of breath; alterations in sense of smell and taste; unconsciousness
Aromatic amines and nitro compounds	CNS depression, methemoglobinemia; some are carcinogenic	Nitrogen oxides, ozone	irritation of eyes, nose, throat, and lung (dry throat with ozone); shortness of breath; bluish pale appearance; rapid breathing and pulse; pneumonia; nitrogen oxides also cause the destruction of red blood cells and cause liver and kidney damage
Anhydrides and isocyanates	irritation of skin, eyes, nose, and throat; asthma; allergic contact dermatitis		
Miscellaneous organic compounds Polychlorinated biphenyls (PCB), polybrominated biphenyls (PBB), tetrachlorodibenzodioxin (TCDD)	chloracne, liver injury; carcinogenic and teratogenic in animals	Carbon monoxide	weakness, confusion, headache, nausea and vomiting, dizziness, drowsiness, jaw stiffness, shortness of breath, seizures, coma, lung edema, pneumonia
Metals Lead compounds	Colic; abnormal red blood cells; injuries to kidney, peripheral nerves (weakness and palsy), and brain (irritability, restlessness, excitement, confusion, delirium, vomiting, visual disturbance); lead acetate is carcinogenic in rats		
Arsenic compounds	Edema, heart damage, low blood pressure, vomiting of blood, bloody stool, skin lesions, injuries of nervous systems, liver and kidney damage, cancers of skin and lung		

In acute cadmium poisoning by ingestion, irritation of the gastrointestinal tract is the major toxicity, causing nausea, vomiting, diarrhea, and abdominal cramps. With chronic exposure by inhalation, however, kidneys and lungs are the target organs. Arsenic compounds damage many organs. They cause skin lesions, decrease in heart contractility, blood vessel damage, and injuries of the nervous system, kidney, and liver. Arsenic compounds also produce skin and lung tumours in humans. Certain nickel and hexavalent chromium compounds, as well as beryllium oxide, are toxic to the lungs and can cause lung cancer.

Acids, such as sulfuric and hydrochloric acids, and strongly alkaline compounds, such as sodium hydroxide, and potassium hydroxide are corrosive to tissues on contact and can cause severe tissue injuries (Table 2). Sulfuric acid, sodium hydroxide, and potassium hydroxide are active ingredients in drain cleaners, the ingestion of which can cause severe chemical burns of the mouth and esophagus.

Hypochlorites are often used as bleaching agents. In low concentrations, as in household bleaches, hypochlorites have little toxicity but may be irritating to tissues; they can, however, be corrosive at high concentrations (Table 2). Cyanide ions poison the oxidative metabolic machinery of cells so that insufficient energy is generated. The effect is as if there were a lack of oxygen for the cells, even though there is plenty of oxygen in the blood (Table 2). Hydrogen sulfide and chlorine are highly irritating to the respiratory tract, with pulmonary edema the major toxic effect (Table 2). Chronic fluoride poisoning is called fluorosis, which is characterized by tooth mottling and increased bone density. These changes, especially of the bone, are related to a change in body calcium caused by fluoride. Silica and asbestos remain in the lungs for long periods of time, and both produce lung fibrosis (Table 2). In addition, asbestos is a well-known human carcinogen.

General air pollutants. Sulfur dioxide, an acidic pollutant, irritates the respiratory tract. It causes violent coughing when it irritates the throat, and may result in shortness of breath, lung edema, and pneumonia when it reaches the lungs.

Both ozone and nitrogen oxides are oxidizing pollutants. Like sulfur dioxide, they cause respiratory irritation; ozone and nitrogen oxides, however, tend to be more irritating to the lung than to the upper respiratory tract.

Carbon monoxide, an asphyxiating pollutant, binds to hemoglobin more strongly than oxygen does. Such binding produces a hemoglobin molecule that cannot carry its normal load of four oxygen molecules. In addition, once carbon monoxide is bound, the hemoglobin molecule does not as readily release to the tissues the oxygen molecules already bound to it. Therefore, tissues lack oxygen, resulting in many toxic effects. Because the brain is especially sensitive to the lack of oxygen, most of the symptoms are neurological. Lack of oxygen is termed asphyxiation, and thus carbon monoxide is an asphyxiant.

DRUGS AND HEALTH CARE PRODUCTS

Poisoning with drugs predominantly involves oral exposures. With drugs, therefore, irritation of the respiratory tract is rare, but anorexia, nausea, and vomiting resulting from gastrointestinal irritation are common.

Painkillers. Painkillers (analgesics) are the most commonly used drugs and account for many poisoning cases. Examples include aspirin and acetaminophen. Aspirin interferes with the oxidative burning of fuel by cells. To get energy, the cells switch to a less efficient way of burning fuel that does not use oxygen but generates a lot of heat. Increased perspiration develops to counteract a rise in body temperature, leading to dehydration and thirst. Aspirin also alters the pH in the body, affecting the central nervous system (Table 3). The major toxicity of acetaminophen is liver damage.

The major toxicity from narcotic analgesics, like morphine, is depression of the central nervous system, especially the brain centre controlling respiration. The cause of death in morphine overdoses is usually respiratory failure. Nausea is caused by morphine's stimulation of the chemoreceptor trigger zone in the brain, and constipation

is caused by morphine's depression of muscular activity in the intestine (Table 3).

Tranquilizers and sleeping pills. Benzodiazepines, such as diazepam, clonazepam, and chloridazepoxide, have a wide margin of safety when used at prescribed doses. Their major toxic effect is depression of the central nervous sys-

Margin notes: Hypochlorites; Carbon monoxide; Benzodiazepines

Table 3: Drugs and Health Care Products

drugs	toxicity, symptoms, and signs
Painkillers	
Aspirin, sodium salicylate	increased perspiration, respiration increased initially, dehydration, acidity in the body, hypoglycemia, CNS depression, respiration decreased, nausea, vomiting, diarrhea, confusion, coma, convulsion, lung edema, death
Acetaminophen	skin rash, decreases in blood cells, liver and kidney injuries, hypoglycemia, coma
Morphine	nausea, vomiting, pinpoint pupil, depressed respiration, delusions, confusion, muscle flaccidity, constipation, coma, death
Tranquilizers and sleeping pills	
Benzodiazepines	increased salivation, muscular incoordination, slurred speech, weakness, seizures, irritability, loss of appetite
Barbiturates	slowed respiration, CNS depression, depressed heartbeat, low blood pressure, shock, kidney failure, lung edema, pneumonia, muscular incoordination, slurred speech, pinpoint pupil, coma, death
Antipsychotic drugs	sympathetic blockade reflex increase in heart rate, parasympathetic blockade, tremors, rigidity, restlessness, jaundice
Nasal decongestants	nervousness, dizziness, tremor, confusion, increased blood pressure and heart rate
Antihistamines	drowsiness, dizziness, ear ringing, blurred vision, lack of coordination, headache, nausea, vomiting, loss of appetite, heartburn, dry mouth and throat, cough, palpitations, decrease in blood pressure, chest tightness, tingling of the hands
Cough medicine	CNS depression
Antiseptics	irritation of esophagus and stomach when ingested
Vitamins and iron pills	
Vitamin A	fatigue, dizziness, severe headache, vomiting, edema, dry and peeling skin, enlarged liver and spleen, teratogenic, red skin eruptions, abnormal hair growth
Iron	nausea, upper abdominal pain, diarrhea, bloody or brown vomit, dehydration, intestinal bleeding, liver damage, drowsiness, acidic condition in the body, rapid breathing, shock
Antidepressants	
Tricyclic antidepressants	parasympathetic blockade, CNS damage, cardiovascular system damage
Lithium salts	thyroid enlargement, edema, increased urination, abnormal heart rhythm, vomiting, diarrhea, tremor, muscle flaccidity, seizures, coma
Drugs of abuse	primarily CNS effects
Cardiovascular drugs	
Digitalis (e.g., digoxin, digitoxin)	gastrointestinal irritation, abdominal discomfort, salivation, fatigue, facial pain, visual disturbances, confusion, delirium, hallucinations
Beta blockers (e.g., propanolol, metoprolol)	constriction of bronchi, nausea, vomiting, diarrhea, constipation, headache, insomnia, dizziness, abnormal heart rhythm
Verapamil	headache, dizziness, gastrointestinal symptoms, edema, rash, abnormal heart rhythm, lowered blood pressure
Procainamide, quinidine	anorexia, nausea, vomiting, confusion, delirium, psychotic behaviour, abnormal heart rhythm, lowered blood pressure
Therapeutics for asthma	CNS stimulation

tem, which results in muscular incoordination and slurred speech (Table 3). For sleeping pills containing barbiturates, chloral hydrate, paraldehyde, and meprobamate, however, the margin of safety is much narrower, and the major toxicity is severe depression of the central nervous system, leading to respiratory and cardiovascular failure (Table 3).

Antipsychotic drugs. Like benzodiazepines, antipsychotic drugs such as chlorpromazine, perphenazine, and haloperidol have a relatively large therapeutic index, rarely causing fatalities. They occasionally may block the action of the parasympathetic and sympathetic nervous systems and thus produce such undesired effects as dry mouth and blurred vision from the former and a drop in blood pressure upon standing in the latter (Table 3).

Cold medications. Nasal decongestants, antihistamines, and cough medicine, which are found in over-the-counter preparations for treating the symptoms of colds, have a low potential to produce toxicity. Nasal decongestants, such as ephedrine, mimic the action of epinephrine by stimulating the sympathetic nervous system, and consequently, an overdose of ephedrine produces symptoms related to stimulation of the sympathetic and central nervous systems (Table 3). Depression of the central nervous system and parasympathetic blockade are two common toxicities of antihistamines such as diphenhydramine (Table 3). Depression of the central nervous system is also the major toxicity of dextromethorphan and codeine, both used to suppress coughing.

Antiseptics. Most antiseptics (*e.g.,* hydrogen peroxide, benzoyl peroxide, resorcinol, benzalkonium chloride, parabens, and cetylpyridinium chloride) produce gastrointestinal irritation if ingested (Table 3). Benzoyl peroxide and parabens applied to the skin may be toxic. Among the most toxic antiseptics are hexachlorophene, benzalkonium, and cetylpyridinium chloride, any of which can cause injuries to internal organs. Systemic toxicity (double vision, drowsiness, tremor, seizures, and death) with hexachlorophene is more likely to occur in babies because the relatively thin stratum corneum of their skin is highly permeable.

Vitamins and iron pills. Deficiencies as well as excesses of vitamins are harmful. Excessive vitamin A (retinol, or retinoic acid), known as hypervitaminosis A, can result in skin lesions, edema, and liver damage (Table 3). Overconsumption by Alaskan natives of polar bear liver, a rich source of vitamin A, has produced acute toxicities, characterized by irresistible sleepiness and severe headaches. Chronic poisoning with vitamin A can cause neurological symptoms, including pain, anorexia, fatigue, and irritability (Table 3).

Excess vitamin C can lead to kidney stones. Apart from irritation of the skin and respiratory tract, the most severe toxicity of vitamin K excess is the increased destruction of red blood cells, which leads to anemia and the accumulation of bilirubin, one of the products of hemoglobin degradation (Table 3). Excess bilirubin can result in brain damage in newborns, a condition known as kernicterus. Because the blood–brain barrier is not well developed in newborns, bilirubin enters and damages the brain. Due to the blood–brain barrier, kernicterus is not seen in adults.

Iron, a metal that is necessary for normal health, can also cause poisoning. The toxicity of iron is a result of its corrosive action on the stomach and intestine when present in high concentrations. As a result, intestinal bleeding occurs, which can lead to the development of shock (Table 3).

Antidepressants. Among tricyclic antidepressants, amitriptyline and imipramine account for most of the fatal cases of poisoning. These drugs have a number of effects, including blockage of the parasympathetic system and damage to the central nervous system, the latter producing symptoms such as fatigue, weakness, lowered body temperature, seizures, and respiratory depression (Table 3). Death is usually caused by damage to the heart. Lithium salts, used to treat manic depression, have a relatively low therapeutic index.

Drugs of abuse. Mind-altering drugs commonly abused include amphetamines, cocaine, phencyclidine, heroin, and methaqualone. These drugs are primarily toxic to the central nervous system; amphetamine and cocaine cause

stimulation of the system (hallucinations and delirium), and heroin causes the depression of the system (depressed respiration and coma). In contrast, phencyclidine and methaqualone are biphasic, producing first depression (drowsiness) and then stimulation of the central nervous system (delirium and seizures). Amphetamines also affect the gastrointestinal tract (anorexia, nausea, vomiting, diarrhea) and stimulate the cardiovascular system (increased blood pressure and heart rate, palpitations, and abnormal heart rhythm). In addition to hallucinations and delirium, cocaine causes euphoria, sexual arousal, confusion, and sympathetic stimulation. Phencyclidine is also known to cause aggression and psychotic behaviour, while methaqualone produces excessive dreaming and amnesia.

Cardiovascular drugs. Digitalis (*e.g.,* digoxin) is a class of drugs used for congestive heart failure, with a very narrow margin of safety. Digitalis overdose usually begins with gastrointestinal symptoms, such as anorexia, nausea, and vomiting, followed by sensory symptoms, such as pain and visual disturbances (Table 3). There are also effects on the central nervous system, characterized by delirium and hallucinations.

The major toxicities of beta blockers (*e.g,* propranolol and metoprolol) result from the blockage of sympathetic effects on the tracheobronchial tree (lung) and heart. Sympathetic stimulation relaxes smooth muscles in the tracheobronchial wall and makes the heart beat faster and more forcefully. Blockage produced by propranolol or metoprolol can cause bronchoconstriction and heart failure (Table 3).

Antiasthmatics. Drugs for treating asthma, such as theophylline and aminophylline, are structurally similar to caffeine. Like caffeine, which is a stimulant, theophylline and aminophylline also stimulate the central nervous system. Therefore, excitement, delirium, rapid breathing, increased heart rate, and seizures occur with an overdose. With excessive stimulation of the heart, palpitations and irregular heart rhythm (arrhythmia) can result, leading to sudden death.

POISONS OF BIOLOGICAL ORIGIN

Biotoxins can be conveniently grouped into three major categories: (1) microbial toxins, poisons produced by bacteria, blue-green algae, dinoflagellates, golden-brown algae, etc., (2) phytotoxins, poisons produced by plants, and (3) zootoxins, poisons produced by animals. The geographic distribution of poisonous organisms varies greatly; poison-producing microorganisms tend to be ubiquitous in their distribution. Poisonous plants and animals are found in greatest abundance and varieties in warm-temperate and tropical regions. Relatively few toxic organisms of any kind are found in polar latitudes.

Knowledge of the evolutionary significance and development of most biotoxins is largely speculative and poorly understood. In some instances they may have developed during the evolution of certain animal species as part of the food procurement mechanism (*e.g.,* in snakes; cnidarians, jellyfishes, and their relatives; mollusks, octopuses, and others; and spiders). Biotoxins may also function as defensive mechanisms, as in some snakes, fishes, arthropods (*e.g.,* insects, millipedes), and others. The defense may be quite complex—as in the protection of territorial rights for reproductive purposes—and inhibitory or antibiotic substances may be produced that result in the exclusion of competitive animal or plant species. Certain marine organisms and terrestrial plants may release into the water, air, or soil inhibitory substances that discourage the growth of other organisms; well-known examples include the production of antibiotic substances by microorganisms. Similar chemical-warfare mechanisms are used in battles for territorial rights among the inhabitants of a coral reef, a field, or a forest. Thus biotoxins play important roles in the regulation of natural populations. Of increasing interest has been the discovery that certain substances, which may be toxic to one group of organisms, may serve a vital function in the life processes of the source organism.

Importance to humans. Venom-producing animals and stinging and dermatogenic (*i.e.,* skin-poisoning) plants ca-

Digitalis

Evolutionary aspects of biotoxins

Excessive vitamin A

Table 4: Representative Toxic Microfungi

	toxin	comments
Claviceps purpurea (ergot)	"ergotaxine," a complex of toxic alkaloids, ergocryptine, ergocornine, ergocristine, and others	causes poisoning in animals and humans; produces vomiting, abdominal pain, numbness, nervous disorders, convulsions, gangrene, and abortion
Stachybotrys alternans	stachybotryotoxin	causes a toxicosis in animals and humans; produces stomatitis (inflammatory disease of the mouth), rhinitis (inflammation of the mucous membranes of the nose), conjunctivitis (inflammation of the inner surface of the eyelid), failure of blood to clot, blood abnormalities, neurological disturbances, and death
Aspergillus flavus and other species, *Penicillium* species	aflatoxin complex (16 or more known toxins)	causes toxicosis in animals and possibly man; toxins damage liver and kidneys; aflatoxin is one of the most potent liver-cancer-producing agents known
Fusarium sporotrichioides and other *Fusarium* species	fusariogenin, epicladosporic acid, fagicladosporic acid	causes alimentary toxic aleukia in animals and man; produces burning sensation of the mouth, tongue, throat, and stomach; causes nausea, vomiting, headache, cold extremities, hemorrhagic spots, convulsions, anemia, gangrene, death
Cladosporium epiphyllum and other species of *Cladosporium*	same as *Fusarium* species	
Pithomyces chartarum (*Sporidesmium bakeri*)	sporidesmin	causes facial eczema (an eruptive severe rash) in cattle; produces sensitization of the skin to sunlight, resulting in scab formation and sores; there may also be severe liver damage
Fusarium species, *Rhizopus* species, *Aspergillus* species, *Penicillium islandicum*, and others	luteoskyrin, "islanditoxin," citrinin, citreoviridin, and others; a large complex of poisons is involved	causes moldy or yellowed rice, which is toxic to animals and man; the effects in man have not been well defined; may cause nausea, vomiting, diarrhea, prostration, liver damage, and death; the effects vary greatly because of the various poisons involved

pable of inflicting pain and sometimes death by means of parenteral contact (*i.e.*, by bringing poisons into the body other than through the digestive tract) constitute environmental hazards. Biotoxic agents may produce their injurious effects by becoming involved in the food supply; ingestion of a poisonous microbial organism, plant, or marine animal or one of their toxic by-products may cause intoxication. An example is that of the shore fishes of many tropical islands; otherwise valuable food fishes are frequently contaminated by a poison called ciguatoxin. The poison, a potent neurotoxin (nerve poison), is accidentally ingested by the fishes in their food; such fish can no longer be used for either human or animal consumption.

Some of the effects produced by biotoxins on humans are of an acute nature, and the injuries they cause are readily discernible. The effects of some of the mycotoxins (poisons produced by fungi) and poisons produced by plants, however, are long-term and chronic; they result in the development of cancerous growths and other chronic degenerative changes that are sometimes difficult to detect.

Microbial toxins. Microbial poisons are produced by the Monera (bacteria and blue green algae) and Protista (algae, protozoa, and others), and the Fungi. Various classifications have been proposed for the microbial poisons, but none is entirely satisfactory. The problems encountered when dealing with these organisms result from a lack of precise knowledge concerning their biological nature and their phylogenetic relationships; in addition, their poisons show great diversity and chemical complexity. The following outline, however, is useful in dealing with this subject.

Moneran toxins. The prefixes "exo-" and "endo-" are retained in classifying the bacterial toxins mainly for historical reasons rather than because they are found either outside or inside the bacterial cell. The main differences in these toxins lie in their chemical structure.

Poisonous proteins from bacteria are sometimes referred to as bacterial exotoxins. The exotoxins are generally produced by gram-positive organisms (*i.e.*, bacteria that react in certain ways to the staining procedure known as Gram staining); at least two bacteria, *Shigella dysenteriae* and *Vibrio cholerae*, that produce exotoxins are gram-negative, however. The exotoxins usually do not contain any nonprotein substances, and most are antigenic; *i.e.*, they stimulate the formation of antibodies. The exotoxins may appear in the culture medium in which the bacteria are growing during the declining phases of growth; in some cases they are released at the time of normal destruction of the cells after death (autolysis). The exotoxins are less stable to heat than are the endotoxins, and they may be detoxified by agents that do not affect endotoxins. They are more toxic than endotoxins, and each exotoxin exerts specific effects which are collectively known as pharmacological properties. Exotoxins are neutralized by homologous antibodies—*i.e.*, the active agents in blood serum produced by a process involving the bacteria against which the serum is to be used.

Endotoxins are antigens composed of complexes of proteins, polysaccharides (large molecules built up of numerous sugars), and lipids (fats). The protein part determines the antigenicity, or quality of being reacted against as a foreign substance in a living organism. The polysaccharide part determines the immunological specificity, or limitations on the types of antibodies that can react with the endotoxin molecule and neutralize it (the immunological reaction). Some of the lipids possibly determine the toxicity. Endotoxins are derived from the bacterial cell wall and, when cells are grown in culture, are released only on autolysis. Endotoxins are not neutralized by homologous

Margin notes:
Entry methods for biological poisons

Bacterial exotoxins

Table 5: Representative Poisonous Mushrooms

	toxin	type of poisoning
Lorchel, or false morel (*Gyromitra esculenta*)	gyromitrin	toxicity to people is variable; causes severe liver damage accompanied by nausea, vomiting, abdominal pain, jaundice, enlarged and tender liver, coma, convulsions; fatality rate about 15 percent
Fly mushroom, or fly agaric (*Amanita muscaria*)	muscarine	symptoms develop rapidly and are severe, consisting of severe gastrointestinal disturbances, delirium, hallucinations, convulsions; rarely causes death
Death cap (*Amanita phalloides*)	amanitine, phalloidine	symptoms develop slowly, about 6–15 hours after eating: extreme abdominal pain, nausea, vomiting, excessive thirst, anuria (absence or defective excretion of urine), prostration, weakness, jaundice, cyanosis, convulsion, death; fatality rate about 50 percent; no known antidote but some treatment available
Boletus miniato-olivaceus	muscarine (?)	causes gastrointestinal and visual disturbances
Jack-o'-lantern fungus (*Clitocybe illudens*)	muscarine	causes gastrointestinal upset, not fatal
Inky cap (*Coprinus atramentarius*)	unknown	some people experience a peculiar type of intoxication after eating this mushroom and then drinking an alcoholic beverage: giddiness, gastrointestinal upset, prostration, and tachycardia (rapid heart action); the alcohol is believed to increase the solubility and absorption of the poison
Entoloma lividum	unknown	causes gastrointestinal upset, usually not fatal
Inocybe patouillardi	muscarine	symptoms are similar to *A. muscaria* poisoning
Lepiota morgani	unknown	causes gastrointestinal upset; fatalities have been reported
Mexican hallucinogenic mushroom (*Psilocybe mexicana*)	psilocybin, psilocin	causes euphoria, loss of sense of distance and size, and hallucinations

Table 6: Representative Poisonous Plants

name and distribution	toxic principle	toxic effects and comments
Plants poisonous to eat		
Rosary pea, or jequirity bean (*Abrus precatorius*); tropical regions	abrin (*N*-methyltryptophan) and abric acid	onset of symptoms may be delayed several hours to two days: vomiting, diarrhea, acute gastroenteritis, chills, convulsions, death from heart failure; one seed chewed may be fatal to a child
Aconite, or monkshood (*Aconitum napellus*); North America, Europe	aconite and a complex of other alkaloids	tingling, burning sensation in tongue, throat, skin; restlessness, respiratory distress, muscular uncoordination, vomiting, diarrhea, convulsions, possible death; an extremely poisonous plant
Corn cockle (*Agrostemma githago*); North America, Europe	githagin, agrostemmic acid (saponins)	dizziness, diarrhea, respiratory distress, vomiting, headache, sharp pains in spine, coma, death; frequent ingestion of small amounts results in chronic githagism (a disease, similar to lathyrism, that results in pain, burning and prickling sensations in lower extremities, and increasing paralysis); milled seeds may be found in wheat flour
Locoweed (*Astragalus* species); Northern Hemisphere	locoine	dullness, weakness, irregular behaviour, impaired vision, edema of eyelids, loss of muscular control, loss of appetite, emaciation, starvation, death in sheep, horses, and cattle
Belladonna (*Atropa belladonna*); United States, Europe, Asia	hyoscyamine, atropine, hyoscine, and a complex of other alkaloids	dryness of the skin, mouth, throat; difficulty in swallowing, flushing of the face, cyanosis (a bluish discoloration of skin due to insufficient oxygen), nausea, vomiting, slurred speech, coma, death; children and animals frequently poisoned by eating fruit
Akee (*Blighia sapida*)	hypoglycin A, B	sudden vomiting, drowsiness, muscular and nervous exhaustion, prostration, coma, death
Rape (*Brassica napus*)	glycosides (isothiocyanates)	pulmonary emphysema, respiratory distress, anemia, constipation, irritability, blindness in cattle
Marijuana (*Cannabis sativa*); United States, Mexico, tropical America	cannabinol, canabidiol, and related compounds	exaltation, inebriety, confusion, followed by central nervous system depression; prolonged, frequent use may produce dullness or mania; ingestion in large quantities or injection of the purified extract may produce death by cardiac depression
Water hemlock (*Cicuta maculata*); northern temperate regions	cicutoxin	abdominal pain, nausea, vomiting, diarrhea, respiratory distress, hypersalivation, convulsions, death; among the most poisonous plants
Poison hemlock (*Conium maculatum*); temperate United States, South America, northern Africa, Asia	coniine, conhydrine, *N*-methyleoniine, coniceine, and other alkaloids	muscular weakness, paralysis of extremities, blindness, respiratory paralysis, death; responsible for many human fatalities; leaves most toxic when plant is flowering
Purging croton (*Croton tiglium*); Asia, Pacific Islands, Africa	croton, croton resin, ricinine	vomiting, violent purging, collapse, death; croton oil is also a skin irritant, causing reddening, swelling, and pustules
Daphne (*Daphne mezereum*); temperate regions	glycoside involving aglycone dihydroxycoumarin	vomiting, burning sensation of the mouth, ulceration of the oral mucosa, diarrhea, stupor, weakness, convulsions, and death
Jimsonweed or thornapple (*Datura stramonium*); temperate and tropical regions	hyoscine, hyoscyamine, atropine	headache, nausea, vomiting, dizziness, thirst, dry and burning sensation in skin, mental confusion, mania, loss of memory, convulsions, death; children are often poisoned by eating seeds or sucking flowers
Larkspur (*Delphinium* species); northern temperate regions	delphinine, delphinoidine, delphisine, and other alkaloids	burning and inflammation of mouth, nausea, vomiting, respiratory distress, itching, cyanosis; one of the greatest causes of death in grazing livestock
Dumbcane (*Dieffenbachia seguine*); widely cultivated in temperate regions, tropical regions	protoanemonine, calcium oxalate	irritation and burning of the mouth, tongue, and lips; hypersalivation, swelling of the tongue, difficulty in swallowing and breathing
Foxglove (*Digitalis purpurea*); Europe, North America	glycosides, digitoxigenin, and others	loss of appetite, nausea, vomiting, slow pulse and irregular heartbeat, diarrhea, abdominal pain, headache, fatigue, drowsiness, convulsions, death
Wild yam (*Dioscorea hispida*); southern Asia, Pacific Islands	dioscorine	discomfort, then burning of the throat, giddiness, vomiting of blood, respiratory distress, drowsiness, exhaustion, paralysis of the nervous system, death; raw tubers are a frequent cause of death in the Philippines
Huanuco cocaine (*Erythroxylon coca*); tropics of both hemispheres	cocaine and other alkaloids	central nervous system stimulation followed by depression, numbness of tongue, paralysis of respiratory centres, cyanosis, respiratory distress, death; leaves are commonly chewed by Indians of Peru and Bolivia as a stimulant
Manchineel (*Hippomane mancinella*); Florida, Central America, South America, West Indies	physostigmine or a similar alkaloid plus a sapogenin	fruit causes gastroenteritis, which may be fatal, and causes ulceration of intestinal tract; sap causes burning of skin, swelling and hemorrhage of the eyes; sap is used as an arrow poison
Black henbane (*Hyoscyamus niger*); North America, Europe, Asia, Oceania	hyoscyamine, hyoscine, atropine, and other alkaloids	similar to belladonna poisoning caused by *Atropa belladonna*; children are poisoned by eating seeds and pods

antibodies and are relatively stable to heat; all of them have the same pharmacological properties.

The Cyanobacteria, or blue-green algae, are among the most primitive and widely distributed of all organisms. They have extreme temperature tolerances. Some strains of a species are toxic; other strains of the same species are not. Water blooms of blue-green algae have been responsible for the death of fishes, waterfowl, cattle, horses, swine, and other animals. Blue-green algae have also been implicated as causes of human intoxications.

Mycotoxins. Fungi are plantlike members of the kingdom Fungi (Mycota) that do not contain chlorophyll. A significant number are known to produce poisons of various types. Toxic fungi can be roughly divided into two main categories on the basis of their size: the smaller microfungi and the larger mushrooms. The toxic microfungi are members of one of two classes: Ascomycetes, or the sac fungi, and the Deuteromycetes, or the imperfect fungi (*i.e.,* fungi in which no sexual reproductive stages are known). The large toxic mushrooms, or toadstools, are mostly members of the class Basidiomycetes, although some Ascomycetes, such as the poisonous false morel (*Gyromitra esculenta*), may attain a size as large as some of the mushrooms.

The ability of certain fungi, such as ergot (*Claviceps purpurea*) and some mushrooms, to produce intoxication has long been known. During the 19th century it was recognized that molds are responsible for such diseases as yellow-rice toxicoses in Japan and alimentary toxic aleukia in Russia. The eruption of so-called turkey X disease in England in 1960 and the resulting discovery of the substance known as aflatoxin (see Table 4) stimulated study of the subject of mycotoxicology. Because mycotoxins have now been recognized as potential cancer-producing agents (carcinogens) that can become involved in man's food supply, they have become important in the study of environmental carcinogenesis.

Poisonous mushrooms, or toadstools as they are commonly called, are the widely distributed members of the class Basidiomycetes, although only a few are known to be poisonous when eaten (see Table 5); some of the poisons, however, are deadly. Most deaths attributed to mushroom poisoning result from eating members of the genus *Amanita*. Wild mushrooms should be eaten only if they have been accurately identified by an experienced person; the safest procedure is to eat only cultivated species. The problem of toxicity in mushrooms is complex; no single rule or test method exists by which the toxicity of a mushroom can be determined. The most poisonous species closely resemble some of the most prized edible species; in addition, toxicity within a given wild species may vary from one set of ecological conditions or from one geographical locality to the next. Moreover, although some mushrooms that are poisonous when fresh are edible when cooked, dried, salted, or preserved in some other way, others remain poisonous in spite of all preparation procedures. It has also been observed that some people may become poisoned by eating mushrooms that apparently do not affect others. As with microfungi, the mushroom poisons vary in their chemical and biological properties from species to species.

Protistan poisons. The dinoflagellates, important pro-

Poisonous mushrooms

Table 6: Representative Poisonous Plants (continued)

name and distribution	toxic principle	toxic effects and comments
Barbados nut (*Jatropha cucas*); tropics	curcin	burning of the throat, bloating, dizziness, vomiting, diarrhea, drowsiness, dysuria, leg cramps, violent purgative action; may be fatal to children
Mountain laurel (*Kalmia latifolia*); North America	andromedotoxin	hypersalivation, tears, impaired vision, tingling of skin, dizziness, vomiting, muscular paralysis, convulsions, coma, death; children are poisoned by eating leaves
Grass peavine (*Lathyrus sativus*); North America, Europe, northern Africa, Asia	β-aminopropionitrile	back pain, weakness in legs, paralysis; has caused death in children
Cassava (*Manihot esculenta*); tropics	cyanophoric glycosides	nausea, respiratory distress, twitching, staggering, convulsions, coma, death
Chinaberry (*Melia azedarach*); North America, southern Africa, Asia	azadarin	stomatitis with violent and bloody vomiting, paralysis
Opium poppy (*Papaver somniferum*); Europe, Asia, tropics	morphine, codeine, thebaine, papavarine, narcotine	central nervous system depression, pinpoint pupils, depressed respiration, cyanosis, coma, death
Pokeberry (*Phytolacca americana*); North America, Europe, southern Africa	phytolaccine	burning, bitterness in mouth, vomiting, purging, spasms, convulsions, death
Castor bean (*Ricinus communis*); United States, tropics	ricin, a toxalbumin	burning of mouth, throat, and stomach, vomiting, diarrhea, abdominal cramps, dulled vision, convulsions, respiratory distress, paralysis, death; one to three seeds may be fatal to children
Black nightshade (*Solanum nigrum*); North America, Europe	solanine, a glycoalkaloid	nausea, vomiting, abdominal pain, diarrhea, trembling, paralysis, coma, death
Plants poisonous by contact		
Euphorbia, spurge (*Euphorbia* species); worldwide	a complex of substances including alkaloids, glycosides, and others	eye irritation, blindness, blistering of the skin, swelling around the mouth, burning of the mouth, unconsciousness, death; milky sap is used as an arrow poison
Spurge nettle (*Jatropha stimulosus*); North America, Europe, Asia	toxin unknown	contact produces instant, intense stinging and itching due to an irritating substance injected into the skin by the stinging hairs; results in a skin eruption of minute red papular (small conical elevations of the skin) rash, which lasts about 30 minutes; a dull purplish discoloration of the skin may remain for several weeks
Shiney-leaf stinging tree, tree nettle (*Laportea photiniphylla*); Australia	5-hydroxytryptamine (and other toxic substances?)	contact with the stinging hairs of this plant produces intense, rapidly spreading pain, reddened rash, and later a severe skin eruption; severe stings may result in intense, unbearable pain; fatalities have been reported; dried leaves may cause intense sneezing
Poisonwood (*Metopium toxiferum*), West Indics, Florida	similar to poison ivy	contact with any part of the tree, especially sap, turns the skin black, causes a rash, blisters, etc., smoke from a burning tree is very irritating, causing illness and temporary blindness
Strophanthus (*Strophanthus* species); Florida, tropical America, Africa	an alkaloid, trigonelline, and a large number of cardiac glycosides and aglycones	vomiting, slow and irregular pulse, blurred vision, delirium, circulatory failure, death; used as an arrow poison
Curare (*Strychnos toxifera*); Central America and northern South America	toxiferines, caracurines, and other alkaloids	haziness of vision, relaxation of facial muscles, inability to raise head, loss of muscle control of arms, legs, and respiratory muscles, death; used as a poison for arrows and for blowgun darts
Poison ivy (*Toxicodendron radicans*, also called *Rhus toxicodendron*); North America	urushiol	skin irritation, swelling, blistering, itching; may be fatal to young children; smoke from burning plant is toxic
Plants that produce photosensitization		
Buckwheat (*Fagopyrum sagittatum*); North America, Europe	fagopyrin, a naphthodianthrone derivative	ingestion of the leaves by animals causes liver dysfunction, thereby resulting in deposition of a photosensitizing pigment in the skin; sunlight then causes redness of the skin, nervousness, swelling of the eyelids, convulsions, and prostration in farm animals
St. Johnswort (*Hypericum perforatum*); North America, Europe	hypericin, a naphthodianthrone derivative	similar to buckwheat
Plants that produce airborne allergies		
Box elder (*Acer negundo*); Northern Hemisphere	oleoresin and a water-soluble antigen	hay fever (respiratory allergy), may also cause an eczematous dermatitis of the exposed parts of the body

ducers of the primary food supply of the sea, are microscopic one-celled organisms that are dependent upon various inorganic nutrients in the water and upon radiant energy for photosynthesis, the process by which they produce their own food supplies. Although dinoflagellates inhabit both marine waters and freshwaters, most species are marine. Dinoflagellates are most often found in cool or temperate waters. During periods of planktonic blooms (times of high concentrations of microscopic organisms in the water) dinoflagellates multiply in large numbers. These planktonic blooms, sometimes referred to as red tide because they discolour the water, are often associated with weather disturbances that may bring about changes in water masses or upwellings. During periods of bloom large numbers of toxic dinoflagellates may be ingested by shellfish; the poisons accumulate in their digestive glands. Animals and humans may in turn be poisoned by eating poisoned shellfish. Certain species of dinoflagellates are capable of producing some of the most toxic substances known. The two species of dinoflagellates most commonly involved in human intoxications have been *Gonyaulax catenella* along the Pacific coast of North America and *G. tamarensis* along the eastern coast of North America. Intoxications from these organisms are known as paralytic shellfish poisoning. The symptoms, which begin with a tingling or burning sensation, then numbness of the lips, gums, tongue, and face, gradually spread. Gastrointestinal upset may be present. Other symptoms include weakness, joint aches, and muscular paralysis; death may result. There is no specific treatment or antidote. The poison, variously called paralytic shellfish poison, mussel poison, and saxitoxin, is a complex nonprotein nitrogen-contain-

Symptoms of paralytic shellfish poisoning

ing compound. Paralytic shellfish poisoning is best avoided by following local public-health quarantine regulations.

Respiratory irritation may result from the inhalation of toxic products in the windblown spray from red-tide areas containing the toxic dinoflagellate *Gymnodinium breve*, which is found in the Gulf of Mexico and Florida; the nature of the poison is unknown. Deaths of large numbers of brackish-water pond fishes because of *Prymnesium parvum* have been reported in Israel; the poison is known as prymnesin.

Plant poisons (phytotoxins). The study of plant poisons is known as phytotoxicology. Most of the poisonous higher plants are angiosperms, or flowering plants, but only a small percentage are recognized as poisonous. Several systems have been devised for the classification of poisonous plants, none of which is completely satisfactory. Poisonous plants may be classified according to the chemical nature of their toxic constituents, their phylogenetic relationship, or their botanical characteristics. The following classification, which is based on their toxic effects, has been found to be useful: (1) plants that are poisonous to eat, (2) plants that are poisonous upon contact, (3) plants that produce photosensitization, and (4) plants that produce airborne allergies (see Table 6).

Plant poisons, or phytotoxins, comprise a vast range of biologically active chemical substances, such as alkaloids, polypeptides, amines, glycosides, oxalates, resins, toxalbumins, and a large group of miscellaneous compounds whose chemical structure has not yet been determined. Alkaloids, most of which are found in plants, are characterized by the presence of nitrogen and their ability to combine with acids to form salts. They are usually bitter

Chemical variability of plant poisons

Table 7: Representative Animals Poisonous When Eaten		
name and distribution	toxic principle	toxic effects and comments
Protozoans—one-celled animals		
Dinoflagellate (*Gymnodinium breve*); Gulf of Mexico, Florida	unknown	irritation of mucous membranes of nose and throat; causes sneezing, coughing, respiratory distress due to inhalation of windblown spray from red tide areas
Dinoflagellate (*Gonyaulax catenella*); Pacific coast of North America	paralytic shellfish poison, saxitoxin ($C_{10}H_{15}N_7O_3 \cdot 2$ HCl)	tingling, burning sensation and numbness of lips, tongue, face, spreading elsewhere in the body; weakness, dizziness, joint aches, hypersalivation, intense thirst, difficulty in swallowing, muscular paralysis, and death; extremely toxic; usually involved with the eating of shellfish that have been feeding on toxic dinoflagellates
Mollusks—octopus, squid, shellfish, and others		
California mussel (*Mytilus californianus*); Pacific coast of North America	paralytic shellfish poison, saxitoxin	these mollusks become poisonous to eat because of feeding on toxic dinoflagellates; symptoms same as for dinoflagellates (*Gonyaulax* species)
Butter clam (*Saxidomus giganteus*); Alaska to California	same as California mussel	
Whelk (*Neptunea* species); Europe, Pacific region	tetramine	nausea, vomiting, diarrhea, weakness, fatigue; dizziness, photophobia (intolerance to light), impaired vision, and dryness of the mouth; poison is believed to be restricted to the salivary glands of the whelk
Turban shell (*Turbo argyrostoma*); tropical Pacific Ocean	poison believed to be related to ciguatoxin	diarrhea, weakness of the legs, fatigue; cold water produces a painful stinging sensation, itching; the illness closely resembles ciguatera fish poisoning
Callista shellfish (*Callista brevisiphonata*); Japan	a histamine-like substance, choline	flushing of the face, itching, urticaria (stinging sensation of skin), sensation of constriction of the chest, abdominal pain, nausea, respiratory distress, asthmatic attacks, paralysis, hypersalivation, numbness of the tongue, throat; recovery usually within 10 days
Arthropods—joint-legged animals: crabs, spiders, and others		
Shore crab (*Demania toxica*); Philippines	unknown	nausea, vomiting, diarrhea, muscular weakness, respiratory distress, difficulty in speaking, hypersalivation, muscular paralysis, convulsions, death
Crab (*Zozymus aeneus*); Indo-Pacific	similar to tetrodotoxin; toxicity of these crabs variable	tingling about the mouth, nausea, vomiting, muscular paralysis, coma, convulsions, death
Asiatic horseshoe crab (*Tachypleus tridentatus*); Southeast Asia	unknown	dizziness, headache, nausea, vomiting, abdominal pain, cardiac palpitation, numbness of the lips, weakness, muscular paralysis, hypersalivation, loss of consciousness, death
Sharks, eels, and other fish		
Greenland shark (*Somniosus microcephalus*); Arctic	unknown; flesh toxic; liver of tropical sharks very toxic and may also cause death	nausea, vomiting, diarrhea, abdominal pain, tingling and burning sensation of the tongue, throat, and esophagus, muscular cramps, respiratory distress, coma, death
Moray eel (*Gymnothorax javanicus*); Indo-Pacific†	ciguatoxin*	symptoms may develop rapidly or slowly; tingling about the lips, tongue, and throat, followed by numbness, nausea, vomiting, abdominal cramps, muscular weakness, paralysis, convulsions, teeth feeling loose, visual impairment, skin rash, hot objects feeling cold and vice versa ("Dry Ice" or "electric shock" sensation); loss of muscular coordination, coma, death in about 12 percent of the cases; known as ciguatera fish poisoning, this is one of the most common forms of fish poisoning
Red snapper (*Lutjanus bohar*); Indo-Pacific†	same as Moray eel	

*Fish poisoning is categorically referred to as "ichthyosarcotoxism," but there are several different forms of fish poisoning, such as ciguatera fish poisoning, clupeotoxism, scombrotoxism, and others. †More than 400 species of tropical reef fishes have been involved in ciguatera fish poisoning. These fish are normally edible but under certain conditions may become toxic.

in taste. It has been estimated that about 10 percent of the plant species contain some type of alkaloid. Only a few of the 5,000 alkaloids characterized thus far do not produce any biological activity; most cause a strong physiological reaction when administered to an animal. Amines are organic compounds containing nitrogen. A polypeptide is a string of three or more amino acids. A few polypeptides and amines are toxic to animals. Some glycosides, which are compounds that yield one or more sugars and one or more other compounds—aglycones (nonsugars)—when hydrolyzed (chemically degraded by the introduction of water molecules between adjacent subunits), are extremely toxic to animals. Toxicity resides in the aglycone component or a part of it. Oxalates are salts of oxalic acid, which under natural conditions is not toxic but becomes so because of the oxalate ion. Resins, a heterogeneous assemblage of complex compounds, differ widely in chemical properties but have certain similar physical properties. Some resins are physiologically very active, causing irritation to nervous and muscle tissue. Toxalbumins are highly toxic protein molecules that are produced by only a small number of plants. Ricin, a toxalbumin from the castor bean (*Ricinus communis*), is one of the most toxic substances known.

Under certain ecological conditions plants may become poisonous as a result of the accumulation of toxic inorganic minerals such as copper, lead, cadmium, fluorine, manganese, nitrates, or selenium. Photosensitization, an unusual toxic reaction resulting from the ingestion of certain plants, may be of two types. The toxic substance may be obtained directly from the plant, which thereupon acts on the skin (primary photosensitivity), or the toxicity may result from liver damage caused by the metabolism of a toxic plant and failure of the breakdown products to be eliminated by the liver (hepatic photosensitivity). In either case the animal reacts by becoming restless; in addition,

the skin reddens, and a severe sloughing of the skin develops. Death seldom occurs.

Poisonous plants exist throughout the world; representative species are listed in Table 6.

Animal poisons (zootoxins). Poisonous animals are widely distributed throughout the animal kingdom; the only major group that seems to be exempt is the birds.

Zootoxins can be divided into several categories: (1) oral poisons—those that are poisonous when eaten; (2) parenteral poisons, or venoms—those that are produced by a specialized poison gland and administered by means of a venom apparatus; and (3) crinotoxins—those that are produced by a specialized poison gland but are merely released into the environment, usually by means of a pore.

Oral zootoxins (see Table 7) are generally thought to be small molecules; most venoms (Table 8) are believed to be large molecules, usually a protein or a substance in close association with one. Venoms, which are produced by specialized poison glands, are injected by means of a mechanical device that is able to penetrate the flesh of the victim. Little is known about the biological or chemical properties of most crinotoxins (Table 9). The term poisonous may be used in the generic sense to refer to all three categories of zootoxins.

Some of the most complex relationships in biotoxicology are found in the marine environment. Certain marine biotoxins, such as ciguatera fish poison, apparently originate in marine plants, are ingested by herbivores and then passed on to carnivores and eventually to humans. The extremely complex mechanism by which this is accomplished is not clear. With the buildup of toxic industrial chemical pollutants in the marine environment, the problems of toxicity in marine organisms are becoming increasingly more serious. There is evidence that under certain conditions chemical pollutants may trigger biotoxicity cycles in marine organisms. The outbreaks in Japan of Minamata

Categories of zootoxins

Table 7: Representative Animals Poisonous When Eaten (continued)

name and distribution	toxic principle	toxic effects and comments
Thread herring (*Clupanodon thrissa*); Indo-Pacific	clupeotoxin, chemical nature unknown	metallic taste, nausea, vomiting, abdominal pain, vascular collapse, hypersalivation, numbness, muscular paralysis, convulsions, coma, death; this form of poisoning develops rapidly and violently; mortality rate is about 50 percent and death may come within a few minutes; this form of fish poisoning is known as clupeotoxism; no known antidote
Castor-oil fish (*Ruvettus pretiosus*); tropical Atlantic, Indo-Pacific	oleic acid	produces a painless diarrhea; poisoning known as gempylotoxism; no treatment needed
Skipjack tuna (*Euthynnus pelamis*); tropical seas Bluefin tuna (*Thunnus thynnus*); subtropical and temperate seas	saurine, a histamine-like substance; scombroid fishes (mackerels, tunas, swordfishes, and allies) contain a chemical constituent in their flesh called histidine; when histidine is acted upon, it forms a histamine-like substance called saurine; this occurs when the fishes are permitted to stand at room temperature for several hours; scombroid fishes are more susceptible to the development of saurine poison than most other kinds of fishes	the symptoms of acute scombroid poisoning resemble those of severe allergy: sharp, peppery taste, headache, throbbing of the large blood vessels of the neck, nausea, vomiting, massive red welts, and intense itching; recovery after 8-12 hours; this is probably the most common and cosmopolitan form of fish poisoning; antihistamines are used for treatment
Deadly death puffer (*Arothron hispidus*); tropical Pacific, Indian Ocean, Red Sea	tetrodotoxin ($C_{11}H_{17}O_8N_3 \pm y\ H_2O$)	tingling of lips and tongue, loss of motor coordination, floating sensation, hypersalivation, numbness of the entire body, muscular paralysis, difficulty in swallowing, weakness, nausea, vomiting, convulsions, about 60 percent fatality in humans; no known antidote
Amphibians California newt (*Taricha torosa*); California	tarichatoxin; poison said to be identical to tetrodotoxin; the eggs of this newt are extremely toxic	effects in humans are unknown; no known antidote
Reptiles Hawksbill turtle (*Eretmochelys imbricata*); tropical seas Leatherback turtle (*Dermochelys coriacea*); temperate and tropical seas	chelonitoxin, chemistry unknown; the flesh of some species of marine turtles is extremely poisonous	nausea, vomiting, diarrhea; burning sensation of lips, tongue, mouth; tightness of the chest, difficulty in swallowing, hypersalivation, foul breath, skin rash, sloughing of the skin, enlargement of the liver, coma, death; fatality rate is high; no known antidote
Mammals Sei whale (*Balaenoptera borealis*); North Pacific and North Atlantic oceans	unknown; livers of many marine mammals are toxic	intense headache, neck pain, photophobia, desquamation (peeling in scales) around the mouth and face, flushing of the face; antihistamines are used in treatment
White whale (*Delphinapterus leucas*); Arctic seas	unknown	flesh is poisonous and has caused fatalities in humans; no known antidote
Polar bear (*Thalarctos maritimus*); Arctic	vitamin A and possibly other toxic substances	intense throbbing headaches, nausea, vomiting, diarrhea, abdominal pain, dizziness, drowsiness, irritability, muscle cramps, visual disturbances, collapse, coma, rarely death

disease were the result of such a cycle: microorganisms, algae, shellfishes, and fishes ingested or absorbed industrial wastes with highly toxic organic compounds containing mercury and were in turn consumed by humans, causing a number of deaths among the population.

The relationships of representative poisonous animals and their position in the total framework of the animal kingdom can best be appreciated by categorizing them according to the group in which they belong. They are further grouped as to whether they are poisonous to eat, venomous, or crinotoxic in Tables 7, 8, and 9.

RADIATION

Radiation, radioactivity, and radioisotopes. Radiation is a flow of energy through space or matter. It takes the form of particles (*e.g.*, alpha and beta particles) or electromagnetic waves (*e.g.*, X rays, gamma rays, and visible and ultraviolet [UV] light). Radiation can be classified as either ionizing or nonionizing depending on its ability to produce ions in the matter it interacts with. Ionizing radiation is more toxic than nonionizing radiation.

Radioactivity is the emission of radiation caused by the disintegration of unstable nuclei of radioisotopes. After disintegration, a radioisotope may become a radioisotope of another element, which will further disintegrate. The disintegration series continues until a stable isotope is formed.

Ionizing radiation. Ionizing radiation is radiation that produces ions in matter during interaction with atoms in the matter. The toxic effect of ionizing radiation is related to the ionization. It is believed that ionization of tissues, composed mainly of water, generates H_2O^+ and H_2O^- ions, which in turn form H and OH radicals. Because radicals are very reactive chemically, biological damage, such as attacks on DNA and proteins, results.

There are two classes of ionizing radiation: particulate and electromagnetic. Alpha particles, beta particles, neutrons, and positrons are examples of particulate ionizing radiation. Gamma rays and X rays are electromagnetic ionizing radiation.

Among particulate ionizing radiation, alpha and beta particles are the forms most commonly encountered in the environment and are biologically the most significant. Composed of two neutrons and two protons and thus containing a 2^+ charge, alpha particles are the heaviest ionizing particles. Although they do not penetrate tissue very well, alpha particles turn many atoms in their short paths into ions, producing intense tissue ionization.

In contrast to alpha particles, beta particles are electrons of little mass carrying only one negative charge. They penetrate up to several millimetres in soft tissues. Their low mass and low charge mean that only moderate ionization is produced in tissues when beta particles collide with atoms in its path.

Gamma rays and X rays are electromagnetic radiation of similar properties, with gamma rays having higher energy than X rays. Gamma rays usually accompany the formation of alpha or beta particles. Neither gamma rays nor X rays carry a charge, and neither have mass; consequently, they can penetrate tissues easily, creating moderate ionization along their paths.

Biological damage is related to the degree of tissue ionization produced by radiation. Thus, a physical dose of alpha particles does not produce the same amount of damage as that produced by the same dose of beta particles, gamma rays, or X rays.

Radiation sources. Radiation is either natural or man-made. Natural radiation includes cosmic radiation, terrestrial radiation, radioisotopes inside human bodies, and radon gas. Cosmic radiation consists of charged particles from outer space, and terrestrial radiation of gamma rays from radionuclides in the Earth. Radioisotopes in human bodies come from the food, water, and air consumed. Cosmic and terrestrial radiation, together with radioisotopes inside human bodies, contribute only one-third of the total natural radiation dose. The remaining two-thirds can be attributed to radon, a radioactive gas released from soil that may reach a high level inside buildings with poor ventilation. Man-made radiation consists of radiation from medical and dental diagnostic procedures, at-

Table 8: Representative Venomous Animals That Inflict a Sting

name and distribution	toxic principle	toxic effects and comments
Cnidarians		
Portuguese man-of-war (*Physalia* species); tropical seas	tetramine, 5-hydroxytryptamine	immediate, intense stinging, throbbing, or burning sensation, shooting sensation, inflammatory rash, blistering of the skin, shock, collapse, in very rare cases death
Sea wasp (*Chironex fleckeri*); northern and northeast Australia	cardiotoxin	immediate, extremely painful stinging sensation, seared reddened lines wherever the tentacles touch the skin, large indurated whealike lesions, prostration, dizziness, circulatory failure, respiratory distress, rapid death in a high percentage of cases
Sea anemone (*Actinia equina*); Mediterranean, Black Sea, etc.	nature of venom unknown	burning, stinging sensation, itching, swelling, redness, ulceration, nausea, vomiting, prostration; no specific antidote available
Mollusks		
Cone shell (*Conus* species); tropical Indo-Pacific region	quaternary ammonium compounds and others	blanching at the site of injection, cyanosis of the surrounding area, numbness, stinging or burning sensation, blurring of vision, loss of speech, difficulty in swallowing, nausea, extreme weakness, coma, and death in some cases; no specific antidote
Spotted octopus (*Octopus maculosus*); Indo-Pacific, Indian Ocean	cephalotoxin, a neuromuscular poison	sharp burning pain, similar to a bee sting, numbness of the mouth and tongue, blurring of vision, loss of tactile sensation, difficulty in speech and swallowing, paralysis of legs, nausea, prostration, coma, and death in a high percentage of cases
Arthropods		
Kissing bug (*Triatoma* species); Latin America, United States	unknown	bite usually painless; later itching, edema about the bite, nausea, palpitation, redness; the bite is of relatively minor importance but spreads Chagas disease caused by a trypanosome (protozoan)
Puss caterpillar (*Megalopyge* species); United States, Latin America	unknown	stinging hairs of the caterpillar associated with poison-secreting glands; contact with the hairs produces an intense burning pain, itching, pustules, redness, nausea, fever, numbness, swelling, and paralysis; recovery usually within about six days
Honeybee (*Apis* species); worldwide	neurotoxin, hemolytic, melittin, hyaluronidase, phospholipase A, histamine, and others	sting produces acute local pain or burning sensation, blanching at the site of the sting surrounded by a zone of redness, and itching; local symptoms usually disappear after 24 hours; severe cases may develop massive swelling, redness, shock, prostration, vomiting, rapid heartbeat, respiratory distress, trembling, and death; it is estimated that 500 stings delivered in a short period of time can provide a lethal dose to a human; bees kill more people in the United States than do venomous reptiles
Bumblebee (*Bombus* species); temperate regions	similar to honeybee (*Apis*) venom	stings are similar to honeybee (*Apis*) stings; bumblebees are not as vicious as honeybees
Yellow jacket, hornet (*Vespula* species); temperate regions	similar to bee venom; also acetylcholine	they can both bite and sting; the sting is similar to that of the honeybee's but more painful; yellow jackets are quite aggressive; stings may be fatal
Wasp (*Polistes* species and *Vespa* species); worldwide	similar to bee venom; also acetylcholine	wasps are less aggressive than hornets, and their sting is similar to the honeybee's but generally less painful than the hornet's; stings may be fatal
Harvester ant (*Pogonomyrmex* species); United States	bradykinin, formic acid, hyaluronidase, hemolytic, phospholipase A, and others	ant stings cause immediate intense burning, blanched area at site of sting surrounded by redness, ulceration, fever, blistering, itching, hemorrhaging into the skin, eczematoid dermatitis, pustules, respiratory distress, prostration, coma, and death in some instances
Fire ant (*Solenopsis* species); United States, Latin America	similar to harvester-ant venom	similar to above; stings are very painful, burning sensation, etc.
Millipede (*Apheloria* species and others); temperate areas	hydrogen cyanide and benzaldehyde	toxic liquid or gas from lateral glands causes inflammation, swelling, and blindness in contact with eyes, and brown stain, redness, swelling, and vesicle formation in contact with skin
Centipede (*Scolopendra* species); temperate and tropical regions	hemolytic phospholipase and serotonin	local pain, swelling, and redness at bite site
Brown spider (*Loxosceles* species); United States, South America, Europe, Asia	cytotoxic, hyaluronidase, hemolytic, and others	bite causes stinging sensation or burning pain, blanching at site of bite surrounded by redness, blistering, hemorrhages into the skin and internal organs, ulceration, vomiting, fever, cardiovascular collapse, convulsions, sometimes death
Black widow (*Latrodectus* species); tropical and temperate regions	neurotoxic	bite may or may not be painful, two tiny red dots at site of bite, localized swelling after a few minutes; intense cramping pain of abdomen, legs, chest, back; rigidity of muscles lasting 12–48 hours, nausea, sweating, respiratory distress, priapism (abnormal, painful erection of the penis) in males, chills, skin rash, restlessness, fever, numbness, tingling; about 4 percent are fatal; antiserum is available
Tarantula (*Dugesiella* and *Lycosa* species); temperate and tropical regions	venom varies, usually mild	most of the large tarantulas found in the United States, Mexico, and Central America are harmless to humans; some of the large tropical species may be more poisonous, but their effects are largely localized
Scorpion (species of *Centruroides*, *Tityus*, and *Leiurus*); warm temperate and tropical regions	neurotoxin, cardiotoxin, hemolytic, lecithinase, hyaluronidase, and others	symptoms vary depending upon the species of scorpion; sting from the tail stinger causes a sharp burning sensation, swelling, sweating, restlessness, salivation, confusion, vomiting, abdominal pain, chest pain, numbness, muscular twitching, respiratory distress, convulsions, death; the mortality rate from stings from certain species of scorpions is very high; antiserum is available
Echinoderms		
Crown-of-thorns starfish (*Acanthaster planci*); Indo-Pacific	nature of poison unknown	penetration of the spines produces a painful wound, redness, swelling, vomiting, numbness, and paralysis
Long-spined sea urchin (*Diadema setosum*); Indo-Pacific	nature of poison unknown	penetration of the spines produces an immediate and intense burning sensation, redness, swelling, numbness, muscular paralysis
Sea urchin (*Toxopneustes pileolus*); Indo-Pacific	nature of poison unknown	bites from the stinging jaws or pedicellariae (small pincerlike organs) produce an immediate, intense, radiating pain, faintness, numbness, muscular paralysis, respiratory distress, and occasionally death
Sharks and rays		
Stingray (*Dasyatis* species); warm temperate and tropical seas	stingray venom, cardiotoxin, chemistry unknown	penetration of the tail spines inflicts jagged painful wounds that produce sharp, shooting, throbbing pain, fall in blood pressure, nausea, vomiting, cardiac failure, muscular paralysis, rarely death; no known antidote; stingrays are among the most common causes of envenomations in the marine environment
Bony fishes		
Weever fish (*Trachinus draco*); Mediterranean Sea	weever fish venom, chemistry unknown	opercular and dorsal fin spines can produce instant pain, burning, stabbing or crushing sensation; pain spreads and becomes progressively more intense, causing the victim to scream with anguish and suffer loss of consciousness, numbness about the wound, swelling, redness, nausea, delirium, difficulty in breathing, convulsions, and death; no known antidote
Scorpion fish (*Scorpaena* species); temperate and tropical seas	scorpion fish venom, chemistry unknown	fin spines can inflict painful stings and intense, immediate pain that may cause victim to scream followed by redness, swelling, loss of consciousness, ulceration of the wound, paralysis, cardiac failure, delirium, convulsions, nausea, prostration, and respiratory distress, but rarely death; no known antidote
Stonefish (*Synanceja* species); Indo-Pacific region	stonefish venom, chemistry unknown	produces an extremely painful sting by means of the dorsal fin spines; symptoms similar to other scorpion fish stings but more serious
Reptiles		
Gila monster (*Heloderma suspectum*); southwestern United States	heloderma venom, primarily a neurotoxin	all of the teeth are venomous; bite causes local pain, swelling, weakness, ringing of the ears, nausea, respiratory distress, cardiac failure; may cause death; no antiserum available

Table 8: Representative Venomous Animals That Inflict a Sting (continued)

name and distribution	toxic principle	toxic effects and comments
Rear-fanged snakes		
Boomslang (*Dispholidus typus*); Africa	coagulates the blood; proteolytic and other enzymes are present	local pain, swelling, hemorrhages; bleeding from nose, mouth, and skin; headache, vomiting, collapse, death; antiserum is available
Front-fixed-fanged snakes		
Death adder (*Acanthophis antarcticus*); Australia, New Guinea	coagulates blood; proteolytic and other enzymes present	effects of envenomation develop slowly (15–60 minutes); nausea, vomiting, faintness, drowsiness, staggering, slurred speech, respiratory distress, hemorrhages, death; antiserum available
Indian krait (*Bungarus candidus caeruleus*); India, Myanmar, Malaya, Indonesia	cholinesterase, protease, and other enzymes present	little pain or local reaction, latent period up to 12 hours; abdominal pain, staggering gait, difficulty in swallowing, stiffness of jaws, coma, respiratory distress, cardiac failure, death; antiserum available
Brown snake (*Demansia textilis*); Australia	cholinesterase, ophio-adenosinetriphosphatase, phospholipase, and other enzymes	latent period up to 12 hours; abdominal pain, vomiting, headache, dizziness, blood in the urine, weakness, respiratory and circulatory collapse, death; this snake is responsible for most of the deaths due to snake bite in Australia; very dangerous
Black mamba (*Dendroaspis polylepis*); Ethiopia, Somalia, Natal, southwest Africa	cholinesterase, L-amino-acid oxidase, ophio-adenosine, triphosphatase, and other substances	local pain, swelling, salivation, paralysis of vocal cords, sweating, vomiting, restlessness, drowsiness, collapse, coma, respiratory distress, death; one of the most dangerous of all living snakes; antiserum available; a large black mamba secretes enough venom to kill 10 men
Coral snake (*Micrurus corallinus*); subtropical South America	cholinesterase, hyaluronidase, L-amino-acid oxidase, and other enzymes	numbness without pain at bite, headache, swelling of face and lips, hyperesthesia (unusual sensitivity of skin), sore throat, drooping of eyelids, photophobia, vomiting, rapid heart rate, backache, irritability, salivation, death; there are about 40 species in the genus *Micrurus;* all species are dangerous; antiserum available for some species but not others
India cobra (*Naja naja*); southern Asia, Indonesia, Taiwan, Philippines	carboxypolypeptidase, cholinesterase, diastase, dipeptidase, polypeptidase, protease, and other enzymes; one of the most complex snake venoms	pain radiating from site of bite, edema, numbness, drooping of the eyelids and head, salivation, difficulty in speech, muscular incoordination, weakness, respiratory distress, blindness, incontinence, convulsions, death; antiserum available
Black-necked cobra (*Naja nigricollis*); Africa	cholinesterase, L-amino-acid oxidase, phospholipase, protease, and other enzymes	similar to poisonings by the Indian cobra; venom sometimes sprayed at eyes; produces an intense irritation, but permanent damage to eyes is rare; antiserum available
Tiger snake (*Notechis scutatus*); Australia	coagulates blood; cholinesterase, hyaluronidase, ophio-adenosine-triphosphatase, phosphatase, and other enzymes	latent period of 15–60 minutes; nausea, vomiting, faintness, sweating, drowsiness, staggering, slurred speech, difficulty in swallowing, drooping of eyelids, respiratory distress, death; antiserum available
King cobra (*Ophiophagus hannah*); India, Myanmar, Philippines, Thailand	cholinesterase, L-amino-acid oxidase, ophio-adenosinetriphosphotase	symptoms similar to those produced by other cobras; symptoms develop rapidly, death often occurs in 30–60 minutes; one of the largest of venomous snakes—obtains a length of 16 feet; antiserum available
Taipan (*Oxyuranus scutellatus*); Australia, New Guinea	lecithinase, phospholipase	symptoms similar to those produced by the tiger snake; its long fangs and potent venom make this one of the world's most dangerous snakes; produces flaccid paralysis, respiratory paralysis, often rapidly fatal; antiserum available
Australian black snake (*Pseudechis porphyriacus*); Australia	L-amino-acid oxidase, lecithinase, phospholipase	local pain and swelling, vomiting, hemorrhages from nose and mouth, prostration, hematuria (presence of blood in the urine), and sometimes death; usually the bites are nonfatal; antiserum available
Sea snakes		
Beaked sea snake (*Enhydrina schistosa*); Indo-Pacific	lecithinase	no local reaction; latent period minutes to hours; giddiness, muscle ache, muscular weakness, drooping of the eyelids, lockjaw, respiratory failure, acute renal (kidney) failure, death; all sea snakes are venomous, but only a few species have caused death in man
Erectile-fanged snakes		
Copperhead (*Ancistrodon contortrix*); eastern and southern United States	cholinesterase, L-amino-acid oxidase, phosphodiesterase, and other enzymes	local pain, swelling, necrosis, nausea, vomiting, shock, petechiae (minute bleeding spots), bloody stools, death; antiserum available
Eastern cottonmouth (*Ancistrodon piscivorus*); southeastern United States to central Texas	cephalinase, cholinesterase, hyaluronidase, lacithinase, and other enzymes	similar to poisoning by the copperhead but more severe; local necrosis more marked; death; antiserum available
Fer-de-lance (*Bothrops atrox*); central Mexico, south into South America	cholinesterase, deoxyribonuclease, L-amino-acid oxidase, protease, and other enzymes	local pain, bleeding from bite, gums, nose, mouth, rectum; blood fails to clot; shock, respiratory distress, hemorrhages into muscles and nervous system, death; antiserum available
Eastern diamondhead rattlesnake (*Crotalus adamanteus*); southeastern United States	cephalinase, cholinesterase, hyaluronidase, and other enzymes	local pain, edema, hemorrhaging into the tissues, dryness of the mouth, vomiting, shock, anemia, tingling sensation, blood in feces, difficulty in speech, yellow vision, loss of consciousness, death; antiserum available
Western diamondback rattlesnake (*Crotalus atrox*); southwestern United States	bradykininogen, cholinesterase, hyaluronidase, L-amino-acid oxidase, and other enzymes	symptoms similar to poisoning by *C. adamanteus*, but neurological symptoms less marked; antiserum available
Cascabel (*Crotalus durissus terrificus*); southern Mexico south to Argentina	cholinesterase, deoxyribonuclease, hyaluronidase, lecithinase, and other enzymes	symptoms similar to cobra bites, except that no edema occurs; antiserum available
Bushmaster (*Lachesis muta*); Costa Rica to northern South America	protease	very few bites recorded and little is known concerning the effects of the venom; severe prostration, rapid death; antiserum available
Taiwan habu (*Trimeresurus mucrosquamatus*); southeastern China, Taiwan	neurotoxin, amino-acid oxidase, hemorrhagin, and other substances	local pain, blistering, bleeding into the tissues, shock, death; antiserum available
True vipers		
Puff adder (*Bitis arietans*); Africa, Saudi Arabia	fibrinolytic, bradykininogen, cholinesterase, L-amino-acid oxidase, protease, and other substances	severe local edema, necrosis and sloughing of the tissues, restlessness, respiratory distress, gastrointestinal hemorrhages, death; antiserum available
Saw-scaled viper (*Echis carinatus*); India, Iraq, Saudi Arabia, Africa	carboxypolypeptidase, cholinesterase, dipeptidase, endopeptidase, and other enzymes	local pain and edema; hemorrhages into the skin, mucous membranes, and gastrointestinal tract; liver damage, shock, death; antiserum available
European viper (*Vipera berus*); Europe, Asia, Japan	bradykininogen, L-amino-acid oxidase	local pain and edema, hemorrhages along lymphatics, very little general reaction, vomiting, abdominal pain, shock, death; antiserum available
Russell's viper (*Vipera russelli*); Asia, Indonesia	carboxypolypeptidase, cholinesterase, dipeptidase, lipase, lecithinase, protease, and other enzymes	rapidly spreading edema with hemorrhages into the tissues, abdominal pain, vomiting; blood does not clot; loss of consciousness, circulatory failure, shock, death; antiserum available
Mammals		
Duck-billed platypus (*Ornithorhynchus anatinus*); Australia	protease and other enzymes	may inflict envenomation by means of the spurs on the hind legs of the male platypus; immediate intense pain, swelling, redness in the area of the sting, faintness, numbness about the wound, restlessness, prostration; no death recorded; recovery is uneventful after a few days
Short-tailed shrew (*Blarina brevicauda*); North America	neurotoxic, proteolytic	the lower incisor teeth are associated with submaxillary poison glands; bites produce localized pain, redness in the area of the bite, shooting pains, and general discomfort of the affected part; gradual recovery after several days; no fatalities recorded

Table 9: Representative Crinotoxic Animals*

name and distribution	toxic principle	toxic effects and comments
Sponges		
Red moss (*Microciona prolifera*); eastern United States coastal waters	unknown	contact with the sponge produces a chemical irritation of the skin, redness, stiffness of the finger joints, swelling, blisters, and pustules
Flatworms		
Flatworm (*Leptoplana tremellaris*); European coastal waters	unknown	poison is produced by epidermal skin glands; no human intoxications recorded; extracts from the skin of these worms injected into laboratory animals produces cardiac arrest
Arthropods—joint-legged animals		
Blister beetles (*Cantharis vesicatorea*); United States	cantharidin	toxic substance does not seem to be produced by special glands but is found throughout the body of the beetle; no discomfort at time of initial contact; after about 8–10 hours large blisters develop on the skin accompanied by slight burning or tingling sensation; swallowing of the beetles may cause kidney damage; cantharidin is used as an aphrodisiac known as Spanish fly—a very dangerous substance to use; ingestion can cause severe gastroenteritis, kidney damage, blood in the urine, priapism, profound collapse, and death
Millipedes (species of *Orthoporus*, *Rhinocrichus*, *Julus*, and *Spirobolus*); temperate and tropical regions	unknown	repugnatorial (distasteful to enemies) fluid may be exuded or forcefully squirted from body pores a distance up to 30 inches or more; contact with the skin causes mild to moderately intense burning pain, redness, and pigmentation of the skin; toxic fluid squirted in the eyes may cause temporary blindness, an inflammatory reaction, and pain
Venomous ticks (species of *Ixodes* and *Ornithodoros*); temperate and tropical regions	unknown	tick bites result in swelling, redness, intense pain, headache, muscle cramps, loss of memory, etc.
Fishes		
Sea lamprey (*Petromyzon marinus*); Atlantic Ocean	unknown	slime of the lamprey is toxic; ingestion may cause diarrhea
Soapfish (*Rypticus saponaceus*); tropical and subtropical Atlantic	neurotoxic	slime of fish is toxic; produces an irritation of the mucous membrane
Amphibians†		
European earth salamander (*Salamandra maculosa*); Europe	skin glands of the salamander are poisonous; contains the alkaloids samandarine, samandenone, samandine, samanine, samandarone, samandaridine, and others	effects on humans not known; affects the heart and nervous system; causes in animals convulsions, cardiac irregularity, paralysis, and death
Toads (*Bufo* species); temperate and tropical regions	bufotoxin, bufogenins, and 5-hydroxytryplanime; poison includes a complex of many substances	produces a poisonous secretion in the parotid glands and skin; handling of some toads may cause a skin irritation; ingestion causes nausea, vomiting, numbness of the mouth and tongue, and tightness of the chest; the poison has a digitalis-like action
Frogs (some species of *Dendrobates*, *Physalaemus*, and *Rana*); northern South America and Central America	skin secretions are poisonous; histamine, bufotenine, physalaemin, serotonin, and other substances; composition varies with the species	skin secretions produce a burning sensation when handled; used by Indians as an arrow poison
Tree frogs (some species of *Hyla* and *Phyllobates*); northern South America, Central America	skin secretions are poisonous; batrachotoxin, steroidal alkaloids, serotonin, histamine, and other substances; bufotenine varies with the species	some frog species produce a burning sensation and a skin rash when handled; skin secretions in the eye may produce a severe inflammatory reaction; if ingested, poison causes vomiting and abdominal pain; batrachotoxin is extremely toxic if injected; used by Indians as an arrow poison

*Animals in which poison glands are present and poison is released into the environment through a pore.   †Poisonous amphibians are sometimes referred to as "venomous," but they do not possess a true venom apparatus. They possess only poison glands.

mospheric tests of atomic bombs, emissions from nuclear plants, certain occupational activities, and some consumer products. The largest nonoccupational radiation sources are tobacco smoke for smokers and indoor radon gas for the nonsmoking population.

Emissions from nuclear power plants contribute only a very small portion of the total yearly radiation received. The low dose reflects the negligible amount of radionuclides released during normal operation, although the amount released can be much higher after a nuclear reactor accident. Not every reactor accident is a disaster, however. The 1979 accident at the Three Mile Island nuclear power station, near Harrisburg, Pa., released only a small amount of radiation (0.8 and 0.015 mSv within a 16- and 80-km radius, respectively), less than the background annual radiation dose. The nuclear reactor accident at Chernobyl in the Soviet Union, in 1986, however, was much more devastating, leading to more than 30 deaths and the evacuation of thousands of nearby residents.

Adverse effects of ionizing radiation.   Ionizing radiation quickly kills rapidly dividing cells. In general, immature blood cells in bone marrow, cells lining the mucosa of the gastrointestinal tract, and cells in the lower layers of the epidermis and in hair follicles are the most rapidly dividing cells in the body. As a result, radiation leads to the decreased production of blood cells, nausea, vomiting, diarrhea, malabsorption by the intestine, skin burns, and hair loss. Because of its relatively selective lethal effect on rapidly dividing cells, however, ionizing radiation is used in the treatment of certain cancers. Some cells in the embryo and fetus also divide rapidly, and thus ionizing radiation can cause malformations and even fetal death.

Ionizing radiation can also produce mutations by altering the DNA, and it can result in cancer.

Toxicities of whole-body ionizing radiation.   X rays and gamma rays irradiate the body uniformly and acutely affect all of the tissues discussed above. At sufficiently high doses, this type of radiation can lead to a condition known as acute radiation syndrome. The most sensitive tissue is the bone marrow, where blood cells are generated. The next tissue affected is the gastrointestinal tract. If the dose is high, the central nervous system is affected and the person becomes uncoordinated and disoriented and experiences tremors, convulsions, and coma. At even higher doses, the skin, eyes, and ovaries and testes are affected. Death may follow from 2 to 35 days after exposure. Exposure to radiation can also result in cancers of the bone marrow (leading to leukemia), lungs, kidneys, bladder, esophagus, stomach, colon, thyroid, or breasts.

Radioisotopes that are absorbed and distributed evenly throughout the body also can result in whole-body irradiation. Examples are tritium and cesium-137, both of which release beta particles that can lead to bone marrow toxicities and even, in the case of cesium-137, to death. The toxicity of tritium is less severe than that of cesium-137 because the beta particles generated by tritium are less energetic and because cesium-137 also releases gamma rays.

Local toxicities of common beta-particle emitters.   Unlike tritium and cesium-137, the isotopes strontium-90, iodine-131, and cerium-144 emit beta particles that are not distributed evenly in the body. Strontium-90 releases only beta particles, while iodine-131 and cerium-144 release both beta particles and gamma rays, but their toxicities are primarily caused by the beta particles. These radioisotopes produce toxicities in the tissues where they are stored or concentrated. Strontium-90 and cerium-144 chemically resemble calcium and as a result are stored in bone. Therefore, these two radioisotopes produce bone cancer and leukemia, which is a result of the irradiation of bone marrow. Iodine-131 is concentrated in the thyroid and produces thyroid damage and tumours.

Local toxicities of common alpha-particle emitters. There are radioisotopes that emit primarily alpha particles, together with some gamma rays. Because the destructive effect on tissues of alpha particles is far greater than that of gamma rays, the toxicities of these radioisotopes are contributed mainly by the alpha particles. Because of the limited penetrability of alpha particles, only tissues in the near vicinity of the isotopic molecules are affected. These radioisotopes typically produce tumours at the storage site.

Most of the common alpha-particle emitters belong to the uranium series, which consists of radioisotopes that form one after another, via a nuclear decay reaction, and release mainly alpha particles. The series starts with uranium-238. The nuclear disintegration of uranium-238 forms radium-226 which disintegrates to form radon gas (radon-222). Radon decays to form a series of daughter nuclides, most of which are alpha-particle-releasing isotopes, such as polonium-210. The radioisotopes in the uranium series are important because uranium is the starting fuel for many nuclear reactors and because daughter nuclides in this series are commonly found in the environment.

The toxicity of uranium-238 depends on the water solubility of the uranium compound. Water-soluble forms mainly cause kidney injury, while the insoluble forms produce fibrosis and cancer of the lung. Because of its similarity to calcium, radium-226 is stored mainly in the bone, and it produces abnormal changes in the bone marrow, including anemia and leukemia, cancers of the bone, and paranasal sinuses. The next radioisotope in the uranium series is radon, radon-222. Although radon is radioactive, its toxicity is not due to retention of the gas by the lungs but rather to the series of radioactive daughter nuclides in particulate form. These particulate daughter nuclides are deposited on the respiratory tract when inhaled, the respiratory tract is irradiated by the alpha particles released, and lung cancer can result.

Other radioisotopes do not belong to the uranium series. For example, radium-224, which is deposited mainly on bone surfaces, has been used in Europe to treat ankylosing spondylitis. Because of its short half-life (3.6 days), it affects only the bone surface and not the bone marrow. Its major toxicity is the production of bone cancer. Like uranium-238, plutonium-239, which is used in some nuclear reactors and in nuclear bombs, primarily releases alpha particles. Animal studies indicate that the toxicity of plutonium-239 is similar to that of insoluble uranium-238 in causing fibrosis and cancer of the lung.

Nonionizing radiation. Nonionizing radiation includes ultraviolet light, infrared radiation, microwaves, and radio frequencies, all of which are electromagnetic waves. The toxicity of radio frequencies is rather low. On the whole, nonionizing radiation is not as toxic as ionizing radiation, and the various forms of nonionization radiation share common target organs; particularly the skin and eyes.

Ultraviolet radiation. The toxicity of ultraviolet light depends on its wavelength. Ultraviolet-A (near UV) has a wavelength of 315–400 nanometres, ultraviolet-B (mid UV) has one of 280–315 nanometres, and ultraviolet-C (far UV) has one of 200–280 nanometres. Ultraviolet-A affects primarily the skin and causes burns at high energy levels. The toxicities of ultraviolet-B and ultraviolet-C are similar, but ultraviolet-C is less toxic because it does not penetrate tissues as deeply. Both ultraviolet-B and ultraviolet-C cause injuries to the eyes and skin. Ultraviolet-B is the major component of sunlight and accelerates the aging of skin by damaging the collagen fibres under it. Ultraviolet-B also is the cause of an occupational disease known as "welder's flash," or "arc eye," which is characterized by photophobia, tears in the eyes, spasm of the eyelids, and eye inflammation. Finally, ultraviolet-B can cause skin cancer, which may be a result of the linking of thymidines, a base in DNA, produced by ultraviolet-B radiation.

Infrared radiation and microwaves. The major mechanism of toxicity of infrared radiation and microwaves is the production of heat in tissues. Infrared-A (wavelength 0.8–1.4 micrometres) penetrates the skin, causing burns and pigmentation. Infrared-A also penetrates the liquid content of the eye to reach the retina and can therefore produce damage to all parts of the eye. In contrast, infrared-B and infrared-C (wavelength 1.4–3,000 micrometres) are almost completely absorbed by the superficial layers of the skin and eyes, and the damage is thus confined to the surface. Microwaves (wavelength 1 millimetre to 1 metre) produce heat in tissues. Because testes and eyes do not dissipate heat well, due to low blood flow through these organs, temporary sterility and cataracts can be produced by microwaves.

Lasers. Lasers are high-energy light beams, visible and nonvisible, generated by atoms at an excited state and further amplified by optics. Like most other nonionizing radiation, lasers can produce skin burns. Visible lasers, with a wavelength from 0.4 to 1.4 micrometres, will cause retinal damage if they enter the eyes and are focused by the lens onto the retina.

BIBLIOGRAPHY

Toxic substances: CURTIS D. KLAASSEN, MARY O. AMDUR, and JOHN DOULL (eds.), *Casarett and Doull's Toxicology: The Basic Science of Poisons,* 3rd ed. (1986), contains in-depth discussions of basic toxicology principles. Analysis of the chemical structure of toxins influencing their effect is provided in STANLEY E. MANAHAN, *Toxicological Chemistry: A Guide to Toxic Substances in Chemistry* (1989). MICHAEL A. KAMRIN, *Toxicology: A Primer on Toxicology Principles and Applications* (1988), is a concise, nontechnical general introduction. ERNEST HODGSON, RICHARD B. MAILMAN, and JANICE E. CHAMBERS, *Dictionary of Toxicology* (1988), explains concepts and terminology and covers organizations and authorities in the field.

Exposure and response to poisons: ROBERT H. DREISBACH and WILLIAM O. ROBERTSON, *Handbook of Poisoning: Prevention, Diagnosis, & Treatment,* 12th ed. (1987), contains concise information on the treatment of poisoning by biological toxins and drugs. AVRAM GOLDSTEIN, LEWIS ARONOW, and SUMNER M. KALMAN, *Principles of Drug Action: The Basis of Pharmacology,* 2nd ed. (1973), describes the principles governing chemical absorption, distribution, and excretion of the substances. MATTHEW J. ELLENHORN and DONALD G. BARCELOUX, *Medical Toxicology: Diagnosis and Treatments of Human Poisoning* (1988), focuses on the poisons derived from biological sources. SIDNEY KAYE, *Handbook of Emergency Toxicology: A Guide for the Identification, Diagnosis, and Treatment of Poisoning,* 5th ed. (1988), surveys almost 200 toxic substances.

Sources of poisoning: GEORGE D. CLAYTON and FLORENCE E. CLAYTON (eds.), *Patty's Industrial Hygiene and Toxicology,* 3rd. rev. ed., vol. 2, *Toxicology,* parts A, B, and C (1981–82), is an extensive compendium of information on the toxicology of industrial chemicals. For concise reference on the subject, see ALICE HAMILTON, *Hamilton and Hardy's Industrial Toxicology,* 4th ed., rev. by ASHER J. FINKEL (1983). Information on chemical ingredients of many commercial products is detailed in ROBERT E. GOSSELIN, ROGER P. SMITH, and HAROLD C. HODGE, *Clinical Toxicology of Commercial Products,* 5th ed. (1984). ALFRED GOODMAN GILMAN et al. (eds.), *Goodman and Gilman's The Pharmacological Basis of Therapeutics,* 7th ed. (1985), is an authoritative source of information on the toxicology of drugs.

The toxicology of food is the subject of JOINT FAO/WHO COMMITTEE ON FOOD ADDITIVES, *Toxicological Evaluation of Certain Food Additives* (1988), including lists of acceptable consumption of flavourings, preservatives, and colours; JOSE M. CONCON, *Food Toxicology,* 2 vol. (1988), a comprehensive survey of food contamination and poisoning; PALLE KROGH (ed.), *Mycotoxins in Food* (1987); and W.F.O. MARASAS and PAUL E. NELSON, *Mycotoxicology: Introduction to the Mycology, Plant Pathology, Chemistry, Toxicology, and Pathology of Naturally Occuring Mycotoxicoses in Animals and Man* (1987). BRUCE W. HALSTEAD, *Poisonous and Venomous Marine Animals of the World,* 2nd rev. ed. (1988), is an exhaustive and profusely illustrated compendium on the toxic marine animals of the world, from protozoans to polar bears.

BRUCE W. HALSTEAD. Director, World Life Research Institute, Colton, Calif.
CURTIS D. KLAASSEN. Professor of Pharmacology, University of Kansas Medical Center, Kansas City.
KING LIT WONG. Senior Research Scientist in Toxicology, Krug International, Lyndon B. Johnson Space Center, Houston, Texas.

WORLD
OF
MEDICINE

Alphabetical review of
recent developments
in health and medicine

Adolescent Medicine

Adolescents growing up in the 1990s are generally articulate and aware, and they are exposed to many stimulating and exciting challenges. They are called upon to integrate into their changing lives an extraordinary array of relationships and behaviors. They may also become overwhelmed and confused by the complexities of contemporary society and by the mixed messages they receive from adults, peers, and the media. Many of their questions, concerns, and needs are health related. The specialty of adolescent medicine was founded approximately 40 years ago in order to increase physicians' understanding, knowledge, and skills so that they might better meet the challenges posed by these young patients. Much has been learned in that time, but a great deal remains to be done so that this knowledge can be applied effectively. In fact, adolescents today constitute the only population group in the United States that has *not* experienced an improvement in health status over the past 40 years.

Less-than-adequate health care

A recent survey of 9th- through 12th-graders, performed in a middle-class suburban community in which over 90% of the students had a private physician, indicated a wide range of unmet health care needs. Despite ready access to medical care, these students reported that they were not being helped in four important areas: (1) sexuality; *e.g.,* care related to birth control and sexually transmitted diseases; (2) body-image concerns, especially perceived weight problems among girls and skin problems in both sexes; (3) worries pertaining to smoking and drug and alcohol use; and (4) depression. The adolescents in this community were quite typical of adolescents across the U.S.—by high-school graduation approximately half had had sexual intercourse; 20–25% were "regular" users of alcohol or drugs; more girls than boys smoked cigarettes; 40% of the girls perceived themselves as overweight; and 4% of the students reported serious and persistent depression.

A subsequent survey of pediatricians confirmed the student-survey findings. Very few pediatricians (approximately 10%) provided comprehensive care to their adolescent patients. Fewer than half routinely discussed sexuality or drug use with teens, and very few questioned their adolescent patients about depression or physical or sexual abuse. Most of the pediatricians cited their inadequate knowledge and skills and their "too-busy" practices of mainly infants and babies as the most pertinent obstacles to providing better care for their teenage patients. Although these student and pediatrician surveys sampled small geographic regions, other regional and national surveys have shown similar deficiencies.

Historical perspective

The medical specialty of adolescent medicine was founded in the U.S. by J. Roswell Gallagher in 1951 when he established the country's first adolescent clinic at Children's Hospital in Boston. Gallagher recognized that the health needs of teenagers were not being optimally met within traditional medical care settings; adolescents were "out of place" both in pediatricians' offices, which focused on babies and young children, and in the offices of most internists and general practitioners, whose patients were mainly adults.

The concept of health care targeted specifically to meeting the physical and emotional needs of adolescents received increased acceptance during the 1960s. During that time "health-risk behaviors" that were common in adolescents became known. Media attention was given to the involvement of young people with drugs and alcohol. And teenage sexual activity and violent, "sensation-seeking," and "authority-challenging" behaviors brought the message to the fore that adolescence was a unique time of life—one that is *not* the healthiest.

In 1968 the Society for Adolescent Medicine was founded by a small group of "pioneer" physicians, mainly from medical school departments of pediatrics and medicine. Their mission then was to begin to define formally the field of adolescent medicine, to establish a curriculum for training physicians to provide more effective care for this age group, and to encourage research into adolescent health and illness. In 1972 the American Academy of Pediatrics officially declared that the purview of pediatricians should extend up to their patients' 21st birthdays. Shortly thereafter, an increasing number of university departments of pediatrics around the country began to recruit "specialists" in adolescent medicine in order to establish clinical and training programs. Nonetheless, by 1978 a task force on pediatric education had found that training in adolescent medicine remained deficient for most pediatricians; the task force stressed that this training needed to be broadened. The recommendation, unfortunately, still has not been universally applied, and many pediatrics training programs today offer minimal exposure to adolescent medicine.

Nonetheless, there was increasing dissemination of information pertinent to the health needs of adolescents in the 1980s, and by 1991 the Society for Adolescent Medicine had approximately 1,000 members. The decade of the '90s will see the establishment of an adolescent medicine specialty examination by the American Board of Pediatric Subspecialties—a move that is viewed by many as the ultimate recognition of adolescent medicine as a discrete clinical specialty.

Defining teen health needs

When does "adolescence" begin and end? And what specifically are the health needs of this age group?

Adolescence is a unique time of life—one that is marked by experimentation and risk taking. According to a 1990 report on adolescent health by the American Medical Association, more than half of teenagers do not use seat belts, and 44% reported that they had ridden in an automobile with a driver who had been drinking or using drugs.

The age boundaries of adolescence may arbitrarily be set at 12 and 21. Alternatively, one may take a broader view and say that adolescence begins with the onset of puberty (which for some girls may be as early as age eight or nine) and ends somewhere in the mid- to late twenties when the individual has established an independent, "mature" life-style.

The specific health problems of adolescents may be categorized as (1) unique to this age group (*e.g.,* acne, scoliosis, anorexia nervosa, delayed puberty); (2) shared with other age groups (appendicitis, ear infections); (3) complicated by a chronic illness (*e.g.,* diabetes) or handicap (*e.g.,* spina bifida) in age-specific ways; or (4) biopsychosocial; *i.e.,* resulting from teenage risk-taking behaviors (smoking, drinking, drug use, unsafe sexual practices) or from being depressed, anxious, or otherwise psychologically compromised. An alternative format for categorizing teen health needs delineates problems that (1) are specific to adolescence (acne, anorexia nervosa, scoliosis, delayed puberty); (2) are exacerbated by adolescence (diabetes mellitus and other conditions requiring vigilant adherence to a treatment regimen); or (3) have their origin in adolescence (drug abuse, infertility, obesity, hypercholesterolemia, schizophrenia).

Whichever way one views the health problems of adolescents, it is apparent that their needs are broad and varied, often quite specific to their age group, and frequently related to their social environment and developmental maturity. The special attraction and challenge of practicing adolescent medicine must include an appreciation and enjoyment of the young person who is experiencing such dramatic physical and psychological transitions, as well as an understanding of the social context (family, school, peer group, community, economic status) in which the young person

resides. This is a very tall order for many health professionals who have neither the training, the time, nor—often—the interest to focus on the adolescent in this way.

Adolescent physical development

The prepubertal child is faced with very dramatic physical growth and body transformations that occur rapidly over a few years. This physical process consists of a marked increase in height and especially weight, changes in body composition, and development of secondary sexual characteristics. The average 10-year-old boy's height will increase 30% and his weight will more than double by age 18. The initial pubertal event in boys is enlargement of the testicles at an average age of 12, followed by growth of pubic hair and enlargement of the penis. Boys are still growing rapidly late in their pubertal development, and some boys continue to grow even after the high-school years. Although the sequence of pubertal events follows a fairly predictable pattern, the age of onset and the rapidity of these changes are quite variable, and those teens falling out of the "average" range may understandably suffer considerable self-consciousness for a time.

The average girl will increase 20% in height during early adolescence—most of it occurring prior to the onset of menstruation. Her weight will typically increase about 70%, or approximately 4.5 kg (10 lb) per year, from age 11 to 14 and then continue to rise more slowly thereafter. While greater muscle mass constitutes much of boys' added weight, girls naturally acquire new curves, comprised of fatty-tissue accumulation in certain areas (especially legs, buttocks, abdomen, and breasts). Girls typically begin to mature physically at a younger age than boys, as a glance at any fifth- or sixth-grade class will show. The initial pubertal event for girls will be either breast budding or the growth of pubic hair at an average age of 11. However, these initial events may occur as early as age 8 or as late as age 13 in healthy girls. The onset of menstruation occurs later in puberty—in the U.S. at an average age of 12½.

In contemporary society, which values muscular males and thin females, adolescents may risk their health to conform to these ideals. The abuse of anabolic steroids by males to increase muscle mass and strength and the starving or binging-purging behavior characteristic of eating disorders that are prevalent among females are behaviors that pose serious health risks for many adolescents.

Psychosocial development

It is useful to think of adolescent psychosocial development as consisting of early, middle, and late stages, which correspond to the junior-high, high-school, and after-high-school years. During each stage, adolescents are working hard on three main "tasks": (1) separating from parents and establishing independence and a sense of self; (2) coming to terms with their sexual identity, which will allow for companionship as well as intimacy; and (3) realizing interests, abilities, and skills that will enable them to formulate a plan for the future. The adolescent works on these tasks within the family framework, among his or her peers, and at school. Most young people will experience greater ease with one task than with another; however, some adolescents have difficulty with all three.

Daniel Offer, a child psychiatrist at Michael Reese Hospital and Medical Center, Chicago, and the University of Chicago Pritzker School of Medicine, surveyed thousands of normal adolescents in the 1970s; widely varying patterns of psychosocial development were evident. Some experienced continuous and steady growth; others seemed to have periods of surgent growth; and only a minority displayed tumultuous growth. Offer concluded that no particular path through adolescence was clearly preferable and that the route taken by an adolescent seemed to result from complex and interacting factors, including child-rearing practices, genetics, life experiences, social environment, and individual temperament.

The toll of health-risk behaviors

The death rate among adolescents due to natural causes (infectious diseases, malignancies, heart disease) has decreased dramatically (90%) since the 1930s, whereas the death rate from violence and injury has remained stable during this time. In fact, today's leading causes of death during adolescence (an estimated 75%) are accidents, homicide, and suicide. A number of factors make adolescents vulnerable to these events. Often they are linked to excessive drink-

ing of alcohol and abuse of drugs. Adolescents who are depressed or anxious are more likely to become victims of this cycle. Many adolescents have been the victims of physical or sexual abuse by a parent, stepparent, other relative, care giver, or other powerful person. Most of these young people have been frightened into keeping their victimization a secret or are too ashamed to tell anyone, yet they suffer grave psychological wounds, which may lower their threshold for partaking in behaviors that jeopardize health.

In addition to causing high rates of mortality, teenage risk-taking behaviors also cause significant morbidity (compromised health status and injury-related disability). Such behaviors include cigarette smoking; various forms of nutritional abuse such as starving, overeating, or self-induced vomiting; alcohol and drug abuse; participation in sensation-seeking activities from skateboarding to motorcycling to driving at high speeds in automobiles; and unsafe sexual

By age 18 more than 50% of U.S. teenagers are sexually active; many do not use birth control. Not surprisingly, there are about one million teenage pregnancies annually, and sexually transmitted diseases in this young population group are at epidemic levels.

Phil Huber—Black Star

Adolescent participation in sensation-seeking activities such as motorcycle racing and driving at high speeds in automobiles contributes to an alarmingly high incidence of accidents, resulting in significant injury-related disability.

practices. Since the 1960s the earlier initiation of sexual activity has resulted in a dramatically increased incidence of unwanted adolescent pregnancies and a marked increase in various sexually transmitted infections, including chlamydia, gonorrhea, herpes simplex, human papillomavirus, and human immunodeficiency virus (HIV), the virus that causes AIDS.

There are, however, encouraging data being reported from the late 1980s. These data indicate a 22% drop in alcohol-related traffic fatalities for drivers under age 21; a modest decline in daily cigarette smoking among high-school students, especially males; a major change in adolescents' perception of the harmfulness of drug use and a related decline in the use of marijuana, hallucinogens, and tranquilizers; and a dramatic (but still inadequate) increase in condom use among adolescents in response to the AIDS epidemic.

Medical checkups: targeted for teens

The medical checkup has become an American tradition for people of all ages. The idea of targeting a comprehensive checkup specifically for adolescents is relatively new. Such an approach, however, provides a crucial opportunity for uncovering a wide range of physical and emotional disorders and dysfunctions that teenagers and their families may be unaware of.

Because there are defined health needs and health problems that are unique to adolescence, the checkup should be designed to evaluate the teenager's health in the broadest terms. The checkup thus should assess physical growth and development, general psychosocial adjustment, possible risk-taking behaviors that may jeopardize health, and any unknown physical or emotional problems or dysfunctions.

A complete physical examination should include measurement of the primary parameters of the adolescent's growth and development (weight, height, pubertal changes). In order to reveal any asymptomatic problems that may require further evaluation or treatment, the exam should include a blood pressure measurement and careful examination of the lymph and thyroid glands, lungs, heart, abdomen, genitalia, skin, muscles, joints, and spine (to check for scoliosis). Basic laboratory testing for a healthy adolescent need not be extensive but should reasonably include a complete blood count, urine analysis, cholesterol measurement, and tuberculosis skin test.

The physical exam should also include updating of immunizations. Most adolescents at age 14 or 15 are due for a booster dose of diphtheria-tetanus toxoid (Td), and by age 12 they should have received a second booster dose of a measles-mumps-rubella (MMR) vaccine. Mumps can be particularly risky to boys, who may become sterile if they are infected after puberty. Rubella (German measles) can be dangerous to young women; if they contract the disease when they are pregnant, it can be transmitted to the fetus.

Vision testing should be done about every two years. About 25% of teenagers need vision correction (most often for nearsightedness). Hearing tests should be done at least once or twice during the adolescent years; many teenagers may be at risk for hearing damage from exposure to loud music.

The most important and potentially most productive part of the medical checkup, however, should be a private discussion between the doctor and the adolescent patient to review in detail such things as the adolescent's usual daily patterns of eating, sleeping, and physical activity and, for girls, any concerns about menstruation. Talking about how things are going at home, with peers, and at school enables the doctor to assess important aspects of the patient's psychosocial development. Some discussion of sexuality and the use of cigarettes, alcohol, and drugs should be pursued in a manner appropriate to the age, maturity, and social life of the individual adolescent.

A meeting between the doctor and the adolescent's parents to discuss their concerns and to obtain past health information about the patient (childhood illnesses, surgery, hospitalizations, allergies, medications, etc.) and the family's health status is another crucial component of the medical history. Most young adolescents are not ready to assume full responsibility for their health care and welcome their parents' participation in their medical evaluation. As the adolescent matures and develops a one-to-one relationship with the doctor, it is hoped that a gradual shift toward independence will be fostered, with the young patient assuming increasing responsibility for matters relating to his or her health.

Since any checkup should be designed to uncover those problems that are most prevalent and potentially serious within a specific population, it is imperative that an adolescent's medical examination target the crucial areas of sexuality; body-image concerns, which may reveal potential eating disorders, skin conditions requiring treatment, and aberrations in growth and development; psychological distress (especially depression and anxiety), which generally arises from difficulties with parents and peers or at school and may be manifested as physical symptoms such as headaches or abdominal pain or may be associated with suicidal thoughts or self-destructive behavior; and abuse of substances including cigarettes, alcohol, and drugs.

When the physician inquires about each of these critical areas, an important message is conveyed to the adolescent patient—that the doctor understands the context of the teenager's life and is available to discuss *any* concerns he or she may have. This author always says to her young patients, "You don't have to be sick to come to see me."

The unmet challenge

Although it is clear that adolescents as a group have special health needs, the provision of appropriate care for these young people remains very much an unmet challenge. In 1990 the American Medical Association

The concept of a teen-targeted medical evaluation is relatively new. In addition to assessing physical health and psychosocial adjustment, the exam should allow young patients to express their concerns about sexuality, body image, drugs and alcohol, and relationships with parents and peers—to talk openly and confidentially about whatever is on their minds.

Children's Hospital, Boston

(AMA) issued the publication *America's Adolescents: How Healthy Are They?* and in it recognized that organized medicine, in partnership with other groups, needs to coordinate future research to enhance both the assessment and monitoring of the health of the country's teenagers. It emphasized that the common roots of adolescent health problems need to be explored and recommended that periodic national surveys be done on the incidence and severity of physical and emotional disorders of this group.

Currently the AMA's department of adolescent health, in collaboration with the Society for Adolescent Medicine, is conducting a two-year study to develop guidelines for adolescent health care services, which will then be disseminated to all physicians in the United States. It is hoped that the provision of these guidelines, as well as the tools and training to use them effectively, will enable greater numbers of adolescents to receive the comprehensive care they need and deserve.

—*Andrea Marks, M.D.*

AIDS

The year 1991 marked the official end of the first decade of the AIDS (acquired immune deficiency syndrome) epidemic. The overall feeling in the scientific community at this historic juncture was one of cautious optimism. Researchers have made significant gains in understanding how the virus works and is spread, and they are now able to prolong the lives of those who are infected. Still, AIDS remains a uniformly fatal affliction, and the number of reported cases continues to grow.

The World Health Organization (WHO) is predicting a dramatic increase in global AIDS infections in the next 10 years. According to WHO estimates, 8 million to 10 million people were infected with HIV (human immunodeficiency virus, the virus that causes AIDS) in 1990; 40 million could be infected by the year 2000. Less developed countries will suffer the most, experiencing as many as 90% of new cases. In 1991 Michael H. Merson, director of WHO's Global Program on AIDS, called attention to an alarming rise in infections in Thailand and India.

Recent WHO statistics show that HIV is spreading especially rapidly among women and children in sub-Saharan Africa and in Asia, where an estimated additional three million women and children are expected to die from AIDS in the 1990s. Women already account for 52% of adult cases in Uganda, for example (compared with 11 and 12% in the U.S. and Europe, respectively). The disease has become the leading cause of death for women aged 20 to 40 in some central African cities.

In the Western Hemisphere more than three million people will have been infected with HIV by the middle

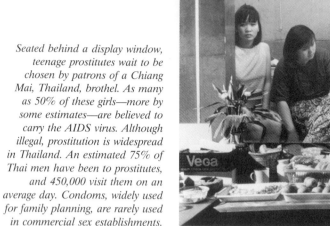

Seated behind a display window, teenage prostitutes wait to be chosen by patrons of a Chiang Mai, Thailand, brothel. As many as 50% of these girls—more by some estimates—are believed to carry the AIDS virus. Although illegal, prostitution is widespread in Thailand. An estimated 75% of Thai men have been to prostitutes, and 450,000 visit them on an average day. Condoms, widely used for family planning, are rarely used in commercial sex establishments.

of the decade, according to a 1991 report by the Pan American Health Organization. The report said that the spread of the epidemic in Latin America is paralleling that that occurred in the U.S. five years ago.

On a worldwide basis, AIDS continues to be overwhelmingly a sexually transmitted disease; 75% of cases are spread through sexual contact, 10% perinatally (from an infected mother to her baby), 10% by intravenous (IV) drug use, and 5% through transfusion of contaminated blood, according to WHO. This report covers events from mid-1990 through the closing of the international conference at the end of June 1991.

Update from Florence

More than 8,000 scientists from around the globe gathered in Florence for the Seventh International Conference on AIDS. Despite the discouraging news about the unrelenting spread of the disease in the Third World, the assembled researchers heard of some promising developments. An experimental Japanese drug, called SP-PB, was reported to shrink the tumors associated with Kaposi's sarcoma, a cancer that afflicts many of those with AIDS. The drug, made from bacteria in the soil, had no toxic side effects in laboratory animals. Samantha McWhinney of the Harvard School of Public Health reported on a study of Massachusetts infants born with HIV. Her findings showed that only half developed the disease within seven years, which indicates that the illness develops more slowly in this young age group than previously believed.

The reports on vaccine development were not as encouraging, however, although some researchers continued to express the belief that a vaccine would be developed by the turn of the century. Half a dozen U.S. biotechnology companies thus far have begun work on experimental vaccines that not only would

protect the uninfected but also would boost the immunity of those already carrying the virus. MicroGeneSys, Inc., has been testing a product called VaxSyn on human volunteers for several years, but other U.S. companies are still testing their vaccines on animals. Jonas Salk, who developed the first polio vaccine in the 1950s, announced in Florence that he planned soon to test an experimental vaccine on himself.

The U.S. epidemic

By mid-1991 some authorities were predicting that the AIDS epidemic in the U.S. had already peaked—*i.e.,* that the annual number of newly diagnosed cases had reached its highest point. (In 1981 the number of cases reported to the U.S. Centers for Disease Control (CDC) was 189; in 1990 it was more than 43,000.) Still, the cumulative total of cases—and deaths—was growing and was expected to continue to do so for some time. In the first decade of AIDS, local, state, and territorial health departments had reported more than 100,000 AIDS deaths to the CDC. Almost a third of these—more than 31,000—were reported during 1990. Overall, one million Americans are believed to carry the virus; about 60% of them may already be suffering from suppressed immunity, although most of them may not recognize any symptoms.

AIDS continues to affect minority groups disproportionately to their numbers in the population. Of the more than 179,000 cases reported to the CDC by mid-1991, some 45% were among whites, compared with about 28% among blacks and 15.5% among Hispanics.

AIDS emerged in the '80s as a leading cause of death among young adults in the United States. It was the third leading cause of death among men 25 to 44 years of age in 1988 and was expected to be vying for first place in that age group during the '90s. The disease continues to be a predominantly male affliction, although the percentage of women with AIDS is growing. Of the reported cases, more than 148,000 have been men; women number more than 16,000; and about 3,000 have been children under the age of 13 at the time of diagnosis. Most deaths from AIDS in the U.S. thus far have occurred among homosexual or bisexual men (59%) and among male heterosexual and female IV drug users (21%).

As many as 80,000 U.S. women of reproductive age could be infected with HIV, according to a study conducted by Marta Gwinn and colleagues of the CDC's Division of HIV/AIDS. The study tracked the prevalence of HIV infection among childbearing women through blood samples drawn from their infants; because antibodies to HIV cross the placenta during pregnancy, their detection in newborns reflects HIV infection in the mothers. The CDC researchers estimated that there had been about 5,800 births to HIV-positive women annually between 1988 and 1990 (based on a survey of 38 states and the District of Columbia, which accounted for 95% of cases of perinatal transmission). Using a transmission rate of 30% *i.e.,* about one-third of all infants born to HIV-infected women are themselves infected—the researchers figured that about 1,800 newborns per year had acquired HIV infection. The highest seroprevalence rates were found in New York (5.8 per 1,000), the District of Columbia (5.5),

Kimberley Bergalis, diagnosed with AIDS in late 1989 at age 21, had no known risk factors for the disease. Public health officials concluded that she was probably infected during a tooth extraction procedure by her dentist, David Acer, who subsequently died of AIDS.

Susan Greenwood—The New York Times

New Jersey (4.9), and Florida (4.5). Of the states surveyed, only Montana and New Hampshire recorded no births to seropositive women.

The incidence of AIDS is most acute within the nation's 13 largest metropolitan areas, their numbers constituting about 55% of the overall cases. Only 5% of U.S. hospitals care for more than half of the cases. During 1991 these overburdened municipal hospitals continued to sound the alarm over an impending crisis in AIDS care. In fiscal 1990 Congress authorized $875 million in emergency relief for those cities hardest hit by the epidemic. However, only $221 million had been appropriated by early January 1991 to pay for much-needed treatment and early-intervention programs.

Health care workers and HIV

In July 1990 the CDC reported the possible transmission of HIV from a dentist who had AIDS to an unidentified patient during an invasive dental procedure. The patient, who subsequently identified herself as Kimberly Bergalis of Fort Pierce, Fla., had no identified risk factor for HIV infection and was infected with a strain of HIV closely related to that of the dentist, as determined by viral DNA sequencing. A follow-up investigation by the CDC subsequently found four more seropositive individuals believed to have been infected by the dentist. Following the initial CDC report, the dentist, David J. Acer, wrote an emotional letter to a Florida newspaper, acknowledging that he had AIDS and denying that he had exposed his patients to the risk of transmission, although he had continued to practice for several years after his diagnosis for symptomatic HIV infection in 1986. In his letter Acer urged his patients, who may have numbered more than 1,700, to be tested for HIV. By the time the letter was published, Acer had died.

The case marked the first time since the start of the epidemic that the CDC had verified HIV transmission from an infected health care worker to a patient during an invasive procedure. Although it was unable to determine exactly how the transmission occurred, the CDC took the opportunity to reexamine the guidelines for prevention of HIV and other blood-borne pathogens in the health care setting. The agency had long promoted adherence to a set of preventive measures, so-called universal precautions, which include prevention of blood contact between health care workers and patients and proper cleaning and sterilization or disinfection of instruments and equipment. The measures called for health care workers to wear protective clothing, including latex surgical gloves, when coming in contact with any patient's bodily fluids, regardless of whether the patient's HIV status was known. In its own assessment of the potential risk of HIV transmission from health care worker to patient, the CDC estimated that as few as 13 or as many as 128 patients already may have been infected by U.S. surgeons and den-

tists—figures based on the estimated number of HIV-infected surgeons and dentists (about 1,500) and the number of surgical and dental procedures each would perform annually (about 500 per surgeon and 3,000 per dentist). It was assumed that a practitioner would work an average of seven years after infection.

For two days in late February, dozens of prominent physicians, civil libertarians, and AIDS activists met with CDC officials in Atlanta to challenge the new calculation of doctor-to-patient HIV risk. Not only was the formula disputed, but doctors were alarmed at the possibility that the government agency would consider the transmission risk great enough to require HIV testing of all health care workers. The American Dental Association (ADA) believed the risk was much lower than the CDC estimates, in part because the CDC classified many dental procedures as invasive when dentists said they were not. Invasive procedures generally are those that involve the doctor's using surgical instruments so as to cause a patient to bleed. Still, the ADA adopted a policy calling on HIV-infected dentists to either stop performing invasive procedures or disclose their HIV status to their patients.

The American Medical Association (AMA), the nations' largest physician organization, representing the interests of more than 250,000 physicians, called in June for routine voluntary screening to "reassure the public," in the words of AMA board member Nancy Dickey. The AMA called on doctors who know they are at risk for AIDS—because of work-related exposure or life-style—to be tested for HIV. The organization also believes that doctors should be free to order HIV tests for patients with verbal consent alone, rather than requiring formal written consent.

In July U.S. Health and Human Services Secretary Louis Sullivan announced recommended new guidelines for health care workers infected with the virus, urging them not to perform medical procedures in which there was any risk of "blood contact" with patients. The guidelines, drafted by the CDC, called for doctors, dentists, and others who perform invasive procedures to be voluntarily tested for both AIDS and hepatitis B; those who are found to be infected should refrain from performing such procedures until they have obtained permission from both a peer review committee and potential patients.

While the debate in the medical community continued, three of the infected patients of the Florida dentist sought legal redress. Bergalis was awarded a $1 million settlement from the late dentist's insurance company and an out-of-court legal settlement from the health insurer that had recommended the dentist.

A related—and equally contentious issue—is the question of how best to prevent health care workers from becoming infected as a result of occupational exposure to HIV. According to one estimate, the HIV-positive proportion of the patient population may be as high as 10% in some health care settings. Although CDC figures show that only 40 health care workers have been infected on the job since the start of the epidemic, many professionals have expressed skepticism about such a low number. Surgeons and others with a high risk of blood exposure are now more scrupulous about wearing protective garb; some wear two pairs of surgical gloves and transparent plastic shields or goggles to protect their eyes from aerosolized blood. Many surgeons would like to see testing of all surgical patients become mandatory. Such a practice, however, would raise major ethical questions about whether those who tested positive had to be told and if a doctor or hospital could refuse treatment. Further, in the emergency setting, where the risk to health care workers is among the highest, there is usually no time for blood tests.

Treatment developments

The year was marked by several promising developments in treatment for both HIV and the opportunistic infections of AIDS. Despite some acceleration in the drug-approval process, however, it still was not rapid enough to suit many patients and their advocates.

Anti-HIV drugs. In a research breakthrough, scientists at Agouron Pharmaceuticals Inc. of La Jolla, Calif., announced in April 1991 that they had mapped the three-dimensional structure of a key protein used by the AIDS virus to infect cells. Ribonuclease H is a fragment of the enzyme reverse transcriptase, which is essential for reproduction of the virus. Researchers replicated a part of the reverse transcriptase molecule that included the ribonuclease H function, and they were able to identify the exact sequence of amino acids that make up the molecule. The discovery provided scientists with a new molecular target for designing a drug that would specifically lock onto ribonuclease H and prevent it from functioning, thereby slowing or halting the progress of the disease.

Preparing to perform a hip operation, an orthopedic surgeon dons an elaborate AIDS-protection suit. Some health care workers would like to see mandatory HIV testing for all hospital patients.

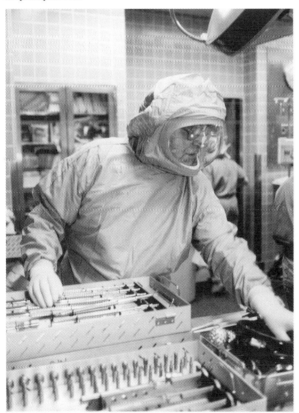

Pamela Price—Picture Group

The only drug now approved in the U.S. for direct treatment of HIV is zidovudine, also known as AZT (azidothymidine; Retrovir). It works by blocking polymerase activity in another part of the reverse transcriptase enzyme molecule. Many AIDS patients cannot tolerate the side effects of AZT, however, and several alternative agents—all still experimental in mid-1991—are under development.

Two of the more promising are ddI (dideoxyinosine; also called didanosine) and ddC (dideoxycytidine; also called zalcitabine), both chemically related to AZT. To the dismay of many AIDS patients and their advocates, these drugs were not moving through the approval process as speedily as had been hoped. (Their predecessor, AZT, was on the market after only three months of testing.) In the belief that their patients could not wait the usual six months to a year that it would take for the new drugs to clear bureaucratic hurdles, a group of medical professionals and AIDS activists took the unusual step of petitioning the U.S. Food and Drug Administration (FDA) to speed their approval. In preliminary studies both drugs appear to improve the immune system's level of CD4+ cells, the infection-fighting cells that are depleted in AIDS.

The three drugs—ddI, ddC, and AZT—are known as nucleoside analogues and work by mimicking the chemical building blocks of DNA, the basic genetic material. The drugs insert a false building block into the growing DNA chain of HIV, thus jamming the mechanism by which the virus replicates. Because such drugs interfere with human as well as with viral DNA, they tend to have toxic side effects. Almost half of all AIDS patients find they must give up AZT after a period of months or years because it damages their bone marrow. Patients are believed to tolerate a combination of nucleoside analogues in low doses better than any single one alone.

About 15,000 HIV-infected people in the U.S. have been taking ddI and ddC as part of community drug trials and compassionate distribution programs. Some have experienced peripheral neuropathy, or painful nerve damage to the hands and feet, according to early reports from the clinical trials. Those taking ddI also suffered from pancreatitis (inflammation of the pancreas). DdI, approved as an investigational new drug (IND) in 1989, has been distributed both to AIDS patients who cannot tolerate AZT and to those whose disease was progressing despite the use of AZT. In 1990 ddC gained the same IND status. In addition, both drugs now have "open label" study status; this means that rather than being restricted to testing in controlled clinical trials, they can be used in studies in which no placebos are given and that generally have no strict enrollment limits.

In January the National Institute of Allergy and Infectious Diseases announced the start of a national clinical trial to compare the effectiveness of ddI and ddC on 400 HIV-infected individuals. The two-year study in 14 cities sought to include those who, many AIDS experts believe, have been underrepresented in previous studies, including women, racial and ethnic minorities, and drug users.

The search for effective anti-AIDS drugs is by no means limited to the U.S. The Pharmaceutical Manufacturers Association says a total of 77 research projects involving 42 medications are being carried out by 40 companies around the world. One promising drug, a nucleoside analogue code-named BCH 189, was discovered by IAF BioChem of Canada and is being jointly developed with the British pharmaceutical company Glaxo. Laboratory and animal studies indicate the drug will have fewer side effects than AZT, ddI, or ddC.

Drugs for opportunistic infections. In August 1990 the U.S. National Commission on AIDS criticized the National Institutes of Health (NIH) for failing to conduct an aggressive research effort to find effective treatments for the leading opportunistic infections associated with AIDS, including *Pneumocystis carinii* pneumonia (PCP), mycobacterium avium tuberculosis, cryptococcal meningitis, toxoplasmosis, cytomegalovirus, and candida yeast infections.

The major breakthrough in the treatment of opportunistic infections came in 1989 with the development of aerosolized pentamidine (NebuPent) for prevention of PCP, a parasitic form of pneumonia that occurs in about 85% of all AIDS patients. Trimethoprim, a sulfa drug, given orally also can prevent most PCP infections, although many AIDS patients cannot tolerate sulfa drugs. Several recent studies suggest that putting patients on prednisone, a steroid hormone, to reduce inflammation in the lungs enhances survival in PCP. A panel of experts from the University of California and the NIH recommended in 1990 that the steroid be added to the list of standard treatments. The panel had reviewed five trials of adjunctive therapy with corticosteroids, and it concluded that such therapy reduces the likelihood of respiratory failure and death in patients with moderate-to-severe cases of PCP.

In January 1991 the FDA approved the drug erythropoietin (Epogen), a recombinant human hormone, for treating anemia in AIDS patients. In February the FDA—with the blessing of the Drug Enforcement Administration—permitted the first distribution of marijuana to AIDS patients to help them cope with the nausea and severe weight loss that afflicts most patients.

Also in January 1991 the Department of Health and Human Services announced that HIV-infected children could begin receiving intravenous immunoglobulin, an antibody-containing serum, which researchers believe will help them avoid life-threatening bacterial infections. A study involving 372 children between the ages of 2 months and 12 years showed a reduced number of bacterial infections and fewer hospitalizations

among those whose immune system cell counts had not fallen below a critical level.

The urgency of developing drugs for children with AIDS became evident in several studies, including one by Children's Hospital of New Jersey in Newark. The study showed that while 37 to 50% of HIV-infected adults live at least a year after PCP diagnosis, only 26% of children live that long.

In March 1991 the National Institute of Mental Health and National Institute of Allergy and Infectious Diseases began a clinical study of the effectiveness of peptide T, a drug that treats the neuropsychological effects of HIV infection. It is hoped that the drug will combat problems of concentration and memory loss in some patients. The study is being conducted by investigators at the University of Southern California.

A drug called ditiocarb sodium, developed by French scientists, was found to be effective in reducing new opportunistic infections in patients already showing symptoms of AIDS, according to a University of Arizona study. There was, however, no statistically significant difference in survival between those who received the drug and a control group. The Arizona investigators noted that further studies would be needed to determine the long-range effectiveness of the drug.

AIDS drug research around the world, in fact, suffered from a number of controversies and scandals throughout 1991. In Romania the government banned a substance that was being used in an unorthodox drug experiment on almost 100 Romanian babies who had become the subject of international attention following the overthrow of the Communist government there. For nearly two months the infants, mostly orphans hospitalized in Colentina Hospital in Bucharest, received injections of a mysterious drug along with a regimen that involved repeated enemas and a strict vegetarian diet. The health ministry stopped the experiment after it was unable to identify the chemical structure of the drug or find out where it was manufactured or whether there was any quality control.

A drug touted in Kenya as a "miracle" treatment for AIDS produced mixed results when tested in Los Angeles in two groups of HIV-infected patients. The drug, called Kemron in Africa, is known as oral alpha interferon (Intron A) in the United States. African researchers had claimed that it not only suppressed AIDS symptoms in some patients but removed all signs of infection in as many as 8 of the 101 men and women who had been treated. Details of the study were published in the *East African Medical Journal* in July 1990. U.S. doctors and researchers criticized the African research as being poorly designed and involving patients who may not have had any symptoms of AIDS. A subsequent study by WHO also found the drug to be relatively ineffective against AIDS.

Alpha interferon, a recombinant form of a natural body protein, has long been promoted as a cure for

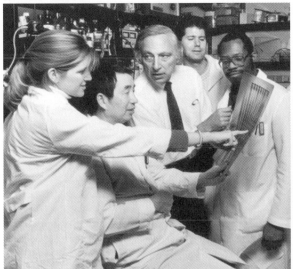

In his 1991 book Virus Hunting, *leading U.S. researcher Robert Gallo, pictured (center) with his lab team, defends himself against charges of misconduct in connection with his claim to have discovered the AIDS virus.*

AIDS. (The drug is used in the treatment of hepatitis B and C.) An injectable form has been used successfully to treat genital warts and Kaposi's sarcoma. While the drug is being studied extensively in the United States, AIDS patients have traveled to Kenya to receive injections or have bought it in liquid form from "underground" sources. One of the Los Angeles studies, which involved 167 patients, found virtually no change in immune function after patients took the drug for five months. However, they suffered no detrimental effects. The second, a study of 40 patients, found encouraging results in 37 of them. The patients reported they had gained weight, improved in their ability to fight infection, and generally felt better.

Controversial treatment. AIDS patients in the United States clamored for information about an unproven heat treatment, called hyperthermia, following the reported death of an American who had gone to a Mexican clinic for the therapy. The patient's blood had been removed, heated, and reinfused in a continuous process that was supposed to kill HIV.

Other controversies

The high costs of certain AIDS treatments were responsible for several controversies surrounding drugs during the past year. A lawsuit filed in March 1991 by a public interest group claimed that the patent on AZT owned by the Burroughs Wellcome Co., sole manufacturer and distributor of the drug in the U.S., should be invalidated because the company's patent application had not fully disclosed the part played by outside researchers in developing AZT. Because AZT is presently the only drug approved by the FDA

as effective in slowing the progression of AIDS, Burroughs Wellcome has a very lucrative monopoly. AIDS activists have long objected to the drug's high cost, which can run $2,000–$3,000 a year. If they could strip the company of its exclusive rights, there would be competition among manufacturers, leading to lower prices. Burroughs Wellcome denies that there was any impropriety in its patent application. In addition, some doubts were raised in 1990–91 about the ability of AZT to delay symptoms when given early in the course of the disease and about the relative efficacy of early AZT therapy in black and white patients. The latter disparity again draws attention to the need for more thorough studies of racial and ethnic differences in the outcome of various AIDS treatments.

Burroughs Wellcome was also criticized for sponsoring a public service campaign urging people who thought they might be infected with HIV to get tested so that they could avail themselves of early treatment. Some AIDS activists regarded the ads as a thinly disguised sales pitch for AZT (which is not mentioned by name), although it is cosponsored by several patient advocacy and physician groups.

Another drug recently involved in a dispute is aerosol pentamidine. The U.S. distributor, Fujisawa Pharmaceutical Co., was accused by AIDS advocates of presenting as a research study a scheme that was really intended to promote sales. Again, the high cost of the treatment was at the heart of the issue. Aerosol pentamidine is not under patent; Fujisawa, which has exclusive rights to sell it in the U.S., charges considerably more than does a French company that markets the drug elsewhere. It was alleged that the Fujisawa study was designed to get U.S. physicians who had been importing the less expensive foreign drug to buy it at home.

Charges of inappropriate or unethical conduct continued to follow a leading U.S. AIDS researcher, Robert Gallo, in 1991. After an initial dispute over who had first identified the virus that causes AIDS, two scientists, Gallo of the NIH and Luc Montagnier of the Pasteur Institute in Paris, had agreed to share credit as codiscoverers. There were lingering reports, however, that Gallo's laboratory in Bethesda, Md., had accidentally or intentionally misappropriated virus samples supplied by the French laboratory. An investigation into the matter was reopened by the NIH in 1990. In a letter to the journal *Nature,* Gallo acknowledged in April 1991 that a virulent strain of HIV that had contaminated the Pasteur Institute's HIV cultures also contaminated his cultures after the French lab sent him samples in 1983. Gallo's collaboration on an experimental AIDS vaccine with French immunologist Daniel Zagury was halted by the NIH after allegations that children in Zaire had been inoculated with the vaccine, which was not approved for testing in humans.

—Sherry Jacobson

Special Report
Southern California Clears the Air
by Robert Reinhold

Daily life in big metropolises poses many dangers, perhaps none more insidious than that from the polluted air that people must breathe. Nowhere is this more true than in the Los Angeles basin, a vast urbanized region—home to 12 million people and 8 million cars, trucks, motorcycles, and other motor vehicles—where geography and weather combine to produce the foulest air in the United States. Trapped by mountains and baked by relentless sunlight, the daily emissions from southern California's automobiles, power plants, furniture factories, and even common house paint and hair spray add up to the worst smog in the nation. Every month petroleum products equal in volume to the massive 1989 oil spill from the *Exxon Valdez* pour into the air above Los Angeles, the nation's second largest city, and its endless suburbs. It has been estimated that air pollution in southern California alone exacts more than $7.4 billion in health, agricultural, and environmental costs annually.

Now, after years of hesitation, authorities in California have begun the toughest assault yet on smog. Their efforts were bolstered by new medical evidence that smog can have devastating health effects not only on children and the ill but also on the healthiest citizens. Most ominously, researchers at the University of California at Los Angeles (UCLA) reported in early 1991 the results of an 11-year study that had found chronic exposure to smoggy air causes not just temporary but permanent lung damage. A few months earlier, in September 1990, the California Air Resources Board, citing cumulative medical evidence that smog can cause serious injury even to healthy, vigorous adults, ordered all local pollution-control districts in the state to issue health alerts at much lower smog levels than previously for the most dangerous pollutant, ozone.

The nation's boldest antipollution plan

The real beginning of the war on smog came on March 17, 1989, when regional authorities in southern California adopted a wide-ranging plan meant to bring air quality in the area into compliance with federal standards by the year 2007. The two main agencies involved, the South Coast Air Quality Management District and the Southern California Association of Governments, proposed more than 100 stiff new rules and regulations for the basin, which includes Los An-

geles, Orange, and Riverside counties and nondesert parts of San Bernardino county.

The regulations would affect nearly every resident and business in the 34,600-sq km (13,350-sq mi) region, from large oil companies to backyard barbecuers. Later stages of the plan envisioned new technologies that would almost entirely eliminate certain sources of bad air; *e.g.,* zero-pollution paint and cars that operate on electric fuel cells. The plan went beyond just emission technology, however. It took the first step in inducing local communities to achieve a better "jobs-housing balance," meaning that new housing should be built in close proximity to workplaces in order to reduce commuting by automobile.

The southern California plan, which served as a model to Washington, was followed in 1990 by a federal Clean Air Act encompassing environmental hazards beyond just urban smog, calling for actions ranging from tightening of national vehicle emissions standards to controls on acid rain. About the same time, the California Air Resources Board, the overarching state agency with ultimate authority on air quality, announced new rules meant to force motor vehicle manufacturers and oil companies to come up with even more efficient engines and cleaner fuels than required under federal law; otherwise, they would not be allowed to sell their products in the state. The board also set emission standards for nonautomobile motors—*e.g.,* those on power lawn mowers, leaf blowers, and generators—the first such standards imposed anywhere in the world. Together the local and state actions in California complemented the federal rules, sometimes surpassing them in stringency.

The broad measures were likely to have effects far beyond the state of California. Given the importance of the California market, manufacturers of products from diesel trucks to nail polish were expected to redesign or reformulate their products to reduce volatile hydrocarbons and comply with California law, meaning that consumers nationally would realize the health benefits—as well as the added financial costs—of the changes. Although in theory Californians welcomed the moves toward cleaner air, there was also mounting concern that the cost of the improvements would disproportionately affect the working class, with many manufacturing plants, such as furniture factories, being forced to move elsewhere.

The vast urban Los Angeles area has 12 million residents, 8 million motor vehicles, and the foulest air in the United States. It also has the nation's most aggressive plan for combating pollution.

What is smog?

Smog is a general term that applies to air pollution, which can vary considerably in content and severity from one region to another. The five main components of this "stew" are ozone, carbon monoxide, fine particulate matter, nitrogen oxides, and reactive organic gases. By almost any measure, the Los Angeles basin, the world's largest single market for gasoline, has by far the worst air quality in the country. About two-thirds of its pollution comes from motor vehicles, the rest from power plants, oil refineries, factories, and residential sources. On average, more than 9,000 tons of pollutants are spewed into the basin's air daily.

The chief villain is ozone, an invisible gas, which in the upper atmosphere is essential for protecting humans from the harmful effects of sunlight but at lower levels aggravates heart and respiratory diseases and diminishes lung capacity. Studies have shown that lung capacity in parts of the Los Angeles basin is reduced by 10 to 15%. Ozone forms when nitrogen oxides from fuel combustion come in contact with reactive organic gases, or ROG, from evaporated petroleum products—such as drying paints, solvents, household cleaners, and inks—in the presence of sunshine. The Air Quality Management District estimates that Los Angeles basin ozone costs each resident of the region $1.60 a day in medical care and damage to vegetation, paint, rubber used in a wide range of everyday household products, and other materials.

Ozone pollution is at its worst in Los Angeles during the summer months, with the long days of hot sunshine and a prevailing wind from the Pacific that pushes stagnant air against the inland mountains. The Los Angeles basin typically exceeds the federal ozone standard nine times as often as the highest-rated area outside of California (the New York metropolitan area).

Nevertheless, there is good news, too. The cumulative impact of car pooling, lower-pollution fuels, and numerous other measures appears to be cutting ozone levels from the peaks they reached 30 years ago; 1990 was the "cleanest" in many a year, with the number of days on which ozone levels exceeded the federal standard of 0.12 parts per million (ppm) of air being 130, down from 155 days in 1989. When a first-stage alert is declared, people with respiratory and heart diseases are advised to stay indoors and avoid strenuous activity, and schools are urged to curtail children's participation in sports and recreation; alerts were down from 54 days in 1989 to 41 days in 1990. (First-stage alerts were declared when ozone reached 0.20 ppm until September 1990, when the level was lowered to 0.15 ppm.) An ozone level of 0.35 ppm results is a second-stage alert, during which all motorists are advised to avoid unnecessary driving and certain industries can be compelled to curtail operations; no second-stage alerts were declared in Los Angeles in 1990.

Carbon monoxide (CO), also an invisible gas—and the chief pollutant in many eastern U.S. cities—damages health by reducing the bloodstream's capacity to carry oxygen. It comes mainly as a by-product of automobile combustion, and in Los Angeles, where 5,430 tons a day are emitted, it is worst during the fall and winter months, when cool air containing this gas hovers close to the ground. In 1989 the basin exceeded the federal standard of 9.4 ppm on 55 days; the peak level reached was 21.8 ppm.

Nitrogen oxides, the pollutants that impart the yellow-brown hue that airline passengers witness over the Los Angeles basin, are worst during the fall and early winter, when the sun is weaker and the process by which ozone is formed is slowed. Nitric oxide and nitrogen dioxide, or NOx, as they are collectively called, are also products of combustion. These pollutants are respiratory irritants that lower resistance

Ozone: worst offenders*			
Los Angeles-Anaheim-		Modesto, Calif.	7.6
Riverside, Calif.	137.5	Parkersburg-Marietta,	
Bakersfield, Calif.	44.2	W.Va.-Ohio	7.2
Fresno, Calif.	24.3	Greensboro-Winston	
New York, N.Y.-N.J.-		Salem-High Point, N.C.	7.2
Conn.	17.4	Pittsburgh, Pa.	7.0
Sacramento, Calif.	15.8	Springfield, Mass.	6.7
Chicago, Ill.-Ind.-Wis.	13.0	Providence, R.I.-Mass.	6.4
San Diego, Calif.	12.3	St. Louis, Mo.-Ill.	6.2
Houston-Galveston-		Portland, Maine	6.1
Brazoria, Texas	12.2	Nashville, Tenn.	5.6
Knox county, Maine	11.1	Huntington-Ashland,	
Baltimore, Md.	10.7	W.Va.-Ky.-Ohio	5.5
Boston	10.0	Kewaunee county, Wis.	5.5
Milwaukee-Racine, Wis.	9.8	Cincinnati, Ohio-Ky.-Ind.	5.4
Muskegon, Mich.	9.4	Portsmouth-Dover-	
Atlanta, Ga.	9.3	Rochester, N.H.-Maine	5.3
Sheboygan, Wis.	9.1	Worcester, Mass.	5.2
Philadelphia, Pa.-N.J.-		Cleveland-Akron-	
Del.	8.8	Lorain, Ohio	5.2
Hartford, Conn.	7.9	Washington, D.C.-Md.-Va.	4.9
El Paso, Texas	7.9		

*average number of days per year national ozone standard of 0.12 parts per million was exceeded in 1987–89
Source: Office of Air Quality Planning and Standards Technical Support Division, U.S. Environmental Protection Agency

A "smoke patrol" officer issues a citation to the driver of a heavy-duty diesel truck. Every month citizens report about 7,000 offending vehicles to the California Highway Patrol on its toll-free hot line.

to infection. The basin is the only area in the United States where NOx levels regularly exceed the federal health standards (by 15% on average). In 1989 the high levels resulted in two health alerts. NOx also contributes to the pollution problems of fine particulates and acid deposition.

So-called fine particulates are contaminants composed of minute particles (of less than 10 micrometers in diameter, finer than a human hair), which come from diesel soot, the wearing out of rubber tires, and other sources. They obscure visibility and are inhaled deep into the lungs. In the Los Angeles area, fine particulates generally are found at twice the allowable level.

Smog and health

Extensive animal and human tests have documented the damaging effects of ozone. The gas inflames, swells, and scars the airways of the lungs, reducing the body's ability to combat infection and expel foreign matter. Particularly vulnerable are those already suffering from respiratory ailments such as emphysema, bronchitis, and asthma (about 10% of the basin's population), but healthy persons and even exceptionally fit athletes suffer, too, according to the Environmental Protection Agency (EPA).

Controlled laboratory experiments found that healthy adults engaging in heavy exercise during ozone exposures that exceeded the federal standard of 0.12 ppm

suffered from coughing, shortness of breath, pain during deep breathing, fatigue, headaches, and nausea, among other symptoms. In one such study, reported by Henry Gong, Jr., in the *Journal of Sports Medicine and Physical Fitness,* it was determined that the higher the rate of breathing, the deeper the penetration of ozone into the respiratory system, even when ozone levels were comparatively low. Gong found that in some cases the reactions were so severe that athletes were unable to complete routine endurance tests. Other studies have found that heat and humidity compound the effects of ozone.

Children are of particular concern for several reasons: their lungs are not fully developed; because of their body size, the amount of air they inhale is proportionately several times greater than that inhaled by adults; and they spend much time outdoors playing hard and breathing through their mouths (breathing through the mouth bypasses the natural filter of the nose, which cuts out 90% of pollutants before they reach the lungs). The EPA found that children experienced persistent loss of lung function after a five-day elevated ozone episode. In a field study at a summer camp where maximum one-hour levels exceeded 0.12 ppm on four of the five days and reached 0.18 ppm on one day, children's lung function failed to return to normal for many days. A 1984 study by Kay Kilburn at the University of Southern California found that children who grew up in the Los Angeles basin showed a 10 to 15% loss in lung function, compared with youngsters reared in cleaner air.

An important question that remains to be resolved is whether the effects of ozone are short term or permanent. Some experts believe that the body ultimately adapts and compensates for the damaging effects of ozone on performance. The EPA, however, has cited studies on animals that have demonstrated significant immune system damage at moderate levels of ozone exposure, as well as a small amount of permanent lung scarring.

Perhaps the most extensive and indicting ozone study to date was reported in early 1991 by a team of researchers at UCLA. They concluded that "pollution is more than an inconvenience." In the words of the principal investigator, epidemiologist Roger Detels, "People who have grown up in these highly polluted areas may expect to have even greater difficulties with respiratory problems as they reach old age." The study attempted to compare the effects of pollution on the health of residents of three basin communities that have different kinds and levels of pollution: Glendora, in the foothills, which has ozone levels that are among the highest in the nation; a neighborhood in Long Beach that is situated downwind from refineries that spew large amounts of industrial nitrogen and sulfur dioxides into the air; and Lancaster, a remote suburb in the high desert with relatively clean air.

Recent studies of exercisers have shown that smog causes shortness of breath, coughing, headaches, nausea, fatigue, and other symptoms and that ozone is particularly damaging, penetrating deep into respiratory passages.

The 11-year study, involving 2,500 nonsmoking residents, found that average lung capacity was significantly lower in Glendora and Long Beach than in Lancaster and that there was little indication of improved lung performance over time. High ozone caused narrowing of the airways in the lungs, resulting in poor delivery of oxygen to bodily organs. What was perhaps most ominous was that a majority of people did not perceive that they were impaired. Even though people's lung capacity was 50 to 75% less than what it should have been, they would say that they were "fine." Detels believes, however, that these people had probably modified their life-styles in significant ways, often thinking that they were experiencing "normal" effects of the aging process.

Less threatening than ozone but nonetheless of serious concern is carbon monoxide, which displaces oxygen in the blood. The federal levels for CO are regularly exceeded in many areas of the basin, particularly where traffic is heavy. The EPA warns that such areas should be avoided by people with angina and other forms of heart disease and those with chronic respiratory diseases like bronchitis, asthma, and emphysema, as well as the elderly, infants, and people suffering from anemia. The agency has set 9.5 ppm as the allowable level over an eight-hour period; above that, sensitive persons may experience untoward effects. For example, healthy young men become exhausted when exercising; heart patients have lowered exercise capacity and suffer angina attacks sooner; and people suffer reductions in vision, learning ability, and manual and motor dexterity, evidenced in activities such as driving. In addition, animal studies suggest that CO might harm the fetus or newborn.

While there is a paucity of reliable data on the long-term effects of NOx at normal outdoor levels, there is evidence that even at low levels NOx can irritate the lungs, cause bronchitis and pneumonia, and reduce resistance to infections.

Fine particulates—known as PM10, for their length (10 micrometers)—are considered especially hazardous because they reach the deepest parts of the lungs. Particulate pollution contributes to respiratory illness, cancer, and premature death. The EPA has estimated that as many as one in 12 of the lung cancer cases among Los Angeles basin residents who are nonsmokers can be attributed to soot from diesel trucks, cars, and buses. Most susceptible to PM10 injury are people with influenza or chronic respiratory and cardiovascular illness, young children, the elderly, and athletes and others who breathe through the mouth frequently. According to a 1986–88 study by Steve Colome, then at the University of California at Irvine, a third of adult asthmatics showed significant decreases in lung function when sulfate particles in the air were high.

Assault on smog: past, present, and future

Fighting smog is not entirely new in southern California. It began during the 1950s, when a number of concerted steps were taken, including the banning of backyard incinerators in 1958. Even before the present antipollution plan was passed in 1989, the region had begun to deal with emissions from motor vehicles, which account for two-thirds of the area's colossal smog problem.

For example, biannual smog-checks have been required on all nondiesel vehicles registered in California for many years—a measure that is estimated to reduce air pollution by 60 tons a day. Vehicles sold in California have long been required to meet much stricter emission standards than those in other states. Furthermore, gas stations have been required to have vapor-recovery systems on their pumps. More recently, both smog officials and private corporations began a campaign to rid the roads of "heaps" and "junkers," the older cars that spew out many times the pollution of new models.

In addition, the California Highway Patrol has a "smoke patrol," eight full-time officers who cruise the freeways looking for smoking vehicles. Heavy-duty diesel trucks account for three-fourths of the citations. A special toll-free number allows residents to report offending vehicles; more than 7,000 complaints are received in an average month.

Meanwhile, the city of Los Angeles began a program to cut the number of trucks—which are responsible for 17% of air pollution from mobile sources—that operate on city streets during peak hours. To discourage automobile use, the Air Quality Management District passed Regulation XV, which requires all companies with 100 or more workers at a single site to develop "trip-reduction plans" as a means of encouraging carpooling and use of mass transit. This rule, first implemented in July 1988, was eventually expected to result in major reductions in NOx, CO, and ROG.

In a metropolis where only 3% of commuters use public transportation, a new light-rail commuter line, the Blue Line, connecting the downtowns of Los Angeles and Long Beach, opened in 1990, the first leg in a 480-km (300-mi) mass-transit system for the region, which authorities hope will ultimately lure commuters away from their cars. Also planned are 644 km (400 mi) of car-pool lanes on freeways and 800 km (500 mi) of bikeways, as well as an electrified, clean-fuel bus system.

Nonetheless, these collective measures were not enough, especially considering the fact that the basin's population is expected to swell by 50% from 12 million to 18 million over the next 20 years. Because of this, the Air Quality Management Plan, adopted by the South Coast Air Quality Management District in 1989 and approved later that year by the Air Resources Board, broadened the sweep of the attack on smog beyond motor vehicles alone. Regulations were imposed for a wide range of other pollutants and polluters: paints, cleaners, sprays, oil companies and other industries, and even the home barbecue. In order for compliance with federal standards to be reached by 2007, emissions of NOx and ROG would have to be reduced by more than 80% from current levels, despite the population increase.

The controversial plan has three tiers. The first tier, set to be implemented during the first five years, consists of 123 new measures, 15 affecting oil companies, 21 aimed at other businesses and industries, 22 concerning paints and solvents, 52 on traffic and transportation sources, and 13 on homes and agriculture. The effects of the measures on southern Californians are both small and large. For example, the air district banned the sale of charcoal lighter fluid for barbecue grills starting Jan. 1, 1992. Only electric starters and propane and natural gas grills will then be allowed, a step that is expected to cut hydrocarbon emissions by two tons a day. The agency also moved to reduce chemicals that evaporate from paint spraying, urging automobile body shops to convert to high-volume, low-pressure spray guns and water-based primers. In 1991 the agency ordered large commercial bakeries in the basin to install devices to capture the ethyl alcohol that arises when bread is leavened. But officials backed off touching one of the sacred mainstays of southern California life—the drive-through restaurant. As a means of reducing carbon monoxide, the plan had originally proposed to ban construction of any new drive-throughs. Instead, it opted for measures to discourage unnecessary engine idling in line.

The second and third tiers are much less specific but call for a ratcheting down of allowable emissions through adaptation of existing technologies, use of cleaner fuels, and ultimately, in the final stage, the introduction of new technologies, such as fuel cells to power motor vehicles. For example, state agencies are sponsoring numerous pilot projects such as the development of an electric vehicle powered by nickel-cadmium batteries, which has already achieved a range of 235 km (147 mi) at a constant speed of 56 km/h (35 mph). The goal of 2% of new cars being electric has been set for 1998. On the industrial side, the world's largest solar-dish-run engine, which would provide zero emissions from nontransportation sources of electricity generation, is being tested. Finally, several backup measures may be imposed if the three-tier approach fails, including stiff parking fees and strict limits on vehicle registrations.

Cost and controversy

Given the enormous implications for daily life and business, the assault on smog in California has not advanced without bitter dissent. The Community Air Quality Task Force, a coalition of business, labor, and government leaders, charged that the air-quality plan would cost the region from 530,000 to 889,000 jobs in such industries as furniture manufacturing, construction, metal fabrication, aerospace, chemicals, plastics, restaurant, and movie and television production. (In mid-1991 there were already unconfirmed reports that about 40 furniture makers had relocated either part or all of their manufacturing operations to Mexico in order to avoid complying with the new rules requiring use of low-emission paints and varnishes.) The task force also expressed concern that the vast majority of the losses would be suffered by lower-paid workers. A study commissioned by the task force and conducted by the Pasadena Research Institute maintained that the state would lose at least $700 million a year in direct sales tax revenues as a result of the proposed new smog rules—more than $2.8 billion when the ripple effect on other businesses was counted.

The air-quality district, however, disputed these findings, saying its own studies had concluded that attaining federal air-quality standards would result in annual benefits, reduced health costs, and other savings amounting to $9.4 billion a year at a price of $2.6 billion a year. It is too soon to know if either side is right. It is certain, though, that the smog and its cost in both health and dollars will remain a major issue in southern California for decades to come.

Back Care

Over a lifetime, 80% of people suffer at least one episode of low back pain. Fifty percent recover within one week, and 90% are free of symptoms within six weeks, regardless of the diagnosis or type of treatment. Unfortunately, more than half have one or multiple recurrences of back pain during the next two-to-three-year interval. Even though the majority who suffer do not seek medical attention, back pain is the second most frequent reason a patient in the U.S. consults a physician, exceeded only by the common cold.

Back pain's causes: more questions than answers

At least 95% of the time, no precise cause for acute low back pain can be identified, regardless of how elaborate the diagnostic workup is. Infrequently, herniation (rupture) of a lumbar disk is the culprit, but even in this case the clinical course of back pain is generally similar to the pattern in patients where the source is alleged to be mechanical—*i.e.*, "strain or sprain." Even when disk material is placing pressure on a nerve and causing sciatica (pain radiating down a leg), the nerve usually wins out, and the process abates with time. This self-repair is probably due to the nerve tissue's being much firmer than the disk material and, once the acute inflammation subsides, the patient becomes asymptomatic, at least for a time.

Many mysteries remain regarding the spine. Why, for example, does pressure on a spinal nerve cause pain whereas numbness results when peripheral nerves (those outside the central nervous system) are compressed?

Risk factors

Unequivocal risk factors for low back pain have recently been identified. Fortunately, they are all manageable. Obesity conveys a twofold increased risk of low back pain, making maintenance of ideal body weight critical. An additional independent risk factor is cigarette smoking—a three-pack-a-day smoker has a 2½-times greater chance of experiencing low back pain than does a nonsmoker! Although the explanation for this association is not sufficiently understood (it could be poorer oxygenation in the back, hardening of the arteries in the spine, or any of a number of other possibilities), the obvious lesson is that persons with back pain should stop smoking, as should others, in order to avoid or prevent back pain (and for many other health reasons as well). People whose occupations require heavy lifting and physical labor were once considered to be at high risk for low back pain. However, such on-the-job physical activity apparently plays less of a role than had been thought. In fact, recent data suggest that sedentary workers are at greater risk for back pain than are heavy laborers.

Diagnosis

For most sufferers of back pain, expensive and time-consuming diagnostic measures are not indicated. For those whose pain persists longer than a month or so, there are now several sophisticated imaging methods for investigating the source of the problem. The practice of instilling dye into the spinal cord (myelography), which is painful and frequently causes significant irritation of tissue, has been replaced by the noninvasive imaging technique computed tomography (CT). Even clearer visualization of the bones, disks, and nerves of the spine can be acquired with magnetic resonance imaging (MRI). Though it is quite expensive and requires that the patient remain virtually motionless for an extended period of time inside a confined, circular chamber—a situation that many patients find claustrophobic—MRI involves no radiation exposure. Unless a tumor or infection is suspected, however, it rarely is necessary to use MRI for evaluation of back pain.

New therapeutic insights

Single episodes of low back pain are almost always self-limited; it is the subsequent and frequently more debilitating attacks toward which treatment should largely be directed. On the basis of a definitive study published in 1986, prolonged bed rest for acute mechanical low back pain is no longer advised; participants in the study who stayed in bed for just two

Several unequivocal risk factors for low back pain have been identified, including lack of physical activity and being overweight. Now, however, it appears that those who are at greatest risk are smokers.

Cathy Melloan

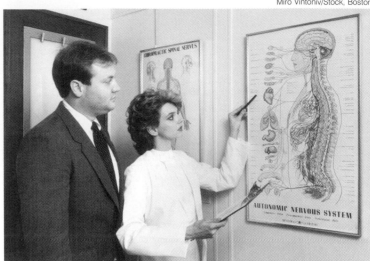

A patient consults a chiropractic practitioner about treatment for back pain. The most extensive trial to date comparing chiropractic and medical therapy for low back pain was conducted in England. For patients with chronic or severe pain, chiropractic treatment was found to be more effective than hospital outpatient management, and the benefit appeared to be long lasting. In general, those with mild to moderate back pain benefit about equally when they receive therapeutic attention in either a medical or a chiropractic setting.

days after the onset of pain did fully as well as those subjected to seven days of bed rest.

Even more encouraging, the utility of exercise therapy is becoming widely accepted. Another important study showed that while an intensive exercise regimen actually increased the degree of back pain during the inceptive month, during the ensuing two months of exercise far greater improvement was noted. (Those doing the prescribed exercises were compared with a control group not engaged in similar exercise.) These findings emphasize the notion that patients should not become discouraged by a degree of increased discomfort early in a therapeutic exercise program.

Treatment frustrations

One of the accepted therapeutic rules is that fewer than 1% of patients with low back pain should be subjected to surgery, regardless of the cause of pain. Yet the efficacy of most other treatments is debatable, primarily owing to a lack of rigorous scientific evaluation. The ineffectual nature of current medical and surgical approaches often leads to additional frustration and depression for the patient with back pain, compounding the original physical problem.

Physicians realize the limitations of current therapies. For them, patients with pain in the back all too frequently become "pains in the neck." The "avoidance approach" that many physicians take toward patients with back pain helps explain the frequency with which patients seek assistance from alternative health care providers such as chiropractors. Adding to patients' confusion is the long-standing discord between physicians and chiropractors—each group viewing the other's approach as ineffectual.

Actually, some of the principles traditionally espoused by both chiropractors and physicians have been fallacious. The fundamental theories regarding chiropractic practice are scientifically unfounded.

Chiropractors consider the spine and its nerves to be responsible for complete governance of visceral organ functions. Certainly the spine in an important part of the anatomy, but the "complete governance" notion is not physiologically valid. Yet stories abound of patients who have found relief at the office of a chiropractor. Physicians' treatments for low back pain also have been ineffective or even injurious. Too often they inappropriately prescribe prolonged bed rest, traction, corsets, steroid injections, chemonucleolysis (injection of an enzyme into a painful disk), or strong analgesic or anti-inflammatory drugs or recommend surgery before other options have been exhausted.

Seeking relief—medical versus chiropractic

In the 1980s two reports appeared in the medical literature indicating that patients with low back pain were more satisfied by chiropractic treatment (largely spinal manipulations) than traditional medical therapy (drugs, rest, physical therapy). British investigators recently finished a herculean study to evaluate this perception further. Eleven medical centers in England recruited patients with low back pain for whom there were no contraindications to manipulation and who had not received treatment in the prior month. Those who volunteered were assigned at random to receive chiropractic treatment (384 patients who received a maximum of 10 treatments, primarily spinal manipulations similar to those used by chiropractors in the U.S., given over a 3–12-month period) or conventional outpatient medical treatment at a hospital (357 patients). All were reevaluated after six months of therapy, and most again at one and two years.

The degree of pain and improvement that patients experienced was graded by means of the Oswestry back pain questionnaire, which gives scores for 10 categories such as intensity of pain and difficulty with lifting, walking, and traveling. The result is expressed on a scale ranging from 0 (no pain or difficulties) to 100% (highest pain or difficulties on all items). At entry into the study, both groups had an average score of approximately 30%, indicating that mild to moderate back disorders existed. Overall, both groups tended to show equivalent degrees of improvement, which ranged between 10 and 15% for the mild patients (Oswestry scores of less than 40%) and 20 and 35% for the chronic or severe patients. Although not evident at 6 and 12 months, at 24 months the severe group receiving chiropractic care had around 7% better scores than their counterparts who received medical care.

Is chiropractic care superior, as the above results suggest, at least for patients with more severe chronic pain? One could surmise that the U.S. Supreme Court tended to think this way, since it cited the British study in a decision in late November 1990 supporting its previous ruling that the American Medical Association's boycott of chiropractors was illegal.

However, a closer look at the study's findings indicates that most patients with nonsevere low back pain receiving therapeutic attention will tend to improve somewhat over a two year period, regardless of the type or source of treatment rendered. The degree of similarity of the treatments given by the chiropractors and hospital clinics in this study is actually surprising. For example, both groups received treatments designated as "manipulations," and some subjects in both groups received exercises as well.

Several major weaknesses of the study make additional interpretation impossible. For example, there is no information as to whether the hospital group received drug therapy for pain or whether over-the-counter analgesic preparations were used by the chiropractic group. The patients in the chiropractic group received about 44% more treatments than the hospital group, which could have contributed to the successful outcome in the former group; the total

costs for their treatments were also higher than those of medically treated patients. Furthermore, the evaluators were not blinded; *i.e.,* they were aware of the treatment assignments. Certainly the chiropractors would have put their "best foot forward," realizing the importance of the outcome for the reputation of their profession. Bias, then, could have influenced the findings in the study. Finally, the medical regimen used by the hospital-based medical group (traction, corsets, manipulation) would be viewed as outmoded and deficient by many medical practitioners. Overall, it appears from this study that patients with mild to moderate low back pain who are given conservative therapeutic attention in either a medical or chiropractic setting benefit about equally.

TENS: a failing grade for a popular treatment

Transcutaneous electrical nerve stimulation (TENS) units are, like many medical devices, widely used despite a limited amount of scientific validation. TENS units are alleged pain-control devices designed with rechargeable batteries and intended for home use. The sufferer places the five centimeter (two inch) round, rubber electrodes over painful areas, and stimulation is delivered in the form of small, barely noticeable electric pulses for around 45 minutes at least three times a day. Skin irritation at the sites of the electrodes is a common problem; otherwise, no side effects ensue.

Elaborate theories have been put forth to explain why TENS may work. One is that when large-diameter peripheral nerve fibers are blocked, pain is severe, and that when those nerve fibers are stimulated, pain is decreased. TENS supposedly provides such stimulation. The proponents of TENS are numerous, and in recent years it has become almost a ubiquitous approach to chronic pain. For example, in 1986 Veterans Administration medical centers spent nearly $2 million for TENS units.

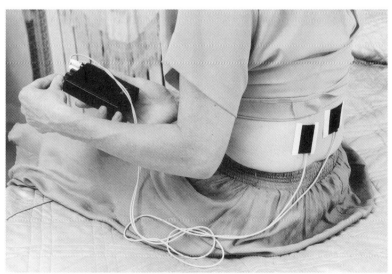

Dan McCoy/Rainbow

Transcutaneous electrical nerve stimulation (TENS) is a widely used form of therapy that is supposed to suppress pain when low-level electrical impulses are applied to the skin over the painful area. Despite the popularity of TENS—a treatment that patients can self-administer at home—its efficacy has never been proved. A recent study of patients with low back pain found no improvement attributable to TENS. The study did find that marked improvement occurred with exercise.

Back care

Despite popularity and the quasi-scientific rationale for its use, there is scant evidence from properly designed clinical trials conducted over many years that TENS is an effective mode of treatment. In the most recent study—one that possessed sufficient academic rigor to be published in the *New England Journal of Medicine*—TENS failed again. Notably, the study reaffirmed what previous investigations had found: that exercise in the management of low back pain *is* effective.

Volunteers were randomly assigned to one of four groups: TENS plus exercise (37 patients), TENS alone (36 patients), exercise and "sham" TENS (36 patients), and sham TENS alone (36 patients). (The latter two groups used devices that looked like actual TENS units but delivered no electric stimulation.) TENS and sham TENS units were applied to the area of maximum pain, and for subjects with sciatica, electrodes were placed over the leg as well. The subjects were unaware of whether they were actually receiving TENS (verified by questioning). The exercise program consisted of a uniform set of 12 sequential exercises performed daily. The regimen was adapted from a YMCA exercise program and was designed to improve the flexibility of the spine, hips, and legs. Compliance was maximized by repeated instruction, feedback, and written information. Treatment was continued for four weeks, during which time participants' progress was evaluated by the investigators twice weekly. Treatment effects were measure by functional status, self-assessment of any improvement, a pain rating, and a physical exam.

In terms of outcome, significant benefit was observed in all four groups, but no improvement attributable to TENS occurred. In contrast, several outcomes revealed beneficial effects of exercise. Most subjects, however, were not continuing to exercise two months after the end of the intervention period, illustrating a frequently occurring paradox in the treatment of low back pain: sufferers' lack of compliance with prescribed long-term exercise therapy despite its evident benefits.

This study's major weakness was the inability to provide a precise placebo counterpart to the exercise group. Although exercise has been shown in many studies to be effective, it cannot be stated with certainty that exercise, rather than increased personal clinical attention, accounted for the improvement. The more convincing conclusion from the study is that patients' time and money can be spent on better things than TENS to ease their low back pain.

Current recommendations

Investigations into new forms of treatment for low back pain continue, such as the use of laser treatments to vaporize water in herniated disks—an experimental approach being studied at Columbia University College of Physicians and Surgeons, New York City. For the present, however, individuals who have experienced a severe episode of mechanical low back pain—and those who wish to avoid this frequent malady—would be wise to make appropriate alterations in certain of their life-style habits.

In particular, they should maintain a regular exercise program that encompasses endurance training; the back is protected more by muscles conditioned to combat fatigue than by muscles capable of achieving maximum strength. No scientific evidence exists to support the widespread notion that sit-ups are harmful for the back; they actually are an excellent way to tone both the abdominal and lumbar musculature. Brisk walking (1.6 km [1 mi] in 15 minutes), stationary or outdoor cycling, various aerobics regimens, push-ups, shallow knee bends, and jogging all confer benefit to the entire body, as well as the back. Achieving and maintaining ideal body weight is also important. An individual approach to achieving this goal is recommended. For most, maintenance of a lower weight

Contrary to widespread belief, sit-ups are not harmful for the back and do not exacerbate back pain; in fact, they provide excellent toning of the abdominal and lumbar musculature.

is virtually impossible without a sustained increase in caloric expenditure provided by exercise. Finally, people should not smoke. As with many matters of health, those who suffer from back pain do have choices.

—*David E. Trentham, M.D.*

Cancer

In spite of many marvelous advances and new forms of treatment, cancer still remains the second greatest cause of death in the United States. More than one million new cases will occur in 1991; about one-half of these individuals will eventually die from the disease. The disease is widespread. One person dies from cancer every minute, and more die from cancer yearly than the combined total of servicemen killed in all the wars fought by the United States thus far. Nearly one of three Americans will develop cancer during his or her lifetime. Even children are not spared. Cancer is the leading cause of death of children between the ages of 3 and 14; approximately 76,000 develop the disease annually.

The cure rate for the most common types of cancer—cancer of the lung, breast, ovary, and large bowel—is not much better now than it was 30 years ago. Approximately 150,000 women will develop cancer of the breast this year (it is the leading tumor type among nonsmoking women), and approximately 44,000 of them will die of the disease. Lung cancer will afflict 150,000 people this year; fewer than 10% of the patients will live five years following diagnosis. The cure rate for cancer of the pancreas is equally poor.

On the bright side, however, the outlook for patients with certain types of neoplasms—such as leukemia and lymphoma (a disease of lymph nodes)—is much better. Here, in many cases, drug treatment is able to kill all the cancer cells. A majority of children with leukemia can be cured. Surgery is not used because the cancer cells originate in blood-forming tissues and the malignant cells—like normal blood cells—spread widely throughout the body. The reason tumors of this type may be cured with drugs, and solid tumors such as cancer of the lung or breast cannot, is not well understood.

The aims of cancer therapies

Why does cancer remain such a lethal disease, and why has the development of a cure remained such an elusive goal? The most difficult problem at present is that once the malignant cells have spread (metastasized) from their original site to distant organs and tissues, and complete surgical removal of diseased tissue is no longer possible, there is no known treatment that can cure the patient.

The ultimate objective of cancer therapy is to cure the disease—to kill each and every last cancer cell in the patient's body. A single residual malignant cell

lodged, for example, in a bone, the liver, or the brain will proliferate just like the original tumor, giving rise to a recurrence. And cells from these metastatic tumors can spread elsewhere throughout the body, eventually overcoming the patient.

After surgery to remove the primary tumor, at the place where the tumor first developed, doctors attempt to kill the remaining cancer cells with radiation and chemotherapy. The unfortunate part of these treatments is that they are not selective. They kill normal cells as well as neoplastic ones. X-rays destroy any cells they encounter. And, since malignant and nonmalignant cells are often mixed or in very close proximity, the amount of irradiation the patient can receive is limited.

In a similar manner, chemotherapeutic drugs kill any dividing cell, normal or malignant. Since many normal cells of the body—essential for life—are dividing, these cells, like the cancer cells, are also killed. Blood-forming cells and immature white blood cells in the bone marrow that prevent infection are examples of critical normal cells that divide continuously, limiting the total amount of drugs that can be used in treatment. Patients undergoing chemotherapy become anemic because immature red blood cells are killed. Because immature white blood cells are destroyed by the chemotherapy, the patients are subject to infection. Hair cells, which proliferate continuously, are a more visible example; many patients undergoing chemotherapy experience excessive hair loss. In most instances, hair regrows when the therapy is discontinued. Blood-forming and white blood cells also gradually return to normal levels after treatment.

In 1991 the U.S. Food and Drug Administration (FDA) allowed the use of granulocyte colony-stimulating factor, a natural hormone of the body that stimulates the formation of white blood cells, to be used in conjunction with chemotherapy. Colony-stimulating factor causes bone marrow to regenerate normal numbers of white blood cells, enabling cancer patients to tolerate intensive chemotherapy and to fight infections that often occur with high-dose anticancer drugs. Many patients are expected to receive the hormone as part of the overall management of their cancer.

Chemotherapeutic treatments are given to the limit of the patient's tolerance in order to kill all remaining cancer cells. Unfortunately, in many cases, a small proportion of the total population of malignant cells develop resistance to the drugs, even before they are administered. (People are frequently exposed to toxic substances in food, in water, and in the air. Cells normally have genes for complex mechanisms to resist toxins. The cancer cells "protect" themselves by using the same genes to resist chemotherapeutic drugs.) These cells survive and eventually regrow.

Since tumors can recur from an extraordinarily small number of malignant cells that have metastasized

Steven Rosenberg at the National Cancer Institute has been using experimental immunotherapies to treat patients with advanced malignant melanoma. The X-ray on the left shows that melanoma has spread to a patient's lungs; two months after treatment with tumor-infiltrating lymphocytes and interleukin-2 (right), most of the cancer had disappeared.

from the original site, numbers that are too small to be found even by the most sensitive methods, doctors may give chemotherapy even when surgery appears to have completely removed all of the patient's cancer cells. Treatment with chemotherapeutic drugs after surgery, when no residual disease is obvious, is known as adjuvant chemotherapy. This approach is commonly used in breast cancer and has prolonged the lives of the majority of patients who receive it, although many are not cured.

For these reasons, doctors strongly recommend early treatment for cancer before the tumor has spread. Periodic examinations, *e.g.,* an X-ray examination of the breast (mammography) and examination of the colon with a flexible tube (colonoscopy or sigmoidoscopy), are safe and relatively efficient. They enable physicians to detect common malignancies before symptoms occur and the tumor has spread. Periodic mammography and clinical examination of the breast have been shown to reduce the mortality from the disease by about one-third in a large group of patients between the ages of 50 and 59. Occasional examination of the stool for blood (a simple test) reduces the chance of dying from colorectal cancer by more than 25%. Since complete removal of the malignancy by surgery is the patient's best hope, periodic examination and prompt consultation with a physician when symptoms first occur are recommended. Yet only 33% of women over the age of 50 have mammography. Similarly, only small numbers of men and women have periodic examinations of the stool or the colon. According to the American Cancer Society, 42,500 cancer-related deaths in 1989 could have been prevented through early detection and treatment.

Unfortunately, in about one-half of all cases, small numbers of cancer cells have spread to distant sites in the body even before the earliest symptoms are noted and surgery can be performed.

Biological therapy: a new weapon

In recent years, biological therapy has been added as a new weapon in the cancer-treatment armamentarium. The great advantage is that, unlike radiation and chemotherapy, the treatment is selective. Only cancer cells are killed by biological therapy; normal cells are unaffected.

Biological therapy takes advantage of the body's own resistance to malignant disease—the natural resistance to cancer cells that certain cells in the body have. This was first shown when it was discovered that tumor growth in patients with severe infection was inhibited; cells resisting the invading bacteria killed the malignant cells as well.

One of the substances secreted during the course of an immune response to infection is interleukin-2. It is a protein secreted by T cells, a class of lymphocytes (white blood cells) found in lymph nodes, the spleen, and peripheral blood. Interleukin-2 increases both the number and the activity of cancer-fighting cells.

Steven Rosenberg at the National Cancer Institute in Bethesda, Md., heads a large group of scientists investigating the possible role of interleukin-2 in cancer therapy. For a number of years, Rosenberg and his colleagues have been removing peripheral blood T cells from patients with malignant melanoma, a highly invasive tumor of the pigment-forming cells of the skin. The T cells are stimulated in the laboratory (*in vitro*) with interleukin-2 and then reinfused by intravenous injection into the patient with melanoma. The activated cells seek out and destroy metastatic melanoma cells. In about 25% of Rosenberg's patients, results are dramatic: partial tumor regression occurs without any other form of treatment.

Since this is an experimental form of therapy, the patients chosen for treatment have large tumors and are terminally ill. In many instances, the cancer cells regrow after a regression has occurred. The treatment, it must be emphasized, is not a cure for the disease.

More recently, Rosenberg has recovered T cells from tumors themselves. These tumor-infiltrating lymphocytes (TIL cells), treated *in vitro* with interleukin-2, "home" to the tumor after reinjection. The TIL cells are more active in killing the malignant cells than non-selected T cells from the peripheral blood. Rosenberg has taken advantage of the homing properties of TIL cells. He has transferred the gene for tumor necrosis factor (TNF) into the TIL cells and then reinfused them into the patient. TNF is a natural "poison" used by lymphocytes to kill cancer cells. Unfortunately, as is the case with chemotherapeutic drugs, some cancer cells develop resistance to TNF.

Physicians are now evaluating the effects of combining biological therapy with chemotherapy and X-ray therapy. Combined treatment may be more effective than any single form of therapy because a cancer cell that is resistant to one form of treatment may be susceptible to another. In the future many more patients will be cured, as treatment today is beginning at earlier stages in the course of patients' illnesses—before the total population of cancer cells has become too large.

Causes: what medical scientists understand today

What causes cancer? There are many known causes (carcinogens)—environmental toxins, chronic infection, recurrent irritation, and hormones, among others. Even substances produced by the body itself can cause the disease. Their common feature is that they stimulate normal cells to divide excessively. Gene mutations responsible for transforming normal cells occur when cells divide. During cell division, the parental cell's DNA is duplicated, and each daughter cell receives one copy. As the duplication takes place, an error sometimes occurs that affects certain critical genes of the cell. While most such errors are recognized and repaired, on occasion the repair mechanism fails, and the error persists as a gene mutation. Cancer results when there is mutation of certain, identified genes (discussed below), which control the response of the cell to external signals that regulate the number of cell divisions. Nondividing cells, such as nerve cells and heart muscle cells, rarely divide and almost never develop tumors.

A notable example of a type of cancer associated with infection is cancer of the liver caused by the hepatitis B virus. Most patients who develop primary liver cancer have this infection. The virus itself does not directly cause the cancer. It slowly and progressively infects more and more healthy cells of the liver, destroying them. The liver undergoes regeneration and repair. Cell division is required for repairing the damaged liver, and the situation becomes one of chronic liver cell death and regeneration. Since there is no known cure for hepatitis B infection, the damage and process of repair is ongoing. On occasion, during cell division, a gene controlling the extent of cell proliferation undergoes mutation and no longer functions properly. A liver tumor results. Hepatitis B is a common infection in East Asia and sub-Saharan Africa; a vaccine is now available that effectively prevents infection, thereby preventing many cancer deaths.

Cancer of the lymph nodes (lymphoma) is a second example of a cancer associated with chronic infection. Lymphoma occurs commonly in patients with AIDS. As treatment for AIDS has improved and survival is prolonged, as many as 25% of AIDS patients now develop this form of malignant disease. The reason for this is that patients with AIDS, like many healthy individuals, are chronically infected with the Epstein-Barr virus (EBV). EBV causes infectious mononucleosis, a relatively short-lived active infection often seen in young adults that persists in chronic form. Like hepatitis B infection, EBV does not cause cancer directly. In immune-deficient patients, however, the EBV virus damages a class of antibody-forming cells known as B cells. The cells are stimulated to proliferate, and chronic proliferation of B cells leads to malignant transformation. In healthy individuals the immune system keeps the virus in check, and the incidence of lymphoma is far less—about 0.5 per 100,000 population.

Noninfectious chronic irritants also cause cell proliferation and cancer. Gallbladder cancer is quite rare; however, gallstones are present in approximately 90% of patients with the disease. The stones irritate the wall of the gallbladder, damaging the cells and stimulating repair. The incidence of cancer of the colon is very high in patients with ulcerative colitis—a chronic inflammatory disease of the colon. As with other irritants, proliferation in cells lining the colon is increased as damage and repair take place. Asbestos is a serious occupational cancer-causing material. It, too, is a chronic irritant and is highly associated with malignant mesothelioma, an otherwise rare chest cancer.

The most common cancer-causing irritant, of course, is tobacco. Tobacco use is directly associated with cancer of the oral cavity, throat, esophagus, and breathing passages of the lung. It is especially dangerous because, in addition to stimulating cell proliferation, substances in tobacco tar are directly damaging

T lymphocytes recovered from a patient's tumor are cultured in a laboratory dish; when such cells are reinfused into the patient's body, they have the potential to become a weapon that can recognize and attack malignant cells, causing tumors to regress.

to DNA. Thus, gene mutation in cells damaged by tobacco is far more likely to take place than might otherwise occur. Lung cancer in smokers is the most common cause of cancer deaths in both sexes.

Hormones—natural body products—also cause cell proliferation. Female hormones (estrogens) are associated with breast cancer and cancer of the uterus, and male hormones (androgens) are associated with cancer of the prostate. The list of cancer-causing substances is long. Their common feature is that they stimulate cell proliferation. Some damage the DNA of the normal cell as well.

Important genetic clues

Cancer may be viewed as a genetic disease at the level of a single cell. The DNA of a critical gene of an individual cell of the patient's body undergoes a mutation—*e.g.*, a certain gene in a cell of a milk-forming gland of the breast or a cell lining a breathing passage in the lung. Mutation in a gene that is normally involved in controlling cell division causes the cell to be unresponsive to the external controls that signal it to stop dividing.

Normally, repair of an injury involves the division of healthy cells. Cell division ceases when the repair is complete. In cancer, each of the daughter cells inherits the genetic change, and the cells divide progressively. As a consequence, a tumor develops. Subsequent genetic changes in the cells' progeny lead to the acquisition of new properties, such as the capacity to survive and proliferate in distant sites and the capacity to resist chemotherapeutic drugs. The malignant cells spread throughout the body. Since even a small tumor contains many millions of cells (a tumor of one cubic centimeter [about 0.06 cu in] contains approximately 10 million cells), numerous genetic changes have occurred, enabling some of the cancer cells to survive even the most vigorous treatment.

Cancer in families. For many years scientists have had clues indicating that cancer is a genetic disease. Only recently, however, have the specific genes that undergo mutation been identified. One of the most significant clues was the observation that the tendency to develop some forms of cancer is inherited, just like eye or hair color.

The tendency to develop cancer of the breast, for example, shows distinct familial characteristics. The probability that a healthy young woman whose mother developed breast cancer at an early age (before menopause) will develop breast cancer herself is approximately 50%. If her mother and sister both developed cancer while they were relatively young, her chances of developing the disease rise to about 80%. The chance that any woman will develop breast cancer at some point in her life, although still disturbingly high, is by comparison much less—about 10%. Breast cancers that occur at an older age (after

menopause) generally do not show a familial tendency.

Some families have a high incidence of various forms of cancer. The Li-Fraumeni syndrome is the name given to a familial tendency to develop a diversity of cancers. The inheritance is dominant; that is, the child of parents one of whom comes from a family that has the Li-Fraumeni syndrome and one who does not is more likely to develop cancer than members of the population at large.

In the early 1970s, Alfred G. Knudson of the Institute for Cancer Research in Philadelphia and Robert DeMars of the University of Wisconsin independently postulated that more than one genetic change was required for a normal cell to be converted to a malignant one. In this theory two changes are required, one in each of two allelic genes that are involved in controlling cell division. (Two copies of each gene are present in an individual cell. One copy is inherited from the mother, and the complementary gene is inherited from the father. These analogous genes are called alleles.) The genes that prevent the cell from transforming from a normal to a malignant one are known as tumor suppressor genes. Each cell contains two allelic tumor suppressor genes. If both are damaged, cell transformation occurs. It is believed that members of families with an inherited tendency to develop cancer inherit one damaged (mutated) tumor suppressor gene. Damage to the second occurs randomly during cell division, and cancer occurs. The chance that this might occur is obviously greater than if both suppressor genes are normal. In that case, both would have to be inactivated in the same cell in order for cell transformation to occur.

Retinoblastoma is a malignant disease of the light-gathering tissue of the eye. Like breast cancer, the tendency to develop retinoblastoma may be inherited. The tumor suppressor gene for retinoblastoma is present on chromosome 13. (In humans there are 46 chromosomes—23 from the mother and 23 from the father. The chromosomes are numbered 1 to 22, plus the sex-determining chromosomes, X and Y. Each pair of chromosomes contains many allelic genes.) If one of the two suppressor genes on chromosome 13 has mutated or has been deleted, a single mutation in the remaining suppressor gene is sufficient to cause the cancer. The cell in the retina, previously inhibited from dividing by external control, is now unresponsive to controls that govern the number and frequency of divisions. The cell then begins proliferating, and a local tumor forms. Since there are millions of cells in the retina, the chance that a mutation may occur in the tumor suppressor gene on chromosome 13 is relatively high. The tumor develops during childhood, and familial retinoblastoma occurs in children. Children of families with a high frequency of retinoblastoma, therefore, undergo frequent examination so that the tumor can be removed before it can spread.

It may happen that a child inherits two defective tumor suppressor genes on chromosome 13. In such cases, the chance of developing retinoblastoma approaches 100%. In rare cases, a child who inherits two such defective genes is born with the malignant disease, multiple tumors having been present in the developing retina.

In other forms of cancer, multiple genetic changes within an individual cell are required for transformation. Most cancers of the colon arise from adenomas, which are premalignant tumors of the colon that frequently give rise to cancer. Bert Vogelstein and his colleagues at Johns Hopkins University, Baltimore, Md., compared the genetic alterations in normal colons, premalignant benign colon tumors, and malignant tumors of the colon and the rectum. They examined three changes in genes known to be associated with cell transformation—on chromosomes 5, 17, and 18. One additional change that was examined leads to the activation of an oncogene known as ras. (The ras gene is responsible for a cell-membrane bound protein that transfers external signals to the cell nucleus, stimulating proliferation.)

Some families have a genetic defect that leads to a high frequency of adenomas of the colon. Individual members of such families have hundreds of colorectal adenomas and a high incidence of colon cancer. The genetic defect associated with this disease is present in the region on the long arm of chromosome 5, known as q21. The gene on chromosome 5 may encode a tumor suppressor gene that functions in a recessive manner. Inactivation of both tumor suppressor alleles is required for cell transformation. Families with a high incidence of the disease have inherited the loss of one of the two suppressor genes. However, more than one safeguard against cancer is present, and multiple genetic changes are required for the cell to be transformed. In addition to genetic alterations of chromosome 5, mutation of allelic genes on chromosomes 17 and 18, along with a mutation of the ras oncogene, are required for cell transformation.

A specific gene has been identified on the short arm of chromosome 17 that is also associated with malignant transformation. The gene codes for a protein known as p53. An alteration of the gene for p53 is the most common finding in human tumors. Approximately 50% of tumors in cancer patients in the United States and Great Britain have an alteration of this gene.

The p53 gene is not well understood. However, it is involved in controlling cell proliferation because transfer of the normal p53 gene into a malignant cell converts the cell to normal growth. A defective gene for p53 cannot control the extent of cell proliferation, and a tumor occurs. Families with the Li-Fraumeni syndrome have a mutation of one of the two allelic copies of the gene for p53. As is the case with colon

Bert Vogelstein, a molecular biologist at Johns Hopkins University, Baltimore, Maryland, has advanced the understanding of certain forms of cancer by showing that malignant tumors of the colon and rectum are caused by a series of genetic changes.

cancer, more than one genetic change is required for a cell with a mutation of the gene for p53 to be transformed. Individual members of families with the Li-Fraumeni syndrome may be cancer free for 25 or more years—the time that is required for multiple genetic changes within an individual cell of the body to accumulate.

Translocated oncogenes: key to diffuse tumors. Not all human tumors involve mutations of cancer suppressor genes, however. In leukemia and lymphoma, it is a translocation of an oncogene from one portion of a cell's DNA to another that leads to cell transformation. Oncogenes control cell proliferation. Normally, their expression is carefully regulated by adjoining portions of DNA known as promoters. In some leukemia and lymphoma cells, an oncogene has translocated away from its promoter to a new site near a promoter that is actively stimulating another gene. In its new site, the oncogene comes under the regulation of the active promoter and is expressed at a high level. A malignancy then develops. Thus, cancer results from the inactivation of tumor suppressor genes in the case of solid tumors and from translocation of oncogenes in the case of diffuse tumors.

Insights into cancer's lethality

Once the cell has transformed, subsequent changes in other genes of the cancer cells generate new, abnormal properties. The cells acquire the ability to invade surrounding tissues and to live in "foreign" sites. Some malignant cells break loose from the primary tumor, enter the bloodstream or lymphatics, and spread to other organs, such as the brain, liver, and bone. Normally, cells of one organ are unable to survive in other organs.

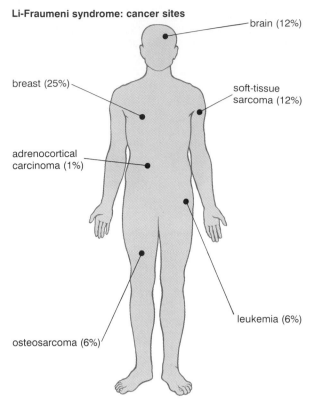

Li-Fraumeni syndrome: cancer sites

brain (12%)

breast (25%)

soft-tissue sarcoma (12%)

adrenocortical carcinoma (1%)

leukemia (6%)

osteosarcoma (6%)

Families with the rare genetic disorder known as Li-Fraumeni syndrome are highly susceptible to several malignant tumors, as shown in the figure. Scientists are now studying individuals from these families to gain a better understanding of the p53 gene; an alteration of that gene appears to underlie the inheritance of their cancers.

The process leading to spread of the tumor is complex, and multiple genetic changes are required. Medical scientists are now able to subdivide metastatic changes into the following steps, each of which may require one or more genetic changes in the cancer cell: detachment of the tumor cell from the primary tumor; invasion through the extracellular environment; invasion of the membrane surrounding small blood vessels; entry into the bloodstream; attachment of the tumor cell to the vascular wall in the vessel of the target tissue; escape (extravasation) from the blood vessel through its membrane to surrounding tissue; and, finally, growth of a new tumor in the target organ.

The target organ itself may contribute to the growth of the tumor, possibly through as yet undefined growth factors that regulate organ development. Isaiah J. Fidler, at M.D. Anderson Cancer Center, Houston, Texas, recently discovered that cancer cells in experimental animals could be selected for their propensity to metastasize to certain organs. Removal and reinjection of melanoma cells metastatic to the lung, for example, led to a heightened number of lung metastases. In his experiments, few lung metastases were found if nonselected melanoma cells were injected.

French scientists from the National Institute of Medical Research in Strasbourg have also contributed new understanding of the metastatic process. The researchers found that newly developed cancers secrete substances that stimulate normal cells nearby to weaken and dissolve the tissue "glue," which acts to keep the cancer cells confined; dissolving the "glue" allows the malignant cells to invade the surrounding tissues.

Tests that predict cancer

The genetic changes in cancer cells—inactivation of tumor suppressor genes and translocation of oncogenes—can now be identified by molecular analysis. In the analysis process, DNA from the tumor is partially digested and "probed" with DNA sequences for genes associated with tumor development. DNA from normal cells of the same patient (conveniently obtained from a blood sample) is also probed. Abnormalities or translocations in cancer-associated genes are detected by differences between tumor and normal cell-derived DNA samples. In certain familial forms of cancer, such genetic aberrations can be identified in normal cells before malignancy develops.

With the advent of molecular techniques that can identify presently healthy individuals who have an increased risk of developing cancer, new problems arise. Health insurance companies may deny insurance to persons who are found by predictive tests to be at high risk, just as they may deny coverage to persons with a high number of motor vehicle accidents. Employers may also want to make use of such tests. They may argue that environmental substances of little risk to normal individuals may cause cancer in persons with inherited defects of tumor suppressor genes. Denying employment to high-risk individuals could lower the company's health insurance premium costs.

Although predictive tests for cancer susceptibility are now only in their infancy, the field will continue to grow, and the tests themselves will become more and more reliable. Consequently, medical ethicists are already debating such questions as: Should the results of genetic tests be made known? Should insurance be denied to individuals found to have genetic defects? Can prospective employees be forced to take a genetic screening test as a condition of employment?

These are important and difficult issues that will take considerable time to resolve. Nonetheless, there is little question that the benefits of genetic screening for cancer are potentially great. Healthy individuals with an inherited predisposition to developing certain forms of the disease can be examined frequently so that any tumor that appears can be removed at the earliest possible opportunity.

—*Edward P. Cohen, M.D.*

Child Health

For child welfare, 1990 was a very special year. Three international agreements gave formal recognition and pledged worldwide commitment to the protection and rights of children. In September, in the largest gathering of world leaders that had ever met to discuss a single topic, 71 heads of state at the World Summit for Children signed a declaration "to give first call" to improving child welfare. By the end of 1990, more than half the countries of the world had endorsed the Convention on the Rights of the Child, which had been adopted by the United Nations General Assembly a year earlier to provide wide-ranging protection for children under international law. It was also the year of a world conference that declared that all children have a fundamental right to education. These pronouncements are the culmination of years of effort by people around the world and represent the recognition that improving conditions for children is the best hope for the world's future.

The leading agency for mobilizing international action for children is UNICEF (United Nations Children's Fund), which earned the Nobel Peace Prize in 1965 for its work in providing resources to care for poor and neglected children. UNICEF continues to promote the ethic of giving priority to children—above all, making children healthy and giving them the skills (through education) to improve their own lot. The achievements of 1990 marked a decade of advances under James P. Grant, the agency's executive director. His leadership has consolidated and expanded the solid reputation of UNICEF as the most activist of the United Nations agencies.

Historical perspective on child health

More was achieved in improving the health of the world's children in the 30 years from 1950 to 1980 than in all prior recorded history. The UN estimate of the mortality of children under five years of age worldwide in 1950 was 251 per 1,000 live births. By 1980 the world average had fallen to 123, more than a 50% decline. In industrialized countries the rate dropped to less than a quarter of earlier figures, and in East Asia it was less than a fifth. In other parts of the world, there was also great improvement but considerable variation (see Table 1).

Child mortality, which is influenced by general socioeconomic conditions, reflects the general health and well-being of populations. Most of the early declines in child mortality were due more to improved nutrition, housing, water supplies, and economic capacity of people to look after themselves than to planned health services.

Between the years 1980 and 1987, under-five mortality rates continued to fall worldwide but at a slower rate than in earlier decades. This was mainly because of a marked decline in the money available for child welfare in the poorest countries of the world, including reductions in spending of 25% on health and 50% on education. Reductions in the gross domestic product (GDP) of 10% in Latin America and 20% in Africa have been particularly damaging—largely because payments on international debts claim 25% of export revenues in less developed Latin-American and African countries. Payments to international banks are over $20 billion more than the total loans and grants for health and other social services received by less developed countries in a year.

Table 1: Child mortality—world picture

	1950		1980		1987	
	under-5 mortality rate (per 1,000 live births)	total under-5 deaths (millions)	under-5 mortality rate	total under-5 deaths	under-5 mortality rate	total under-5 deaths
world total	251	24.8	123	15.5	108	14.7
industrialized countries	84	1.6	20	0.3	18	0.3
less developed countries	295	23.2	138	15.2	120	14.4
Africa	332	3.8	191	4.2	172	4.5
West Asia	334	0.7	118	0.4	99	0.4
Southern Asia	344	7.7	200	7.0	158	6.1
East Asia	273	7.3	51	1.1	45	1.1
Southeast Asia	258	2.2	123	1.4	104	1.3
Central and South America	201	1.5	91	1.1	79	1.0

Source: UN Population Division and UN Statistical Office estimates

Child health

The slowdown in health improvement for children occurred at a time when expectations were high that a reduction in mortality would accelerate—*i.e.,* following the historic International Conference on Primary Health Care at Alma-Ata, Kazakh S.S.R., in 1978, sponsored by the World Health Organization (WHO) and UNICEF. The situation would have been even worse if UNICEF and the U.S. Agency for International Development (USAID) had not mobilized resources for a "revolution" in child survival and development (CSD) in the 1980s.

The watershed conference at Alma-Ata defined three pillars of primary health care (PHC), establishing an infrastructure for sustainable health care. These were: first, to provide high-quality, simple, low-cost health interventions as close as possible to the homes of those who are in greatest need; second, to promote community involvement so that people can largely support and control their own health care; and third, to ensure cooperation and communication with other sectors—a measure that was based on the recognition that health depends on much more than health services.

CSD helped to focus the general principles of PHC by concentrating efforts on specific priorities and establishing that decisions about priorities should be based on the prevalence and severity of health problems and the availability of potential control measures that are inexpensive, acceptable, and simple enough to be applied at the village level. Normally decisions about priorities should be made at the local level, but some health problems are so universal that economies of scale can be achieved through major international programs that establish crucial priorities as well as raise needed resources.

Improving the lot of children: a plan of action

The declaration adopted at the world summit in New York City on Sept. 30, 1990, began:

We have gathered at the World Summit for Children to undertake a joint commitment and to make an urgent universal appeal—to give every child a better future.

The children of the world are innocent, vulnerable and dependent. They are also curious, active and full of hope. Their time should be one of joy and peace, of playing, learning and growing. Their future should be shaped in harmony and cooperation. Their lives should mature, as they broaden their perspectives and gain new experience.

But for many children, the reality of childhood is altogether different.

Emphasizing the plight of the poorest children in the less developed countries, the world leaders at the summit agreed on the technical feasibility of achieving seven overarching goals (with 22 specific subtargets). Almost all countries of the world have made the commitment to achieving these goals by the year 2000. The main goals—aimed at child survival, development, and protection—are:

1. Reduction of infant and under-five mortality by one-third or to a level of 50 (infants) and 70 (under-five) per 1,000 live births, respectively, whichever amounts to the greater reduction.

2. Reduction of maternal mortality by half.

3. Reduction of severe and moderate malnutrition among under-five children by half.

4. Universal access to safe drinking water and to sanitary means of excreta disposal.

5. Universal access to basic education and completion of primary education by at least 80% of primary school age children.

6. Reduction of adult illiteracy rates to at least half of the 1990 levels, with emphasis on female literacy.

United Nations Secretary-General Javier Pérez de Cuéllar addressed the World Summit for Children at UN headquarters in New York City on Sept. 30, 1990. This was the largest gathering of world leaders ever to meet over a single topic; 71 heads of state signed a declaration giving "first call" to improving the lot of the world's poorest children.

John Sotomayor/The New York Times

A Kurdish child receives a cholera vaccination from a French army medic in a refugee camp on the Iraqi-Turkish border. During and after the Persian Gulf war, unsanitary living conditions in many remote camps led to the occurrence of deadly diseases among those forced from their homes. At the World Summit for Children, one of seven main goals agreed upon by world leaders was the protection of children in especially difficult circumstances, particularly in situations of armed conflict.

7. Protection of children in especially difficult circumstances, particularly in situations of armed conflict.

The important question now is: how can these agreed-upon goals be implemented? About 15 million preventable deaths of children occur each year, which is 10 million less than in 1950. The dominant causes of death are synergistic interactions between common infections and malnutrition. Three types of infections—diarrheas, respiratory infections, and immunizable childhood diseases—each cause about a third of these deaths. Resistance to these common infections is greatly compromised by various forms of malnutrition, often producing a downward spiral in which an acute infection causes deterioration in nutritional status, which in turn increases susceptibility to other infections. In addition to pervasive calorie protein malnutrition (or protein-energy malnutrition), which causes weight loss, weakness, apathy, wasting, and diarrhea, many millions of children also suffer from debilitating micronutrient deficiencies, especially of vitamin A, iodine, and iron. Combinations of these problems, which are often life-threatening, are nearly universal among poor children.

To remedy the bleak health status of so many of the world's children, three types of health interventions need to be balanced. First, some health measures are so commonly needed that society can justify imposing them on all people; immunization and community-wide water systems and sanitary improvements are obvious examples. Second, to prevent death from common infections, early diagnosis and treatment are essential—*e.g.,* oral rehydration for diarrhea and antibiotic therapy for pneumonia. And third, long-term sustainability of health improvements requires changes in health habits of mothers and in conditions in the home—*e.g.,* breast-feeding, appropriate feeding during weaning,

basic hygiene and cleanliness, and the prevention of exposure to toxic materials such as cigarette smoke.

UNICEF uses the label GOBI-FFF for: growth monitoring, oral rehydration, breast-feeding, and immunizations—interventions that require immediate emphasis; and family planning, female literacy, and food—interventions that will require attention over a longer term. For almost a decade, international funding has focused mainly on two of these interventions—immunization and oral rehydration.

According to WHO's Expanded Program on Immunization (EPI), established in 1974, coverage of infants in the less developed world against the six main immunizable diseases (measles, whooping cough, diphtheria, tetanus, poliomyelitis, and tuberculosis) rose during the past decade from about 15% in 1980 to about 70% in 1989. It is estimated that about two million deaths are being prevented by immunization each year. At the same time, however, an equivalent number of deaths are still occurring from these diseases. The highest prevalence of deaths occurs among children from the poorest families, who tend to be among the 20% of the population not yet reached.

Oral rehydration therapy (ORT) is a simple, low-cost way of preventing death from watery diarrhea. It uses a properly balanced solution of water, sugar, and salts and is easily administered by mothers. Owing to statements from villagers about increased use of ORT during the 1980s, WHO estimates that about one million lives are being saved annually.

Progress is also being made in controlling the third main cause of infections—childhood pneumonia. This is being accomplished by early diagnoses made by village workers using simple indicators such as rapid respirations and by prompt treatment with low-cost, broad-spectrum oral antibiotics such as sulfamethox-

Child health

azole/trimethoprim, which costs about 15 to 20 cents for a full course of treatment.

Even though progress in promoting child survival continues, the great challenge now is to ensure the sustainability of programs. This will require increasing the local capacity of poor nations to solve their own problems and support their own services. Moreover, the pace of improvement will have to be stepped up to keep ahead of population growth.

The UN estimates that the total number of lives being saved by CSD is essentially equivalent to the expected increase in the number of under-five deaths that would have occurred as a result of population increase, leaving the total deaths per year at about 15 million. If the world summit goals are to be reached, the annual number of child deaths will have to be reduced from 18 million to 7 million by the year 2000.

It is increasingly accepted in less developed countries that mortality and fertility are intimately linked. Family planning helps bring down death rates for children and their mothers. Reducing infant mortality leads to lower rates of overall population growth;

A young mother raising four children on welfare visits the grave of her infant son in rural Mississippi. Rates of infant mortality are extremely high among U.S. women who are caught in a web of poverty and lack both education and access to proper health care.

Greg Campbell/The New York Times

because parents can expect children to survive, they are more likely to have smaller families. There is a great need, therefore, for family-planning services and access to safe, low-cost contraceptives.

A crucial investment

UNICEF's annual report on *The State of the World's Children* (1991) stated that meeting the goals established at the World Summit for Children would be "one of the greatest practical investments which the human race could now make." What is needed now to improve the lot of children in the less developed countries, who fare the worst, is for world leaders to match these goals with an investment of about $20 billion a year. This is an amount equivalent to what the world spends on the military. The proposed distribution would be $3 billion for health, $3 billion for nutrition, $5 billion for education, and $9 billion for water and sanitation. Two-thirds of the money would be provided by the less developed countries themselves, leaving only $7 billion needed in foreign aid (approximately the amount that less developed countries are now paying every 10 days to developed countries as interest on their international debt). For this limited expenditure, all the children of the world would share the basic rights to health and happiness promised at the summit.

Education: critical link to health

As already noted, one of the seven major goals of the world summit's declaration on children was universal access to basic education. Half a year earlier, in March 1990, the World Conference on Education for All met in Jomtien, Thailand, in recognition of the need to do for primary education what PHC was doing for health. In nearly half the less developed countries, the goal of universal primary education has been receding. With current levels of funding, there is no prospect of education goals being able to keep up with the rate of population growth. Although less developed countries have been spending twice as much on education as on health, they also spend twice as much on the military as on education. The result is that in 1990 one in four adults could not read and write; moreover, two-thirds of those were women. Only 55% of children in less developed countries had completed four years of primary education. Half as many girls as boys were literate even though female literacy has consistently been shown to be among the strongest positive influences on birthrates and child health.

As with PHC, there are many examples around the world of effective community-based primary education. However, only 1% of foreign aid to education goes into primary education. Most of the money goes into higher education, despite the fact that primary education has been shown to give more consistent economic returns and greater equity.

The health of U.S. children

In the U.S. the decade of the 1980s was marked by neglect and regression in programs to help poor children. This is indicated by the increased numbers of people living below the poverty line (with a rising percentage being women and children) and the systematic cutting back on virtually all social services.

The high infant mortality rate (IMR) is a critical national problem. During the past two decades, efforts were stepped up to reduce the IMR, partly because U.S. officials were embarrassed about the fact that during the 1960s the country's infant mortality was exceptionally high for an industrialized country (see Table 2).

Presently, the U.S. IMR is still unacceptably high, especially when compared with the rates of other developed nations such as Japan, Sweden, Switzerland, Norway, The Netherlands, and Canada. Moreover, the IMR among U.S. blacks is twice that of whites. Among the major underlying problems are very high rates of teenage pregnancies; a high incidence of low-birth-weight babies (under 2,500 g [5.5 lb]), who have a 40 times greater chance of dying during infancy than do normal-weight babies; complications of drug use during pregnancy; and perinatal transmission of AIDS and other sexually transmitted diseases. All of these problems must be addressed, and substantial services must be provided that target young women, especially those in minority groups. The U.S. public health initiative known as Healthy People 2000, which established nationwide goals and objectives for crucial health improvements for the whole population during the 1990s, emphasizes maternal and infant health services and calls for the reduction of infant deaths from the present 10 per 1,000 live births to 7 by the end of the decade.

The clearest statement of the tremendous unmet needs of children in the U.S. came in the report of the National Commission on Children, which was released in June 1991. A 34-member bipartisan commission, which had been created by Congress in 1987 and was chaired by Sen. John D. Rockefeller IV (Dem., W.Va.), worked for more than two years to produce a comprehensive evaluation of the health and well-being of the nation's children. The report provides a blueprint from which Congress has the opportunity to frame major policy changes during the coming decade.

The report contained many sobering statements indicating that general conditions for children deteriorated greatly during the 1980s. Twelve million children, or one in five, live in poverty. One in four lives with a single parent. More than eight million children have no health insurance coverage. Many U.S. children, the report stated, "will reach adulthood unhealthy, illiterate, unemployable, lacking moral direction and a vision for a secure future. This is a personal tragedy for the young people involved and a staggering loss for

Table 2: U.S infant mortality: improving too slowly				
year	deaths per 1,000 live births		
	white	black	all races
1960	22.9	44.3	26.0
1964	21.6	42.3	24.8
1965	21.5	41.7	24.7
1970	17.8	32.6	20.0
1980	11.0	21.4	12.6
1985	9.3	18.2	10.6
1986	8.9	18.0	10.4
1987	8.6	17.9	10.1
1988	8.5	17.6	10.0
Source: National Center for Health Statistics, 1990			

the nation." Among other things, the report noted that teenage suicide rates are at an all-time high, having tripled in the past three decades, and it decried the widespread use of drugs and alcohol among young people. Succinctly put: "Today, children are the poorest Americans."

The members of the commission emphasized their concern about deteriorating family values, pointing out that the nation's welfare policy "often unwittingly undermines the formation of stable nuclear families." Dismay was expressed over the ironic situation in which "a nation captivated by youth is leaving so many of its young behind."

While there was agreement about the extent of the problems, there was no consensus about what should be done. The majority report suggested solutions that will cost more than $50 billion a year, or $293 billion over the next five years (most going into a $1,000-per-child income tax credit). Congress may find ways of reducing this cost by focusing more sharply on families in need. A $7.7 billion proposal for employer- and government-provided health insurance for all pregnant women and children up to 18 years of age will be considered, along with many other proposals for health insurance reform. The other recommendations included parents having a choice in the selection of their children's schools, several educational reforms, and expansion of the Head Start and Job Corps programs. Social problems on the whole were addressed mainly through exhortation; e.g., "We recommend that parents be more vigilant and aggressive guardians of their children's moral development." Such statements have been criticized as being platitudes that are not likely to result in meaningful action.

It was likely that the commission's proposals would be debated for many months. The report of the National Commission on Children indicates that there are potential remedies for the unsatisfactory status of U.S. children—especially poor children—but that progress at best will be incremental.

—Carl E. Taylor, M.D., Dr.P.H.

Special Report
Joint Replacements: Great Strides
by Charles-Gene McDaniel, M.S.J.

In the 1940s a comical song called "Dry Bones" told how the toe bone is connected to the foot bone, the foot bone to the ankle bone, the ankle bone to the shin bone, and on to the neck bone, which is connected to the "head bone." During the decades since then, medical science has advanced to the point that, except for the last, any of those connecting "bones" (*i.e.,* joints) can be replaced by artificial ones. In fact, "toe bones" are one of the most recent developments in orthopedic implants.

The replacement of joints crippled by severe arthritis, other diseases, or injury has grown phenomenally since the first artificial hip was implanted in 1962 in England. Improved surgical techniques and the development of better materials mean that now—in addition to hips—artificial knees, ankles, elbows, shoulders, and finger and toe joints are implanted with a stunning degree of success. In the U.S. alone, more than 556,000 joints are replaced annually.

The 50 million Americans who suffer from arthritic diseases are the major beneficiaries. The National Institutes of Health has designated 14 hospitals in the U.S. as arthritis centers, where expert joint replacements are considered the leading advance of the past two decades in treating the most common forms of this disease. Such replacements have resulted in substantial improvement of joint function and reduction of pain in 90% of cases. Generally, the best candidates for joint replacement are those whose arthritis does not respond to medication, those whose joint pain is severe enough to awaken them at night or limit walking endurance to about a block or less, and those who have X-ray evidence of joint degeneration.

Replacing ravaged hips

Among the most frequently replaced joints are hips, which, because they are larger than other joints, are relatively easily replaced. At present, the life expectancy of a new hip joint is 15 years, but researchers say that number will soon double as even better implant materials and fixatives are developed. Because of the present life expectancy of most artificial hip joints, orthopedic surgeons generally prefer to wait until the patient is around age 60 before implanting a prosthesis so as to minimize the need for subsequent replacements.

There are exceptions, however. The dancer Edward Villella, as a principal with the New York City Ballet for some two decades, drew gasps from thrilled audiences with his breathtaking leaps, power, and technique. But wear and tear and a series of injuries caused him to suffer excruciating pain for five years. In 1980 he went to London to have a hip replacement. After recuperating, he resumed performing for a time, dancing the lead in *Afternoon of a Faun* and *Apollo* before officially retiring from the stage and eventually becoming artistic director of the Miami (Fla.) City Ballet. Still, he is able to teach and demonstrate "everything except big jumps."

A study reported in 1991, while limited, appears to confirm that young patients are indeed candidates for hip replacement. Forty-three patients in their twenties, thirties, and forties had the operation between 1971 and 1978. Thirty-one hips in 25 patients were still

After his hip replacement, Edward Villella danced demanding principal roles several times before retiring from the stage to become the Miami City Ballet's artistic director. Even now he can demonstrate everything but the "big jumps."

functioning well after an average of 15 years; in 11 of 12 who required revision surgery (replacement of the prosthetic joint), the first prosthesis had worked well for 10 to 15 years. Four of the patients had died of unrelated causes, and two were lost to follow-up.

The hip, one of the body's largest weight-bearing joints, is a ball-and-socket arrangement. The head of the femur, the long bone in the thigh, is the ball, which fits into the acetabulum, the socket attached to the pelvis. The bones are covered with cartilage that acts as protective tissue. The joint surfaces may be destroyed by fatigue, overuse, congenital problems, inflammatory arthritis, bone disease, and deterioration caused by unequal length of the legs. Debris from the process of wear and tear inflames the lining of the joint and leads to cysts and joint destruction.

The artificial hip joint has the same basic parts as the natural hip. It consists of a stem (usually made of a superalloy such as titanium-aluminum-vanadium), which is inserted into the femur, and a prosthetic ball (often metal), which fits into a cup (usually made of high-density polyethylene plastic) that replaces the damaged socket.

A hip prosthesis can be implanted with or without cement. About half of all hip-implant components in the U.S. use no cement. One common technique uses cement to hold the prosthetic stem in the femur and screws to attach a porous cup to the acetabulum, into which bone or fibrous tissue quickly grows to provide fixation. In general, cemented joints have a faster healing time; later, however, loosening may occur, requiring repeated surgery. Uncemented joints, most often used in younger patients, are slower to heal but are expected to grow stronger as natural bone grows around them. The long-term biological effects of implants without cement are not known, but for unknown reasons, these implants are associated with a higher incidence of pain than are cemented joints.

Although today's artificial hips can tolerate considerable stress, there are limits, and some patients are not suitable candidates. Obese patients, for example, are not good candidates for the implants because of the undue stress imposed by their weight. Orthopedic surgeons caution that hip replacement creates a "good hip" but not a "normal hip," so for most recipients there is some limitation on activities.

After initial recovery from the surgery, there is generally a period of one or two days of bed rest in the hospital. Postoperative rehabilitation for a new hip generally requires that patients use crutches for 6 to 12 weeks, followed by a gradual transition, over one to two months, until they are walking with normal gait without crutches or a cane. Most patients regain full strength and energy in three to five months, when ordinary activities can be resumed; walking, sitting, climbing stairs, entering a car, and even participating in nonimpact sports ordinarily cause no problem. In

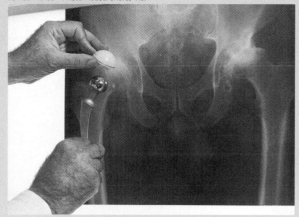

An orthopedic surgeon holds a titanium prosthesis in position against the X-ray of a patient needing a total hip replacement. The artificial joint has the same ball-and-socket arrangement as the natural hip and is designed to bear the body's weight, allowing full and pain-free mobility.

fact, patients are advised to exercise frequently; swimming and exercising on a stationary bicycle are often recommended. To minimize stress on the hip when it is not in use, patients are instructed not to cross their legs while sitting and to sleep on their backs.

The late George Halas, former football player and founder of the Chicago Bears football team, was among the early recipients of bilateral hip replacement (both joints). In 1968, at age 73, "Papa Bear" Halas went to England to have one hip replaced; he returned in 1969 for the other. The operation had not yet been approved in the United States because the safety of the cement that was used had not been established by the Food and Drug Administration. Methyl methacrylate cement was approved in the early 1970s, and now hip replacement is performed an estimated 120,000 times a year in North America and is deemed by far the most successful surgery for patients with advanced osteoarthritis and rheumatoid arthritis of the hip. About 25 to 40% of all those who require the procedure need to have both hips replaced.

New knees

About as many knee replacements as hip replacements are done each year in the United States, with results deemed equal to or exceeding those of hip replacement in terms of the relief of patients' pain, improved function, and survival of the implant. Knees, however, are a more complex, less stable joint.

Knee pain and stiffness result from the same causes as hip problems: osteoarthritis (the breakdown of cartilage), rheumatoid arthritis (inflammatory joint disease), bone disease, injury, wear and tear, and poor alignment of the leg bones. The total knee consists of three parts—the femoral component, covering the thigh bone, the tibial component covering the top of

273

the shin bone, and the patellar component, covering the underside of the patella, or kneecap.

Among those who had a successful knee implant was the singer Pearl Bailey, who suffered from degenerative arthritis; the protective cartilage that acts as a shock absorber had been damaged so that the bones rubbed together—a very painful condition. At age 72 Bailey underwent implant surgery lasting less than an hour to receive a new left knee made of plastic and metal. Sadly, Bailey was unable to truly enjoy her new knee; she had a long-standing heart condition, from which she died in August 1990, less than a month after her implant operation.

Replacement of a knee involves removal of the diseased patella and the ends of the femur (thigh bone) and the tibia. The artificial joint is affixed to the bones of the upper and lower leg with screws or cement; alternatively, in younger patients the procedure is done without cement, and the bone is allowed to grow into the implant's porous surfaces.

The general principle has been to leave as much of the supporting tissue of the knee intact as possible, including the ligaments. Now, however, even the ligaments themselves can be replaced with a synthetic, Teflon-like material. Formerly, damaged ligaments had to be replaced with grafts from a tendon in the patient's kneecap, which meant sacrificing human tissue. Athletes are the most common recipients of artificial ligaments; rugged sports such as football, basketball, soccer, rugby, tennis, and skiing can cause the knee's ligaments, particularly the anterior cruciate ligament, to tear. Although ligaments have been replaced in patients for a number of years at about a dozen medical centers, they are still a very new implant development. Whether over the long term the implants can withstand the wear and tear of athletics has not been determined.

Recovery from knee-implant surgery emphasizes physical therapy—from wiggling the toes in the first days after the procedure to performing gentle knee exercises and then to walking (aided, then unaided). Special strengthening and range-of-motion exercises are part of the recovery process.

Back on their feet

An innovation developed by an Arizona podiatrist now makes it possible to relieve the suffering of patients with painful, twisted arthritic toes. The procedure involves fitting a cap made of high-grade silicone elastomer over the metatarsal joint, which connects with the phalanx, or toe bone. The cap, known as a lesser metatarsal cap, is held in place by a shaft extending from the center of the bone. Formerly, silicone rubber toe implants were used, but these did not cover the joint and left sharp edges that often resulted in bleeding and irritation, contributing to abnormal bone growth following their implantation. The cap solved

274

this problem; it creates a smooth, cushiony surface between the joint and the phalanx, eliminating the potential for irritation. Before it is put in place, the metatarsal heads are trimmed and smoothed. No cement is needed for securing the cap because natural body tissue grows to hold it in place. The cap also reduces postoperative bleeding and swelling, which helps patients get back on their feet in a remarkably short time.

One of the early recipients of the metatarsal toe caps was Dorothy Y., a middle-aged woman suffering from polyarthritis (affecting many joints). Before her implant operation, taking steps "felt like walking on rocks." Her toes were crossed, and thick callus pads had formed beneath all of them so that none would touch the floor. After replacements for all 10 toe joints, 9 were deemed "successful," and she is now able to get around with relative ease. Most people have this procedure as outpatients. Within three weeks they are usually wearing shoes and walking almost normally.

Fingers restored

Not only did Dorothy Y. have implants to relieve her painful toe condition, she also had silicone rubber joint

A patient whose arthritis prevented her from walking without excruciating pain had all 10 toes fitted with silicone metatarsal toe caps, invented by Arizona podiatrist Kerry Zang. After her surgery she was able to get around with ease.

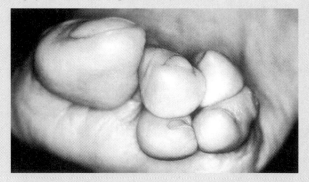

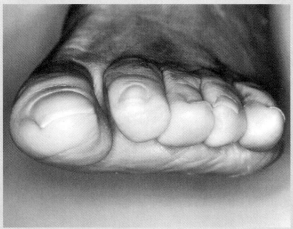

Photographs, Kerry Zang, D.P.M.

implants to replace the deformed joints of six of her fingers—four on the right hand, two on the left. These joint replacements are anchored by stems inserted in the metacarpal bone that joins the hand and the phalanges, which extend beyond the joint. At present, prostheses are not available for diseased thumbs— a considerably more complex joint. While Dorothy Y. cannot extend her fingers to the same degree that undiseased fingers extend, she does have greater extension than she had prior to the implants. Perhaps more important, she no longer has pain.

As is true with all other artificial joints, finger joint replacements do not have the strength of those nature originally provided, and replacement procedures are not suitable for all patients. Pianist Byron Janis had his concert career interrupted at age 45 because psoriatic arthritis had caused the last two joints of all 10 of his fingers to become fused, reducing the span of his hand from 10 keys to 8. Unfortunately, Janis was not a suitable candidate for joint replacement. While implants would reduce his pain, they could not withstand the pounding motions of piano playing.

Shoulders, elbows, and wrists

Replacement of diseased or damaged joints in the upper part of the body has proceeded more slowly—in part because a relatively small number of people need complete replacement of the large upper joints and in part because these joints are complex. However, engineering developments now enable replacements for shoulder, elbow, and wrist joints that are deemed good to excellent for long-term pain relief and restoration of movement and function.

Before a satisfactory artificial shoulder could be devised, a technique was needed for preserving muscle attachment to the joint and retaining support of the ligaments. In a procedure similar to hip replacement, the artificial shoulder is secured to a bone, in this case the humerus in the upper arm, either by biological ingrowth or with methyl methacrylate.

One of the complicating factors with elbow replacement is that many of the muscles moving the hand and wrist are attached to or near the elbow. Some early efforts failed because the prostheses came loose from the humerus and the ulna, a bone in the forearm. The problems, however, were overcome with a modified implant. This implant is now considered one of the most successful, with recipients often forgetting which elbow has had surgery.

Wrist replacements are an even more recent development. The present version of this artificial joint is anchored in the radius, another bone in the forearm, and in the second and third metacarpal bones, which are attached to the fingers. Orthopedic surgeons report that relief of pain in wrist-implant patients is almost universal, as are improvement in function and ease of movement.

Computer-designed joints

Until fairly recently, artificial joints were created after a designer had studied the patient's X-ray films and painstakingly drawn a model. A technician then created a replacement by using an assortment of machine tools and finishing the prosthesis by hand. On average, the process took about 12 weeks. Now even better artificial joints are available with custom-made, computer-designed prostheses. With computer-aided design and manufacture, a joint can be produced in two weeks or less, at a cost that is about 20% lower than previously.

The new prosthesis-creation process works this way: standard X-rays of the joint (or joints) in question as well as a computed tomography (CT) scan, which can detect bone abnormalities, are taken. The computer "reads" these and combines the data. The physician adds other data that can affect the design, such as the patient's weight, age, and level of physical activity. The computer then selects a design from the hundreds it has stored in its memory and displays the appropriate one on the screen. If there is no appropriate model in its memory, the computer has the capacity to generate one that is suitable for the patient. By rotating the design and viewing it on the computer screen from different angles, the orthopedist is able to make sure that the computer-chosen prosthesis will provide the best possible fit for the patient's bone structure. Once the design has been settled on, a punched tape bearing the specifications for the artificial joint is generated by the computer. This tape then is entered into a computer in the machine shop that programs lathes and milling machines to create the custom prostheses from blocks of titanium and other materials.

Future developments

At present, most joints of the human skeleton can be replaced. Perhaps the biggest surprise for some artificial-joint recipients who are enjoying their new lease on life and their newfound mobility comes when they are stopped in airports because their implants have set off the metal detectors!

Orthopedic surgeons and engineers continue to refine the wide array of function-restoring implants; they are developing new and better materials that are likely to enable more patients in the future, especially younger ones, to benefit. For example, E.I. du Pont de Nemours & Co. and the Revra DuPuy company are collaborating on developing new polyethylene bearings that promise longer life for a variety of prostheses, and doctors at the University of Chicago are now devising ready-made joint implants that are connected to segments of artificial bone for replacement in young victims of bone cancer. Surely other innovations can be expected; at least for the foreseeable future, however, there will be no artificial "head bone."

Death and Dying

The battle over the control of decisions about how and when individuals will die is one that grows fiercer each year. Several recent developments have piqued public interest and intensified the conflict. In the U.S. the participation of physicians in two widely publicized patient suicides came to national attention in 1990 and 1991. In the U.K. physicians and ethicists also considered the concept of assisted suicide. And a new U.S. law that took effect in 1991, dubbed "medical Miranda," calls for patients to be informed of their rights when it comes to dying. Of all the developments, however, the most important was the U.S. Supreme Court's first decision on a "right-to-die" case, delivered in June 1990.

The case of Nancy Cruzan

In January 1983, 25-year-old Nancy Cruzan was thrown from her car in an accident on an icy country road in her home state of Missouri. Although rescue workers were able to restore her heartbeat and breathing, she never awoke from her trauma. In time she was diagnosed as being in a persistent vegetative state (PVS). People in PVS are believed to have no capacity to see or hear or to think or have emotions. The condition is possible only because of the way in which the human brain is organized. The capacities for human experience (thoughts, feelings, emotions) and expression depend on an intact upper brain, whereas only the brain stem, running along the back of the neck, is required for the lungs, heart, and homeostatic mechanisms of the body to function. A person whose upper brain is completely destroyed but whose brain stem is intact can live for years in PVS without any capacity for experience or communication.

Several years after her accident, Cruzan's family became convinced that she would not recover and requested that the tube feedings on which she depended be stopped. The Missouri Rehabilitation Center in Mount Vernon, where she was a patient, refused to do so without a court order, so the Cruzan family went to court. After their petition was granted and upheld by Missouri's lower courts, the Missouri Supreme Court reversed the decision and turned down the Cruzans' request. The family appealed to the U.S. Supreme Court, which agreed to hear their petition— the first such case to reach the nation's highest court.

The decision in *Cruzan* v. *Director, Missouri Department of Public Health,* came on June 26, 1990, upholding the Missouri law that required "clear and convincing evidence" that a person would have wanted life-sustaining treatment removed before such a wish would be honored. The immediate effect of the ruling caused considerable distress among right-to-die advocates, but a more careful reading showed that implications of the full ruling were not as cut-and-dried as they first appeared. The court ruled that a restrictive law such as Missouri's, requiring a heavy burden of proof, did not violate the U.S. constitution. However, states could choose to have much less restrictive policies, which would still pass constitutional muster.

Other important points were strongly implied by the decision, although the court did not rule on them expressly. First, the right to refuse medical treatment may well be constitutionally protected. Second, the right to refuse treatment continues to exist even after the individual can no longer speak for himself or herself. Third, artificial nutrition and hydration are not distinct from other forms of medical treatment and may be forgone under proper circumstances. Fourth, how close the individual is to death is not the crucial

The U.S. Supreme Court delivered its first decision on a "right-to-die" case on June 26, 1990. The court ruled that Nancy Cruzan's parents might be allowed to have her feeding tube removed if there was "clear and convincing evidence" that she would not want to live in her persistent vegetative state. In December 1990 such evidence came in the testimony of other people who had known Nancy. When, to the relief of her family, a Missouri judge allowed the tube removed on December 14, protesters began a vigil outside the Missouri Rehabilitation Center, where Nancy was a patient, but their petitions seeking reconnection of her tube were denied by a federal district court. She died 12 days later.

point. The prospect that Cruzan could possibly survive for several decades after her accident was not seen as important.

The Supreme Court's decision was little comfort to the Cruzan family, but the case was far from over. Other people who had known Nancy prior to her accident came forward with additional testimony about her wishes not to be kept alive in a condition such as the one she was in. The attorney general of Missouri withdrew from the case, leaving as parties to the case the family and Cruzan's court-appointed guardians, all of whom believed that she would not want treatment continued. With the additional testimony, the judge ruled that the Missouri law's standard of clear and convincing evidence had been met, and he allowed the family to have her tube feedings stopped. On Dec. 14, 1990, the tube was removed, and on December 26 Nancy Cruzan died peacefully, with her family in attendance—and protesters outside.

More than any other event, the Cruzan case led to a dramatic increase in interest in so-called advance directives—documents that are prepared when persons are still competent and that serve to direct their care once they lose competency. This interest arose from the Supreme Court's endorsement of the individual's right to refuse medical treatment and its apparent approval of the concept of such directives.

People's fears that they may lose control over their own fate upon entering a hospital or nursing home appear to be widespread. Increasing numbers of individuals want some say in what happens to them at such times. In the U.S. most people (over 80% of elderly Americans) die in institutions, and it is estimated that 70% of deaths in institutions involve explicit decisions to forgo life-prolonging treatments.

Physician-assisted suicide: two cases

Some individuals are unwilling to wait until they are in a hospital or nursing home; they seek help from a physician to die sooner. In June 1990, the same month as the Cruzan decision, Jack Kevorkian, a retired Michigan pathologist, attached a machine he had constructed to Janet Adkins, a 54-year-old woman from Portland, Ore., who was in the early stages of a disease believed to be Alzheimer's dementia. The disease had advanced far enough to be noticeable and distressing to her but not so far as to severely incapacitate her—it was later reported that she beat her son at tennis the week before her death—or to make her indisputably incompetent to decide what she wanted to do. She learned of Kevorkian's drug-delivering "suicide machine" and arranged to go to Michigan with the intent of using it on herself. (Michigan was chosen because it had no law against assisting in a suicide.) After a brief conversation in the Volkswagen bus in which the apparatus had been set up, Kevorkian, who was the sole witness to the act,

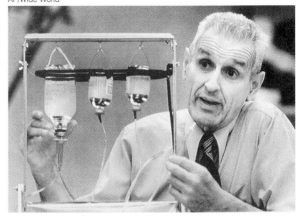

Jack Kevorkian, a retired Michigan pathologist, poses with his suicide device that was used by Janet Adkins, a 54-year-old woman from Oregon with suspected Alzheimer's disease, who chose to die rather than face decline into dementia.

says he inserted an intravenous needle into Adkins' arm, and she then pressed a switch to activate the machine, which released a sequence of saline solution, thiopental, and lethal potassium chloride into her bloodstream. She was dead in less than six minutes.

The story fascinated the nation. Adkins' husband and children expressed great sadness but also support for her actions. She was described as a person who valued greatly her ability to lead a full and vigorous life. The prospect of progressive decline into dependence and dementia was anathema to her.

Kevorkian became an instant celebrity, appearing on many talk shows and being interviewed by countless journalists. To Kevorkian the widespread publicity meant that he had finally gained the platform he had long sought from which to express his bitterness with the American medical establishment and his views about the right of individuals to control their own deaths. Kevorkian's business card reads: "Bioethics and Obitiatry. Special Death Counseling. By Appointment Only." *Obitiatry* is his own term for the medical management of death. (The media have called him "Doctor Death.") He once had proposed conducting experiments on condemned prisoners and then executing them in a way that would best preserve their organs for study.

The dispute immediately following Adkins' death led to the seizure of the suicide machine, a temporary injunction banning its use, and a first-degree murder charge against Kevorkian (the latter was then dismissed). However, a further ruling by a Michigan judge in February 1991 barred Kevorkian from using the machine or building another.

The most interesting feature of the case was the public and professional response to it. On one side, there was a surge of public support for what Adkins had done. A *New York Times*/CBS poll found that 53%

of respondents believed that physicians should be permitted to assist severely ill persons who want to end their lives. On the other side, groups concerned with the right to die, including strong proponents of individual decision making, were highly critical of Kevorkian. He had violated many of the principles that are supposed to govern such decisions: he had known Adkins for only a few hours; he had no independent confirmation of her competency; he did not know if this decision was consistent with her most cherished values; and he seemed to be as interested in promoting his personal views as in helping Adkins. Proponents of the right to die were not pleased that this incident rapidly became the most famous example of its kind.

Physicians, on the other hand, seemed to be of two minds. Organized medicine, for the most part, disparaged Kevorkian's actions and opposed physicians' taking an active role in their patients' suicides. On the other hand, some physicians argued that there were times when it might be appropriate for a physician to assist a patient whom they knew well to end a life that had become unbearable; Kevorkian's assistance to Adkins, however, did not reflect the compassionate and informed aid, growing out of a long relationship, that they had in mind. Such a case did appear only eight months later.

In March 1991 an account of a physician's assisting a patient in killing herself was published in the *New England Journal of Medicine.* Timothy E. Quill, from Rochester, N.Y., told the story of his 45-year-old patient Diane—presumably not her real name—who had been diagnosed with a form of leukemia that is usually but not always fatal. The treatment for it is lengthy and toxic, involving two stages of chemotherapy followed by whole-body irradiation and bone marrow transplantation. Approximately 25% of patients who undergo such treatment have a successful outcome—*i.e.,* a long-term cure. Most, however, die during treatment, and the side effects of treatment are severe. Without the treatment, death could be expected to come rapidly, but the individual generally feels relatively well until close to the very end. Diane, against her family's initial wishes, chose not to undergo treatment for her leukemia. She opted instead to spend time with her husband and son at home.

Because Diane feared that her death would be lingering, she asked Quill for help in ending her life when she could no longer bear the suffering. He then advised her to get information from the Hemlock Society, an organization that supports the option of active voluntary suicide for the terminally ill. When, a week later, she asked Quill to prescribe barbiturates to help her sleep, he wrote the prescription despite feeling uneasy about the implications of his action; he knew that barbiturates were an ingredient in a Hemlock Society recipe for suicide.

Phil Matt/The New York Times

Physician Timothy E. Quill of Rochester, New York, wrote a moving account of his agonizing choice to help one of his patients "over the edge into death" when it was clear that her leukemia was likely to be fatal and would cause her great pain and suffering.

Diane did not commit suicide right away; she lived for more than three months after her diagnosis. She used the time to become closer to her family and friends. Then, when the effects of the leukemia began to dominate her life with pain and weakness, she said good-bye to her family, her friends, and her physician and asked her husband and son to leave her alone for an hour. When they returned she had died— at home—in apparent peace. Quill wrote that "Diane taught me about the range of help I can provide if I know people well and if I allow them to say what they really want. . . . I wonder how many families and physicians secretly help their patients over the edge into death in the face of such severe suffering."

Quill's role in the assisted suicide of Diane is at the other extreme from Kevorkian's role in Adkins' death. Quill knew his patient for eight years and believed that her decision was entirely consistent with the values she had expressed during that time; she had a rapidly lethal and painful disease, the treatment for which was sometimes successful but more often resulted in significant suffering before death; and Quill, at least in his published account, showed great sensitivity to his moral obligations as a physician.

Quill's article reignited the debate that had been sparked by Kevorkian's actions. In the judgment of proponents of physician-assisted suicide, Quill had done virtually everything correctly—the opposite of Kevorkian. On July 26, 1991, this view was supported by a grand jury in Rochester, which said Quill was innocent of any wrongdoing, and on August 16 the New York State Department of Health said it would not bring professional misconduct charges against him. It is likely that the public debate on assisted suicide as well as the debate within the profession will continue for some time.

Assisted death: a British view

In September 1990 a respected group of physicians and ethicists in the United Kingdom came to certain conclusions about physicians' and patients' roles in decisions about dying. The Working Party on the Ethics of Prolonging Life and Assisting Death of the Institute of Medical Ethics published the report "Assisted Death," in which they raised two difficult questions: whether in cases of coma, severe incapacity, or unrelievable pain, doctors "are morally bound to continue with life-prolonging treatment" and "whether and in what circumstances it is ethical to hasten [patients'] deaths by administration of narcotic drugs." This report dealt only with cases where such assistance was requested by conscious, competent patients. It did not consider unconscious or severely incapacitated patients.

The working party's report considered and dismissed several objections to assisting death and stressed the difficulty in drawing a clear line between "killing" and "letting die." It focused on the physician's duty to relieve suffering and asserted that the duty to prolong life applies not in every instance but only where the quality of life is such that the patient wants it prolonged.

The British group's conclusion appears to endorse both physician-assisted suicide and active euthanasia. The report stated: "A doctor, acting in good conscience, is ethically justified in assisting death if the need to relieve intense and unceasing pain or distress caused by an incurable illness greatly outweighs the benefit to the patient of further prolonging his life." Should this become accepted practice, the U.K. would join The Netherlands as the only Western countries where physician-assisted death is openly tolerated.

"Do not resuscitate"

The dramatic scenes on television of physicians and nurses rushing to the bedside of a hospitalized patient who has stopped breathing and whose heart has stopped, or of ambulance paramedics saving the lives of sudden heart attack victims who have collapsed on the street, are very familiar. The procedure used to revive patients on the brink of death is called cardiopulmonary resuscitation (CPR) and may include massaging the heart, injecting drugs, or administering powerful electric shocks intended to get the heart beating again. When it works, it can save a life, but it works much less often in real life than on television.

Approximately one-third of CPRs are successful in the short run—that is, they restore a heartbeat. The other two-thirds of patients die despite the effort to resuscitate them. Of the third in whom a heartbeat is recovered, only one-third to one-half leave the hospital alive. The rest succumb to their illness.

It is generally accepted that not all persons who suffer cardiopulmonary arrest should get CPR. Many people do not want it, and in other cases it is almost certainly futile. A physician can enter a "do not resuscitate" (DNR) order on a patient's chart, indicating that no attempt should be made to revive that patient in the event of cardiac arrest.

Although the concept of not resuscitating patients has been well accepted in ethics, law, and medicine, the implementation of DNR orders has been troublesome. For example, although roughly two-thirds of patients indicate their desire to talk with their physician about life-sustaining treatment, studies consistently find that only one in five patients who have DNR orders ever discussed that decision with the physician; physicians are more likely to have spoken with relatives of the patient. Part of the problem may be that physicians are reluctant to talk with patients about dying until the patients are so sick that they are no longer competent to consent to the accepting or withholding of treatment. Physicians also tend to be poor judges of patients' preferences about resuscitation. Studies indicate that doctors' predictions about what their patients would prefer are highly inaccurate. Furthermore, there is some evidence indicating that patients may view their quality of life more positively than physicians typically do.

One study showed that wide differences existed in the rate at which DNR orders were written for diseases with similarly grave prognoses. Roughly half of patients with AIDS and lung cancer had DNR orders. Patients with two other equally grim diseases—ad-

Life-sustaining treatment: preferences of 126 nursing home residents					
situation and treatment	treatment	no treatment	have doctor decide	have family decide	do not know; other
	percentage of total sample				
critical illness					
hospitalization	58	4	15	22	< 1
intensive care	46	6	26	19	3
cardiopulmonary resuscitation	47	21	30	3	0
surgery	32	15	23	25	6
artificial ventilation	35	17	22	20	7
terminal illness					
hospitalization	29	15	22	28	6
intensive care	23	27	19	26	4
cardiopulmonary resuscitation	20	47	29	4	0
surgery	14	34	18	23	11
artificial ventilation	20	40	12	21	8
permanent unconsciousness					
hospitalization	20	25	20	29	6
intensive care	17	37	16	26	4
cardiopulmonary resuscitation	19	44	31	6	0
surgery	8	42	17	24	9
artificial ventilation	13	49	11	21	6
tube feeding	16	49	14	18	3

From Marion Danis, M.D., *et al.*, "A Prospective Study of Advance Directives for Life-Sustaining Care," *New England Journal of Medicine,* vol. 324, no. 13 (March 28, 1991), pp. 882–888

vanced cirrhosis and severe congestive heart failure—had DNR orders 16 and 5% of the time, respectively. The study's authors did not speculate on whether patients with AIDS and lung cancer have too many DNR orders written or patients with cirrhosis and heart failure too few, but they did comment that their findings "should encourage physicians to determine the preferences of patients about life-sustaining treatments more equitably."

The American Medical Association's Council of Ethical and Judicial Affairs published updated guidelines for DNR orders in April 1991. The new guidelines stress that resuscitation *should* be attempted unless (1) the patient does not want it, (2) it is not in the patient's best interest, or (3) it would be futile. Physicians are urged to discuss CPR with patients before the patients' illnesses destroy their abilities to think and communicate and not to substitute their own judgments about a patient's quality of life for the judgments made by

In July 1990 an organizer of the Death with Dignity citizens' campaign seeks signatures for Initiative 119, which would make Washington state the first in the U.S. to legalize some form of euthanasia.

Lance Muresan/The New York Times

patients or their surrogates. The exception to the rule that patients' judgments should be honored is when CPR would be futile. The physician should discuss the content of a DNR order with patients or the patients' surrogates and allow them to obtain a second opinion or to transfer care to another physician.

Developments in U.S. law

In the spring of 1990, a campaign called "Death with Dignity," or Initiative 119, began in Washington state; signatures were gathered to force the legislature to consider a bill that would make two major changes in the state's laws. First, it would make it much easier for patients with conditions such as PVS to forgo life-sustaining treatment. Second, it would allow physicians to assist in the death of a patient who, in the opinion of two physicians, had less than six months to live; upon being diagnosed with a fatal illness, patients would have to expressly indicate that they would want such assistance. In these cases a living will would not suffice. While some commentators have complained that the proposed Washington bill would force physicians to *take* rather than *save* lives, the bill's supporters seemed likely to get enough signatures to compel the legislature to respond.

Finally, in another development, in November 1990 a new federal law was passed, scheduled to take effect in December 1991. The Patient Self-Determination Act requires that health care facilities, including hospitals, nursing homes, health maintenance organizations, and home health care agencies that receive Medicaid or Medicare funds, inform their patients at the time of admission of their rights to refuse treatment—hence the law's unofficial name, "medical Miranda." Institutions will have to create specific, written policies on refusal of treatment and the use of advance directives. The written, signed instructions of advance directives, which take effect if a person becomes incapacitated and unable to communicate, concern various types of medical treatment to be used or withheld (*e.g.,* CPR, mechanical breathing, artificial hydration and nutrition, major surgery, kidney dialysis, chemotherapy, and transfusions). The patient's records must indicate whether an advance directive exists, and the facility must ensure compliance with such directives, consistent with state law. Furthermore, institutions must educate their staffs and the communities they serve about advance directives.

The purpose of the act is well described by its title, and the general goal seems laudable. Federal officials, however, have been slow to write the specific rules that health care institutions will be expected to follow, and it is unclear how rapidly the new law will be implemented or whether, in light of many patients' and physicians' reluctance to talk about death, it will have its intended impact.

—*Thomas H. Murray, Ph.D.*

Diet and Nutrition

If anyone doubts that Americans are obsessed with what they eat, a quick glance at the comic pages of the local newspaper will offer proof positive: Beetle Bailey, Garfield, Ziggy, and a host of other characters regularly make observations about dieting, obesity, cholesterol, and food fads. Comic strips are a window on the culture—a look into contemporary concerns and preoccupations—and food, nutrition, and health are certainly on many people's minds. Cartoonists poke fun at consumers who endlessly perambulate the supermarket aisles, patiently reading labels and trying to make healthy choices in the face of ever changing dietary guidelines. They even see comic possibilities in the food industry, underscoring the contradictions inherent in a business that promotes superpremium ice cream rich in butterfat and, at the same time, nondairy-based coffee creamers low in fat and free of cholesterol.

Today's consumer: fed up with advice?

During the 1980s U.S. consumers were deluged with dietary recommendations. The American Heart Association, the National Cancer Institute, the National Cholesterol Education Program's Population Panel, the U.S. surgeon general, and the Committee on Diet and Health of the National Research Council, among others, published guidelines for improving the nation's eating habits.

Taken together, these recommendations were designed to help people choose foods that would aid in lowering their risk of coronary heart disease, cancer, stroke, obesity, high blood pressure, diabetes, and osteoporosis. The guidelines were similar in many respects, although they differed slightly in wording and emphasis. In some instances the recommendations were quite specific: reduce total fat intake to no more than 30% of total calories; reduce cholesterol intake to less than 300 mg per day. In other cases they were very general: avoid too much fat; avoid too much sodium.

Consumers have become increasingly frustrated with this plethora of guidelines and, acknowledging this fact, in 1990 nine major government and voluntary health groups convened a conference to discuss recommendations for a diet that could apply to all healthy Americans over the age of two years. The result was a report entitled "The Healthy American Diet." Many nutritionists saw this event as a major step toward eliminating confusion about dietary recommendations and helping people to make wise choices. Even so, these new guidelines are very general, including statements such as "Eat a nutritionally adequate diet" and "Increase consumption of complex carbohydrates and fiber." When it comes to specifics, confusion still reigns for consumers who, mindful of all the dietary advice meted out over the past decade, are trying to make concrete dietary changes. What constitutes an "adequate" diet? Which foods are the best sources of complex carbohydrates? How much fat is "too much"?

One problem is that consumers still do not know how to translate overall dietary guidelines into everyday meal plans. Many researchers are now addressing this issue. The Treatwell eating-pattern guidelines, developed by a group at the University of Massachusetts Medical School in Worcester, constitute one such attempt at a practical daily plan. These guidelines suggest that people eat at least one serving of a high-fiber cereal every day and one or more servings of fruit at each meal; they also recommend choosing fish, turkey, chicken, and lean cuts of red meat and limiting the amount of meat to six ounces or less a day.

Nutritional revisionism

A group of U.S. doctors who call themselves the Physicians Committee for Responsible Medicine proposed in 1991 that the basic four food groups be changed from the traditional (1) meat, (2) dairy products, (3) grains, and (4) fruits and vegetables to (1) grains, (2) vegetables, (3) legumes, and (4) fruits. Meat and dairy foods would be considered options but would have a much smaller role in the diet. This suggestion was not well received by nutrition experts within the medical and dietetics communities, many of whom pointed out that meat and dairy products are major sources of essential nutrients, such as high-quality protein, calcium, zinc, iron, and the B vitamins. They feel that given the increasing number of fat-modified meat and dairy products available in supermarkets, consumers should easily be able to choose healthy, low-fat foods from the traditional four groups.

Even the U.S. Department of Agriculture (USDA) has acknowledged the need for some simplification of the dietary guidelines, however. Its proposed "Pyramid Food Guide"—issued in 1991 but withdrawn shortly afterward—was considered by many authorities to be a step in the right direction. The pyramid was also based on the four-food-group concept. Its foundation was the group containing breads, cereals, rice, and pasta, from which the greatest number of servings per day—6 to 11—was to be chosen. The next step up the pyramid was fruits and vegetables (3 to 5 servings daily), followed by milk, yogurt, and cheese (2 to 3 servings) and, topping the pyramid, meat, fish, poultry, dried beans and peas, eggs, and nuts (2 to 3 servings). Many nutritionists were disappointed when the USDA decided that the pyramid needed more field testing and was not ready for release.

Another source of exasperation on the part of consumers arises from the fact that nutrition is not a static discipline; the "state of the art" varies with new research and evolving ideas. Thus, in 1990 many people who had given up butter for margarine, thinking they

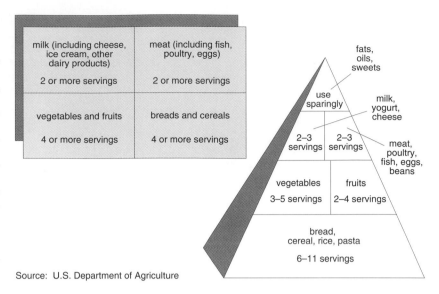

milk (including cheese, ice cream, other dairy products)	meat (including fish, poultry, eggs)
2 or more servings	2 or more servings
vegetables and fruits	breads and cereals
4 or more servings	4 or more servings

Source: U.S. Department of Agriculture

had improved their diets by substituting a vegetable fat for one of animal origin, learned that certain fatty acids in margarine, especially in the solid, stick form, may be just as saturated as those in butter. To add to the confusion, not all saturated fatty acids are alike in their health effects. Stearic acid, a saturated fatty acid found in beef tallow, butterfat, and cocoa butter, does not raise blood lipid levels the way other saturated fatty acids do. Food choices of consumers and dietary recommendations from the experts change constantly as new foods and ingredients become available in the marketplace and as the understanding of the relationship between diet and health is refined.

Less fat, more obesity

Are consumers heeding the advice of experts to make healthy food choices? Yes and no. Many of the 2,167 consumers queried in a marketing survey several years ago indicated that they were aware of the link between

". . . We've just updated the four basic food groups . . ."
Walt Handelsman; reprinted by permission of Tribune Media Services

good nutrition and a reduced cancer risk. Eighty-two percent said that their interest in nutrition had grown over the previous year and that they believed eating fresh fruits and vegetables such as broccoli and cabbage reduces cancer risk. That changing attitudes have been translated into changes in consumption is supported by figures from the USDA. Between 1970 and 1985, per capita consumption of fresh fruits and vegetables increased by 23%, fruit juice by 20%.

"Light" dairy products—that is, those with a lower calorie, fat, cholesterol, or sodium content than regular products—are among the fastest-growing segments of the market. One indication of this trend is the burgeoning of low-fat and nonfat yogurt products. Low-fat yogurt was introduced in the late 1970s, nonfat yogurt in 1988; today the two constitute 80% of the entire yogurt market. Other popular "light" dairy products include low-fat cottage cheese, reduced-fat natural cheeses, and nonfat "ice cream."

It would seem, then, that consumers *are* paying attention to what they eat. A January 1990 Gallup Poll conducted for the International Food Information Council and the American Dietetic Association reported that 74% of those interviewed said they were eliminating fats from their diets; 7 out of 10 were eliminating saturated fats and reducing cholesterol. The cholesterol consciousness of the 1980s apparently motivated many people to make significant changes to improve their health.

Despite the growing demand for reduced-fat and low-calorie food products, however, the incidence of obesity hit an all-time high during the 1980s, especially among younger age groups—the number of obese teenagers increased by 50% during the decade. A clue to this apparent paradox can be found in a survey conducted by the Simmons Market Research Bureau, New York City, of the foods ranked most popular by different groups of consumers categorized by age. Those over age 55 reported that they liked newer products such as low-fat/low-calorie/low-cholesterol cheeses, nondairy cream substitutes, and sugar substitutes, along with traditional foods such as canned corned beef and dried fruits. Consumers in the 18- to 24-year-old market segment, by comparison, listed among their favorites fried chicken, cookie mixes, sloppy joes, pizza made from scratch, and other traditionally high-fat foods.

A similar pattern emerged from studies of the growth in the snack-food industry, which increased 88%—to annual sales of approximately $10 billion—between 1979 and 1988. A 1987 survey of consumer attitudes conducted by the Snack Food Association showed that more than half of the buyers were 20 to 44 years of age; fewer than 10% were over 65. These data suggest that young adults are not as zealous as their elders in counting calories or grams of fat. It is the older generation that is apparently leading the move toward lighter and leaner food products.

Retooling of the food industry

The food industry is driven to a large extent by consumer demands. When physicians and other health professionals urged people to "get the fat out," consumers clamored for reduced-fat and cholesterol-free foods. The industry immediately rushed to fill that demand with a broad array of new products. This trend was evidenced in 1991 by the convening of the second annual Conference on Fat and Cholesterol Reduced Foods. More than 400 participants attended the meeting, held in Atlanta, Ga., which focused on innovations in food product development.

Meat: getting leaner. The meat industry has undergone enormous changes over the past 25 years. In response to the demand for leaner meat products, livestock producers have altered breeding and feeding practices to reduce the fat levels of animals brought to market. The average fat content of beef has decreased by 6% over the last quarter of a century; pork fat has been reduced by 23% and fat in lamb by 9%.

Innovations in the meat industry have not been limited to improving the image and nutritional profile of traditional products. Some livestock producers are introducing totally different items. One of these is *strauss,* a fancy new name for one of the oldest and largest living flightless birds—the ostrich. Described as the "health meat of the nineties," strauss is popular in Europe, especially Germany and Switzerland. While the demand for "ostrich burgers" is virtually nonexistent at the moment, the market has enormous potential. Ostrich meat, which is red, unlike most fowl, is high in protein and low in cholesterol; the taste is reminiscent of tender, juicy roast beef. The challenge will be to find a way to gain the American public's acceptance of this unusual product.

Fake fats: flourishing. Other novel food products are also appearing on grocery-store shelves. These foods are engineered with the taste, the texture, and what food technologists call the "mouthfeel" of traditional products, but they are lower in fat and caloric content. They are made with so-called fat substitutes, ingredients designed to replace a portion of the fat found naturally in foods. One of these is Olestra (formerly called sucrose polyester), which was developed by Procter & Gamble about 20 years ago. If approved by the Food and Drug Administration (FDA), Olestra could potentially replace 35% of the fat in shortening and oils used in the home and 75% of the fat in oils used for deep-fat frying in institutional food service operations.

Simplesse, a fat substitute developed by the Nutra-Sweet Co., is already on the market in a few products, notably imitation ice cream and frozen dessert novelties. It has been approved for use in many other foods and will eventually make its way into dairy products such as yogurt, cheese spreads, cream cheese, and sour cream, as well as oil-based foods such as salad dressings, mayonnaise, and margarine. Simplesse is a cholesterol-free fat replacement made from milk and/or egg-white protein by a process called microparticulation. It provides about 1 to 2 calories per gram (compared with 9 calories per gram in regular

High in protein and low in cholesterol, ostrich meat has gained acceptance in Europe. Will consumers in the United States soon find "ostrich burgers" on the menu?

Douglas Burrows—Gamma/Liaison

fats) and is thus very low in calories as well as in fat. Because milk and egg protein coagulate at very high temperatures, Simplesse cannot be used in cooking oils or in products that will be fried or baked. Further, food products containing Simplesse may cause allergic reactions in persons with allergies to egg or milk proteins.

Many other fat substitutes are being developed from ingredients as diverse as corn starch, potato starch, oats, and natural fats. Reduced-fat foods will clearly come to occupy an important place in the food industry and in the U.S. diet. What is unclear, however, is how these products will affect eating habits and health. Will dieters compensate for the calories they "save" by eating more high-fat products? Will fat substitutes prove to be an effective alternative for people trying to lower their cholesterol levels? Will the dietary counseling provided by dietitians need to change to allow for the new complexity of the food supply? Researchers are certain to begin exploring this area of human nutrition in the near future.

Fiber. The consumer enthusiasm for oat bran that was so evident a few years ago has waned, while interest in other dietary fibers is accelerating. Among those being studied for their positive effects on blood cholesterol are psyllium and pectins. Psyllium, a fiber from the seed husk of the plant *Plantago ovata* and the chief ingredient in bulk-forming laxatives (*e.g.,* Metamucil), is now being added to some breakfast cereals. Water-soluble forms of dietary fibers such as pectins have also been in the spotlight because they have been shown to have a beneficial effect on cholesterol

levels and control of diabetes. Pectins are found naturally in a variety of fruits and vegetables such as apples, citrus fruits, strawberries, squash, potatoes, green beans, and carrots and are added to some processed foods to enhance texture and consistency. Other brans such as corn and rice bran are also being investigated as potentially beneficial.

Food labeling: "new and improved"

The information on package labels is supposed to help consumers make healthy choices, but in many cases reading this small print only adds to their confusion. The FDA is now considering several proposals for improving food labels. Labeling reform found a strong advocate in David A. Kessler, who took over the post of FDA commissioner in December 1990. A graduate of both Harvard Medical School and the University of Chicago Law School, Kessler promised stepped-up enforcement of existing laws and the introduction of stricter regulations to protect the public from misleading claims made by food processors and manufacturers.

Currently about 60% of all processed packaged foods have nutritional information on the label. Under existing regulations—which were formulated nearly 20 years ago—nutrition labeling is voluntary unless the manufacturer adds a nutrient to the product or makes any health claim other than advertising that the food is low in sodium. Under new regulations, nutrition labeling would be required for all foods that are "meaningful sources" of calories or nutrients. "Meaningful sources" are defined as foods that provide 2% or more of the "Reference Daily Intake" (a proposed new labeling standard based on an adjustment of the recommended dietary allowance, or RDA) for protein and 26 vitamins and minerals.

Other features of the proposed new regulations include a precise and standardized definition of terms describing cholesterol content (*e.g.,* "low-cholesterol," "cholesterol-free") and the addition of information about the percentage of calories per serving from fat and saturated fat, as well as the cholesterol and dietary fiber content of a standard serving. Purveyors of fresh produce and seafood would be required to post nutritional information—in the form of signs, tags, booklets, or the like—wherever the foods are purchased by consumers.

In the U.S., three bills relating to nutrition labeling are now being considered by Congress. One of these, proposed by Rep. Henry A. Waxman (Dem., Calif.), was passed by the House of Representatives in July 1990. It would require the mandatory labeling of fresh produce and seafood as well as packaged processed foods. Health claims related to foods could be made only after the FDA reviewed scientific evidence supporting a claim and determined it to be valid. Two bills that have been introduced in the Senate, proposed by

In May 1991, five months after taking office as commissioner of the Food and Drug Administration, David Kessler cracked down on the use of certain misleading terms on food labels—e.g., the adjective fresh, *referring to juice products made from concentrate, and the claim "no cholesterol" on vegetable oils, which contained none to begin with.*

Howard Metzenbaum (Dem., Ohio) and Orrin Hatch (Rep., Utah), call for mandatory nutrition labeling on all processed packaged foods and regulation of health claims made on food labels.

While these regulations, if passed into law, would help consumers understand the nutritional content of the foods they eat, important gaps remain. For example, the new legislation would apply only to foods regulated by the FDA; all fresh meat and poultry products and some frozen foods, however, fall under the jurisdiction of the USDA. These two agencies have different definitions for terms such as "low-fat" and "lite." Thus, a "lite" cheese pizza, which would be regulated by the FDA, must have 33% fewer calories than a standard pizza, whereas a "lite" sausage pizza, under USDA regulation, need have only 25% fewer calories, 25% less fat, or 25% less sodium.

In some cases, labels that seem to provide a service to consumers actually serve only to obfuscate and confuse. In a single serving of luncheon meat such as turkey bologna, for example, claiming to be 95% fat free, 70% of calories in a single serving may come from fat. The phrase "95% fat free" means that by weight the product is 5% fats and 95% other ingredients. All this is beside the point to people who are trying to reduce or monitor their fat intake; they should be primarily concerned with how much fat a given product contains per serving and what percentage of the total calories per serving comes from fat. Continued improvement and refinement of nutrition labels are needed if consumers are to get information that will truly serve their needs.

Some of these improvements have been called for by Commissioner Kessler. Within five months of assuming his new post, he cracked down on several manufacturers whose labels were deemed to be deceptive. Procter & Gamble, the manufacturer of Crisco Corn Oil; Best Foods, the maker of Mazola Corn Oil; and Great Foods of America, which makes HeartBeat Canola Oil, were pressed to remove the words "no cholesterol" from these products' labels. (Although vegetable oils do not in fact contain cholesterol, the oils are a liquid form of fat, which has been linked to heart disease. The fact that they contain no cholesterol does not make them "heart healthy" foods.) Some weeks previously Kessler had ordered the impounding of 24,000 half-gallon cartons of Citrus Hill Fresh Choice orange juice, also a Procter & Gamble product, forcing the company to remove the word *fresh* from that product's label. Under pressure from the FDA, three major pasta sauce manufacturers also agreed to drop the word *fresh* from the labels of their precooked products.

Demographics and diet

The changing demographics of the U.S. population is another factor influencing the direction of food in-

regular hot dog	
nutrition information per serving	
serving size	1 link (57 g)
calories	180
protein	6 g
carbohydrate	2 g
fat	17 g
cholesterol	35 mg
sodium	580 mg

"lite" hot dog—80% fat free	
nutrition information per serving	
serving size	1 link (57 g)
calories	130
protein	7 g
carbohydrate	1 g
fat	11 g
cholesterol	30 mg
sodium	630 mg

Labels can deceive; a product that claims to be 80–90% fat free may derive more than 70% of its calories from fat. Consider the so-called lite hot dog. To calculate the number of calories from fat per serving, multiply 11 (grams of fat) by 9 (the number of calories in a gram of fat): 99. To get the percentage of calories from fat, divide 99 by 130 (total calories per serving): 0.76; then multiply by 100: 76%. The same formula would show that 85% of the regular hot dog's calories derive from fat.

dustry trends. People who live alone now account for 25% of all U.S. households, and this figure is expected to climb to about 33% by the year 2000. The concept of the traditional family has changed, too. In 1970, 71% of all households included married couples; by 1987 the figure had dropped to 58%. Today close to 50 million women work in jobs outside the home; by the year 2000 an estimated 84% will hold regular jobs away from home. In addition, the U.S. is a nation growing older. Currently, one in three adults is over the age of 50. By the year 2000, 74 million baby boomers, aged 35 to 50 years, will reach their maximum earning potential and will, therefore, have more money to spend on food. Finally, the population is becoming more ethnically diverse as the Hispanic, Asian, and black segments increase.

In their search for food products to appeal to these many different groups of consumers, manufacturers will continue to emphasize leaner, healthier foods and the development of novel ingredients, more microwavable foods, new beverages, more ethnic and convenience foods, self-chilling cans and other serving innovations, and packaging designed to extend shelf life. If anything can be predicted about diet in the '90s, it is that consumers will demand—and get—a greater variety of foods than has ever before been available.
—*Diane H. Morris, Ph.D., R.D., and James M. Rippe, M.D.*

Special Report

Brave New Specialty: Interventional Neuroradiology

by Gail McBride

In the past 15 to 20 years, a handful of daring physicians, stimulated by advances in medical technology, have been staging a small revolution. At a few medical centers across the world, radiologists who specialize in the brain and spinal cord can now guide tiny, flexible tubes (catheters), metal coils, and other "mini" devices into minuscule blood vessels of the brain. Their goal: to correct possibly life-threatening abnormalities that either are beyond a surgeon's reach or would bleed too much if surgery were undertaken.

Patients with bizarre symptoms that arise because some parts of their brains are either starved for or overwhelmed by blood are sedated or anesthetized while the radiologists delicately "intervene" to remove various obstructions to normal blood flow or to close off abnormal openings or outpouchings of blood vessel walls (aneurysms), which may cause hemorrhages. To do the latter, they inject materials through catheters that will cause blood to clot.

Because this work takes place inside people's brains and uses devices guided from outside the body, the risk of failure or of causing a second problem while trying to correct the first one is high. But when all goes well, people get their lives handed back to them.

A dramatic operation, a life restored

The case of Bob Myers is a good example. In 1960 Myers suffered two brain hemorrhages caused by an arteriovenous malformation (AVM)—abnormally connected arteries and veins embedded in spongelike tissue—in his brain. In 1963 he underwent brain surgery, in which a surgeon attached tiny metal clips to major blood vessels leading to the AVM in order to block blood flow to it and halt the bleeding. All had gone relatively well until 1980, when he began to have left-sided weakness, double vision, slurred speech, and other problems.

In 1988 Myers started going downhill rapidly. He and his wife, Rhoda, made the rounds of doctors, most of whom assumed that his previous AVM had started swelling or bleeding again to cause his current symptoms. Surgery was deemed too dangerous because of the bleeding risk.

Then Myers learned of Eric Russell, an interventional neuroradiologist at Chicago's Northwestern University Medical School. Russell did a brain angiogram—an X-ray of blood vessels made visible by injection of a contrast substance into the bloodstream. The angiogram showed that instead of an AVM, Myers had another blood vessel problem called an arteriovenous (AV) fistula. This is an abnormal connection between a vein and one or more of the arteries that carry oxygen-laden blood pumped from the heart. The abnormal connection "short-circuits" hundreds of smaller vessels that normally carry oxygen-rich blood from arteries to body tissues, then collect it later, depleted of oxygen, for funneling back into veins and thence to the lungs (for more oxygen) and heart again (for recirculation).

Part of Myers' brain simply was not getting enough oxygen. This included the cerebellum, which coordinates movement. Moreover, certain veins, whose walls are thin compared with those of arteries, had become massively dilated from carrying blood under pressure. In turn, these veins exerted pressure on the brain stem and other critical areas. The brain stem, which connects the cerebral hemispheres to the spinal cord and the rest of the body, controls many functions, speech and vision among them.

Russell believed that he could close Myers' AV fistula with an "interventional" procedure. First, however, surgeons put a tube into Myers' brain to drain off cerebrospinal fluid that was putting pressure on other structures. For reasons not entirely clear, Myers got worse, sinking into a semicoma. Russell acted immediately, asking Rhoda Myers to sign a consent form for the interventional procedure. She signed. It was her husband's only hope.

Russell and his team began by inserting through one of two large, paired arteries in the groin area a hair-thin catheter with a silicone balloon on its tip, which he gradually inched up through Myers' body into the brain, through smaller and smaller brain arteries, navigating tortuous curves as he went. All the while, he was watching an angiographic "road map" on a television screen where X-ray images of the blood vessels of the brain containing the tiny catheter were shown superimposed over images of skull bones. As contrast solution (and blood) flowed in and out of the vessels being navigated, Russell would squirt more of the contrast medium through the catheter and "freeze" the resulting images on the screen. This process is called real-time digital subtraction angiography and has greatly helped interventionalists' work.

Russell hoped to position the balloon in the fistula, inflate it, inject a hardening substance into it, then detach it and withdraw the catheter. This procedure would obliterate the abnormal opening between the arteries and vein. Reaching the spot, Russell inflated the balloon and was trying to detach it when, as the catheter was being withdrawn through the abdomen, it broke! Immediately, the doctors placed a new catheter into the other large groin artery, lassoed the remaining piece of old catheter with a wire loop, and slowly pulled it and the balloon out.

The next day, armed with a balloonless catheter and platinum minicoils, Russell tried again, once more guiding the catheter through blood vessels of the brain. Reaching the fistula, he began discharging the minicoils (measuring two to four millimeters) through the catheter into the opening, where the coils disturbed the blood flow and, in so doing, caused the formation of a large, permanent blood clot that blocked the opening. He also placed coils in other strategic areas to help divert more blood to oxygen-starved areas of the brain. Gradually during the procedure, as blood that had gushed through the fistula was diverted to oxygen-starved brain tissue, Myers woke up. Soon he was talking and moving!

That was December 1988. Myers then spent three weeks at the Rehabilitation Institute of Chicago undergoing intensive physical and occupational therapy to get his balance, movement, speech, and other functions back. In March 1989 he went back to work as a Xerox repairman. In June the Myerses went to Hawaii and had the best vacation of their lives.

An evolving subspecialty

Interventional neuroradiologists are accustomed to treating patients like Myers for whom there is no other option. In years to come, most patients with a neurological problem involving blood vessels may be helped by an interventional procedure. In the United States this could have a major impact on morbidity and mortality, inasmuch as stroke—the most common cerebrovascular problem—is the third-largest killer and a major cause of long-term disability.

Russell, who repaired Myers' complex problem, acquired his skill at New York University Medical Center, which is one of the main U.S. centers for these procedures. There Alejandro Berenstein and In Sup Choi train other interventional neuroradiologists. Operating in a special unit of the hospital, the NYU physicians do 15 to 18 interventional procedures each week—70% in the brain, the rest in the spinal cord, face, or neck.

Many procedures done at NYU are for AVMs, Myers' early problem. In the 1970s Charles Kerber, professor of radiology at the University of California at San Diego, was the first to inject a type of Krazy Glue into the middle of a brain AVM and its "feeding" vessels to promote the formation of a clot, or embolus, that

prevented more blood from entering the AVM. Since then, this procedure has been done many times, sometimes with various substances other than glue; *e.g.,* polyvinyl alcohol foam particles. The usual aim is to block blood flow so that the tangled mass of vessels will shrink and can be more easily removed by surgery or by a radiation therapy device called a gamma knife. Occasionally the injection procedure alone will "cure" the AVM.

In somewhat similar fashion, tumors of the brain, spinal cord, or head and neck, which are fed by many blood vessels, can be partly treated by embolization methods. Using tiny coils, balloons, or various particles, interventionalists induce clotting in the blood vessels so the tumors will shrink and be less bloody when surgeons try to remove them. Other brain and spinal cord problems, too—some resulting from accidents or injury—can be handled with these techniques. The most excitement, however, has come from successful treatment of intracranial aneurysms.

Aneurysms "defused"

Rupture of an aneurysm, a stretching and outpouching of part of a blood vessel wall, causes about 28,000 subarachnoid hemorrhages (bleeding over the surface of or into the brain) in the U.S. each year. People who survive, or those whose aneurysms are detected by certain symptoms before they burst, usually undergo surgery. During surgery the aneurysm is clipped at its neck to prevent more blood from flowing into it. A clot forms inside, reducing the aneurysm's pressure and preventing it from bursting. About 18,000 such operations are done each year.

Sometimes, though, the aneurysm is too deep in the brain or behind bone, where surgeons cannot reach it. In these cases interventional neuroradiologists steer their balloon tipped catheters into the artery bearing the aneurysm, occluding it so that no more blood can enter.

In another, more risky technique, they carefully push a balloon into the aneurysm itself. The balloon is gradually inflated, has a substance injected into it that hardens in 30 minutes, and is then detached (an innovation pioneered by Grant Hieshima, leader of a team of interventional neuroradiologists at the University of California at San Francisco). In time, blood clots between the balloon's outer surface and the aneurysm's inner surface, removing the threat of rupture.

Thus far, this approach has been attempted by only a few neuroradiologists. UCSF is one of the few centers in the U.S. where this daring procedure has been performed numerous times over nearly a decade—where "ballooning" of aneurysms is no longer considered experimental. In the Soviet Union many physicians consider the balloon procedure far preferable to surgery.

In March 1989, at a meeting of the American Society of Neuroradiology, Soviet neurosurgeon Viktor Shcheglov of Kiev reported results of balloon treatment of intracranial aneurysms in 617 people with symptoms of leakage. In 91% of the patients, doctors managed to occlude the aneurysm with the parent artery remaining open; the remaining 9% of patients were treated by occluding the parent vessel. Overall, results were better than with surgery.

More daring yet: treating spasms and strokes

Another remarkable development that shows great promise is the use of balloons to stop blood vessel spasm, which commonly occurs after aneurysm rupture or successful aneurysm surgery and makes it impossible for enough blood to reach vital brain areas. It often causes death.

The new, deceptively simple treatment, pioneered by Soviet neurosurgeon Y.N. Zubkov of Leningrad, involves steering a tiny catheter with a balloon on its tip into the artery and inflating the balloon briefly, then withdrawing it. For some reason, the artery remains open and, unless there has been irreversible brain damage, patients often get better.

In the past several years, the interventional neuroradiologists at UCSF have treated over 20 patients with blood vessel spasm—many of them successfully. The number of cases is still small because patients must be treated within 24 hours of the onset of the spasm; otherwise it is too late to do much good. The NYU team has treated at least eight patients, three "with spectacular results." At the University of Washington, interventional neuroradiologist Joe Eskridge has also rescued many patients with blood vessel spasms: "I've had people come in comatose, unresponsive, and on respirators; three days later, they're normal." Of the more than 35 patients Eskridge has treated, two-thirds have improved.

Brain arteries narrowed by atherosclerosis or by blood clots are another matter. These cause 80% of strokes, but few interventional neuroradiologists in the U.S. have tried to prevent or treat strokes by eradicating the clots or opening up the arteries. One exception is Fong Tsai, chairman of radiology at the University of Missouri at Kansas City. Since the early 1980s Tsai has been doing balloon angioplasty on certain occluded brain arteries. All patients either have already suffered strokes or have had warning symptoms of them, such as transient ischemic attacks. Many have not been helped by treatment with anticoagulants or have been unable to tolerate bypass surgery in the brain.

Tsai has treated more than 200 patients this way with no serious complications. Some improve right away; others who have already had a stroke may have problems that need to be followed for some time; some who have had transient ischemic attacks no longer get them. He attributes their improvement to the interventional procedure.

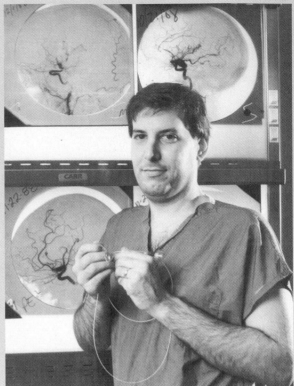

Armed with a balloon catheter and guided by images on television screens that provide a "road map" of the brain's blood vessels, interventional neuroradiologist Joe Eskridge, at the University of Washington, will be able to obstruct a patient's arteriovenous malformation, a tangle of arteries and veins that can cause stroke or other major neurological damage.

The future

Interventional neuroradiologists clearly represent a unique breed of subspecialist. They must be willing to take calculated risks and be able to tolerate significant stress. No matter how expertly trained, interventional neuroradiologists are always faced with the fact that each brain is different and therefore unpredictable. They must be highly resourceful—often inventing ingenious new methods and tools as they go along. Furthermore, despite rapid advances in equipment and materials in the past few years, arteries can be punctured, catheters can break, balloons can dislodge, and so forth.

Nonetheless, interventional neuroradiology has already made many neurosurgical operations much safer, helped perfect others, and eliminated still others. Neurosurgeon Charles Wilson, chairman of the department of neurosurgery at UCSF, has said of this new approach: "It's an incredible advance."

Still, "what we have now are . . . imperfect solutions," says neuroradiologist Stephen Hecht of the University of California at Davis. "In 15 years we'll look back and think this was primitive."

Environmental Health

In the more affluent parts of the United States and other economically developed countries, the classic public health problems—malnutrition, epidemic disease, unsanitary food and water, air pollution from coal smoke, and extremes of climate—have largely been solved. People have come to expect the air they breathe and the water and food they ingest to be pure and safe. Society as a whole has become increasingly intolerant of actions that may cause discomfort to individuals or harm their health—for example, smoking in public places and assaults on the ears from boom boxes. People now expect their government to take appropriate action to reduce certain health risks to negligible levels; *e.g.,* to protect the food supply from toxic substances and to enact and enforce environmental-quality standards.

There is a major problem, however: both government and society have insufficient knowledge, as well as too little money and too few trained personnel, to reduce *all* environmental health risks to levels that will fully satisfy the public. Compounding the problem is the extent of widespread misinformation on the nature and severity of the risks of various environmental exposures, as well as a general mistrust of government's ability to address and solve problems. A recent report entitled "Reducing Risk: Setting Priorities and Strategies for Environmental Protection," prepared by the Environmental Protection Agency's (EPA's) Science Advisory Board, an extramural public advisory group, addressed these issues. Government, the report noted, is more likely to legislate and regulate on the basis of perceived risk than on risks as established by any vigorous quantitative evaluation or expert judgment. It concluded that in terms of the number of people affected and the impact on public health, major risks in the U.S. today are associated with ambient air pollutants (such as ozone, benzene, lead, and acidic particles), hazardous substances in indoor air (*e.g.,* radon, environmental tobacco smoke, volatile organic compounds) and drinking water (lead, chloroform, microorganisms, nitrates, etc.), and workplace exposures. The general public, on the other hand, tends to be more concerned about problems judged by the Science Advisory Board to be of lower relative risk. ("Relative risk" refers to the ratio of the rate of incidence of disease among those exposed to a pollutant to that among those not exposed.) These include toxic-waste dumps, oil spills, radiation from nuclear plants, and radioactive wastes. The board's recommendations are being used by the EPA in establishing priorities for research planning and regulatory timetables in order to achieve the maximum risk reduction consistent with the agency's resources and legal mandates.

Among the recent developments in environmental health, the following current public health concerns are addressed below: exercising in polluted air, asbestos removal, low-level ionizing radiation, and residual environmental lead.

Exercising in polluted air

Large numbers of health-conscious people engage in regular exercise (*e.g.,* jogging, cycling, brisk walking) outdoors. In doing so, they of necessity inhale much larger volumes of air each minute than when they are engaged in more sedentary activities. They also inhale more of the air into the deeper recesses of the lungs. Furthermore, during exertion people often supplement their normal nasal breathing with oral breathing to reduce the added effort of inspiration via the nasal

A New York City jogger may be unknowingly exposing his lungs to harmful levels of ozone, one of several pollutants in urban smog. Because an exerciser takes in larger-than-normal volumes of air, he or she also inhales greater quantities of pollutants with each breath. City dwellers who exercise outdoors would be well advised to work out in the early morning hours, when the concentration of ozone and other noxious substances in the air is at its lowest.

Allsport

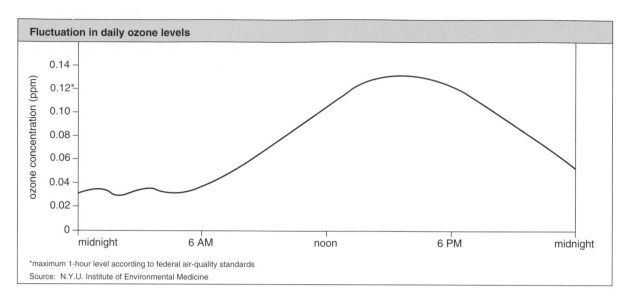

Fluctuation in daily ozone levels

*maximum 1-hour level according to federal air-quality standards

Source: N.Y.U. Institute of Environmental Medicine

passages. As the amount of air inhaled is increased, so is the amount of air pollution deposited along the respiratory tract. Because the nasal passages filter out more pollution than the oral passages, penetration of pollutants to the more sensitive deep lung airways increases with the switch to oral breathing.

From laboratory studies in which healthy volunteer subjects were exposed to air containing ozone at concentrations equal to or greater than those occurring normally in outdoor air, it has been learned that ozone exposures can have several detrimental effects on respiratory function: increased flow resistance (increased work of breathing), reductions in maximal lung volume and flow rates (reduced peak performance), increased frequency of respiratory symptoms such as cough, chest tightness, and pain on deep inspiration, development of deep lung inflammation (release of inflammatory cells into lung airways), and enhanced lung permeability (easier access for other toxicants). The extent of these responses varies considerably among healthy individuals and increases with increasing concentration of ozone, duration of exposure, and level of exercise (ventilation rate).

At the current level of the National Ambient Air Quality Standard for ozone of 0.12 parts per million (ppm) as a maximum concentration average for one hour per day, there were no observable effects on lung function in healthy young adults at rest, some small changes in some subjects after one hour of vigorous exercise, and much greater changes in most people after six hours of moderate exercise. The lung function responses of 10–12-year-old boys were similar to those of young men, except the children did not exhibit the increased prevalence of symptoms that the adults did. Other population subgroups—smokers, older people, and those with chronic lung disease—were less severely affected by increased ozone levels.

Children and young adults engaged in normal outdoor recreational activity have also been studied to determine the effects of air pollution on their lung function and respiratory symptoms. In studies of 8–13-year-old children at summer camps in forested areas of western Pennsylvania and western New Jersey and adults in a forested area of New York, for example, functional decrements in proportion to ozone concentrations were greater than those seen in controlled-exposure studies indoors. Differences in exposure duration and exercise intensity were taken into consideration. It was suggested that the coexistence of acidic aerosol in the outdoor air at these sites had increased the effects of the ozone. Both ozone and acidic aerosol are formed in the air from primary pollutant precursors (hydrocarbons and nitrogen oxides for ozone and sulfur dioxide for acidic aerosol) and tend to be higher in relatively clean forested areas than in cities, where they are neutralized by primary pollutants (nitric oxide for ozone and ammonia for acidic aerosol). Both ozone and acidic aerosol are produced in the atmosphere during daylight hours, and their concentrations drop markedly late in the day and at night. Thus, people who want to avoid the respiratory deficits associated with exercising in polluted air should exercise before about 10 AM, when the daily rise in pollution usually begins.

The wisdom and necessity of asbestos removal

Asbestos, a naturally occurring group of mineral silicates in fibrous crystalline forms, was hailed as a miracle fiber earlier in this century. Asbestos fibers have excellent mechanical and insulating properties and under most conditions are highly resistant to heat and chemical corrosion. Thus, they have been widely used for insulation and fireproofing and were incorporated into composite materials such as asbestos-

290

cement tiles and pipes, motor vehicle brake and clutch linings, and vinyl-asbestos floor tiles. Unfortunately, asbestos fibers also proved to have unique properties in terms of toxicity. Many of the workers who inhaled relatively high concentrations of asbestos fibers over many years developed asbestosis (a diffuse form of lung fibrosis), lung cancer, or cancer of the pleural or peritoneal membranes (mesothelioma). These chronic diseases, usually occurring many years or even decades after initial occupational exposure, are often progressive and fatal. In recent years it has been found that maintenance and custodial workers in schools and other public buildings are exposed to airborne fibers from friable (*i.e.,* easily crumbled) asbestos and damaged asbestos-containing materials, which they may disturb during their work. Many such workers develop pleural plaques, which are markers of exposure and may restrict lung function and be precursor lesions for mesothelioma.

Reviews of the workers' experiences and laboratory studies of animals have indicated that cancer risk from asbestos exposure generally fits linear, nonthreshold dose-response models (*i.e.,* any dose causes a response, and the response is directly proportional to the dose). One can therefore assume that any exposure to airborne asbestos fibers produces some added risk of cancer. The risks of occupational exposure have traditionally been defined in terms of the number of fibers longer than five micrometers (μm) that occur per milliliter of air (f/mL), as measured by a technique called phase-contrast optical microscopy (PCOM), and this measure has been used in the development of risk models. It has been known for some time that only a minority of fibers are longer than five micrometers. On the other hand, it has also been known that long fibers are much more toxic than shorter ones. Recent analyses of animal and *in vitro* studies and data from autopsies of asbestos workers confirm the critical relationship of fiber toxicity and carcinogenicity to fiber length and justify retaining the five-micrometer criterion for assessing the risk of asbestos exposure.

Fiber concentrations in schools and public buildings are usually measured by a different method from the one used to measure industrial levels. This technique, transmission electron microscopy (TEM), has a much better resolving power than PCOM. Since fibers thinner than 0.05 μm are seen by TEM while only fibers thicker than about 0.25 μm are seen by PCOM, the TEM analyses generally show higher fiber concentrations, even when the counts are restricted to long (5 μm or longer) fibers. Nonetheless, building concentrations are much lower than those that occurred in industries such as asbestos mining and milling and textile manufacture, where disease incidence was high. Historic occupational exposures to workers in these industries were often in the range of 5–20 f/mL. The permissible exposure limit for workers exposed to asbestos on the job was 2 f/mL from 1976 to 1986; in 1986 it was lowered to 0.2 f/mL. In 1990 the Occupational Safety and Health Administration (OSHA) proposed that it be reduced to 0.1 f/mL.

There are few published data on fiber concentrations in outdoor air or in schools or other public

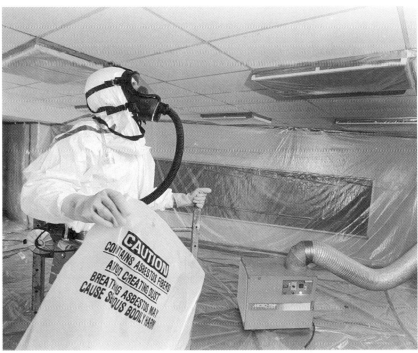

A worker removes asbestos in a Philadelphia school. While many people now view asbestos in public buildings as a serious hazard, environmental health experts warn that removing asbestos-containing material may pose more risk than leaving it in place. Many factors should be considered before removal is undertaken, including the friability of the material, the type of fibers it contains, and the existing level of airborne fibers.

buildings. In 1991 a review panel of the Health Effects Institute-Asbestos Research (a private, nonprofit corporation) gathered all available concentration data and reported that airborne concentrations of asbestos fibers of the dimensions that are most relevant to human health (*i.e.,* fibers longer than 5 μm) show averages on the order of 0.00001 f/mL in outdoor rural air (except near asbestos-containing rock outcroppings) and up to about 10 times higher in the outdoor air of urban environments. However, outdoor urban airborne concentrations above 0.0001 f/mL have been reported in certain circumstances as a result of local sources; for example, downwind from, or close to, frequent vehicle braking or activities that involve the demolition or spray application of asbestos products. The same range of average airborne fiber concentrations is found for the ambient indoor air of public buildings, including those buildings in which damaged, loose, friable asbestos-containing material is present and has been disturbed. Individual measurements often exceed 0.001 f/mL, but almost all building averages are substantially lower.

For an average exposure level of 0.0001 f/mL, cancer-risk models predict an increase in risk of about 0.002%. This corresponds to a lifetime risk of about one chance in 1.6 million in men and one in 800,-000 in women. In the U.S. about one smoker in 10 develops lung cancer, as does about one nonsmoker in 200. For mesothelioma, which is not influenced by smoking, the incidence is about one in 5,000. Thus, the potential health risk from airborne asbestos in buildings is quite small.

In most situations public concern over asbestos in indoor environments has focused primarily on the potential risks to building occupants—students, teachers, and office workers, in particular. However, the potential risk to custodial and maintenance workers—those who would be at greatest risk of exposure to friable asbestos—should be the primary consideration

in determining whether remedial action needs to be taken. The average measured levels of airborne asbestos fibers in most asbestos-containing buildings are now so low that no increase over naturally occurring outdoor levels has been demonstrated directly. Asbestos-removal activities, on the other hand, sometimes cause a considerable and persistent increase in measured levels. On the basis of the available data, it is impossible to be certain whether removal will in practice reduce lifetime exposures of the general occupants of a building—or whether the removal process may actually *increase* their exposures.

Low-level radiation: risks reassessed

Ionizing radiation, like asbestos, is known to cause cancer in highly exposed humans. Leukemia can develop within a few years after exposure, the peak incidence occurring within about 10 years. Other cancers develop later, with most appearing 20 or more years after exposure begins. At relatively high levels of exposure to external radiation, the human and laboratory-animal data are consistent with a linear, nonthreshold exposure-response model. However, these data cannot be used to establish response to the very low dosage levels the general public receives. For internally deposited radionuclides, such as the decay products of radon gas, the data supporting a linear dose-response relationship are also uncertain.

An average resident of the U.S. receives approximately 300 millirem (mR) of radiation annually; this comes from a variety of sources, including radiation naturally present in the environment, which is called background radiation. The largest fraction is from radon and its decay products. In December 1990 the U.S. Nuclear Regulatory Commission lowered its recommended limits on radiation exposures for the general public from 500 millirems per year (mR/yr) to 100 mR/yr. This limit excludes background radiation, diagnostic radiation (such as that from chest X-ray exams), and occupational exposures. It includes exposures attributable to consumer products, the nuclear industry, and radioactive-waste repositories.

A February 1991 National Research Council report recommended a modified risk model for general population dosage to radon decay products. The new model had the effect of reducing the estimated risk of death from radon exposure by about 30%. When applied to the current EPA estimate that radon causes about 20,000 excess (*i.e,* more than could normally be expected) lung cancer deaths each year in the U.S., this model reduces that number by about 5,000. These estimates of excess deaths are based on estimates of radon levels in homes as well as on one dose-response model, and further modifications of the numbers of excess cancers may be made when the national survey of radon levels in homes that is currently taking place is completed.

Asbestos risk in perspective	
cause of death	annual death rate (per million)
asbestos in school buildings	0.02–0.37
floods	2
airplane accidents	6
drowning (ages 5–14)	27
home accidents (ages 1–14)	60
smoking (long-term)	1,200

Adapted from H. Weill and J.M. Hughes, "Asbestos as a Public Health Risk," *Annual Review of Public Health*, vol. 7 (1986), pp. 171–192

Children are at greatest risk from the ingestion of leaded paint, but adults may be exposed to lead from such sources as leaded crystal and dishes treated with lead glazes. Garden soil, house dust, and drinking water can also contribute to exposure to this potentially toxic metal.

Concern about the effects of low-level radiation were intensified with the release in March 1991 of a study of cancer mortality among 8,318 workers at Oak Ridge (Tenn.) National Laboratory hired between 1943 and 1972 and followed medically through 1984. Only 638 (7.7%) had individually measured cumulative doses (total doses over all years of occupational exposure) above five rems. After adjusting for age, socioeconomic status, and other risk factors, the authors of the study concluded that external radiation (with a 20-year lag to account for the delayed appearance of cancer) was associated with a 4.9% increase in cancer mortality for each rem of cumulative exposure. This risk factor was 10 times higher than that for the most recent analysis of the atomic bomb survivors in Hiroshima and Nagasaki, Japan. Risk factors not taken into account in the analysis could be responsible, at least in part, for this figure. These could include concurrent exposures to chemicals or higher-than-normal tobacco usage among those more highly exposed to radiation. Other recent studies of nuclear workers have generally failed to find any correlation between individually monitored radiation exposures and cancer risk. Further studies of nuclear workers are clearly needed to help resolve this ambiguity.

Another major study released in March 1991 indicated that cancer rates among residents of 107 U.S. counties containing or adjacent to those containing nuclear facilities were not higher than rates in other counties. The facilities studied included 52 nuclear electric power plants, 9 facilities operated by the Department of Energy, and 1 former commercial fuel-reprocessing plant. Over 900,000 cancer deaths occurred in these counties from 1950 through 1984, and 1.8 million cancer deaths occurred in the adjacent counties in the same regions that served as controls.

According to the report in the March 20, 1991, *Journal of the American Medical Association,* deaths due to leukemia and other cancers were not found to be more frequent in study counties than in control counties. For childhood leukemia the relative risk, comparing the study counties with their controls, was 1.08 before plants became operational and 1.03 after start-up. For leukemia mortality at all ages, the respective values were 1.02 and 0.98. Thus, the start-up of nuclear plant operations did not increase cancer mortality in the surrounding areas during the time period studied. Considering the very low incremental radiation doses to the population from the operation of these facilities, the results are not surprising, but they are reassuring nevertheless.

Residual environmental lead

The health effects associated with widespread environmental exposures to lead continue to be of major concern. As lead antiknock compounds were removed from gasoline in the 1970s, there was a parallel reduction in the blood lead levels of the general population. At the same time, understanding of the subtler forms of lead poisoning greatly improved. Blood lead concentrations below 30 micrograms per deciliter (μg/dL), once thought to be harmless, were shown to be associated with a variety of neurobehavioral effects in children and with increased blood pressure levels in adults.

The residual lead in the soil from past fallout from auto exhaust contributes to the lead content in foods, as does the use of lead-glazed earthenware to hold foods, leaded glass to hold wines and liquors, and lead in solder used to seal food cans. Other sources of exposure are lead in drinking water (from leaching of lead in pipes and from the solder in copper tubing) and lead in dust and chips from deteriorated leaded paint. In a report published in 1991, researchers Joel Schwartz and Ronnie Levin found the presence of lead paint in the environment to be a significant predictor of the probability of a child's having lead poisoning. They used data from more than 200,000 screening tests of children performed between 1976 and 1980. The reduction in the sale of leaded gasoline during the period of the study reduced mean blood lead levels and increased the percentage of children whose lead toxicity could be attributed to paint. Following this reduction, the relative risk of lead toxicity, given lead paint exposure, was 5.70 during the winter and fall, rising to 12.81 in the spring and 15.8 in the summer, which the researchers suggested was due to increased exposure to window wells where leaded paint had been heavily used for enamel trim.

Evidence is accumulating that the neurobehavioral effects of low-level lead poisoning in children persist into later life. There is also concern that lead accumulated in the bones provides a source of future exposure to other organs or to a fetus during periods of altered maternal mineral metabolism; *e.g.,* as calcium metabolism changes drastically in women during pregnancy and lactation. It is likely that lead sequestered in the bones is released into the prospective mother's bloodstream, with potential toxic effects on both the fetus and the mother.

While the evidence for the association between blood lead concentration and blood pressure in adults has become firmer in recent years, its significance to the incidence of cardiovascular disease has been more speculative. Using electrocardiogram data from the second National Health and Nutrition Examination Survey, Schwartz has now shown a highly significant association of lead with pathological changes in the heart muscle. The results suggest that if the mean blood lead level of the population were halved, there would be about 24,000 fewer myocardial infarctions (heart attacks) per year, and incidence of all cardiovascular disease would be reduced by over 100,000 cases. Thus, the proportion of cardiovascular disease in the U.S. attributable to blood lead concentration is small, but compared with most other environmental toxins, lead makes a relatively large contribution to the development of such disease.

The EPA regulates lead under a variety of statutes, and because of concern that its various programs had different and inconsistent targets and strictness standards, it requested a study by the Science Advisory Board to examine the evidence that lead is a carcinogen and determine the extent of the differences between its control programs for lead in air, drinking water, and solid wastes. The EPA study group agreed that lead is a carcinogen in rodents. However, given the limited state of understanding of the contribution of lead to tumor formation, and considering the fact that the animals studied were exposed to very high levels, the study concluded that there was not a sufficient basis for assigning levels of cancer risk to specific human exposures.

The study group also reviewed the manner in which scientific data on lead were utilized by the EPA in determining acceptable levels of exposure to lead in drinking water and ambient air. It concluded that the EPA had taken a generally sound, although not fully consistent, approach. However, there were problems and inconsistencies noted in the establishment of target blood lead levels and definition of populations at risk, among others. The group recommended that the EPA develop a national policy on blood-lead-level reductions (particularly for children) and address environmental exposure to lead on the basis of preventing adverse neurological effects in children. Basing regulatory strategy on the observable neurobehavioral effects in an especially vulnerable human population can avoid the problems inherent in extrapolating from animal studies and from studies using unrealistically high exposures; this approach appears likely to provide an acceptable degree of protection for the entire population.

—*Morton Lippmann, Ph.D.*

Gastrointestinal Disorders

Nearly 2,300 reports by scientists and clinicians from the United States and abroad were presented at the Digestive Diseases Week program, which met in May 1991 in New Orleans, La. The meeting, an annual event, is attended by nearly 7,000 physicians from around the world and is sponsored jointly by the American Gastroenterological Association, the American Association for the Study of Liver Diseases, the American Society for Gastrointestinal Endoscopy, and the Society for Surgery of the Alimentary Tract. Some of the topics that were of major concern are highlighted below.

Getting rid of gallstones

Interest continues in two recently developed nonsurgical treatments for gallstones—one, a method for dissolving stones using bile acids or various solvents; the other, a technique for fragmenting them with ultrasonic lithotripsy. The drug lovastatin (Mevacor), introduced in 1987 for lowering blood cholesterol levels, has also been found to reduce cholesterol levels in bile. In animal experiments lovastatin has been shown to facilitate the dissolution of cholesterol gallstones, and it may thus become a useful addition to bile acid therapy.

The likelihood of stones recurring following either dissolution with bile acids or fragmentation with lithotripsy is a continuing problem. (There are as yet no definite statistics on recurrence rates after successful lithotripsy.) An Italian study reported in 1990 showed a high rate of reappearance of stones after complete dissolution with either of the two bile acids now in use; recurrent stones were common, especially in patients who had multiple gallstones at the onset of treatment. The Italian researchers found that only 50% of recurrent stones dissolved during a second course of therapy and that there was no response to therapy after a second recurrence. Clearly, dissolution treatment has a limited usefulness at present and should be confined to patients who are either poor operative risks or unwilling to undergo surgery.

Surgical removal of the gallbladder (cholecystectomy) is still the definitive treatment for symptomatic gallstones. However, it is a major operation that requires hospitalization for 7 to 10 days and a lengthy recuperative period. Because of these disadvantages, considerable interest has been aroused by a novel form of cholecystectomy in which the gallbladder is removed completely with the aid of a laparoscope (a fiber-optic device) introduced into the abdomen at the navel through a very small incision. A laser probe for cutting and forceps for grasping are inserted through three tiny 0.6–1.25-cm (0.25–0.5-in) incisions at the right rib margin. The laparoscope allows the surgeon to view the gallbladder and its main artery and duct and to guide the movements of the forceps and laser probe inside the abdomen. In one study of 25 patients who underwent laparoscopic cholecystectomy, hospitalization was required for an average of only two days, and patients were able to return to work in less than one week. This operation, developed by surgeons in Nashville, Tenn., is becoming the operation of choice for patients with uncomplicated gallstone disease.

Ulcers: an infectious disorder?

There have been significant recent advances in the understanding, detection, and treatment of peptic ulcers. Such ulcers were once thought to be caused solely by the excess secretion of acid by the stomach, but in recent years there has been growing enthusiasm for the theory that a bacterium plays a part in the causation of chronic gastritis (inflammation of the mucous membrane that lines the stomach) and some forms of peptic ulcer. In late 1989 an international bacteriology journal officially renamed the organism; the new name, *Helicobacter pylori,* is taxonomically more precise than the original designation, *Campylobacter pylori.* The relationship of *H. pylori* to all peptic ulcers—duodenal and gastric—is steadily becoming more apparent, infection having been found in the stomach linings of 90–95% of patients with duodenal ulcers and in almost every case of gastritis of the lower stomach, or antrum. Several studies have shown that duodenal and gastric ulcers recur frequently and fairly quickly if *H. pylori* infection persists in the stomach following treatment with acid-blocking agents, which are cur-

rently the most widely prescribed antiulcer drugs. On the other hand, recurrence is rare when the bacterial infection is eradicated with antibiotics.

Bismuth-containing compounds (such as the over-the-counter preparation Pepto-Bismol) are effective in at least temporarily controlling *H. pylori* infections. Many investigators feel that more permanent results are achieved when antibiotics, such as amoxicillin, tetracycline, and metronidazole, are used in varying combinations in addition to bismuth salts. Gold sodium thiomalate, an antiarthritic drug with characteristics similar to bismuth, has also been shown to be effective in eliminating *H. pylori* and may become a useful therapeutic agent.

The detection of *H. pylori* in stomach tissue biopsies has become quite simple with the use of a sensitive and specific test that indirectly determines the presence of urease, an enzyme unique to *H. pylori,* among the various bacteria that may be present in the stomach. The organisms may also be detected microscopically under the protective layer of mucus lining the wall of the stomach, but this process takes more time and requires a special tissue-staining procedure. The standard staining methods used to identify other microorganisms generally are not sensitive for the *Helicobacter* species.

Scientists now have a better understanding of the process by which ulcers cause their damage. Another enzyme secreted by *H. pylori,* phospholipase, is believed to be responsible for the injurious effects of the organism on the stomach. Phospholipase is capable of destroying the protective layer of fatty substances called phospholipids that overlies the cells lining the stomach and duodenum (epithelial cells). This action would permit the mucous membrane to be easily damaged by gastric acid and pepsin. Further, lysolecithin, a substance produced in this enzymatic reaction, is now also known to be capable of causing tissue injury.

Ulcer drug developments

While the work on *H. pylori* makes it appear more and more likely that peptic ulcer disease is caused primarily by infection rather than by excess secretion of acid, the use of acid-blocking agents is still strongly indicated in the early treatment period to reduce the injurious effects of acid on the mucous membrane of the stomach. Recent data indicate that there are no major differences between the four currently available histamine (H_2)-blocking agents (cimetidine, ranitidine, famotidine, and nizatidine) in regard to efficacy or side effects. A change of brands may be helpful for people who develop uncomfortable side effects to one or another of these drugs.

However, not all patients with peptic ulcer disease respond to H_2-blocking agents. In 1989 omeprazole (Prilosec), the first drug of a new class of agents for

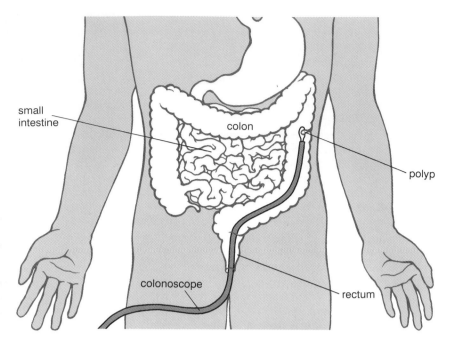

small intestine

colon

polyp

colonoscope

rectum

A fiber-optic instrument known as a colonoscope can be used to examine the entire 1.5–1.8-meter (5–6-foot) length of the colon for the presence of cancerous tumors or of polyps, growths that may develop into cancer. Some polyps that are found during such an examination can be removed by means of a wire snare on the colonoscope.

treating gastrointestinal disease, became available in the U.S. It is very effective in promoting the healing of peptic ulcers, particularly those not responsive to the H_2-blocking agents. H_2 blockers act by adhering to specific receptors on the outer membrane of acid-secreting cells located in the body of the stomach, thus preventing histamine from stimulating the cell to produce acid. Omeprazole, however, combines with the acid pump (the mechanism that produces increased acid secretion) on the secretory surface of the cell and thereby markedly reduces all stimuli to the secretion of acid, including histamine, gastrin, and acetylcholine. The drug is taken orally only once daily and, although expensive, it is well tolerated.

Continued administration of either the H_2 blockers or omeprazole, at reduced dosages, has also been shown to prevent recurrences of peptic ulcers for up to at least three years after healing. Ulcers do reoccur in some cases, however, and it is possible that ongoing *H. pylori* infection may be a factor.

Reflux redux

Reflux esophagitis is an inflammatory disease that results from weakness of the valvelike mechanism, or sphincter, at the lower end of the esophagus, just above the stomach. This weakness allows gastric secretions to flow backward (reflux) into the esophagus and damage its sensitive mucous membrane. The resulting inflammation may lead to mucosal bleeding, ulceration, and stricture (abnormal narrowing). Patients complain of heartburn, trouble in swallowing, and occasional pain in the chest on swallowing. Until recently medical treatment consisted of antacids, H_2-blocking agents, weight loss, and avoidance of certain provok-

ing substances, such as coffee, chocolate, acidic or alkaline foods, alcohol, and tobacco. In many cases, however, the H_2 blockers do not reduce gastric acid enough to be fully effective. In these instances, the newer acid-suppressing agent omeprazole, discussed above, has been shown to be much more effective. It is administered in a single daily dose that can be reduced for maintenance therapy after healing has taken place.

Certain medications that increase the contraction strength of the lower esophageal sphincter may also be useful in the treatment of reflux esophagitis. Among these are bethanechol (Urecholine), metoclopramide (Reglan), and cisapride, a new drug not yet available in the United States (marketed as Prepulsid in Europe). There is also evidence that erythromycin, a broad-spectrum antibiotic, increases contraction strength in the lower esophageal sphincter.

While such drug treatment is usually effective, it must be followed continuously in order to prevent recurrent symptoms. For some patients this regimen may become onerous. In these cases effective surgical treatments are available, although they involve a major procedure. An operation may be more strongly indicated in esophagitis patients who develop cellular changes (dysplasia) in the mucous membrane of the esophagus (Barrett's epithelium)—changes that may be indications of a future cancer. Where dysplasia has been present for an extended length of time, it is unlikely that mucosal cells will revert to normal as a result of drug treatment. Under these circumstances, surgery is strongly indicated to prevent the further progression of the dysplastic process, although it will not reverse the preexisting dysplasia.

Cost-effective cancer screening

Like many other forms of cancer, colon cancer is highly treatable if found early. The same is true of polyps, growths that develop in the lining of the intestine and may progress to cancer. Currently, there are three diagnostic techniques used to identify existing and potential colon cancers—chemical tests of the stool for invisible (occult) traces of blood, sigmoidoscopy, and colonoscopy. While colonoscopy, which examines the entire 1.5–1.8-m (5–6-ft) length of the colon, rarely fails to reveal any existing lesions, it is expensive and must be performed under sedation. Sigmoidoscopy, using a flexible, 60-cm (24-in) instrument, is a less invasive procedure (the instrument allows visualization of the last 60 cm of the colon), but there is always the possibility that cancerous or precancerous growths may lie beyond its reach. Tests for occult blood, on the other hand, are inexpensive and are available in kit form for home use. They are problematic, however, in that they produce a high rate of false-positive results, necessitating additional procedures to verify the accuracy of the original test. Further, they sometimes produce false-negative results, thus missing a certain percentage of existing cancers.

There is, at present, little agreement about which of these tests should be used or how frequently. This debate was a focus of concern at the New Orleans meeting. At the heart of this issue are the relative costs and efficiency of the available diagnostic tools. Several studies conducted in the past couple of years have addressed these questions. In one of these, Australian investigators reported that a new test, Heme-Select, was more successful in detecting tiny amounts of blood in the stool of patients with small and large polyps than was the more widely used Hemoccult II. The incidence of false-positive results was not evaluated, however.

Another project, which investigated the effectiveness of a mass stool-screening program, confirmed the view that a significant number of colonic cancers may not be detected by occult blood testing alone in patients who have no other symptoms; the findings suggest that some sort of direct visualization, probably with the flexible sigmoidoscope, should be done regularly in healthy patients over the age of 50 at least once every five years. As many as 90% of all colonic cancers are located within the range of this instrument. This recommendation was confounded, however, by the results of another investigation in which healthy men over the age of 50, who had had negative stool tests, were examined by sigmoidoscopy. On a subsequent examination with the colonoscope, nearly 30% of those who had negative sigmoidoscopies to 60 cm were found to have polyps above that level.

Until a definitive detection procedure is determined, the current recommendations of the American Cancer Society are probably still the most cost effective. They call for annual testing for occult blood in the stool (using the most sensitive and specific method available) after age 40 and a sigmoidoscopy every four to five years after age 50. A full colonoscopy should be performed if any stool specimens are positive for occult bleeding. Some early lesions may be missed for a year or two with this approach, but it is highly unlikely that colonic cancers will not be detected at an operable stage. Since most cancers and large polyps bleed at some time, and because a very large percentage of cancers and large polyps are located within the reach of the sigmoidoscope, they are fairly certain to be detected by this process. Regular routine use of full colonoscopy as a screening test for asymptomatic patients over age 50 is unlikely ever to become cost effective.

—*Harvey J. Dworken, M.D.*

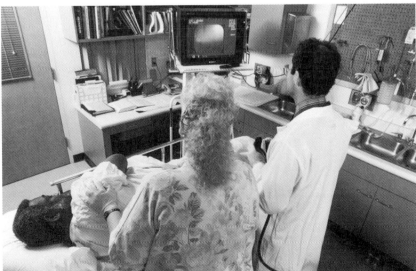

A patient undergoes colonoscopy while a physician and a technician monitor the progress of the exam on a television screen. Because the procedure is invasive—requiring sedation—and costly, it is unlikely to become a routine screening test for those without symptoms.

Special Report

The Serious Business of Child's Play

by Charles-Gene McDaniel, M.S.J.

Play is the highest development in childhood, for it alone is the free expression of what is in a child's soul.
—Friedrich Froebel (1782–1852),
originator of kindergarten

When six-month-old Dena plays peek-a-boo with her mother, she is doing more than merely having fun; she is learning some of the earliest lessons of life—lessons that will remain with her throughout adulthood. She is learning to trust another person, learning that people and objects continue to exist even when they cannot be seen.

Play, a highly complex phenomenon, is not only important for human development, it is essential. The dividends of childhood play are reaped throughout life, contributing to creativity and emotional health in adulthood. Children who do not have the opportunity to play are slow to develop. In extreme cases they may end up mentally unbalanced or retarded. They may even die at a very young age.

Humans are not unique among the Earth's creatures in their ability and need to play. Ethologists, scientists who study animal behavior, have observed that all mammals and birds play, while reptiles, amphibians, fish, and insects do not. Kittens play with balls as a prelude to later predatory activity. Puppies wrestle and "worry" shoes and other objects; kids, lambs, colts, and calves frolic. Among human beings the quality and type of play vary among cultures and social classes.

Play denigrated

Contemporary psychologists and other child development experts tend to agree that the opportunity for free play, unprogrammed and without adult interference, at least in early childhood, is important for optimal intellectual development and social adjustment. "We forget that play is the work of childhood," points out Kathryn Hirsh-Pasek, professor of psychology at Temple University, Philadelphia, who has studied the role of play in child development. Above all, she emphasizes the importance of adults' respecting children's play and letting them explore and learn on their own.

Her view, while shared by many experts, runs counter not only to the ideas of many parents but also to the Puritan practices that were embedded in the early history of the United States and many other Western countries. In Victorian England children were looked upon as "little adults" and were expected to behave accordingly. It was not until after the Industrial Revolution and the subsequent adoption of laws forbidding child labor that many American children had time to play—*i.e.,* time to be children. Well into the middle of the 20th century, this was a luxury that was not available to youngsters raised on farms; as soon as they were old enough, it was necessary for them to contribute to the demanding work of farming.

Hirsh-Pasek, like many of her fellow child development specialists, laments the fact that many middle-class parents today are demanding that children achieve like adults—the phenomenon of the "hurried child." These parents are seemingly unaware that such a pressure-cooker approach to raising their children may have untoward consequences. Some parents and educators are concerned that scholastically American children are falling behind children in other parts of the world, most notably Japan. What they fail to consider is that Japanese children pay a price for their high academic achievement. The high suicide

Soon after birth most babies engage in playful activities. Touching, gazing, cooing, and being cuddled are their first games; their own bodies and those of their parents are their first toys.

Suzanne Arms-Wimberley

298

Suzuki Method musical training is designed to develop ability and character at a very early age. But some child development experts wonder if these talented young performers are being deprived of vital lessons that can be learned only through unprogrammed play.

rate among young people in Japan, attributed in large measure to the highly competitive educational system, has become a source of great national concern.

Some parents take a deadly serious, rigorously purposeful approach to play. This is particularly true of the generation of "baby boomers," many of whom postponed childbearing in order to pursue careers. These parents have fewer children, often only one, and they have great expectations for them. Their children learn that they must "work" early and hard to get ahead in life. Often such parents are disdainful of the normal stages of babyhood—the "goo-goo" baby talk and playing peek-a-boo and pat-a-cake; they consider "unprogrammed" play—any play that is not purposeful—to be a waste of time.

For some parents, having "superkids" is a status symbol, as important as financial success and having material possessions. Such parents are personified in "stage mothers" and "Little League fathers," whose own self-identity is heavily tied to their children's achievements. Without considering that children's development and talents vary, they push their children to be athletic, musical, artistic, and so forth; it is crucial to them that their children be high achievers. Yet it is just as important for four-year-old Craig to sit on the kitchen table pretending it is a boat and "rowing" with a broom as it is for him to learn to count before he reaches school age. While it may not be obvious to parents with high expectations for their offspring, Craig and other children who engage in pretend activities are learning crucial lessons.

Studying play

What is play? A whole range of children's activities are considered play, including what some experts catego-rize as exploration. However classified, these activities are vital to children's well-being and learning. Most parents naturally play with children almost from birth, responding to their cues and providing them with progressively more sophisticated challenges, starting with rattles and colorful moving objects hung over cribs.

The study of play has a long history. During the past two decades investigations into the nature of play have intensified; these studies have been facilitated to a great extent by video cameras, which make it possible for child development researchers to record the play activities of children and then study the film in order to appreciate the nuances of their play. The benefits of active play for physical development and coordination are obvious. It is the cognitive and social development benefits that are less well understood and generally underappreciated. Research continues, especially in these latter areas.

Effects of neglect

The condition of neglected infants and children in overcrowded, understaffed orphanages in Romania became known to the world after the recent overthrow of the Communist government. The Nicolae Ceausescu regime had set the goal of increasing the population by several million, only to find some 140,000 children abandoned by parents who could not care for them. It was not merely neglect that produced underweight, retarded children but also the lack of a consistent, caring adult who would feed, diaper, and bathe the children—and *play* with them.

Decades earlier, when orphanages were more common in the modern industrialized world, the eminent Swiss-Hungarian psychologist René Spitz and others observed similar conditions in orphanages throughout Europe. Owing to the large numbers of orphans, caretakers could barely attend to the most basic needs of the babies; there was no time to play with them, and there were certainly no toys in their cribs for stimulation. Spitz observed that the infants typically were frightened and sad and would cry when adults came near them. Even when provided with adequate food, they ate poorly. In a short while they became weak, emaciated, and inactive and were uninterested in their surroundings. In this compromised state of health, many became ill with infections, and some died; many others were retarded, even though they had been normal at birth. By age two, unlike their normal, healthy counterparts, they were unable to walk, talk, or feed themselves.

Such neglect in overcrowded orphanages is extreme and rare in the contemporary world, where, in fact, there is a shortage of adoptable babies. Neglect today takes different forms but is still common. Children may be neglected by their families for a variety of reasons, including poverty, ignorance, indifference, or pursuit of careers by both parents.

299

Researchers have found that neglected children from extremely deprived families living in disorganized, overcrowded ghetto apartments do not develop concepts of time and space in the way that children who are not so deprived do naturally. They lack the range of vocabulary and curiosity, and they do not seem to know how to play.

By contrast, some parents may be able to provide for their children lavishly, showering them with toys and other material possessions, but are unable to provide the emotional nurturing and the stimulation for playing that children need. So-called nonempathic parenting is one of the less obvious forms of neglect, but its effects can be dramatic. Another prevalent kind of neglect today is leaving children at home alone because both parents work full time outside the home. "Latchkey" children who spend most of their time in an empty house lack encouragement to play and often develop emotional problems at an early age.

Infancy's curriculum

Soon after birth, most babies engage in playful activities. While being fed by bottle or breast and cuddled by their mothers, babies pause to look at their mother's face and touch her. Such touching, gazing, and wiggling of feet are babies' first games, and their

From the time they begin to crawl, toddlers need an environment that is conducive to playing—where they can be energetic, noisy, and messy. Pieces of their parents' world are often their favorite playthings.

Cathy Melloan

mothers' and their own bodies are their first toys. Stimulated by parental cooing and talking while they are fed, changed, and bathed, babies begin to babble, then identify sounds with people and objects—"Ma-ma," "Da-da," "rat-tle." Recently reported research from Canada has shown that even deaf babies "babble" with their hands in the same rhythmic, repetitive fashion as hearing infants babble with their voices. The manual babbling, in apparent imitation of the sign language of deaf parents, occurs at about 10 months of age, the same age at which hearing children begin to put together sounds that resemble words.

From the time children can crawl, they begin to explore, and virtually any object becomes a toy, serving not only to amuse but to educate (*e.g.*, pots and pans found in low kitchen cupboards, mother's slippers, father's galoshes). During infancy and as toddlers, children learn to differentiate between textures and the sensations of various objects: the hardness of their high chair compared with the softness of stuffed animals and sofa cushions; the mushiness of their cooked cereal and applesauce compared with the firmness of a teething biscuit; the slipperiness of water compared with the grittiness of sand; and the heat of the kitchen stove that causes sudden pain when touched compared with the sharp cold of an ice cube.

At this stage, young children come into conflict with watchful parents who want to keep them from harm—from touching a hot stove or falling down stairs. While too-watchful parents can deprive the child of important learning experiences, this is the time when young children learn that there are necessary limits on exploration if they are to remain safe and happy. Establishing such boundaries on play also teaches meaningful lessons—about trust, caution, fear, and wariness.

All this has been called "the hidden curriculum of infancy." As youngsters explore and "play" with almost anything in their midst, they are learning about time, space, and distance—they find out how much time and energy it takes to crawl across the floor. They learn about cause and effect—what they can do to things and what happens to them as a result—and thus how to control their environment. These are life-long lessons that are remembered even when many of the lessons learned later at school are forgotten.

Acquiring "social intelligence"

Psychologists say that much of the "social intelligence" that children bring with them to the playground is related to how they were treated at home. Those who have strict and punitive parents tend to be aggressive. Children whose parents talk to them about emotion tend to be more willing to share toys, to play compatibly with others, and to be more sensitive to other children's feelings.

The crucial social intelligence that children derive from early experiences governs their ability to cope in

In preparing an elaborate tea party for a toy rabbit, a three-and-a-half-year-old tries on the role of gracious hostess; her creativity knows no bounds as she entertains her guest and makes the event a pleasurable one.

life. Recognizing the importance of this acquired skill, the U.S. National Institute of Mental Health (NIMH) recently funded a three-year collaborative study. Researchers at Duke University, Durham, N.C., Vanderbilt University, Nashville, Tenn., the University of Washington, and Pennsylvania State University are working with children who have not developed social skills to help them overcome their inability to interact with others in appropriate ways.

The importance of these skills may not be obvious. But extensive research has shown that low social competence has distinctly adverse effects. In a study of 200 kindergartners, all of whom started at the same developmental level, it was found that those who were rejected by their classmates as poor playmates did only half as well on tests of academic readiness when tested at the end of the year. The unpopular children—those that others did not want to play with—were unhappy about going to school and had an increasing number of absences as the year wore on. A second study showed that unpopular children who were rejected in third grade had poor academic standing in sixth grade, and another found that children who were the most unpopular at age 7 or 8 were twice as likely as other children to be "social misfits," to have been arrested or to have dropped out of high school by age 18.

From playing comes the development of "friendship skills," like taking turns, cooperating, joining a group, controlling anger, and resolving conflicts. The aim of the NIMH project is to devise ways to help children who do not have these skills, in the hope of making

them not only happier children but more competent adults.

The Swiss psychologist Jean Piaget (1896–1980) is credited as the originator of the theory linking play and social functioning. He believed that children are intrinsically motivated to engage in social interactions and that when youngsters resolve conflicts among themselves, they learn how to manage the environment competently.

Today's technological developments are considered by some psychologists to be a detriment to acquisition of such social intelligence. They argue, for example, that video games cannot teach the subtle cues of body language and the social pleasures that children learn through free play with other children. Video games are not the only culprit. Television and the telephone take away from the time children have to spend playing. Crime and drugs on the street also are responsible for keeping children indoors instead of playing freely outside.

Fantasy and curiosity

One often-misunderstood aspect of children's play is that of the imaginary playmate. It is common for children to pretend that a toy animal is a living pet or that a doll is a sister or brother or a best friend. Sometimes the imagined playmate is entirely in the youngster's mind—invisible to others—but a true companion to the child. These characters often are named and referred to by the child in conversation. With such imaginary playmates, children learn responsibility as they imagine that someone is depending on them. Studies have shown that children who invent playmates are more likely to be cooperative during play with others and more predisposed toward social interaction.

In addition to imaginary companions, children often create elaborate fantasy worlds, which psychologists consider highly sophisticated forms of play. The reasons for inventing fantasy worlds vary. Some children create fantasies to widen their worlds—to expand their realm of exploration. Others may devise complex imaginary worlds to escape from their problems. They may be lonely or feel inadequate except when they can take refuge in their fantasy world.

Childhood curiosity stimulates playing and exploring; these in turn stimulate more curiosity. Every parent is familiar with the three-year-old who endlessly asks, "Why?" That ceaseless curiosity is the basis of creative thinking, which in later years enables artists to create and scientists to pursue unanswered questions with the goal of understanding the universe and controlling it for the good of humankind.

Providing for play

To what extent can parents provide for their children's play? Authorities emphasize that playing comes naturally to children; it is self-motivated. Parents can and

Youngsters learn to cooperate, to share, and to resolve conflicts from playing. These important "friendship skills" contribute to their ability to get along with others as adults and live happy, productive lives.

should guide and encourage play, but for the play to be most meaningful, it should also be self-directed—the "rules" should be set by the child, not imposed by the parents.

Once children are actively mobile, they need an environment that is conducive to playing; they need space to explore and, ideally, at least some of the time, they need places where their playing can be energetic, noisy, and messy. Making mud pies and dashing around yelling are valuable endeavors.

What about toys? Certainly the toy industry is a booming one; annual sales in the U.S. are well over $1 billion. Authorities' views on the value of commercial toys vary, but most agree that children will play with what they have access to, whether it is the kitchen broom or an expensive computer game.

Providing the environment and encouragement to play is more important than providing lots of toys. British psychologist Penelope Leach, a world-renowned child development authority, says that commercially produced toys have a place in children's play and pleasure but points out that many of the "most-used playthings" are pieces of the parents' world.

Of course, parents should always make sure that a store-bought toy is safe. In addition to checking for safety, Leach offers the following tips for purchasing toys: Parents should make sure that they (or their children) are not being misled by advertising. In other words, will the toy do what one expects it to? The toy should be a practical plaything for the individual child. It should "fit" with the child's current play. Furthermore, a toy should be something that the child is free to use as he or she pleases; it should not be too delicate or too costly, and it should not be something that is irreplaceable.

Playing and emotional well-being

Sigmund Freud, the founder of psychoanalysis, believed that healthy emotional functioning is dependent upon play, which serves as a way for children to express feelings that they may or may not be able to verbalize. Some child therapists today observe their young, troubled patients playing with dolls in order to determine what might be the source of their problems. Play therapy using dolls may also be used to forfend emotional problems. Play therapists in hospitals use dolls to prepare pediatric patients for surgery so that they will be less traumatized by this frightening experience. At Children's Hospital of Philadelphia, dolls are used to teach young cancer patients about chemotherapy; before they start on a course of chemotherapy, they are able to administer "play" injections to toy patients.

Can children play too much? Children can become overwhelmed if they have too many activities, too many toys, or too many playmates at once. Similarly, children may be given toys that are too advanced for their age level and thus go unused. Or they may use inappropriate toys inappropriately: a baseball bat in the hands of a two-year-old becomes a weapon for pounding the furniture—or the family dog.

Leach emphasizes that as children get older they still need time to play for the sake of their well-being. Often, however, their lives become so full of structured activities that spontaneous "just-for-fun" play ceases. Yet, says Leach, if older children are "driven from one achievement to the next, on an ever tighter schedule, we cannot be surprised if they become as harassed as striving executives and ready, in adolescence, either to break away from all achievement to look for a peace of their own, or to join their ulcer-ridden elders in the nearest bar."

Life is most meaningful when all aspects of behavior are integrated, as they are in children's play. Play unifies the mind, body, and spirit. Those children who have the opportunity to play in the consistent care of loving adults usually develop into healthy adults, capable of growth and change, who can make maximum use of their intelligence and talents.

Genetics

The revolution in human genetics that began a little more than a decade ago is now moving from the laboratory to the clinic. Rapid-fire advances in technologies that were perfected in the 1980s—making possible the location and isolation of genes from a sample as small as a single cell—are beginning to spawn new treatments for cancer and hereditary diseases as well as methods for averting congenital defects even before pregnancy begins. The identification of genes implicated in hereditary disorders is progressing at a rapid pace. Not only are medical geneticists able to identify the precise regions of DNA that are involved in diseases due to defects in a single gene, they are now beginning to gain deeper understanding of the complexities of diseases such as atherosclerosis, early-onset Alzheimer's disease, and certain types of cancer, which result from the cumulative effects of several genetic aberrations.

Human gene therapy: early report

At the Clinical Center of the National Institutes of Health (NIH), Bethesda, Md., on April 5, 1991, W. French Anderson told the Recombinant DNA Committee of the NIH that the first use of human gene therapy to treat a genetic defect was proving effective. The patient was a four-year-old girl who was born with severe combined immunodeficiency (SCID), the disease that had condemned David, the Houston, Texas, youngster known as the "bubble boy," to life in sterile isolation. The girl has a defective gene for the enzyme adenosine deaminase (ADA), and her immune system is therefore unable to combat infections. Previously she had been undergoing enzyme replacement therapy with the drug pegademase, which enabled her immune system to function at about half the normal efficiency.

At the time of their report, Anderson and colleagues R. Michael Blaese and Kenneth Culver had been treating the child for six months with infusions of her own lymphocytes (white blood cells that "mastermind" the immune system) into which working copies of the ADA gene had been inserted. In each of six half-hour sessions, she had received intravenous infusions of a solution containing about one billion such altered cells. The treatment had to be repeated once a month because, like all body cells, lymphocytes die and must be replaced. Anderson told the NIH committee that the altered cells, along with the ongoing ADA treatments, had succeeded in raising the girl's immune function to near normal levels, allowing her to mingle freely with other children and enabling her to recover rapidly from a bout of influenza. A 10-year-old girl with SCID, who had begun the treatment in January 1991, was also reported to be doing well.

Also in January, Anderson, in collaboration with Steven Rosenberg, an oncologist at the National Cancer Institute, began gene therapy in two patients with malignant melanoma (a form of skin cancer that readily invades other organs), each of whom had advanced disease that had failed to respond to drugs. They were treated with infusions of a version of their own cells that had been cultivated from excised tumors. These cells, called tumor infiltrating lymphocytes, or TIL cells, specialize in invading and attacking tumors. The TIL cells were fortified with extra copies of the gene for tumor necrosis factor (TNF), a protein secreted by lymphocytes that kills cancer cells.

The above cases represent the first successful instances of the therapeutic use of genetically altered cells. (In an earlier experiment altered cells were used to monitor the progress of a cancer treatment.) The researchers emphasized that this approach does not permanently alter patients' genetic makeup or correct their genetic deficiencies. Rather, it employs lympho-

At the Clinical Center of the National Institutes of Health in Bethesda, Maryland, a 10-year-old girl—one of two young patients in the first trial of human gene therapy—casually glances at a book while receiving an infusion of genetically altered white blood cells. The procedure is supervised by pediatrician Kenneth Culver. The patient, who suffers from adenosine deaminase deficiency, was reported to be doing extremely well in the early stages of the new treatment. At first, "it made me feel funny having new genes in my body," she said of her role as a medical pioneer, "but I'm used to it now."

cytes to deliver proteins in somewhat the same way capsules are used to carry drugs; like drug treatments, such gene therapy has to be repeated as often and for as long as it is needed.

Preimplantation genetics

Applying DNA technology to *in vitro* fertilization (IVF) has given rise to the science of preimplantation genetics, which makes possible the selection of embryos without known genetic defects for implantation in the prospective mother's uterus. Conventional IVF involves treating a woman with hormones that trigger the release of several oocytes (eggs), collecting these oocytes, fertilizing them in the laboratory with the prospective father's spermatozoa, and implanting the fertilized eggs in her uterus. Preimplantation diagnosis inserts an additional step in which either oocytes or embryos are screened for genetic defects prior to implantation.

At the first International Symposium on Preimplantation Genetics, held in Chicago in September 1990, geneticists and obstetricians discussed their experiences with the technique thus far. Alan Handyside and colleagues of Hammersmith Hospital in London reported that they had used preimplantation genetics to select embryos for women who, because they carry a defective copy of a particular gene on one of their two X chromosomes, are carriers of so-called X-linked diseases such as muscular dystrophy or hemophilia. Male children born to these women inherit one maternal X chromosome, along with one Y chromosome from their fathers; they therefore have a 50% chance of acquiring the X chromosome that bears the defective gene. To eliminate any risk of having a son with an X-linked disease, some couples choose to abort all male fetuses. The Hammersmith physicians have developed a technique to enable carriers of X-linked diseases to become pregnant with female fetuses only (who will have a normal gene on the second X chromosome). After IVF the fertilized oocytes are allowed to divide three times to produce eight-cell blastulas, early-stage embryos that are essentially tiny fluid-filled orbs with an outer covering of cells called blastomeres. At this stage doctors can remove a single blastomere without damaging the blastula and extract the DNA from that blastomere for analysis.

The blastomere DNA is added to a solution and heated so that the two strands of the helical DNA molecule separate. To that solution the doctors then add two DNA probes—short synthetic stretches of DNA that attach to specifically targeted sequences of DNA. The probes are designed to attach to either end of a segment of DNA that is unique to the Y chromosome. Next, an enzyme called a polymerase is added; it creates copies of the segment between the probes. The duplication process, called the polymerase chain reaction, or PCR, can produce a million copies of the segment within an hour. Thus, if the Y chromosome is present, it will be manifested by a millionfold amplification of the segment bounded by the probes. If it is absent, there will be no reaction.

When screening for X-linked disorders, Handyside and colleagues select for implantation only blastulas without Y chromosomes. Although they have produced several successful pregnancies this way, they plan eventually to replace the Y-chromosome probes with PCR probes for specific genetic defects such as Huntington's disease. If they can eliminate only blastulas that have defective genes, they can select male as well as female embryos that are apparently healthy.

Other researchers are using techniques that screen for defects in unfertilized oocytes. Yury Verlinsky and colleagues at Illinois Masonic Medical Center in Chicago have focused on identifying maternally carried diseases by examining the polar body—the set of chromosomes discarded when the oocyte undergoes meiosis, the process of division by which the cell reduces its full complement of 46 chromosomes to half, or 23. (With the 23 chromosomes contributed by the sperm, the fertilized oocyte will attain the full number.) The polar body migrates to the zona pellucida, the clear envelope encasing the oocyte, where it can be removed without harming the oocyte.

The investigators can then subject the polar body DNA to PCR analysis to screen for dominant, single-gene defects—*i.e.,* those in which, of the paired genes normally present, a single defective gene is enough to cause disease. If the polar body contains a defective gene, they can assume that the oocyte contains an undamaged gene. They then select for fertilization and implantation only oocytes that have shed the defective gene into the polar body.

Cancer therapy that makes "antisense"

Researchers are developing a new approach to cancer therapy that involves preventing oncogenes—mutant or defective versions of genes that regulate cell growth and division—from producing the proteins thought to be responsible for the malignancy. In essence, this strategy disrupts the process whereby the genetic information is translated into proteins.

Scientists have long known that only one strand of the double-stranded DNA molecule—the so-called sense strand—codes for the synthesis of a protein. (Not all regions of this strand are active in the coding process; some are noncoding, or "junk," regions.) At the beginning of the protein-production process, the two strands of DNA separate, and enzymes called polymerases "read" the information on the noncoding, or "antisense," strand. The polymerases use this information to construct a complementary RNA copy of the active regions of the sense strand. This "messenger RNA" (mRNA) is a surrogate for the sense strand with all noncoding regions eliminated.

Normally the mRNA travels from the nucleus to the cell's cytoplasm, where small beadlike structures called ribosomes use it as a template to assemble a given protein. However, like any single strand of DNA, mRNA is irresistibly attracted to its complement. Should it encounter a complementary strand of antisense mRNA, it will pair with that strand to form a double-stranded molecule, which cannot serve as a template. Thus, antisense mRNA for a given gene can be used to prevent the translation of mRNA's instructions for that gene and, consequently, to block the production of the protein encoded by the gene.

To create antisense mRNA, researchers insert thousands of copies of a particular gene into a cell's nucleus by means of one of several approaches, such as injecting DNA into the nucleus or transferring it via a virus that has been stripped of its ability to cause disease. In most cases the copies of the gene that are accepted into the cell's DNA strand will be incorporated haphazardly throughout it: some will be backwards, others "flopped" so that the antisense strand is in the position normally occupied by the sense strand. These flopped DNA copies are isolated and fitted with promoters that enable them to generate antisense mRNA. They are then inserted into vectors, or carriers, that transport them back into the cell.

In March 1990 Jack A. Roth and colleagues at the M.D. Anderson Cancer Center in Houston reported that they had used antisense mRNA of the *ras* oncogene to suppress the growth of human lung cancer cells in mice. The researchers chose the *ras* gene because it is known to play a role in the formation of lung, kidney, colorectal, and other types of malignant tumors. The group transplanted the antisense version of the *ras* gene into cultured human lung cancer cells that were producing the mutant *ras* protein. When they analyzed the cells a few days later, they determined not only that the cells contained large amounts of antisense *ras* mRNA but that the production of the *ras* protein had declined to one-third the previous level. They then injected a million of these antisense-treated lung cancer cells into one group of mice and the same number of untreated lung cancer cells into another group. They found that the tumors engendered by the antisense-treated cancer cells grew much more slowly than those arising from the untreated cells.

Several other teams of investigators are creating short synthetic segments of antisense RNA that would interfere with the production of proteins coded for by oncogenes but not with the synthesis of proteins encoded by normal forms of the gene. Treatments based on these antisense molecules would selectively inactivate genes responsible for runaway cell growth and proliferation while sparing normal, rapidly dividing cells, such as hair follicles and the epithelial cells lining the digestive system, which are often destroyed by conventional chemotherapy.

Preventing tumor formation

Cancer researchers continue to discover genes now categorized as antioncogenes, or tumor-suppressor genes. This class of genes codes for proteins that maintain normal cellular growth and, when damaged or deleted, can initiate tumor formation.

In November 1990 a team from Osaka (Japan) University reported that they had isolated a gene on chromosome 9 that is mutated in patients with one form of xeroderma pigmentosa, a type of skin cancer. The gene codes for a protein that is apparently involved in the repair of DNA that has been damaged by ultraviolet radiation. Previously, damage to another DNA-repair gene had been linked to another form of the disease. Because xeroderma pigmentosa is a recessive disorder, people who develop either of the two forms must have two defective copies of the gene.

In March 1991 two teams of researchers, one led by Bert Vogelstein of John Hopkins University, Baltimore, Md., the other by Raymond White of the University of Utah, located two neighboring genes on chromosome 5 that are thought to play pivotal roles in initiating the formation of colon polyps, which, though benign, often precede the development of colorectal cancer. In March Vogelstein and White reported that they had found one gene, called MCC (for "mutated in colorectal cancer") because it is altered in colon tumor cells. In August they announced the discovery of the second, named APC ("adenomatous polyposis coli"), which appears to be mutated in all body cells of people with familial adenomatous polyposis, a condition that if untreated can progress to colon cancer before the patient is 30 years old. The researchers believe that both are tumor suppressor genes. When both copies of these genes are mutated, as in people who have colorectal cancer, the absence of any controlling factor allows cell growth to proceed unabated.

Photomicrographs show the well-ordered cells lining a healthy colon (left) and the chaotic disorganization of cells within a cancerous colon tumor. In 1991 geneticists discovered two genes responsible for initiating this irregular growth.

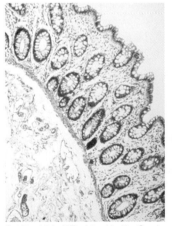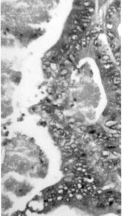

Bert Vogelstein, M.D., Johns Hopkins Oncology Center

Genetics

Retinitis pigmentosa: new findings

In 1990 two teams of researchers shed new light on the genetic defects responsible for a leading cause of blindness, retinitis pigmentosa, a hereditary condition in which a buildup of pigment in the cells of the retina, the part of the eye that registers light energy, gradually narrows the visual field. Most patients with retinitis pigmentosa are legally blind by age 40.

There are two forms of the disease. The less severe, which affects one in 3,500 people worldwide, appears to be autosomal (that is, caused by a defect on any chromosome other than the X or Y). People with this form of the disease usually retain some vision until about age 40. The other form, which affects one in 20,000 males, is thought to be an X-linked condition (*i.e.,* to result from a defect on the X chromosome); it usually results in blindness by age 30.

Maria Musarella and colleagues at the Hospital for Sick Children in Toronto reported that they had found a large deletion in an X chromosome of a patient with several X-linked disorders, including Duchenne muscular dystrophy and retinitis pigmentosa. When they determined what region of the chromosome was missing by comparing it with a normal X-chromosome, they found that it contained a gene that codes for a protein in the retina. They are now working to isolate the gene and to determine the structure and function of its protein product.

Thaddeus Dryja and colleagues at the Massachusetts Eye and Ear Infirmary in Boston reported that they had identified four mutations in the gene for rhodopsin—a protein found in the rod receptors, which are responsible for night vision—in 27 patients with the autosomal form of retinitis pigmentosa. The mutations were not present in 106 people with normal vision or 123 other patients with the same form of the disease. The Boston researchers concluded that in the 27 patients, and possibly others as well, retinitis

pigmentosa is a result of one of four mutations in the rhodopsin gene, which is located on chromosome 3. They speculate, however, that many other mutations, perhaps in other genes, will also be implicated in retinitis pigmentosa.

Polygenic disorders

Research into the genetics of several diseases has already yielded evidence favoring the involvement of many genes. Following the announcement in 1990 that alcoholism is apparently associated with a gene that codes for the neurotransmitter dopamine, several research groups reported that they were unable to find evidence for such an association. Similarly, since the 1987 publication of reports linking Alzheimer's disease to genes on chromosomes 19 and 21, further research has failed to substantiate such connections. A team from St. Mary's Medical School in London reported in February 1991 that they had associated a mutation in the gene for the precursor protein for amyloid—a substance that accumulates abnormally in the brains of Alzheimer's patients—with the disease in members of two families with a history of early onset (*i.e.,* disease before age 65). However, the researchers emphasized that the defect, located on chromosome 21, was not present in DNA from hundreds of other persons with the disease.

Cumulatively, these and similar studies were beginning to indicate that neurological and psychological disorders with a genetic component are likely to involve several physiological pathways. While some severe and early-developing forms of disease, such as early-onset Alzheimer's disease, may be the result of a defect in a single gene, late-onset forms may require the malfunction of several genes. Unraveling the genetics of these multifactorial disorders is likely to be a long and complex process.

Progress in Marfan syndrome

Since around the turn of the century, when the French pediatrician Antonin Marfan first described a young patient with long, spidery fingers (arachnodactyly) and other skeletal abnormalities, the galaxy of anomalies now known as Marfan syndrome has been a medical puzzle. In the ensuing decades physicians continued to add to the list of skeletal, cardiac, and ocular defects seen in affected individuals, noting that the severity of the disease varies markedly among patients. They also determined that many characteristics of the syndrome—such as dislocations in the lens of the eye and distension of the aorta, the blood vessel that carries oxygenated blood from the heart—were attributable to an underlying defect in the connective tissues. It is this defect that is responsible for the elongated bones, weakened blood vessels, and other problems seen in Marfan patients. Meanwhile, geneticists, having identified Marfan syndrome as an

This calf's long, thin hind legs and weak joints and tendons are signs of a form of Marfan syndrome, an inherited connective tissue disorder. By studying this animal model of the disease, scientists hope to be able to aid human patients.

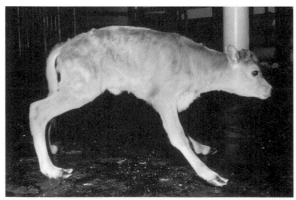

Kathleen Potter, D.V.M., and Thomas E. Besser, D.V.M., Washington State University

autosomal dominant defect, have probed the genome in search of the gene responsible, eliminating sites on all chromosomes except 8 and 15. By mid-1990 these two lines of investigation—into the underlying defect and chromosomal site—had begun to converge.

First, in July scientists at the University of Washington and Johns Hopkins University reported that a protein called fibrillin, part of the structural matrix of the connective tissues, is abnormal in many people with Marfan syndrome. In some patients cells do not make sufficient quantities of fibrillin, while in others the protein may be produced but is not properly incorporated into the matrix.

Then, in October, a team of molecular geneticists at the National Public Health Institute in Helsinki, Fin., reported that they had traced a gene responsible for Marfan syndrome in five families to a region of chromosome 15. Although they did not identify the gene itself, they narrowed its location to a region defined by three genetic markers.

Finally, in July 1991 researchers from Johns Hopkins and the Shriners Hospital for Crippled Children in Portland, Ore., identified the fibrillin gene on chromosome 15. They subsequently found that mutations existed in the fibrillin gene in two patients who had developed Marfan's spontaneously rather than inheriting the defective gene—confirming that defects in the fibrillin gene are responsible for the syndrome. These discoveries are expected to lead to a definitive diagnostic test.

Meanwhile, a panel of experts named by the U.S. National Museum of Health and Medicine decided in May 1991 to approve a proposal to create a genetic profile of Abraham Lincoln. The plan called for extracting and analyzing DNA from bone and hair samples that were taken at the autopsy of the 16th U.S. president and are now held at the museum. Through the use of PCR, it is theoretically possible to amplify the DNA from a single cell and to determine whether known genetic mutations are present. The process will work, however, only if Lincoln's tissues contain undegraded DNA. Although tissue samples from other historical figures are available, Lincoln's were chosen because there are no surviving descendants who would be affected by such an investigation. Moreover, medical researchers are especially interested in determining whether Lincoln, who had the tall, lanky frame and long fingers associated with Marfan syndrome, actually had the disorder.

The Genome Project at age two

Under the joint aegis of the NIH and the Department of Energy (DOE), the Human Genome Project completed its second official year in September 1991. There are six official NIH-funded centers, located at Baylor University, Houston; the Massachusetts Institute of Technology; the University of California at San Francisco;

Paul Hosefros/The New York Times

In May 1991 a scientific committee headed by medical geneticist Victor A. McKusick approved a plan to test tissue samples from the remains of Abraham Lincoln to see if the 16th U.S. president might have been afflicted with Marfan syndrome. Investigators hoped to be able to recover usable DNA from the 125-year-old specimens of Lincoln's hair, blood, and bones held in the Washington, D.C., National Museum of Health and Medicine.

the University of Michigan; Washington University, St. Louis, Mo.; and the University of Utah. DOE has designated centers at two of its California installations, the Lawrence Berkeley and Lawrence Livermore laboratories. Each center has a specific goal, such as mapping a given chromosome.

During 1991 the Working Group on Ethical, Legal, and Social Implications of the NIH's National Center for Human Genome Research sponsored 19 conferences to discuss society's responsibility in handling the information produced by the genome project. The conferences were designed to familiarize the public with legal and ethical issues likely to be generated, including public screening for genetic diseases as well as the ownership and confidentiality of genetic information.

—*Beverly Merz*

Health Care Financing

Almost everyone who reads the newspapers today is aware that health care costs in the United States are increasing rapidly. As insurers and the government have responded to these rising expenditures by instituting a variety of cost-containment initiatives, many people have been affected by their actions. In order to understand the recent preoccupation with controlling health care costs, it is necessary to study the reasons behind the recent growth in spending, review precisely

Health care financing

where the health care dollar is being spent, and examine the impact of several recent cost-containment initiatives on quality of and access to care.

Impact of rising costs

Spending on health care services has risen rapidly since 1960. Expenditures for all health care services increased from $30 billion in 1960 to $610 billion in 1990. On an individual level, per capita health expenditures increased from $200 in 1960 to $2,400 in 1990. Thus, the average American worked from January 1 to February 14 simply to pay his or her share of the nation's health care bill.

Economists are concerned with the increase in this spending in relation to the growth in the overall economy. For this reason, increases are typically compared with the gross national product (GNP)—the total value of goods and services produced by the country's residents. Health care spending as a percentage of GNP has increased every year since 1960, when the figure was 5%. This increased to 7% in 1970, 9% in 1980, and over 12% in 1990.

Policymakers are concerned that this increased spending may constrain the nation's ability to provide other goods and services. In 1988 11.1% of GNP went for health care, compared with 6.4% for education and 6.2% for defense. The percentage spent on education and defense declined slightly between 1970 and 1990; on health care it increased significantly.

Government officials are concerned that this spending is growing much faster than that on other governmental services. From 1970 to 1990 the rate of increase in health care spending by the federal government rose faster than rates not only for national defense but also for social security and other government programs. State officials worry because the Medicaid program, which provides health care services to low-income beneficiaries, is now the second largest state government program (after education) and is taking

resources from other state programs such as law enforcement, road construction, and recreation.

Private industry fears that these rising costs are constraining its ability to provide wage increases since much of the increase in personnel costs is being spent on health care services. Industries that face international competition are especially concerned since such costs are significantly higher in the U.S. than in other industrialized nations. The cost of the average American automobile, for example, now includes almost $800 in health care benefits that car companies pay to workers. By comparison, the cost of such benefits attached to the price of a car built in Japan and paid to Japanese workers is less than $400. It is not surprising that unions are concerned about the effect of health care costs on their bargaining position, and in recent years corporate attempts to limit medical benefits have been a main issue behind United Automobile Workers' strikes.

Health economists and health services researchers have become concerned about rising costs for two additional reasons. First, the United States is spending significantly more on health care than any other industrialized country, whereas most of the indicators used to compare the health status of the population show that that country is below the level of many other industrialized countries. In 1988 the United States spent 11.2% of its gross domestic product (similar to GNP but excluding imports and exports) on health care, compared with less than 9% in Canada, Sweden, and Germany and less than 7% in Japan and the United Kingdom. At the same time, comparisons of longevity (life expectancy at birth) and infant mortality (deaths during the first year of life), two measures that are commonly used for comparing the health status of populations, show that the U.S. is below more than half of the 24 major industrialized countries. These comparisons of expenditures and health status raise important questions about whether the United States

Over 350 angry workers and retirees from Connecticut demonstrated outside the state capitol to let it be known that skyrocketing health insurance rates were placing them in dire straits. As the president of the United Automobile Workers Local 1604, which represents retired autoworkers, put it, "Employees have to make a decision: either buy food or buy health insurance. That's a life-threatening situation."

Tony Bacewicz/Hartford Courant

is getting proper value for the dollars it spends on health care.

A second reason is that studies also suggest that some of the services being provided may be inappropriate or medically unnecessary. One recent study examined a sample of medical records of patients having one of three procedures—coronary angiography, endoscopy, and carotid enterectomy. A panel of physicians developed criteria to determine when a particular procedure was appropriate, indeterminate, or clearly inappropriate, and then it reviewed some 4,500 medical records. The panel found that 17.3% of the coronary angiographies (X-ray examinations to visualize the arteries that supply the heart muscle), 10.5% of the endoscopies (visualization of the organs of the upper gastrointestinal tract), and 28.5% of the carotid endarterectomies (surgical removal of plaque from neck arteries supplying blood to the head) were clearly inappropriate.

Other studies have examined variations in hospital admission rates to determine the appropriateness of admissions. They showed wide variations in rates that cannot be explained by demographic, health-status, or economic factors. For example, it was revealed that physicians in Boston were twice as likely to perform a carotid endarterectomy as physicians in New Haven, Conn., but only half as likely to do coronary bypass surgery. Another study showed that in Maine the likelihood of a woman's having a hysterectomy by the time she reached 70 years of age ranged from a low of 20% in one community to a high of 70% in another. When researchers investigated the reasons for the variation, they concluded that health status, demographic factors, and income could not explain much of the variation; rather, an unquantifiable residual "medical-practice factor" appeared to be the only valid explanation.

Who pays?

Federal and state governments provide 42% of the U.S. health care dollar, primarily through the Medicare and Medicaid programs. Medicare pays for acute care services (primarily hospital and physician) for most citizens over the age of 65. Medicaid provides both acute and long-term care (primarily in nursing homes) to low-income citizens who meet certain eligibility criteria. Private health insurance, usually provided by employers as a fringe benefit, mainly covers acute care services. Out-of-pocket expenditures are incurred for services not covered by insurance (over-the-counter drugs, for example) and for medical care for the 31 million individuals with no health insurance. During the 1980s health care expenditures increased at approximately the same rate for all of these payers, although the increase for Medicaid was slightly lower, suggesting that no payer is more successful than any other at controlling costs.

Spending the health care dollar

Almost two-thirds of the health care dollar is spent on hospital and physician services. During the 1980s spending by all of the major care providers increased by approximately 10% per year, although physician expenditures—at 12%—increased slightly more. The more rapid increase in physician expenditures was caused primarily by numerous cost-containment initiatives designed to move patients out of the hospital and into ambulatory settings as soon as possible.

Fundamentally, three factors are responsible for the growth in health care spending—aging of the population, inflation, and service intensity. The least important factor—responsible for approximately one percentage point per year—is the growth and aging of the population. Overall inflation and any additional inflation specific to the health care industry are responsible for most of the spending growth, averaging 7.5% per year during the 1980s. However, neither of these components lends itself to the control of rising health care costs.

The component receiving most of the attention is the one that cannot be explained by either of these two factors—so-called service intensity. It includes, for example, the cost of new technology, additional standard laboratory and radiological tests ordered by physicians, more frequent visits by more patients to physicians, and the cost of treating new illnesses. This service-intensity component has increased steadily by 1 to 4% per year in the past decade. Increases in service intensity are the costs that government policymakers, corporate executives, union leaders, and health services researchers focus on when they try to control medical costs.

Cost-containment initiatives

Because price times quantity equals cost, most cost-containment initiatives are designed to control either the price or the quantity of health care services. In general, the public payers (Medicare and Medicaid) have concentrated on controlling price, while the private payers (Blue Cross and commercial insurers) have concentrated on quantity. In addition, a number of proposals aim to reduce health care spending by comprehensively changing the financing and delivery of services.

Price controls. The major cost-containment initiative in the 1980s was the development and implementation of the Medicare Prospective Payment System (PPS). In 1983 Congress changed the method of paying hospitals from a cost-based reimbursement system, which essentially paid hospitals their own costs for providing patient care, to a PPS, which established a set of predetermined payment amounts for every Medicare patient in the hospital. Patients can be classified into one of approximately 475 diagnosis-related groups (DRGs); the number continues to increase as

Signe Wilkinson/Philadelphia Daily News

medical practice changes. Associated with each DRG is a payment reflecting the cost of treating the patient that is relative to the cost of treating patients in other DRGs.

Implementation of the Medicare PPS has been monitored very closely to determine what effect it is having on health care costs, access to medical care, and the quality of that care. Results suggest that in response to the PPS, the average length of hospital stays has declined, nursing home and home health agency visits have increased, more services are performed on an outpatient basis, and the rate of increase in Medicare inpatient hospital costs has declined. At the same time, it does not appear that access to or quality of care has declined or that overall medical costs have been affected. Although the overall hospital profit margins in the 1980s were twice what they had been in the 1970s, they started to decline during the latter part of the decade.

States have used various types of PPSs to control hospital and nursing home payment rates in the Medicaid program. States were first permitted to use these systems in 1981, and by 1989, 38 states had adopted some form of PPS. At the end of the 1980s and early in the 1990s, many of these states were in federal court defending the adequacy of their payment rates from challenges by hospitals or nursing homes. The litigation involves interpretation of congressional language requiring states to set rates that pay the "cost of economically and efficiently operated providers." Most of the litigation centers around the meaning of the term *cost* and the definition of an "efficient provider." Initially hospitals lost these cases, but more recently they have begun to win in some cases.

In 1989 Congress passed a fundamental reform of the methodology for paying physicians, to be phased in gradually from Oct. 1, 1991. The legislation has three major components. The first is the development of a fee schedule, known as the Resource-Based Relative Value Scale, which establishes a payment for each service a physician provides. The fee schedule is based on the time and skill level required for performing that service compared with the other services a physician provides. The second component sets a global budget (known as a volume performance standard) for Medicare spending on physician services. If the total spending for physician services in the Medicare program exceeds a preestablished global budget, then the fee levels will be reduced in the subsequent year. The third component limits the amount that the Medicare beneficiary pays for physician services out of his or her own pocket. Commonly known as balanced billing, it limits how much the physician can charge the Medicare beneficiary above the amount established by the Medicare fee schedule.

Limiting the quantity of services. One of the major initiatives that was designed to control the quantity of services is utilization review. Under this system, the insurer requires the care provider to furnish information about the services that will be (or have been) provided. The insurer has a set of medical appropriateness criteria that have been developed for that specific condition; on the basis of those criteria, the insurer may allow or deny payment for those services. As private insurers have begun to apply more stringent criteria, the number of disputes that have arisen between insurers, patients, and physicians over the medical necessity of a particular procedure has increased. The fundamental question is who should decide about the medical necessity of a procedure—the physician or the insurer.

In the early 1990s the courts began to be in the forefront of decision making about medical appropriateness. The most visible cases involve the decision by insurers to deny coverage for individuals with various types of cancer who want to receive autologous bone marrow transplants. This procedure is employed in cases in which the huge doses of chemotherapy and radiation needed to overcome a tumor could kill the patient by destroying the bone marrow, where blood cells are manufactured. Some of the patient's marrow is removed, stored while the patient is under-

310

going treatment, and then reinjected into the bloodstream. The reinfused marrow migrates to the bone and begins making cells again. The special advantage of this approach is that the body will not reject the transplant, as could happen with bone marrow from a donor. The insurers argue that the clinical efficacy of this procedure has not been proved for certain cancers and that the insurance contract denies coverage for experimental procedures. They do not want to pay for the very expensive (over $100,000) procedure until its benefit has been demonstrated. The courts are being asked to decide whether this procedure is still experimental and therefore not part of the standard insurance contract. These are difficult decisions when all other procedures have been tried; autologous bone marrow transplants are frequently the patient's last hope for survival. In reviewing these cases, the courts have reached contradictory opinions, and this issue will be in litigation for the next several years.

During the 1980s many corporations, in an attempt to control the number of unnecessary services being provided, increased the level of cost sharing. They felt that increasing the level of either the deductible or the coinsurance would heighten individuals' awareness of the cost of medical care and lower their utilization of services. Many corporations increased the amount of coinsurance during the mid-1980s, but this trend abated as employees became concerned about the amount they were paying for health care. In the late 1980s, there were several strikes in response to attempts by corporations—such as Nynex, the New York "Baby Bell"—to make their employees pay more.

Competitive initiatives

In the 1980s numerous attempts were made to introduce more competition into the health care system on the basis of standard economics textbook reasoning—more competition lowers prices, drives out ineffective providers, and increases consumer satisfaction. Most studies of the health care delivery system suggest that in reality, competition usually means that hospitals, physicians, and other providers deliver more services, thereby increasing the cost to consumers.

The U.S. Department of Justice also became more involved in health care in the late 1980s. The department began challenging mergers of not-for-profit hospitals, arguing that they are anticompetitive. The court rulings on this issue appear to be contradictory; in cases where the facts and motives have appeared to be similar, some mergers have been allowed while others have not.

Comprehensive proposals

In addition to the numerous initiatives designed to control the price or the quantity of medical services, there are also several proposals to revise the entire health care system. Probably the most well known

are calls for national health insurance. While most of these are designed primarily to assure universal health insurance coverage, many have promised to lower the administrative costs of the medical system. The theory is that administrative costs would be lower if a single insurer could process all the information on patient care, with fewer administrative staff having to be hired by providers to respond to each insurer's own forms and policies.

A second proposal is to allocate health care resources on a more systematic basis. The state of Oregon has established a plan for setting priorities for services for low-income citizens. All possible medical services were identified; the relationship of cost and benefits of each was computed; and each service was ranked in order of desirability of funding. Those below the priority score—determined by the amount of money available—would not receive funding. If approved by the federal government, the plan would be implemented.

In addition to the significant ethical and procedural problems with that proposal, there are major analytic ones. For example, conditions that have widely varying degrees of seriousness and thus require different treatment have been classified within single categories. Also, some of the priority scores that have been developed have come under criticism, and the list of priorities has already had to be revised. The latest list was issued in February 1991 (see Table). Another concern is that Oregon is attempting to have this system apply to all low-income patients—not sim-

To cope with company medical costs exceeding $1 billion annually, Nynex Corp., a "Baby Bell" telephone company, proposed making employees pay a greater portion of their insurance premiums—a solution that workers found unacceptable.

Neal Boenzi/The New York Times

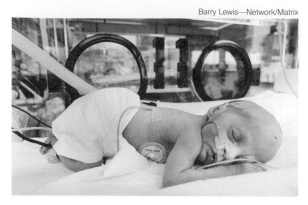
Barry Lewis—Network/Matrix

A controversial cost-containment plan in Oregon set priorities for health care warranting coverage. In the revised list of about 800 services, treatment of extremely low-birth-weight babies (under 1,500 grams [1.3 pounds]) received one of the lowest rankings.

ply the current Medicaid patients—without increasing the amount of funding. Thus, most Medicaid beneficiaries would probably receive fewer benefits, and some conditions would go untreated.

Future outlook

Most health care spending involves the provision of medical services. Therefore, to control costs it would

---

Oregon health services priorities

original list (May 1990)	revised list (February 1991)
ranked as most economically worthwhile to treat	
bacterial meningitis	pneumonia (several types)
phenylketonuria	tuberculosis
non-Hodgkin's lymphoma	peritonitis
septicemia	foreign body in throat
meningococcal meningitis	appendicitis
candidiasis	hernia with obstruction, gangrene, or both
salmonella	ectopic pregnancy
Wilms' tumor	acute orbital cellulitis
bacterial infection (general)	croup syndrome
listeriosis	injury to major blood vessels of upper extremity
least worthwhile	
pulmonary artery atresia	gynecomastia
thyrocalcitonin	kidney cyst
unspecified artery disorder	terminal HIV disease
varicose veins without inflammation	chronic pancreatitis
varices of other sites	superficial wounds
acute osteomyelitis	constitutional aplastic anemia
femoral hernia without obstruction	prolapsed urethral mucosa
transsexualism	blockage of the retinal artery
umbilical hernia with obstruction	extremely low birth weight anencephaly
vulval varices	

Source: Oregon Health Services Commission

---

be necessary to limit the price or the quantity of those services. However, attempts to impose such limitations are facing significant ethical, analytic, legal, and political constraints.

None of the proposals to date for controlling medical costs is without some increased risk or inconvenience. For cost containment to be truly effective, people must be willing to give up something, and so far, at least, the American public has not been willing to make major sacrifices. The most reasonable speculation, therefore, is that health care costs are likely to continue to increase in the 1990s.

—*Gerard F. Anderson, Ph.D.*

Health Care Law

● In 1981 two-and-a-half-year-old Justin Barnhart died of untreated Wilms' tumor, a cancer of the kidney. His parents, members of the Faith Tabernacle Church, relied on God to cure the boy's illness. They were convicted of involuntary manslaughter and endangering the welfare of a child.

● Four-year-old Shauntay Walker died of bacterial meningitis in California in 1984 after a 17-day illness. Laurie Walker, Shauntay's mother, called in a Christian Science practitioner but refused to take the child to a doctor. Laurie Walker was convicted of involuntary manslaughter.

● In 1986 seven-year-old Amy Hermanson died of juvenile-onset diabetes. Her mother said that Amy had been healed by a Christian Science practitioner but that the girl herself had chosen to pass on. Both parents were sentenced to 15 years' probation; a four-year prison sentence was suspended on the condition that they agree to provide their two surviving children with necessary medical care.

● David and Ginger Twitchell, a Massachusetts Christian Science couple, were convicted of involuntary manslaughter in 1990 and sentenced to 10 years' probation after their two-year-old son, Robyn, died of a surgically treatable bowel obstruction. Instead of seeking medical care, the Twitchells had relied on prayer to heal Robyn.

In the past decade 21 sets of parents have been convicted in U.S. courts for failing, on religious grounds, to provide their children with lifesaving medical care. For at least 100 years, faith healing—treating illness with prayer—has been practiced by members of several U.S. religious groups, including the Faith Tabernacle Church, the Faith Assembly, and—the largest and best known denomination—the Church of Christ, Scientist. Although their specific practices vary, all share the belief that healing comes only from God and that resorting to medical treatment is a sign of lack of faith. Few people doubt that prayer, or at least a "positive attitude," can contribute to recovery from illness. How far it should be relied on, however, is a matter of considerable dispute.

The controversy takes on additional dimensions when the individual forgoing medical care is a child and the decision to rely on faith alone is made by a parent on the child's behalf. Prosecutors, child advocates, and physicians argue that parents who fail to provide their children with lifesaving medical care are imposing their religious beliefs on their children, who may die as a result. Church members counter that such accusations are tantamount to being persecuted for one's religious beliefs.

The right to refuse

Throughout the United States the law is clear that competent adults can refuse medical care of any kind, including lifesaving treatment, for themselves for any reason. The most common example of exercise of the right to refuse treatment is the refusal of blood transfusions by Jehovah's Witnesses on the grounds that certain passages in the Bible forbid it. Reasons having nothing to do with religion are equally valid, however. For example, in a 1980 case a man was found to have the right to refuse to remain on a mechanical ventilator that was sustaining his breathing simply because he did not like it. Even though he was certain to die without artificial respiration, he had the right to decide what, if any, medical treatment he would undergo—and, therefore, to refuse care.

The right to refuse treatment is, in fact, part of every American adult's autonomy and right to self-determination. As articulated in 1914 by Benjamin Cardozo (later an associate justice of the Supreme Court): "Every human being of adult years and sound mind has a right to determine what shall be done with his own body." Where children are concerned, however, a more protective attitude prevails. This is because the children, not the parents, suffer the consequences of the parents' decisions.

Parental obligations and prerogatives

In the U.S. children enjoy special status under state law because they are considered neither old enough nor wise enough to make decisions in their own best interest. In particular, children generally do not have the legal right to make decisions about their own medical treatment. Anyone who has tried to clean the badly scraped knee of a resisting three-year-old knows that children do not always appreciate the need for medical care. It is for this reason that states, acting as *parens patriae* (Latin, meaning "parent of the country's people")—in their role as protector of the welfare of children and the mentally disabled—require a parent (or guardian) to provide necessary medical care for a child. This safeguard presumably enables the child to survive to adulthood and have the opportunity then to make his or her own decisions.

Christian Scientists Ginger and David Twitchell relied on prayer to cure their two-year-old son of an obstructed bowel. After the child died, a jury found the Twitchells guilty of involuntary manslaughter.

The parents' obligation to provide their children with necessary medical care is so well established in common law that specific laws codifying this duty have not been thought necessary. In many individual cases, however, the court has ordered medical treatment for children when the parents objected for religious reasons or preferred an alternative or less orthodox healing method. For example, in Massachusetts in 1978 traditional chemotherapy was ordered for two-year-old Chad Green, a leukemia patient, in spite of his parents' preference for laetrile (an unproven drug) and vitamin therapy because the court found that chemotherapy offered the possibility of a cure. In determining whether to require medical treatment, courts take into account the likelihood that a treatment will succeed, the risk of death or permanent injury to the child without treatment, and any risks posed by the treatment itself. The court must act in the best interests of the child, not the parents. In the case of Chad Green, the court said, "Where, as here, the child's very life is threatened by a parental decision refusing medical treatment, this State interest [in protecting the welfare of children] clearly supersedes parental prerogatives."

Where the child's life is not at stake, or the only available treatment is itself risky or experimental, parents have more leeway. Juliet Cheng acted on this principle when she objected to joint surgery for her daughter Shirley, a seven-year-old with severe juvenile rheumatoid arthritis. The mother was not convinced that surgery would achieve more than traditional Chinese remedies, although a Connecticut court disagreed. In a later proceeding, however, an expert panel found the

In 1978 a court ordered that two-year-old leukemia victim Chad Green (pictured at right with his mother, Diana) undergo conventional chemotherapy. His parents favored a regimen of laetrile—an unproven drug— and vitamins. When experts feel that alternative therapies may be as valuable as established ones, however, courts have supported them. Thus, Juliet Cheng (far right) was able to reject joint surgery for her seven-year-old daughter, Shirley, who had severe arthritis; Cheng wanted to try traditional Chinese remedies first.

surgery to be unnecessary. A Delaware court affirmed the same principles in a 1991 decision. A physician recommended a radical type of chemotherapy for a three-year-old who was dying of Burkitt's lymphoma. The treatment had only a 40% chance of success. The child's parents refused on religious grounds, and the court found that the treatment—which would be painful, would have terrible side effects, and could itself cause the child's death—was not necessary.

Parents retain many other prerogatives. The U.S. Supreme Court has upheld parents' rights to choose where their children go to school and what languages they learn. Clearly, while these are important elements of child rearing, they do not directly affect the child's health. Where there is a conflict between the parents' preferences and the child's very life, U.S. courts agree that the child's life is the foremost consideration, regardless of the reasons for the parents' decision.

The same rules apply when parents act—or fail to act—out of deeply held religious beliefs. Thus, the same court that permits a woman to refuse blood transfusions for herself will order transfusions necessary to save the life of her child. In most cases, where Jehovah's Witnesses refuse blood transfusions for their children, they are willing to consent to other treatments, such as surgery, that would save the child's life. In such a case, the hospital may petition a court to order the blood transfusion. The court will do so if it can be shown that the transfusion is necessary.

Of course, the child's life can be saved only when the illness is discovered in time to be treated. The more troubling cases are those where a child dies without coming to the attention of the state or the medical profession. It is these cases that have become the subject of criminal prosecution.

"Free exercise"—or involuntary manslaughter?

Some people feel that criminal prosecution of parents who have just lost a child only compounds the pain

of a tragedy. No one questions the motives of parents who rely on faith healing or prayer. In several recent cases, Christian Science parents, including both the Twitchells and the Hermansons, did summon specially trained and accredited practitioners to pray for their children in accordance with the teachings of their church. These parents were not unmoved by the child's plight. Rather, they turned for help to what they believed to be the best source of healing, which was not medicine.

Motivation, however, is not a defense against a charge of involuntary manslaughter or reckless endangerment. If the prosecutors in these cases really thought that the parents had wanted their children to die, they would have charged the parents with intentional murder. Involuntary manslaughter is the crime of causing someone's death by acting in a way that is likely to cause death—without deliberately meaning to kill the other person. Causing someone's death by failing to provide the care one is obligated to provide remains a crime, although the punishment is less severe than that prescribed for intentional murder.

Still, in most such cases, because the U.S. Constitution protects freedom of religion, the parents believed that they had no legal obligation to take the child to a doctor. The First Amendment provides that "Congress shall make no law respecting an establishment of religion, or prohibiting the free exercise thereof." This so-called free exercise clause protects the right of these parents—and all others—to put religious beliefs into practice. Because it was their religious beliefs that compelled them to eschew medical care for their children, criminal prosecution would, they reason, violate the free exercise clause.

Beliefs versus conduct

There are, of course, limits to what one may do in the name of religion. In the 1940 case of *Cantwell* v. *Connecticut,* the Supreme Court explained that the free exercise clause upholds two types of freedom: the freedom to believe and the freedom to act. "The first is absolute," the court said, "but, in the nature of things, the second cannot be. Conduct remains subject to regulation for the protection of society." In the U.S. people are guaranteed complete freedom of religious belief, and it is not the province of the law to decide which beliefs are valid and which are not. Rather, the law concerns itself with conduct, whatever the reasons motivating it.

Thus, the law does not allow religious beliefs to excuse conduct that endangers other people. For example, a hypothetical religious belief holding that an infant should not eat anything for the first six months of its life would not excuse parents from complying with the duty to provide necessary care, including feeding the child. Human sacrifice may have been an accepted religious practice at one time, but it is not a practice protected by the Constitution.

It is not always possible to neatly separate beliefs and actions. Nonetheless, the court has recognized that some beliefs may be translated into action without state interference. A state must have a compelling reason to regulate conduct that is motivated by and rooted in a legitimate and sincerely held religious belief. Thus, an employer may not require an employee to work on designated sabbath days. Usually, religious beliefs compelling an individual to refrain from work on a particular day can be accommodated relatively easily and without danger to anyone.

On the other hand, in the 1944 decision of *Prince v. Massachusetts*, the Supreme Court held that a Jehovah's Witness church member was not entitled to have her child distribute religious literature door to door in violation of the child labor law even though her religious beliefs required that the child do so. The court made clear that "neither rights of religion nor rights of parenthood are beyond limitation." The state

may protect the well-being of children, whether parents' claims of control are grounded in conscience or religion. In an often-quoted passage, the court said:

The right to practice religion freely does not include the liberty to expose the community or the child to communicable disease or the latter to ill health or death. . . . Parents may be free to become martyrs themselves. But it does not follow that they are free, in identical circumstances, to make martyrs of their children before they have reached the age of full legal discretion when they can make that choice for themselves.

Limits of religious exemption

Even though parents are not constitutionally entitled to treat their children in all respects as their religion requires, 43 states have enacted legislation exempting parents from child neglect or support laws when these conflict with their religious beliefs. These so-called religious exemption laws vary from state to state, but most provide that parents will not be deemed to have neglected their children simply because they provide them with spiritual healing in accordance with the tenets of a recognized church or religious denomination. Most of these laws, enacted at the behest of the Christian Science Church, require that a sick child be treated by a practitioner duly accredited by the church.

Many members of churches that practice spiritual or prayer healing believe that the religious exemption laws protect parents from being prosecuted for *any* crime in connection with a child's injury or death, including manslaughter and child endangerment. However, religious exemption laws tend to accommodate prayer treatment only insofar as it does not place a child at risk of serious harm. All but one court have found that the exemption laws have very narrow application. In Pennsylvania, California, and Massachusetts, for example, courts have interpreted the religious exemption law to mean that parents will not be accused

This youngster and his six sisters and brothers, all members of one Philadelphia fundamentalist Christian family, were stricken with measles in February 1991. They had never been vaccinated against the common, preventable childhood disease because their parents' religion eschews childhood immunization and other forms of medical care. Several Philadelphia children died of measles during this same outbreak. Here, the question arises: Should parents who fail to protect their child from a communicable disease be subject to prosecution if the child dies of the disease?

Bill Cramer/The New York Times

of neglecting their children simply because they offer the child spiritual healing. The principle involved here is that parents cannot be accused of neglect merely because they treat their children in a manner different from the majority's child-rearing practices. But if a child is seriously ill or in need of medical care to save his or her life, the parents, in failing to provide such care, can be considered to have neglected the child's most basic needs.

Religious exemption laws are often part of a state misdemeanor statute requiring parents to provide financial support for their children. In most cases, however, courts have found that the religious exemption in a child-support law is not a defense in the distinctly different and more serious crime of manslaughter or child endangerment. Thus, even if parents are not liable for nonsupport or neglect for the act of choosing prayer instead of medical care, they may be liable for child endangerment or manslaughter if the child suffers serious harm as a result of their failure to provide medical care.

Prayer: an alternative?

Since religious freedom has not proved an effective defense against prosecution for the death of a child, some religious groups are now advancing the idea that treatment by prayer is a reasonable and effective alternative to medical care. Representatives of the Church of Christ, Scientist, argue that both the law and the media have ignored the successes of prayer. They point out that medical treatment offers no guarantee of cure and, further, that parents are not held liable when the efforts of orthodox medicine fail to save a sick child.

If society is to ensure the well-being of children who are unable to protect themselves, how is it to judge whether prayer is less or more effective than medicine or equally so? Are years of sincere religious belief enough, or must objective scientific evidence provide the answer?

Some churches are now seeking new laws that would recognize spiritual healing as legally equivalent to medical care in the treatment of children. Such laws may not fare any better in court than existing religious exemptions. The first part of the First Amendment's religious freedom guarantee prohibits the government from making any law respecting the establishment of religion. This so-called establishment clause prohibits discriminating among religions or granting a preference to one religion. The language in many religious exemption laws specifies that the spiritual treatment must be provided "in accordance with the tenets and practice of a recognized church or religious denomination by a duly accredited practitioner thereof." In practice, this provision limits the exemption to members of the Christian Science Church and, some would argue, creates a special preference.

Recently, critics of religious exemption laws have claimed that the exemptions violate the equal protection clause of the Fifth Amendment to the Constitution. This is because the law denies the same state protection offered all children to those children whose parents qualify for the exemption. Moreover, all other parents who deny their children necessary medical care are subject to prosecution, whatever their reason for failing to provide that care.

Children's lives at stake

Child advocates have now begun an effort to repeal state religious exemption laws. They argue that religious beliefs should not be accommodated when they allow children to die. Supporters of the exemption laws counter that this is an attack on unpopular religious beliefs or on the efficacy of prayer itself. Repealing the religious exemption laws would not, of course, repeal the right to pray or to use spiritual methods of healing. To the extent that a person's religion forbids the use of medical care for children, however, it would inhibit religious practices.

Proponents of repeal feel that the law should make it clear that parents have an obligation to provide medical care when a child is at risk of serious harm or death. They are concerned that if parents believe that they have no duty to take a child to a doctor, the child's illness will not be discovered in time to save his or her life. Although all states require that cases of child neglect be reported to state health officials, children who are treated at home with prayer alone may not come to the attention of authorities and may die before effective treatment can be ordered. Prayer practitioners may not believe that a child is dangerously ill or that medical care can or should be sought, and they are unlikely to report the case to authorities. Church members, on the other hand, are concerned that parents will be prosecuted for believing, mistakenly but in good faith, that a child's condition is not serious. For them the question is one of how to judge when the need to provide medical care has arisen.

All parents are held to the same standard of reasonableness in providing care for their children. In the cases that have been prosecuted thus far, there was no question that the child's condition was obviously life-threatening and that effective medical care, with a well-documented record of success, was available to treat the condition.

When it comes to children, the law and parents certainly have one concern in common—the best interests of the child. Still, disagreements about what is acceptable care are inevitable. When such disputes arise, should religious reasons for refusing medical care count more than cultural, philosophical, or personal ones? When a child's life is at stake, the law says no.

—*Wendy K. Mariner, J.D., LL.M., M.P.H.*

Medical Research: The Forgotten 51%

by Jean A. Hamilton, M.D.

Although women typically live longer than men, this does not mean that they necessarily enjoy better health. In fact, women in the United States have higher rates of illness and disability than do men. If men and women were physiologically identical, then there would be no reason to consider the possibility that males and females have differing health care needs or that the sexes require separate study. Of course, they are not the same, and some of their differences in physiological functioning may be critical to understanding sex-related differences in health and illness. In addition, psychological and social influences on health may be sex-linked and may contribute to sex differences in morbidity and mortality.

Understanding differences in the health status of subgroups within the population is necessary in order to ensure that health care decisions and research are appropriate. Subgroups can be defined by a variety of demographic variables, including age, socioeconomic status, ethnicity or race, and gender. If subgroup differences are ignored, health care delivery will not be equitable, and portions of the population will be needlessly exposed to overtreatment, undertreatment, or simply the wrong type of treatment.

A male data base

Historically, there has been a preference among researchers for studying men. In fact, some have observed that the existing clinical data base is constructed overwhelmingly from studies of a single, minority subgroup: white, young or middle-aged, middle-class males. The research bias in favor of males is reflected in studies of disease processes, definitions of illness and disability, methods for evaluation and diagnosis, clinical trials of promising new treatments and methods of prevention, and patient participation in treatment decisions.

These biases suggest that the clinical data base may not be relevant as a guide for making appropriate health care decisions about females. Scientists refer to this problem in terms of whether the data can be "generalized" to other groups. In other words, can the data from males be applied to females in general? Or are they applicable only to a subgroup of females under narrowly defined conditions?

Recognizing that the public health implications of an overly narrow clinical data base can be profound,

the U.S. Public Health Service (PHS) convened a task force to study women's health issues. In its report, issued in 1985, the task force concluded that significant gaps in knowledge about women's health existed and that these gaps had led to inadequate clinical attention to the health needs of women. The task force recommended that a systematic effort be made to address issues related to gender bias in research and clinical practice. Such conclusions were notable because the PHS, which is charged with overseeing the health of the public at large, had itself identified women's health as an area of concern, implying that it had failed to protect the health of 51% of the population.

Documenting the gender gap in research

Despite unambiguous findings and clear recommendations for change, the task force report has had little impact on research or clinical practice. The National Institutes of Health (NIH), which is a part of the PHS, is the main federal agency for supporting biomedical and behavioral health research. The NIH suggested as early as 1986 that researchers include women in their studies, but the policy was not communicated to the field until mid-1989 and is not applied consistently even today.

Meanwhile, data documenting the gender gap in research have continued to accumulate. A report prepared by an NIH advisory committee on women's health issues found that only 13% of the annual NIH budget in 1987 went to research on women's health. Congressional and public interest were spurred by the publication in 1988 of the "Physician's Health Study," which assessed the protective effects of aspirin against cardiovascular disease in 22,071 men and no women. Controversy about using that and other studies conducted only on men as a guide to treatment decisions for women was evident in editorial opinions published in leading medical journals, such as the *New England Journal of Medicine* in 1989 and the *Journal of the American Medical Association* in 1990.

In order to assess what the NIH had done to address gaps in knowledge about women's health since the 1985 report, several lawmakers requested that a study be done by the General Accounting Office (GAO). The overwhelming conclusion, as expressed by one GAO official, was, "In brief, we found that NIH has not adequately implemented its policy." The

THE AIDS PUZZLE

WHERE DO WOMEN FIT?

An Australian poster poses some important questions about how women fit into the AIDS picture. The diagnostic criteria for AIDS were not established with the female population in mind, yet the epidemic is spreading rapidly among women.

study noted that even when research protocols included women, analyses typically were not conducted in a way that would reveal sex-related differences and that no procedures had been put in place to monitor compliance with NIH policies. The latter omission was taken as evidence of a lack of seriousness about the issue on the part of NIH officials.

Given the distinctly male data base and the obvious biases in both research and practice, the question arises: Are women harmed as a result? In the absence of a systematic and comprehensive survey of gender bias, it is necessary to rely on selected examples to answer this question.

Unreliable diagnoses

Biases are evident in the ways in which women's illnesses are diagnosed. The diagnostic criteria for AIDS (acquired immune deficiency syndrome), for example, were not determined with women in mind. Although HIV infection was first observed in the U.S. predominantly in males, international data indicated considerable risk for females as well. Originally women were primarily viewed as vectors for the AIDS virus rather than as patients. It would not have been difficult, however, to anticipate that women with AIDS would

be subject to different opportunistic infections (rare or ordinary infections that take on life-threatening proportions in people with compromised immunity) than men. In fact, females with AIDS have high rates of virulent vaginal infections and pelvic inflammatory disease. Furthermore, because the criteria were blind to gender considerations, women with HIV infection, who generally do not "fit" the male pattern, continue to be excluded from social security benefits and from entry into treatment trials. There can be no doubt that these women have been harmed by existing gender biases.

Another indication that diagnosis of female diseases may not be reliable is that some commonly used diagnostic tests may have greater validity for males than for females. For example, the cardiac stress test, involving exercise on a treadmill to assess heart function, is not as sensitive or specific for heart disease in women as it is in men.

Yet even when a stress test suggests that there may be an underlying heart problem in a woman, further tests to confirm the finding often are not done. A report in 1987 in the *Annals of Internal Medicine* found that after an abnormal stress test 40% of male patients were referred for cardiac catheterization, compared with only 4% of females. Other studies also have suggested that women are denied as full a workup as men typically receive. The detection of lung cancer, for example, is greater in males than females, in part because of a higher index of suspicion and higher rates of utilization of laboratory tests.

Women also can have somewhat different laboratory indicators for illness. There is evidence that high-density lipoprotein (HDL)-cholesterol levels are an important predictor of heart disease in women but not in men, yet this gender-specific information has not been incorporated into the mainstream of clinical practice.

Treatment inequities

Once a diagnosis has been made, women may receive less vigorous treatment than do men. For example, despite the fact that female patients with kidney failure have slightly better survival rates than males, a 1988 report in the *Archives of Internal Medicine* found that women are less likely to receive a kidney transplant.

In some cases, gender stereotypes about illness impair access to appropriate treatment. For example, a specific type of chest pain, angina pectoris, is more often associated with myocardial infarction (heart attack) in males than in females; as a result, angina in females may often be discounted. This practice harms women because initial heart attacks in women are associated with high death rates.

Two reports in the July 25, 1991, issue of the *New England Journal of Medicine* documented the pervasive pattern of treating women with coronary heart disease (CHD) less aggressively than men. One study analyzed discharge data on 49,623 patients in

318

Massachusetts and 33,159 patients in Maryland hospitalized for known or suspected CHD. In both states women were less likely to undergo either diagnostic angiography or revascularization—bypass surgery or balloon angioplasty (see Table, page 320).

It is also the case that some treatments are associated with a poorer outcome in women, but rarely have the reasons for this been investigated. For example, for unknown reasons, women have higher death rates after coronary bypass surgery than do men.

Not only are women discriminated against by not receiving optimal health care during their vital years, but they also receive less-than-equal treatment when it comes to dying. A paper by Steven H. Miles and Allison August in *Law, Medicine, and Health Care* demonstrated a clear gender bias in "right-to-die" cases. For example, the verbally expressed wishes of previously competent male patients without advance written directives (a "living will") were more often considered "rational," whereas women's verbal wishes were more often considered "unreflective, emotional, or immature."

Pharmacological research

There is no question that women have been underrepresented in pharmacological treatment trials—a practice suggesting that medical science does not have adequate knowledge about appropriate drug use in women. As one example, young women have not been included in clinical trials seeking pharmacological treatments for Raynaud's disease, even though 60–90% of reported sufferers of this peripheral vascular disorder, characterized by pallor, pain, and extreme coldness of the fingers and toes, are young women.

It is also clear that optimal drug dosages for men may differ from those for women. Nevertheless, women have been categorically excluded from most trials that initially assess a drug's safety and dosage (so-called phase I trials). They are included sometimes in phase II trials and often in phase III trials, but most frequently women receive drugs once they are marketed in the absence of studies adequate to assess gender-related differences.

Psychiatrist Mary V. Seeman at the University of Toronto has documented that symptoms in female patients with schizophrenia can be controlled with lower dosages of antipsychotic (neuroleptic) medications than those recommended on the basis of phase I studies in men. By taking neuroleptic dosages appropriate for male schizophrenics, women often are overmedicated and put at risk for side effects. Moreover, women are at high risk for the most serious adverse effect of neuroleptics, tardive dyskinesia, a central nervous system disorder characterized by involuntary movements. Such unexpected toxicity after a drug is marketed occurs when the medication is prescribed for patients who were not included in the early stud-

ies. It is ironic that the exclusion of women from early testing does not prevent, but only delays, their exposure to medications that may, in fact, harm them.

Possible menstrual cycle effects on medication requirements have been all but ignored, both in research and in clinical practice. Nonetheless, significant menstrual cycle effects have been demonstrated for subgroups of women using lithium and other antidepressants; clonidine, an antihypertensive; phenytoin, an anticonvulsant; propranolol, a beta-adrenergic blocker used in treating hypertension, angina pectoris, and migraine; and methaqualone, a sedative-hypnotic. As an example, women with clinical depression may experience exacerbations of depression premenstrually. Therefore, they may need higher medication dosages in that part of their cycle but lower doses the rest of the time. Moreover, menstrual variations in response to a number of drug therapies suggest that to get the desired effects, suitable administration may require giving medications in conjunction with physiological and symptomatic changes during the cycle.

In December 1990 a panel of over 100 experts at a symposium convened by the National Women's Health Resource Center (NWHRC) in Washington, D.C.— "Forging a Women's Health Research Agenda"—

Many commonly used diagnostic tests are not reliable indicators of disease in women. Exercise stress testing on a treadmill, for example, is not as sensitive or specific for assessing coronary disease in women as it is in men.

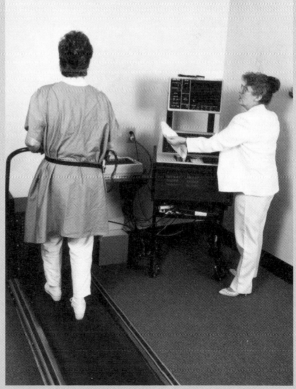

C.C. Duncan—Medical Images, Inc.

summarized what is known about gender differences in clinical pharmacology. The panel strongly recommended that women be included to a greater extent in clinical pharmacology trials and that research on gender effects in pharmacology become a priority. Without gender-sensitive research, the panel said, women will continue to be needlessly undertreated or overtreated with drugs.

Rationale for exclusion

There have been at least four overt obstacles or objections to including women in clinical trials but particularly in those studying pharmacological interventions. Concerns about the risk to a fetus should a woman become pregnant during a trial is one. These concerns have merit, but blanket exclusion of women in their reproductive years from the early phases of drug testing assumes incorrectly that all women are equally at risk for pregnancy.

Clearly the goal should be to include women with the least risk of pregnancy; ideally these would be women who have had a tubal ligation or hysterectomy, women who are not sexually active, and postmenopausal women. In most cases a highly sensitive radioimmunoassay to determine the presence of human chorionic gonadotropin in a blood or urine sample can rule out early pregnancy immediately prior to drug trials. To further reduce the risk of pregnancy, the use of mechanical contraceptives should be discussed with the subject and her sexual partner, and the consent process should advise the woman to inform the investigator if her plans for contraception change during the study.

Although potential liability for harm to the fetus cannot be waived by informed consent, legal scholars have argued that pharmaceutical companies and those conducting a trial need only show that they have taken reasonable precautions so that the risk is negligible. It is unrealistic to expect the potential risk to a fetus to be zero since such a standard is not required for living persons. In this regard, it is relevant that in 1991 the U.S. Supreme Court ruled in the Johnson Controls case that women cannot be uniformly excluded from the workplace because of the risk of toxic exposure to a potential fetus. The company's "fetal protection policy" was deemed by the court a violation of the Civil Rights Act of 1964 and the 1978 Pregnancy Discrimination Act amendments. While this decision came out of the specific way employment law has developed in the U.S., it may have implications for decisions about the inclusion of women in early phases of drug testing.

It is encouraging that a number of university institutional review boards (IRBs) have recently approved drug studies in women of childbearing age; e.g., the State University of New York at Buffalo, the University of Arizona, and the University of Nebraska at Omaha. The consent and protection procedures approved by these IRBs may serve as models for further study and refinement.

The complexity of including women in research is a second common reason cited for their exclusion. Including both sexes increases the sample size and complicates the analysis of the data. Because there may be menstrual-cycle-related effects in women, special assessment measures are needed. In recent years, however, accurate hormone measurements and increasing consensus on definitions and methods have helped to advance the field of menstrual-cycle research, so that methodological concerns should be less of a barrier to pharmacological research in women. Given the high rates for self-reported premenstrual symptoms, drug studies should take the phase of the cycle into account in order to avoid confusion about whether symptoms represent intervention-related side effects.

A further impediment to including women in trials is that, in general, female subjects report more symptoms overall than do men. In a drug trial these might be mistaken for drug side effects.

While serving on the 1985 PHS Task Force, this author noted that including women in prospective studies of illnesses that are more common in men would require a very large sample of women in order to observe their less-frequent occurrence of the disease in question—a requirement that could more than double the cost of the research.

The cost of bringing a new medication to the public has been estimated at $125 million. In the United States alone, pharmaceutical companies invested $7.3 billion in research and development in 1989—more than the $6.8 billion spent by the NIH on all other biomedical research. The prospect of substantially increasing these costs, needless to say, appears staggering, but the inclusion of women in every clinical trial is no more needed than was blanket exclusion. The aforementioned NWHRC report outlined a rational method to target drugs (and disease processes) that require intensive, gender-related study—an approach that would help to keep costs at a feasible level. A step in the right direction was taken in March 1991 when the National Academy of Science's Institute of Medicine held a preliminary meeting to examine the issue of including women in clinical trials.

An important study quashed

A major trial was recently proposed to assess the effects of low-fat diets on breast cancer, a disease that strikes 10% of women in the U.S. and kills 50% of those afflicted. The Women's Health Trial was designed to be one of the largest female clinical trials ever undertaken, involving 24,000 women, and to be conducted over 15 years at a cost of $107 million. Even though there have been strong suggestions for many years that high-fat diets may be an important risk factor for subsequent development of breast cancer, the National Cancer Institute deemed the trial too costly.

Yet the proposed study had been widely compared to the trials conducted on men to assess the role of low-cholesterol diets in coronary artery disease, which were amply funded by the NIH. Physicians did not just "guess" that low-cholesterol diets would probably be helpful, and surely patients at risk for heart disease would not be motivated to change their diets unless a clear benefit was demonstrated. A guess concerning the effects of diet on breast cancer is not good enough either.

Prevailing stereotypes

Scientists, of course, are not immune to cultural stereotypes, even though the idea of being biased is contrary to the self-image of most scientists, physicians, and other health care professionals. Even the best-intentioned and "objective" scientist may be prone to "blind spots."

The American Medical Association's *Guides to the Evaluation of Permanent Impairment*, for example, has been criticized for its stereotyping of women. A 1990 *Harvard Law Review* article by attorney Ellen Pryor observed that according to the *Guides,* an impairment of the male reproductive organ results in 5–10% "whole-person impairment," whereas injury to the female reproductive organs does not qualify for such impairment status. Disability in a woman, Pryor noted, is defined in terms of whether she remains "able to do kitchen work, go shopping . . . and care for her house." By contrast, men are defined as impaired if they are unable to play "18 holes of golf regularly."

Remaining barriers

While a number of technical issues have been resolved, major barriers to advancing women's health research remain. These include the continued devaluation of women in society, the low status of women in science, political controversy about female reproduction, and a lack of funding from public and private sources.

Despite important gains over the past decades, women continue to hold unequal social roles. There is little doubt that this devaluation affects the visibility

Lise Beane

In the spring of 1990, activists with the Women's Community Cancer Project lobbied outside a medical conference on breast cancer in Cambridge, Massachusetts, for legislation, research, and appropriate health care services. Despite the huge toll taken by breast cancer, its causes are still not known, nor are ways to prevent it. Recently a major study designed to determine the effects of diet on the development of breast cancer was proposed but did not receive government funding because it was deemed too costly.

Since becoming director of the National Institutes of Health in April 1991, Bernadine Healy has taken a number of important steps toward making female health a new national priority.

of women's health problems and the seriousness with which they are addressed.

Evidence of such unequal status was reflected in the rejection of a nationally prominent female researcher for tenure at Uniformed Services University of the Health Sciences, Bethesda, Md., in the mid-1980s. A male department chairman commented that although the investigator was widely published and well-respected in her field, the focus of her work, "women's health," was a "desultory" area of investigation.

Many experts have come to believe that some of the profound gaps in knowledge about women's health would not have occurred had women been better represented among senior scientists and policymakers. The situation for women at the NIH and at the Alcohol, Drug Abuse, and Mental Health Administration (ADAMHA) is instructive because these are the premier training grounds in the U.S. for investigators in the health sciences. Only 14% of top staff positions at the NIH are filled by women, and the situation is no better at ADAMHA.

In 1984 the National Institute of Child Health and Human Development (NICHD) held a workshop to identify barriers to clinical research careers for women. Among those determined were: the predominance of men in senior positions; the assignment of women to a disproportionate share of teaching (at universities) and patient care (at medical centers); discriminatory treatment, such as exclusion from peer networks; lack of alternative careers paths; and lack of access to training and funding opportunities.

Even though women's health is not limited to reproductive functioning, controversy related to female reproduction, including abortion, has been a significant barrier to public and private funding. This political con-

troversy has had a chilling effect overall on women's health research because reproductive endocrinology is not well integrated into basic and clinical science training programs. Florence Haseltine, director of the Center for Population Research at the NICHD, has pointed out that because obstetrics and gynecology has been notoriously underfunded and the NIH lacks an in-house program of research, potential interdisciplinary research on women's health has been neglected. One consequence is that women in the U.S. are deprived of the development of new contraceptive technologies.

Closing the gap

In addition to seeking enhanced funding for obstetrics and gynecology research, some experts have called for the creation of a new academic discipline that focuses on women's health. Physician Karen Johnson, an expert on women's mental health issues, has proposed a new medical specialty that would have a core curriculum in internal medicine but a major emphasis on women's psychology and physiology.

A model academic program was established in 1988 at the University of Melbourne, Australia. The university's Centre for Women's Health in Society offers a graduate diploma in women's health, and it funds and directs a variety of research programs related to women.

By 1991 a number of important steps in the right direction had been taken. At the December 1990 symposium sponsored by the NWHRC, a research agenda established four priority areas: female cardiovascular illness, menopause (with a special focus on osteoporosis), breast cancer, and clinical pharmacology related to female health. In July 1990 a women's health equity bill was introduced in the U.S. Congress. In September 1990 an Office of Research on Women's Health was created at the NIH.

Then in April 1991 Bernadine Healy became the new NIH director; shortly thereafter she announced a $500 million initiative for women's health research. In the last week of July, Healy commented on gender disparities in health care in leading medical journal editorials. "Our responsibility now is to establish a science base that will permit reliable diagnoses, as well as effective treatment and prevention strategies to provide care to women, based on 'appropriate biological or medical indications,' " she said in the *Journal of the American Medical Association.* And in the *New England Journal of Medicine,* she wrote that the NIH is now committed to making "women's health a priority, not just in the interest of women but for the well-being of the American people."

It remains to be seen whether serious levels of funding will be forthcoming from private and public sources. Ultimately, the proof of success will be measured in terms of dollars devoted to research.

Collegiates Conquer Dyslexia

by Gertrude M. Webb, Ed.D.

For the first time in my life, at 21 years of age, someone was unraveling the mystery of dyslexia for me—helping me understand what had been so baffling ever since I first got to school—why I had had such trouble trying to say what I wanted to say. So often I could solve problems faster and better than anyone else, yet when I had to write or verbalize the answers to the problems I had solved, I simply could not make myself understood. And how I struggled—and failed—when it came to learning sequential information, like lists of capitals of states or numbers in a row! I was simply at a loss as to how to master those disassociated bits of information. Oh, how I tried—studying them for innumerable hours and freezing with fright when I was faced with these tasks in tests!

My problems meant that I received very confusing feedback: responses such as "I'm having difficulty understanding you, Andrea." "Sometimes you seem so bright, yet sometimes I can't understand you at all." "The way you express your ideas is so mixed up." "What is the trouble, Andrea? Can't you do better?" Such befuddling responses from teachers, peers, and family members, too, made me question my own intelligence. What a roller coaster my feelings rode while I tried to figure out how smart or dumb I really was!

That was in 1979. It was then that Andrea was accepted into a unique program for adult dyslexics at Curry College, Milton, Mass., a private, four-year, co-educational liberal arts college with an enrollment of just over 1,200. After undergoing tests that indicated the ways she took in information from her world and processed it, she began to see exactly where her strengths and weaknesses lay. The testing revealed how Andrea expressed her ideas both verbally (in words) and visually (in images). Her ability to put ideas together using common sense, to make practical judgments, to reason abstractly, and to organize visually were strengths; her difficulties were in the language arts and showed up as deficits in speaking, reading, and writing. In addition to her language problems, the trouble she had getting her hands and eyes to cooperate resulted in her near-illegible handwriting.

Confusing p's and q's and other manifestations

After the testing, Andrea had the opportunity to meet with peers and instructors in Curry's special program for students with dyslexia, where she learned about the wide range of manifestations dyslexia can have. Some students had not begun talking until late in their preschool years. For some their first production of language had been terribly garbled. Many described being pulled out of class for extra help in their first

grades at school; this was when they began to feel "different," the beginning of a sense of inadequacy. Typically, they could not distinguish letters—b's from d's, or p's from q's—or they inverted them (u for n). Some could not match the sounds of letters like j, m, or s to the letters they saw on paper. Others reported reversing letters or whole words when they tried to write, writing them as though they saw the letters in mirrors (qob for dog). They also read words backwards (was for saw).

Still others reported having great trouble trying to tell time; they could not "read" what the little and big hands on a clock were saying. Many experienced frustrations when they tried to follow directions, especially when they were given a series of instructions to follow, such as: "When the bell rings, put your workbooks and pencils away; then go to the coat closet; get your outside clothing; get in line and wait there until I tell you your bus is here—and don't forget your lunch boxes." Words, words, words, how jumbled they all got!

The school-related problems dyslexics have are wide and varied. Some have only occasional trouble in one area, while others experience most of the difficulties described by the Curry students, and for them everything about learning is a constant battle. The quintessential difficulty for dyslexics is in learning to read. Their own sense of inadequacy is then profound. For them there is nothing funny about the ordeal; learning to read seems an impossible dream.

As noted, Andrea performed well in tasks requiring spatial organization. As a result, she could design, imagine, and create original images. Geometric

The passage below demonstrates how a printed page may appear to a student with dyslexia; letters and words may be rotated, reversed, transposed, joined, or incorrectly separated. Moreover, words in a line of print may appear to float rather than adhere to the line. Because so much energy must go into the decoding process, comprehension is often minimal.

n","saidB   y. "W   r
 "Comeo   ets   ehav di cku i o n.
                        eto   pth sc
  eqon'   not   fqodc
W   thavea   her cano   orn."

"Come on," said Betsy. "We have to pick up this corn. We don't have another can of popcorn."

Courtesy of Richard D. Lavoie, Riverview School, East Sandwich, Mass.

shapes and numbers were her "friends." However, some dyslexics, in addition to their difficulty in areas of language, have spatially related difficulties: they confuse front and back, up and down, below and above, and, most commonly, left and right. These problems evidence themselves in attempts to solve math problems and in other tasks at school. Students who have both spatial and language problems are sometimes called "double dyslexics"; learning coping strategies is considerably more vexing for them than it is for students whose difficulties are confined to the language areas. Fortunately, the number of double dyslexics is comparatively few. Indeed, when Andrea learned the possible degrees of severity of dyslexia, she felt lucky. "I think of the man who felt sorry for himself because he had no shoes until he met a man who had no feet," she said.

Defining dyslexia

Definitions of *dyslexia* vary. Literally translated from its Greek derivation, it means "difficulty in the use of words." Around the turn of the century, the term *word blindness* was used. Other terms that have been variously applied are *amnesia visualis verbalis, script blindness, congenital reading retardation,* and simply the broad description *learning disability.* The American Psychiatric Association's *Diagnostic and Statistical Manual of Mental Disorders,* third edition, revised, lists dyslexia as "developmental reading disorder." The criteria for the diagnosis are: (1) the individual has a reading level well below average, (2) the problem interferes with academic achievement and daily living tasks that require reading, and (3) the difficulty is not due to a defect in visual or hearing acuity or to a neurological disorder.

One definition that is particularly useful, in that it describes the scope of the problem and also suggests that the difficulties can be overcome, was proposed by the eminent British neurologist Macdonald Critchley in the late 1970s:

A learning disability which initially shows itself by difficulty in learning to read, and later by erratic spelling and by lack of facility in manipulating written as opposed to spoken words. The condition is cognitive in essence, and usually genetically determined. It is not due to intellectual inadequacy or to lack of sociocultural opportunity, or to faults in the technique of teaching, or to emotional factors, or to any known structural brain defect. It probably represents a specific maturational defect which tends to lessen as the child grows older and is capable of considerable improvement, especially when appropriate remedial help is afforded at the earliest opportunity.

Estimates of the number of persons with dyslexia vary from 3 to 35% of the population; the most reliable figures come from one of the early medical researchers in the field, Richard Eustis, at Children's Hospital in Boston. From his exacting studies he estimated in 1955 that 8–10% of the total population had dyslexia while only 3% had such severe problems that their needs could not be met in a usual school setting. These estimates are probably still relevant. There has been little dispute concerning dyslexia's prevalence by gender; males are affected about three times more often than females.

As a rule, childhood dyslexia precedes adult dyslexia; that is, adult dyslexia is not a phenomenon arising suddenly at age 20, 30, or later. However, it is often undetected during childhood years. Andrea's case is instructive. She was seen as a slow learner yet also as an overachiever (for she tried so hard, attending summer school each year to maintain her grade level); she was a willing worker, a really "good kid" as described by her teachers, who, not knowing what to do to help her, gave her passing marks and said, "Let's move her up to the next grade"—even though she had not mastered all of her classwork.

Fortunately, schools and regular classroom teachers are now studying appropriate strategies to help dyslexic children within the regular classroom; moreover, they know enough to call for the help of special educators when more support is needed. It is this author's hope that within the next decade dyslexic children will no longer have their sense of self-worth damaged owing to the ignorance of a teacher who concluded that they were "stupid."

Insights into cause

A specific cause of dyslexia is not known. However, obstetricians have recorded trauma at or immediately before or after birth, resulting in damage to the language centers located in the left hemisphere of the brain. Other theories propose that prenatal chemical imbalances or emotional trauma in infancy may result in damage to the neurological system that causes specific language difficulties.

In the late 1970s researchers in Boston studied the brain of a dyslexic child who had been killed in an accident. They found that in the left side of the brain the organization of nerve cells was distinctly abnormal, while no abnormality was seen on the right side—findings that have been confirmed in subsequent studies.

One of the pioneers of dyslexia research was Norman Geschwind, professor of neurology at Harvard Medical School. To support Geschwind's research, the Orton Society, an organization memorializing the work in the field of learning disabilities by Samuel Orton in the early 1900s, funded a program at Beth Israel Hospital in Boston to which brains of deceased dyslexics are donated. Geschwind's untimely death in 1987 left his colleague, neurologist Albert Galaburda, to carry on. By early 1991 nine brains of dyslexics had been examined in the Beth Israel laboratory. Findings indicate differences in the relationships of the left and right hemispheres of the brains, which are presumed to have contributed to language difficulties.

The part of the brain known as the temporal plane, or planum temporale, makes up a major portion of the speech and language area (known as Wernicke's area). In nondyslexic individuals the planum temporale is larger on the left in approximately 65% of cases and larger on the right in about 11%; in the remaining 24% the planum temporale is symmetrical–*i.e.,* about equal in size on both sides of the brain. Brains of dyslexics studied at autopsy have consistently shown the symmetrical pattern. Researchers have concluded that many cases of dyslexia may result from disturbed development of the normally larger left-sided language region.

Possible familial, genetically based causes of dyslexia have been proposed by a number of investigators, dating from 1905. Several of the more recent studies have attempted to define the mode of inheritance. Researchers at the University of Colorado at Denver and Yale University School of Medicine studied the school records of 117 pairs of identical and fraternal twins, many of whom had a reading disability. Such studies of the comparative incidence of disability in identical twins (who come from the same egg) and fraternal twins (from separate eggs) are particularly useful in revealing probable genetic differences. The Colorado and Yale investigators found that in the identical twin groups both twins were affected in 85% of cases, whereas with the fraternal twins both were affected in only 55% of cases. These findings are consistent with a genetic basis for reading disability.

Additional research on the brain's role in dyslexia is being done by Frank Duffy and colleagues at Children's Hospital in Boston. Using electroencephalographs that graph, or "map," the responses of the brain when presented with specific tasks, they have proposed a system for classifying dyslexics according to electrical activity in the brain.

A unique college program

While the medical research looks to the probable causes of dyslexia, dedicated educators have long been challenged by the paradox of the seemingly bright dyslexic student and his or her poor academic performance. This author, being so challenged, helped establish a pioneer program to meet the needs of language-disabled adults who had struggled through their school years without any remedial help. Begun in 1970, the Program for Advancement of Learning, affectionately known as PAL, is for "college-able" but "language-disabled" students and is part of the curriculum of Curry College.

Students who are accepted by Curry and PAL usually are aspiring to a liberal arts college education. Many wonder if they really can succeed after a history of school difficulties. Andrea also wondered this. She was willing to work hard, but she had worked hard before. In Andrea's case her PAL instructor encour-

Gertrude M. Webb, Ed.D.

Students in the PAL program at Curry College, Milton, Massachusetts, are provided with "tools" to help them conquer reading difficulties. By plotting the central ideas in a textbook chapter on paper, then graphically interconnecting parts of the whole, they learn to make sense of material that may at first seem a complete jumble.

aged her to focus on what the testing had revealed as her strength: her ability to reason and solve problems. She was taught how to apply those abilities to successful learning in her course work. All PAL students are admitted to the program because the admissions committee believes they can succeed in this setting. The students are valued for their *abilities*; no matter how defeated they have felt in the past, most come to accept that their teachers are betting in their favor—with good reason.

Like most dyslexics, Andrea suffered from a failure to read at the expected level. In attempting to read, adult dyslexics often can grasp main ideas, especially when the content is personally meaningful. It is the mass of details that throws them. Critchley has noted that because dyslexics were such poor and slow readers in school, they have a great "reluctance to read" as adults. He described the extent of the reluctance with the example of the "established executive" whose school days were plagued by dyslexia; now he will go to great lengths to "avoid studying printed reports, memoranda, briefs, parliamentary white papers, and the like." He will probably contrive for a junior colleague or personal assistant to extract the salient points or read the documents to him.

Andrea's PAL instructor challenged her to use her abstract-thinking ability to conquer her reluctance to read and to apply that ability in the reading assignments for her classes. For example, before reading a chapter entitled "Nuclear Energy" in a textbook on current scientific issues, she was asked to write down the title in the center of a blank piece of paper and draw a circle around it. She was then asked to speculate about what the chapter might contain—in other words, what did she already know about the subject? Andrea's response was that nuclear energy had been initially designed to help humankind advance, that somehow its purposes had altered, and that it was now threatening humankind's destruction. She was instructed to put each of these categories on the paper, circle them, and then join each category she had named to the already centered chapter title. She called these categories "for man's good," "history," and "for man's destruction." The instructor also suggested that Andrea put several blank circles on the paper in which to include information she had not yet thought of. Then when she read the chapter, she was able to find the information that belonged in each category. A major section of the chapter was about the components of nuclear energy, so she designated an additional circle as "components." What a different approach to reading this was! Andrea was amazed at how relating ideas in this graphic way helped her comprehend complex material and how meaningful it all suddenly became.

One of Andrea's areas of difficulty was the mastering of unrelated information, such as the elements in the periodic table; she recalled having struggled in junior high school trying to memorize the names and dates of the battles of the Civil War. Her PAL instructor introduced her to the world of mnemonics—a technique for improving one's memory known since the days of Aristotle but for Andrea a great revelation—a tool that enabled her to conquer numerous former problems.

Like many of her peers, Andrea needed help with organizational tasks; she had difficulty sequencing things. Strategies to help her in this area included putting stories together using cartoons, constructing time-management calendars, keeping date books, and utilizing any number of other self-prompting "tools."

As Andrea's empowerment as a student was developing, many new strategies were introduced for her to "try on for size," evaluating their usefulness, applying them or not on the basis of her own judgments. Andrea, like the other students in PAL, realized that her thinking was truly being respected; further, it was being challenged, and she was expected to use it.

Early in the program the students begin to understand the concept of language as an integration of listening, speaking, reading, and writing. PAL students are encouraged to form study groups as they learn new methods of coping with their former language difficulties; their discussions help them individually clarify their own thinking. They are also taught how to pose questions, and they learn the differences between factual, conceptual, and problem-solving ones. Many PAL students who need to concentrate on writing-improvement strategies, spelling, or strengthening their weak vocabularies benefit from using a word processor. Some students initially conquer their reading difficulties with taped textbooks, which do not replace printed books but are used as a supplement—an aid.

From the outset, students in the dyslexia program are always treated as Curry students first and participants in PAL second. The only special treatment they get is at exam time. The PAL students have the option of taking untimed exams. A stress-free setting for taking exams can make a great deal of difference. However, as the students make progress, they are encouraged to take their exams in the usual setting along with their Curry classmates. As PAL students' sense of competence and self-worth strengthens, their learning is energized; they are willing to take risks, accept new challenges.

Triumphing

Experts continue to disagree about the etiology and definition of dyslexia. It is generally agreed, however, that the earlier a person gets remedial help, the better; the prognosis is usually best if the problem is diagnosed before the third grade. Nonetheless, even adult dyslexics who have struggled all their lives *without* help can overcome their reading and language difficulties. Curry College is one of several institutions of higher learning that have special supportive programs for learning-disabled adults. There are also several organizations that can be helpful to adult dyslexics. One of these is the Association of Learning Disabled Adults, a self-help network based in Washington, D.C.

One of the first lessons that PAL students learn is that they must not be their own enemies. The French writer Alexander Dumas said it particularly well:

A person who doubts himself
Is like a man
Who would enlist in the ranks of his enemies
And bear arms against himself.
He makes his failure certain by himself
Being the first person to be convinced of it.

Students remain in the PAL program for as long as they need it. After a year and a half, Andrea felt secure enough to continue without PAL support and went on to complete the work for her baccalaureate degree, with a major in fine arts and a minor in behavioral sciences.

Andrea recalls the shared feelings of accomplishment among those who had started in PAL together. At graduation she was joined by approximately one-third of the class who had started with her in the program (her former "PALS"). As Andrea put it: "We felt as great as Hans Christian Andersen, Thomas Edison, Winston Churchill, Nelson Rockefeller, Woodrow Wilson, and other famous language-disabled heroes must have felt when their work was finally recognized."

Hearing Disorders

Sounds of sufficient loudness and duration can cause temporary or permanent hearing loss. Such loss may range from mild to profound; it is often accompanied by tinnitus (ringing in the ear). The harmful effect of repeated sound overstimulation is cumulative and currently cannot be remedied by medical or surgical treatment. The phenomenon of noise-induced hearing loss has been appreciated for more than 100 years and is reflected in such expressions as "boilermaker's ear." Epidemiological studies have confirmed that workers exposed to loud noise on the job experience gradually decreasing auditory acuity. Despite the fact that such hearing loss is preventable, today's noisy home and recreational environments are placing increasing numbers of people at risk.

In 1990 the U.S. National Institutes of Health convened a consensus conference to consider issues related to noise-induced hearing loss. After receiving reports from experts in the field, a panel of scientists and lay people drafted a statement detailing what is currently known about the problem and posing questions for further study.

Types of hearing loss

Damage to the ear from exposure to potentially injurious sounds may be classified as either acoustic trauma or noise-induced hearing loss. The pattern of damage that results from a specific exposure depends on the frequency (in cycles per second), intensity (*i.e.,* loudness, in decibels), duration, and scheduling (*i.e.,* continuous or intermittent) of the exposure, as well as the susceptibility of the ear involved.

Current U.S. Department of Labor regulations set the boundary between acceptable and damaging noise in the workplace at 85 decibels (dB) for continuous exposure during a full workday. The decibel is a measurement unit for expressing the intensity of a sound. The decibel scale is an exponential one; a change of only a few decibels can represent a significant change in loudness. Because individual susceptibility to the damaging effects of loud sounds varies, it is difficult to predict the precise magnitude of hearing loss that will result from specific exposures. Therefore, criteria for determining risk are based on the average responses of large numbers of individuals.

Acoustic trauma. Exposure to intense sounds of short duration, such as a burst of gunfire, can produce immediate, severe, and permanent hearing loss, called acoustic trauma. By means of direct mechanical destruction, high-intensity sound waves can damage virtually any structure in the ear, from the tympanic membrane, or eardrum, and ossicles (middle ear bones) to the delicate sensory and neural structures (*e.g.,* the organ of Corti) in the fluid-filled compartments of the inner ear.

Temporary threshold shift. Moderate exposure to potentially damaging noise may cause a temporary hearing loss, called temporary threshold shift (TTS), which will resolve when the individual is no longer exposed to the loud sounds. The precise anatomic and physiological changes that occur in the inner ear during TTS are not fully understood, but they are believed to affect the delicate auditory nerve endings and sensory cells of the inner ear; the latter are called hair cells because of the bundles of hairlike projections, called stereocilia, that range along their upper borders.

Noise-induced permanent threshold shift. With continued exposure, the hearing loss of TTS gradually becomes permanent. The magnitude of this so-called noise-induced permanent threshold shift is determined by subtracting from the individual's hearing loss the amount of loss to be expected in an age-matched sample of the population that is not exposed to the noise. Microscopic changes observed in the inner ears of patients with this kind of hearing loss seem to indicate that the most vulnerable structural elements are the hair cells themselves. In addition to showing permanent damage to the stereocilia, electron microscopic studies have demonstrated degeneration of the rootlet structures that normally anchor the stereocilia to the hair cell. The number of hair cells affected increases with repeated noise exposure. Although there is at present no evidence to suggest that degenerated hair cells in humans are ever replaced, recent studies in birds have documented hair cell regeneration after initial loss following noise exposure. This finding holds potential for future treatment or prevention strategies in humans.

"The shot heard . . ."

Impulse noises, such as gunfire or the explosion of firecrackers, are characterized by very high sound intensity levels of short duration. The initial acoustic pulse of a gun discharge may last only a few milliseconds, but the peak sound level may range from 132 to 170 dB, with clear potential for immediate and permanent injury to sensitive inner-ear structures. Large-caliber rifles and shotguns are particularly hazardous.

Impulse noise is one of the most important causes of noise-induced hearing loss in the population at large, which is more likely to be exposed to a single damaging event than to continuous hazardous levels of noise day after day. Recreational hunting is one activity that poses a significant threat to the hearing of some segments of the population—among industrial workers, for example, 69% of whom reportedly are hunters. Furthermore, those who both work in noisy industries and engage in sport shooting may develop hearing losses due to gunfire noise over and above those sustained in occupational exposure. The ear most often affected is on the side opposite the shoul-

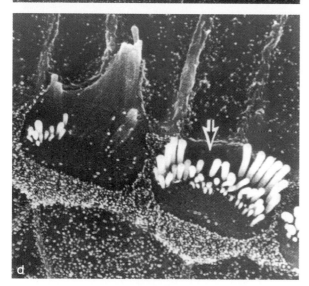

Noise-induced damage is graphically visible on scanning electron micrographs of stereocilia, the hairlike projections on the sensory cells of the inner ear. After relatively minor damage, normal stereocilia (a) appear ruffled (b); with greater trauma, many become bent (c). Fusing and destruction of stereocilia (d) are associated with profound hearing loss.

der the rifle rests on; the ear closest to the shoulder supporting the butt of the gun is slightly protected from the full blast of the muzzle. In frequent shooters, differences in the degree of hearing loss sustained by their two ears can range from 15 to 30 dB.

Hazards of popular music

While an explosion poses an obvious hearing risk to an unprotected ear, other potentially damaging environmental sounds may be less readily apparent. Parents and policymakers have expressed concern about potential hearing loss that might result from youngsters' exposure to rock music, "boom cars," motorcycles, and personal stereos.

Some recent scientific studies have focused on noise sources encountered during leisure-time activities, rock concerts in particular. Amplified sound as loud as 105 to 115 dB is typical at a rock concert (as compared with sound levels of about 95 dB in a discotheque). Earlier generations of amplifiers were in the 20,000- to 30,000-w range, but current large concert speakers are equipped with 100,000- to 500,000-w amplifiers. The sounds produced by such electronic systems are well above the discomfort level for most people. Not only the audience but also the musicians, stagehands, ushers, and concessionaires at such events risk noise-induced hearing loss from prolonged exposure to these very high sound levels. Some rock musicians whose hearing has been impaired have launched a campaign to warn concertgoers about the potential danger of loud music. Most people can experience the short periods of exposure during a typical concert without suffering permanent hearing loss, but practically everyone exposed to such sound levels will have some degree of *temporary* loss, often accompanied by tinnitus.

Personal stereos, which have been on the market for about a decade, are capable of producing sound levels in excess of 110–115 dB. Because they are portable and are often used to drown out annoying background noises in the work or leisure environment, exposure time can be quite prolonged. Furthermore, because headphones conduct the sound directly into the ear of the person wearing them, others—parents, for example—may not be aware of the loud sounds to which the listener is being exposed. Listeners may compensate for the occurrence of TTS, which should serve as a warning sign, by simply turning up the volume to even more hazardous levels.

There is, however, a distinction to be drawn between the sound levels that such devices are capable of delivering and the levels at which a typical listener utilizes them on a daily basis; several studies of the preferred listening levels of typical personal stereo users found that most adjust their devices to safe volumes. The NIH consensus panel suggested that consideration be given to product labeling to

Leaf blowers and other motorized lawn and garden equipment can produce sound at levels known to cause permanent hearing loss. Users would be well advised to wear some sort of hearing-protection device.

alert unsuspecting consumers, particularly parents of young listeners, about the potential hazards associated with prolonged, inappropriate use of personal stereos. Several manufacturers are already voluntarily providing such information. Persons who experience a "full" feeling in the ear, muffled hearing, or tinnitus following use of such devices should modify their listening habits to avoid possible permanent damage.

Sound levels attained in many so-called boom cars, containing very powerful stereo amplifiers and speakers, may exceed 120 dB. The intensity of the sound that can be heard by individuals standing some distance from a boom car with its stereo playing and windows closed provides an indication of what the occupants must be experiencing. People riding in such cars for extended periods of time are at significant risk of suffering permanent noise-induced hearing loss.

Equipment to be wary of

Many commonly used household devices also are capable of producing hazardous sound levels. Outdoor lawn-care equipment such as gasoline-powered leaf blowers can produce maximum levels of 110 to 112 dB at the ear level of the person operating the machine. Calculated by federal standards, the average level of such devices is 102.6 dB. Thus, a 1½-hour daily exposure to this noise level would violate federal workplace noise standards. Sound levels approaching 116 dB have been reported with different types of chain saws. Clearly, hearing protection should be worn by anyone using such loud devices as chain saws, unmuffled lawn mowers, leaf blowers, power saws, heavy-duty vacuums, and rug-cleaning machines. Most casual users will not exceed allowable exposure periods; nonetheless, caution is warranted because of individ-

ual differences in susceptibility to damage. Persons living in rural settings, where many noisy devices may be used on a daily basis, appear to be particularly at risk for noise-induced hearing loss. One indicator of the presence of hazardous background noise is difficulty experienced by the user when attempting to communicate with another person in the presence of the noise source. If the two cannot make themselves understood even when shouting, the noise is probably reaching damaging levels.

Some cordless telephones have recently been identified as posing a significant risk of acoustic trauma. In one study, analysis of the ring signal of several cordless models revealed sound levels of approximately 140 dB, well above allowable exposure levels. Individual cases of immediate and permanent hearing loss have been reported in persons who failed to switch off the ring signal before placing the receiver to their ears.

Recreational vehicles such as all-terrain vehicles, snowmobiles, go-carts, and motocross bikes have also been implicated in noise-induced hearing loss, as have firecrackers and cap pistols. The NIH panel reiterated the need for early education about noise and hearing loss, beginning in elementary school.

Aging, medications, and hearing loss

The contribution of noise exposure to the gradual loss of hearing associated with the aging process, called

Some cordless telephones pose a risk of acoustic trauma from extremely loud ring signals that sound directly in the ear of the person answering the call. One can avoid this by switching off the ring signal before placing the receiver to the ear.

presbycusis, is not totally clear. However, studies of certain primitive peoples, culturally isolated from most hazardous noise sources, suggest that noise may play a significant role in the age-associated hearing impairment that is seen among older people in industrial countries. While some degree of hearing loss may be an inevitable effect of aging, it makes sense that the contributions of a preventable factor such as damaging sound levels should be more intensively investigated.

When administered at certain dosage levels, some medications have been shown to be ototoxic—that is, they produce damage to the hair cells and nerves of the inner ear and thus hearing loss. The most widely known of these drugs are some anticancer drugs, most notably cisplatin, and certain antibiotics (e.g., streptomycin, kanamycin, gentamicin) used to treat specific life-threatening infections. Laboratory studies indicate that a combination of noise exposure and ototoxic drugs produces more hair cell loss and hearing loss than either the noise or the drug alone. The exact mechanism of interaction is unknown. Physicians must exercise extra caution to protect patients who are taking such drugs from potentially damaging noise exposure. Such patients should have frequent audiometry testing, and drug-dosage levels should be carefully monitored.

Noise in infancy—and before

Concern has also been raised regarding possible dangers of noise-induced hearing loss during prenatal development and in the neonatal period. There is strong evidence that noise in the mother's environment reaches the inner ear of the fetus. These findings are based on observations of fetal heart-rate changes, eye blinks, overall body movements, and electrophysiological data recorded during examinations to assess fetal viability. Follow-up studies of infants who experienced such sound stimulation in utero have not provided conclusive evidence of any hearing damage when compared with unexposed infants, however. Nonetheless, some animal species have been shown to undergo a period of heightened susceptibility to acoustic trauma during fetal development.

Another area currently being investigated is the potential hazard of exposure to high sound levels in neonatal intensive care units. Many of the infants being treated in such units are also concurrently receiving potentially ototoxic drugs. Noise levels inside incubators vary from 60 to 80 dB. Loud, high-frequency warning sounds are sometimes produced by monitoring equipment. Forceful closing of incubator cabinet hoods and tapping on the outside of the transparent cover can also result in significant impulse noises in the interior space. Respirators and other life-support

The endangered ear		
type of noise	sound level (decibels)	effect
"boom car" jet engine shotgun rock concert	over 125	beyond threshold of pain; potential for hearing loss high
discotheque, "boom box," thunderclap	over 120	hearing loss likely
chain saw, pneumatic drill, jackhammer, symphony orchestra snowmobile garbage truck, cement mixer	100–120	regular exposure of more than one minute risks permanent hearing loss
farm tractor newspaper press subway, motorcycle	90–100	15 minutes of unprotected exposure potentially harmful
lawn mower, food blender	85–90	continuous daily exposure for more than eight hours can cause hearing damage
diesel truck average city traffic noise	80–85	annoying; constant exposure may cause hearing damage
dishwasher vacuum cleaner, hair dryer	60–80	intrusive but not harmful
kitchen garbage disposal normal conversation quiet office refrigerator humming	below 60	comfortable; safe level
whisper leaves rustling	below 30	barely audible

Source: National Institute on Deafness and Other Communication Disorders, National Institutes of Health, January 1990

equipment can increase the noise in the ambient environment by 5 to 25 dB. Significantly, high-risk infants may be exposed to these noise levels for weeks or even months at a time without intermittent periods of quiet. The effects on hearing of these long-term noise exposures have yet to be determined. Follow-up studies of these young patients are complicated by the fact that many of the circumstances that lead to admission to the neonatal unit (*e.g.,* prematurity, low birth weight) are independently associated with a higher incidence of hearing loss. Without waiting for conclusive evidence concerning the risk of early noise-induced hearing loss, organizations of physicians and nurses who specialize in neonatal care have begun to advocate noise-reduction programs in hospital nursery units.

Noise-reduction devices

Hearing-protection devices have been developed for use in environments where hazardous noise levels are unavoidable. Specially designed noise-reduction ear muffs are now worn by shooters at target ranges and by airport personnel working around jet engines. Others who are concerned about noise exposure can purchase ear plugs, made from compressible, spongelike materials that reduce noise levels, at drug and sporting goods stores. (These plugs are not the same as ear plugs made to keep water out of the ears of swimmers, and they should not be used interchangeably.) Each type of hearing-protection device should have a rating on the label that indicates how much noise reduction can be achieved if it is worn according to instructions. Individuals with normal hearing who wear such protection in noise levels greater than approximately 85 dB will still be able to hear loud speech, machinery, and important warning sounds.

Acoustic engineers and other specialists are working to develop strategies for eliminating noise from certain environments. Noise-canceling sounds can be generated in some instances; this feature is already employed in headphones used by airline pilots, and similar devices may eventually become available to the public. Consumers should be aware that the vast majority of noise-induced hearing loss is preventable if hearing-protection devices are worn consistently during exposure to potentially damaging sounds.

Infant hearing loss: new guidelines

In most cases, hearing loss in newborns and infants is an "invisible" disorder. The hearing-impaired child may begin to babble in a seemingly normal way and, unless subtle signs of hearing loss alert parents and others to the problem, detection of the loss may be delayed until the child fails to develop normal speech and language. Because late detection of hearing loss may lead to significant delay in the development of communication skills and to later problems in school,

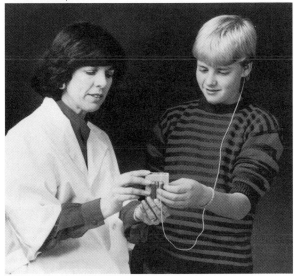

A profoundly deaf youngster—who could not be helped by a conventional hearing aid—may be able to hear sounds and to identify some spoken words with the aid of the Nucleus 22 Channel Cochlear Implant, approved in 1990 for use in children.

early identification of educationally significant hearing loss is important.

In 1990, stimulated by recent medical advances that have increased the survival of markedly premature, low-birth-weight, and other severely compromised newborns, the Joint Committee on Infant Hearing (composed of representatives from a number of U.S. professional associations with an interest in child health) issued a revision of its earlier guidelines. The criteria used to identify infants at risk for impaired hearing (*e.g.,* respiratory distress, certain infections, family history of deafness) were expanded, and recommendations were made for the identification and management of hearing-impaired newborns (less than 28 days old) and infants (29 days to 2 years).

Cochlear implants for children

The cochlear implant is a device that provides electrical stimulation to surviving nerve fibers in the inner ears of deaf persons who do not have enough residual hearing to benefit from conventional hearing aids. One such implant, used in adults in the United States for several years, was approved by the U.S. Food and Drug Administration (FDA) in 1990 for use in profoundly deaf children and adolescents. The safety and efficacy of the device for children were established during four years of intensive clinical investigation, which included data from 80 children who had worn the implant for at least 12 months. Because implantation of the device may eliminate any residual hearing, an NIH consensus panel previously recommended a minimum trial of six months of other rehabilitation mea-

331

sures and conventional amplification devices; only if these have no benefit should the cochlear implant be considered.

Although a cochlear implant does not restore normal hearing, it does provide specific benefits, including improved detection of environmental sounds, enhanced lipreading performance, some ability to identify spoken words, and improved speech. A few children who have the device are able to recognize words in conversation without the aid of lipreading. The FDA intends to continue monitoring children who receive the device so that any unanticipated problems can be rapidly detected, and the manufacturer has agreed to collect yearly follow-up data on each patient for five years after implantation.

—*Patrick E. Brookhouser, M.D.*

Heart and Blood Vessels

Over the past several years, major advances have occurred in both the understanding of the mechanisms responsible for heart and vascular diseases and the approach to their treatment. These advances have been due in part to the application of new technologies and in part to the insights derived from the powerful tools provided by molecular biology. Quite recently, a new approach to cardiovascular research has been taken by some investigators: the goal is to find effective therapies for cardiovascular diseases; the strategy is to get back to basics—*i.e.,* to understand the molecular and cellular mechanisms responsible for the evolution of the disease and to use this knowledge to inhibit the pathological processes. The application of cellular and molecular biology approaches has provided numerous insights into the pathogenesis of coronary atherosclerosis and other cardiac diseases.

Hypertrophic cardiomyopathy: genetic discoveries

A disease that has benefited from such research is hypertrophic cardiomyopathy (HCM), characterized by an inappropriate thickening of the heart muscle. In most patients, if not all, the disease is inherited and is transmitted as an autosomal dominant trait; 50% of the offspring of an affected person will carry the abnormal gene. Although patients may live normal lives without any symptoms or limitations, most will ultimately develop light-headed spells, fainting episodes, chest pain, or shortness of breath; the most seriously affected individuals can die suddenly and without warning. HCM is one of the most common diseases responsible for the untimely deaths of young people, including competitive athletes, who were considered to be in superb health.

Several groups of investigators have attempted to identify the gene responsible for HCM. Recently, linkage analysis studies (a technique that determines whether a specific site on a chromosome seems to

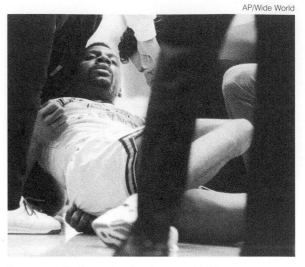

Recent genetic discoveries that have provided better understanding of hypertrophic cardiomyopathy, an inherited enlargement of the heart muscle, may lead to better treatments. In the future, untimely deaths, as that of star basketball player Hank Gathers, might be prevented.

track only with those family members who have the disease) have proved fruitful, although the results are somewhat surprising. In some affected families a mutation has been found on the gene that encodes the protein known as cardiac myosin heavy chain, which is involved in muscle contraction. This gene is located on chromosome 14. However, in other families whose members appear to have the same disease, at least as assessed clinically, a second and different mutation affects the gene. In still other families the abnormal gene is located on some chromosome other than 14. Thus, different mutations affecting the same gene and different mutations affecting two completely different genes can lead to the development of what until now was considered a single disease entity.

Given these breakthroughs, it will soon be possible to carry out blood tests—even as early as the fetal stage—to determine which subjects in an affected family have or will develop the disease. Finally, knowing the genetic abnormality will ultimately lead to more effective treatment.

Number one public health problem

Atherosclerotic coronary artery disease is a major health problem and the leading cause of morbidity and mortality in Western civilization. This pathological process usually begins in childhood and manifests itself clinically in adulthood by acute myocardial infarction (heart attack), angina pectoris (chest pain lasting minutes, precipitated by exertion), and occasionally evidence of congestive heart failure and rhythm disturbances. The underlying process leading to these events is a narrowing of a blood vessel (coronary artery) that supplies the heart muscle. The narrowing is caused by a fibrofatty plaque (atheroma) gradually developing in the arterial wall, narrowing its cavity (lumen) and thereby interfering with the flow of blood necessary for normal heart function. A typical atheromatous plaque consists of many elements, including smooth muscle cells, scar tissue, lipid droplets, cholesterol crystals, calcium deposits, and large foam cells, which are cells whose cytoplasm is filled with cholesterol esters and free cholesterol.

Fissuring or rupture of an atherosclerotic plaque is associated with the formation of a blood clot, which can cause an abrupt occlusion of the coronary artery. The consequences of sudden cessation of blood flow to the area of the heart muscle supplied by the occluded artery are usually catastrophic—severe angina pectoris, heart attack, or sudden death.

Reducing the risk factors for atherosclerotic coronary artery disease (*e.g.,* stopping cigarette smoking or treating hypertension and high serum cholesterol levels) is a very important intervention. This can retard the progression of disease, and often it can prevent its development. Unfortunately, however, such intervention is not sufficient to eliminate the disease. Therefore, major efforts have been undertaken to develop new modes of therapy targeting occluded atheromatous (stenotic) coronary arteries.

Visualizing and characterizing coronary arteries

Currently, the best available technique for evaluating the extent and severity of coronary artery disease is contrast coronary angiography. In this method, a catheter (a long, flexible, hollow tube through which pressures can be measured and agents injected) is

Coronary angiography is currently the "gold standard" for evaluating coronary artery disease. A catheter is advanced through a peripheral artery to the root of the aorta; radiopaque dye is then injected into the coronary artery, and X-rays are taken to provide a picture of obstructed areas.

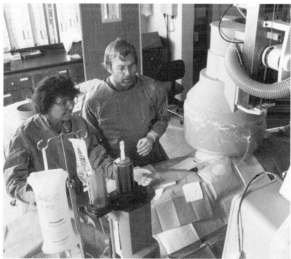

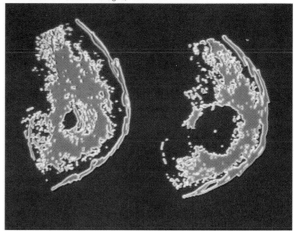

Intravascular ultrasound is a new imaging method that enables the sophisticated assessment of atheromatous plaque within the arterial wall. Severe occluding is seen in the artery (above left); the healthy artery on the right is unobstructed.

advanced through a peripheral artery to the root of the aorta at its origin near the heart and then is directed into a coronary artery. Radiopaque dye is injected into the coronary artery through the catheter, and X-rays are taken so that a moving picture image of the coronary arteries is obtained. This technique, which provides a negative "contrast" image of the lumen of the coronary artery, allows detection of areas of narrowing or obstruction. However, it is not possible to visualize the arterial wall itself, and it is difficult to determine whether the narrowing is due to a clot or to an atheroma.

Recently, intravascular ultrasound has emerged as an imaging modality that provides a new perspective on the anatomic features of atherosclerotic coronary artery disease. Ultrasound employs the transmission of high-frequency sound waves to surrounding tissues. These sound waves are reflected, collected by a receiver, and processed so that images of the surrounding tissue can be constructed. Computer processing permits sophisticated image analysis. In the past, ultrasound has been applied to imaging many different organs of the body, including the uterus (in order to view the growing fetus) and the heart (in order to characterize the heart muscle and valves).

Now, high resolution ultrasound transducers are being applied to the tip of a cardiac catheter (similar to the catheters employed in contrast coronary angiography). Instead of serving as a conduit for injected contrast material, this catheter provides an intravascular ultrasound image from which accurate measurements can be made of the lumen area (and thereby of the degree of coronary arterial narrowing) and from which the composition of the atheromatous plaque within the arterial wall can be assessed. Studies are in progress to determine how reliable this instrument is in making such determinations and whether the information so derived can be helpful in making clinical decisions.

Dissolving the blood clot: therapy for heart attack

The most ominous consequence of atherosclerotic coronary artery disease is the development of a myocardial infarction. This clinical event is caused by sudden, complete occlusion of a coronary artery, which results in cessation of blood supply to the portion of heart muscle (myocardium) that is supplied by this artery. The myocardium is totally dependent on a continuous supply of oxygenated blood to function and survive. When deprived of blood (and thus of oxygen and other essential nutrients), the myocardium will not be able to function normally and, if the amount of residual blood flow is very low, the affected heart muscle will die during the first few hours following coronary occlusion.

Myocardial infarction generally develops when a blood clot forms at the site of an atheromatous coronary artery plaque. Administration of pharmacological agents capable of dissolving the blood clot (thrombolytic agents) within the first several hours after onset of arterial occlusion can restore patency of the artery and thus reestablish blood flow to the injured portion of the myocardium. Exciting research performed over the past few years has shown that a large percentage of the clots responsible for precipitating the acute infarction can be dissolved by thrombolytic agents, resulting in up to a 40% decrease in mortality rate.

Currently, there are several groups of thrombolytic agents in clinical use. All are direct or indirect activators of the native human fibrinolytic system (converting plasminogen to plasmin, which is the blood product capable of dissolving clots). Debate now centers not on whether these drugs can reduce mortality from heart attack—unequivocal data demonstrate that they can—but on which drug and which treatment program is best (most beneficial to the patient and most cost-effective). A study published in 1990 demonstrated in a head-to-head comparison of tissue plasminogen activator (t-PA) and streptokinase that the two drugs produced equivalent effects. The study has been challenged, however, and new studies are being initiated in the hope of arriving at the best possible therapy for the heart attack victim.

Recurrent narrowing of coronary arteries

Since its first clinical application in 1977, angioplasty of the coronary arteries has become a critically important modality for treating patients suffering from atherosclerotic coronary artery disease. In this widely accepted nonsurgical technique, a small balloon-tipped catheter is positioned within a stenotic segment of the coronary artery and then inflated, thereby compressing the plaque and dilating the artery. In addition to balloon angioplasty, other transcatheter modalities for performing angioplasty have been developed in the attempt to restore coronary blood flow without resorting to surgery. These include the excimer laser, which delivers short pulses of laser energy at ultraviolet wavelength and is capable of removing atherosclerotic plaques, and atherectomy devices, with which the actual removal of atherosclerotic material from the interior of the arterial wall is possible by means of a rotating surface that either cuts or pulverizes the tissue. Also used are endovascular stents, which are small tubular meshlike devices that are delivered to the stenotic arterial site collapsed over a balloon catheter. As the balloon is inflated, the stent expands. The balloon is then deflated and removed, leaving the stent as an internal scaffold that keeps the vessel open.

The initial success rate for opening a narrowed artery and improving blood flow to the heart muscle is over 90%. Unfortunately, however, as the follow-up data on the patients treated with these newly developed techniques have been analyzed, it has been found that 25–50% of the patients develop recurrent narrowing (restenosis) of the previously treated arterial site within six months.

Several pharmacological approaches to reducing the incidence of restenosis have been attempted, but so far to no avail. However, a great advance in understanding the restenosis process was made when it was found that the primary cellular mechanism responsible for restenosis is "activation" of the smooth muscle cells that normally reside in the media of the coronary arteries.

Mechanisms responsible for restenosis. The coronary artery has three layers of cells. The *intima* consists of one layer of endothelial cells that line the entire inner surface of the vascular tree. Endothelial cells form an uninterrupted smooth surface, creating a highly selective permeable barrier between blood elements and the arterial wall. The *media* consists of several layers of smooth muscle cells that form the muscular wall of the artery. In the normal coronary artery, smooth muscle cells function as contractile elements that regulate wall tension and diameter; these cells very rarely proliferate. The *adventitia,* which consists of fibroblasts, elastic fibers, and collagen, makes up the outermost layer of the artery.

The process leading to arterial restenosis mainly involves medial smooth muscle cell response to the injury created by the angioplasty procedure. Balloon inflation stretches the narrowed arterial segment, disrupting endothelial cell continuity and damaging the endothelial and smooth muscle cells. Platelets from the bloodstream that do not attach to intact endothelium adhere to the damaged endothelial surface. The platelets, damaged endothelial cells, and damaged smooth muscle cells release a number of products, among which are growth factors (substances that promote growth of cells). The smooth muscle cells begin to synthesize not only more growth factors but also receptors, which reside on the surface of the cell and are responsible for mediating the effects of the growth factors.

Exposure to certain growth factors, especially when there are an increased number of cell receptors that bind these factors, causes marked changes in the injured vascular smooth muscle cell; the cells lose their normal contractile characteristics and become secretory cells that proliferate rapidly and migrate to the intima. Excessive proliferation and migration of the activated smooth muscle cells lead to the development of a new cell layer (*neointima*) between the media and intima, which encroaches on the lumen. This process of proliferation and migration of vascular smooth muscle cells to form the neointima is the fundamental process leading to vascular narrowing and recurrent narrowing. Since it is projected that approximately 400,000 angioplastics will be performed in 1992 in the United States alone, restenosis represents a major public health problem.

Coronary restenosis and cancer: an intriguing link. The process of cell migration and excessive proliferation, which eventually leads to restenosis, is remarkably similar to the process involved in cancerous growth; one of the major differences is that the excessive proliferation of the smooth muscle cells eventually ceases, and the cells resume relatively normal function. The excessive growth of cancer cells cannot be turned off, and their continued growth is what ultimately leads to the death of the organism that harbors such uncontrolled cells. This uncontrolled growth is in part related to the fact that cancer cells often manifest, or "express," excessively high levels of growth factors and their receptors—the processes leading to such overexpression are not subject to the normal control mechanisms. Cancer investigators are using the powerful tools of molecular biology and recombinant DNA technology in attempts to control these processes and design interventions that can selectively kill the cancerous cells.

The power and ubiquitous applicability of molecular biology can be illustrated through examination of one way that investigators in the field of cardiology are freely adapting strategies involving techniques that were initially used to fight cancer. The numerous proteins that are present in living organisms are the essential constituents of all cellular processes; they are encoded by unique segments of DNA, the genes. Modern molecular biology techniques have allowed scientists to isolate and duplicate (clone) large numbers of genes. When a gene is cloned, it is possible to identify ways in which it can be turned on and off and to study its gene product—the specific protein that it encodes. The ability to isolate genes and syn-

Photographs, Howard Sochurek/Medical Images, Inc.

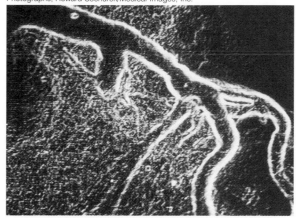

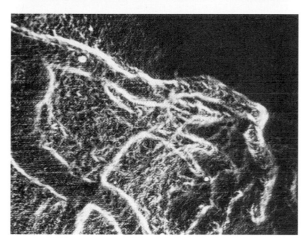

The missing trace of a blood vessel (top image, lower left) signals an occluded left coronary artery; after balloon angioplasty (above) blood flow is restored. Unfortunately, 25–50% of patients who undergo such treatment experience restenosis (recurrent narrowing). Researchers are now applying the tools of molecular biology to solve this problem.

thesize their gene products has revolutionized scientific research. Investigators are just now beginning to realize the potential of using such proteins as potent medicines.

Before a desired protein can be obtained through expression of its gene, the gene has to be placed in an environment that will be conducive to the extraordinarily complex process that is involved in protein expression. One way this can be done is to put the gene into bacterial or yeast cells, which then function as "factories" to produce the gene product.

Not only can scientists now isolate genes, clone genes, and express single gene products, they can also combine or fuse two genes that encode different proteins. When such fused genes (called recombinant genes) are expressed, a new protein is produced that is composed of both of the gene products but now in the form of a single molecule. These novel proteins are called "fusion," or "chimeric," proteins. Proteins

335

can be created that actually have two functions, each inherent in one of its two subunits. Transformed bacterial cells can be used as factories to produce large quantities of these fusion proteins, just as they are used to produce the proteins of single genes.

Anticancer strategy. One group of gene products that has been of great interest comprises the very potent toxins produced by certain bacteria. Examples are diphtheria, shigella, and pseudomonas toxins, designed by nature to kill cells. The genes encoding these proteins have been isolated and cloned, and their recombinant proteins have been expressed.

Pseudomonas exotoxin (PE) is naturally produced by the bacterium *Pseudomonas aeruginosa,* and it exists, at least in part, to protect the bacterium from harmful products present in a hostile environment. The toxin is composed of three parts, which carry out the various cell-binding and cell-killing functions of the molecule. It is possible to manipulate the DNA that encodes the toxin in such a way that one part of the gene can be deleted from the other two parts. Specifically, a truncated PE gene can be expressed, which results in a novel protein (referred to as PE40, owing to its molecular size of 40 kilodaltons) that has powerful cell-killing functions but cannot seek out or bind to cells.

Rapidly growing cancer cells often display large numbers of certain receptors that, when stimulated, enhance their rate of proliferation. It was reasoned that if PE40 could be programmed to recognize and bind to those surface receptors, cancer researchers would have a way of selectively killing these cells.

Such programming has been made possible by the tools of DNA technology. By fusing the truncated gene encoding PE40 with a gene encoding a molecule that can bind to one of these receptors (a ligand), a recombinant fusion toxin is expressed that is able to recognize and attach to cell surface receptors as well as to enter and kill the cell. These types of chimeric toxins have been produced by expression of gene fusions (composed of the genes for growth factor ligands and for PE40) in bacteria. Examples of growth factors used in such ways include transforming growth factor α (TGFα) and acidic fibroblast growth factor (aFGF). TGFα-PE40 and aFGF-PE40 have been found to kill human tumor cells growing either in culture or in laboratory animals that have had human tumors implanted in them. Investigations are under way to determine whether such fusion toxins will be useful in treating patients with cancer.

Novel approach to restenosis. Cardiology investigators recognized that this strategy for cancer therapy might be applicable to the problem of arterial injury due to restenosis. As noted above, the process of restenosis in some ways is like cancer in that there is a period of time during which smooth muscle cells proliferate. When the proliferation is excessive, such

that the large mass of smooth muscle cells that develops encroaches on the vessel lumen, blood flow to the heart muscle is compromised.

Earlier studies had demonstrated that when smooth muscle cells proliferate, they overexpress certain growth factors, as well as the receptors to which these growth factors bind. Experiments were therefore carried out to determine whether TGFα-PE40 and aFGF-PE40 have the ability to kill rapidly proliferating smooth muscle cells. When these cells were placed in a culture plate and were stimulated to grow rapidly, the cells were found to be extraordinarily sensitive to the cytotoxic effects of both toxins.

While these results were exciting, it was recognized that if these toxins killed all smooth muscle cells, they would not be therapeutically useful—*i.e.,* it would be lethal to the patient. This strategy could be successful only if the rapidly proliferating cells, in preference to quiescent "normal" smooth muscle cells (which had not been injured and were not stimulated to proliferate rapidly), were targeted by the toxins. This was found to be the case; cytotoxicity was 30 times less when cells were in a quiescent state than when they were rapidly proliferating. Additional studies indicated that the receptor to which TGFα-PE40 bound was 40 times more common on the surface of rapidly proliferating cells than on quiescent cells, thereby accounting for the greater sensitivity of rapidly proliferating cells to the toxin.

These studies, conducted on smooth muscle cells in a culture dish, raise the intriguing possibility that the use of recombinant techniques to produce "killer" molecules, which selectively target actively proliferating cells, might be applied to the problem of restenosis following coronary angioplasty. It remains to be seen, however, not only whether the selective cytotoxic effects achieved in culture dishes can be achieved in experimental animals but also whether they can be achieved without the complication of important deleterious action either in the healing response to vascular injury or on nonvascular cells and tissues.

The future

The application of molecular biology techniques to the problem of restenosis of coronary arteries is only one example of an evolving strategy that cardiovascular investigators are pursuing. Whether or not this particular approach proves successful, there is little question that the knowledge and powerful tools derived from molecular biology will be extensively applied to many cardiovascular problems in future years, and heretofore unrecognized opportunities for advancement in the understanding and treatment of heart disease will emerge.

—*Shmuel Banai, M.D.,*
Stephen E. Epstein, M.D.,
and Clay B. Siegall, Ph.D.

Special Report
The World Within: Understanding Autism
by Peter E. Tanguay, M.D.

Since 1938, there have come to our attention a number of children whose condition differed so markedly and uniquely from anything reported so far, that each case merits—and, I hope will eventually receive—a detailed consideration of its fascinating peculiarities.

—Leo Kanner

In 1943 when the German-born U.S. physician Leo Kanner published his paper describing 11 cases of children who showed "autistic disturbances of affective contact," he was already the well-known author of the first American textbook of child psychiatry and an esteemed psychiatrist in the department of pediatrics at Johns Hopkins Hospital in Baltimore, Md. The term *autistic,* from the Greek *autos* ("self"), implied that these youngsters had a unique self-absorption and lack of interest in the world around them. The word was already well known in psychiatry, having been used to describe one of the cardinal features of schizophrenia. Although Kanner published his observations in an obscure journal, it was his hope that others might be inspired to share his fascination with children suffering from this puzzling disorder. They did so to a degree Kanner never could have imagined. In the almost 50 years since he named and described the condition, thousands of books and papers have been published about autism, and millions of dollars have been spent on studies of the syndrome.

Rare but fascinating disorder

Why, one might ask, has there been such avid interest, especially given that autism is a rare condition, much less common than reading or language disorders in children, for example, or schizophrenia or depression in adults? Perhaps it is because autism strikes at the heart of what it is to be human: to be able to relate emotionally to others and to communicate socially. Like Kanner, many investigators have become so absorbed by the enigmatic condition that they have spent their entire research careers studying it.

What has been learned about autism since Kanner's time? It is now known that one in 2,500 people is autistic and that the syndrome occurs about three times more often in males than in females. The prevalence of the syndrome has been found to be similar wherever it has been measured, including Japan and countries in Europe. It occurs equally often in the lower and upper socioeconomic classes, though until the 1970s it had been thought to be more frequent in the latter group. Likewise there are neither racial nor ethnic differences in the prevalence of autism.

What is autism?

Understanding autism was very much on the mind of the actor Dustin Hoffman in late 1987, when he had been selected to play Raymond Babbitt, an autistic adult, in the film *Rain Man.* While considering whether he would undertake the part, Hoffman consulted with several autism experts, this author among them.

A disorder of communication. One aspect of the condition that these authorities emphasized to Hoffman is that the symptoms of autism are thought to represent a failure in social communication. Normally, people communicate information and feeling through more than words and grammar alone. They constantly change the pitch and intensity of their speech, following rules that they learn instinctively while growing up speaking a particular language. These so-called prosodic changes communicate crucial meanings; for example, one's tone of voice might indicate that what one is saying is to be taken at its face value or, alternatively, that it should be taken ironically.

Facial expressions also help to convey feelings such as anger, sadness, guilt, and fear. In addition, there is gesture: sympathy and concern are communicated by a warm embrace; horror, surprise, or embarrassment is conveyed by spontaneously covering the mouth with a hand. Waving the hands and arms adds punctuation to verbal communication. Also essential are the social rules of communication; *i.e.,* ways to start and end a conversation, introduce a new topic, and enter into an ongoing dialogue. Finally, and perhaps most important of all, everyone knows that other people have thoughts that differ from their own, and they become adept at learning what these thoughts might be from watching the subtle cues others send by means of their tone of voice, facial expressions, and gestures.

Children learn these communication skills amazingly early. Babies are born with the ability to express common emotions through universal facial expressions; by three months of age they are able to engage in highly emotionally charged games in which they react and respond as their caretakers display exaggerated facial expressions, gestures, and changes in tone of voice. By 12 months babies know to look to their mother's face when they are uncertain about how to act; many of their actions derive from the emotional message they read in her expression.

While normal infants are adept at these communication skills, children with autism are much less so. In some instances, children with autism seem not to have the slightest awareness of how to communicate their wishes, feelings, and needs, nor do they know how to interpret messages from others. As they grow up, some autistic persons do learn to communicate with good grammar and correct syntax, and their social communication may be only slightly impaired. Even so, their conversation usually has a rote, mechanical quality.

Most children with autism are not diagnosed until 18 months of age or later, though in retrospect, parents often realize that what they took to be an infant's particularly placid and undemanding character was the first manifestation of the condition. The parents may initially take the child to the pediatrician out of concern that the baby may be deaf or because they have noticed that he or she is not interested in playing games such as pat-a-cake and peek-a-boo. They may perhaps observe that the child's eyes do not follow them when they are within sight, that the child does not point to objects to call attention to them. Most children with autism start to speak late, and many do not speak at all.

Other noted features. Children with autism often show other unusual behaviors, such as repeatedly flapping their hands in front of their faces or wiggling their fingers before their eyes. They may be extremely sensitive to or upset by certain sounds or become agitated by minor changes in their everyday routines

or surroundings. And, as they learn to speak, they may continually repeat the words addressed to them, a symptom called echolalia.

An actor masters a role

Once Hoffman had learned about autism from the specialists, he then turned to the *real* experts—autistic people themselves. So that he could himself learn to be autistic, he spent hours trying to understand how they as individuals see the world. Because Raymond, the autistic man in the film, was not mentally retarded, Hoffman got to know similar persons, including Temple Grandin, a woman diagnosed as autistic when she was a child but who has since earned a doctorate in animal sciences and is a livestock-handling consultant in Colorado. Her book about her growing up, *Emergence: Labeled Autistic,* provides a unique "insider's" view of the world of the autistic.

With his perspective thus sharpened, Hoffman traveled to Cincinnati, Ohio, where the first scenes of the film were to be shot. Initially his costar, Tom Cruise, cast as Raymond's younger brother, Charlie, found that playing opposite Hoffman was highly disconcerting. Cruise would speak his lines, expecting a social response from Hoffman. He got none. Remarkably, Hoffman *was* autistic! The film, of course, was a huge success, and Hoffman won an Academy Award for his performance.

Was the portrayal of Raymond Babbitt in the film accurate? To a certain degree it was not. Raymond was not mentally retarded, but 70% of people with autism are. Mentally retarded persons, even those who are quite retarded, can express their feelings normally and can communicate socially unless, of course, they are both autistic and mentally retarded. Further, Ray-

When asked to put four pictures into a sequence so that they tell a story, autistic children were able to successfully order the pictures of an escaped balloon and a trip to the sweet shop (top and center). However, they were puzzled by the bottom group of pictures, in which understanding the events requires an appreciation that what goes on in the mind of another person may conflict with one's own beliefs and expectations. Thus, in the story of the last piece of candy, the autistic children were unable to comprehend the boy's surprise on finding the box empty.

From *Autism* by Uta Frith; © 1989 Basil Blackwell Publishers, Oxford, England

In his Academy Award-winning performance as Raymond in the film Rain Man, *actor Dustin Hoffman convincingly portrayed the autistic person's lack of expression and responsiveness.*

mond was a savant—a word derived from the French *savoir*, meaning "to know," used to describe those very rare individuals who perform astounding feats of mathematical calculation or memory. Raymond could correctly multiply numbers in his head at great speed (faster and more accurately than any normal person could); he could correctly count several hundred toothpicks as they spilled out of a box onto the floor; and he could remember with amazing accuracy what cards had been dealt at the blackjack table in a Las Vegas casino. Very few people with autism are capable of such feats. And, it should be noted, no one has any idea how savants accomplish their awesome acts of brilliance.

Evolving understanding

As previously noted, it was in 1943 that Kanner first called attention to the syndrome of autism. Had the disorder previously gone undetected? What were these persons called before the term *autistic* was applied? Many were undoubtedly simply considered to be retarded, and their inability to function socially went largely unnoticed. Occasionally they may have been singled out. In 1898, in the *Journal of Nervous and Mental Disorders,* psychiatrist Martin Barr reported what he called "an extraordinary case of echolalia." His description was of a person who might well be called autistic today. Barr attributed the young man's handicaps to "transcortical motor aphasia," a condition in which a lesion disconnects various parts of the brain involved in the understanding and production of speech, leading to a loss of speech. The idea, enunciated almost 100 years ago, is surprisingly similar to some of the contemporary neuropsychological theories invoked to explain autism.

In the book *Autism: Explaining the Enigma,* child

psychiatrist Uta Frith proposes that the "wild" boy found and educated by French physician J.-M.-G. Itard in 1801 (the subject of the 1970 film *L'Enfant sauvage* by François Truffaut) may have been autistic. Others have also remarked on this. Frith suggests that some of the "holy fools" of Russia, Christian mystics who wandered about in rags and were said to have prophetic powers, may have been autistic. In the 1950s and 1960s there were some, such as Lauretta Bender and Barbara Fish, child psychiatrists from New York University, who believed that autism and schizophrenia might be the same disease. Studies since then have shown that they are not.

Children who have certain specific brain disorders may appear to be autistic. Roughly 5% of children with the chromosomal abnormality called fragile-X syndrome have symptoms of autism to at least a moderate degree. Rett syndrome, a neurodegenerative disease occurring almost exclusively in females, may in the course of its development resemble autism. Because of this, it has been suggested that all girls with autism should be suspected of having Rett syndrome until proved otherwise. Other conditions that may cause a child to appear autistic are certain serious untreated inborn errors of metabolism, such as phenylketonuria (PKU) and tuberous sclerosis. Autism has also been reported to occur as an aftereffect of encephalitis (inflammation of the brain).

"Bad" parenting: not to blame

Research has provided some general clues to the cause of autism but no specific ones. What is now known for certain is that "bad mothers" do not cause their children to become autistic. The pernicious belief that autism represented withdrawal from a world perceived as rejecting and anxiety provoking was held by many experts for several decades after Kanner's initial description of the disorder. Kanner himself went from believing that autism was biologically caused to believing that it was due to parental rejection, only to return to a biological explanation in later years. Even today the so-called bad mother hypothesis remains popular among clinicians in some countries in Western Europe, though not in England.

Among the more potent forces who helped to discredit this belief were the parents of the autistic. In 1964 Bernard Rimland, a U.S. psychologist with an autistic son, published a book in which he challenged the then-prevailing idea that the condition was caused by psychological trauma. Rimland's was the first book to present evidence that autism is a biological disorder of the brain. Shortly thereafter, a small group of parents founded the National Society for Autistic Children, later changed to Autism Society of America. The society has been a powerful force in bringing about better educational and treatment programs for children and adults with autism.

Search for biological causes

Several studies have confirmed that genetic factors play a part in autism. It has been estimated that a couple who have had one autistic child have about a one-in-50 chance of having a second—*i.e.,* a chance 50 times greater than for parents who have not had an autistic child. Twin studies show that if one fraternal twin is autistic, the chance that the other will be similarly affected is low; among identical twins, on the other hand, the chances that the second twin will be autistic, or will suffer from some type of mental retardation or severe language disorder, is as high as 70 to 80%.

A few recent studies using sophisticated medical imaging techniques such as computed tomography (CT) and magnetic resonance imaging (MRI) have reported finding structural (anatomic) abnormalities in the brains of persons with autism. However, different investigations have located the abnormalities in different areas of the brain, in part because most studies have focused on only a single part of the brain. Several investigators have reported abnormalities in certain areas of the cerebellum and associated brain systems. It has also been reported that the upper brain stem appears smaller in some persons with autism; this is an area of the brain in which there are complex centers for control of attention and for the integration of sensory input with higher cortical operations. Still other researchers have reported various specific lesions and defects in the cerebral hemispheres in some autistic subjects. However, with the exception of Eric Courchesne, a neuropsychologist at the University of California at San Diego, who has found cerebellar abnormalities in most of his autistic subjects, the majority of investigators studying brain structure in autism report abnormalities in only 10–15%.

Why have scientists failed to consistently identify a specific brain defect in autism? It may be that current techniques for examining the brains of living subjects are insufficient to detect such abnormalities. Another possibility is that the abnormalities in brain function occur at the molecular level, in the form of defective activity of the chemical substances that transmit nerve impulses.

Although there was a heavy emphasis on the study of neurobiochemical activity in autistic persons during the 1970s and early 1980s, this research produced only one finding that has stood the test of time: roughly 50% of autistic subjects have higher than normal levels of the neurotransmitter serotonin in their bloodstream. Despite considerable effort, no one to date has been able to explain the relationship of this finding to brain function. More recently, positron emission tomography (PET) has been used to create images of metabolic brain activity in autistic subjects, with mixed results. One study found that autistic persons had signs of increased activity in most areas of

An autistic youngster who attends classes at a public school receives special help from a therapist. Such programs seek to provide academic education in keeping with the child's intelligence level and to offer appropriate social stimulation.

the brain; a second found that this increase was seen to only a mild degree and only in frontal areas. Clearly much more work needs to be done.

Enlightened treatment

Because the core deficits in autism are in social communication, it is very important that an autistic child be placed in an environment where there are people who provide a liberal dose of social stimulation—through conversation, games, or informal play—and who try to elicit social responses from the child. Such programs can best be organized by school districts as part of their regular preschool, grade school, or high school classes. Programs should also have as a goal an academic education that is in keeping with the child's IQ level. Structured programs tend to be more effective than unstructured ones.

Mainstreaming—the integrating of handicapped children into regular classes—is a major issue in the field of autism treatment. Some of its proponents argue that virtually all autistic children of school age should attend classes with normal children and, as adults, should live in integrated, urban group homes such as halfway houses that are not solely for autistic persons. Mainstreaming advocates feel that special schools and classes are stigmatizing and that residences in which there are only handicapped persons are substandard and even dehumanizing. Those with opposing views hold that each person with autism is a unique individual and that, while mainstreaming and urban living may be ideal for some, these options are not the best solution for all. They believe that a wide range of options should be provided so that each family may select the one that is appropriate.

Programs for autistic persons, especially those who are retarded, are usually designed to reinforce desired behaviors through various rewards specific to the individual. Self-stimulatory behaviors (e.g., rocking, hand flapping, body twirling) should be discouraged, as they have been shown to interfere with learning social and cognitive skills. Many of the more successful programs, especially those for children under the age of five, actively involve the parents and other family members in the home. Parents, working in partnership with educators and psychologists, learn what types of play and games work best to help the child attend to social cues. A model program of this sort, called Project TEACH, was developed in the early 1970s by Eric Schopler at the University of North Carolina. The project continues today, with an expanded emphasis on treating young adults.

Magda Campbell, a child and adolescent psychiatrist at New York University, has spent much of her professional career studying the effects of various medications on the symptoms of autism. She has shown that certain tranquilizers, specifically haloperidol (Haldol), judiciously given, with the dose adjusted carefully on an individual basis, may reduce maladaptive behaviors and may make it easier for some children with autism to learn. She stresses that the effects of medication vary from child to child and that it should be used primarily as a temporary adjunct to a well-designed educational and social program. In the mid-1980s claims were made that fenfluramine (Pondamin), a stimulant similar to the amphetamines, could lead to dramatic improvements in children who were autistic, but extensive studies since then have shown that fenfluramine is not effective in autism.

Whatever the chosen treatment, the emotional needs of the parents and siblings must be balanced against the special needs of the autistic person. Support from other parents, as well as sibling-to-sibling support, available through the local chapters of the Autism Society of America, can be helpful in guiding the family to its own most appropriate course of action. A recent best-selling novel, *Family Pictures* by Sue Miller, provides an intergenerational perspective on the life of a family with a retarded autistic son. Although the boy, Randall, is present only in occasional interludes in the story's action, his presence is always intensely felt. Long after he has gone to live in a group home, a grown sister reflects, "If anyone had asked me about our family—where we all were and so forth—I might have said there was one still at home. . . . Psychologically [Randall] was still there. Among them. That he was always the one who needed them, needed their protection. The one who had to be arranged for, even a thousand miles away." The presence of a severely mentally handicapped individual always has profound emotional effects on other family members. The effect is not always negative, however—witness the brother or sister who becomes a teacher of handicapped children as a result of having a retarded sibling.

Dealing with self-destructive behavior

A small number of autistic children, usually ones who are quite retarded, may engage in repetitive head-banging, self-biting, or self-hitting. Children have been known to lose their eyesight and to develop scars and disfiguring lesions as a result of this behavior. Some go so far as to endanger their own lives. No medications are known to have a direct effect in stopping these activities. Potent tranquilizers may reduce such behavior by making the child lethargic and impairing consciousness, but these effects obviously make it very difficult for the child to take any active part in social treatment programs.

Autistic persons who engage in these behaviors often do not speak, and it has been suggested that the self-injurious actions are in part a result of severe frustration over inability to communicate. Ingenious programs designed to aid them in communicating may help. In one family the parents took photographs of the important objects and people in their son's everyday environment. They put the pictures in albums and on a bulletin board so that their son could point to the photos in order to communicate his needs or wishes. Once, when the father was to be away from home for several days, his photo was pasted on the calendar over his return date; each morning the boy crossed off another day in anticipation of the father's return. The parents felt that this system for helping the son to communicate kept him from engaging in self-destructive behavior.

A new ending for *Rain Man*

In the film *Rain Man*, a court eventually took Raymond away from Charlie and returned him to the protected environment of the institution where he had spent much of his life. Many moviegoers were disappointed with this ending and wrote letters to newspapers saying so.

What alternative endings might there have been? One possibility might be that Raymond would return to the institution for a time to say farewell to his friends there. Then, with the substantial sum of money Raymond had inherited, he and Vernon, the devoted staff member with whom he had developed a strong relationship, would go to live in an apartment in California near Charlie. Charlie would join the Autism Society of America, where he would learn even more about the condition and how he could best continue to help Raymond. Raymond would find work, perhaps as a stock boy in a local video rental store; he would have a "job coach" who would help him learn how to behave socially with his fellow workers.

In one of the movie's earlier versions, the final scene was of Charlie and Raymond lazily fishing on a riverbank on an idyllic summer day. Such a happy ending—after all—would not have been entirely unrealistic.

Hepatitis

The word *hepatitis* is derived from the Greek words *hepar* ("liver") and *itis* ("inflammation"). It therefore refers to any inflammation of the liver, regardless of cause. Descriptions of a disease similar to viral hepatitis were contained in the Babylonian Talmud (*c.* 5th century AD). Beginning in the 8th century, periodic epidemics of hepatitis were described, many of which occurred during wars. After World War II, studies using human volunteers demonstrated that at least two agents caused viral hepatitis. These were called the hepatitis A and B viruses. Since that time three more—named C, D, and E—have been identified. Hepatitis can also be caused by medications and toxins that affect the liver, especially alcohol, and by bacterial, fungal, and parasitic infections. The five known hepatitis viruses are the main infectious causes, however. Significant progress in understanding these viral infections has been made over the past 25 years, resulting in improved detection, treatment, and prevention of this worldwide disease.

Symptoms and diagnosis

The liver is the largest and heaviest solid organ within the body. It functions as both a "factory," converting the nutrients in food into energy, and a "waste-management plant," modifying various chemicals (including many drugs) and excreting them into the gastrointestinal tract through the bile ducts. When the liver is inflamed, these functions are impaired or cease altogether. In rare cases, viral hepatitis leads to the massive destruction of all liver cells, resulting in death.

The signs and symptoms of hepatitis are similar regardless of the cause. They include fatigue, loss of energy and appetite, weakness, muscle aches, decreased sense of smell and taste, fever, nausea, vomiting, abdominal pain, and, less commonly, rash, joint pains, and arthritis. As any of these findings may be present in other disorders, and none is a specific indication of hepatitis, the illness may be unsuspected or misdiagnosed. Some patients with hepatitis become jaundiced, developing a yellow discoloration of the skin and the whites of their eyes, tea-colored urine, and clay-colored bowel movements.

Even in patients who are symptom free, evidence of either active or prior hepatitis infection can be detected by laboratory tests. Routine tests may include an evaluation of the liver enzymes called aminotransferases. When the liver is inflamed, these enzymes are released from liver cells into the bloodstream, providing a sensitive indicator of liver disease. Another test for hepatitis involves an assay of the amount of bilirubin, a yellow pigment, in the blood. Bilirubin is a normal breakdown product of hemoglobin, the protein that carries oxygen and imparts the red color to blood. Bilirubin is released into the bloodstream from red blood cells at the end of their normal life-span. Healthy liver cells modify bilirubin and excrete it into the bile. When the liver cells are diseased, however, bilirubin cannot be modified or excreted, and it accumulates in the bloodstream, causing jaundice.

Although the nonspecific tests mentioned above identify inflammation of the liver, they do not identify the cause. Specific diagnostic tests for the viral agents outlined below are thus necessary. The incubation period (time from infection to onset of illness), modes of transmission, outcome of infection, and appropriate preventive measures are different for hepatitis A, B, C, D, and E. While it is likely that other hepatitis-causing viral agents exist, these five account for the majority of cases of infectious liver disease in the world.

The murky waters of the Tiber River were cited as a source of hepatitis A virus during an outbreak of the disease in Rome in the late 1980s. Some of the city's residents called the contaminated waterway an "open-air sewer."

Infants and young children infected with hepatitis A often exhibit no symptoms. Anyone who is responsible for the care of children in diapers is at risk of getting or spreading the virus that causes the disease. To protect both themselves and their young charges, attendants in day-care centers should wash their hands thoroughly after each diaper change or wear a fresh pair of disposable gloves for each. Another crucial safeguard in such settings is the disinfection of diaper-changing areas.

Hepatitis A

Hepatitis A is the most common type of hepatitis worldwide. It is rarely fatal; infected persons recover completely after one to four weeks of illness. Occasionally the illness recurs within three months after the initial episode. Those who have been infected develop antibodies that protect them against further episodes of hepatitis A.

Hepatitis A virus (HAV) is contracted enterically—by the ingestion of contaminated food or water—and is spread by poor personal hygiene and inadequate sanitation. After ingestion, the virus enters the bloodstream and reproduces in the liver. Illness occurs an average of 28 days after exposure. The virus passes from the liver into the feces prior to the onset of illness; thus, the disease usually has spread within a community by the time the first case is recognized. Antibodies to HAV generally can be detected in the patient's blood at the beginning of the illness, thereby revealing the type of virus responsible.

Older people who become infected with HAV have more severe disease than do younger ones. For example, only 5% of children under the age of eight who are infected with HAV develop jaundice, compared with up to 90% of adults. In many less developed countries that still have inadequate water and sewerage systems, virtually everyone in the population is infected early in life. Because such early infection usually is not associated with illness and because it confers protection against future HAV infection, large outbreaks of symptomatic hepatitis A do not occur in these countries. With industrialization and improved sanitation, on the other hand, childhood infection declines, and increased numbers of people reaching adulthood are susceptible to the virus. The potential for exposure to HAV in less developed countries remains significant, and infection in susceptible adults leads to symptomatic disease. This creates a paradox: as the frequency of infection in the community (*i.e.,* number of people with antibodies to HAV) decreases, the number of cases of symptomatic illness due to HAV increases. Among people in developed countries, the spread of the virus occurs as a result of contact with infected individuals—particularly within households and in day-care centers where young children have not yet been toilet trained—and travel in less developed countries.

Researchers are currently working on two different types of vaccines for HAV—inactivated and live virus vaccines. Because the virus grows slowly in the laboratory, both are expensive to produce. However, it is likely that an inactivated virus vaccine will become commercially available within the next few years. Recombinant DNA technology is beginning to show promise in vaccine development and may prove less costly than conventional methods. Until a vaccine is available, short-term protection against hepatitis A is afforded by injections of gamma globulin (antibody-rich human blood protein), which can be given as a preventive measure to persons who are strongly suspected of having been exposed.

Hepatitis B

Unlike hepatitis A, hepatitis B causes chronic infection as well as acute illness. Worldwide, it is a significant cause of chronic liver disease, including cirrhosis (replacement of functioning liver cells with fibrous tissue), and, according to the World Health Organization, it is the ninth major cause of death. Hundreds of millions of people are chronically infected with the hepatitis B virus (HBV). Such persons are about 100 times more likely to develop liver cancer (hepatocellular carcinoma) than those who are uninfected. This makes HBV second only to tobacco as a known human carcinogen. Fortunately, effective vaccines have been developed to prevent HBV infection.

The time between exposure to the virus and the onset of symptoms is between 40 days and six months. Although the illness is often indistinguishable from hepatitis A, it tends to be somewhat more severe and

343

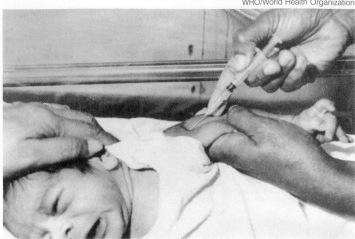

In Singapore, Saudi Arabia, and most countries of the Western Pacific region, all newborns are routinely immunized against hepatitis B. Infants born with the hepatitis B virus have high rates of lifelong, chronic infection; female children who are infected may pass the disease on to their own offspring. Mass immunization of newborns aims to break this vicious cycle. Because the incidence of hepatitis B in the U.S. has been increasing and adults at risk have not taken advantage of the vaccine, some health officials are now recommending routine childhood immunization.

protracted. As mentioned above, some people will develop chronic infection, resulting in either persistent infection without evidence of active liver disease or active liver disease that progresses to cirrhosis.

HBV (and related hepatitis viruses found in animals) has several unusual features, including the method of reproducing its genome (genetic material). The HBV genome is a partially double-stranded, partially single-stranded circle of DNA. (The other four known types of hepatitis viruses have RNA rather than DNA genomes.) Once an HBV particle has infected a cell, it employs the cell's own synthesis machinery to make numerous RNA copies of the viral DNA via a process called transcription. It then uses a viral enzyme known as reverse transcriptase to transcribe this RNA back into new copies of the viral genome, which are released from the cell in the form of new virus particles. The usual flow of genetic material in living cells is DNA to RNA; thus, the RNA-to-DNA step used by HBV is the reverse of normal. The only other viruses known to employ this reverse process are the so-called retroviruses, a group that includes the human immunodeficiency virus (HIV), which causes AIDS.

The infectious HBV particle consists of a "core" of DNA and protein surrounded by an "envelope" composed of a different protein. Large amounts of this envelope protein are produced during infection. The protein can be readily detected in the blood and serves as a marker of active infection. Antibodies to the core and envelope proteins can also be detected in the blood, and the type of antibodies present in an individual indicates whether the infection occurred recently or some time in the more remote past.

HBV is spread when skin or mucous membranes are penetrated by contaminated blood or other bodily fluids. In the United States and other developed countries, transmission occurs primarily through sexual contact with infected individuals or during intravenous (IV) drug use. Use of contaminated or improperly sterilized needles and instruments in such procedures as ear

piercing, tattooing, shaving, or acupuncture can also result in transmission. Furthermore, male homosexuals, heterosexuals who have multiple partners, and health workers with occupational exposure to blood are at risk of acquiring hepatitis B, as are infants born to infected women.

While the number of hepatitis B cases in the U.S. remained constant between 1981 and 1988, hepatitis B acquired through homosexual activity and in health care work decreased by 62 and 75%, respectively. Among homosexuals this decrease was presumably related to modification of high-risk sexual behaviors, undoubtedly because of fears about possible exposure to HIV. In health care personnel the decline was probably a direct result of immunization with hepatitis B vaccine and more careful attention to the standard precautions used when handling blood samples, needles, surgical instruments, and the like.

During this same period, however, HBV infections acquired through IV drug use increased by 80%, making this the most common mode of transmission. Simultaneously, hepatitis B acquired via heterosexual exposure increased 38%, paralleling recent increases in cases of heterosexually acquired syphilis. These data indicate that the current approach of vaccinating only those considered to be at high risk for hepatitis B has not been effective in reducing the incidence of disease. Universal childhood vaccination was therefore recommended by an advisory committee of the U.S. Public Health Service in 1991 as a more efficacious strategy for preventing this sometimes fatal liver disease in adulthood. The state of New York passed a law in 1990 requiring that all pregnant women be screened for HBV in hopes of identifying and treating newborns at risk.

Of all those infected with HBV, 5 to 10% become chronic carriers of the virus. The likelihood of becoming a chronic carrier is greater in individuals who have asymptomatic disease. As with hepatitis A, infants and young children usually have asymptomatic infection.

Consequently, infants infected at birth have high rates of both asymptomatic infection and subsequent development of chronic infection.

In Asia and sub-Saharan Africa the usual method of transmission is from an infected mother to her infant during birth (*i.e.,* vertical transmission) or shortly after. If the child is female and infected, she will probably become chronically infected and may subsequently transmit the virus to her own children. In these regions, 5 to 20% of the population are chronically infected.

A comparison of the geographic distribution of liver cancer with the prevalence of chronic HBV infection illustrates the link between these two diseases. There is also experimental evidence to support the theory that HBV plays a part in the development of liver cancer. Laboratory animals infected with a virus closely related to hepatitis B develop liver cancer. In humans the role of other cofactors in the development of liver cancer remains to be determined; however, environmental carcinogens and alcohol ingestion are suspected of contributing. Liver cancer usually does not develop until 20 to 50 years after infection.

The method by which HBV contributes to liver cancer is unknown. The virus may either directly trigger cancer development by a mechanism yet to be determined or indirectly induce cancer by causing persistent inflammation of the infected liver. The HBV genome does not appear to contain a cancer-causing gene (oncogene), and the long latency period between infection and the appearance of liver cancer further argues against the existence of such a gene. In some forms of cancer, the insertion of viral DNA into the chromosome of the infected cell occurs at a specific location known to affect the normal control of cell growth. Extensive studies of HBV-infected liver cells and cancerous liver cells indicate that the DNA of the hepatitis B virus is integrated into the chromosome of the cancer cell, but it is inserted at random sites. Thus, specific disruption of genes controlling liver cell growth should not occur as a direct result of HBV infection.

Two types of hepatitis B vaccine are currently licensed for use in the U.S. The first was made by purifying HBV particles from the blood of infected persons and inactivating the virus by several chemical treatments. This HBV vaccine was the first human vaccine to be derived from human blood. Recombinant DNA technology has also produced a vaccine that is based on the envelope protein of the virus. It was the first recombinant-DNA-based vaccine to be licensed for use in humans. Several other recombinant-based hepatitis B vaccines are under development. As noted above, the groups at highest risk for HBV have not generally taken advantage of the available vaccines; fewer than 40% of U.S. health care personnel have been vaccinated, for example. Vaccines therefore have not yet had a significant impact on the overall incidence of hepatitis B. More widespread use is critical for eradicating this disease. In less developed countries mass vaccination immediately following birth will be necessary to reverse the mother-to-infant cycle of infection. Following exposure to the virus, a combination of gamma globulin (from persons with high levels of HBV antibodies) and vaccination can prevent up to 90% of HBV infections if they are given rapidly. The drug interferon alpha has been shown to produce long-term remissions in up to one-third of patients with chronic infection.

Hepatitis C

Following the discovery of the hepatitis A and B viruses in the late 1960s and early 1970s, S.M. Feinstone and colleagues at the U.S. National Institutes of Health described another type of hepatitis that occurred in as many as 7 to 10% of blood transfusion recipients. Over 90% of these cases were not caused by either the hepatitis A or B virus; hence, the term "non-A, non-B" hepatitis was coined. Although extensive work with an animal model of infection demonstrated that it was caused by another protein-enveloped virus, the major causative agent remained a mystery until 1988, when, using recombinant DNA methods, scientists succeeded in cloning the genome of the non-A, non-B hepatitis virus. Since that time a diagnostic test has been developed to detect antibodies to the virus in a patient's blood. An antibody test is also used by most U.S. blood banks to screen donor blood. The virus has been named the hepatitis C virus (HCV). In the U.S. alone it is responsible for some 150,000 to 300,000 cases per year.

HCV is predominantly blood borne, although it appears that other modes of transmission can occur. One study of blood drawn from persons who had developed posttransfusion hepatitis indicated that 45 to 88% of cases were caused by HCV. In addition to transmission via transfusion, it is also spread by other forms of blood exposure. High-risk groups include hemophiliacs, drug addicts, dialysis patients, and medical personnel. HCV has been found in people who have no known history of any such exposure as well, indicating that at least a percentage of transmission occurs through household or sexual contact. Additionally, transmission can occur from mother to infant at or around the time of birth. HCV appears to be transmitted much more efficiently by blood exposure than by other routes, however. With the development of improved diagnostic tests for HCV, a clearer understanding of the transmission and extent of hepatitis C will undoubtedly emerge in the next few years. Unfortunately, the current test often does not detect the disease until months after the onset of illness. Moreover, it may miss the diagnosis completely. Thus, many persons with posttransfusion hepatitis who do not test positive for HCV may, in fact, have hepatitis C. Newer diagnostic tests, which appear to be more sensitive than the existing one, are being developed and will be available for widespread use soon. Nevertheless, the possibility exists that other, as yet unidentified agents may occasionally cause posttransfusion hepatitis.

The clinical manifestations of hepatitis C are more insidious than those of hepatitis A and B, and a more indolent and prolonged course is the norm. In fact, approximately 75% of persons with hepatitis C do not develop jaundice, and it is common for the infection to go undiagnosed. In spite of the mild initial illness, 50 to 70% of infected persons develop chronic hepatitis, and up to 25% of infected persons ultimately develop cirrhosis of the liver. End-stage liver disease may already be present by the time the infected person first seeks medical care. Among persons with liver cancer, 40 to 70% of those with no evidence of HBV infection are positive for HCV. Thus, hepatitis C may also have a direct or an indirect role in the development of liver cancer. Chronic hepatitis C is one of the most common reasons for liver transplantation in adults. As with chronic hepatitis B, treatment with interferon alpha reduces disease activity, although the beneficial response is often transient. No HCV vaccine has yet been developed.

Hepatitis D (delta hepatitis)

In 1977 Mario Rizzetto and co-workers at the Ospedale Molinette, Turin, Italy, described a new protein found in patients with hepatitis B, which they called

Now that a diagnostic test has been developed for hepatitis C, liver specialists have confirmed that this blood-borne virus can be transmitted via donor organs and that it may be a significant cause of posttransplantation liver disease.

L. O'Shaughnessy—Medichrome/The Stock Shop

the "delta" protein. Subsequently, it became clear that this protein was not an HBV protein but rather was produced by a separate virus, called the delta agent. In the spirit of naming viral hepatitis agents alphabetically, this one was designated hepatitis D virus (HDV).

Hepatitis D must be considered in the context of hepatitis B because it can reproduce only in cells that are actively infected with HBV. HDV is an RNA-containing "defective" virus. Consequently, hepatitis D can occur as a "coinfection," being transmitted concomitantly with hepatitis B virus, or it can "superinfect" a person who already has chronic hepatitis B. HDV is transmitted by sexual contact or by exposure to contaminated blood. When HDV is transmitted with HBV, the illness resembles other forms of hepatitis; however, the infection tends to be more severe. Death results in as many as 20% of people with combined hepatitis B and D, compared with fewer than 1% of those who have hepatitis B alone. Coinfection with HDV and HBV does not increase the risk of developing chronic hepatitis B.

As in coinfection, when HDV infects someone already actively infected with HBV (superinfection), the outcome is more severe than with other forms of hepatitis. When chronic hepatitis B is complicated by HDV infection, a bout of acute hepatitis occurs, followed in almost all cases by the development of chronic delta hepatitis. Reports indicate that up to 80% of persons with chronic delta hepatitis develop cirrhosis and complications of chronic liver disease. In contrast, only 15 to 30% of individuals with chronic hepatitis B experience these complications. HDV does not appear to be linked to liver cancer, perhaps because infected individuals tend to die from complications of liver disease before the passage of the 20 to 50 years usually required for liver cancer to develop.

Diagnosis of HDV infection should be considered in persons with severe hepatitis B, in persons with chronic hepatitis B who develop acute hepatitis, or in persons with rapidly progressive HBV-induced liver disease. If active hepatitis B is not detected, HDV infection cannot be present. Antibodies to HDV can be detected in the blood of individuals with chronic HBV and HDV infection. However, in individuals with acute HBV complicated with HDV coinfection, the antibody response to HDV is not very brisk and is often short-lived. Thus, the diagnosis can be missed by current tests.

Hepatitis D is common in certain regions of the world, especially in Mediterranean areas and the Middle East. Up to 40% of Middle Easterners chronically infected with HBV will have evidence of HDV infection. The distribution of HDV is not uniform in these high-prevalence areas, however, and lower rates are found within them, particularly in southern Italy and northern Africa. Hepatitis D is uncommon in the United States, South America, and northern Europe. In these areas

HDV infection has occurred mainly in groups receiving multiple transfusions and in IV drug abusers. It is not known why hepatitis D is found more commonly in some groups with high rates of hepatitis B (e.g., transfusion recipients) than in others (such as homosexual men and health care workers). HDV infection appears to be rare in Asia, in spite of the high prevalence of chronic hepatitis B. Hepatitis D can also cause epidemics, usually in isolated populations in less developed regions of the world, although it is not understood how the virus is introduced into these populations.

Prevention of hepatitis B will automatically prevent hepatitis D. Thus, hepatitis B vaccination and hepatitis B immune globulin are effective in preventing coinfection with HDV. Persons with chronic hepatitis B remain at risk for superinfection by HDV and should be counseled about the dangers of HDV and advised to avoid behaviors associated with transmission of the virus (e.g., drug abuse, sexual promiscuity). No proven therapy lessens the severity or slows the rate of progression of hepatitis D, but the results of some small studies indicate that interferon alpha may inhibit the virus and improve liver cell function. This effect appears to be transient, however, and further study is needed. Liver transplantation for patients with chronic hepatitis D has been reported to be successful in some individuals. Because of the side effects, costs, and experimental nature of this form of treatment—and because of the scarcity of donor organs—more study is needed before transplantation can be widely considered.

Hepatitis E

In the early 1980s scientists from different parts of the world identified a fifth viral cause of hepatitis. Prior to that time, several large outbreaks of hepatitis caused by contaminated drinking water had been carefully evaluated. Tests indicated that neither hepatitis A nor hepatitis B was involved. Viral particles were subsequently isolated from the stool of infected individuals, and scientists were able to produce hepatitis in chimpanzees by infecting them with these specimens. Outbreaks of human disease in different parts of the world were ultimately found to be related to the same heretofore unknown virus. It was called hepatitis E virus (HEV) for epidemic, or enterically transmitted, hepatitis.

In the short time since hepatitis E was first recognized, much has been learned about the virus, largely from the chimpanzee model. Infected chimpanzee liver specimens provided HEV genetic material, which led to the cloning of the virus in 1990. The virus contains RNA but is not related to the other RNA-containing hepatitis viruses (HAV, HCV, and HDV).

The clinical manifestations of hepatitis E are similar to those of the other forms of viral hepatitis except that severe infection and death are more common. Approximately 1% of HEV patients will die; the mortality rate is particularly high in pregnant women (up to 40%). The time from infection to illness averages 40 days, slightly longer than in HAV (the other enteric form). Secondary spread of HEV within families is unusual, perhaps because much less virus is present in the stool of persons with HEV than in those with HAV.

HEV has been documented in Asia, India, Africa, Peru, and Mexico and may be the most common cause of jaundice and acute hepatitis in these locations. It has not been found in outbreaks of hepatitis in the United States or western Europe. Methods to detect antibodies to HEV proteins, now only experimental, show promise and should lead to a clearer understanding of the natural history and epidemiology of this disease.

—*Jack Thomas Stapleton, M.D.*

Neurology

Exciting discoveries and steady incremental progress each contributed to recent advances in understanding disorders of the brain and other parts of the nervous system. Alzheimer's disease received a major share of attention as medical researchers continued to seek an improved picture of its prevalence and causes and to search out new avenues for diagnosis and treatment. Studies of the nerve-cell death common to a variety of neurological diseases led to a unifying concept of the process and suggested fresh therapeutic approaches. Breakthroughs in uncovering the genetic basis for muscular dystrophy and neurofibromatosis brightened prospects for gene therapy as a means of abolishing or alleviating these presently incurable diseases.

Alzheimer's disease: new gains

Alzheimer's disease is a common, gradually progressive dementia—*i.e.*, a severe decline in intellectual abilities—characterized by accumulation in the brain of two kinds of structural abnormalities, called neuritic plaques and neurofibrillary tangles. Research directed toward understanding this condition has made considerable gains in recent years, ranging from the development of diagnostic tests and trials of new medications to insight into the disease mechanism. While a cure is not yet within reach, researchers in the field are optimistic that one will be found.

One of the more important recent developments involves recognizing the prevalence of Alzheimer's disease in the community. The disease was once thought rare but is now known to be one of the most common afflictions of the elderly. A surge of interest among physicians, scientists, and the public came in the late 1970s and early '80s when epidemiological studies showed that the number of people who have dementia of the Alzheimer's type increases dramatically with age. As early as 1976 a group led by Robert Katzman of the University of California at Los Angeles calculated that Alzheimer's disease is the fourth leading killer among elderly Americans and suggested that the number of affected individuals is nothing short of an epidemic. Initial studies indicated that 5–15% of the population over age 65 have dementia and that a majority of this group have Alzheimer's disease.

A more recent, somewhat controversial study headed by Denis A. Evans of Brigham and Women's Hospital and Harvard Medical School, Boston, suggests that even these sobering statistics are too low. After giving a brief memory test to more than 3,000 persons living in a Boston community, followed by a more extensive examination of some of them, they concluded that of everyone in this group over age 65, 10.3% had probable Alzheimer's disease. Of those between age 65 and 74, 3% had Alzheimer's; of those between 75 and 84, 18.7%; and, remarkably, of those over age 85, 47.2%. In other words, the chance is about 50-50 that a person who lives to be 85 will develop Alzheimer's disease. These numbers emphasize the scope of the problem and suggest that because people are living longer on average, more and more individuals will become Alzheimer's victims.

For the most part, doctors cannot predict who those victims will be. Nevertheless, there are rare families in which Alzheimer's disease seems to be inherited in a dominant fashion; thus, in every generation about half the family members get the disease. The symptoms of Alzheimer's in these individuals are identical to those of anyone else afflicted, although frequently they begin at a relatively early age, in the fifties or sixties. In 1987 Peter St. George-Hyslop, James Gusella, Rudy Tanzi, and co-workers at Massachusetts General Hospital, Boston, reported on the genetic analysis of four such families, suggesting that a gene located on chromosome 21 was associated with developing Alzheimer's disease. This news was exciting because it had been

known that another disease that is caused by a problem with chromosome 21, Down syndrome, also strongly predisposed to development of Alzheimer's. In any case, it was assumed that members of those families prone to developing Alzheimer's would all have the same gene defect. Further study of more families throughout the world, however, led to a surprise: not all families showed linkage of their disease to chromosome 21.

In a study published in 1991 by John Hardy of St. Mary's Hospital Medical School, London, 2 families (out of 25 families studied) had a specific mutation in a gene carried on chromosome 21 that is responsible for a protein called the amyloid precursor protein (APP). This is the first identified gene to be associated with Alzheimer's disease pathology. The finding is especially intriguing because amyloid, formed from a fragment of APP, builds up in the brains of all patients with Alzheimer's disease as a component of neuritic plaques. Why the mutation, which amounts to a change of one amino acid building block in APP, would lead to accumulation of the amyloid fragment and why that process in turn would lead to dementia remain targets of intensive research.

Diagnosis of Alzheimer's disease is based primarily on a characteristic clinical picture of worsening memory loss, problems in verbal expression, personality changes, and other signs of failing intellect that lead, over a 5–10-year period on average, to a profound dementia. Such symptoms suggest Alzheimer's, but a variety of other illnesses can mimic the disease. Because effective therapy exists for some of these other illnesses, doctors will call for tests, including computed tomography (CT) of the brain and blood chemistry studies, to look for other causes of memory loss. An absolute diagnosis of Alzheimer's disease can be made only through examination of brain tissue under a microscope, an evaluation not usually possible until after death. Consequently, there is high

Retired engineer George Rehnquist, whose wife, Lucille, is afflicted with Alzheimer's disease, has campaigned to persuade the U.S. Food and Drug Administration to approve the drug tacrine as a treatment for the disease. Originally a promising drug candidate, tacrine was later shown in trials to provide no substantial benefit to patients and to carry a risk for liver damage. Recently medical experts, officials, and families of Alzheimer's victims have taken issue over whether, in view of the inexorably deadly nature of Alzheimer's disease and the present lack of treatments, even marginal benefits from tacrine therapy outweigh its potential toxic effects.

Robert E. Kollar/The New York Times

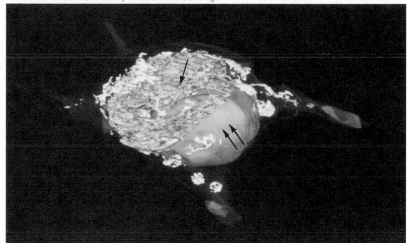

Mark H. Ellisman, M.D., University of California at San Diego

A supercomputer-generated image of a nerve cell from the brain of an Alzheimer's disease victim details the location of abnormal fibrous material (the neurofibrillary tangle; single arrow) that may be responsible for displacing the cell nucleus (double arrows) from its normal position. Such three-dimensional images, made by means of computer image analysis and electron microscopy of individual brain cells, are providing fresh insight into the defects in cellular structure seen in Alzheimer's patients and the ways those defects lead to the symptoms characteristic of the disease.

interest in developing a laboratory test that can accurately diagnose Alzheimer's disease in the living patient. It was reported in 1990 that a new test based on Alz-50, an antibody identified by Peter Davies of the Albert Einstein College of Medicine, Bronx, N.Y., can differentiate chemically between brains affected by Alzheimer's and nonaffected brains. The assay measures the amount of a substance called Alzheimer's disease associated protein (ADAP) in brain tissue, and it may be able to do the same in samples of cerebrospinal fluid obtained from patients via a lumbar puncture (spinal tap). Although the exact identity of ADAP is still controversial, most evidence suggests that it belongs to a family of cellular proteins, called tau proteins, that had earlier been identified as a major constituent of neurofibrillary tangles.

Neurofibrillary tangles, along with neuritic plaques, accumulate in the brains of patients with Alzheimer's disease and destroy neurons (nerve cells) in various parts of the brain, including the hippocampus and basal forebrain. Because both the hippocampus and the basal forebrain are believed to be important in memory function, damage in these areas is thought to contribute to the memory impairments of Alzheimer's disease. Basal forebrain neurons make a neurotransmitter (a chemical carrier of signals between neurons) called acetylcholine, and so the lack of acetylcholine, a deficiency found in the brains of Alzheimer's victims, may contribute to the symptoms of the disease. Accordingly, several medications intended to increase the amount of acetylcholine in the brain have been tested for efficacy in treating symptoms. Perhaps the most noted is tacrine (tetrahydroaminoacridine) because of a 1986 study that suggested that the drug led to a marked improvement in symptoms of Alzheimer's disease. Subsequent studies, unfortunately, failed to show any substantial benefit, and in 1991 a U.S. Food and Drug Administration report raised questions about the data on which the original report was based. As of

mid-1991 a very large independent study on tacrine being run by a consortium of medical schools was still in progress.

Another drug used for many years to treat Alzheimer's disease is Hydergine, a combination of compounds known as ergoloid mesylates, but its benefits have remained controversial. In a study reported in 1990 that compared the effects of a newer preparation of the drug (Hydergine-LC) with those of a placebo in 80 elderly individuals with Alzheimer's disease, no improvement was noted after 24 weeks.

Although the results from current drug trials are not particularly encouraging, new trials are being planned that will explore other avenues of therapy. Nerve growth factor (NGF), a substance made by the body that is necessary for survival of basal forebrain neurons, is widely regarded as a promising candidate for therapy, although it needs to be tested more extensively in experimental animals and in human volunteers before clinical trials are possible. Another medication that may prove useful in slowing the progression of Alzheimer's disease is Deprenyl (selegiline), which in recent clinical trials has been shown to retard another chronic neurodegenerative illness, Parkinson's disease. Finally, medical researchers are studying the details of the normal fates of the amyloid precursor protein and of tau proteins in order to learn why these molecules accumulate abnormally as plaques and tangles in Alzheimer's disease.

Preventing nerve-cell death

A large number of disorders having neurological involvement are characterized by death of neurons. In some, like stroke or low blood sugar, cells die rapidly. In others, like Parkinson's disease or Huntington's disease, there is a slow, relentless death of neurons over many years. The loss of particular populations of neurons is responsible for the particular symptoms of the latter two diseases. In Parkinson's disease loss

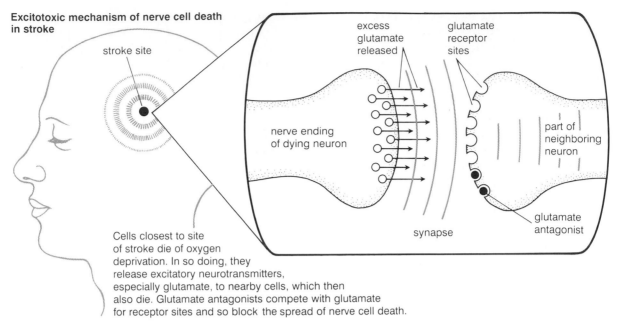

Excitotoxic mechanism of nerve cell death in stroke

stroke site

excess glutamate released

glutamate receptor sites

nerve ending of dying neuron

part of neighboring neuron

synapse

glutamate antagonist

Cells closest to site of stroke die of oxygen deprivation. In so doing, they release excitatory neurotransmitters, especially glutamate, to nearby cells, which then also die. Glutamate antagonists compete with glutamate for receptor sites and so block the spread of nerve cell death.

Although diminished blood flow to local areas of brain tissue is directly responsible for some of the cell death in stroke, an excitotoxic mechanism involving neurotransmitters may extend the destruction to cells of adjacent tissue. Drugs that interfere with this mechanism show promise in limiting stroke-caused brain damage.

of nerve cells that use dopamine as a neurotransmitter results in slowing of voluntary body movements, rigidity, and a characteristic tremor at rest. In Huntington's disease nerve cells are lost in areas of the brain controlling movement. Victims develop random jerky movements of the head and extremities, an effect termed *chorea,* from the Greek for "dance."

The cause of nerve-cell death in these diseases and how to prevent it are among the greatest challenges facing neurologists. Recent evidence has led to a unifying concept, called excitotoxicity, about the mechanism of cell death. According to this idea, excitatory neurotransmitters (those that stimulate neurons into activity) can cause nerve cell death in some disease states. The major excitatory transmitter in the brain is the amino acid glutamate (glutamic acid). It normally is released locally at synapses, the connections between neurons, where it travels from the neurons that release it to molecular receptors on the target neurons. In disease states glutamate can be released in abnormally large amounts. Under these circumstances it causes calcium to build up inside nerve cells, an effect that ultimately causes cell death. This mechanism is now thought to play a role in the cell death that accompanies stroke, low blood sugar, and several degenerative diseases of the nervous system. Drugs that are antagonists to glutamate—*i.e.,* that compete with glutamate at synapses for access to glutamate receptors—have been developed, and these have been shown to block nerve cell damage in models of stroke in experimental animals. Attempts to test these drugs in humans are just beginning.

An interesting example of a toxic exposure to an excitotoxin occurred in 1987 on Prince Edward Island in Canada. People ate mussels contaminated by algae that produce an excitotoxin known as domoic acid. They later developed gastrointestinal symptoms and seizures, and many had to be hospitalized. A small number suffered permanent memory loss and a loss of neurons in a region of the brain critical for the formation of new memories. Similar results have been obtained with this compound in experimental animals.

A possible role for excitotoxins in Huntington's disease has been suggested by the finding that injections of excitotoxins into the brains of experimental animals cause damage in a way that bears a striking resemblance to the disease process; the injections destroy those neurons that degenerate in Huntington's and spare those that resist degeneration. Research on Parkinson's disease received a boost in the early 1980s from the observation that some drug addicts who had injected themselves with an impure synthetic narcotic developed Parkinson's disease. The contaminant, dubbed MPTP, was isolated and found to produce Parkinson's disease in monkeys. The mechanism by which it kills nerve cells, however, has remained unclear. Recent research has shown that the cell death caused by MPTP can be prevented with glutamate antagonists, suggesting that the process occurs by an excitotoxic mechanism. Another study has demonstrated that MPTP-induced cell death also can be prevented with a newly characterized growth factor called brain-derived neurotrophic factor. Such results from animal models of neurological diseases may lead to treatments that halt nerve-cell death in both stroke and degenerative diseases.

Another neurological abnormality in which excitatory neurotransmitters like glutamate play a role is epileptic seizures. Seizures are caused by an abnormal firing of neurons in the brain. Once a group of neurons fires, the electrical activity then spreads to the rest of the brain, causing loss of consciousness. The phasic jerking movements of the extremities seen in seizures are caused by an alternation of electrical discharges and suppression of activity. Excitatory neurotransmitters increase the electrical discharges, while inhibitory neurotransmitters block the discharges. Several anticonvulsant medications now in use, for example, phenytoin (Dilantin) and phenobarbitol, work by increasing inhibition of the abnormal discharges. An interesting observation is that glutamate antagonists are potent anticonvulsants in experimental animals. They also prevent nerve-cell death, which can accompany seizures. These drugs therefore represent a potential new therapeutic avenue for treating epilepsy.

A different new approach to stroke therapy involves compounds that dissolve blood clots and thus remove clot blockage in blood vessels supplying the brain—the cause of most strokes. Trials are under way to determine if prompt administration of tissue plasminogen activator (t-PA), a naturally occurring clot-dissolving protein in blood, can improve the outcome in stroke. The hope is that restoration of blood flow to the brain will lead to return of function in areas of the brain in which neurons are not functioning properly but have not yet died. Ultimately therapy may involve both a clot-dissolving drug and a glutamate antagonist.

A recent advance in stroke prevention is the recognition that many patients with abnormalities in heartbeat rhythm are at high risk for stroke. When the heart muscle does not contract rhythmically, blood flow slows, raising the likelihood that clots will develop in the heart. The clots then travel through the blood vessels and lodge in a narrow region, blocking the vessel and causing a loss of blood supply and tissue damage. This mechanism of stroke is common in patients who have an abnormal heart rhythm known as atrial fibrillation. New work has shown that if these patients are placed on drugs that inhibit clotting, their risk of stroke can be dramatically reduced. Although such therapy increases the risk of bleeding into the brain or other tissues, with proper management the reduced risk of stroke greatly outweighs the increased risk of bleeding.

Muscular dystrophy: advances in genetics

Duchenne muscular dystrophy is a severe X-linked genetic disorder (one carried on the X, or female-determining, chromosome) that affects one of every 3,000–5,000 boys. Marked by skeletal muscle degeneration,

it is caused by defects in an immense gene on the X chromosome that was first isolated in 1987 by Louis M. Kunkel of Harvard Medical School and co-workers. The biological function of dystrophin, the protein that is encoded by the gene, is unknown, but its location has been narrowed to the cytoplasmic (inner) face of muscle-cell membranes, where it has direct contact with several other membrane-associated proteins. Recent studies carried out in mice that have dystrophin gene defects suggest that dystrophin plays a role in governing cellular calcium levels and contributes to the stability of muscle fibers. Dystrophin also has been found in the brain, where its production is controlled by a different regulatory portion of the gene, called a promoter, than that used in muscle. The presence in the gene of two separate promoters, one responsible for expression (translation of genetic instructions into protein) in muscle cells and one for nerve cells, suggests that dystrophin may be regulated differently in brain and muscle. Kunkel suggested that dystrophin's role in the brain may involve the formation of synapses, thus perhaps explaining the presence of intellectual impairment in some Duchenne patients.

A second, much milder form of muscular dystrophy, Becker muscular dystrophy, also involves mutations in the dystrophin gene. Most mutations responsible for either form involve deletions in the sequence of molecular subunits, called nucleotide bases, that make up the gene. It has been suggested that while Duchenne patients possess deletions that totally disrupt the way in which the instructions for synthesizing dystrophin are "read" from the gene sequence, Becker patients may make an altered protein that functions in a compromised manner. This distinction has been supported by the observation that whereas Duchenne patients either lack dystrophin or contain very low levels of the protein in their muscle cells, Becker patients produce dystrophin that is abnormal in size or somewhat reduced in quantity. In 1990 Kay Davies of the Institute of Molecular Medicine, Oxford, and colleagues described the gene deletion in a Becker-afflicted family whose affected members have very mild muscle symptoms. The deletion removed almost half of the gene's protein-coding sequence, resulting in production of a shortened protein but one that still took up its proper place in the muscle cell membrane.

These results are encouraging with regard to the prospect of gene therapy, since the very large dystrophin gene may be replaceable with a more manipulable "minigene." In 1991, using genetic engineering techniques, Thomas Caskey of Baylor University, Waco, Texas, and colleagues reported success in inserting a full-length version of the mouse dystrophin gene into cultured cells, thereby providing a system in which the gene's function can be directly studied. This achievement also opens the way for testing gene therapy approaches in an animal model. A challenge

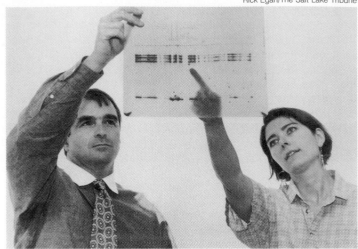

Raymond White and postdoctoral fellow Joanna Groden examine an autoradiogram, the result of a laboratory technique used to sort and identify genes and gene fragments. In 1990 independent teams led by White at the University of Utah and Francis Collins at the University of Michigan identified and characterized the gene whose mutant form is responsible for neurofibromatosis.

for future research is to determine which portions of the large dystrophin protein are most crucial for proper muscle function.

Neurofibromatosis: more pieces in the puzzle

Von Recklinghausen neurofibromatosis (NF1) is a common genetic disorder passed on as an autosomal (non-sex-linked) dominant trait and characterized by patches of pale brown skin pigmentation (café-au-lait spots) and tumors called neurofibromas. The rate of new mutations leading to NF1 (*i.e.,* the birthrate for individuals who are the first in their family to have neurofibromatosis), at one in 10,000, is among the highest for genetic disorders. Interestingly, according to a 1990 report by Bruce Ponder of the University of Cambridge and colleagues, the new mutation was of paternal origin in 12 of 14 families studied.

In 1987 researchers traced the NF1 gene to chromosome 17. Three years later Francis Collins and co-workers at the University of Michigan announced that they had identified a large gene deriving from a region of chromosome 17 in which multiple deletions and chromosomal translocations had been reported in NF1 patients. The gene was isolated by means of a strategy in which large segments of this crucial region of chromosome 17 were inserted into artificial chromosomes, which were then propagated in yeast cells as a way of purifying and replicating the large gene segments. The gene so obtained was found to be disrupted in three NF1 patients. In addition, a patient identified as having a new NF1 mutation possessed extra DNA in the NF1 gene. The high spontaneous mutation rate of NF1 may be due to the large size of the NF1 gene.

The protein encoded by the NF1 gene, as determined by a team led by Raymond White at the University of Utah School of Medicine, contains a region similar to those seen previously in a family of proteins (GTPase activating proteins, or GAP) involved in the control of cell growth. This discovery suggests neurofibromatosis may be the result of the loss of proper regulation of cell growth due to the deletion or altered activity of the NF1 gene. Elucidation of the exact function of the gene should lead to a greater understanding of the disorder and new approaches to therapy.

Hyperkalemic periodic paralysis

Also known as Gamstorp's disease, hyperkalemic periodic paralysis is an autosomal dominant genetic disorder characterized by recurrent episodes of muscle weakness and paralysis attacks. Paralysis is due to the inability of the muscle to be excited into action and is associated with elevated levels of potassium in the blood serum. Attacks often follow exposure to cold, rest after exercise, fasting, or ingestion of foods that are high in potassium. Studies have indicated that in patients with this disorder an influx of sodium into muscle cells can be triggered by only a slight increase in potassium levels outside the cells. Normally such an increase would be too small to open a specific channel in muscle cells that allows the entry of sodium; the unusual response suggests an abnormality in the protein or proteins in cell membranes that control sodium and potassium traffic in and out of the cell.

On the basis of this information, Bertrand Fontaine and co-workers at Harvard Medical School studied the gene that encodes part of a protein, the alpha subunit of the human-muscle sodium channel, which is responsible for sodium entry into muscle cells. In 1990 the gene was traced to the long arm of chromosome 17 and then shown to be tightly linked to the site presumed to carry the genetic defect for hyperkalemic periodic paralysis. Thus, it is likely that the gene for the sodium channel alpha subunit contains the defect responsible for the disease.

—Bradley T. Hyman, M.D., Ph.D.,
M. Flint Beal, M.D.,
and Rudolph E. Tanzi, Ph.D.

Special Report

A Thoroughly Modern Malady

by Robert Keene McLellan, M.D., M.P.H.

In Wimberley, Texas, in the rolling hill country southwest of Austin, there is a unique and growing community of people who have taken refuge from what they call a "chemical world." Anyone who visits there must comply with elaborate restrictions—such as removing all traces of perfume or after-shave lotion and dressing in clothes made only of undyed natural fibers. To bring in a newspaper or magazine from the outside world is forbidden—even mail must be aired on a clothesline before it can be taken indoors. Conversations between visitors and residents are often conducted out of doors and at a distance. The goal of these measures is to prevent contamination of the community by any vestiges of man-made chemicals. These are people who suffer from a malady known variously as multiple chemical sensitivity (MCS), environmental illness, or "20th-century disease."

Few current problems in occupational and environmental medicine arouse more heated debate than this poorly understood condition. At one extreme are physicians who feel that MCS is no more than a popular explanation for chronic, vague symptoms that are patently psychological in origin. At the other extreme are practitioners of an unorthodox medical specialty called clinical ecology. Clinical ecologists opine that MCS is a "new" medical problem—one unique to the 20th century—that is the result of physiological abnormalities created in susceptible people when they are exposed to certain chemicals. Although this dispute shows no sign of abating, a consensus has been reached in the medical community that persons with MCS have real problems, which are often chronic and severely debilitating, and that as patients they deserve compassionate medical attention. Irrespective of the uncertainties about MCS, there are considerable clinical and some research data to provide informed physicians with a foundation for the rational evaluation and treatment of patients with this controversial disorder.

Symptoms and sufferers

At present there is not adequate scientific evidence that MCS is indeed a new disease. Similar conditions were certainly described in earlier times although called by different names. In 1881 the U.S. neurologist George Miller Beard wrote of a syndrome characterized by "special idiosyncrasies in regard to food, medicine, and external irritants." Beard attributed the disorder to modern civilization, specifically steam power, print and telegraphic communications, science, and the changing role of women. The French writer Marcel Proust may have been the most celebrated historical figure to suffer from an MCS-like disease. After his mother's death Proust became increasingly reclusive and obsessed with his health. His social withdrawal was paralleled by a growing concern about the effects of various seemingly trivial environmental exposures on his delicate constitution. In *Marcel Proust: His Life and Work,* Leon Pierre-Quint quotes him as follows:

My dear friend, . . . shall I be causing you much inconvenience if I ask you to take the handkerchief out of your jacket? You know I can't bear any perfume. . . . The last time you were so good as to come and see [me] . . . I was obliged to take the chair you sat in and keep it out in the courtyard for three days; it was impregnated with the scent."

A porcelain-walled trailer provides protection from the "chemical world" for a woman in Wimberley, Texas. She visits with her daughter, who remains outside, by intercom.

Daemmrich—Stock, Boston

The complaints of present-day MCS patients are so characteristic that they are now recognized as constituting a syndrome—*i.e.,* a complex of potentially related symptoms that tend to occur together. The most prominent complaints are usually neuropsychological—fatigue, dizziness, headache, impaired memory, inability to concentrate, inexplicable mood swings. Other common symptoms include palpitations (rapid heartbeat); shortness of breath; chest tightness; irritation of the mucous membranes of the eyes, nose, and throat; and intestinal distress marked by bloating, cramps, and diarrhea. The symptoms are puzzlingly out of proportion to any physical findings of disease, which typically are lacking. The illness is generally chronic, although some patients experience remissions. Many, however, become progressively more incapacitated, yet they show no evidence of physiological decline—except as may arise out of extreme treatments, such as severely restricted diets.

The term *multiple chemical sensitivity* is often used inappropriately in both lay and professional publications to describe the complaints of a highly diverse group of people who feel that various aspects of the environment make them ill. Within the group are: (1) chronically ill individuals who, because their disease is undiagnosed, have latched on to MCS as the latest fad explanation for their problems but who may be suffering from any of many elusive illnesses, such as chronic fatigue syndrome, multiple sclerosis, depression, or panic disorder; (2) patients with underlying medical problems that make them unable to tolerate airborne pollutants; such conditions may lead to symptoms commonly associated with MCS—*e.g.,* asthma associated with hyperventilation; (3) patients with disorders resulting from exposure to neurotoxic substances (for example, brain damage due to carbon monoxide poisoning); these disorders also produce symptoms commonly linked to MCS; (4) patients with respiratory conditions—caused by either infection or toxic exposures—that have rendered them exquisitely sensitive to the irritant effects of low levels of chemicals in the immediate environment; (5) persons with *any* illness that goes away when exposure to supposedly offending environmental substances ceases; and (6) individuals who have developed an apparently exquisite and debilitating intolerance to common substances or environments that cannot be wholly explained by traditional psychological, medical, or toxicological principles.

Though no agreement has yet been reached on a clinical definition of MCS, specialists in occupational and environmental medicine generally reserve the diagnosis for the last subgroup.

The "typical" patient

According to the above definition, the "typical" MCS patient is one who was relatively healthy, or at least

MCS sufferers: a patient profile*	
age range	27–78
female	23
male	3
married	23
single	3
years of education (mean)	14.6
occupation	
white-collar, clerical	13
teaching	6
small business, managerial	3
professional	3
homemaker	1
*26 patients in study	

Adapted from Donald W. Black, M.D., *et al.,* "Environmental Illness," *JAMA,* vol. 264, no. 24 (Dec. 26, 1990), pp. 3166–70. Copyright 1990, American Medical Association

functioning well in society, until the occurrence of a defined environmental exposure. This event causes symptoms, usually symptoms that are consistent with the particular exposure—*e.g.,* a person who works around formaldehyde may develop breathing problems or irritated skin and burning eyes. Subsequently, however, the symptoms recur, provoked by lower concentrations of the offensive agent. A progressive generalization of the illness then occurs. The patient experiences distress in more and more environments and with more substances. The environments and agents that trigger symptoms may include everything from shopping malls to detergent aisles of grocery stores, recently remodeled buildings, passing whiffs of perfume, new carpeting, vehicular exhaust, natural gas, newsprint, and pesticides. Some MCS patients complain that strong electromagnetic fields precipitate their symptoms.

Published estimates of the prevalence of MCS are nothing more than wild guesses. The syndrome is not rare, however. Virtually any practicing occupational medicine specialist or allergist has seen several such individuals. One review of medical records of all patients seen at two university-based occupational medicine clinics between 1984 and 1986 revealed that 1% of patients met the diagnostic criteria for MCS. Persons seeking medical care for MCS have been predominately female, Caucasian, middle-aged, and above average in socioeconomic status, but cases are by no means restricted to this narrow demographic group. Children and elderly people and workers in a wide range of occupations are known to be affected.

Many hypotheses

Drawing conclusions based on the research to date is difficult because of the poor scientific methods that have been employed by most investigators, especially their failure to use a consistent, clear definition of MCS. It is possible that many of the hypotheses are correct; their diversity may simply reflect the heterogeneity of the MCS patients who have been studied.

Considerable medical literature on the health effects of exposures to low doses of chemicals lends credence to the possibility that MCS is a unique physiological disorder. Knowledge of the toxic properties of a substance usually allows a reliable prediction of health effects based on dose. Sick building syndrome (SBS)—a condition that occurs in indoor environments where the air is constantly recirculated—is probably a predictable effect of exposure to very low levels of volatile organic chemicals, dust, or biological agents. Some theorists believe that MCS may be an extreme form of SBS; like MCS, SBS commonly affects productivity, and its victims have prominent neuropsychological and respiratory complaints yet no physical evidence of disease. However, MCS sufferers differ from those with SBS in that they also report food intolerance, symptoms that occur in diverse environments, and often significant disability.

Decreased tolerance. For every environmental agent, there is a part of the population that is particularly intolerant. People with MCS may represent the extreme on this continuum. Aside from the effects of genetic and constitutional (*e.g.,* age, sex) factors, a wide variety of acquired problems are known to decrease an individual's tolerance of environmental exposures. These include nutritional deficiencies, disturbances of normal chronobiological rhythms (such as in jet lag), past or concurrent chemical and drug exposures, immunologic sensitization to specific chemicals, and allergic respiratory disease.

Altered immunity. Another set of hypotheses to explain MCS is based on the fact that chemicals sometimes have unpredictable effects. The classic unpredictable response is allergy. The scent of the wood of the western red cedar is pleasing to most people, but some mill workers exposed to a natural chemical in the sawdust develop asthma. This kind of allergic response is specific to a single substance, however, whereas MCS appears to be very nonspecific. It is, of course, possible that people complaining of multiple chemical sensitivities are actually responding to a single, ubiquitous agent, as yet unidentified.

Alternatively, the immunologic phenomenon of cross-reactivity may explain reactions to surprisingly different substances—for example, an industrial product and a vegetable that contain similar chemical components. In one case, a worker with asthma caused by exposure to isocyanates used in the manufacture of a man-made foam material developed asthmatic symptoms on eating radishes (which are known to contain isocyanates). It has also been proposed that MCS represents some other form of immune system disturbance. It is well known that environmental agents affect the immune system and can trigger such pervasive disorders as arthritis. There is, however, no credible proof that patients with MCS suffer from an immunologic disorder.

Idiosyncratic reactions. Yet another hypothesis is that these are idiosyncratic reactions—unpredictable responses to synthetic chemicals. There are many examples of this phenomenon. Indomethacin, for example, a commonly used antiarthritic medicine, causes depression in some individuals. Though such reactions are usually specific to a single compound, some patients have adverse reactions to low doses of disparate drugs.

Cumulative effects. One perplexing observation is that in some MCS patients, sensitivity to a specific agent is inconsistent over time. Many scientists conclude that this is proof that the disorder, at least in these individuals, is probably psychological. Clinical ecologists have postulated two explanations for this phenomenon. One is that it is the sum of all environmental stressors—toxic, immunogenic, and psychological—rather than any specific agent that leads to symptoms. This idea suggests that each patient has a threshold for the combined effect of all stressors. If a person is close to this threshold, a minute exposure—the proverbial last straw—may lead to symptoms, whereas at another time, when the sum of all exposures is lower, a higher dose of the same agent may be well tolerated. There are indeed well-described ex-

Paul Bierman-Lytle uses only nontoxic products in his work as an architectural designer. He became interested in sick building syndrome when he realized that many construction materials made him "cough, sneeze, and feel generally lousy."

Kristine Larsen

Even a passing whiff of scent may provoke symptoms in persons who suffer from multiple chemical sensitivity. Such people would like to see laws prohibiting the indiscriminate spraying of perfume in department stores, a popular promotional tactic. A chemically sensitive consumer (right) wore a mask to testify at a public hearing in New York City on legislation that would ban fragrance strips from magazine and direct-mail advertising.

amples of a person's response to a chemical being influenced by the sum of many environmental factors; for example, alcohol ingested on an empty stomach upon awakening is more intoxicating than when consumed with dinner.

State of adaptation. Clinical ecology also postulates that the patient's "state of adaptation" will affect his or her response; chronic exposure to a substance produces chronic illness without obvious relation of exposure to symptoms. Theoretically, removal from the ongoing exposure will then change the response so that acute effects can be identified when exposure recurs. A parallel example of this phenomenon has been documented in addiction studies. An alcoholic, for example, will respond less dramatically to two shots of whiskey than will a person who has been abstinent for several months.

Conditioned response. Psychophysiological reactions represent another class of unpredictable responses to chemicals. One theory suggests that MCS is no more than the result of classic behavioral conditioning to a chemical stimulus. Thus, symptoms that are originally linked with the sensory perception of a noxious substance are subsequently provoked by exposure to a similar but less potent stimulus. Over time, the triggering stimulus becomes generalized to include a variety of agents. Another intriguing theory has grown from observations of the profound physiological effects of minute concentrations of chemicals when mediated by the olfactory system. Mere whiffs of perfume provoke shortness of breath in many asthmatics. This effect is prevented in many individuals when the olfactory route of exposure—*i.e.,* the nose— is blocked. Contrary to expectation, patients with MCS do not in general have a sense of smell more acute than normal; in fact, diminished or distorted olfactory acuity has been found in at least some MCS patients.

Studies show that these disturbances are linked with occupational exposures to chemical solvents and are often associated with a range of neuropsychiatric abnormalities.

Psychological factors. Several reports have noted a high prevalence of psychological disorders in MCS patients that either predate or coexist with the onset of the illness. These disorders could explain the multiplicity of complaints in MCS. For example, depression often leads to poor concentration. Indeed, personality styles, and perhaps psychological problems secondary to MCS, may account for some of the unexpected intensity of complaints and associated debility. Some people's personalities may predispose them to overinterpreting and amplifying symptoms originally associated with a toxic exposure, particularly if it was a frightening occurrence. Physicians often see people who, although satisfactorily recovering from heart attack, become "cardiac cripples" in their anxiety over basically innocuous symptoms that they fear may indicate another impending attack. In the MCS patient, similar fears may lead to secondary psychological difficulties such as anxiety or depression or phobias about all chemical odors.

Most investigators would agree that any physiological abnormalities identified must be major if they themselves are to adequately explain the total debility of many MCS patients. It seems likely that MCS, like most chronic diseases, ultimately will be found to be multifactorial, and psychosocial factors will undoubtedly be recognized as playing a critical part in the natural course of the illness.

Diagnosis

Given the uncertainties regarding the nature and causes of MCS, it is not surprising that there is also a diversity of opinion about how best to diagnose and treat the problem. As with other poorly understood syndromes, there is presently no proven "cure" for MCS. Nonetheless, there are several basic principles and techniques that are likely to be helpful by virtue of their proven usefulness in related medical problems.

First, and most important, patients complaining of MCS should be rigorously evaluated by a primary care physician to rule out the presence of other identifiable medical and psychological disorders. If such disorders are not found—or their treatment does not relieve symptoms that otherwise fit the profile of MCS—the patient may benefit from further evaluation by a specialist. Generally speaking, specialists in allergy, occupational medicine, or clinical ecology are likely to be the most knowledgeable about MCS. If there has been a clear history of a toxic exposure, the occupational medicine specialist is best equipped to consider the possible long-term effects of that exposure. (Most occupational medicine physicians belong to the American College of Occupational and Environmental Medicine; the organization of clinical ecologists is called the American Academy of Environmental Medicine.) In some cases, a multidisciplinary evaluation and treatment team is appropriate; members would include physicians, psychologists, nutritionists, and social workers.

Beyond the traditional diagnostic techniques used to evaluate medical or psychological problems that may be associated with MCS, there are no widely accepted laboratory tests to confirm or deny that a patient has the syndrome. A clinical ecologist is likely to use such techniques as monitoring reactions to sublingually administered drops of chemical mixtures, measuring the levels of environmentally persistent chemicals in body tissues, evaluating the extent of the intestinal colonization with candida (a common body fungus), and testing aspects of immune function. None of these techniques, however, has been scientifically established as relevant to the MCS patient's complaints.

Many procedures may be appropriately performed by a specialist looking for underlying abnormalities in MCS—among them allergy testing, controlled dietary manipulation, nutritional assessments, lung-function tests, olfactory acuity testing, and neuropsychological examinations. The latter are performed by a psychologist; their purpose is to look for physiological or psychological explanations, or both, for symptoms such as memory loss or poor concentration.

Most physicians interested in MCS feel that the best diagnostic test involves the use of an environmental chamber where subjects can be exposed to low levels of common chemicals in a scientifically controlled manner and monitored for objective reactions. Only a few such chambers exist, however, and there are still unresolved technical issues about their use in testing MCS patients.

At the present time, the diagnosis of MCS is based not on the results of any specific laboratory test but rather on the following minimum clinical criteria: (1) complaints involve more than one organ system and are predictably exacerbated in diverse environments or with exposure to diverse substances that are tolerated by the vast majority of people; (2) the syndrome has been present for at least three months; (3) there are no obvious medical or psychological explanations of the symptoms; and (4) the patient has sought medical care for the symptoms or has made significant changes in life-style in an attempt to relieve symptoms.

Treatment: a realistic approach

It is not uncommon for MCS sufferers to make drastic life-style changes in an attempt to reduce their exposures to offending substances. For example, many patients quit work or withdraw from social life. A realistic approach to treatment attempts to prevent these kinds of extreme responses.

The overall goal of treating patients who meet the diagnostic criteria of MCS is to improve their social functioning and level of comfort without necessarily expecting resolution of all symptoms. A long-term relationship with a physician who attempts genuinely to understand the patient's social background, psychology, and biology is more likely to be therapeutic than a more narrowly focused, short-term relationship.

A woman uses a special reading box equipped with an exhaust fan to protect herself from the chemicals in paper and ink, while foil covering the walls shields her from fumes given off by building materials.

Miguel Luis Fairbanks

Coping skills. As with any chronic illness, patient education is a key to increasing the patient's independence from the medical system. The chief goals of this education are to emphasize the benign course of MCS—it is not a progressive or degenerative disease—and to teach techniques for avoiding secondary emotional problems and social debility. These techniques help the patient to focus on the activities and situations he or she is able to tolerate rather than on those that provoke symptoms. Every effort should be made to maintain gainful employment and continue with the usual household duties. As with most chronic illnesses, there are organizations (such as the National Center for Environmental Health Strategies in Voorhees, N.J., and the Human Ecology Action League in Atlanta, Ga.) that can provide support, camaraderie, up-to-date legal and scientific information, and practical tips for coping with the disorder.

A behavioral psychologist may be able to provide patients with tools for gaining greater control over their reactions to environments (or agents) that provoke symptoms. One such technique involves behavioral deconditioning. During purposeful and graduated exposures, the individual employs relaxation techniques to interrupt such responses as rapid heartbeat or stomach cramps. Another approach involves the pairing of pleasing odors such as the scent of cinnamon with learned relaxation responses. Sniffing the cinnamon can then be used to block reactions in situations that typically provoke symptoms.

Avoidance. A mainstay of treatment is the development of strategies to prevent—or at least reduce—exposures to offensive environmental agents and, where necessary, to improve the individual's tolerance of these agents. Optimizing the quality of the indoor air in which MCS patients live and work is an intuitive though unproven approach to care. Avoidance of offending substances provides relief, and prolonged avoidance is reported by some patients to improve tolerance and, ultimately, enables them to return to a normal life-style.

In general, the rationale and design of an appropriate avoidance program follow principles similar to those helpful to people with standard respiratory allergies. The patient's home, and in particular the bedroom, can be made into a safe haven from suspected offensive environmental agents with a few not-too-drastic modifications—*e.g.,* replacing carpeted floors with wood or tile, using unscented laundry detergents, and filtering the indoor air to reduce pollutants.

Though not definitive, the trend in the United States has been to consider MCS as a bona fide handicap protected from discrimination in federally subsidized housing and in the workplace. Employers and landlords are therefore required to make "reasonable accommodations" to meet the special environmental needs of MCS patients.

Other measures. Other treatment strategies focus on improving patients' environmental tolerance or at least improving their overall sense of well-being. All underlying physiological problems should be corrected if possible—for example, the regular use of lubricating drops for dry eyes and nose may relieve irritation of these tissues, treatment of medically diagnosed nutritional deficiencies may relieve fatigue and improve mental functioning, and treatment of common allergies may increase tolerance to airborne irritants. An exercise program that maximizes both cardiovascular conditioning and flexibility can be expected to further contribute to an improvement in overall well-being.

Although there is no scientific evidence of any therapeutic benefit in eating "organic" foods, there is sound nutritional justification for a dietary regime that restricts highly processed foods and encourages a wide range of fresh foods. There is increasing evidence that foods cause symptoms that reach beyond classic allergic responses and into the realm of neurobehavioral effects. When food-related symptoms are confirmed by controlled dietary manipulation, elimination of specific foods may be warranted.

Some caveats

Avoidance regimes are not without potentially disastrous consequences to the individual—among them, increasing social withdrawal and possible malnutrition—to say nothing of the financial costs to society of recognizing MCS as a handicap deserving of legal protection. Some patients go to great extremes to avoid chemical exposures, though there is little evidence that such measures are actually helpful. They may live alone in porcelain-lined trailers in remote areas, cover their walls and furnishings with aluminum foil to contain chemical emissions, or wear gas masks to protect themselves in public. They may also subsist on bizarre, nutritionally incomplete diets. The most therapeutic program of avoidance is one that creates a healthy environment and diet suitable for all family members, rather than a regime of deprivation that leads inexorably to social alienation.

Numerous treatment methods other than those described above have been employed by persons suffering from MCS, many of them unproven and potentially risky. The latter include elaborate "detoxification" regimes, long-term therapy with antifungal drugs, removal of mercury amalgam dental fillings, and "immunotherapy" with low doses of chemicals.

The professional conflict about MCS has historically been fueled more by polemic than by knowledge. Scientific research is just now beginning to address some of the knotty questions posed by this puzzling disorder. In the meantime, MCS patients and their families deserve medicine's best efforts to provide care and comfort while avoiding the creation of further medical, social, or economic complications.

Occupational Health

In 1991 the record keeping on U.S. workplace illness and injury was taken over by the Occupational Safety and Health Administration (OSHA); previously this had been handled by the Bureau of Labor Statistics.

In 1989, the most recent year for which provisional figures are available, there were 8.6 cases of job-related illness and injury per 100 full-time workers in the U.S., unchanged from the previous year. The majority were injuries—only 0.3 work-related illnesses per 100 workers were recorded, a figure recognized by public health authorities as being well under the actual number. All told, there were more than six million work-related injuries, of which almost three million were serious enough to cause the loss of productive work time. Approximately 54 million workdays were lost as a result. Eight industries accounted for about one-fourth of all injuries reported. They included motor-vehicle manufacturing and, in the nonmanufacturing sector, eating and drinking establishments, grocery stores, hospitals, department stores, and hotels and motels. There were in addition at least 3,300 work-related fatalities, although this number, too, is thought to be unrealistically low. About 50,000 more cases of occupational illness were reported than in the previous year, trauma accounting for approximately one-half and skin diseases for about one-quarter of all cases. It should be noted that these numbers represent private industry alone and do not reflect death, illness, or injury of workers in government agencies.

Children at work—illegally

A particularly ominous trend evidenced by statistics on work-related injuries is the growing contravention of child labor regulations. According to figures from the General Accounting Office (GAO), there was a 250% increase in the violation of child labor laws at the end of the 1980s as compared with the beginning of the decade. Increasingly, minors are being discovered working under sweatshop conditions—putting in longer-than-allowed hours, missing school, and risking exposure to toxic solvents and dangerous machinery. Even the more common places of childhood employment, such as fast-food establishments, have recently been found to be violating child labor laws. The GAO statistics indicated that 48 minors were killed and 128,000 injured in work-related accidents in 1987–88.

In one 24-state sample of worker's compensation claims filed on behalf of children, compiled by the National Electronic Injury Surveillance System, nearly 24,000 such claims were reviewed. Of these, 30% involved 16-year-olds, and about 60% involved 17-year-olds; the remaining 10% represented injuries to workers aged 13–15. Males accounted for a predominant portion of the claims, and more than 300 claims were made by individuals younger than 14. Among the injuries reported were a significant number of lacerations and puncture wounds, sprains and strains, burns, and fractures and almost 150 amputations. Some states also reported fatalities. California, for example, recorded 12 work-related deaths in workers under the age of 18. Although these rates are high, on a worldwide basis injury and fatality statistics for children could be expected to be much higher, especially in less developed countries, where children make up a greater percentage of the labor force.

Putting a price on life and health

OSHA recently began to levy larger fines against employers than in previous years, not only in cases of

An inspector from the New York State Department of Labor finds an 11-year-old girl working alongside her mother in a Manhattan clothing factory. The end of the 1980s was marked by an enormous increase in reported violations of child labor laws.

Keith Meyers/The New York Times

Gloyce Qualls, a worker at the Johnson Controls battery plant in Milwaukee, Wisconsin, celebrates the 1991 U.S. Supreme Court ruling that struck down the company's mandatory exclusion of women of child-bearing age from jobs that could expose their unborn children to health hazards. Several years earlier Qualls had undergone voluntary sterilization rather than give up a high-paying production line job, in which she was exposed to fumes from molten lead. The high court declared that women—rather than their employers—should be the ones to decide if they would work in potentially hazardous jobs.

child labor violations but in many other settings. In addition, it has become public policy to settle fines for a larger percentage of the actual amount than had been the case in the past. Traditionally, even large fines were settled for a few pennies on the dollar. Under the new policy, the agency will attempt to collect closer to 50% of the total, assuming that settlements can be agreed upon and companies cooperate with the agency. The largest fine ever levied—$3,480,000—was against an ARCO facility in Texas for a 1990 fire; BASF was ordered to pay $1,060,000 for an explosion in a Cincinnati, Ohio, plant in 1990. Both incidents resulted in loss of workers' lives. OSHA is also attempting to improve workplace conditions through education, including the publication of a new periodical called the *Job Safety and Health Quarterly.*

Deaths continue to be reported each year from trench cave-ins and accidents in confined spaces such as chemical tanks. The death of a Texas worker in a trench cave-in 1989 resulted in a $55,100 fine; criminal penalties, including a jail term for the company president, were still pending. In a highly unusual accident, an employee of a Kentucky water-supply company drowned while trying to clear a clogged pipe at the bottom of a water basin in a filtration plant. The fine assessed for this incident was only $490. In the area of worker's compensation, a court decided that the family of a policeman who died as a result of an encounter with a deranged individual could not sue for loss of life; police work, the court ruled, must be considered inherently dangerous.

Legal issues

In a much-anticipated decision, the U.S. Supreme Court ruled in March 1991 that employers cannot exclude fertile women from jobs that could potentially cause harm to a developing fetus. The court ruled that such employment policies violate federal antidiscrimination statutes and declared that it should

be up to the woman herself to decide if she would take a job that might expose her unborn baby to a possible health hazard. The ruling overturned a controversial 1989 decision by a lower court that had upheld the right of Johnson Controls, a major manufacturer of automotive batteries in Milwaukee, Wis., to ban women from jobs that entail exposure to lead. A decision in favor of such a "fetal protection" policy could have had the ultimate effect of excluding all women of childbearing age from any job that might pose a threat to the fetus, thus making up to 20 million existing industrial jobs, many of them high paying, unavailable to most women. The high court's ruling did not address the issue of employers' long-term legal liability for birth defects.

Two important decisions involving drug testing at the workplace were handed down by the Supreme Court in recent sessions. The first upheld the right of the Federal Railway Administration to require blood and urine specimens from railroad employees who are involved in accidents. In a second case the court upheld the right of the U.S. Customs Service to require urine testing for employees involved in the interdiction of illegal drugs, those whose jobs make it necessary for them to carry firearms, and those who handle classified material. The ruling in the railroad case pointed out that "special needs" of public safety take precedence over the Fourth Amendment prohibition against search without probable cause. A notable recent ruling was in the settlement of the *Exxon Valdez* oil-spill case, where a court found the captain of the vessel not guilty of substance abuse.

Infectious agents in the workplace

Recent surveys show that workers at high risk for exposure to HIV (human immunodeficiency virus) and hepatitis B infection, such as laboratory and hospital personnel, are often poorly trained and not knowledgeable about appropriate disease-prevention measures.

Despite the fact that an effective vaccine against hepatitis B is available, a number of health care workers at risk for the disease have not been immunized.

Exposure to infectious agents is not limited to workers in health fields. The state of Minnesota reported an outbreak of psittacosis (a bacterial infection of birds also known as parrot fever) among workers in a turkey-processing plant. The disease is transmissible to humans, in whom it is manifested by a pneumonia-like illness. While psittacosis had been known to infect wild bird populations, including turkeys, this case indicates that commercially raised poultry may also carry the infectious organism. An unusual outbreak of ocular infections was reported in a Massachusetts computer-fabrication facility that relied heavily on the use of microscopes. Workers typically shared microscopes, and investigators found a positive correlation between the risk of infection for any individual and the number of hours of microscopic work done each day. With the institution of hygienic practices similar to those used in medical settings, such as washing the lenses between uses, there were no further outbreaks during a one-year follow-up.

Toxic metals and irritant gases

Occupational exposure to heavy metals is not uncommon. Recent reports documented a number of cases of illness due to mercury and lead. One such report involved a work crew employed in the demolition of a bridge in western Massachusetts in 1988. More than half of the crew developed lead poisoning while using acetylene torches to cut apart pieces of the bridge, which over the years had been painted repeatedly with lead-based paint. Lead poisoning in demolition crews had been seen and documented previously and could easily have been prevented, in this case by the proper use of devices such as respirators or special hoods that supply workers with uncontaminated air. There is concern that the problem may become more common as bridges built in the United States in the 19th and early 20th centuries age and are either torn down or renovated.

Excessive lead exposure and cases of lead poisoning were also reported in workers repairing car radiators and lead automotive batteries. In some instances general environmental contamination had also taken place when batteries were burned as a fuel source, and in a few cases children nearby were harmed. Small-scale home workshops where lead is used—in the glazing of pottery or recycling of car batteries—are common in less developed countries and put not only workers but their families at risk. Such situations are not new; particularly notable cases have been reported in Nigeria and in Trinidad and Tobago.

The Zinc Corp. of America was recently fined more than $600,000 for violations of the federal lead standard, including improper respirator selection, lack of engineering controls, and failure to provide a lead-free lunchroom facility. In other reports on occupational exposure to metals, investigators in Japan found a higher-than-expected rate of lung cancer among chromate workers, while authorities in The Netherlands found no apparent acute changes in pulmonary function among welders exposed to zinc-coated steel. In the U.S., occupational medicine specialists launched an investigation of the effects of beryllium, a toxic metal used in the manufacture of nuclear weapons, on the health of workers exposed to beryllium dust at weapons plants in Colorado, New Mexico, and elsewhere.

Among the more unusual reports from 1990–91 concerning workplace exposures were two incidences of illness associated with toxic and irritant gases. In Minnesota an outbreak of respiratory illness occurred among more than 100 ice hockey players and spectators at a recreational arena. The disorder was attributed to high levels of nitrogen dioxide, resulting from a malfunctioning ice-resurfacing machine. The outbreak pointed up the potential of long-term low-level nitrogen dioxide exposure to increase the risk

Even at low levels previously believed safe, carbon monoxide in the air—from automobile exhaust and cigarette smoke—has been found to be harmful. Toll booth workers may be at particularly high risk for occupational exposure.

Julie Houck—Stock, Boston

of respiratory infection and chronic obstructive pulmonary disease. At high levels nitrogen dioxide has even been known to be fatal. The authors of the study, published in the *Journal of the American Medical Association,* emphasized the importance of regular checking and maintenance of ice-smoothing equipment and proper ventilation of ice hockey arenas.

In a large multicenter study reported in November 1989, the common, toxic air pollutant carbon monoxide was found to have adverse effects at levels that had previously not been thought of as particularly harmful. Carbon monoxide is found in numerous occupational settings. In the bloodstream it binds with hemoglobin—the oxygen-carrying component of the blood—to form carboxyhemoglobin, thus reducing the amount of oxygen available to the body tissues. Smoking also raises the blood level of carboxyhemoglobin. Normally, smokers have levels of between 4 and 8% carboxyhemoglobin in their blood; this study showed that 5–10% of nonsmokers had levels above 2%. Further, it provided evidence of adverse short-term effects on exercise performance in individuals with coronary artery disease who were exposed to low levels of carbon monoxide. People in a number of different kinds of workplaces, particularly those with high automotive emissions—such as toll booths and tunnels—and those where there is much cigarette smoking, may have high blood levels of carbon monoxide.

Noise, radiation, and computer hazards

Noise exposure continued to be an area of concern in occupational health, and some large fines were levied for violation of federal noise standards. A case of special importance was that against the Budd Co., a German-owned U.S. business that manufactures subway cars, which was fined more than $3 million for violation of federal noise guidelines. Activities such as jackhammering, metal stamping, and aircraft maintenance and the operation of heavy equipment such as bulldozers present a particularly high risk for noise-induced hearing loss.

Following on the heels of the National Research Council's 1989 revised risk estimates, which indicated that low levels of radiation may be much more carcinogenic than previously believed, several studies were published that examined radiation risks in specific occupational settings. One of these examined deaths from cancer among workers at the Oak Ridge (Tenn.) National Laboratory, a weapons production and nuclear research facility. Comparing white male workers who had been exposed to radiation with those who had not, the investigators found higher death rates from all types of cancer among the exposed workers. The entire worker population had an unusually high death rate from leukemia, 63% higher than would be expected in a comparable unexposed group. Concern about radiation went beyond the workplace in a February 1990 report from Great Britain of an unusually high incidence of leukemia among children of men who worked at the Sellafield nuclear reprocessing plant.

It has been well documented that radiation exposure is greater for people at high altitudes than for those on the ground. Flight personnel would thus be expected to have high levels of exposures. A U.S. Department of Transportation report, published early in 1990, found that some flight crews have greater radiation exposure than the average worker at a nuclear power plant. The report also included estimates of the risk of cancer, depending on the number of flights per year, for both crews and passengers. To date, however, there have been no reports of elevated cancer rates among airline crews.

The potential hazards associated with work at video display terminals (VDTs) continued to be a focus of interest. In 1989 the mayor of New York City vetoed a strict VDT control bill, but a similar measure was passed by the San Francisco Board of Supervisors in December 1990. The San Francisco ordinance will require adjustable equipment, so as to relieve eye and musculoskeletal strain, as well as scheduled work breaks away from the computer keyboard. It applies to all workers who spend more than half of their workday at a computer.

The fears that VDTs may pose a hazard to pregnant women were allayed by the results of a 1991 federal government study that compared two groups of women employed as telephone operators. The study found no increased risk of miscarriage in those who worked at VDTs. Carpal tunnel syndrome and other repetitive trauma disorders continue to be associated with work at VDTs, however. Harder to evaluate or quantify are the allegations of undue stress by workers in a variety of industries, ranging from airline reservations to mail-order sales. The growing capability of supervisors to monitor the speed and efficiency of workers' transactions via electronic means has led many employees to describe their computerized workplaces as "electronic sweatshops."

Needed: more expertise

Reports from researchers at the Mount Sinai School of Medicine in New York City, published in the *American Journal of Industrial Medicine,* highlighted the dearth of physicians trained in occupational medicine and, in particular, the uneven distribution of such specialists over the heavily industrialized state of New York. Further, very few U.S. physicians in primary care practice have sufficient experience in dealing with occupationally related illnesses. To try to rectify this situation, the National Institute for Occupational Safety and Health (NIOSH), working with the Agency for Toxic Substances and Disease Registry, has funded a pilot program at several medical schools in the southeastern U.S.—among them, those at the Universities of Kentucky, Alabama, and South Florida and at Duke University, Durham, N.C.—in which occupational medicine specialists will train family practice physicians and internists in the field of occupational medicine. Should this effort prove successful, it is anticipated that similar cross-training programs may be established elsewhere around the country.

—Arthur L. Frank, M.D., Ph.D.

Pharmaceuticals

In November 1990 a new commissioner was appointed to head the U.S. Food and Drug Administration (FDA): David A. Kessler. A 40-year-old pediatrician and attorney, Kessler previously taught food and drug law at Columbia University School of Law, New York City, while serving as medical director of the Jack D. Weiler Hospital of the Albert Einstein College of Medicine. On accepting the position as commissioner, Kessler announced that he views his role as helping to revitalize the FDA as a strong and effective regulatory agency.

New head for a beleaguered agency

Since an industry-wide scandal involving generic drug approvals was first disclosed in 1989, the public had raised questions about the agency's ability to carry out its mission. In March 1990 the Department of Health and Human Services established an ad hoc advisory committee to examine the agency's mission, responsibilities, and structure; Kessler served as one of 15 consultants on the committee until his nomination as commissioner. The committee, which issued a final report in May 1991, determined that the FDA needed to bolster its enforcement activities. In his written testimony to the Senate Labor and Human Resources Committee, which confirmed him as commissioner, Kessler likewise said one of his primary goals would be to "emphasize strong enforcement of the law." In his public statements and in testimony at hearings before Congress, he repeatedly expressed his belief that greater resources were needed so that the agency could enforce laws. He also has said that the majority of the FDA's enforcement budget should be earmarked for the field investigators rather than the compliance office in the agency's Rockville, Md., headquarters. Moreover, he lost no time in hiring an additional 106 criminal investigators.

It soon became evident that the new commissioner had Congress on his side; the House of Representatives passed legislation in June 1991 to appropriate $761.9 million for the FDA for fiscal year 1992, begun Oct. 1, 1991. The total was 11% over that appropriated for fiscal 1991. Kessler has worked Capital Hill shrewdly, cultivating the support of individual members of the Senate and House. He knows Congress' importance to the FDA from experience; Kessler was a consultant to Sen. Orrin G. Hatch (Rep., Utah) in the

When David A. Kessler became commissioner of the Food and Drug Administration in November 1990, he took on the job of revitalizing a sorely beleaguered agency. "What I care about most is restoring . . . credibility and integrity. . . . We are going to enforce the law," he announced.

early 1980s, when the senator was chairman of the Labor and Human Resources Committee, which has jurisdiction for health legislation in the Senate.

Congress appeared eager to help Kessler take action to strengthen the FDA in the wake of the generic drug scandal. Findings from the investigations were broadly seen as having shaken the public's confidence in the FDA's ability to protect the public health. The investigations also raised doubts about the validity of scientific data submitted to the agency by pharmaceutical manufacturers, the ethics of an unknown number of FDA staff, and the ability of the agency to police not only the industries it is charged to regulate but its own employees. Kessler said plant inspections to verify the accuracy of information submitted by manufacturers would replace the honor system, under which the FDA previously had assumed that data submitted on drug testing reflected actual studies performed. Criminal investigations by the Justice Department have removed from the agency the handful of employees who had taken illegal payments from drug companies in exchange for preferential treatment of those companies' product marketing applications.

Kessler also has made a point to improve the speed and forcefulness with which the agency regulates prescription drug advertising. In May 1991 the FDA demanded that Bristol-Myers Squibb issue "Dear Doctor" letters to correct statements about its line of anticancer drugs that had been published in a company-sponsored magazine distributed to oncologists; the drugs had been promoted by the manufacturer for unapproved uses. On July 10, 1991, the FDA also demanded that Allergan Pharmaceuticals, Inc., correct advertising that promoted Betagan (levobunolol), prescription eye drops for the treatment of glaucoma, as superior to other companies' ophthalmic solutions.

Under the Food, Drug, and Cosmetic Act, the FDA is responsible for ensuring that drug manufacturers' promotional activities are balanced and truthful. However,

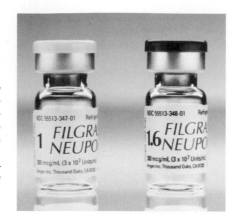
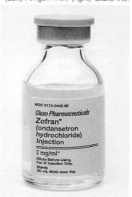

Two drugs approved by the FDA early in 1991 are for cancer patients undergoing chemotherapy. Filgrastim (Neupogen) is the first of a new class of infection-fighting drugs known as colony-stimulating factors; the drug helps immunocompromised patients marshal defenses to resist potentially life-threatening infections associated with reduced white blood cell counts. Ondansetron (Zofran) is an antiemetic agent for alleviating chemotherapy-induced nausea and vomiting—common side effects associated with cancer treatment.

it has not always been possible to strictly regulate physician participation in industry-sponsored activities or to distinguish between events that are promotional in intent and those that are nonpromotional scientific exchanges. In an article in the July 18, 1991, issue of the *New England Journal of Medicine,* Kessler sought the cooperation of physicians in order to guarantee that "scientific and educational activities . . . retain their rigor and intellectual credibility." He pledged that the FDA "is determined to ensure that the promotional activities of pharmaceutical firms are identifiable as such and that they conform to laws."

Congress has also taken a renewed interest in the regulation of pharmaceutical advertising. In December 1990 the Senate Labor and Human Resources Committee held two days of hearings to discuss guidelines that were recently adopted by the American Medical Association and the Pharmaceutical Manufacturers Association regarding appropriate limits on industry gifts to physicians and doctors' honoraria for participating in industry-sponsored symposia.

Another major objective that the new commissioner announced early in his term was to clear the substantial backlog of applications for new drugs and biological products awaiting approval. Computerization of the agency's drug applications files and speeding up of the approval process of drugs for fatal diseases were being considered as remedies for the problem.

New drugs

As the federal agency authorized by law to review new drug products for safety and effectiveness before they are marketed, the FDA approved 23 new chemical compounds in 1990 and 10 in the first six months of 1991 for marketing in the United States. The FDA ranks its approval of each new pharmaceutical by the therapeutic advance that, in the opinion of the agency, the product represents. The average time required for the FDA to complete its review of each of the 23 new drugs approved in 1990 was 27.7 months.

An AA rating is assigned to compounds whose review is given a high priority because they are intended for treatment of AIDS, which currently has no cure. Fluconazole (Diflucan) was the sole product approved in 1990 with a 1AA rating. The "1" indicates that fluconazole is a new chemical compound, never before marketed as a pharmaceutical in the U.S. Fluconazole is a synthetic, broad-spectrum antifungal agent for treating two fungal infections that afflict many persons with AIDS—cryptococcal meningitis and candidiasis. The product was approved on January 29 after a premarket review of just 11 months.

1A approvals. New compounds considered by the FDA to represent an important therapeutic gain over other products already marketed for the same diseases or conditions are rated 1A. Products with A ratings are given the second highest priority of review. In 1990 the average review time for 1A drugs was 17.5 months. These included: idarubicin (Idamycin), approved for the treatment of acute myeloid (nonlymphocytic) leukemia in adults; colfosceri palmitate (Exosurf Neonatal), a synthetic lung surfactant for infants who have or are at risk of developing respiratory distress syndrome or who show evidence of pulmonary immaturity; levamisole hydrochloride (Ergamisole), which is used with 5-fluorouracil as an adjuvant treatment after surgery in patients whose colon cancer has spread to adjacent lymph nodes, a regimen that can substantially reduce the risk of dying from recurrent colon cancer; eflornithine hydrochloride (Ornidyl), a treatment to alleviate inflammation of the brain and the membranes surrounding the brain and spinal cord that constitute the meningoencephalitic stage of the sleeping sickness infection caused by *Trypansoma brucei cambiense;* and altretamine (Hexalen), for palliative treatment of persistent or recurrent ovarian cancer.

Early in 1991 the FDA approved Amgen Inc.'s filgrastim (Neupogen), a granulocyte colony-stimulating factor (G-CSF), for use in cancer patients undergoing chemotherapy to help fight life-threatening infections that are associated with a significant reduction of white blood cells. Depending on the dose, which is calibrated individually according to body weight, the hospital's cost for the drug ranges from $756 to

$2,408 for one regimen of 7 to 14 days, according to Amgen. Neupogen is the first of the neutrophil (white blood cell)-stimulating factors to be approved by the FDA. Some medical scientists consider the discovery of this new class of infection-fighting drugs to be as important as the discovery of antibiotics.

Immunex Corp.'s sargramostim (Leukine) is the second approved colony-stimulating factor. Cleared for U.S. marketing on March 5, 1991, Leukine is a granulocyte-macrophage colony-stimulating factor (GM-CSF), which is comarketed by Hoechst-Roussel Pharmaceuticals under the brand name Prokine. The drug is expected to enhance the safety and recovery of cancer patients who require bone marrow transplants. Hoechst-Roussel states that a hospital's average cost for a 21-day course of Prokine is $2,520 per patient. A cost-benefit study sponsored by the company suggested that sargramostim therapy could lead to a decrease of $10,000 to $15,000 in medical care costs, resulting largely from shorter hospital stays.

A number of colony-stimulating factors are expected to follow filgrastim and sargramostim to market. Essentially, these agents help immature white blood cells (leukocytes) within the bone marrow become mature, functioning cells; thus, they help the body produce leukocytes greater in number and more efficient in fighting disease.

A 1A "orphan" drug approved in 1990, pegademase is an enzyme-replacement therapy for patients diagnosed as having severe combined immunodeficiency (SCID) and whose bodies fail to produce adenosine deaminase (ADA). SCID due to inherited ADA deficiency is an illness that afflicts only about 40 patients worldwide each year, or about one per million births (not all SCID patients lack the enzyme ADA); such patients are at high risk of developing life-threatening infections and without extraordinary isolation measures rarely survive beyond two years of age. Pegademase is currently intended for use in only 19 patients in the U.S. In clinical trials all patients showed considerable improvement—reductions in opportunistic infections and normal frequency of and recovery from ordinary childhood infections. The drug does not cure SCID, however; patients will need to receive it for life. The annual cost for the drug is projected to range from $60,000 to $350,000 per patient.

Under the Orphan Drug Act, which became law in 1983, the FDA makes grants to pharmaceutical companies for drug development of products needed for the treatment of life-threatening disorders that typically affect only a small number of patients. (An orphan disease is defined as a rare disorder that afflicts fewer than 200,000 persons.) Early 1991 saw the approval of two additional orphan products with 1A ratings.

On April 5 the agency approved an orphan drug for Type I Gaucher disease, a hereditary malformation of blood cells that is characterized by an enzyme deficiency and that seriously affects a total American patient population of 2,000 to 3,000 people, largely of Eastern European Jewish descent. Symptoms of the disease include enlargement of the spleen and liver, abnormal pigmentation of skin, anemia, and bone lesions. The drug, alglucerase (Ceredase), manufactured by a relatively new biotechnology company, Genzyme Corp., works as a "targeted" enzyme-replacement therapy that is given by intravenous infusion over one to two hours, usually once every two weeks. The company estimates that the cost for maintenance therapy will range from $20,000 to $60,000 per patient per year. However, the National Gaucher Foundation has estimated that severely ill patients may need to pay up to $200,000 per year for the drug.

Fludarabine (Fludara) was also approved in April; it is for the treatment of patients with B-cell chronic lymphocytic leukemia—a condition diagnosed in about 8,000 patients in the United States each year. The alkylating agent, given intravenously, is an orphan product whose use is limited to patients who have not responded to other therapies or whose disease has progressed despite treatment with a standard alkylating chemotherapeutic drug.

1B approvals. The FDA's 1990 approvals included

Enzon, Inc.

Eight-year-old Laura Boren was the first patient treated with pegademase, an orphan drug for patients with inherited adenosine deaminase deficiency, a condition that afflicts only about 40 patients worldwide each year. She is speaking with physician Michael Hershfield (center) of Duke University Medical Center, Durham, North Carolina, and Abraham Abuchowski, the scientist who pioneered the technology that enabled the enzyme-replacement therapy to be developed.

four 1B drugs—new compounds that in the agency's view represent only modest therapeutic gains over similar products on the market but that nonetheless have potentially important advantages; for example, they offer greater patient convenience, elimination of an annoying though not dangerous side effect, or significant cost savings. The 1B drugs approved were dapiprazole hydrochloride (Rev-Eyes), eye drops to reverse the effects of mydriatic (pupil-dilating) agents used in ophthalmologic examinations; moricizine hydrochloride (Ethmozine), a treatment developed in the U.S.S.R. for life-threatening cardiac arrhythmias (irregular heartbeats); olsalazine sodium (Dipentum), used to maintain remission of ulcerative colitis in patients who cannot tolerate the standard drug therapy, sufasalazine; and technetium $99_{m_{Tc}}$ teboroxime (CardioTec), a myocardial perfusion agent used to distinguish abnormal heart muscle in patients with suspected coronary artery disease.

Early in 1991 ondansetron (Zofran) was approved with a 1B rating for the prevention of nausea and vomiting (emesis), one of the unpleasant side effects associated with cancer treatment. It is the first of a new

The orphan drug alglucerase (Ceredase) will initially help about 2,000 to 3,000 patients with Type I Gaucher disease. These patients, mostly of Eastern European Jewish descent, have an inherited malformation of blood cells and lack the enzyme glucocerebrosidase.

Genzyme Corporation

class of 5-HT$_3$ receptor antagonists to be approved for U.S. marketing. Ondansetron, discovered and marketed by Glaxo, works by blocking the receptors on the vagus nerve, which relays messages to a center in the brain that triggers vomiting. In studies of patients receiving highly emetogenic chemotherapy, 65% had total or near-total elimination of nausea and vomiting. The drug is also very effective in children; odansetron completely controlled vomiting in 58% of pediatric patients on various chemotherapeutic regimens, and 77% had complete or near-complete control. Glaxo estimates that of the one million new cancer diagnoses in the U.S. each year, 500,000 patients will undergo chemotherapy; of that number, about half will experience nausea and vomiting.

Two orphan 1B drugs were approved in early 1991. On January 17 the FDA approved gallium nitrate (Ganite) for treatment of hypercalcemia (excess calcium in the blood) in cancer patients. Although gallium nitrate has a limited market, the manufacturer, Fujisawa Pharmaceutical Co., estimated that the potential patient population for the product is 100,000 to 150,000. Consequently, the FDA gave special consideration to the marketing application in an effort to speed its review; Ganite was approved less than 22 months after Fujisawa submitted its marketing application.

Succimer (Chemet) was approved on January 30 for the treatment of lead poisoning in children. The drug is an orally active heavy metal chelating agent that increases the urinary excretion of lead while sparing other essential trace elements such as zinc, calcium, and iron. Unlike the standard treatment for lead poisoning, which had required hospitalization and a series of painful injections, Chemet 100-mg capsules can be taken on an outpatient basis. The recommended course of treatment is 19 days. The FDA emphasizes that identification and removal of the lead source should accompany the therapy because the drug cannot prevent future poisoning.

A new nonsteroidal anti-inflammatory drug (NSAID), etodolac (Lodine), was approved on Jan. 31, 1991, for the management of the stiffness, inflammation, and other symptoms of osteoarthritis and as a general-purpose analgesic, for the relief of pain. Etodolac's twice-daily regimen may prove to be a key to its usefulness among a crowd of NSAIDs already on the market—many of which need to be taken up to six times a day for an optimal therapeutic effect. The drug has also been shown to cause less gastric damage than similar agents used in the treatment of rheumatic symptoms and is as well tolerated in older (over age 65) as in younger adult patients, according to the manufacturer, Wyeth-Ayerst.

1C approvals. Twelve of the 23 drugs approved in 1990 had 1C ratings—representing new chemical compounds with little or no therapeutic gain over existing products. Estazolam (ProSom) was approved for short-term management of insomnia. Two agents, halobetasol propionate (Ultravate) and fluticasone propionate (Cutivate), are used to relieve inflammatory and pruritic (itching) manifestations of corticosteroid-responsive skin diseases. Technetium 99$_{mTc}$ Sestamibi (Cardiolite) is a myocardial imaging agent for distinguishing normal from abnormal myocardium and localizing abnormal heart muscle tissue in patients with suspected myocardial infarction (heart attack). Technetium Tc 99 mertiatide (Technescan MAG3) was approved as a renal (kidney) imaging agent. Pipercuronium (Arduan) is an adjunct to general anesthesia that provides skeletal muscle relaxation during surgery. Both doxazocin mesylate (Cardura) and isradipine (DynaCirc) are agents for reducing high blood pressure; doxazocin is a twice-a-day alpha-adrenergic blocking drug and isradipine is a once-a-day calcium-channel blocker. Ofloxacin (Floxin) is a quinolone antibiotic for several bacterially caused sexually transmitted diseases and for infections of the lower respiratory tract, urinary tract, and skin. (Quinolones are rapidly bactericidal and are effective against a number of organisms that are resistant to other types of antibiotics.) Bepridil hydrochloride (Vascor) is a therapy for chronic stable angina (chest pains associated with physical exertion). Sermorelin (Geref) is used in evaluating the ability of the pituitary gland to secrete human growth hormone and thereby helps determine whether short physical stature in children is due to growth hormone deficiency. And finally, nafarelin (Synarel) was approved in a nasal-spray form as a treatment for the gynecologic disorder endometriosis, in which tissue grows outside the uterine cavity, causing painful menstruation (dysmenorrhea), painful sexual intercourse (dyspareunia), and, in some cases, infertility.

In January 1991 the FDA approved ramipril (Altace) for treatment of high blood pressure. Ramipril is the latest in a group of cardiovascular agents known as ACE (angiotensin converting enzyme) inhibitors. ACE inhibitors have been shown to be especially effective in lowering blood pressure in patients with low or absent levels of the hormonal substance renin, which is released by the kidneys. One advantage of Altace is that it is taken only once daily.

New formulations. Chemical compounds previously marketed in the U.S. in different formulations are assigned a "3" status. Ratings of 3C were given to two new formulations of ciprofloxacin (Cipro), a broad-spectrum quinolone antibiotic. (Cipro tablets had been approved in 1987 as the first quinolone antibacterial with a broad spectrum of uses: for infections of the lower respiratory tract, skin, bones, joints, and urinary tract.) Cipro I.V., approved on Dec. 26, 1990, is the first parenterally administered quinolone to become available in the United States for use in hospitalized patients. A week later Ciloxan ophthalmic solution became the first quinolone antimicrobial approved for

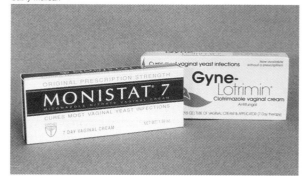

Gyne-Lotrimin (clotrimazole) and Monistat 7 (miconazole nitrate), both formerly prescription antifungal medications for treating vaginal yeast infections and candidiasis, recently became available as over-the-counter products.

ocular use, as treatment for bacterial conjunctivitis and corneal ulcers.

Another 3C reformulated product approved in 1991 was Voltaren Ophthalmic. The 0.1% solution form of the NSAID diclofenac sodium (Voltaren) is for the treatment of postoperative inflammation in patients who have undergone cataract surgery—the first such agent approved for that use. The manufacturer, Ciba-Geigy Corp., which estimates that more than one million cataract operations are performed annually in the United States alone, has established a new division to market the product: Ciba Vision Ophthalmic.

Prescription to OTC status. The FDA granted a different type of approval for two so-called crossover drugs in November 1990 and February 1991, when it cleared for over-the-counter (OTC) sale clotrimazole (Gyne-Lotrimin) and miconazole nitrate (Monistat 7). Both are longtime prescription antifungal products used to treat vaginal yeast infections or candidiasis. As OTC products they are available in cream and suppository forms. In early 1991 the FDA was considering some 20 other prescription drug products for OTC status—for treatment of problems ranging from acne to bee stings to ulcers.

New biologics

The FDA defines "drug" broadly as any "article" that affects bodily functions; the federal Food, Drug, and Cosmetic Act designates that a drug is a product "intended for use in the diagnosis, cure, mitigation, treatment, or prevention of disease" or "intended to affect the structure or any function of the body." The FDA also approves "biological products," which are defined by the Public Health Service Act as "any virus; therapeutic serum; toxin; antitoxin; vaccine; blood, blood component, or derivative; allergenic product or analogous product; or arsphenamine or its derivatives (or any other trivalent organic arsenic compound) applicable to the prevention, treatment, or cure of diseases or injuries of man." The FDA distinguishes drugs from biological products before they are tested in clinical studies. Thus, when a company presents data from laboratory (*in vitro*), animal, and other preclinical studies and requests permission to begin study in humans, the agency at that point determines whether the compound is a drug or a biological product and forwards the application either to the Center for Drug Evaluation and Research or to the Center for Biologics Evaluation and Research.

A significant new biological product was approved in 1990: gamma interferon (Actimmune) to treat chronic granulomatous disease, a rare inherited disorder in which the victim's white blood cells cannot resist infection. Actimmune is an orphan product with an estimated initial patient population of 250 to 400 people. (About 50 new cases of chronic granulomatous disease are diagnosed each year.)

Besides Actimmune, key biological products approved in 1990 included human cytomegalovirus (CMV) intravenous, for attenuation of primary cytomegalovirus disease associated with kidney transplantation; BCG (Bacillus Calmette-Geurin) live (TheraCys) and BCG tuberculosis vaccine (TiceBCG) for the treatment of carcinoma *in situ* of the urinary bladder; T.R.U.E., an allergen patch test for diagnosing contact dermatitis; coagulation factor IX (AlphaNine) for control of bleeding in patients deficient in this vital clotting factor; and epoetin alfa (Procrit) for the treatment of anemia in AIDS patients taking the drug AZT.

Vaccines approved during 1990 included two for immunization of infants as young as two months of age against *Haemophilus influenzae*, type B: HibTITER and PedvaxHIB. In addition, a new inactivated polio vaccine was developed by the French company Institut Merieux and approved for use in the U.S. in December.

Four biologic diagnostic tests also were approved in 1990: a blood test that determines the presence of antibodies to human immunodeficiency virus, type 2 (HIV-2), indicating potential infection; an assay for confirming HIV-I infection; and Ortho HCV Elisa Test System and Chiron HCV C100-3 Antigen, both to detect the presence of antibodies to type C hepatitis virus.

Alzheimer's drug: unresolved questions

One of the most important marketing applications that was still being reviewed by the FDA in early 1991 was for tacrine (tetrahydroaminoacridine), which the Warner-Lambert Co. had proposed to market under the trade name Cognex as a treatment for loss of memory and cognitive functions associated with Alzheimer's disease. Because Alzheimer's disease is a debilitating condition for which no cure or adequate treatment exists, the FDA and the National Institute on Aging helped design an expedited study protocol. Unfortunately, the quickened review process left unan-

swered many questions about the drug's efficacy, and an advisory committee convened by the FDA to review the tacrine study data was therefore unable to recommend approval. The advisory committee's acting chairman called the shortcuts in study design "a gamble" and said the committee might have been better able to recommend approval if the studies had demonstrated "clean, clear-cut" evidence of improvement in patients' cognitive function.

Warner-Lambert had presented data from two key clinical trials. The committee agreed that only one portion of one study showed some statistically significant "small effect," as measured by an objective cognition assessment; ostensible positive results of a second pivotal study, the panel said, were "confounded" by complicating factors, such as the subjects' use of concomitant drug therapy. However, rather than require Warner-Lambert to conduct a new battery of clinical trials, the FDA asked the company in March 1991 to continue study of the drug through an "expanded access" clinical study program. Intended for fatal or irreversible debilitating illnesses for which adequate treatments do not exist, the FDA's expanded access protocol would allow many heretofore untreated patients to receive tacrine before approval—at the same time making it possible for the company to receive broader and more rapid data collection. If tacrine becomes available under such a program, the disadvantage for Warner-Lambert is that it will not be able to sell the product; the mixed blessing for patients is that although distribution will be relatively limited and the product will not have the imprimatur of FDA approval, those who receive the drug will obtain it at no charge during the study program.

"Orphan" developments

As noted above, several of the new therapies approved by the FDA in 1990 and 1991 were orphan drugs, products intended for the treatment of illnesses with limited patient populations. The orphan drug review procedure established by the 1983 Orphan Drug Act for the most part has been a great boon. By early 1991 the FDA had designated 442 products as orphans and had approved 54 of them. Rep. Henry A. Waxman (Dem., Calif.), a principal author of the act, agreed that "by all accounts the act has been a great success," but he also cited a few cases in which it was *too* successful. In 1990 he tried to amend the law to correct what he considers the "unintended effect of increasing prices for otherwise profitable drugs." Specifically, he was referring to three products: Amgen Inc.'s epoietin (Epogen), an antianemia drug that costs patients about $8,000 per year; Lyphomed's aerosolized pentamidine (NebuPent), which is used to treat *Pneumocystis carinii* pneumonia and which costs AIDS patients more than $1,000 annually; and Genentech Inc.'s Protropin and Eli Lilly & Co.'s Humatrope, both genetically engineered human growth hormone agents for treating growth failure in children. Protropin and Humatrope are slightly different chemically, but they are similar in that they cost $10,000 to $30,000 annually.

Because orphan products generally have relatively small markets and little potential to generate revenues, one intention of the act is to provide incentives for manufacturers to develop and market products to treat rare diseases. Such incentives include research and development tax breaks, research grants, and lessened requirements for FDA approval. The key incentive, however, has turned out to be market exclusivity, a seven-year period in which the initial manufacturer can market its orphan product free from competition. At the time the law was enacted, many older products abandoned by their original manufacturers and no longer marketed (hence the term *orphans*) had been identified as possibly useful treatments in rare diseases. Because such products were older, they lacked patent protection, and because their potential uses involved limited markets, it was not cost-effective for manufacturers to invest in the clinical study required for bringing them to market for new uses— particularly if other companies were free to market competitive versions of any successful product.

Recognizing that new products with potentially large markets can be approved initially as orphans for narrow therapeutic uses, Waxman proposed two major changes in the law. One was that profitable orphan products that are developed simultaneously share market exclusivity, thus ensuring price competition. Waxman reasoned that the existence of more than one company interested in developing an orphan product was prima facie evidence of a product's potential profitability. Further, he proposed that market exclusivity be withdrawn if an orphan drug's intended patient population grew beyond the 200,000-patient threshold.

Lilly, Genentech, Amgen, and Lyphomed all opposed the proposed amendments and the concept of shared exclusivity because they had each beaten their competitors in a race to approval and obviously wanted to retain the spoils of their successful research. Waxman reluctantly accommodated their arguments by making his shared exclusivity proposal prospective—*i.e.,* it would apply only to new products designated as orphans after July 1990. However, Lyphomed remained opposed to the bill, anticipating that the population of AIDS patients who became infected with *Pneumocystis carinii* pneumonia in the future might grow beyond the 200,000-patient limit for orphan status. The legislature passed the amendments in October 1990, at the close of the 101st Congress, but Pres. George Bush vetoed the bill on November 9, after intense lobbying by Lyphomed.

Waxman called the veto "shocking" and decried the

Capsule-tampering episodes				
year	drug	poison	locale	deaths
1991	Sudafed 12-Hour	cyanide	Washington	2
1986	Extra-Strength Excedrin	cyanide	Washington	2
1986	Contac, Teldrin, Dietac	rat poison	Orlando, Fla., and Houston, Texas	0
1986	Tylenol Extra Strength	cyanide	Yonkers, N.Y.	1
1982	Tylenol Extra Strength	cyanide	Chicago	7

lost opportunity to "inject competition" into the $100 million-per-year drug markets. He vowed to reintroduce orphan law amendments in the 102nd Congress, but as of mid-1991 he had not done so.

Abuse and tampering

Two over-the-counter cough and cold products that have been marketed for years attracted a degree of notoriety during 1990 and 1991. One of these was Robitussin-DM, marketed by the A.H. Robins division of American Home Products. Reports from poison control centers since mid-1989 have indicated that an increasing number of adolescents have abused Robitussin-DM cough syrup by quaffing entire bottles to obtain a mildly psychoactive effect from the ingredient dextromethorphan. Robins responded in April 1991 by introducing unit-dose vials of the product.

Burroughs Wellcome recalled one million packages of its Sudafed 12-Hour controlled-release decongestant capsules from the market in March 1991 after it received three reports of cyanide poisoning, including two deaths, from Washington state. The events appeared to be a replay of previous OTC-drug-tampering crimes in which the perpetrator replaced the contents of capsule products with poison, returned them to their packages, and replaced them on store shelves for sale. Such tampering first occurred when Tylenol capsules were filled with cyanide in 1982 in the Chicago area. At that time the manufacturer, Johnson & Johnson, withdrew all Tylenol capsules and replaced them with "caplets"—small, capsule-shaped tablets. (More recently the company has introduced one-piece capsules.)

Sudafed's manufacturer also replaced its product with a new dosage form—Sudafed 12-Hour coated tablets; tablets and one-piece or sealed capsules make tampering much more difficult. Although the FDA has considered banning all capsules for OTC products, it is not likely to do so. A major advantage of capsule medications is that for many people they are easier to swallow. It has also been noted that capsules may confer a therapeutic placebo effect to some patients because they resemble prescription medications.

—*Louis A. LaMarca*

369

Special Report
Examining Health in Eastern Europe
by Donald P. Forster, M.B. B.S., M.Sc.

The recent political changes in Eastern Europe have stimulated an increased interest in appraising the social systems of the former Communist states. This is partly because the information for such analyses is now more readily available and partly because, in the wake of political transition, changes in the industrial economy and in the educational and health systems inevitably follow. The scene is therefore set for the evaluation of what may be called a "natural experiment," comparing the old order with the new.

The health legacy
Health or lack of health is determined, broadly speaking, by three factors—namely, the quality of the health care service and of the environment on the one hand and the appropriateness of the life-style of the people on the other. In any country each of these influences on health is related, to a greater or lesser extent, to a nation's economic well-being. This has probably been of more importance in Eastern Europe than in the West since in the former the state exerted central control over both policy and finance.

The assessment of health poses certain problems. Its measurement is difficult, at least when the objective is to compare countries in a reliable way. A valid but indirect method of approaching this task is to use measurable, negative indexes of health, usually in the form of death rates. Data provided by most countries to the World Health Organization (WHO) show that mortality rates for all causes of death were similar in Western and Eastern European nations until about the mid-1960s. In the period since then, mortality rates have shown virtually no improvement in Eastern Europe—for example, in Hungary, Czechoslovakia, and Poland—yet have shown reductions of 20 to 25% in the Western European and North American democracies; East Germany tended to hold a position intermediate between the Western nations and other Eastern European countries.

These findings are reflected in the life expectancy from birth. The average increases in life expectancy in the Western nations from the mid-1960s to the late 1980s were 4.5 years in men and 4.7 years in women. Over the same period in Hungary, Czechoslovakia, and Poland, little change occurred in male life expectancy, while an improvement of only 2.2 years on average was seen in females.

Deaths can be separated into those that are avoidable through appropriate, direct medical care given at the right time and those that are not avoidable through such means but are determined primarily by environmental factors and individual human behavior. Examples of the former include deaths caused by acute appendicitis, hypertension (high blood pressure), and diseases that are preventable by immunization. A good example of the latter is death from lung cancer caused by cigarette smoking, exposure to toxic contaminants, or both. Automobile fatalities constitute another example in this category. Using these two categories, recent studies have demonstrated that the lack of improvement in health in Eastern Europe in the last 15 to 20 years has been due mainly to an increase of about 15% in death rates from conditions that are influenced by environment and lifestyle. In addition, the reductions in Eastern Europe's death rates from conditions avoidable through medical intervention have fallen far short of rates achieved in the West.

Health care systems
The post-World War II health care systems of Eastern Europe were all based broadly on the Soviet model. In general, the health services were well endowed with staff and hospital beds. However, with few exceptions, the quality of the technology in the hospitals was poor. A team of medical personnel from Gloucestershire Royal Hospital in England visited hospital facilities in

Life expectancy from birth: East and West (in years)							
		males	females			males	females
Hungary	1955–59	64.5	68.9	West	1955–59	66.3	71.3
	1965–69	66.9	72.0	Germany	1965–69	67.5	73.5
	1988	66.1	74.2		1988	72.3	79.1
Czecho-slovakia	1955–59	66.6	71.6	England	1955–59	67.9	73.5
	1965–69	67.0	73.5	and Wales	1965–69	68.6	74.5
	1988	67.7	75.3		1988	72.7	78.4
Poland	1955–59	62.1	67.8	United	1955–59	66.7	73.0
	1965–69	66.7	73.1	States	1965–69	66.8	74.1
	1988	67.1	75.7		1987	71.6	78.6
East Germany	1955–59	66.2	70.8	Canada	1955–59	67.7	73.1
	1965–69	68.1	73.2		1965–69	68.9	75.5
	1988	69.7	76.0		1987	73.3	80.2

Source: World Health Statistics Annuals, World Health Organization, Geneva

the town of Brasov, Rom., in 1990. Reporting on their visit in the *British Medical Journal,* they referred to a meeting with one pediatrician who had commented that his most sophisticated piece of equipment was a stethoscope. Visiting the Romanian operating theaters was, in their words, "like stepping back 50 years." In addition, Eastern European countries lacked modern Western pharmaceuticals. For example, death rates from peptic ulcer, a condition that is eminently treatable with modern drugs, have been reduced by at least two-thirds during the last 30 years in the West but not more than one-third in Eastern Europe. On the positive side, however, the comprehensive state health care systems of Eastern Europe always attained high immunization rates, mainly through compulsory schemes.

Within the official health care systems of Eastern Europe, low salaries were prevalent and incentives for doctors and other medical staff were meager. East German doctors, for example, earned less than $1,000 a month—about the same as bus drivers. The relatively low status of medicine compared with occupations such as engineering directly reflected the pecking orders established by the governments, which favored investment in industry. World Bank figures suggest that the percentage of the gross domestic product spent on health care in Eastern European nations was consistently less than in the countries of the Organization for Economic Cooperation and Development.

Even before the political upheavals of 1989 and the mass exodus from East Germany, there was a "brain drain" of doctors from the East. In fact, Czechoslovakia was already training doctors for East Germany in the early 1980s. Evidence of the exodus is seen in the fact that there are now 30% more patients per physician in the former East Germany than in what was West Germany. In addition, the departures of vast numbers of nurses to West Germany added to the drastic shortages of experienced medical personnel in the East.

The medical professions within several of the former Eastern bloc countries have encountered difficulties in starting up independent medical organizations, largely because of a lack of experience. Although the two Germanys theoretically favor uniting their physicians' associations, many obstacles must be surmounted before this can be accomplished. The differences between the Eastern and Western systems are marked, and more than 40 years of rigorous state control in the East cannot be cast off easily or overnight.

A veil of pollution

In the postwar era the Eastern European regimes promoted heavy industrial development. The industrial economy of Eastern European nations was protected from competition from the Southeast Asian countries; it also benefited little from technological advances.

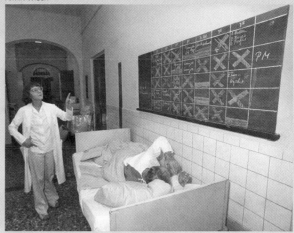

Armin Wiech

Crosses mark canceled operations at St. George's Hospital, Leipzig. With the political upheavals of 1989, doctors and other experienced medical staff from this and other East German cities fled to the West in droves.

Continued emphasis on heavy industry—most of it occurring in outdated plants—led to environmental pollution of major proportions, a problem that was long denied officially by the Communist regimes. Some principal culprits are dust and sulfur dioxide, from the burning of poor-quality brown coal, and heavy metals such as lead, mercury, and cadmium, the mining and processing of which has contaminated the atmosphere and water. The situation was not helped by the failure to set and adhere to safety limits for industrial emissions.

Even in the aftermath of the 1986 accident at the Chernobyl nuclear power plant in the U.S.S.R., there have been relatively few objective published studies from Eastern Europe on the health effects of pollution. However, in Poland, whose pollution problems are considered among the worst in the world, evidence is beginning to emerge of wide-ranging health consequences from decades of environmental devastation, particularly in the Silesian mining area. High and increasing infant mortality rates and a high incidence of congenital defects in children up to age four are among the effects that have been noted. It is believed that ecological conditions are at least partly responsible. The Polish Academy of Science claims that a third of the country's 38 million people live in "areas of ecological disaster." It is hoped that further studies of the scope of the pollution and its effects will determine the extent to which the environmental contamination can be eliminated.

Ways of life

As already noted, the effects of the environment on health have been compounded by life-styles in Eastern Europe. Smoking rates in Poland and Hungary are among the highest in Europe, and there is no doubt

Shoppers queue to buy sausages in Budapest, and smokers in Zabrze, Poland, light up. Diets high in saturated animal fats and smoking rates that are among the highest in Europe undoubtedly have contributed to the low health status of Eastern Europeans.

that smoking has been partially responsible for the increase in coronary heart disease mortality of 40% or more in those countries since the mid-1970s. State-produced cigarettes are cheap (about 35 cents a pack) and strong (without filters). They carry no health warnings, and the harmful effects that are so well known in the West are not widely recognized in the East. Furthermore, international tobacco companies are now beginning to capitalize on what is perceived as a vast new market for their products, which are viewed as status symbols by Eastern Europe's large population of smokers.

Alcohol consumption is high in Hungary and the former East Germany. This is clearly reflected in the fact that mortality rates from cirrhosis of the liver in Hungarian men and women are the highest in the developed world.

There are relatively few objective data about the relationship of diet and disease in the East. Overall, the proportion of total fat in the average diet in Eastern European countries does not appear to be excessively high compared with diets in Western Europe. However, in the East the average diet is such that the proportion of polyunsaturated fats in the total dietary fat is low, while saturated animal fats appear to constitute the main component. The high levels of coronary heart disease mortality found in Eastern Europe would be in accord with such a diet.

All the Eastern European countries have had limited access to fresh fruit and vegetables—important sources of fiber. Epidemiologists have estimated that about 35% of cancer deaths may be due to dietary factors, and research has suggested a link between colorectal cancer and diets that are low in fiber, though the evidence is not conclusive. It may be that a significant proportion of cancer deaths in former

Eastern bloc countries are at least partly attributable to the relative lack of fiber in their diets.

Differences in health and their possible explanations have been explored by demographer Peter Jozan in Budapest. In the early 1980s the variations in male mortality rates between the 22 districts of Hungary's capital city were examined; variations were found to be as wide as those among Western European industrial cities. For example, the life expectancy for males in the "best" district was 69.7 years, yet it was only 64.2 years in the "worst" district. In a statistical analysis it was found that 64% of the variation in life expectancy could be explained by differences in occupation (measured as the proportion of manual workers), in educational levels (number of grades in school completed), and in housing—specifically in terms of overcrowding (measured as persons per 100 rooms). Although these results do not necessarily imply cause and effect, they do suggest that the interplay of lifestyle and environment has been important in explaining mortality in one Eastern European city.

Population policies

In the West the debates and controversies about contraception and abortion policies center on issues of morality, the rights of the unborn child, and the safety and welfare of the mother and family. By contrast, the focus of abortion and contraception policies of former Communist states was on population control. In Hungary, for example, a liberal legal abortion policy was introduced as early as 1956. By 1973 concern about the low birthrate had given rise to restrictions on therapeutic abortions. The procedure was then authorized only if a woman had two living children unless there were other relevant circumstances—for instance, being single or living in poor social conditions.

In Romania abortion on request became legal in 1957. But then in 1966 contraception became illegal, and therapeutic abortion was permitted only for women aged 35 and older with five or more children or if the mother's life was threatened. These conditions were made more restrictive by Nicolae Ceausescu's regime in 1985 and were liberalized again only after the regime's fall in December 1989. The apparent purpose of this dark period in Romania's history was to increase the population by some seven million to eight million persons by the turn of the century. During these draconian times, women of childbearing age were expected to procreate, and they were regularly subjected to compulsory pregnancy examinations. Failure to accede entailed the forfeit of rights to state benefits.

The consequences of Romania's 1966 antiabortion law were a reduction in known legal abortions and an unquantifiable increase in "back-street" abortions. As a result, maternal mortality associated with abortion rose fivefold, according to official figures for the years 1966 through 1983; in the latter year this maternal death rate was 25 times higher than that in neighboring Hungary and over 100 times greater than the abortion-related death rate for England and Wales. The official figures undoubtedly underestimated the real situation; in fact, even the collection of the official data was curtailed in 1984, presumably because the picture they painted was too scandalous for public scrutiny.

The stringent antiabortion measures in Romania gave rise to a temporary increase in births. Further difficulties were caused, however, by the Ceausescu drive to repay foreign hard currency debts, partly through the export of food. The harsh fiscal measures made it difficult for parents to support children. What resulted was an overwhelming number of unwanted, orphaned babies who were also malnourished. In 1990 more than 600 institutions were said to house as

many as 130,000 children under age 18 in the most deplorable conditions.

Now that the harsh population policies have ended, Romanian women are again turning to abortion as the primary form of birth control. The women abort largely because contraceptives are not widely available or are too costly for most to obtain. In 1990 about one million abortions were performed on 600,000 women.

AIDS in the East

In Romania it was a short step from the consequences of the misguided population policy to the outbreak of AIDS (acquired immune deficiency syndrome). Thousands of sickly, unwanted babies housed in pediatric wards and orphanages were subjected to a long-outmoded medical practice—that of unnecessarily injecting frail newborns with adult blood. This was done with reused syringes and contaminated blood supplies. Furthermore, in a situation where both food and milk supplies were restricted, it was common practice to feed malnourished babies intravenously—also with dirty needles. It is believed that AIDS was spread by the constant reuse of needles without adequate sterilization.

WHO sent a team to investigate the pediatric AIDS epidemic in Romania once it had been exposed. Supplies of sterile needles were also dispatched in hopes of halting the outbreak. At the same time, WHO became concerned that the new mobility of the adult populations of Eastern Europe would lead to a rapid and uncontrolled spread of the AIDS virus. Reports of widespread prostitution and heroin use in several of the former Communist-ruled countries prompted WHO to regard Eastern Europe as "the new frontier for the AIDS epidemic."

Anticipated changes

It is apparent that improvements in Eastern European health will not flow from any single intervention. In-

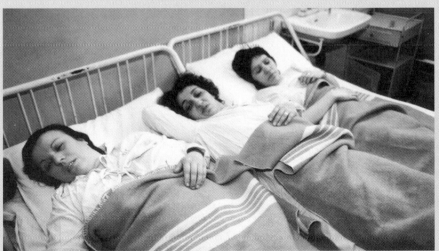

Anthony Suau—Black Star

Women rest after abortions at a clinic in Cantacuzino, Romania. Now that the harsh population policies of the Ceausescu regime have been lifted, women in Romania, who have little access to contraceptives, are turning to abortion as their primary form of birth control. In 1990 about three abortions were performed for every live birth.

Czechoslovak schoolchildren in the town of Mezibori must wear face masks when air quality is poor. Throughout Eastern Europe the promotion of heavy industrial development in the post-World War II era led to environmental pollution of major proportions. Czechoslovakia is one of several countries that are now committed to cleaning up their filthy air and contaminated land and water sites.

troduction of a market-oriented economic system will be a necessary accompaniment of other changes. In the short term, substantial subsidy from the West may be required. As an example, lower incomes in the eastern part of the unified Germany will mean a lower yield in per capita contributions to health insurance, compared with contributions from the western part. Consequently, West German pharmaceutical companies were required, as part of the German unification treaty, to offer a 55% discount in drug costs to patients from the former East Germany. The terms of this agreement have since been altered so that the pharmaceutical industry and the federal government share the cost of the subsidy. Similar subsidies and incentives may also be needed in order to persuade doctors to work in these less wealthy areas in the eastern part.

The types of innovation and the speed at which innovations are introduced are going to vary, given the marked differences among the national cultures and governments; Hungary, for example, has a right-of-center government, while the ideologies within the Czechoslovak government cover a wide range. Nevertheless, nationally based health insurance systems have been proposed in both countries. No doubt the stimulus for this radical change in health services, toward payment of doctors and hospitals on a fee-per-item-of-service basis, is to motivate greater health care activity—*i.e.,* more services and increased use of them. This clearly needs to be supported by attention to quality control and improved equipment.

Policies must also be put in place for environmental correction. Czechoslovakia in particular is now taking steps to clean up its long-polluted environment. Pollution there has taken a major toll on health and

is associated, in part, with life expectancies that are five to seven years shorter than those in Western industrial nations. The wide-ranging cleanup plans include seeking financial assistance from the European Commission for projects such as improving safety in aging nuclear reactors and creating facilities for the treatment of hazardous waste. Such environmental concerns will be at the center of the market economy reforms in Czechoslovakia, even at the cost of delaying some economic growth.

East Germany was left with a legacy of pollution from silver and uranium mines concentrated around the eastern border area adjacent to Czechoslovakia. The now-unused mines are emitting potentially toxic levels of radon gas; lakes contain uranium-laced radioactive sludge; and large waste piles of many toxic materials pose further health hazards. Early in 1991 the Bonn government announced that it would finance a $3.6 billion program to clean up the waste.

Each of the Eastern European countries needs active health-promotion policies to counteract the unhealthy life-styles seen in recent years. Health researchers and educators in the East should now benefit from no longer having to protect the state system from criticism. Indeed, much of the potential improvement in health will depend on the new openness—that is to say, the exposure of policies and services to criticism by the public and experts alike.

It has been some 15 to 20 years since the health record of the Eastern European nations began to diverge from Western standards and deteriorate to the currently low levels. Though many of the requirements for intervention have been identified and are being actively pursued, only some of these will have effects in the short term.

Psychology

In the United States over the past quarter century, there have been drastic changes in the composition of the psychological community. In the early 1960s the membership of the American Psychological Association (APA) was evenly divided between psychologists with academic-scientific interests (experimental psychologists) and those with clinical-health service interests (clinical psychologists). By 1981 nearly two-thirds of the membership was in the latter category. Corresponding changes occurred in graduate training; from 1970 to 1984 the number of experimental psychology doctorates awarded declined, while those in clinical psychology doubled.

Rifts and changes

One consequence of this shift was an increasing estrangement of experimental psychologists from the APA; not only have large numbers dropped their membership, but relatively few of the new graduates have become members. There had been a prevailing opinion that the APA was too much concerned with the interests of clinicians, especially those in private practice, to the neglect of academic-scientific interests.

A number of organizational changes were proposed to make the APA more attractive to academic-scientific psychologists. The most recent of these proposals was that three "assemblies"' be established, each with a relatively high level of autonomy, to replace the existing 40-odd, mostly small, special-interest divisions. Namely, these were to be an experimental-applied assembly, a clinical practice assembly, and a public interest assembly. This proposal, strongly supported by the experimentalists, was decisively defeated by a mail vote.

There were two important consequences of that vote, however. First, the governing bodies of the APA moved quickly to augment services for academic members, providing substantial financial support for a scientifically oriented board, a "science directorate," to be parallel with a "practice directorate." An example of the new efforts aimed at appealing to experimental psychologists was the initiation of a "science weekend" at the annual convention. The weekend at the 1990 meeting had as a theme "the scientific bases of psychological interventions." Other support came in the sponsorship of a number of distinguished scientist lectures, the establishment of grants-in-aid for experimental psychology graduate students working on their dissertations, and coverage of graduate students' convention-travel expenses.

A second consequence of the rejection of the assemblies plan was the immediate formation of a new national organization, expressly designed to serve scientific interests. For several decades the independent Psychonomic Society has provided a kind of home for experimental psychologists. It has well-attended annual meetings and a number of prestigious journals. However, its membership is limited to well-established researchers—to the exclusion of recent graduates aspiring to research-oriented careers.

The new, more comprehensive organization, formally initiated at the 1988 APA convention, was called the American Psychological Society (APS). Presently there is a high degree of overlap in the membership lists of the APA and the APS (three-quarters of the APS members have retained APA membership). Several APA past presidents actively worked in the formation and publicizing of the APS. Both organizations are now taking an active political role, especially in lobbying for financing of research and training. At present the relationship between the APA and the APS is a somewhat uneasy one; it remains to be seen how that situation will evolve. Currently both professional organizations appear to be in good shape.

In 1992 the APA celebrates its centennial, at which time its new 11-story headquarters in Washington, D.C., is scheduled to be occupied. With nearly 400 employees and a 1991 operating budget of more than

Brad Bower—Stock, Boston

A heated issue in psychology today is whether psychologists should be allowed to prescribe a limited number of psychoactive drugs. Some clinical psychologists oppose the idea because they believe that not having access to medications has enabled them to develop dynamic "talking" therapies and to be more effective psychotherapists.

$40 million, it is fiscally sound. Moreover, a recent survey of APA members (described more fully below) found an unusually high level of satisfaction with the organization (*e.g.,* 90% of those questioned rated the APA positively for providing guidance that had been helpful in professional advancement); this is especially significant because 34% of those polled were primarily affiliated with a university or other academic institution, and only 28% were in private practice.

By mid-1991 the APS had over 11,000 members, far fewer than the APA's 100,000-plus members (and several thousand associate members). Given the growing discrepancy in numbers between academic-scientific and health-service providers in psychology, the APS has not done badly. It has a highly motivated membership, a strongly supported annual convention, and a growing publication program. Its flagship bi-monthly journal is *Psychological Science,* edited by Harvard University psychologist William K. Estes, and a second journal, *Trends in Psychological Science,* to consist of brief reviews of work in selected scientific research areas, is planned. Hence, in spite of its youth, the APS seems to be firmly established.

Should psychologists prescribe drugs?

Perhaps the "hottest" issue in clinical psychology in the past few years has been the question of whether properly trained psychologists should be permitted to prescribe medications. First seriously suggested by U.S. Sen. Daniel Inouye (Dem., Hawaii) in a 1984 address to the Hawaiian Psychological Association, this proposition initially received a chilly reception from psychologists, including many clinical psychologists. Recently, however, the response has become increasingly positive. The complex implications are evident in the pro and con arguments.

Pro. The initial impetus for the proposition, and still probably the most important reason for favoring it, is that important segments of the population are simply not getting the treatment they need. The elderly, the rural population, and military personnel are grossly underserved by mental health services. For example, the 700,000 active-duty troops in the U.S. Army are served by 180 psychiatrists and 120 psychologists. Granting clinical psychologists the right to prescribe from a limited formulary of some dozen drugs would mean that more patients who could benefit from medications would be able to receive them.

A second, more general argument for granting clinical psychologists prescription privileges is that it would enable them to more effectively treat clients who need temporary psychoactive medications (mainly antidepressants and antianxiety agents) in order to permit an orderly introduction of other psychotherapeutic measures. Viewed in this way, having prescription-writing privileges would be a logical extension of the clinical psychologist's practice.

Finally, it would not be unique for clinical psychologists in the U.S. to prescribe medications, as a number of other nonphysician groups of health professionals presently have at least limited prescription privileges. These include psychologists within the U.S. Indian Health Service, nurse-practitioners in 34 states, physician assistants in 28 states, pharmacists in the state of Florida, and dentists, podiatrists, and optometrists in all 50 states. Therefore, proponents ask, why not include properly trained psychologists also—especially in light of the degree to which their present training prepares them to understand and treat their clients behaviorally?

Con. Many psychologists believe that accepting prescription-writing privileges would be an endorsement of the so-called medical model, which is intrinsic to psychiatric treatment. Avoiding such an alleged capitulation, against which many psychologists have long struggled, seems to be the strongest argument against the proposal. A related argument is that giving even limited prescription privileges to psychologists would substantially eliminate the last remaining important de facto distinction between psychiatrists and clinical psychologists and that the consequent blurring of professional identities is undesirable.

Some psychologists also think that not having direct access to the use of psychoactive medications has resulted in more creative approaches to psychotherapy. They believe that maintaining the status quo in this regard should help ensure the continuation of such an advantage.

Growing support. What are the prospects for federal and/or state approval of prescription privileges for U.S. psychologists? They are surprisingly good, it now seems, in light of the early ambivalence within the field of psychology itself. An independent Washington, D.C., opinion-poll firm recently surveyed the APA membership on a variety of issues. Extensive telephone interviews with 1,505 randomly selected APA members were conducted during December 1990. For the first time, a majority of those questioned supported the prescription proposition; 68% said they "strongly support" or "somewhat support" proposed legislation that permits licensed clinical psychologists who undergo additional training to prescribe some psychoactive drugs for their patients. The same respondents even more strongly supported a pilot project that is presently under way within the Department of Defense, in which military psychologists are receiving training to prescribe therapeutic drugs. Over five times as many positive as negative responses were obtained—78% in favor of the project, and only 15% against it, the remainder expressing no opinion.

The objective of the Defense Department's project is to assess the desirability of a more systematic and permanent program. The study was endorsed by Congress in 1989, and a blue-ribbon advisory panel was formed by the U.S. surgeon general in 1990 to work out a detailed plan. The panel agreed on a formal training curriculum. A four-month academic program was then started at Ft. Sam Houston in San Antonio, Texas, in September 1990, to be followed by eight months of intensive "hands-on" training at Walter Reed Army Medical Center in Washington, D.C.

The relatively bright prospects of the prescription-privileges proposition have been expressed by one key player, Patrick DeLeon. DeLeon is a clinical psychologist who for many years has served as a legislative assistant to Senator Inouye; his qualifications include a law degree. As reported in *Clinical Psychiatric News* (June 1989), DeLeon "walked into the lion's den at the annual meeting of the American Psychiatric Association with a provocative prediction: psychologists are going to be given the right to prescribe psychotropic medications." In spite of the "heated protest" from the floor that these remarks elicited, DeLeon commented that "prescribing is no big deal—except for turf reasons" and predicted that psychologists' prescription privileges will evolve in steps over several years.

Hawaii was the first state in which the prescription issue was openly debated. In 1990 state legislators adopted a resolution that supported open discussion of the matter in order to "address the issue of the unserved mental health needs of Hawaii's people and the possibility of allowing appropriately trained psychologists to prescribe psychotropic medications in diagnosis and treatment."

During the August 1990 annual convention, the APA council of representatives voted 118–2 to finance a "task force on prescription privileges." Among the envisioned benefits of so enlarging the role of the clinical psychologist were improved health services for elderly and rural residents, more appropriate approaches to women's health needs, and new ways of addressing needs of the homeless.

At present, an acknowledged "sticky" problem is the need for responsible programs for training psychologists in the use of psychoactive medications. Because of the lack of existing training facilities capable of both hands on supervision and competency certification, DeLeon has supported a collaboration of psychologists with schools of nursing in the 34 states in which nurses are currently authorized to prescribe. In fact, there is a firm basis for such a collaboration, as nearly one-fifth of doctoral-level nurses have degrees in psychology.

Of course, it is impossible to foretell the roles that psychologists and psychiatrists will have as health professionals if, in fact, prescription privileges are granted to psychologists on anything resembling a national scale. There will surely be continued erosion of the differences between the two professions. To some extent it is likely to accentuate the adversarial feelings that psychiatrists have toward psychologists, as the

B.F. Skinner, who was one of the most influential psychologists of the 20th century, died of leukemia in August 1990 at age 86. Skinner was first and foremost a behavioral psychologist who helped shape behaviorism as a science and a philosophy.

former feel their "turf" being increasingly encroached on. However, there is not likely to be much change in the generally superior ability of psychiatrists to deal with more serious mental disorders. Traditionally, this has been an important advantage of psychiatric training. Whether the traditional superiority of the clinical psychologist in the research arena will also persist remains to be seen; the answer may largely depend on how effectively research training is emphasized by independent, clinically oriented schools of psychology that are now training increasing numbers of practicing psychologists. These schools grant the doctor of psychology degree, but they do not require a research dissertation.

B.F. Skinner: passing of a pioneer

B.F. Skinner, probably the most prominent and the most controversial psychologist of the last half of the 20th century, died of complications from leukemia on Aug. 18, 1990, at the age of 86. Little more than one week earlier, at the APA's annual convention in Boston, he had received a "Citation for Lifetime Contributions to Psychology," the first such recognition to be awarded by the organization. As the APA president, Stanley Graham, said when presenting the award: "[Skinner] initiated a revolution in thinking in psychology and continues to have an enormous influence on the field today." At the Boston meeting Skinner delivered a dramatic 15-minute address, speaking clearly and without notes, in spite of the ravages of his fatal disease, to an appreciative overflow audience of 1,500.

Skinner's contributions spanned a remarkably wide range, from such eminently practical devices as teaching machines and "Air-Cribs" for babies to pragmatic "treatments" based on schedules of reinforcement and to theoretical formulations on evolutionary determinants of behavior. First and foremost, however, Skinner was a behavioral psychologist—a pioneer who helped shape behaviorism as a science and a

One of B.F. Skinner's many innovations was the Air-Crib, a germ-free mechanical baby tender, which he believed would provide an optimal environment for a child's growth and development during the first two years of life. His daughter Deborah, pictured in 1945 at 13 months of age, was the device's first "guinea pig."

philosophy. His "operant conditioning" theories were couched in a radical behavioristic position that denied scientific status to "mentalistic" concepts. He adamantly denounced "the mysterious world of the mind," which he called "an unwarranted and dangerous metaphor." Skinner was especially antagonistic to the emergence in the 1970s of cognitive theory and research in psychology. He elicited a gasp from his last audience at the APA convention when he called cognitive science "the creationism of psychology" and described the departure from the APA of some cognitivists as "not a secession but . . . an improvement."

Skinner's theoretical emphasis was on the emission of behavior rather than on responses to stimuli. Early in his career he abandoned the reflex concept developed by the Russian physiologist Ivan Pavlov. His own operant conditioning was developed as a kind of complement to Pavlovian, or classical, conditioning; the pivotal difference between these two paradigms is whether behavior to be learned is emitted with no apparent stimulation (Skinnerian) or is elicited by overt stimuli (Pavlovian).

Skinner is perhaps best known for the development of the operant conditioning chamber for use with small animals, mainly rats and pigeons; this device is widely known as the "Skinner box," although it was not so called by Skinner himself. His use of rats and pigeons as learning subjects in a progressively regulated reinforcement procedure ("shaping") is illustrative of the kind of research Skinner carried out. Withholding reinforcement until the desired behavior is emitted causes the probability that the behavior will occur to be increased and thus shapes behavior. The power of such shaping is seen in what Skinner called "superstitious behavior" (named from the similarity of the behavioral process—which is based on random reinforcements—to that commonly noted in human superstition). For example, if an experimenter randomly reinforces a pigeon (with access to grain),

the pigeon will then consistently raise its right wing, or lower its head, or do whatever it happened to be doing in the operant chamber when the first few random reinforcements were given. A more familiar example of shaping is the training of pigeons to play Ping-Pong (reinforcements were given for batting a Ping-Pong ball back and forth)—an achievement for which Skinner said he did not wish to be remembered.

Skinner's *Verbal Behavior* (1957) was perhaps his most important book, or at least it was apparently so regarded by Skinner himself. In this work he developed the thesis that verbal behavior is essentially like other behavior rather than being unique and invariably determined by genetically given principles. The latter position has been strongly argued by linguist Noam Chomsky, whose highly critical review of *Verbal Behavior* was very influential and was widely regarded as a devastating blow to Skinner's theoretical framework. Nevertheless, interest in Skinner's approach to the problem has recently begun to be revived.

Skinner himself did not respond to this attack. It is interesting that over his 60-year career in psychology, he rarely took note, at least publicly, of opposing or alternative perspectives. He had enough confidence in the correctness of his own positions to be able to ignore the alternatives.

A comprehensive list of Skinner's applications of behavior analysis to practical problems would have to include the improvement of education, mainly through the substitution of positive reinforcers, such as praise, for negative reinforcers, such as punishment, and the use of programmed instruction and teaching machines; the education of the severely retarded; the treatment of behavioral problems, mainly by means of behavior-modification techniques; the rearing of infants, exemplified by the invention for one of his own children of a soundproof, germ-free, temperature-controlled, automated baby crib—which he considered an optimal environment for a child's growth and

378

development in the first two years of life; the betterment of society, as envisioned in his popular utopian novel, *Walden Two* (1948), and in his more controversial book, *Beyond Freedom and Dignity* (1971), in which he questioned the value of some of society's most revered concepts and challenged society to improve itself by applying his own radical principles as replacements; and a host of less well-publicized contributions in other areas (*e.g.,* business management, thinking and perception, military systems, and, in his later years, gerontology).

Burrhus Frederic Skinner, more familiarly known as Fred, was indeed "a giant of our discipline," as he was acclaimed by Raymond Fowler, editor of the *American Psychologist* and chief executive officer of the APA. His contributions to both the theory and the practice of psychology will no doubt have an incalculable, continuing influence on the field.

—*Melvin H. Marx, Ph.D.*

Sexual and Reproductive Health

Recent events have had both medical and social impacts on the reproductive health and freedom of women in the United States. Although some progress has been made in a few areas, the overall situation for American women is a bleak one—considerably bleaker than for women in many other developed countries. There has been an alarming increase in the incidence of sexually transmitted diseases (STDs), including the reemergence of infections that had been under control—most notably, syphilis—and several newer viral STDs, for which there is presently no effective form of therapy. This situation has led to near epidemics of pelvic inflammatory disease (PID), resulting in many cases of infertility and ectopic pregnancy.

The methods of contraception currently available to U.S. women, with a single exception, are essentially those that have been available since the 1960s. By comparison, women in many other countries have considerably more options. Moreover, fears and anxieties regarding several current methods (sometimes without basis in fact) have contributed to the approximately three million unplanned pregnancies that occur each year—more than half of which end in abortion. For years the U.S. has had higher pregnancy and abortion rates than any other industrialized country. More than one million of the unwanted pregnancies that occur each year are in the teenage population. Lobbying by antichoice groups has played a role in blocking the development of contraceptive agents; it has also narrowed access to legal pregnancy termination.

The *Webster* v. *Reproductive Health Services* decision of the U.S. Supreme Court on July 3, 1989, opened the door to state-by-state removal of the freedom of choice granted by the *Roe* v. *Wade* decision of 1973. Shortly after the *Webster* decision, the repercussions were being felt nationwide, and the women most severely affected are those who are indigent, live in rural areas, or reside in states (such as Utah and Louisiana) that have made or would make abortion virtually unattainable for the majority of women in those states. On April 28, 1991, an antiabortion law in Utah, which had been rushed through the state legislature earlier in the year, took effect. When originally enacted, it had sanctioned the death penalty for any woman in the state who had an illegal abortion and for her doctor, but the law was "clarified" before taking effect to remove the possibility of a murder charge. Louisiana enacted one of the nation's strictest abortion measures in June 1991. The Louisiana law states that "life begins at conception" and permits abortion

Walt Handelsman; reprinted by permission of Tribune Media Services

only if the life of the mother is at risk or if a woman is a victim of rape or incest and reports the crime to authorities. Louisiana doctors who perform abortions could face prosecution under the new law.

Nationally, prospects for obtaining safe, legal abortions became even dimmer on May 23, 1991, when the Supreme Court ruled 5–4 to uphold government regulations that bar federally funded family-planning clinics from discussing abortion with patients (or even answering patients' questions about options). The ruling affects about 4,000 clinics across the country that serve some 4.5 million women, largely those with low incomes. Many physicians see the decision as a direct attack on their right to discuss treatment options with patients.

Poor and disadvantaged women in the U.S. continue to be the victims of substandard medical care in other ways as well. This is particularly evident in the inadequate prenatal care they receive, resulting in the country's unacceptably high infant mortality rate.

Some startling new evidence concerns male reproductive health. Several recent studies now suggest that toxic damage to sperm may be responsible for a

In a May 1991 ruling the U.S. Supreme Court barred federally funded family-planning clinics from even mentioning abortion to clients. Many physicians see the so-called gag rule as an infringement on their right to discuss treatment options with patients.

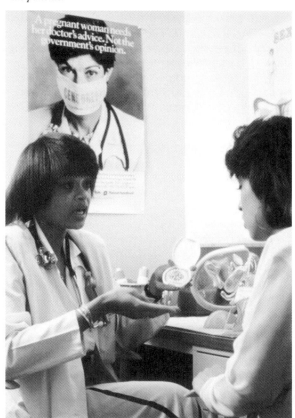

Michael L. Abramson/Time Magazine

sizable number of the 250,000 U.S. babies born each year with birth defects. Previously the cause of some 60–80% of birth defects was unknown; while birth defects related to exposures in women—*e.g.,* from cigarettes, alcohol, thalidomide, and diethylstilbestrol (DES)—have accounted for some of the total, sperm were assumed to have an all-or-nothing effect on the induction of pregnancy and no impact on fetal abnormalities. The research in this area is not yet conclusive, but both animal studies (which show that defects in offspring may result when males are exposed to more than 100 different chemical substances) and human epidemiological studies (which link fathers' occupations to birth defects in children) now lend strong credence to an important role for sperm. Such findings could lead to new laws regulating toxic exposure of males at the workplace.

STD epidemic

Not too many years ago, the term *venereal disease* (VD) was used to describe those medical conditions that resulted from the transmission of organisms at the time of sexual intercourse. These diseases were only five in number (syphilis, gonorrhea, chancroid, lymphogranuloma venereum, and granuloma inguinale) and, in almost all instances, could be diagnosed and treated successfully. Now, however, at least 20 organisms that can be transmitted sexually are recognized, and they are known to result in at least 50 different STD syndromes.

There are several reasons for this increase—in some instances to epidemic proportions, with more than 12 million cases occurring annually in the United States alone. The most important causes are changes in social and sexual behavior. In the U.S. the average age at first intercourse has declined progressively over the past several decades. In addition, it is common for young people to have many sexual partners. These situations have been accompanied by low usage of effective contraception, particularly the barrier methods that protect against both pregnancy and STD transmission.

To complicate matters further, several of the common STDs have long incubation periods and few or no symptoms, thus permitting their unknowing transmission to other individuals. Yet another factor that has allowed the rapid and uncontrolled spread of infection is the great increase in world travel. Finally, the newer viral STDs—such as human papillomavirus, human immunodeficiency virus (HIV), hepatitis B, and genital herpes—remain difficult to diagnose accurately and in most instances impossible to treat effectively.

Return of "the shadow on the land"

Syphilis was first described in Europe in the early 16th century and subsequently spread worldwide. In the 1930s U.S. Surgeon General Thomas Parran began a campaign, emphasizing partner notification and rigorous treatment, to wipe out this infection, which he called "the shadow on the land." With the development of penicillin in the 1940s, it seemed that the conquest of syphilis was a reasonable and achievable goal. Indeed, syphilis cases declined by 99%, and for several decades the disease appeared to be under control. Now, however, the U.S. is experiencing the highest rates of syphilis in 40 years.

The Centers for Disease Control (CDC) in Atlanta, Ga., estimated that there were 50,223 cases of primary and secondary syphilis in 1990, a rate of 20 cases per 100,000 population—up 9% from 1989 and representing the highest rate since 1949. It is clear that a large portion of this increase is occurring in urban-dwelling blacks—a rise attributed to poverty and social conditions. Rates among blacks more than doubled from 52.6 to 121.8 per 100,000 between 1985 and 1989. Rates among Hispanics were high but essentially remained stable.

In the late 1970s and early 1980s syphilis rates were highest among homosexual and bisexual men. Owing to the increasing threat of AIDS, however, the sexual practices of this population group have altered considerably, which has resulted in a marked drop in their rates of syphilis.

The connection of syphilis to AIDS is now well recognized. Since any open genital sore will allow the transmission of HIV (the AIDS virus) to occur more readily, the lesions of syphilis (as well as of herpes, chancroid, and other STDs) provide an easy route of access and thus increase the risk of spreading AIDS. Furthermore, the evidence is mounting that HIV infection alters the clinical course of syphilis and the response to treatment. Intensive early therapy and novel approaches to treatment are needed when individuals have concurrent infections.

Syphilis is caused by a spiral-shaped organism (spirochete) known as *Treponema pallidum*. The disease has three clinical stages. In the first stage (primary syphilis), a painless sore (chancre) appears about three weeks after exposure; it is usually found on the genitalia but can occur at any point of sexual contact. Whether treated or not, the lesion will disappear after two to six weeks. About six to eight weeks later, the spirochetes spread via the bloodstream throughout the body, resulting in the second stage of the disease (secondary syphilis). This is most often characterized by a rash, but the patient may also develop swollen lymph nodes, headache, sore throat, weight loss, and malaise. During this second phase, multiple body organs may be damaged, including the brain, eyes, liver, and kidneys. Even if untreated, the patient will usually become relatively asymptomatic again (a latent period) but will remain infectious for about another two years. After a variable length of time (from one to as many as 20 years), the infec-

This poster from the 1940s warned U.S. servicemen that any woman—even the "girl next door"—could be a "VD" carrier. In the 1990s syphilis, which for decades was under control, has reemerged at epidemic levels.

tion reaches the third stage (tertiary syphilis), which can cause irreversible systemic damage to the skin, central nervous system, cardiovascular system, brain, bones, liver, and other organs.

It is also possible to transmit syphilis to a fetus during pregnancy. When the baby is born, it may be asymptomatic or the disease may be suspected because the infant has a runny nose, rash, anemia, or other systemic symptoms. However, no symptoms may develop for weeks or months. Late congenital syphilis (with symptoms appearing after the third month of life) may result in meningitis, deafness, slow-developing hydrocephalus, and permanent damage to bones, teeth, the spleen, and liver.

There are many reasons for the increasing number of cases of syphilis that are not being detected or reported at early stages. For one thing, routine testing of all U.S. hospital patients was discontinued when it appeared that syphilis was under control; only New York state has resumed testing because of the recent rise in incidence. Moreover, there have been sharp cutbacks in funding for public health services, which have had the primary responsibility for STD control and treatment. The majority of today's syphilis cases, however, are the result of the changing social, economic, and behavioral factors already described. One predominant reason for the present high rates, especially in minority groups, is the widespread practice of trading sex for drugs—crack, in particular. In addition, many substance abusers, particularly teenagers, do not use any form of contraception.

The very nature of the disease itself adds to the complexity of the present problems. Syphilis has been called "the great imitator" because in all three of its stages it can appear in the guise of many other diseases—a circumstance that has led to many missed or incorrect diagnoses. Moreover, physicians today have been lulled into a false sense of security because it appeared that the disease was in check; thus, they often do not think of syphilis initially when a patient manifests symptoms that present a diagnostic problem. When the diagnosis is missed, the disease will inexorably progress to the next stage. Another confounding problem in controlling the current epidemic is that the traditional method of partner notification has become a much less effective form of control since many individuals with syphilis are substance abusers and, in return for drugs, have frequent sex with individuals whom they are unable to identify once the diagnosis has been made. A recent study in Portland, Ore., for example, showed an average of five nonidentifiable sexual partners among 146 syphilis-infected heterosexual adults.

It is estimated that if the current trends continue, annual rates of as many as 130,000 cases of syphilis will be seen in the late 1990s. This figure does not account for the well-recognized fact that at least 25% of cases of syphilis are not reported to health authorities.

PID: rampant and ravaging

Pelvic inflammatory disease is a loosely used term that refers to inflammation or infection of the female genital tract that occurs primarily as a result of one or more STDs. Many physicians feel that the term lacks specificity and have suggested that several terms related to the particular portions of the reproductive tract involved in the disease process would more appropriately describe the condition.

Many different organisms have been incriminated in these infections. The two that are of primary importance and that often occur together are *Neisseria gonorrhoeae* and *Chlamydia trachomatis*—both bacteria. Gonorrhea has been recognized for years as a primary cause of PID, and adequate forms of antibiotic therapy have been developed. Despite the development of several drug-resistant gonorrhea strains, the number of cases in the U.S. has plateaued at about 1.4 million per year. Chlamydia, on the other hand, is a more recently recognized infection that is increasing rapidly; in fact, it is now the most prevalent STD, with four million cases in the U.S. annually.

The majority of women infected with these bacterial diseases remain virtually asymptomatic for considerable periods of time. When symptoms of gonorrhea and chlamydia infection do start to develop, women most commonly experience pelvic pain of varying degrees of severity, which can be exacerbated by sexual intercourse and various athletic activities.

Once an attack has progressed to become more severe, patients become more and more symptomatic. They develop fever and an increase in pain as the infection first involves the uterus, then spreads to adjacent pelvic tissues (or structures). When treatment for gonorrhea is delayed or inadequate, serious illness— *e.g.,* arthritis, meningitis, or septicemia (infection of the bloodstream)—as well as PID may result. In their most severe forms, PID infections result in pelvic abscesses

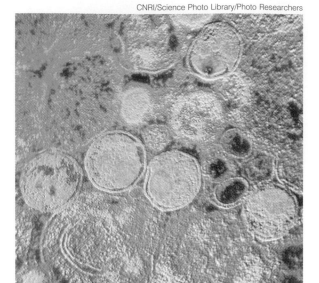

Sexually transmitted infections caused by Chlamydia trachomatis *are a major cause of serious pelvic inflammatory disease in women; if untreated, these infections can result in permanent sterility. Moreover, chlamydia is now thought to be responsible for 50–80% of cases of ectopic pregnancy.*

that can involve the fallopian tubes, the ovaries, or both. This is a potentially very dangerous situation since the rupture of such abscesses can result in endotoxic shock (caused by poisonous substances present in bacterial organisms) or even death.

Chronic PID can lead to temporary or permanent infertility or life-threatening ectopic pregnancy. Current estimates are that some 250,000 women are rendered permanently sterile by complete tubal occlusion annually. When tubes are only partially blocked, fertilization can occur; however, because the fertilized egg is unable to pass down the tube, an ectopic pregnancy (implantation within the tube) can result. Such a pregnancy can rupture through the wall of the tube, often producing major blood loss or passage of the egg into the abdomen, where in rare cases it continues to develop. A ruptured ectopic pregnancy almost always requires emergency surgery to remove the damaged tissue; in some cases a portion of the tube can be spared, but often the surgery renders the woman permanently sterile on the affected side.

The rate of ectopic pregnancies in the U.S. has been increasing steadily. In 1970 there were 18,000 such pregnancies reported to the CDC; by 1987 there were 88,000. It is now believed that many of these (an estimated 50–80%) are due to chlamydia infections that have gone unrecognized. Because the incidence of undiagnosed PID is already so high and is apparently increasing, and because untreated infections can cause such extensive reproductive ravages, the CDC recently convened a panel of experts to review the data on PID. The experts saw the need for better diagnostic measures, new programs to educate physicians, nationwide screenings, better treatments, and considerable further research into PID's causes.

One long-implicated cause of PID—the intrauterine device (IUD)—has recently been exonerated, at least by one study. Researchers from the University of Washington's department of biostatistics and the Center for Research on Population and Security (Research Triangle Park, N.C.) found that IUD users were not at increased risk of pelvic infection. Earlier research condemning IUDs and litigation against several manufacturers had led to the removal of all but two devices from the U.S. market. (In other countries, particularly China, IUDs continue to be one of the most widely accepted forms of contraception—used by an estimated 84.5 million women worldwide.) While the findings of the recent study are persuasive, further research is necessary; moreover, for the present, IUDs are still not recommended for women with a history of PID or ectopic pregnancy or who are at high risk for STD.

Fertility potential of older women

For centuries it had been believed that once a woman stopped ovulating and reached menopause, she would be unable to bear children. However, major innovations in the induction of pregnancy have now changed that. A report in the *New England Journal of Medicine* in October 1990 described the successful pregnancies of four postmenopausal women—one of whom had twins. They had been "primed" for pregnancy by hormonal therapy. Their husbands' sperm was used to fertilize ova obtained from younger, premenopausal women, and the fertilized ova were then released into the uterine cavities of the older women. The chances of fetal abnormalities occurring with this procedure are low because the ova are donated by younger women.

To those working in the field of obstetrics and gynecology, this accomplishment is generally viewed as having great medical interest. For the individual women involved, it represents a near miracle. However, the risks to the fetus and the mother associated with pregnancy and delivery increase progressively with advancing age—mortality being six times greater for women aged 40–50 years as compared with women in their twenties. Furthermore, the personal, social, and psychological impact of births to older and postmenopausal women have not been determined. It remains to be seen what the overall long-term risks and benefits of such procedures will be. In an editorial, Marcia Angell, one of the *New England Journal*'s editors, commented: "The limits on childbearing years are now anyone's guess; perhaps they will have more to do with the stamina required for labor and 2 AM feedings than with reproductive function." At present, it seems unlikely that numerous pregnancies of this type will be undertaken.

Contraception developments

For many years the field of contraception research and development has been seriously underfunded in the U.S., and American women have had dwindling birth control options. Furthermore, once a leader in this area, the U.S. has now lost its position of prominence. This circumstance has resulted in a situation that is detrimental to women the world over who depend on the U.S. pharmaceutical industry and the Food and Drug Administration (FDA) for the development, testing, and approval of safe and effective therapeutic drugs and devices, including contraceptives.

A long-awaited new contraceptive. The introduction in late 1990 of the subdermal hormonal implant known as Norplant was notable because it was the only major new form of pregnancy prevention to become available in the last 30 years. This particular form of contraception had been under investigation in the U.S. since 1966; 16 other countries had previously approved the method. It is considered one of the most effective contraceptives ever marketed—with a failure rate of less than 1%. The six flexible capsule implants (each about the size of a matchstick) are introduced under the skin of the upper arm and protect against unwanted pregnancy for at least five years. Studies have shown that after removal of the implants, 86% of women who attempt to conceive become pregnant within one year.

The major clinical disadvantage of Norplant is that considerable irregularity in bleeding cycles has occurred in many users, particularly in the first months after implantation. About 2–7% of women discontinue use of the implants within the first year because of this problem. Norplant is also a relatively expensive form

In 1990 Norplant became the first new form of contraception available to U.S. women in 30 years. The six matchstick-size capsules, implanted under the skin of the upper arm, provide protection against pregnancy for five years.

Wyeth-Ayerst Laboratories

of contraception when viewed from the perspective of the initial outlay of $500–$700. When costs are pro-rated over the five-year duration, however, the method is somewhat less expensive than monthly packs of oral contraceptives. Despite the implant's reliability for contraception, unless the user is in a long-term mutually monogamous relationship, she still needs to use condoms for protection against STDs.

Six-year IUD. Although not a new method, another contraceptive was approved by the FDA late in 1990; the copper intrauterine device ParaGard, with a wear time of six years, is now the longest-acting reversible contraceptive on the market. ParaGard had been previously labeled for four years of continuous use. This highly effective form of family planning shares with Norplant the advantage of requiring only one act on the part of a woman for the acquisition of safe and effective long-term contraception. While ParaGard is lower in cost and is associated with much lower rates of abnormal bleeding than Norplant, its use is usually restricted to women who have had at least one pregnancy, are in a mutually monogamous sexual relationship, and have no history of PID or ectopic pregnancy. The only other IUD currently marketed in the U.S. is Progestasert—a progesterone-releasing device that must be replaced yearly.

RU-486: continuing controversy. The so-called abortion pill, mifepristone (RU-486), is a safe and 95–98% effective method of pregnancy termination when

At a July 1991 rally in New York City, pro-choice activists expressed outrage over the increasingly limited number of pregnancy-prevention options available to U.S. women. In particular, the French "abortion pill," RU-486, has encountered fierce opposition from antiabortion groups.

Najlah Feanny—SABA

used in conjunction with an injection of the hormone prostaglandin. RU-486 is not only a safe, nonsurgical early abortifacient—considerably less risky than surgical abortion, particularly in the second trimester—it also shows considerable promise as an effective mode of treatment for a number of other conditions. These include endometriosis; cancers of the breast, brain, and prostate; Cushing's disease, a disorder of the adrenal cortex; and even glaucoma.

RU-486 was introduced in France in 1988 for use up to the seventh week of pregnancy; in France this method is now used in about one-quarter of all abortions. In April 1991, after the death of one woman, the French government banned its use by heavy smokers and women over age 35. China has approved the pill but has not marketed it. In July 1991 the U.K. authorized the use of RU-486 up to the ninth week of pregnancy. It will be available under the provisions of the 1967 Abortion Act—only at National Health Service hospitals and clinics and with the signatures of two doctors. Because the agent continues to arouse controversy, the French manufacturer has decided not to market the pill in other countries at this time.

Owing to the intensive lobbying efforts of antichoice groups, it is unlikely that RU-486 will be generally available at any time in the forseeable future in the U.S. In the past year, however, several major medical groups, including the American Medical Association, the American Public Health Association, and the American College of Obstetrics and Gynecology, have spoken out against the political invasion of medical progress and in favor of U.S. trials of mifepristone. And in May 1991 the New Hampshire state legislature moved toward approval of a resolution offering the state as a clinical testing site for RU-486.

It is estimated that throughout the world 200,000 lives are lost to surgical abortions each year. The wide availability of RU-486 to women, especially in less developed countries, would therefore be a great boon.

World picture

In the U.S. the options for effective contraception and safe pregnancy termination have narrowed; STDs are epidemic; infant mortality rates are unacceptably high; and women in lower socioeconomic groups receive increasingly substandard health care. This dismal picture is for women in one of the world's wealthiest developed countries.

In the less developed countries, the picture is far grimmer: some 20–45% of all deaths of women of reproductive age are the result of complications of pregnancy, childbirth, and unsafe abortion practices. The Washington, D.C.-based Worldwatch Institute estimated that worldwide in 1991 one million women would die and 100 million would be maimed in a "global epidemic of reproductive health problems."

—*Elizabeth B. Connell, M.D.*

Skin and Hair Disorders

Skin is the largest organ of the human body, accounting for about one-sixth of the body's weight. It performs a protective function, guarding the internal structures from contact with the environment, and is vital to the maintenance of bodily health. Hair also performs a few protective functions, but it is largely ornamental and is not considered essential to human life.

Recent advances in treating skin disorders

For several decades the incidence of genital warts has been increasing steadily. These warts, caused by human papillomavirus, usually develop after sexual contact with an infected person. They represent a continuing challenge because the warts may be very resistant to therapy and may recur even after apparently successful treatment. In addition, epidemiological studies have shown a significant association between genital warts and the occurrence of cancer of the cervix.

Vaginal, cervical, and rectal warts are usually treated by physical modalities, such as surgery, cryotherapy, or lasers. External genital warts in both men and women are generally treated with topical agents such as podophyllin, a plant extract obtained from *Podophyllum peltatum* or *Podophyllin emodi.* Standard treatment with podophyllin, however, has several drawbacks. The concentration of the active substance, podophyllotoxin, varies considerably in the extracts, making standardization of the therapy difficult. In addition, until recently the agent had to be applied in a physician's office and washed off by the patient after a few hours in order to minimize the risk of adverse effects such as severe local irritation. However, the active compound, podophyllotoxin, has been purified and is now available in a standardized 0.5% solution (Condylox) for the treatment of genital warts. There is no longer a need to wash off the agent after application, and patients can treat themselves at home. This new approach to the problem of genital warts appears to offer a considerable advantage over traditional therapy.

Atopic dermatitis or atopic eczema is a common chronic skin disorder that tends to run in families; it is often associated with respiratory allergies such as asthma and hay fever, and it generally begins in childhood. The hallmark of this condition is patches of dry, red, and itchy skin that usually worsen during the wintertime. Traditional therapies for atopic dermatitis include the use of emollients and nondetergent soaps, ointments containing moderate to potent corticosteroids or tar, and oral antihistamines to relieve the itch. Some patients also benefit from ultraviolet light treatments similar to those used to treat psoriasis.

According to the results of several early trials in the United States and Germany, interferon gamma, a new agent, may prove useful in the treatment of severe atopic dermatitis. Interferons are a large family of proteins that are released from animal or human cells infected with a virus. Their biological function is believed to be the protection of other cells in the body against infection with the same virus. Some types of interferon have been used previously with some success in dermatologic conditions such as warts and certain skin cancers. In several preliminary studies, patients treated with interferon gamma experienced a clear reduction in skin inflammation and itching.

Another innovative experimental therapy in dermatology is extracorporeal photochemotherapy (photopheresis). This treatment is actually a variant of PUVA (a combination of oral psoralen and ultraviolet light A [UVA]) photochemotherapy. In photopheresis, blood is removed from the patient, and the white blood cells are separated from the red blood cells and plasma in a cell separator. The patient's white blood cells are then exposed to psoralen *in vitro* and irradiated with UVA light. The irradiated white blood cells are then washed and reinfused into the patient's body. The therapy was initially developed for the treatment of widespread cutaneous T-cell lymphoma (CTCL), a cancer of T lymphocytes in which there is a propensity of the cells to infiltrate the skin. Remarkable results have been reported in patients with CTCL treated with photopheresis, especially when it has been combined with other treatments. It is currently thought that the success of photopheresis in CTCL is due to the malignant cells' being altered by their exposure to psoralen and UVA in such a way that the natural immune defenses of the body recognize these cells as abnormal and destroy them. Therefore, this treatment would constitute a form of vaccination against the patient's own cancer. This concept has stimulated therapeutic trials of the technique in other conditions in which white blood cells are thought to attack tissues of the body, such as graft rejection and several autoimmune diseases.

New systemic therapies for psoriasis

In psoriasis, a chronic skin disorder that affects 1 to 2% of the U.S. population, there is accelerated production of epidermal cells (the epidermis is the outer layer of the skin) and inflammation of affected areas. The disease is characterized by the presence of red, scaly patches most commonly on the knees, elbows, buttock folds, and scalp and behind the ears; in some patients lesions are widespread. The primary causes of the condition are still unknown. Although there is currently no cure, several types of treatments can control the disease by temporarily slowing the excess replication of skin cells and reducing the inflammation. A common form of treatment is the application of topical medications—creams, ointments, and solutions that contain potent derivatives of hydrocortisone (cortisol), anthralin, or coal tar—to affected areas. Used singly or in combination, these agents can lead to the clearing of individual lesions. However, chronic therapy with potent topical corticosteroids can lead to localized skin atrophy (thinning, loss of strength, and inelasticity) or occasionally to hypopigmentation (loss of skin color). Anthralin and crude coal tar can cause irritation in the form of contact dermatitis or reddish-brown discoloration of the skin.

For more widespread forms of psoriasis, ultraviolet light treatments such as UVB (ultraviolet light B) and PUVA are effective and relatively safe. UVB and PUVA treatment will lead to clearing of psoriasis in 85 and 90% of patients, respectively. Both forms of therapy are complicated by accelerated photoaging of the skin (changes in the skin caused by chronic exposure to ultraviolet light—in this case an artificial source—including wrinkling, loss of elasticity, prominence of blood vessels, hyperpigmentation, and dryness). PUVA therapy also has been associated with an increase in the incidence of squamous cell carcinoma and cancer of the scrotum. Men who receive PUVA treatment thus should shield their genitals.

Severe psoriasis often requires systemic treatment with drugs that are given orally or by injection, either alone or in combination with ultraviolet light. Most of these therapies carry the risk of considerable toxicity; therefore, careful patient selection and close monitoring for adverse effects are necessary. It is important to remember that psoriasis is a chronic disease; although systemic treatments can cause impressive initial clearing, none of the currently available treatments cures the disease. As a general rule, these systemic treatments should not be used during pregnancy except when absolutely necessary.

One systemic drug that has been used for years is methotrexate, a highly potent agent used to treat cancer. Because the doses used for treating psoriasis are lower than those for cancer, many of the side effects of cancer chemotherapy (nausea, vomiting, and hair loss) are avoided. Methotrexate is effective in controlling widespread plaque-type psoriasis. It can also be a highly effective therapy for patients who suffer from arthritis associated with psoriasis. The major drawback of methotrexate, even in low doses, is its toxicity for the liver. Therefore, a liver biopsy is sometimes recommended at the beginning of treatment, and a biopsy should be obtained when a total dose of approximately two grams of methotrexate has been taken. Since the usual dose of methotrexate is approximately 7.5 to 15 mg per week, a liver biopsy would be needed every three to five years if the drug were taken continuously (which it rarely is). Because low-dose methotrexate may also lower the blood count, notably in older patients, blood testing must be done periodically, especially at the beginning of therapy.

New analogues of methotrexate with less toxicity for the liver are now under study, but they have not yet been approved for the treatment of psoriasis.

Retinoids—potent therapeutic agents derived from vitamin A that have been found to offer an effective oral therapy for a variety of skin diseases—are another class of drugs used in the treatment of psoriasis. Because of their potential toxicity, however, they require careful consideration by the physician before use and are generally not appropriate for patients with minimal psoriasis, who can be treated quickly and effectively with traditional therapies.

The retinoid etretinate, developed and commercialized during the last decade, is effective in the treatment of two severe variants of psoriasis: pustular psoriasis, characterized by fever, malaise, widespread psoriasis, and the formation of pustules within psoriatic lesions, and erythrodermic psoriasis, manifested by total-body redness and scaling. Etretinate and other retinoids have revolutionized the treatment of these forms of psoriasis; in most patients the agents produce a rapid and complete clearing.

The synthetic retinoids, however, are teratogenic; they can cause serious birth defects if they are present in a woman's body during pregnancy. Etretinate is stored and accumulates in fatty tissue and can be detected in the blood of patients several years after last being taken. Except in the most unusual circumstances, it should not be used in women of childbearing potential. Other common adverse effects include cutaneous and mucous membrane side effects, such as chapped lips, nosebleeds, irritation of the eyes, dry skin, peeling of palms and soles, and hair loss. Systemic side effects include elevation of blood lipids; muscle, joint, and/or bone pain; hyperostosis (calcium deposits) in the spine; liver toxicity; and calcification of ligaments. Thus, frequent blood sampling to monitor potential side effects, especially in the beginning of therapy, is essential.

Several pharmaceutical companies are actively investigating the potential usefulness of other retinoids in dermatologic disease. One of the major goals is to discover an oral retinoid that has the same therapeutic efficacy as etretinate but is eliminated from the body more rapidly. A metabolite of etretinate, acitretin, has been marketed in Europe for a few years. It seems to have a therapeutic- and side-effect profile similar to that of etretinate and was thought to be more rapidly cleared after cessation of therapy. However, its manufacturer recently temporarily withdrew it from the market and then reintroduced it with new guidelines for extended posttherapy contraception, thus seriously casting doubt on claims that it is rapidly eliminated. More studies are needed to assess more exactly the duration of its teratogenic risk. Investigation is under way on arotinoids, a new class of synthetic retinoids significantly more potent than etretinate.

Photographs, John J. Voorhees, M.D., University of Michigan

 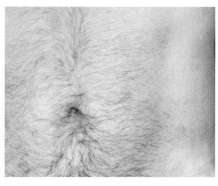

Marked improvement of psoriasis is seen after eight weeks' treatment with cyclosporine at the lowest dosage, three milligrams per kilogram of body weight. Because side effects can be severe, the oral immunosuppressant is used only in patients whose conditions are unresponsive to other therapies.

Cyclosporine, which is derived from the soil fungus *Tolypocladium inflatnum gams*, is an immunosuppressive agent that has been used since the late 1970s to prevent graft rejection in organ-transplant recipients. The mechanism of action of the drug in a variety of conditions is related to its ability to inhibit immune responses in the body that are mediated by T-helper lymphocytes, a particular type of white blood cell. Several studies have detailed significant improvement of severe psoriasis during cyclosporine treatment. The drug is taken orally once or twice daily, usually in daily doses of 3 to 10 mg per kilogram of body weight. Although the therapy is very effective in the majority of patients, most of them experience a relapse upon withdrawal of the drug. It is uncertain whether the risks associated with cyclosporine allow for the use of the drug in long-term maintenance therapy. Relatively common side effects include renal failure, hypertension, nausea, anorexia, diarrhea, liver toxicity, elevation of blood lipids, hypertrophy of the gums, joint pains, excessive hair growth, headaches, seizures, and other signs of central nervous system toxicity. Prolonged use of this immunosuppressive drug is also known to increase a patient's risk of developing a malignancy, particularly lymphoma and cutaneous squamous cell carcinoma. Only patients with very severe psoriasis who do not respond to or cannot tolerate more conventional treatments should be considered for cyclosporine therapy because its long-term toxicity still has not been completely defined; moreover, there is a rapid relapse of psoriasis after the drug is stopped, and the therapy has a high cost. Although a topical formulation of cyclosporine may cause fewer side effects, current evidence indicates that the penetration of the drug through the skin is inadequate for the treatment of psoriasis. The use of cyclosporine injected into the dermis under psoriatic lesions is currently under investigation.

FK-506, a compound produced by *Streptomyces tsukubaensis*, was discovered in 1984 in Japan during a search for new immunosuppressive and cancer chemotherapeutic agents. The drug has been shown to be considerably more potent and less toxic than cyclosporine in the prevention of graft rejection after organ transplantation and has also been found to be a promising agent for the treatment of severe psoriasis in several experimental protocols. Published results of these studies are not yet available, however.

FK-506, a new immunosuppressant derived from a soil fungus, was discovered and developed in Japan. In several experimental protocols the agent has shown promise as a treatment for severe psoriasis—one that is more potent but less toxic than cyclosporine.

Fujisawa Pharmaceutical Co., Ltd.; photograph, Isao Itani

Photographs, Hideo Uno, M.D., University of Wisconsin, Madison

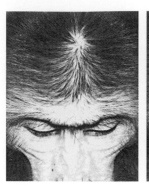

The stump-tailed macaque monkey has a predictable pattern of hair loss, which has provided scientists with a "speeded-up" model of the balding process in humans. Shown (left to right) are macaques at four years, with fully developed scalp hair; five years, with early balding; and seven years, with advanced balding.

During the past five years, several reports have been published suggesting that oral and topical vitamin D derivatives may be useful additions to the therapeutic armamentarium for psoriasis. Although the mode of action of these compounds has not yet been established, several observations have indicated that vitamin D and its analogues can modify epidermal growth and certain activities of T lymphocytes. Several clinical trials are currently under way to assess the magnitude of the benefit and the risk for side effects with this treatment.

Pattern baldness

Pattern baldness (androgenetic alopecia) is the most common form of hair loss, affecting approximately half the male population and about one-third of women. Its development is determined mainly by genetic factors, age, and normal androgenic hormonal stimulation. Androgens are hormones, produced and secreted in the testes in men (and by the ovaries and the adrenal glands in women), that are responsible for many male secondary sex characteristics; *e.g.,* muscle development, hair growth, particularly in the beard area, and deepening of the voice. To understand pattern (or male-pattern) baldness, one needs to know a few basic facts about normal hair growth.

The quest for ways to induce new hairs to grow on a balding pate is age-old. Unfortunately, most alleged remedies for hair loss are expensive and completely worthless.

Historical Pictures Service

The process of hair growth and loss. Each normal hair goes through a growth cycle. For about three years growth is vigorous and relatively steady. Then, for about three months, the follicle, which generates the hair, goes into a resting phase. These nongrowing hairs are only loosely attached to the scalp and can be pulled out with minor traction during washing or combing. When the follicle starts producing a new hair, the old one is obligatorily pushed out, and the cycle resumes; normally about 75 to 100 scalp hairs are lost per day through the shedding of resting hairs. While some hair follicles appear able to continue this process indefinitely, others are inclined to shut down as people age. In men these follicles are located predominantly on the temples and at the crown of the head. In women they are distributed more diffusely across the top of the scalp.

As people age, the periods of active growth of their hair follicles get shorter, and the diameter and pigmentation of their hair decrease. Ultimately, fine, short, colorless hairs remain. This process must affect at least half the follicles in any given area of the scalp before thinning becomes noticeable.

Pattern hair loss in men occurs predominately on the top of the head (vertex) and at the frontal hairline. Male-pattern hair loss not uncommonly begins in young men when they are in their early twenties. It may eventually lead to the confluence of both bald areas, leaving only a peripheral fringe of scalp hair. The clinical diagnosis is usually obvious because of the characteristic pattern of the hair loss. No medical diseases produce similar patterns of hair loss in men.

In women the pattern of thinning may resemble that seen in men, but usually a diffuse thinning of the hair occurs. Several conditions can cause similar diffuse thinning of the hair, including iron deficiency and an overactive or underactive thyroid gland. Therefore, in women a detailed history, physical examination, and diagnostic workup focusing on hormonal abnormalities, nutritional deficiencies, and other conditions are indispensable for excluding other causes of the loss. Female patients with pattern hair loss may have increased hair growth in other body areas (for example, in the beard area, under the arms, and on the lower abdomen) and other signs of androgen excess. Because these women may have diseases of either the adrenal glands or ovaries (including benign and malignant tumors), they should have a thorough medical evaluation.

Hair loss and the quest for treatment

In spite of the fact that some degree of pattern hair loss accompanies the normal process of aging, it can have profound effects on self-image and social interactions. Many patients with pattern hair loss seek treatment to enable them to regrow lost hair or to prevent further hair loss. Many remedies, including electrical stimulation and the application of a variety of exotic substances, have been promoted for pattern baldness and have been eagerly tried by balding clients. The majority of these treatments are expensive, however, and have proved completely worthless.

Minoxidil. Both the medical literature and the popular press have given much attention to the agent minoxidil—originally a drug used in the treatment of high blood pressure. Minoxidil 2% topical solution (Rogaine), approved in the U.S. in 1988 as a prescription drug for male-pattern baldness, is the first and only available Food and Drug Administration (FDA)-approved topical medication for the treatment of hair-loss conditions. Minoxidil's mechanisms of action are not yet understood. Several studies have shown that about 20% of men who use it twice daily for 6 to 12 months experience cosmetically significant hair growth on the top of the scalp (crown)—but not at the hairline. These patients will grow a sufficient amount of normal-appearing hair to cover the bald area. In the remaining minoxidil users, only small amounts of thin hairs are produced or balding follows its genetically determined course.

In successful cases maximal hair growth is usually obtained after about one year. The hair growth can be maintained in most patients if minoxidil application is continued. In several studies, however, minoxidil-induced hair growth was lost in a significant proportion of patients even when twice-daily applications

were continued. If treatment, which costs about $60 per month, is discontinued, there will be a gradual loss of the new hair growth. Many patients conclude that the effects of long-term minoxidil application are not cosmetically meaningful enough to continue treatment. The candidates most likely to have successful regrowth of hair are young men with hair loss that is of recent onset, is mild, and is located on the crown. Topical minoxidil has also shown some promise for the treatment of male-pattern alopecia in females, but additional data are needed to assess the magnitude of the benefit. There is no evidence that minoxidil is useful in causing hair growth on a receding frontal hairline, and whether topical minoxidil slows the rate of hair loss in pattern baldness has not been conclusively determined.

The most common adverse effects of minoxidil (affecting 2 to 3% of users) are allergic or irritant contact dermatitis (clinically similar to a mild case of poison ivy) and itching of the scalp. Although small amounts of the drug are absorbed systemically, no major side effects have been documented. However, a small increase in heart rate has been noted in some patients. Individuals with coronary artery disease or heart failure are at higher risk for the development of systemic side effects; therefore, minoxidil should be used with caution in patients with either condition.

Oral antiandrogens. In some women in whom an increase in androgens has been documented, agents that suppress the production or action of male hormones, such as spironolactone, cyproterone acetate, and flutamide, may be effective in the treatment of baldness. These drugs have not yet been approved for this purpose by the FDA. Their use should be considered investigational since well-controlled studies have not been completed. Cyproterone acetate is currently available in several European countries but not in the United States.

Transplants and implants. An alternative approach to the problem of pattern baldness is surgical treatment, which generally yields more substantial and permanent results. Hair transplantation by multiple punch

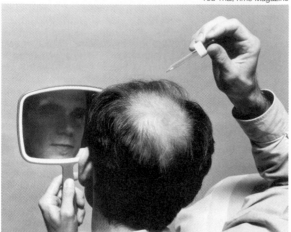

Minoxidil (Rogaine) is the only approved prescription treatment for male-pattern baldness. About 20% of men who use the topical solution twice daily for 6 to 12 months experience cosmetically significant hair growth on the crown.

autografts, described by Norman Orentreich in the late 1950s, is the most common method of hair-replacement surgery. A "punch" is a small anesthetized cylinder of skin that is removed with a sharp forceps shaped like a small cookie cutter. In this method grafts containing viable hair follicles from the relatively unaffected areas of the scalp are transplanted to the bald areas. The success of hair transplantation is therefore based on the principle that the transplanted hair follicles will behave as they did in their original location and thus permanently grow hair. The standard graft is a four-millimeter cylinder of skin that contains between 8 and 15 hairs. Skin cylinders 3.5 mm in diameter are removed from the recipient site in carefully plotted patterns and replaced with the grafts. The first grafts are inserted toward the front of the head to design the frontal hairline; subsequent grafts gradually cover the more posterior areas. In the past 40 years, the original transplantation technique has undergone considerable refinement. One advance was the development of the power punch forceps, which yields more uniform and qualitatively better grafts than the original hand-held instruments. Another innovation addressed a common problem of hair transplantation: the tendency of grafting to produce a hairline that was thick and abrupt. "Minigrafts," containing three to eight hairs, and "micrografts," consisting of just one or two hairs, enable surgeons to design a more naturally appearing frontal hairline.

The extent of present and probable future hair loss should be determined in evaluating a candidate for hair-replacement surgery. A detailed family history, a careful examination, and good planning are essential so that hair is not transplanted from a donor site that is destined for future baldness. The best candidates for hair transplantation have sufficient donor hair of adequate density. Also, individuals with thick, curly, and light-colored hairs will usually have better cosmetic results. It is more difficult to obtain satisfactory results in women who suffer from pattern alopecia because their pattern of hair loss is more diffuse.

Potential complications of hair transplantation include postoperative bleeding, tissue swelling, bruising, and infection. Loss of the transplanted hairs may occur in the months following the procedure; however, new hairs that are not sensitive to androgens gradually regrow. Inadequate growth is usually due to poor technique. Although it is performed as an outpatient procedure under local anesthesia, the whole process is tedious, requiring many sessions for satisfactory results. At least several hundred grafts are needed, at an approximate cost of $20 to $40 per graft, and because hair transplantation for baldness is considered cosmetic surgery, it is not reimbursed by medical insurance.

The implantation of synthetic fibers or human hair from donors has been advocated by some practitioners, but these techniques lead invariably to complications. Common problems are foreign-body reactions, in which the body encloses the synthetic fibers with inflammatory cells and fibrous tissue, infection, scarring, and often rejection of the grafts. Therefore, synthetic implants are not recommended.

Scalp reduction and "flap" surgeries. Patients with extensive male-pattern baldness, who are often not good candidates for hair transplantation because donor sites do not yield enough grafts for sufficient coverage of bald areas, may benefit from so-called scalp reduction. Bald skin patches on the crown are sequentially excised. Then hair-bearing skin is stretched over the areas, significantly reducing the degree of baldness. This technique yields satisfactory results either alone or in combination with punch graft hair transplantation. Plastic surgeons have used so-called tissue expanders successfully in this procedure to create more stretchable and elastic skin; these are fluid-filled sacs that are temporarily placed under the scalp and inflated to stretch the hair-bearing area and thereby enable more complete coverage of the excised bald area.

Finally, another surgical approach is the detachment and transposition of hair-bearing flaps to create a dense frontal hairline. The flap is a wedge of hair-bearing scalp skin that remains attached at one side. The free edge of the flap is swung around to the area along the frontal hairline where bald skin of similar size has been excised. The flap is then sewn into place. This method is technically more difficult than hair transplantation or scalp reduction, requires general anesthesia, and can be associated with significant complications such as tissue death.

—Serge A. Coopman, M.D.,
and Michael Bigby, M.D.

Special Report
Arthritis: The Aerobics Advantage
by Karen J. Connell, M.S.

Arthritis sufferers who lived in the early part of this century had only very limited treatment options. At that time arthritis was an unknown quantity. Imprecise terms such as *rheumatism* were used to describe almost any ailment that chronically affected the muscles, bones, or joints.

People with arthritis were strongly discouraged from participating in vigorous activities for fear that they might aggravate their joint problems and hasten the disease process. Rest was the cornerstone of therapy. Wealthy patients often sought their ease at spas, where "treatments" included daily immersion in the hot natural mineral waters, application of mud packs, and drinks of the spring water. Those who could not afford the luxury of a rest cure would probably be told by the doctors to "go home and live with it" and to lie down—or at least restrict physical activity—whenever possible.

Today the picture is very different. More than 100 specific forms of arthritis have been identified and named; drugs have been developed to help control pain, inflammation, and the progression of the disease; and seriously affected joints can be replaced with artificial implants. In addition, it is now known that there is much that individuals with arthritis can do for themselves, and they are encouraged not to passively accept the restrictions imposed by the disease. In the late 1960s and early '70s, the burgeoning interest in physical fitness and the recognition by health professionals of the mental and physical benefits of vigorous exercise prompted a reconsideration of the traditional views on exercise for people with arthritis.

Proven benefits of exercise
Over the past 15 or so years, researchers in the Scandinavian countries and the United States have studied the effect that vigorous stationary cycling has on people with arthritis. Their results have consistently indicated that such aerobic exercise is both safe and physically beneficial. (Aerobic exercise stimulates cardiovascular function and enhances the body's ability to use oxygen.) More recently, investigators have begun to examine the effects of weight-bearing aerobic exercise, including brisk walking and dance-based aerobics.

In 1989 physical therapist Marian Minor and her colleagues at the Arthritis Rehabilitation Center, University of Missouri, reported the results of a study that compared the effects of brisk walking and aerobic aquatics (aerobic exercises performed in water) with the effects of nonaerobic exercise emphasizing stretching and flexibility. Participants were people diagnosed with rheumatoid arthritis or osteoarthritis. At the end of a 12-week program, the aerobic exercisers showed a much greater improvement in cardiorespiratory endurance, a decrease in the amount of time it took them to briskly walk a distance of 15 meters (50 feet), a lowering of depression and anxiety, and an increased level of overall physical activity in their everyday lives. Also in the 1980s the late rheumatologist Susan G. Perlman and her colleagues at Northwestern University's Multipurpose Arthritis Center in Chicago reported similar results from a program for people with rheumatoid arthritis that included dance-based low-impact aerobic exercise. None of the participants in either program found that their arthritis became worse as a result of participation in vigorous activity. In fact, in the Northwestern program most of the rheumatoid arthritis patients experienced a significant decrease in both joint pain and swelling.

Although research into the specific advantages of various kinds of exercise continues, there is now a substantial body of evidence confirming many physiological benefits of vigorous activity for people with arthritis. Less studied have been the potential effects of physical activity on daily functioning, psychological well-being, and general quality of life. Moreover, little attention has been given to investigating whether the benefits of exercise to people with arthritis might be enhanced by a combination of a physical program and other activities, such as education about the disease process and how to cope with it.

Education + exercise = "Educize"
The Perlman study mentioned above was the first to investigate the effects of a program combining aerobic exercise and patient education. The program was based on the premise that such a regime would offer more comprehensive and lasting benefits than a program of solely physical exercise or one devoted only to education.

In the early 1980s Perlman's curiosity was piqued by the fact that many of her patients wanted to join in the "aerobics craze," à la Richard Simmons or Jane

An Educize instructor leads a class member through a gradual warm-up routine to ensure that any stiff joints and taut muscles will be adequately prepared for the subsequent aerobic workout.

Fonda, then sweeping the U.S. She began to question whether, despite conventional wisdom, people with arthritis might benefit from a low-impact aerobic routine. In the face of skepticism and even scorn from some of her colleagues, she began to explore how aerobic exercise and some flexibility and muscle-strengthening resistance training could be modified so as to be safe for people with arthritis. Working with an exercise-dance specialist, a physical therapist, and an occupational therapist, Perlman developed a program for a small experimental group of patients. These initial patients were so enthusiastic and seemed to benefit so much both physically and psychologically that Perlman decided to initiate a formal study of an exercise-combined-with-education program.

In 1982 this author, a medical educator, began working with Perlman, supported by a grant from the National Institutes of Health, to further develop a program that was appropriately dubbed "Educize." It was reasoned that adding a discussion session to the exercise program might help to ensure that participants fully understood the modifications they needed to make in the exercise routine to prevent injury or exacerbation of their disease. The discussions encouraged active problem solving as a way to help participants address everyday problems imposed by their arthritis.

Over the six-year period from 1983 to 1989, the Educize concept was refined. During the first three

years, two of the original collaborators conducted the exercise and discussion portions. Between 1986 and 1989, the group developed and tested a program to train hospital-based health professionals—nurses and occupational and physical therapists—to lead the class sessions.

The first official Educize "students" were 53 rheumatoid arthritis patients. They ranged in age from 27 to 84 years, the majority being 40 and over and 33% being over 60; 95% were women. All participants experienced some functional limitations as a result of their disease, and 45% had moderate to severe limitations. The original programs spanned a 16-week period; participants met twice weekly for two hours, with one hour devoted to exercise and one to discussion. Currently the Educize program is open to people with most arthritic conditions, typically including rheumatoid arthritis, osteoarthritis, systemic lupus erythematosus, fibromyalgia (also called fibrositis), and low back pain. Participants range in age from the mid-twenties to mid-eighties. After completing 12 weeks of twice-weekly two-hour sessions, participants "graduate" and have the option of joining an ongoing twice-weekly "maintenance" program.

Sadly, in December 1989 Educize's innovator, Perlman, died. The program's present success is a tribute to her unremitting devotion to helping arthritis patients overcome their pain and their limitations.

The workout

A typical Educize class includes 15–20 minutes of warm-ups in seated, then standing, positions. Gentle stretching and rotating movements concentrate on loosening tight muscles—in the back, neck, shoulders—and joints—shoulders, hips, ankles. The warm-up is followed by an aerobic dance segment that increases over time from 5 to 20 minutes per class. The purpose of the aerobic activity is to promote cardiovascular efficiency and conditioning; class members work to raise their heart rate to 60–70% of their estimated maximum (or an equivalent level of perceived exertion). The concluding segment of the workout consists of 15–20 minutes of exercises conducted on a floor mat, promoting flexibility and muscle strengthening and including relaxation training.

The aerobic portion of the class focuses on the continuous use of the large muscle groups, thus creating an increased demand for oxygen. Routines are built on walking and traditional dance steps; movement of the feet is accompanied by coordinated arm motions. Participants are taught how to adjust the intensity of their workout—for example, limiting the range of motion or decreasing the speed of movements to lower the intensity.

In low-impact aerobic dance exercise, one or both feet must maintain contact with the floor at all times. This is in contrast to traditional aerobic dance, where routines usually involve moves such as jumping, jogging, and hopping. For people with arthritis, soft, light, low-impact movements minimize wear and tear on the joints, especially those of the lower body (hips, knees, ankles), which have the potential to be stressed or injured. Following the aerobic workout, a cool-down segment gradually reduces the heart rate and body temperature toward resting levels, thus preventing faintness. The cool-down includes muscle-strengthening exercises and progressive relaxation.

Participants are encouraged to try out modifications that help them compensate for their arthritis-imposed limitations. An individual with poor balance may stand with both feet farther apart than usual to provide a wider base of support. Another might hold on to the back of a chair for support to compensate for leg weakness or do some exercises while sitting to avoid stress on a swollen knee or ankle. Gentle thigh slapping can substitute for hand clapping and finger snapping, thus minimizing stress on arthritic finger joints. Participants also learn to take responsibility for creating and leading the exercise routine.

Overcoming obstacles—creatively

The approach to discussion employed in Educize is based on the problem-solving theory of the U.S. educator and philosopher John Dewey. The instructor helps class members explore ways they might use the physical benefits derived from the program to overcome arthritis-related problems in their everyday lives. One participant, for example, might aspire to travel or return to work; another's goal might be to

build enough strength and endurance to spend the day at a shopping mall; for some it might be simply to perform an ordinary activity such as getting into the bathtub or out of a chair without help or to sit on the floor and play with a grandchild.

Whatever the problem or goal, participants are encouraged to develop for themselves various methods of overcoming physical limitations. They critique each other's ideas and develop ways to test them, both in the group and at home. The results of personal "experiments" are shared and critically analyzed in the group. Refinements and reformulations of ideas follow, and new experiments are undertaken.

Measuring the benefits

Educize research has investigated the effects of the program on participants' physiological condition, ability to function, psychological state, and quality of life. Results indicate no deleterious effects on arthritis symptoms or disease progression. In fact, most people find that joint pain and swelling decrease while mobility and stamina improve. Further, depression and fatigue decrease significantly. Participants report benefits to their general health and improvements in their ability to function—to walk several blocks, climb stairs, bend, lift, and stoop. They find they are less hampered by their arthritis and better able—as well as more determined—to carry on activities important to them despite the fact that they still experience a certain amount of discomfort.

Whether a dance-based vigorous exercise program that did not include the problem-solving discussion

Moving to the beat of lively music, an Educize class launches into a vigorous low-impact aerobic workout. The idea that people with arthritis can benefit from aerobic exercise—which focuses on improving cardiovascular conditioning—is a relatively new one that is rapidly gaining adherents among both health professionals and patients.

Rehabilitation Institute of Chicago

would produce comparable benefits has not been formally studied. However, it is reasonable to infer that the "education" component enhances the exercise program's effects.

Some studies have failed to confirm that vigorous exercise has measurable psychological benefits in older adults—even when they experience concrete physiological gains. However, Educize participants who are 60 years of age or older *do* evidence psychological benefits similar to those seen in younger participants.

One of the primary problems with all exercise programs is adherence—*i.e.*, sticking with it. The existing literature suggests that, on average, no more than 50% of middle-aged or elderly adults who begin a therapeutic exercise program are still participating six months later. A 1987 study suggested, for example, that approximately 50% of elderly individuals who begin exercising will drop out before the 10th week of a 20-week program. In sharp contrast, no more than 20% of those who begin an Educize program typically drop out and, despite the two-hour class length, better than 75% of participants attend at least 75% of the classes.

"Impossible" dreams

Program leaders consistently observe that the Educize experience seems to stimulate in participants a renewed sense of possibilities. They often find ways to pursue personally important goals they had either set aside or abandoned because of their arthritis.

Many seemingly impossible goals have been realized by Educize program members: one woman was able to return to work after more than two years of debilitation; an elderly man who had advanced rheumatoid arthritis affecting his hips and shoulders was able to resume swimming; a middle-aged woman with severe osteoarthritis in her feet and ankles was able to ice skate; and a 50-year-old with advanced disease in her wrists, hands, ankles, and feet fulfilled a 12-year dream to once again scale the rocky waterfalls at Ocho Rios, Jamaica.

Who can participate?

Experience suggests that most people with arthritis—even those who have other coexisting medical problems—can participate safely and effectively in Educize or any well-constructed exercise program. So far, the only people excluded have been those with cardiovascular problems—a resting heart rate greater than 100 or a resting blood pressure greater than 160/95; those who have had joint surgery within the previous six months; individuals who are wheelchair bound; and those with a hearing impairment that would preclude participation in group discussions. All participants are required to complete a medical history form and to obtain written permission from their primary physician.

Instructors: qualifications and training

There are several basic criteria that make for a successful instructor, including (1) at least two years of nursing or other practice experience, including some work with people with arthritis; (2) special interest in working with persons who have a chronic illness; (3) certification in cardiopulmonary resuscitation; (4) some experience with movement, as from participation in an aerobic exercise or dance class; and (5) a strong commitment to helping patients find ways to help themselves rather than relying on health professionals for "answers."

Educize instructors are trained to help each participant safely perform all aspects of the low-impact aerobic workout; to enhance each participant's ability to assess and manage arthritis-related problems, such as joint pain, swelling, and instability, as well as fatigue, weakness, and fear of injury; and to assist each participant in creating ways to use Educize to enhance his or her quality of life. Instructors are well versed in measures to ensure safety in an exercise program, the influence of various medications on heart rate and exercise performance, and principles of problem-solving education. Training includes a supervised practicum of at least six weeks' duration.

An idea whose time has come

Like other chronic diseases, most forms of arthritis must be managed over a long period of time. Since drugs and surgery have a major impact on only a small percentage of the 50 million Americans with arthritis, most must rely on education to help them learn to cope with the disease. Strategies that enable people to maximize their abilities and to overcome pain, functional limitations, and other arthritis-related problems offer an especially attractive way to help offset the devastating effects and the financial and personal costs of the disease.

Educize, with its "whole person" versus "injured parts" philosophy and its demonstrated effectiveness, seems a particularly timely program worthy of wider dissemination. It has already helped many who would otherwise have succumbed to pain and disability. This approach is a relatively new one, however, and at present is limited in its availability. Further information on the program is available from the Northwestern University Multipurpose Arthritis Center (303 E. Chicago Avenue, Chicago, IL 60611).

There are other organized exercise programs for arthritis sufferers around the U.S., such as the PACE (People with Arthritis Can Exercise) low-impact aerobic exercise program. Information about such programs and about a variety of educational activities for people with arthritis can be obtained from the Arthritis Foundation (1314 Spring Street NW, Atlanta, GA 30309) or any of its local chapters, listed in the telephone directory.

Smoking

In the 1991 Persian Gulf war, Allied bombs decimated the Iraqi military machine and killed between 100,000 and 200,000 Iraqis. During the same six weeks, another weapon of mass destruction claimed from two to three times as many lives around the world, a toll it repeated with regularity every six weeks thereafter. Developments in the Gulf transfixed the global community; the other source of devastation went virtually unnoticed. Indeed, this other technology was the object of a campaign of promotion and glamorization, funded to the tune of over $3 billion annually in the United States alone. The weapon? The cigarette.

According to the most recent estimate from the U.S. Centers for Disease Control (CDC) in Atlanta, Ga., smoking killed 434,000 Americans in 1988. The World Health Organization (WHO) places the global toll of tobacco in the vicinity of 3 million deaths per year and estimates that the annual figure will rise to 10 million by the year 2020. Further, given current trends in smoking around the world, WHO estimates that fully 500 million people now alive—a tenth of the globe's population—will die as a direct result of the consumption of tobacco products. A vast proportion of the deaths will be among the populations in the world's poorer nations.

Several salient points are made by these figures. One is the anticipated enormous growth in the global toll of tobacco. In part, this toll reflects the general tendency for tobacco consumption, and particularly cigarette smoking, to increase as societies become more affluent; in part, it reflects the aging of larger proportions of the population into the middle and older years, when tobacco takes its greatest toll. But the heavy toll also results from a concerted effort by a global tobacco industry, concentrated in six multi-national companies based in the U.S. and the U.K., to promote smoking in countries not yet familiar with aggressive, Western-style marketing campaigns. Often these marketing tactics are directed at segments of the population that traditionally have eschewed tobacco, such as Asian women.

There is also a less obvious point to be made by the figure of 434,000 U.S. smoking-related deaths—one involving fewer than 1% of the total. These are lung cancer deaths in *nonsmokers* as a result of passive smoking—inhalation of the smoke from other people's cigarettes. In the late 1980s and early '90s, increasing attention has focused on the health consequences of passive smoking. Recent epidemiological studies and sophisticated reviews of the existing body of research have confirmed that passive smoking is indeed a cause of lung cancer in adult nonsmokers; hence the CDC's inclusion of these deaths in its estimate of the death toll attributable to smoking. At the same time, new research is indicting passive smoking as a cause of numerous other diseases in adults exposed to the smoke of spouses and co-workers and in the offspring of smokers as well. A major study published in 1991 estimates that passive smoking may kill as many as 53,000 Americans annually, a large majority from heart disease. If that number is accurate, passive smoking is the nation's third largest cause of avoidable premature death, lagging behind only active smoking and alcohol consumption. The toll of passive smoking then would exceed that of all automobile accidents and would be comparable to the combined total of deaths from homicide and suicide.

Marlboro Man abroad

In a two-year period, exports of U.S. cigarettes doubled, with most of the increase occurring in Asian countries. Fueled by the demand for exports, cigarette

Robert Landau—West Light

The death count changes nearly once a minute on this electronic billboard over a major thoroughfare in Los Angeles. Although cigarette smoking in the U.S. has been declining for more than a decade, tobacco-related diseases still kill more than 400,000 Americans annually.

production has been increasing in the United States in recent years, despite a continuing decline in domestic consumption. The export demand has reversed the decrease in production that had begun in the early 1980s as a result of declining demand at home. The success of Philip Morris and its corporate colleagues in invading Asian and Eastern European countries has forced the public health community to reconceptualize the notion of tobacco's "Tar Wars." Years ago, that expression connoted the tobacco giants' battling for market share in the U.S. by developing and promoting lower-tar-and-nicotine cigarettes. Today the battle is not to lower tar but to spread it around, especially in Asia, Africa, the Soviet Union, and Eastern Europe.

The American tobacco giants have been aided and abetted in this effort by the White House and Congress. Appealing to section 301 of the 1974 Trade Act, the Office of the Trade Representative in the White House, urged on and actively supported by members of Congress, has threatened trade sanctions against countries that fail to remove barriers to the importation and marketing of American cigarettes. Ironically, this push to expand markets for American cigarettes and tobacco has coincided with the war on illicit drugs. Thus, at the same time that the federal government threatened sanctions against countries that exported

Japan's cigarette business was essentially closed to foreigners until the Office of the U.S. Trade Representative forced the market open in 1987. Now sales of U.S. cigarettes total over $600 million annually, and the promotion of American brands knows no bounds.

Robert Wallis—J.B. Pictures

their illicit drugs to U.S. shores, it also threatened sanctions against countries that tried to impede the export of America's principal drug to their shores.

Exploiting the Asian market. In particular, in the late 1980s the U.S. trade representative threatened trade sanctions and reprisals against several Asian countries. In a remarkably short period of time, this policy succeeded in getting Japan, South Korea, and Taiwan to repeal bans on imports, reduce tariffs, and even amend and eliminate public health laws and restrictions on cigarette advertising.

Most notably, in 1986 the Japanese market was forced open, and an advertising war erupted. Virtually unknown prior to that time, cigarette advertising rapidly emerged as a mainstay of commercial broadcasts. Within two years, cigarettes had become the second-most-advertised product on Japanese television, with ads up 10-fold in numbers since the forced entry of the Marlboro Man. Much of the advertising is directed at women, a group that traditionally has not smoked in Japan. Surveys indicate that female college students in Japan today are four times as likely to smoke as their mothers.

In Taipei, Taiwan, adolescent smoking has risen an estimated 28% since the entry of the multinational tobacco companies. In one ploy, teenage patrons of a popular discotheque were offered free entrance in exchange for empty Winston packs. In South Korea a ban on print advertising of cigarettes was repealed. Smoking among Korean boys is reported to have increased by two-thirds; among girls, the increase exceeds 400%.

The most recent trade action, initiated in April 1989, was the demand that Thailand repeal a cigarette-import ban, a preexisting tariff, and the Thai law banning cigarette advertising. Unlike the previous section 301 trade actions, which caught the health community unawares, this one galvanized both U.S. and international health professionals and organizations, who aggressively opposed the U.S. action in Thailand. Ultimately, the federal administration sent the matter to Geneva for resolution by the General Agreements on Tariffs and Trade (GATT), the international trade body. Late in 1990 a GATT panel ruled that the Thai import ban had to be lifted. However, the panel also concluded that priority could be given to human health in issues of trade liberalization of harmful products like cigarettes. The panel affirmed a nation's right to attempt to discourage smoking through advertising bans, high excise taxes, and other policy measures. In December the U.S. trade office dropped its section 301 action against Thailand.

Eastern Europe and the Soviet Union. Asia is not the only target of the multinational cigarette companies. Long in Latin America and Africa, the multinationals rushed into Eastern Europe and the Soviet Union immediately following *perestroika* and the ef-

Most smokers start young. The Belgian magazine Spirou *received applause from the World Health Organization for carrying the antismoking message loud and clear to its young readers in a special issue devoted to smoking and its hazards. The cover read: "I decided to quit before I started!"*

fective dismantling of Communism in the Eastern bloc countries. Smoking rates are high in these countries, and cigarettes are deemed to be of low quality.

Foreign companies quickly "divided up" the East German cigarette industry, with Philip Morris acquiring the rights to tear down a Dresden tobacco plant and replace it with a new factory manufacturing 10 billion Marlboros annually. Ad bans that were still in place in the Eastern European countries were openly flouted. In Warsaw trolleys were festooned with the Marlboro logo; a "Marlboro week" was held in Budapest; and hot-air balloons bearing the Camel logo filled the skies over Prague. U.S. brands of cigarettes are reportedly quickly becoming a status symbol, especially sought by Eastern European teenagers.

In September 1990, Philip Morris and R.J. Reynolds announced new deals with the Soviet Union to produce 34 billion cigarettes, a figure subsequently revised upward. The potential of the Soviet market for American cigarettes is suggested by anecdotal reports that during a cigarette shortage in the Soviet Union in the summer of 1990, a single pack of Marlboros fetched a price of $30 on the black market. Prior to the shortage, the black market cost of Marlboros was $7 or $8 a pack.

International ramifications. The international invasion by the world's principal tobacco companies is not new. The multinationals have been in Latin America for decades; the British-American Tobacco Company (BAT) inaugurated its tobacco growing, processing, and marketing activities in Kenya in 1907. Nevertheless, prompted by declining cigarette consumption in the developed world (at an annual rate of 1–1.5%) alongside expanding consumption in the less developed nations (2% per annum), the cigarette manufacturers have stepped up their invasion. Their weapons

include not only the most aggressive marketing tactics but the use of political influence—the latter being levied both by the multinationals' home countries (as in the actions of the U.S. trade representative) and by the governments of the host countries.

In the case of the U.S., the new international sales push means that a country once renowned for its humanitarian concerns abroad is now being viewed by many overseas as exporting its epidemic of lung cancer to Asians, Africans, and Eastern Europeans. When historians look back on the concluding decades of the 20th century, this phenomenon will constitute a dark chapter in U.S. contributions to world health.

Passive smoking: clear and present dangers

The first official public recognition of the potential hazards to health associated with involuntary inhalation of "second-hand" tobacco smoke came in the 1972 U.S. surgeon general's report on the health consequences of smoking. That report inaugurated an era of research and subsequent public debate that redefined the issue of smoking in the U.S., and increasingly in other developed countries as well. The "antismoking campaign" took a crucial new turn, for the first time including a legislative initiative designed to protect the rights of nonsmokers.

The 1972 report documented the chemicals emitted by the burning cigarette and discussed their possible pathological effects. Given a dearth of explicit scientific evidence at the time, however, the principal conclusions were that environmental tobacco smoke irritated healthy nonsmokers' eyes and throats and could exacerbate symptoms in people with heart and lung diseases. It was during the two decades following publication of that report, and particularly in the past decade, that a substantial body of scientific knowledge concerning the health consequences of passive smoking has been assembled.

That passive smoking causes disease in nonsmokers should hardly be surprising. The burning cigarette has been characterized as a "prolific chemical factory," producing over 4,000 chemical compounds, at least 43 of which have been identified as carcinogens. In fact, "sidestream" smoke (the smoke emitted into the atmosphere from the burning end of the cigarette) contains many of these chemicals in greater concentrations than does "mainstream" smoke (the smoke inhaled through the cigarette by the smoker).

Lung cancer connection confirmed. The most notable early contributions to this literature were three studies published in 1981, from Japan, Greece, and the U.S., which identified elevated risks of lung cancer in the nonsmoking wives of men who smoked. The data from Japan and Greece showed an elevated risk for lung cancer that was statistically significant. Subsequent analyses of other data from several countries have supported this finding, and by 1986 the epidemiological evidence was sufficient for the U.S. surgeon general to conclude, "Involuntary smoking is a cause of disease, including lung cancer, in healthy nonsmokers." In a report issued the same year, a prominent panel of scientists convened by the National Academy of Sciences concurred.

The association of lung cancer with passive smoking has been confirmed in several authoritative reviews of the evidence since then, including the report of a scientific panel of the Environmental Protection Agency (EPA), released to the public in 1990. This report was particularly noteworthy because several of the panelists had formerly served as consultants to tobacco-industry-related organizations.

The practical import of the EPA report is that it should lead to the declaration of environmental tobacco smoke (ETS) as a "class A carcinogen," which means that ETS should be regulated in the workplace. Such a ruling ought to give impetus to further expansion of workplace smoking restrictions. Several surveys of employers have documented rapid growth both in the number of firms restricting smoking in the workplace and in the severity of the restrictions.

Endangered hearts. Estimates of the numbers of lung cancer deaths produced by inhalation of ETS vary slightly from one study to the next. The most recent estimate by the CDC placed the total at close to 4,000 deaths in 1988. However, while lung cancer

There is mounting evidence that parents' smoking harms their children. A study reported by Yale University researchers in late 1990 estimated that 17% of lung cancer in nonsmokers is the result of childhood exposure to parental tobacco smoke.

Is smoking around children a form of child abuse?

Tobacco smoke is not just an annoyance; it hurts more than feelings.

The Environmental Protection Agency (EPA) says, "Passive smoking induces serious respiratory symptoms in children. Asthmatic children are particularly at risk. Children of smokers have significantly higher rates of hospitalization for bronchitis and pneumonia, and a number of studies report that chronic ear infections are more common in young children whose parents smoke. Also, lung development is slower in children exposed to environmental tobacco smoke (ETS). Lung problems caused by ETS exposure in childhood can extend into adult life."

Please don't smoke around children.

Thank you.

GASP OF COLORADO
Group to Alleviate Smoking Pollution

has proved to be the easiest disease to associate with passive smoking, as it was with active smoking, it may not be the most important. A review of the scientific evidence relating ETS to heart disease, published in 1991, concluded that the heart disease toll of passive smoking could be an order of magnitude greater than the cancer total. Authorities concluded that the relative risk of ETS-related cardiovascular disease was likely to be similar to that of lung cancer, approximately 1.3, meaning that a passive smoker's risk of heart disease (or lung cancer) death exceeded by 30% that of the average person not exposed to ETS. The huge potential impact of ETS on heart disease was derived from the high prevalence of heart disease in the nonsmoking population (which experiences a much lower prevalence of fatal cancers than does the smoking population). Combining the estimated heart disease deaths produced by passive smoking with lung cancer and other ETS-related deaths suggests that the toll of passive smoking could exceed 50,000 deaths a year.

This shocking conclusion awaits confirmation through further research and analysis. It raises the prospect, however, that a common, even mundane, environmental exposure could be killing Americans at a rate never imagined in connection with any other environmental agent.

Children: not spared. If the possible number of heart disease deaths caused by ETS has challenged scientists and public health officials, the emotions of the public were stirred by yet another new finding. In the Sept. 6, 1990, issue of the *New England Journal of Medicine,* a group of scientists based at Yale University reported that the children of smokers had an increased risk of developing lung cancer when they became adults, even though they themselves had never smoked. The researchers estimated that parental smoking could account for approximately 17% of the lung cancers experienced by nonsmokers.

This finding was not the first to address adverse health effects of parents' smoking on children. Best known are the consequences of smoking during pregnancy—low-birth-weight babies, intrauterine growth retardation, and failed pregnancies. Additional research, much of it dating from a decade ago, has established that the children of smokers have increased rates of respiratory infections and reduced rates of growth in lung function, with "dose-response" effects documented—*i.e.,* the risk of adverse health effects increases with the intensity of exposure.

Anything to keep them smoking

Tobacco continues to exact a horrible toll in the United States, but over time that toll will recede, simply because smoking is on the decline, as it has been without interruption for the past two decades. The enormous profitability of cigarettes, however, assures

Bombarding television viewers 1989 Marlboro Grand Prix	
type of exposure to Marlboro logo or name	number of exposures
small raceway sign	4,998
large billboard	519
Marlboro car	249
start-finish overpass	57
crew member in Marlboro jumpsuit	31
graphic of standings	18
Marlboro helmet	11
Marlboro car driver in jumpsuit	10
Marlboro jacket	7
Marlboro cap	5
sign on large screen	4
wife of Marlboro car driver in jumpsuit	4
Marlboro umbrella	3
Marlboro trophy	2
Marlboro written out	1
Marlboro patch on driver's wife's neck	1
Marlboro shirt	1
awards-presentation backdrop	1
spoken mention	11
total	5,933

From Alan Blum, M.D., "The Marlboro Grand Prix," *New England Journal of Medicine*, vol. 324, no. 13 (March 28, 1991), pp. 913–917

that the tobacco industry will not willingly relinquish its control over America's population of smokers. In recent years the industry has been mounting a multi-pronged advertising, public relations, economic, and political campaign in order to maintain as much of its market as possible.

Perhaps the most conspicuous advertising and promotion thrust on the part of the tobacco industry at present is the sponsorship of sporting events. Alan Blum, professor of family medicine at Baylor University College of Medicine, Houston, Texas, recently reviewed the sports sponsorship activities of Philip Morris and R.J. Reynolds. Blum concluded that in sponsoring automobile and motorcycle racing, the "big two" U.S. tobacco companies not only promoted their products to fans at the event but also reached a vast television audience—thereby quite effectively circumventing the congressional ban on broadcast advertising of cigarettes. Blum reported that "in an effort to verify the extent of television exposure of cigarette brands in spite of the ban," an observer, "a medical student with a moderate interest in automobile racing," had viewed the July 16, 1989, hour-and-a-half broadcast of the Marlboro Grand Prix six times (on videotape). Almost 6,000 exposures to Marlboro—either sightings of the Marlboro logo or spoken mention of the brand name—were recorded; thus, Marlboro cigarettes were effectively being advertised and promoted to TV viewers almost 50% of the time that the race was on the air.

Recent advertising campaigns for new brands of cigarettes have targeted specific demographic groups. The new cigarette Uptown was aimed at African-Americans. The Uptown campaign in 1990 drew the wrath of Louis Sullivan, secretary of health and human services, who expressed outrage at the manufacturer, R.J. Reynolds, for its "slick and sinister advertising," for "deliberately and cynically . . . promoting a culture of cancer." Sullivan noted that black Americans already die from smoking-related diseases at higher rates than do whites: "Uptown's message is more disease, more suffering, and more death for a group already bearing more than its share of smoking-related illness and mortality."

Less than a month after the test-marketing of Uptown was canceled, owing to widespread protests, R.J. Reynolds tried again. This time it introduced Dakota, a cigarette aimed at young "virile females" aged 18–24 who have a high school education or less; work in entry-level service or factory jobs; enjoy drag races, monster trucks, and going to clubs and bars; and aspire to get married and have a family in their early twenties. This campaign, which exploited a young population group whose rates of smoking and lung cancer have been rising dramatically and steadily over the past two decades, also drew fire from the public health community.

Another conventional marketing tool is pricing. Until a decade ago, the U.S. cigarette industry, a six-firm

U.S. Secretary of Health and Human Services Louis W. Sullivan joined the protest against Philip Morris for its sponsorship of the Virginia Slims women's tennis tour. He has repeatedly urged all *athletes to reject tobacco-industry support as "blood money."*

Patsy Lynch

WARNING...
YOU MUST BE ABLE
TO REACH COIN
SLOT TO OPERATE
THIS MACHINE...

oligopoly, avoided price competition. In 1981 one of the firms introduced unbranded "generic" cigarettes that were sold for reduced prices in black-and-white packages with no-name labels. Soon thereafter, competition erupted in the "branded generics" category, brand-name cigarettes (*e.g.,* Viceroy and Raleigh) that also sold for reduced prices. More recently, "sub-generic" brands have emerged (*e.g.,* Richland); they are sold at approximately two-thirds the price of the "regular" branded generics. The "price-value" segment of the market (as it is called within the industry) grew from 4% in 1983 to 15% in 1989, and its expansion continues.

Offering cigarettes at lower prices serves a vital function from an industry perspective. It enables the preservation of nicotine dependence among the most price-conscious smokers—*i.e.,* those who might quit (or not start) if prices remained uniformly high. While price competition preserves market profits, it also risks reducing unit profits—a matter that has become an industry-wide concern in the 1990s. The tobacco-company ideal would be to successfully discriminate between smokers who are price sensitive and those for whom price is not an issue, with the former remaining smokers owing to the availability of so-called off-price brands and the latter continuing to purchase the full-price brands.

If *pricing* and *promotion* are standard marketing techniques, the tobacco industry is well known also for a third marketing "P," *public relations.* Among its recent efforts was a campaign supported by the Tobacco Institute, which represents the tobacco industry, purportedly intended to discourage smoking by children. The campaign included espoused support of a few ostensibly restrictive policy proposals, such as supervising cigarette vending machines in locations frequented by minors and requiring billboard ads for cigarettes to be 150 m (500 ft) from schools and playgrounds. However, the measures, which the institute called "broad-based initiatives," in fact represented considerably less restrictive alternatives to already existing policies.

Critics labeled the Tobacco Institute's campaign transparent and cynical. The cynicism reflects the obvious dependence of the industry on the initiation of smoking by children. The dominant realities of cigarette smoking are the early age of initiation and an unparalleled rate of addiction. Surveys indicate that as many as half of all smokers begin smoking by the age of 16; no more than one out of 10 smokers begins smoking after age 20. Nicotine-addiction rates, variously estimated at 90 to 95% of smokers, exceed those observed for virtually all other drugs, including heroin, cocaine, and alcohol.

On the legislative front, the industry has initiated a thus far modestly successful attempt to pass state laws prohibiting discrimination in hiring based on the applicant's smoking status. These laws do not challenge the right of employers to prohibit smoking on the job. Of all the industry strategies adopted in recent years, this campaign may be the only one to have divided the antismoking community. Some members of the community believe that such protection is warranted, recognizing that smoking is an addiction and therefore—like any other drug problem—deserving of compassion and treatment. Others oppose the legislation in part because it appears to attempt to elevate smoking to the protected status afforded race, sex, age, and religious affiliation.

Tobacco's future toll

A true "smoke-free society by the year 2000," the goal envisioned for the United States by former surgeon general C. Everett Koop, is unlikely—despite its rhetorical appeal. Increasingly, however, laws and social mores will cause smokers to find themselves ostracized and physically isolated. Over time, both the number of the country's smokers and the health toll of smoking will recede.

As smokers and smoking dwindle in the U.S. and in other developed countries, their numbers in the poorer nations of the world will rise ever more rapidly. In many parts of the globe, appreciation of the hazards of smoking falls short of that realized in the U.S. over 40 years ago. Smoking has been called the "brown plague" of the 20th century in the developed countries. This plague, which has been spread by greed, will wreak its havoc throughout the world during the next century.

—*Kenneth E. Warner, Ph.D.*

400

Special Report

Burgeoning and Beleaguered: Psychoanalysis in the '90s

by Arnold D. Richards, M.D.

Psychoanalysis, the science of mind and method of treatment founded by Sigmund Freud in the 1890s, today enjoys a paradoxical status. On the one hand, psychoanalysis has flourished; it has grown into an important and respected profession with practitioners and training institutes throughout the world. The 7,500-member International Psycho-Analytic Association (IPA), the oldest and in some respects the most prestigious of its professional organizations, today has 39 branch societies in 30 countries. The American Psychoanalytic Association, an IPA affiliate, has 3,030 members and 27 accredited institutes for the analytic training of physicians, psychologists, and social workers. Also influential in the United States are the psychoanalysis division of the American Psychological Association, with about 3,200 members, and the American Academy of Psychoanalysis, whose membership of 800 is limited to physician-analysts. The Committee on Psychoanalysis of the National Federation of Societies for Clinical Social Work has 700 members.

In Europe and Latin America psychoanalysis is in a period of expansion; there were 1,500 analysts-in-training in Argentina alone in 1990. Worldwide, the scientific research tradition of psychoanalysis was marked by the establishment in 1989 of the Mary S. Sigourney

Award Trust, intended to recognize outstanding contributors in the field. Its first winners, named in 1990, were Jacob Arlow, a prominent psychoanalytic theoretician and clinician; Harold Blum, the former editor of the *Journal of the American Psychoanalytic Association* and the current head of the Freud Archives; and Otto Kernberg, who has published widely on the subjects of character pathology, particularly the borderline syndrome and "object relations" theory.

Further, the 1980s witnessed a burgeoning interest in psychoanalysis in the academic world as scholars in the humanities (literature, history) and social sciences (anthropology, sociology) appropriated psychoanalytic principles and theories to explain data in their domains. Biographers and historians, in particular, continue to make extensive use of psychoanalysis in their research and writing; each year sees the publication of new "psychobiographies" and "psychohistories."

Scientific status in question

Offsetting these positive developments, however, is a tendency within certain academic, scientific, and intellectual circles to depreciate psychoanalysis as outmoded and irrelevant. The question has been raised whether psychoanalysis in its current form is a scien-

The Mary S. Sigourney Award Trust was established for the purpose of recognizing outstanding contributions to the field of psychoanalysis. The award's first recipients, in 1990, were (below, left to right) Jacob Arlow, Harold Blum, and Otto Kernberg.

Photographs, American Psychoanalytic Association

tific discipline at all or can even aspire to be. Using the natural sciences as a paradigm against which to judge psychoanalysis, philosophers of science such as Adolf Grünbaum have offered major critiques of the scientific status of psychoanalytic data and hypotheses. These, however, have been met by spirited defenses by such analysts as Marshall Edelson, author of *Psychoanalysis: A Theory in Crisis* (1988). Edelson and others contend that psychoanalysis is an enterprise that advances hypotheses and that those hypotheses are subject to refutation.

Much of the scientific criticism of recent years has come from workers in cognitive science and neuroscience. These critics, many of whom are themselves psychoanalysts, hold that many of Freud's clinically derived insights are refuted by recent work in cognitive development, sleep research, and brain functioning and that those not actually refuted can more usefully be formulated in the language of one or another of these "hard" sciences.

In the 1990s, questions about the scientific status of psychoanalysis have converged with negative assessments of Freud himself by a new generation of historians and biographers. These critics have been especially given to inferences, some more plausible than others, about the impact of Freud's personal psychology (*e.g.,* his relationship with his parents) on his theoretical formulations (*e.g.,* the Oedipus complex). Together, the various critiques of psychoanalysis as a science and the findings and conjectures about Freud's personal life have decidedly lowered the public perception of psychoanalysis.

New and rivaling theories

The paradoxical status of contemporary psychoanalysis, as both successful and beleaguered, finds its echo in internal debates over the nature of the discipline. Psychoanalysis as conceived by Freud was a psychology of conflict, in which instinctual drives of a sexual and aggressive nature collide with the requirements of reality, including the demands of the individual's conscience. Psychopathology, in the form of neurotic symptoms, is the expression of unconscious conflict between drives and the various forces opposing their expression. Instinctual wishes deemed unacceptable by an individual are repressed out of awareness or otherwise disguised or transformed. The symptoms are "compromise formations" whereby repressed drives gain expression in a way that disguises their true meaning.

Over the past two decades, a number of psychoanalytic theories have challenged this Freudian conception. In modern object relations theory, for example, the traditional emphasis on biologically grounded drives gives way to an emphasis on issues of bonding and attachment, especially between the infant and its mother. Drive-related strivings, or wishes for pleasure

from body zones (oral, anal, and genital), are understandable only in terms of how these wishes connect the infant to its mother, father, and other caretakers and how they are gratified by them. Psychopathology, according to this theory, results not from the repression of instinctual wishes but from a tendency to internalize and then repeat early patterns of interaction within one's family constellation.

A number of the more recent psychoanalytic theories focus on the concept of the self. The most prominent of these is "self-psychology," pioneered by the late Heinz Kohut, a Chicago psychoanalyst noted for his ground-breaking works *The Analysis of the Self* (1971), *The Restoration of the Self* (1977), and *How Does Analysis Cure?* (1984). Self theories tend to view early development in terms of a programmed unfolding of a series of functions that together constitute the "self"; the emphasis is on maturational potentials inherent in the self and on the individual's relative success or failure in realizing these potentials. Because self theories construe early development as an agenda with successive stages to be traversed, they tend to view psychopathology not in terms of conflicts (the traditional position) but rather in terms of deficits (*i.e.,* failures to negotiate particular developmental challenges).

Another prominent theory is "interpersonal psychoanalysis." This approach, while not denying the existence of unconscious motives, places greater emphasis on the development of patterns of interpersonal relatedness and the way in which such patterns can become distorted and maladaptive. The interpersonal approach, like the object-relational, focuses on the repetition of these maladaptive patterns in later life; it differs from the object-relational approach in deemphasizing both the linkage of such patterns to instinctual drives and the subsequent internalization of such patterns in the patient's mind.

Two other influential psychoanalytic theories deserve mention. Although both claim many adherents in Europe and South America, they have relatively limited followings in the United States. Kleinian psychoanalysis, associated with the work of the British analyst Melanie Klein, emphasizes the role of intense envy and destructiveness in early life. Lacanian psychoanalysis evolved from the work of the French analyst Jacques Lacan, who stresses that the unconscious is structured like a language and therefore must be decoded like one.

In the early 1990s, this coexistence of rival theories—sometimes not so peaceful—shows little sign of abating. This state of theoretical pluralism is both good and bad. Theoretical disagreement, so evident in the animated dialogue at psychoanalytic congresses and in the pages of professional journals, can be constructive. It suggests that analysts are willing to learn from one another in ways that call into question the convictions of the past. The comparative assessment of different theories, in calling attention to basic methodological and clinical issues, can have a revitalizing effect on the profession. The downside of pluralism, however, is seen in the organizational developments that often accompany the growth of rival theories. Hand in hand with the productive exchanges promoted by emerging theories comes a push toward factionalism. Here the case of self psychology—with its own membership societies, annual conferences, and publications—is instructive. Such institutional autonomy can inhibit meaningful dialogue.

Intriguing contributions from neurobiology

Among the most important research questions today is the relation of psychoanalytic concepts to biological and neurological processes. To the extent that neurobiological findings can provide support for certain psychoanalytic theories over others, research in this area promises a way of adjudicating the competing claims of rival psychoanalytic theories. As neurobiological processes are found as markers of psychological processes, they will argue for those psychoanalytic theories that allow for, and make use of, such processes.

There now exists a body of literature on the neuroanatomic structures and neurophysiological processes that may underlie certain core psychoanalytic concepts. This literature includes neurophysiological demonstrations of unconscious mental processes; neuroanatomic distinctions, for example, between the right brain (the locus of nonverbal, creative thinking—Freud's "primary process") and the left brain (the site of verbal, logical thought—Freud's "secondary process"); research on the neurophysiological pathways of emotional expressions (e.g., fear, panic, anger, and rage); and research on the impact of perceptual environmental experience on neurological development, as, for example, the effect of visual stimuli on the maturation of the brain pathways and structures necessary for sight. The notion of "neuroplasticity" (critical periods during which certain experiences are necessary for optimal brain development) has been proposed as a conceptual link between neurobiological functioning and mental activity, including unconscious mental processes. In a recent book typifying this genre of interdisciplinary research, the neuroscientist Jonathan Winson proposed a "neural representational system" in which the Freudian unconscious is equated with biogenetically ancient mechanisms that involve rapid eye movement (REM) sleep and are located in the hippocampus and related structures of the limbic system of the brain.

The widening scope of analysis

Another area currently being researched is the relationship of psychoanalysis to other therapies that rely on the acquisition of insight. As a method of psychotherapy, psychoanalysis has always been a particularly demanding and costly undertaking, requiring four or five visits a week for several years. This requirement is related to the way in which the psychoanalytic process is engaged. Only through frequent visits can the patient (the analysand) become comfortable with the method of free association, overcome resistances to in-depth psychological exploration, and make contact with painful, unconscious conflicts. Moreover, only by seeing the analyst at frequent intervals can the analysand form a regressive "transference neurosis," in which strong emotions associated with significant figures in the patient's life (e.g., parents, siblings) can be transferred onto the analyst and hence relived in the analytic relationship.

Presently, there is considerable interest in the ways in which psychoanalytic principles can be applied to less intensive or long-term forms of psychotherapy. Clinical researchers are exploring, for example, the role of transference in psychotherapy of short duration ("brief psychotherapy"). Likewise, clinical research is being conducted on the application of psychoanalytic principles and techniques to what is called "psychoanalytic psychotherapy." In this form of therapy, the patient sees the therapist from one to three times weekly and during the treatment sessions may sit facing the analyst rather than lie on the couch with the analyst out of view.

While there is a general consensus that psychoanalysis proper is the treatment of choice for patients with intact personalities who suffer from various conflicts and inhibitions, psychoanalytic psychotherapy is often the preferred treatment modality for more seriously disturbed individuals—those suffering from borderline personality disorders or psychosis. For these patients the regression and the contact with unconscious mental processes that are intrinsic to the psychoanalytic procedure can be stressful to the point of producing a disorganizing effect; such patients frequently lack the ego strength and capacity for sustained introspection that are prerequisites of successful analysis.

An influential minority of psychoanalysts now believe that even for relatively healthy patients with moderate symptomatology who are able to withstand the emotional rigors of analysis, psychoanalytic psychotherapy can result in lasting personality change. These analysts believe that interpretation of unconscious conflicts, especially as expressed in the transference, will result in transformative psychological insights, regardless of the frequency of visits or whether the analysand sits facing the analyst or is recumbent on the couch—features they regard as extrinsic to the analytic method.

For most analysts, however, the frequency of visits and the recumbent position (in which the analyst is not seen) remain necessary adjuncts to the use of free association, the quintessential technique that facilitates controlled regression, the transference neurosis, and the achievement of fundamental insights about oneself and one's interpersonal relations. Traditionally oriented psychoanalysts still believe that only out of these processes can radical personality change emerge.

In Freud's time psychoanalysis was believed to be inappropriate for the most seriously disturbed psychotic and borderline patients. Psychotic individuals have major problems with reality testing; they have the problem of treating their fantasies as reality and acting accordingly. Often they must live in controlled therapeutic environments in which their daily lives are regulated. Individuals with so-called borderline disorder manifest both neurotic and psychotic symptomatology without fitting distinctly into either diagnostic category. Some ego functions are fairly well preserved in the borderline state, but other ego functions show impairment, resulting in reduced flexibility and adaptability and interference with the individual's overall evaluation of reality.

Many psychoanalysts believe, however, that for some individuals with borderline disorder, obsessive-compulsive disorder, or clinically significant depression, psychoanalysis (or psychoanalytic psychotherapy) can be effectively combined with pharmacological therapy. Powerful psychotropic drugs often can help control strong emotions to the point that seriously disturbed patients may begin to explore, psychoanalytically, the unconscious conflicts and fantasies that make them behave as they do.

Psychopharmacology, then, is one of a whole family of treatment adjuncts that make psychoanalytic work possible with borderline patients and even some psychotic patients. These adjuncts, technically termed "parameters," include such noninterpretive interventions as the provision of support, guidance, and educational counseling. Collectively, these measures can make the therapeutic environment safe and nonthreatening for seriously disturbed individuals; they help to provide what analysts call a "holding environment." Such an environment serves as a preparation for psychoanalysis, helping patients feel sufficiently secure, coherent, and integrated to undertake the demanding psychoanalytic work.

Leo Stone, a former director of the New York Psychoanalytic Institute's low-cost psychoanalytic clinic, has emphasized that analysts needed to adapt their methods to accommodate patients far more disturbed than the neurotic patients Freud had in mind when he developed his theories and procedures at the turn of the century. The introduction into the therapeutic setting of the types of parameters described above constituted what Stone termed the "widening scope" of psychoanalytic treatment.

The psychoanalyst's training

Psychoanalytic training—what it consists of, how long it takes, what qualifications it requires—looms as one of the crucial issues now before the field. Traditionally, most psychoanalysts were medical doctors who first specialized in psychiatry and then enrolled in psychoanalytic training institutes. In the United States, in the quarter century following World War II, psychiatrists who were also psychoanalysts chaired a large number of medical school psychiatry departments and thus, in large measure, were able to determine the content of psychiatric training. As a result, many young psychiatrists proceeded to psychoanalytic institutes as the natural culmination of their professional education.

In the 1970s, however, psychiatry as a medical specialty began to diverge from a psychoanalytic orientation. Today the newer perspectives of biological psychiatry and psychopharmacology increasingly dominate the psychiatric landscape and consequently have gained ascendancy in psychiatric training programs. Thus, the percentage of psychiatrists who enter psychoanalysis is much smaller than it was several decades ago. Offsetting this trend, however, are the increasing numbers of nonmedical psychotherapists, notably clinical psychologists and clinical social workers, who are presently pursuing psychoanalytic training.

Since 1987 nonphysicians, psychologists, and social workers have been accepted for full clinical training at institutes affiliated with the American Psychoanalytic Association. In 1989 three nonmedical U.S. institutes were admitted to the IPA: the Institute for Psychoanalytic Training and Research (New York City), the New York Freudian Institute (with branches in New York City and Washington, D.C.), and the Psychoanalytic Center of California (Los Angeles). In 1991 the IPA admitted a fourth nonmedical institute: the Los Angeles Institute and Society for Psychoanalytic Studies. These recent developments suggest that psychoanalytic training under the aegis of the IPA will be increasingly open to qualified applicants from all the healing professions; it betokens a more unified profession, one subject to common standards and less given to acrimony among rival factions.

Among these common standards, none will be more important than the establishment of an appropriate and relevant training experience to be shared by all mental health professionals aspiring to become psychoanalysts. Traditionally, medical-psychoanalytic training has entailed a personal psychoanalysis (a "training analysis") at a frequency of four or five sessions weekly. At the same time, the psychoanalytic candidate conducts several actual analyses under the supervision of senior faculty members. Only through such a training analysis can the candidate-analyst experience what psychoanalysis offers—a therapeutic experience yielding insight conducive to major personality change. And only through the supervised cases can the candidate receive an adequate introduction to the psychoanalytic method, with its unique integration of the investigatory and the clinical. Any training program that dilutes these requirements (by offering training analyses and supervised cases conducted at a frequency of fewer than four sessions weekly) compromises what is most distinctive about psychoanalytic treatment.

It remains to be seen how successful the IPA will be in establishing uniform training requirements among the heretofore independent training institutes currently being brought within its fold. In the United States an ideal scenario would see the American Psychoanalytic Association and groups newly accredited by the IPA enter an alliance aimed at upholding the value of an in-depth analytic experience as the foundation of training.

The patients: who can benefit?

Of course, this vision of psychoanalytic training presupposes the availability of psychoanalytic patients—individuals willing to make the sacrifices required for so intensive and long-term a treatment. Drug therapy and the less costly, less demanding, and less time-consuming forms of psychotherapy have proved effective in ameliorating the symptomatic distress of many people. In recent decades, fewer and fewer people have been willing to accept the sacrifices that psychoanalytic treatment entails. Because so few patients now enter psychoanalysis, the vast majority of analysts spend more time treating patients in psychotherapy than in conducting psychoanalysis proper. With rare exceptions, only the most senior members of the profession are able to practice psychoanalysis full time.

What makes a patient a suitable candidate for long-term analysis? Arlene Heyman and Gerald Fogel, members of the American Psychoanalytic Association's Committee on Public Information, offer the following generalizations about who can benefit from psychoanalysis:

The person who is best able to use psychoanalysis to advantage is a fairly sturdy individual, although he or she may feel far from sturdy at the time of seeking treatment. Indeed, this person may have already achieved some important satisfactions—in work, with friends, or through special interests and hobbies—but nonetheless is unable to appreciate life fully.

He or she may be hampered by long-standing symptoms—depression or anxiety, or sexual incapacities, or physical problems without any demonstrable underlying physical cause. One person may have private rituals or compulsions or repetitive thoughts of which no one else is aware. Another might be troubled by a sense that things always seem to turn out in unpleasant ways, by patterns of failure or disappointment which can not have been brought about by chance. For instance, a woman might become aware that she is always working at a job which is below her capacities—

Paul Merideth—Tony Stone Worldwide

The classic psychoanalytic position—patient lying on couch, analyst out of view—facilitates free association and transference, processes that enable the patient to uncover and gain insights into unconscious sources of conflict.

either procrastinating about seeking, or finding reasons somehow to refuse, more challenging positions. Or a man may observe that he falls in love only with other people's wives or with women who are in some other important respect unavailable. Some people seek analysis because the way they are—their character—limits their choices and pleasures. One might have difficulty being spontaneous and feeling close to others; another might be suffering and complaining inordinately, despite the fact that his lot in life does not seem objectively bad.

Whatever the problem—and each is different—that a person brings to the psychoanalyst, it can be properly understood only within the context of that person's strengths and life situation. Hence, the need for a thorough evaluation to determine who will benefit—and who will not—from psychoanalysis.

The future

Despite competition from other therapies, psychoanalysis continues to offer something uniquely valuable—the possibility of renewed psychological growth that can make life significantly more fulfilling. For individuals burdened by the past, whether in the form of painful symptoms, troubling fantasies and beliefs, or restrictive and unsatisfying human relationships, psychoanalysis can result in a new level of conflict-free functioning, with little subsequent need for psychological help. Psychoanalysis enables people with a variety of pathological dependencies—on symptoms, other people, or restrictive life-styles—to achieve long-term autonomy and self-reliance.

Whether psychoanalysis thrives in the future depends largely on whether the basic values of the psychoanalytic enterprise are prized by the culture at large. Specifically, only if self-understanding and psychological growth are transmitted to the generations as social and personal ideals warranting commitment and deserving of sacrifices will the discovery of Freud prosper in the century to come.

Surgery

Minimally invasive therapy became the driving force behind changes in general surgery in the late 1980s, transforming what had traditionally been a field of tried and true techniques into one of the most rapidly changing branches of medical practice. The operation that opened the door to this remarkable metamorphosis was laparoscopic laser cholecystectomy.

Revolution in gallbladder surgery

Cholecystectomy, or removal of the gallbladder, is one of the most common operations performed by general surgeons, accounting for over half a million operations per year in the United States. Although most commonly seen in the middle and late adult years, gallbladder disease affects all ages. Most gallbladder disease results from the formation of stones—insoluble masses, most often of cholesterol—within the gallbladder. It is usually manifested as pain under the right rib cage—pain that may be brought on by consumption of fatty foods. For the past century, surgery has been performed through a large incision under the right rib cage, and it is considered the "gold standard" for management of gallstones and gallbladder disease. Unfortunately, the pain that occurs following the surgery is intense, requiring that patients remain hospitalized for three to seven days for pain control and normalization of bowel function. Most patients need to refrain from routine activities for another four to six weeks to allow the incision to heal.

Laparoscopic laser cholecystectomy eliminates the need for the painful incision but still allows for removal of the gallbladder and stones. The first such operation was performed in the United States by this author in Nashville, Tenn., in 1988. Around the same time, surgeons in France, Philippe Moret in Lyon and François Dubois in Paris, reported success with similar procedures. Owing to the simplicity of the method pioneered in the U.S., the so-called Reddick technique has become the most common method of performing laparoscopic cholecystectomy around the world.

The operation is usually performed under general anesthesia. Four small punctures are made in the abdominal wall, each measuring 0.6–1.25 cm (0.25–0.5 in). One of the punctures, in the navel, is totally hidden. The other three are placed under the right rib cage. Small tubes (trocars) are placed through the incisions to give access to the abdominal cavity. The abdomen is filled with carbon dioxide gas, which pushes the abdominal muscle wall up and the intra-abdominal organs down, thus allowing a space in which the surgeon can operate. Carbon dioxide does not support combustion and is rapidly absorbed after the procedure, thereby making it safer to use than air. It does, however, cause some mild discomfort postoperatively until it is eliminated by the body.

A telescope-like instrument called a laparoscope is placed through the navel trocar and operating instruments through the other three portals. A video camera attached to the laparoscope allows the surgeon and operating team to visualize the gallbladder at a 16-power magnification on a television screen, making identification of anatomic structures easier than it is through the classical open surgical approach requiring a large incision. Initially, a laser was utilized for dissection of the gallbladder because of its accuracy and safety. However, some surgeons have chosen to perform the dissection with electrocautery because it is a less expensive method than laser excision and does not require specialized laser surgery skills.

Although some gynecologic laparoscopic equipment was available when laparoscopic cholecystectomy was developed, much of it had to be modified and new tools had to be designed to make this operation feasible. The instrument most needed was a round "clip applier" that would pass through the laparoscopic trocars and allow the surgeon to quickly tie off, or clip, blood vessels. Without the clip applier, surgeons would have to perform tedious suturing, which not only would be difficult to learn but would add significantly to the time required for completing the operation. This author and surgical nurse Wayne Miller developed the first such instrument prior to performance of their initial cholecystectomy; the instrument was subsequently refined by the United States Surgical Corp. into an automatic, multiloading device that has the ability to apply multiple clips to bleeding arteries and tissues. Known as the Endo-Clip Applier, it is currently used by most laparoscopic surgeons around the world.

The entire laparoscopic cholecystectomy operation is viewed indirectly via the television screen. The surgeon places the instruments through the trocars and proceeds as if playing a video game. The gall-

Most gallbladder disease results from the formation of stones within the organ; the stones themselves are insoluble masses, most often composed of cholesterol. This diagnostic X-ray shows an extremely severe case of gallstones.

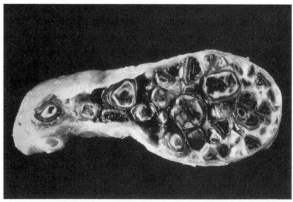

John A. LaGuidice, M.D., Walter J. Hogan, M.D., and Joseph E. Green, M.D.

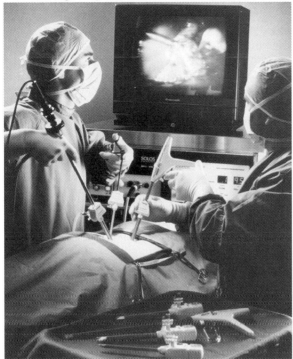

The laparoscope—a telescope-like device attached to a miniature video camera—has revolutionized gallbladder surgery, enabling surgeons to view anatomic structures at 16-power magnification on a TV screen while operating through small punctures in the abdominal wall.

bladder, which is a balloonlike storage organ for bile, is grasped with small pliers through two of the portals, and the laser and clip applier are passed through the other trocar. The major blood vessel (cystic artery) and drainage tube (cystic duct) from the gallbladder are controlled with the clip applier, and the laser is used to remove the gallbladder from its attachments to the liver. The laser effectively coagulates the many small blood vessels found in the liver bed as it cuts the gallbladder away.

Once the gallbladder has been freed of its attachments, it is pulled through the umbilical incision. Occasionally the stones are too large to be removed through the small opening and must be crushed from the outside prior to removal, but this maneuver can be easily accomplished with the use of a crushing clamp placed through the neck of the gallbladder. Finally, each incision is closed with absorbable sutures placed beneath the skin and covered with a waterproof dressing, allowing the patient to resume normal activities after the surgery.

In Tübingen, Germany, a group of surgeons at University Hospital developed another laparoscopic approach to gallstone surgery. Their method enables them to open up the gallbladder, remove the stones, and then reclose the organ without removing it. Though it shows promise, this "organ-preserving" surgery is still experimental.

Spreading like wildfire

Although all general surgeons are skilled in the classical removal of the gallbladder, until recently very few were versed in the techniques of laparoscopy. Therefore, a massive training effort was needed to properly educate the surgeons of the world.

Traditionally, surgery is taught during a five-year residency on a one-to-one basis with an experienced senior surgeon personally assisting a less experienced surgeon through his or her first few attempts at any operation. Owing to the small number of surgeons skilled in laparoscopy and the large numbers needing the training, previous teaching methods were inadequate.

This author initially taught a handful of interested surgeons the technique by having them assist him in his operating theater; however, the demand for training became overwhelming. As the print and television media informed the public about the advantages of laparoscopic cholecystectomy, patients began demanding the operation from their surgeons. Indeed, the laparoscopic approach to gallbladder surgery was spreading like wildfire. Surgeons who could not perform laparoscopic surgery soon found their practices dwindling. Perhaps for the first time in history, an informed public became the driving force behind an operation, and a frenzy developed among surgeons to learn this procedure.

Initially, a two-day intensive laboratory training course was established in Nashville. The course was unique in that it used pigs, rented from farms, as a training model for laparoscopic removal of the gall bladder. These animals offered several advantages over more commonly used laboratory animals, such as rabbits and dogs. They were available in large numbers; there was little sentimental attachment to the animals since they were not considered pets and were generally raised for slaughter; and since removal of the gallbladder did not harm the pigs, they could be sent back to farms and allowed to grow to market size. (Interestingly, it was noted that the pigs gained weight faster after gallbladder removal—thus increasing their market value.)

Soon, however, the demand for training far exceeded the abilities of the Nashville lab. Numerous other courses sprang up across the United States; most were patterned after the Nashville course and were taught by graduates of that training program. One such course, at the Advanced Laparoscopy Training Center in Marietta, Ga., soon became the most sophisticated training program in the country. A teaching facility that would accommodate 40 training surgeons per course was established by gynecologist William Saye, who had collaborated with this author

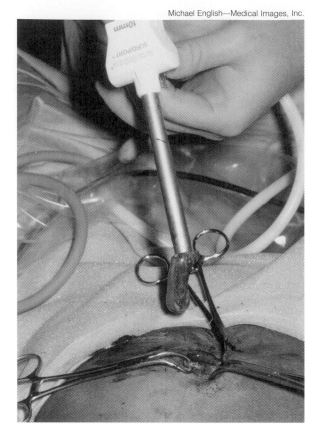

In laparoscopic cholecystectomy the gallbladder—a balloonlike organ attached to the liver—is freed of its attachments, then pulled with special laparoscopic graspers through an incision in the navel measuring less than 1.25 centimeters (0.5 inch).

on the initial design of the laparoscopic cholecystectomy procedure.

The courses at the Marietta facility consist of instruction in laparoscopic principles in general and detailed training in the procedure of laparoscopic cholecystectomy specifically. Special plastic boxlike devices ("trainers"), which are covered by membranes and resemble the human abdomen, were developed to allow surgeons to learn hand-eye coordination prior to performing actual surgery in the animal lab. The first day of training includes lectures, videotapes showing the technique, live demonstrations, and practice on the training boxes. The training then advances to the laboratory, where the trainees are able to remove gallbladders of pigs. During the laboratory period, they learn not only the surgical technique but also the intricacies of the high-technology instruments that are used.

In a period of eight months in 1990, well over 1,000 surgeons from most of the 50 U.S. states and 11 foreign countries received training at the Marietta facility. By the end of 1990 more than 20,000 laparoscopic cholecystectomies had been performed in the United States alone.

Laparoscopy's evolving applications

Now that most surgeons (about two-thirds of surgeons in the U.S.) have learned the basics of laparoscopy and realize its many benefits, they are turning their efforts toward converting other commonly performed general surgical procedures into minimally invasive ones. Appendectomy, long performed through a 5–10-cm (2–4-in) incision in the right lower abdomen, is now routinely managed laparoscopically through incisions in the umbilicus and below the pubic hairline, giving a much improved cosmetic result and decreasing the possibility of adhesions. An additional advantage is that the pelvic organs and intestine can be easily examined for other evidence of pathology; 20% of all patients who appear to have appendicitis actually have other disease instead.

Surgeons are striving to use the laparoscope when they perform other common operations, although many of these techniques are in their infancy. Hernia repair shows considerable promise, and work on intestinal resection and ulcer surgery is just beginning.

Inguinal hernias are outpouchings in the abdomen near the groin; in the U.S. an estimated 550,000 persons undergo operations for this problem annually. The operation has required a painful incision and an uncomfortable repair that involved sewing muscle attachments together. Pioneering work by surgeons Leonard Schultz at Abbott-Northwestern Hospital, Minneapolis, Minn; Albert Spaw at the Laparoscopic Laser Center of Baptist Hospital, Nashville; John Corbitt at JFK Medical Center, Atlantis, Fla.; Miguel Valez at Anaheim (Calif.) Memorial Hospital; and Mark Talamini at the Johns Hopkins Hospital, Baltimore, Md., has shown that inguinal hernias can be safely repaired through the laparoscope. In the still experimental procedure, laparoscopic hernia repair is most often done by patching the defect in the abdominal wall with a tension-free synthetic mesh screen. This approach causes less pain than other hernia operations and should allow the patient to return to normal activity much faster.

Robert Bailey and Karl Zucker of the University of Maryland School of Medicine, Baltimore, have revised an ulcer surgery technique that was originally performed in France. The French method involved cutting the stomach muscle. The improved technique cuts only the nerves to the stomach that promote acid secretion, making the operation safer. Although by early 1991 this operation had been performed only a handful of times, it holds promise as a procedure that may become more widely used.

The revolution of laparoscopy in general surgery has spilled into other surgical specialities. Gynecologists, who once ruled the laparoscopic world, have experienced a rejuvenated interest in laparoscopy, repairing damaged fallopian tubes, performing hysterectomies, removing ectopic pregnancies, and doing "belly button" sterilizations. By employing the laparoscope, urologists have found that they can determine the stage of prostatic and urologic cancers; they can also remove diseased kidneys through small incisions by severing and pulverizing them in the body and then suctioning out the tissue.

Future directions

Laparoscopic laser cholecystectomy has opened the door to minimally invasive surgery and has created a revolution in many surgical disciplines. An editorial in the March 27, 1991, *Journal of the American Medical Association* called laparoscopic cholecystectomy "a remarkable development." The advantages are universal. The economic impact of major surgery is lessened since hospital stays are shorter and patients can return to work much faster. Many of the procedures can be done as outpatient surgery. This benefits insurance companies, which must pay for hospitalization; patients, who no longer have to miss work for extended periods of time after surgery; and employers, who no longer have to temporarily replace workers who have had major surgery. Cosmetic benefits are obvious since major incisions are not necessary.

With the miniaturization of surgical instruments and improvements in video optics, the 1990s will see the development of many new minimally invasive techniques. Eventually these innovations may totally eliminate the need for major surgery.

—*Eddie Joe Reddick, M.D.*

Systemic Lupus Erythematosus

Rheumatic diseases include a wide variety of illnesses that affect connective tissues—ligaments, tendons, bone, cartilage, muscle, blood vessels, and other structural elements of the body that share a common embryological origin. Rheumatic diseases have diverse causes. Errors in the chemical structure of proteins may produce defective, injury-prone connective tissues. For example, production of abnormal forms of the protein collagen, a major structural element in connective tissues, can result in accelerated osteoarthritis or in increased elasticity of tissues and consequent susceptibility to injury. Alternatively, the primary cause of a rheumatic disease may stem from a biochemical abnormality, as in gouty arthritis, which is characterized by excessively high levels of uric acid in the blood.

One rheumatic disease in which the mechanisms of injury (but not the underlying cause) are particularly well understood is systemic lupus erythematosus (lupus or SLE). People afflicted with lupus form antibodies against the body's own constituents, triggering widespread self-injury by the immune system. The mechanisms of tissue injury and diverse clinical manifestations of systemic lupus have fascinated physicians for more than a century, and recent gains in diagnosing and treating lupus illustrate the progress being made in combating rheumatic diseases.

Incidence and predisposing factors

Although anyone can be affected by SLE, 90% of patients are women who develop the disease after the onset of puberty and before menopause. In the U.S. lupus strikes between one in 1,000 and one in 6,000. It is more likely to occur in members of certain races, particularly blacks and Chinese. In addition to race and sex, other inherited characteristics, especially variations in genes that control immune responses, predispose an individual to the disease. The fact that not every identical twin who develops lupus has an affected twin suggests that environmental factors play a major role in triggering the illness. Sunlight, certain prescription drugs, hormonal therapy including the use of birth control pills, and possibly viral infections may all influence disease expression. Abnormal blood tests suggestive of lupus are more frequent than expected in genetically unrelated family members (*e.g.,* spouses, in-laws) and in laboratory workers who process blood from SLE patients, suggesting the presence of a transmissible agent. People with lupus have abnormal numbers of the circulating white blood cells known as lymphocytes, which exert powerful controls over the immune response. The end result appears always to be overactivity of B lymphocytes (B cells)—a type of lymphocyte that produces antibodies—characteristically resulting in production by cells derived from B cells of antibodies directed against the body's own tissues.

A disease of many guises

Symptoms that often lead to diagnosis of SLE include rashes (especially in sun-exposed areas), arthritis, inflammation in the membranes surrounding the lungs and heart (pleurisy and pericarditis), fatigue, fever, and weight loss. Severe lupus characteristically affects the kidneys, nervous system, and circulating blood cells. Several organs may be involved, either simultaneously or sequentially. Disease manifestations may either wax and wane spontaneously or progress inexorably unless treated. Because the symptoms of lupus can mimic literally hundreds of other illnesses, it is sometimes difficult even for experts to identify early cases without the help of specialized blood tests. Decades ago, when such tests were not available, only patients with advanced disease and a poor prognosis were reliably identified. Modern diagnosis and treatment of lupus can be said to have begun about 1950 with the introduction of the first laboratory test that signaled the presence of abnormal antibodies in affected individuals.

Antibodies are relatively large protein molecules assembled from subunits to form a "binding site" capable of attaching to only one molecular target, or antigen. Antibody attachment results in specific alterations in the shape of the remainder of the antibody molecule, which in turn becomes capable of activating additional immune responses. Normal humans have approximately a million kinds of circulating antibodies directed at different targets. Antibody production is markedly enhanced by exposure (or sometimes reexposure) to an antigen; for example, a disease-causing bacterium. However, by virtue of a complex system of checks and balances that is as yet incompletely understood, exposure of the immune system to the body's own tissues does not simulate the development of autoantibodies, or antibodies to "self" antigens, in normal people. It is not known why lupus causes this immune system breakdown, which characteristically results in the formation of autoantibodies. Nevertheless, medical scientists have gathered considerable knowledge about the nature of these autoantibodies and the ways in which they produce disease.

Role of antibodies: a clearer picture

Abnormal antibody production in SLE patients can produce illnesses in at least three distinct ways. First, autoantibodies may attach to antigens on material, including genetic material, that originates within cells and that is released into the bloodstream during the normal process of cell death and disintegration. Complexes of such intracellular material and antibodies, called immune complexes, become trapped in bodily tissues, particularly in those organs that filter blood to produce urine or other bodily fluids.

For example, SLE patients frequently have large amounts of circulating antibodies to DNA, the molecule that transmits the genetic code. Release of DNA into the bloodstream can result in the formation of circulating immune complexes of DNA and anti-DNA antibodies, which have a strong propensity to lodge in the kidney. This may lead to a series of immunologic attacks on kidney cells. Disruption of kidney function may manifest itself as leakage of protein or blood into the urine, inability to excrete waste products, or severe high blood pressure. In the early stages, when kidney disease is most easily treated, it may produce no symptoms and remain unnoticed unless appropriate investigations are performed. Because the damage is caused in large part by deposition of immune complexes, early and aggressive drug treatment to reduce antibody formation can be extremely valuable in some patients.

In addition to injuring the kidney, immune complexes may be deposited throughout the body and produce a wide range of symptoms, including skin rashes, arthritis, pleurisy, central nervous system disease, and diffuse damage to blood vessels.

A second way that lupus causes illness involves a direct antibody-mediated attack on cell-membrane

antigens. The most accessible targets for blood-borne autoantibodies are, not surprisingly, circulating blood cells. Red blood cells, platelets (cell-like blood components important in clotting), and white blood cells (including certain lymphocytes that are active in controlling immune responses) can all be affected. A major problem for SLE patients is the reduction of the numbers of circulating platelets (thrombocytopenia), brought on in most cases by the attachment of antibodies to the surfaces of circulating platelets, a process that marks these platelets for ingestion by tissue-bound macrophages (scavenging white blood cells) in the liver and spleen. The drop in circulating platelets can become severe enough to pose a serious risk of bleeding.

Because antibodies are the cause of most cases of thrombocytopenia in lupus, initial treatment is usually directed at stemming the production of antibodies and slowing the pace of immunologically mediated injury with prednisone (a steroid drug with potent anti-inflammatory and immunosuppressant effects) and other immunosuppressive drugs. It is also possible to lower markedly the rate of platelet reduction in some patients by removing the spleen, the home of most of the macrophages that ingest antibody-coated platelets. In addition, platelets can sometimes be "tagged" with toxic drugs that appear to inhibit macrophages from damaging them, and the immune system can be "confused" by intravenous administration of large quantities of antibodies harvested from donated blood, which appear to compete with antibody-tagged platelets for ingestion and destruction in the liver and spleen.

Direct antibody-mediated attack has also been proposed as a mechanism for some forms of the brain damage seen in central nervous system lupus. In this case, antibodies directed at the surface of either nerve cells or supporting cells known as glial cells may produce injury.

Lupus is now known to cause illness a third way—through the production of autoantibodies affecting the coagulation system. The result, hypercoagulability of the blood, shows itself in the tendency for some people with lupus to develop blood clots in arteries and veins. The clots in turn can produce a variety of maladies including blockage of vessels in the legs, lungs, brain, or eyes and interruption of critical blood supply to the placenta in pregnant women, which results in recurrent spontaneous abortions. A sensitive assay for the antibodies (called anticardiolipin antibodies), together with certain other tests, can identify those SLE patients at high risk for clots and fetal loss.

In the past almost all of the manifestations of SLE were attributed to inflammation resulting from the presence of antibodies directed against intracellular or cell-surface antigens. Many of the effects stemming from hypercoagulability—*e.g.*, strokes, fetal loss, and pulmonary blood clots—were either not recognized as features of lupus or inappropriately managed with anti-inflammatory agents. The recent recognition of noninflammatory lupus that affects coagulation has led to appropriate use of anticoagulants—rather than drugs directed at the immune system—with improved therapeutic effects and fewer side effects.

Criteria for diagnosing lupus

The hallmarks of lupus are the simultaneous involvement of several organ systems, the presence of autoantibodies in the blood, and the reduction of the number of circulating blood cells. Although the American College of Rheumatology's criteria now used for diagnosing lupus were created for the purposes of standardizing selection of patients for research studies, they have proved to be an extremely useful clinical tool. In fact, studies have shown that the vast majority of patients with lupus can be distinguished from those with other rheumatic diseases on the basis of these criteria and that the vast majority of patients who do not have lupus are successfully excluded. Of course, in the early stages of the disease, it is possible for one or two characteristic symptoms to be present, an insufficient number to sustain a definite diagnosis. Patients who meet two criteria are considered to have "possible" lupus, patients with three criteria to have "probable" lupus, and patients with four to have "definite" lupus.

The skin and mucous membranes are the site of several disease manifestations of lupus and, in fact, a diagnosis can be made from disorders of the skin and mucous membranes alone. Inflammatory changes may also affect the joints, the lining of the heart and lungs, and the kidneys and may, in part, be responsible for central nervous system disease, discussed below. Although nervous system manifestations can be quite varied, presence of seizures or psychosis has traditionally been considered typical of lupus. Additional categories of disease manifestations include antibody-mediated cytopenias (depressed numbers of circulating blood cells) and autoantibodies.

Lupus in pregnancy: cautious optimism

Because of the tendency of SLE to affect young women, the disease inevitably is associated with problems during pregnancy. In fact, for many years it was believed to be extremely hazardous for any woman with lupus to become pregnant. Today it is possible to make several better informed statements regarding the association of lupus with pregnancy.

First, there is probably a slightly increased tendency of lupus to flare during pregnancy. The statement is somewhat controversial, however; some researchers feel that there is no increased risk.

Second, like many other rheumatic diseases, lupus tends to show increased activity after the end of pregnancy. Apparently, the hormonal and immunologic adjustments that allow the maternal immune system to tolerate the fetus (which is in part composed of foreign antigens derived from the father) comes to an abrupt end, resulting in a "rebound" of immunologic activity. It is now standard practice for women with lupus to be observed carefully after childbirth and treated early and aggressively, usually for a brief time, if increased activity is noted.

Third, the potential toxicity to the unborn child of drugs conventionally used to treat lupus may cause considerable difficulties in managing disease manifestations that would otherwise be well controlled. For example, aspirin, other anti-inflammatory drugs, antimalarial drugs like hydroxychloroquine, and powerful immunosuppressive drugs like azathioprine and cyclophosphamide may be variously used in patients showing different manifestations of lupus. None of these, however, is employed during pregnancy except under very unusual circumstances. In addition, many drugs used to treat such complications of lupus as high blood pressure, headaches, seizures, or pain must also be discontinued. As a result, even though the underlying disease activity may be no different during pregnancy, patients may feel worse. In unusual cases it may be necessary to withhold important therapeutic drugs and accept a certain amount of irreversible organ damage until the child is born. Obviously the management of pregnancy in such individuals is fraught with extremely difficult choices to be made jointly by the physician and patient.

Finally, there is much new knowledge about factors that increase the risk of fetal loss or injury. Throughout pregnancy, perhaps most importantly during the second trimester, antibodies that are associated with hypercoagulability confer risk of sudden fetal loss. Unfortunately, in some women with this risk factor, spontaneous abortions may occur repeatedly—as often as five or six times. (Because the risk of spontaneous abortions in women without lupus is at least 25%, it is considered wise to await three spontaneous abortions in an SLE patient before diagnosing this syndrome.) Attempts have been made to treat the condition with large doses of prednisone throughout pregnancy; with heparin, an injectable anticoagulant; or with daily small doses of aspirin, which inhibits platelet aggregation. No single method is known to be highly efficacious or superior to the others, but anticoagulation with heparin or aspirin appears to be much less harmful to the mother than nine months of treatment with high-dose steroids.

There is also increased risk for offspring of women who have circulating antibodies to a "self" antigen known as the Ro/SSA antigen. These antibodies appear capable of crossing the placenta and affecting the fetus in later development and at birth. The major consequence appears to be antibody-mediated injury

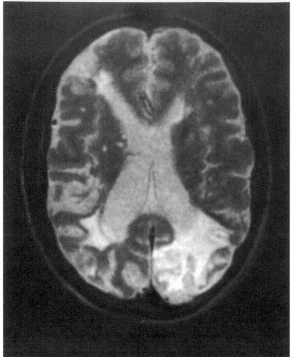

Magnetic resonance imaging (MRI) is allowing neurologists to locate abnormalities in the brains of individuals with lupus who are suspected of having had multiple strokes. In the MRI scan of a lupus patient, above, bright areas in the lower right and upper and lower left identify regions of brain death presumably due to deprivation of blood supply.

to the conduction system of the fetal heart, blocking the normal transmission of electrical signals from one part of the heart to another. This injury may cause slowing, or sometimes cessation, of the heartbeat. When present in newborns, it can occasionally require a pacemaker. Transmission of the Ro/SSA antibody across the placenta also appears to be responsible for neonatal lupus syndrome. Affected babies usually develop mild symptoms of lupus, particularly facial rashes, that tend to resolve as soon as the antibodies transmitted from the mother are removed from the fetal circulation.

Gestation is a hazardous time for any unborn child and more so for the child of an SLE patient. The majority of pregnancies in such patients, however, are successful, and the majority of children born are normal.

Progress in diagnosing central nervous system lupus

In 50–75% of people afflicted with lupus, abnormalities of the brain, spinal cord, or peripheral nervous system develop some time during the course of the disease. Clinical manifestations vary and include seizures, strokes, impairment of intellectual function, headaches, difficulties with vision or hearing, major psychiatric disorders, spinal cord injury, and disruption of the sensory and motor functions of peripheral nerves extending from the brain and spinal cord into the body. Fortunately, many patients develop only mild, reversible symptoms, and of those who develop severe manifestations, about 70% improve partially or completely.

Because of its complexity, central nervous system lupus has been described as one of the last frontiers of clinical medicine. It is certainly one of the more difficult aspects of systemic lupus to diagnose and manage. For many years immune-complex–mediated inflammation of the brain's blood vessels was thought to be the major cause of brain injury. More recently the role of clotting, which results in vessel blockage and loss of blood supply to areas of the brain, has been appreciated. However, detailed studies of the brains of patients who have died with central nervous system lupus have found neither vessel inflammation nor clots in 75% of cases. Although the majority of symptoms remain unexplained, one contributing factor may be the presence of antibodies directed against components of the surfaces of brain cells. Furthermore, some antibodies appear capable of interfering with the chemical transmission of signals at synapses, the junctions between nerve cells. Because there are many chemical messengers with different functions, each of which may be widely distributed in the brain, selective interference with a particular type of transmission presumably could produce characteristic functional abnormalities in the absence of obvious localized brain injury. Finally, in severe lupus, impaired functioning of the kidney or other organs, drug side effects, infections, or other coexistent problems can cause major nervous system abnormalities even if the brain is not under direct immunologic attack.

Diagnosis and management of central nervous system lupus are further complicated by the frequent inability to identify the specific area in the brain that is actually diseased, even when symptoms obviously originate within the nervous system. Although some neurological problems—for example, a stroke affecting movement of the right arm and control of speech—may be rather precisely localized in the brain on the basis of symptoms, other neurological symptoms seen in lupus—such as headache, psychosis, or depression of intellectual function—are not predictably associated with specific brain abnormalities. For this reason it is necessary to combine the results of several diagnostic procedures to make the best possible assessment of active disease. At the present time the two best clinical tests are analysis of spinal fluid for evidence of inflammation and magnetic resonance imaging (MRI), a sensitive procedure for identifying localized or diffuse brain-substance injury. Another relatively new imaging technique, positron emission tomography (PET), permits observation of metabolic activity in the brain and localization of areas of the brain that function abnormally, even in the absence of detectable anatomic abnormalities.

When SLE patients develop new neurological symptoms, it is often useful to analyze a specimen of cerebrospinal fluid, obtained by a lumbar puncture (spinal tap). Since cerebrospinal fluid surrounds the brain and spinal cord, its composition reflects their state of health; abnormalities can provide evidence of brain injury and inflammation. Probably the most important cerebrospinal fluid abnormality in lupus is the presence of increased numbers of white blood cells, signifying an inflammatory process at work. Some patients also have excessive amounts of antibodies in the fluid, indicating exaggerated immune responses presumably resulting from active lupus.

Since the early 1980s diagnosis of central nervous system lupus has been greatly aided by MRI of the brain. Although patients may develop symptoms that appear likely to be the result of lupus-caused brain injury, there may be other possible causes that need to be eliminated. In the past there was no reliable method of pinpointing areas of brain injury, although anatomic abnormalities could be detected by computed tomography (CT) in about half the cases. The sensitivity of CT scans of the brain is limited by the use of X-rays, which are affected much more by bones than by soft tissue and are deflected by the skull during examination of the brain. The introduction of MRI, which identifies abnormalities in soft tissues on the basis of water content and the relationship of hydrogen atoms to the surrounding chemical environment, has made it possible to take detailed pictures of soft tissues. Because MRI surveys tissues in three dimensions, it is possible to scan the entire brain and display abnormalities from various perspectives. In addition, it is possible to "tune" the MRI in individual situations to provide maximum contrast between normal and abnormal tissues.

Today MRI makes it possible in the vast majority of cases to identify abnormalities in the brains of SLE patients who experienced neurologists suspect have had strokes. Heretofore this had not been the case for patients whose symptoms (*e.g.,* depression, psychosis, or headache) made brain damage difficult to localize on the basis of a clinical examination. Interestingly, many patients with progressive and severe intellectual impairment are revealed by MRI to have multiple small strokes as the underlying cause. In addition, patients who have only transient difficulty, say with speaking or moving an arm or leg, will show corresponding brain abnormalities in MRI surveys done during their affliction but not in subsequent scans done weeks or months later. This suggests that some patients with lupus have reversible injury to the brain, a phenomenon that is considered unusual; this is impossible to verify or disprove without examining the affected tissues microscopically. Finally, comparison of MRI surveys before and after courses of therapy provides an invaluable measure of the disease course and response to treatment.

It is now possible to assess brain function (as opposed to structure) by means of PET scanning, which uses radioactively labeled molecules that are metabolized in the brain. The molecules can be any of a variety of substances—*e.g.,* oxygen, sugar molecules, or amphetamines—that are incorporated into living brain tissue. Before injection into the patient, the molecules are treated so that they will emit positrons, subatomic particles whose interaction with matter in the brain produces harmless radiation that is picked up by an

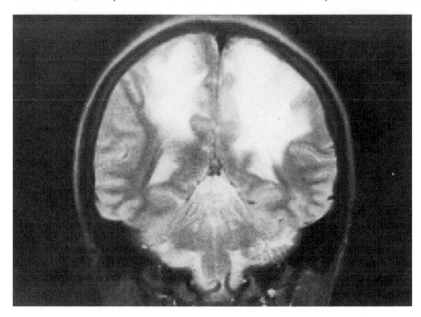

In patients with lupus who suffer only transient neurological difficulties— e.g., in speaking or moving a limb— MRI can reveal corresponding brain abnormalities. In the vertical MRI scan at left, the bright regions in each hemisphere represent an unknown form of brain injury to a patient who experienced a recent seizure. The person recovered, and the brain abnormalities did not appear in later scans.

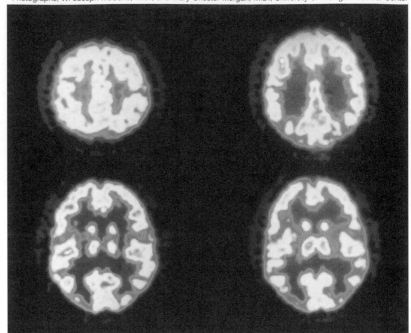

Positron emission tomography (PET) can help assess function in healthy and diseased brain tissue by mapping concentrations of tracer compounds as they are metabolized by working brain cells. The PET images at right represent four horizontal sections through a healthy living brain as it takes up radioactively labeled sugar (glucose) molecules. Varying intensities (usually represented by colors) in the patterns correspond to different rates of glucose uptake. In a normally functioning brain, the patterns are symmetrical.

array of detectors surrounding the patient. Like MRI, PET scanning enables reconstruction of an image of the brain in three dimensions.

Studies of SLE patients have been performed with use of the radioactive isotope oxygen-15, which shows blood delivery to brain tissues, and fluorodeoxyglucose, a sugar that is incorporated into cells during active metabolism. Results suggest that PET scanning is much more sensitive than MRI or any other known

technique in detecting abnormalities in SLE patients. Indeed, virtually all such scans performed on patients during active central nervous system disease have shown at least subtle abnormalities, while some have shown major abnormalities. In addition, many patients with normal results on neurological examinations and no clinical evidence of brain disease still have subtle abnormalities on PET scans. It remains to be learned whether the abnormalities revealed by PET scanning

PET images of the brain of a patient showing severe intellectual impairment due to lupus contrast sharply with the set above. Numerous areas of abnormality and asymmetry in the patterns reveal that multiple strokes have occurred.

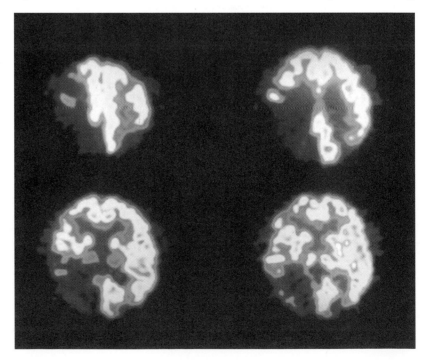

are clinically important or reflect actual abnormalities of the brain and whether they will prove to be a good indicator of early central nervous system disease when MRI shows nothing abnormal.

Advances in treating severe lupus

The outlook for patients newly diagnosed with systemic lupus has never been better. The 10-year survival of such patients is at least 90% and probably higher. The prognosis is better still for persons in whom the disease is suspected but not proved. Proper rest, appropriate exercise, weight control, and avoidance of smoking and foods containing large amounts of cholesterol or saturated fat are important for every lupus patient. Avoidance of sunlight through proper dress and sunscreens is important for many patients. Regular surveillance for signs of subclinical disease—such as the appearance of protein or cells in the urine or low blood counts—aids prompt treatment.

Anti-inflammatory drugs like aspirin, ibuprofen, and naproxen are important for managing fever, inflammation, and malaise. Another important class of drugs for treating lupus is the antimalarial agents, particularly hydroxychloroquine. When administered over several weeks to months, they appear to reduce the activity of lupus affecting the skin, hair, joints, pleura, and pericardium. Treatment of virtually all severe manifestations of lupus due to immune complex disease or antibodies against cell-surface antigens includes the use of prednisone. Unfortunately, short-term administration of prednisone can be complicated by serious infections, and long-term administration of high doses markedly accelerates the process of aging, resulting in such adverse effects as cataracts, osteoporosis, thinning of muscle and skin, a higher incidence of hypertension and diabetes, and atherosclerosis. Even if the disease activity is controlled, patients requiring long-term treatment with high doses of prednisone may do better with the addition of an immunosuppressive agent, described below. Prednisone does not adequately control immunologically mediated manifestations of lupus in some patients. Patients with severe kidney disease, for example, may have progressive increases in protein loss and reduction of the ability to clear waste products in spite of high doses of prednisone. Such people are candidates for vigorous treatment with immunosuppressive agents.

There has been considerable recent improvement in the immunosuppressive approach to treating lupus. Presently it is possible in most patients to control almost all immunologically mediated symptoms with immunosuppressives, at least for a few years, if treatment is begun early enough. Because these agents show considerable cumulative toxicity over the long term, they are much more satisfactory for treating acute, fulminant disease than chronic, slowly progressive disease. In cases in which prednisone can control symptoms but prolonged therapy is required, a combination of the immunosuppressant azathioprine with lower doses of prednisone provides the opportunity for less cumulative steroid toxicity.

Even in the face of treatment with prednisone and azathioprine, lupus may worsen in some patients or may show very severe, progressive manifestations like progressive kidney disease. These patients are candidates for treatment with intravenous cyclophosphamide. An immunosuppressive agent, cyclophosphamide acts both by inhibiting the synthesis of DNA, thus interfering with cell division, and by directly modifying the responses of lymphocytes to immunologic stimuli. Its effects are particularly potent in diseases involving autoantibodies, such as lupus. Like azathioprine, it is best used in combination with prednisone. Cyclophosphamide, however, produces severe side effects, among them ovarian or testicular failure, suppression of bone marrow function, and accelerated development of cancer including bone marrow tumors, skin cancer, and bladder and urinary-tract cancer.

The variability of kidney disease in different patients with lupus and the relatively small number of patients with severe kidney disease at any single medical center had made it impossible, until recently, to prove that the use of immunosuppressive agents actually improves the long-term outlook for kidney disease. In randomized, controlled, long-term studies of a large group of patients at the National Institutes of Health, Bethesda, Md., administration of cyclophosphamide intravenously once every three months, in combination with oral prednisone, was shown to provide superior results after 5–10 years compared with prednisone alone. Supplementing the cyclophosphamide with intravenous fluids to produce a high urine output appeared to eliminate problems with bladder toxicity and urinary-tract cancer over that period.

More recently, monthly administration of cyclophosphamide intravenously was tried as initial therapy. Early results have been extremely gratifying. Almost all patients with kidney disease who were selected for treatment had reduced amounts of cells and protein in the urine and improved kidney function after six months. In addition, even patients who had remained ill with multiple disease manifestations after treatment with high doses of prednisone or azathioprine showed improvement of their symptoms and needed less prednisone during that period. Disease manifestations like thrombocytopenia and certain forms of central nervous system lupus also appeared to respond, although the results were preliminary. Detailed laboratory studies of immune responses before and after treatment with intravenous cyclophosphamide supported the clinical evidence that the drug can dramatically reverse progressive, immunologically mediated damage that has resisted treatment with prednisone.

—*W. Joseph McCune, M.D.*

HEALTH INFORMATION UPDATE

Instructive and practical
articles about common
and not-so-common
health concerns

"Where's the Beef?"
by Diane H. Morris, Ph.D., R.D.

"Where's the beef?" growled the disgruntled fast-food patron as she examined the dubious hamburger patty she had just been served. This snappy question, delivered by a pugnacious octogenarian, launched one of the most popular and successful advertising campaigns of the past decade. The message underscored the U.S. public's expectations about their beloved hamburgers—that the portion should be hearty, the beef hot, juicy, and good tasting.

Americans have definite expectations not just about hamburgers but about meat in general. It must be satisfying, nutritious, and safe to eat. In most U.S. families, meat is still the centerpiece of the meal. Meat has, however, acquired a somewhat tarnished image over the past few years as headlines have focused on studies linking a high-fat diet to increased risk of heart disease and certain kinds of cancer. Families today are eating more meatless meals and are substituting chicken and fish for red meat—a category that includes beef, pork, lamb, and veal.

Long a staple of the "three-square-meals-a-day" approach to nutrition, meat now seems to have fallen out of fashion with health-conscious consumers. Has a "verdict" on meat been reached? Can meat, particularly red meat, constitute an integral part of a healthy, nutritious diet? Which cuts of meat are most nutritious? Which cuts are highest in fat? How much meat can one eat when following a cholesterol-lowering diet?

Meat eating: historical view

Thousands of years ago, hunters and gatherers roamed the Northern Hemisphere in search of food. Hunting expeditions were organized around the trapping and killing of large game, including mammoth, buffalo, deer, moose, and bear.

When food was plentiful, the diet consisted primarily of meat—as well as waterfowl and fish. This meat-based diet was supplemented with berries, wild roots, greens, and, in the New World, corn in season. Over the winter months, however, food stores usually dwindled, reaching a crucial low point by late winter and early spring. During months of food scarcity, hunters sought the fattest animals for food; in fact, they would bypass lean prey in favor of fatter animals, even when the hunters themselves were starving. A similar phenomenon was documented in more recent recorded history. During the winter of 1805, explorers Meriwether Lewis and William Clark made the following notation in their journal: "Captain Clark returned last evening with all his hunting party. During their excursion they had killed 40 deer, 3 buffalo, and 16 elk; but most of the game was too lean for use."

It was also traditionally claimed that high-fat meat was more satisfying and nourishing than its lean counterpart. In his 1923 report on the Canadian Arctic expedition, anthropologist and Arctic scholar Diamond Jenness wrote of the Eskimo, or Inuit, people: "Men and dogs will half-starve on a diet of lean caribou-meat, however plentiful, whereas half the quantity of blubbery seal-meat will satisfy their desires and keep them well nourished." Thus, animals with a high body-fat content have long been prized and were hunted selectively during times when food was scarce.

Today, of course, the situation is very different. In the U.S.—and most other developed countries—a wide variety of foods are available year-round, and survival is not tied to the success of hunting for game. While some subgroups within the U.S. population are still at risk for malnutrition, the emphasis for many Americans has shifted from a concern about not getting enough calories and nutrients to the problem of eating too much. A primary public health concern today is the high intake of dietary fat, particularly saturated fat and cholesterol.

417

Meat consumption: a downward trend

How much red meat is currently being eaten by people in the U.S.? According to figures from the National Live Stock and Meat Board, Americans are not the ravenous consumers of red meat they are often perceived to be. After the amount of fat, bone, and tissue removed in the trimming of retail cuts of meat and in losses from cooking was calculated, it was determined that U.S. consumers eat about 113 g (4 oz) of red meat a day on average, a moderate level of consumption for the population of a developed country.

Have meat-consumption patterns changed in recent years? Yes, according to most indicators. One measure of consumption is what the food industry calls "per capita disappearance" data. Per capita disappearance refers to the amount of a food product *available* in the food supply on an individual (perperson) basis; it does not provide information about the amount of food actually eaten. In 1985 (the latest year for which figures are available), the per capita disappearance of red meat, poultry, and fish reached an all-time high of 84 kg (185 lb), edible weight. (Edible weight is the portion of the animal carcass that can be eaten, excluding all bones but, in the case of red meat, including the thin strip of fat usually sold on retail cuts.) Between 1965 and 1985, poultry registered the largest change in per capita disappearance, with chicken increasing 72% and turkey 62%. Fish disappearance also reached a record high in 1985, increasing 34% over the 1965 figure. The per capita disappearance of red meat as a category had changed very little during the two decades from 1940 to 1960, although the disappearance of two specific products, veal and lamb, declined by more than 50% during that time. These trends in meat-consumption patterns appear to be continuing.

A similar pattern is reflected in another measure of U.S. dietary patterns, the Continuing Survey of Food Intakes by Individuals, conducted by the U.S. Department of Agriculture (USDA). This large national survey of the food intake of children under 5 years of age and adults aged 19 to 54 obtained information about changes in people's eating patterns from 1977 to 1985. Participants reported eating less beef, luncheon meats, and pork in 1985 than in 1977. Fish consumption by all groups increased between 1977 and 1985. Another index of consumption, expenditures for poultry and fish at the grocery store, increased by more than 100% between 1976 and 1988, according to *Supermarket Business* magazine. Thus, even though they are still putting red meat on the dinner table, consumers seem to be heeding the recommendation to eat more fish and poultry.

Why eat meat?

Meat and meat products are nutrient-dense foods—that is, they provide substantial amounts of nutrients

Where's the protein?		
	portion	protein (g)
meats		
chicken breast	4 oz cooked*	36
fish, haddock	4 oz cooked	25
hamburger	4 oz cooked	30
tuna (canned, oil- or water-packed)	4 oz	33
turkey breast	4 oz cooked	30
nonmeat foods		
hard cheese	1 oz	8
cottage cheese	¼ cup	8
kidney beans, canned	½ cup	6
lentil or bean soup	1 cup	6
milk, low-fat	1 cup	8
nuts	1 oz, ¼ cup	8
peanut butter	2 tbs	8
tofu	4 oz	8
yogurt	1 cup	8

*4 oz cooked = about 5–6 oz raw weight

for the number of calories per serving. Furthermore, the protein in meat is highly digestible. In addition, meat protein is a high-quality protein in that it contains adequate amounts of the essential amino acids, the building blocks of protein that cannot be manufactured by the body and must be supplied in food.

An "average" young man, weighing 72.6 kg (160 lb), requires about 58 g of protein daily; a 58.1-kg (128-lb) woman needs about 46 g. This translates to roughly two ounces of protein, the amount that would be found in 170–255 g (6–9 oz) of meat. Pregnant women need about 10 g more of protein daily than nonpregnant women. Growing children need more protein than adults. Healthy diets provide about 10 to 20% of calories from protein.

Meat is a good source of the B vitamins, particularly thiamin, riboflavin, niacin, vitamin B_6, and vitamin B_{12}. These vitamins play specific roles in the utilization of carbohydrate and fat, two of the body's fuel sources, and in other metabolic processes. Vitamin B_{12} deserves special mention. Meat and other animal products (*e.g.,* dairy foods, eggs) are virtually the only dietary source of vitamin B_{12} for humans; plant foods lack vitamin B_{12}.

Meat and meat products are also important sources of at least two minerals, iron and zinc. Until 1979 meat was the main source of iron in the U.S. diet. Since that time, however, with the increased fortification of foods such as flour and baked goods, grain products have become the primary source of dietary iron. The advantage of obtaining dietary iron from meat and meat products is its high "bioavailability." That is, the iron found in meat—called "heme" iron because it is

A proud cattle breeder displays a prize Hereford specially developed for its leanness. Changes in livestock breeding and feeding practices are now producing animals with a higher proportion of muscle to fat than their predecessors; at the supermarket this translates into cuts of meat that appeal to today's health-conscious consumer.

chemically bound to the blood protein hemoglobin—is rapidly absorbed and utilized by the body. The iron in grain products, vegetables, nuts, beans, and peas is "nonheme" iron and is poorly absorbed in the absence of meals containing meat. An 85-g (3-oz) serving of lean beef, pork, lamb, veal, or poultry provides from 6 to 15% of the U.S. recommended dietary allowance (RDA) for iron.

Meat is also an excellent source of zinc, a mineral found in virtually all cells of the body and required for many cellular functions. As with iron, the zinc in red meats and some seafoods has a higher degree of bioavailability than that found in plant products. An 85-g serving of lean beef provides about 40% of the U.S. RDA for zinc. A similar amount of pork provides about 20%; lamb, a little less than 30%; and poultry, about 12%. The zinc content of fish ranges widely, from a low of about 2% in 85 g of tuna packed in water to a high of 43% in a comparable portion of Alaskan king crab.

Leaner animals, leaner cuts

The increased demand for poultry and lean red meat has had far-reaching effects on the methods of livestock production. Over the past two or three decades, breeders have responded to market forces by changing breeding and feeding practices to reduce the body fat of meat animals while preserving taste and palatability. For example, compared with practices of former years, livestock today is slaughtered at a younger age, when the animals are relatively lean and have a greater proportion of muscle tissue to fat. Cattle, hogs, and lambs have been crossbred with lean stock to produce animals with less body fat and more muscle mass—beef carcass fatness has been reduced about

6%, pork about 23%, and lamb about 9% over the last 20 to 25 years. Thus, animals taken to market today are considerably leaner and more muscular than animals bred in the 1950s and '60s.

Another significant change can be seen in the meat-display case at the supermarket. Today's red meats are trimmed of virtually all external fat. In 1989 Jeffrey Savell of Texas A&M University coordinated the National Consumer Retail Beef Study, an industry-wide program designed to evaluate consumer preferences. Savell and his colleagues found that the average fat thickness for retail cuts of beef across the country was less than 3.2 mm (⅛ in). More than 40% of the retail cuts sampled had no external fat. The study showed that when retail cuts of beef had either no external fat or less than 6.4 mm (¼ in) of external fat, consumers purchased more beef than they had previously and gave high ratings for taste and texture.

These twin market trends—toward leaner meat products and better trimmed retail cuts—have resulted in an improved nutritional profile for red meats, particularly beef and pork. While meat and meat products are still significant sources of fat, in the U.S. accounting for about 57% of the fat available for consumption, the contribution of fat from animal products to the overall diet is on the decline.

High cholesterol: is meat to blame?

Most consumers now know that diets high in saturated fats increase the blood levels of cholesterol and low-density lipoprotein, the so-called bad cholesterol. On the other hand, diets containing polyunsaturated and monounsaturated fats lower blood lipid levels.

What many consumers do not realize is that animal fats are made up of a mixture of saturated and un-

Where's the fat?

red meats	total fat (g)	saturated fat (g)	calories	cholesterol (mg)
veal top round (roasted)	2.9	1.0	127	88
pork tenderloin (roasted)	4.1	1.4	133	67
beef top round (broiled)	4.2	1.4	153	71
beef eye of round (roasted)	4.2	1.5	143	59
pork sirloin chop, boneless (broiled)	5.7	1.5	156	78
pork loin roast, boneless (roasted)	6.4	2.4	160	66
lamb leg (roasted)	6.6	2.3	162	78
pork loin chop, bone in (broiled)	6.9	2.5	165	70
beef tenderloin (broiled)	8.5	3.2	179	71
frankfurter, beef and pork (boiled)	24.8	9.1	272	42
pork sausage, country-style (cooked)	26.5	9.2	314	71
poultry				
turkey breast, skinless (roasted)	2.7	0.9	133	59
chicken breast, skinless (roasted)	3.0	0.9	140	72
turkey thigh, skinless (roasted)	6.1	2.1	159	72
chicken thigh, skinless (roasted)	9.3	2.6	178	81

	total fat (g)	saturated fat (g)	calories	cholesterol (mg)
chicken breast, skin on (fried)	11.2	3.0	221	72
duck, skin on (roasted)	24.1	8.2	286	71
fish and seafood				
lobster meat (cooked)	0.5	<0.1	83	61
scallops, bay or sea (raw)	0.6	<0.1	75	28
cod (broiled)	0.7	0.1	89	47
shrimp (moist heat cooked)	0.9	0.2	84	166
flounder (broiled)	1.3	0.3	99	58
crab, Alaskan king (steamed)	1.3	0.1	82	45
oysters (eastern, raw)	2.1	0.5	59	47
tuna, white (canned in water)	2.1	0.6	116	36
trout, rainbow (broiled)	3.7	0.7	128	62
tuna, light (canned in oil)	7.0	1.3	168	15
salmon, sockeye (broiled)	9.3	1.6	184	74
other				
tofu/bean curd	4.1	0.6	65	0
eggs (hard-boiled)	9.5	2.8	134	466
American cheese food (pasteurized process)	20.9	13.1	279	54
cheddar cheese	28.2	17.9	343	89
peanuts (roasted in shell)	41.4	7.3	495	0
peanut butter	43.5	7.2	502	0

all 3-oz portions

saturated fats. Beef fat, for example, contains roughly equal proportions of monounsaturated and saturated fat, with small amounts of polyunsaturated fat. The saturated fat in beef is composed largely of two fatty acids, stearic acid and palmitic acid. Recent studies show that these two saturated fatty acids actually have different effects on blood cholesterol. Palmitic acid, which makes up about 27% of the total fatty acids in beef, raises blood cholesterol. Stearic acid, which is also found in cocoa butter and other edible fats and oils, makes up about 19% of the total fatty acid profile of beef and evidently does not affect blood cholesterol levels one way or the other. Obviously, fats of different types affect the body differently, and scientists still have much to learn about the properties of various types of fats.

But what about the cholesterol content of meat? Does it contribute significantly to elevated blood cholesterol levels? Cholesterol is found only in products of animal origin—meat, eggs, and dairy products. It is also found normally in the human body and is synthesized by the liver. Dietary cholesterol—that eaten in food—is responsible for elevated cholesterol levels in some individuals, but it is not the cause in others. Thus, eliminating meat (and other sources of cholesterol) from the diet is not a foolproof way of lowering one's cholesterol level, and for some people it may not be at all effective.

Furthermore, lean beef or pork has a cholesterol content comparable to that of chicken (without skin), so substituting chicken for "red" meat does not nec-essarily reduce cholesterol intake. Many people now avoid shrimp and other shellfish because these foods are high in cholesterol; however, shellfish is very low in saturated fat, which is the more important influence on blood cholesterol level.

Is it appropriate for red meat to be included in a cholesterol-lowering diet? Definitely, according to the American Heart Association (AHA) and other groups interested in promoting healthy diets. The AHA's "Eating Plan for Healthy Americans" recommends choosing poultry, fish, and *lean* red meat, noting that consumers should be careful to trim the visible fat from all meat.

A recent study supports this recommendation. Kerin O'Dea and her colleagues at Deakin University and the Royal Melbourne Hospital in Melbourne, Australia, determined that adding beef fat to an otherwise low-fat diet raised blood cholesterol levels in a group of 10 healthy adults. It was the beef *fat,* however, not the actual lean beef itself, that was the culprit. The Australian researchers concluded that a low-fat diet—including lean cuts of meat, trimmed of visible fat and low in saturated fat—could be effective in lowering elevated blood cholesterol levels.

Safety concerns—drugs and hormones

Some of the changes in livestock breeding and feeding that enabled producers to offer leaner cuts of meat have raised other safety and health concerns. Chief among these changes is the use of antibiotic drugs and bovine somatotropin (bovine growth hor-

Steve Kagan/The New York Times

A McDonald's customer samples one of the first McLean Deluxe burgers (with only 10 grams of fat). While responding to evidence that high-fat diets are unhealthy, fast-food chains are still hoping to please the hamburger-loving public.

mone). Antibiotics were originally added to animal feed to reduce the risk of infectious diseases spreading among crowded herds of livestock. An unanticipated effect of this practice was the development of larger, more muscular stock. Some public health authorities claimed that giving low, "subtherapeutic" doses of antibiotics (primarily penicillin and the tetracyclines) to poultry and livestock promoted the development of antibiotic-resistant strains of bacteria and ultimately caused illness in humans. However, in reviewing hundreds of studies, the National Academy of Sciences found no data linking antibiotics in animal feed to any actual cases of human disease. Despite the fact that antibiotics have been given a clean bill of health, nearly all U.S. cattle feeders have discontinued the practice. Cooking meat thoroughly, for the proper time and at recommended temperatures, kills all disease-causing bacteria in meat products.

A more recent controversy has developed over the use of bovine somatotropin, which can now be produced in huge quantities by means of recombinant DNA technology. When the hormone is implanted in cattle, it enhances growth and produces leaner beef with less fat. It also stimulates milk production in dairy cattle. The implant itself is usually placed in the animal's ear, which is discarded after slaughter.

Bovine somatotropin occurs naturally in cattle and, together with other hormones, is present in minuscule amounts in meat and milk, whether the animals received implants or not. The question of the drug's safety was addressed recently by a consensus panel convened by the National Institutes of Health, which concluded that meat and milk from hormone-treated cattle are safe for human consumption.

A cancer risk?

Another dietary safety issue is the possible contribution of meat to an increased risk of colon cancer. In December 1990 Walter C. Willett and his colleagues at Harvard Medical School, Boston, published the results of a study of nearly 89,000 women aged 34 to 59. It was a prospective study—*i.e.,* the women, who were asked to answer a questionnaire about their diets, were healthy at the time and had no history of cancer. They were followed medically for about six years. The women who reported eating beef, pork, or lamb as a main dish every day developed colon cancer more than twice as often as those who said they ate these foods less than once a month. Consumption of chicken (without skin) and fish was associated with a lower cancer incidence. The researchers concluded that a diet high in animal fat increases the risk of colon cancer, and they recommended that consumers substitute fish and chicken for high-fat meats.

What do these findings mean for consumers who enjoy the taste of meat and wish to include it in their diets? First, it is in the very nature of such large prospective epidemiological studies that they typically describe associations between factors—in the above case, consumption of a diet high in animal fat and development of colon cancer—but do not imply a cause-

Is fast food "fat food"?					
menu item	serving size (g)	calories	protein (g)	total fat (g)	cholesterol (mg)
Arby's					
roast beef (regular)	147	353	22.2	14.8	39
grilled chicken deluxe	208	373	17.3	19.5	20
turkey deluxe	221	399	26.6	20.2	39
Burger King					
Whopper	270	614	27	36	90
hamburger	108	272	15	11	37
BK Broiler chicken sandwich	168	379	24	18	53
Chicken Tenders	90	236	16	13	46
Fish Tenders	99	267	12	16	28
Kentucky Fried Chicken					
chicken breast (center), Original Recipe	115	283	27.5	15.3	92.5
chicken breast (center), Lite 'n Crispy	86	220	—	11.9	57
Kentucky Nuggets (6 pieces)	96	276	16.8	17.4	71.4
McDonald's					
Big Mac	215	560	25.2	32.4	103
hamburger	102	260	12.3	9.5	37
McLean Deluxe	206	320	22	10	60
Filet-o-Fish	142	440	13.8	26.1	50
Chicken McNuggets (6 pieces)	112	270	20	15.4	56

and-effect relationship. That is, the finding that a diet high in animal fat is *associated with* an increased risk of colon cancer does not mean that such diets *cause* colon cancer. There are many other variables involved.

Furthermore, subjects of the study were "free-living" women (*i.e.,* they were not under the control or supervision of the researchers) who were eating a typical U.S. diet in which 38 to 46% of total calories were derived from fat. It is not known whether the findings can be generalized to apply to men or to people who consume less fat in their diets. Finally, the researchers focused on the role of various types of meats in the development of colon cancer; the study itself was not designed to tease apart the health effects of high-fat versus lean red meats. Given all of these considerations, the study does not warrant an approach that would eliminate all meat, but it does suggest continued caution about diets high in fat, especially animal fat, and a move toward a more moderate intake of meat and meat products.

The shrinking hamburger

For those who may still be unconvinced that U.S. consumers have begun to recognize fatty meats as undesirable, one need only point out the latest trend in the fast-food business, the reduced-fat hamburger. In the spring of 1991 McDonald's became the first national chain to introduce such a product, their McLean Deluxe, which has only half the fat (10 g) of the Quarter Pounder (20.7 g). It uses a manufacturing process that substitutes water for some of the fat. The addition of chicken sandwiches to fast-food menus also reflects the public's interest in reducing the intake of red meat. Of course, the cooking process is important, too—a grilled skinless chicken fillet is quite another thing from a deep-fried leg or breast eaten with the skin. Likewise, a fried fish sandwich, especially if served with mayonnaise or tartar sauce, is not as healthy a choice as it might at first seem.

The message on meat

In the past few years, revised dietary recommendations have been published by the U.S. surgeon general, the USDA, the National Institutes of Health, and such organizations as the American Heart Association and the American Cancer Society. While the wording of their dietary guidelines differs slightly, the overall message is virtually identical: eat more dietary fiber, and eat less fat. All of these groups recommend the inclusion of lean red meat, poultry, and fish in the daily diet as good sources of protein, iron, vitamins, and minerals. All recommend cutting down on the consumption of high-fat foods, particularly those high in saturated fat and cholesterol, and focusing instead on eating more foods high in dietary fiber, such as fruits, vegetables, beans and peas, and whole grains and cereals.

How can one eat the healthiest possible diet and still include red meat, poultry, and fish? The following are three basic guidelines.

Control portion size. It is important to keep in mind that an 85-g serving of meat is only about the size of a deck of playing cards. For children and most adults, only two servings, or about 170 g, of lean meat are needed daily. When combined with a variety of fruits, vegetables, whole grains and cereals, and low-fat dairy products, these two servings of low-fat meat provide all of the protein and other nutrients needed for a healthy, balanced diet.

Select only lean cuts and trim all visible fat. Lean beef cuts include top round, bottom round, tenderloin, round tip, and sirloin steak. Select the "choice" or "select" USDA grades rather than "prime," as these have less marbling within the meat and hence less fat. When buying pork, choose tenderloin, loin center, or leg cuts and trim all visible fat. All kinds of poultry and fish are good choices. Regardless of the meat selected, it is best to use low-fat cooking methods such as braising, broiling, stir-frying, and roasting. For those who enjoy barbecuing but are concerned about the possible health risks of carcinogens that form when meat is cooked at high temperatures, a good strategy is to choose only lean meats for grilling and cook them to medium or medium rare rather than well done.

One physician, Donald Small, and his colleagues at the Boston University School of Medicine recently published a "recipe" for extracting fat from ground beef to reduce its saturated fat and cholesterol content. It was the first time the prestigious *New England Journal of Medicine* had ever published a recipe! Although this method is on the right track, many consumers may find the extraction process—which involves cooking the meat in vegetable oil and then rinsing it in water—to be more trouble than it is worth, especially as lean cuts of meat are already widely available. In addition, Small's technique can be applied only to ground meat, not to steaks, chops, or roasts.

Consider the entire dietary pattern. Meat and meat products are by no means the sole sources of fat, saturated fat, and cholesterol in most people's diets. Whole-milk dairy products, including ice cream and yogurt, are major sources of fat, as are vegetable oils, solid margarine and butter, some baked goods, most desserts, and many frozen entrees. It is often necessary to read all the fine print on the food label to ferret out the high-fat food products and locate low-fat ones.

While dietary changes are warranted for many Americans, taking meat off the table entirely is not necessary. Lean red meat (and poultry and fish) can be included in a low-fat, low-cholesterol diet. Consumers who grew up on hearty portions of beef still can have their meat and eat it, too—in moderation.

Women and Coronary Disease
by Marc K. Effron, M.D.

The myth that women are immune from heart attacks is being rapidly dissolved as new reports emphasize the importance of heart disease in women in today's aging society. Coronary artery disease is characterized by the buildup of cholesterol-laden cells in the arteries supplying critical blood to the heart muscle. Severe obstruction of these coronary arteries can lead to angina pectoris (episodic chest pain), myocardial infarction (heart attack with damage to the heart muscle), or sudden cardiac death. The medical and economic consequences of coronary disease are enormous.

Cardiovascular disease, including heart disease, hypertension, and stroke, accounts for 500,000 female deaths in the United States each year. This compares with 220,000 female deaths from cancer. A woman's chance of dying from breast cancer is one in 11 and from any cancer one in 4. Her chance of dying from heart disease is one in two.

The high frequency of coronary disease in women is not matched by a similar high frequency of major treatments for the disease. The latest available figures (from the American Heart Association) indicated that in the United States In 1987, 244,000 women and 268,000 men died of heart attacks; nevertheless, in 1988 only 83,000 coronary bypass operations were performed on women, compared with 220,000 such operations on men. Coronary angioplasty, a procedure that utilizes a catheter to dilate the coronary arteries by the insertion and inflation of a balloon, was performed on only 60,000 women, as compared with 160,000 men.

It is disadvantageous that most information on prevention, diagnosis, and treatment of coronary artery disease is based on studies performed on men. Most studies have either excluded women or included them in such low numbers that meaningful conclusions about coronary artery disease in the female population could not be reached. This limited participation by women in research trials is due in part to age limits on enrollment (men are more likely to have manifestation of coronary artery disease at an earlier age), sponsorship of several major studies by the Veterans Administration (with its predominantly male population), and possibly residual bias among medical scientists that coronary disease is a male problem. Whatever the reason for the paucity of studies involving women, the male data may not be fully applicable to female patients.

Distinctive clinical manifestations

Coronary disease is the leading cause of death in men over the age of 40 but does not become the leading cause of death in women until age 60. It seems that women are largely protected from atherosclerosis until menopause.

Age at onset of clinical symptoms is not the only difference between the two sexes. The cardiac chest pain described by women may not be as severe or may not be sensed as true pain. Alternatively, women may simply have a different way of communicating the symptoms of coronary disease. The angina that women experience may not be reproducibly provoked by exercise, as it usually is in men. Indeed, silent myocardial infarction, occurrence of a heart attack without any chest pain, is more common in women than in men.

Women have a higher death rate during and following an acute myocardial infarction. Recent findings from a study done by researchers at the University of Massachusetts Medical School, Worcester, listed mortality within six weeks of a heart attack as 4% in men but 9% in women. Following a heart attack, women are also more likely to suffer a second attack within a year, experience angina pectoris, or develop congestive heart failure, a fluid buildup in the lungs from a weak heart.

Risk factors: male-female differences

Risk factors are those habits or medical conditions known to be associated with and possibly directly causative of coronary disease. However, not all risk factors apply equally to both sexes. There are a number of subtle risk factor differences that can have great importance in the prevention of coronary heart disease in women.

Smoking. Cigarette use is an exceptionally strong contributor to coronary disease in women; 70% of myocardial infarctions in women under age 50 are associated with smoking. Given this augmented danger, the increased popularity of cigarettes among women over the past four decades is an especially troubling development.

Cholesterol. High serum cholesterol is a well-known risk factor for coronary disease in both sexes. Most studies have focused on heart attack risk associated with low-density lipoprotein (LDL)-cholesterol—the so-called bad cholesterol—in men. It has been known for some time that high-density lipoprotein (HDL)-cholesterol ("good" cholesterol) is an independent predictor of coronary risk. The correlation is inverse; the lower the HDL-cholesterol, the higher the risk of coronary artery disease. HDL-cholesterol may, in fact, be a more important determinant of coronary risk in women than in men.

It is more common to find women with high total cholesterol and no coronary disease. Such women often have a particularly high HDL-cholesterol level. Dietary changes that emphasize lowering the total cholesterol or LDL-cholesterol may not be beneficial to women. Exercise and weight reduction may be more important measures than diet in preventing female coronary disease; both can favorably elevate the HDL-cholesterol level.

Obesity. Obesity is an independent risk factor for coronary disease in women. In a recent study of female nurses aged 30 to 55 years who were monitored for eight years, 40% of coronary events (heart attacks and angina pectoris) were attributed to obesity. In the women with severe obesity, defined as 30% or more over ideal body weight, 70% of coronary events were attributed to being overweight.

Diabetes. Diabetes mellitus can lead to coronary disease in both women and men. The coronary arteries of people with diabetes are often diffusely narrowed by atherosclerosis along their entire length. This makes catheter and surgical treatment of the coronary problem very difficult. Careful control of blood glucose levels may minimize the vascular damage in those patients.

Hypertension. Hypertension has long been recognized as an important risk factor for coronary artery disease. It appears, however, that high blood pressure is a risk factor that may not lead to heart disease in women to the extent that it does in men.

Stress. Stress, too, is regarded as a coronary risk factor, but it is difficult to quantify and evaluate. If emotional stress is an independent contributor to coronary disease, then there are special concerns for women. Presently, at least 55% of working-age women are in the paid work force in the United States. Whereas men typically relax after a workday, women are more likely to experience increased stress as they switch to the demanding domestic roles of mother and homemaker. Consequently, they may have elevated adrenaline and blood pressure levels that persist into late evening hours.

Special female risk factors

Systemic lupus erythematosus (SLE) is a generalized inflammatory condition of unknown cause with multiple sites of organ damage. SLE is more common in women than in men, with onset in adolescence or young adulthood. Artery inflammation may be part of the clinical presentation. True atherosclerosis may also appear and lead to angina and heart attack; possibly, inflammatory damage to the arterial walls leads to later atherosclerosis. Thus, women with longstanding SLE must be regarded as being prone to coronary problems.

Premature menopause is also regarded as a special risk factor for coronary disease in women. HDL-cholesterol levels decrease and LDL levels increase after menopause. This change in serum lipids corresponds to the increasing presence of coronary disease in women aged 50 to 60. These changes do not occur in women who are given oral estrogen replacement, however, as estrogen boosts the level of HDL-cholesterol. In one study, those women taking estrogen had only half the risk of dying of cardiovascular disease that women not receiving estrogen replacement therapy had.

Another potential risk factor for coronary disease in women is oral contraceptive use. Most birth control pills are a combination of estrogen and progesterone analogues. However, a wide variety of formulations are in general use, and the hormonal potencies of the various chemical analogues differ. The physiological effects of such preparations outside the reproductive system thus may be quite diverse.

Oral contraceptive use by women aged 40 to 50 years may pose an increased risk of myocardial infarction and of other thromboembolic events such as deep vein thrombosis and pulmonary emboli (blood clots that have migrated to the lungs). Cigarette use may synergistically augment these risks in older birth control pill users. These effects may result from augmented blood coagulability rather than from any direct provocation of atherosclerosis.

Oral contraceptives can, however, alter the pattern of lipids that are a recognized determinant of coronary atherosclerosis. Combination pills with a low dose of the progesterone analogue norethindrone increase the HDL-cholesterol level by 10%. The combination pills with high-dose norethindrone have no effect on HDL levels. Alternatively, combination pills with low- or high-dose levonorgestrel, another progesterone analogue, are associated with decreased HDL levels. Some, but not all, pills containing low doses of progesterone may thus reduce coronary risk and may be preferred for long-term use. Other formulations may actually increase the coronary risk.

Combination oral contraceptives also alter the metabolism of glucose. Blood glucose may rise to abnormally high levels after eating, and the body may become somewhat resistant to the action of insulin secreted by the pancreas. These abnormalities of glucose metabolism vary with the type and dose of progesterone component of the contraceptive pills but can mimic the changes seen with diabetes mellitus. Such subtle diabetic changes may promote the development of coronary artery disease. If lipid and glucose metabolism are altered enough to potentiate coronary atherosclerosis in women using oral contraceptives, then the health implications are very great since millions of young women worldwide are users of birth control pills. Short-term effects and safety are quite good. Long-term cumulative effects on the heart are less clear.

Diagnostic testing

The predictive value of a diagnostic test depends in part on the prevalence of disease in the population being tested. Lower incidence of disease in a population leads to a higher rate of false-positive results. This phenomenon causes particular problems in the early detection of coronary disease in women. For example, if one assumes that a falsely abnormal stress electrocardiogram will occur in 10% of normal women tested and that the prevalence of coronary disease in the tested population at age 50 is only 5%, then for every 100 such women tested, there would be about 15 positive or abnormal test results. Ten of these 15 abnormals would be false positives (actually normal patients), and only 5 of the 15 positives would be true positives.

Clearly, the diagnosis of coronary disease in middle-aged women, a population with a low disease prevalence, is affected by the potential for inaccurate test results. Although stress electrocardiography by treadmill testing has significant limitations in women, when a thallium scan (a test that uses an injected radioactive isotope to assess myocardial blood flow) is added to the stress test, the accuracy improves slightly. Yet the false-positive and false-negative rates still are often inadequate for definitive decision making in many women with suspected coronary problems.

The gold standard for diagnosis of coronary artery disease is the coronary arteriogram. This invasive test is often performed on an outpatient basis with at least six hours' observation at the hospital following the procedure. The risk associated with coronary arteriography is low but not insignificant. Serious complications may occur in about one of every 1,000 individuals tested. Although a coronary arteriogram is expensive, its cost is usually justified by its diagnostic accuracy. If women were more readily referred for coronary arteriography, the cumulative expenses of the less accurate stress tests and noninvasive scans could be avoided. Until a more precise noninvasive method becomes available, more coronary arteriography should be performed earlier in women patients when there is a reasonable suspicion of coronary disease.

Treatment response

Differences between women and men in therapeutic outcomes may not all be due to sex per se but can sometimes be attributed to differences in body size, degree of illness, and age at time of treatment.

Thrombolytic therapy. Thrombolytic treatment describes a procedure frequently performed within hours after an acute myocardial infarction, when a blood clot may suddenly cause total occlusion of a previously narrowed coronary artery. Sustained chest pain ensues, and damage to heart muscle progresses quickly. A potent clot-dissolving enzyme or enzyme activator (*e.g.,* streptokinase, tissue plasminogen activator) is administered intravenously, dissolving the clot that has acutely occluded the coronary artery and reestablishing blood flow to the myocardial tissue. The heart attack is interrupted, and damage is minimized.

As an acute intervention, thrombolytic therapy has equal benefits in women and men. Reduction of the myocardial infarction size is similar, but there is a higher incidence of bleeding complications in women. The more frequent hemorrhagic problems in women, however, may not be due to sex alone. In research studies of thrombolytic agents—trials whose participants were male—fixed-dose regimens were used. The clinical doses used relative to body mass are therefore more potent for women than for men. Perhaps an adjustment of drug dose based on body size could retain the benefits and reduce the hemorrhagic risk of thrombolysis.

Angioplasty. The immediate success rate of percutaneous transluminal coronary angioplasty for opening narrowed coronary arteries is lower in women. Bal-

Women who have had heart attacks can derive important benefits from structured cardiac rehabilitation programs. Unfortunately, such programs often are oriented more toward men and thus discourage women from participating.

Chris Walker/Chicago Tribune

loon angioplasty in women may be less successful because of the more advanced age of the patients, worse angina preceding the procedures, and higher rates of hypertension and diabetes, processes that may alter the properties of the artery wall. Moreover, the vessel size may be slightly smaller in women. However, when angioplasty is immediately successful in women, the long-term patency (open state) rate is similar to that in male patients; 70–75% of successfully dilated arteries will remain open several months after balloon angioplasty.

Drug therapy. Beta-blocking drugs, such as propranolol and metoprolol, have been shown to reduce the occurrence of fatal and nonfatal myocardial reinfarctions when given to acute myocardial infarction patients. Women and men appear to benefit equally from this simple and cost-effective therapy.

Aspirin is another drug therapy that is given following acute myocardial infarction. Aspirin decreases the adhesiveness of the blood platelet cells to vessel walls and can prevent thrombus formation. When aspirin is given to acute myocardial infarction patients, it lowers the rate of stroke (occlusion of blood vessels to the brain) and recurrent heart attack. Despite the effectiveness of aspirin after acute myocardial infarction, not all studies of aspirin therapy for atherosclerotic disease have shown equal benefits for both sexes. Some aspirin studies show effectiveness only in men and not in women. Other studies, such as one large trial using aspirin to prevent an initial myocardial infarction, did not include women at all.

Many other drug therapies for coronary disease have not been directly evaluated for applicability in women. Therapy for women remains largely based on extrapolations of research results in men.

Bypass operations. Coronary artery bypass surgery has proliferated as a major treatment for coronary disease in men and women. Segments of the saphenous vein of the leg are transposed as conduits from the aorta to the coronary artery. The internal mammary artery, which normally is situated along the inside of the chest wall adjacent to the sternum, can also be surgically transposed to bypass a diseased coronary artery. Coronary bypass surgery is usually reserved for patients with severe multivessel coronary disease, those with disease of the left main coronary artery, and patients with less extensive disease for whom other treatments have not been effective in controlling symptoms of angina.

Surgical mortality for coronary bypass is higher in women. One large hospital's experience shows a mortality of 4.6% for women and 2.6% for men. The women, who were an average of six years older than their male counterparts, tended to have worse symptoms of heart disease prior to their operation. Angina at rest was more common in women, as was a recent history of worsening angina. Congestive heart failure was also more common in women preoperatively, complicating their postoperative recovery.

Once coronary bypass surgery has been completed, patency of the bypass grafts is an important determinant of surgical success. Graft patency is lower in women. One study suggests that early graft closure in women is due to the smaller size of their coronary arteries, accounting for their higher surgical mortality. Another study, however, found no such correlation.

Cardiac rehabilitation. Cardiac rehabilitation, a physical exercise program that enables myocardial infarction patients to achieve full functional recovery, with the supplementary goal of reducing the risk of future coronary events, is effective and beneficial for both women and men. Studies indicate that such programs can achieve similar increases in physical work capacity in both sexes. Unfortunately, however, women do not derive the benefits from cardiac rehabilitation to the same extent that males do. Women show less adherence to the exercise prescription; their attendance wanes more often; and rehabilitation goals are not met as often as with men. Social factors are probably very important in this setting; the programs may be more oriented to men and thus more likely to retain a male following.

Future directions

Coronary artery disease differs in many ways between the sexes. Risk factors must be weighed differently. Clinical manifestations and responses to therapy are not the same. The future management of women heart patients should include special attention to what may be atypical warning symptoms prior to myocardial infarction.

Physicians' alertness to the coronary risk in women should be accompanied by more aggressive diagnostic and treatment approaches. Moreover, most differences in therapeutic results between the sexes are not so great as to justify withholding these major therapies from women. Clinical practice must be based on individual assessment and not on stereotypes.

Through medical research, specific questions on coronary disease in women can be asked and eventually answered. The U.S. National Institutes of Health has recently opened the Post-Menopausal Estrogen Progestin Intervention trial. This is the first large prospective study of coronary risk factors in women; specifically the effects of hormone replacement therapy on coronary risk factors will be assessed.

There is a great need for more clinical research on coronary artery disease in women. This will require cooperation among multiple research institutions and inclusion of women at an older age than is standard in male trials. In research, as in clinical practice, the male stereotype must be replaced by a new focus on coronary disease without sexual bias.

Hypochondria
by Brendan A. Maher, Ph.D.

In 1771 the first edition of the *Encyclopædia Britannica* described "the hypochondriac passion": a disorder characterized "by such a train of symptoms that it is a difficult task to enumerate them all; for there is no part of the body, that is not soon or late a sufferer by its tyranny." After describing the varieties of symptoms encountered in this disorder, the writer concluded with the observation that fear of disease and death rendered the patients "fickle, impatient, and prone to run from one doctor to another."

Hypochondriasis had been known to the medical profession for more than 2,000 years before the encyclopaedist wrote the foregoing account. The Greek physician Galen, writing in the 2nd century AD, was the first to use the term *hypochondriasis,* although the disorder itself had been described by the Greeks more than five centuries earlier. Galen believed that it was the overproduction of bile by the spleen, an organ lying directly below the cartilages of the lower ribs, that produced hypochondriasis. The Greek *hypo,* meaning "below or under," and *chondros,* meaning "cartilage," thus were combined to form the single term that is still in use today. The Greeks' explanation of the condition has vanished, but the term survives as an accepted label for a disorder that has been common throughout history and, indeed, continues to be a prevalent psychiatric problem today.

What is hypochondriasis?

Hypochondriasis (or hypochondria, the colloquial term) is a psychological disorder. The *Diagnostic and Statistical Manual of Mental Disorders,* third edition, revised (*DSM-III-R*), defines hypochondriasis as a disorder that has certain essential features. The criteria for its diagnosis include:

- preoccupation with the fear of having, or the belief that one has, a serious disease, based on the person's interpretation of physical signs or sensations as evidence of physical illness
- appropriate physical evaluation does not support the diagnosis of any physical disorder that can account for the physical signs or sensations or the person's unwarranted interpretation of them, and the symptoms are not those of panic attacks
- the fear of having, or the belief that one has, a disease persists despite medical reassurance
- the duration of the disturbance is at least six months

Hypochondriacal concerns include a wide spectrum of bodily functions. Sometimes the individual is preoccupied with the possibility of disease in a specific single organ, such as the heart or lungs. Alternatively, he or she may worry about one or more of an array of minor symptoms: sweating; rapid or slow heartbeat; coughing; choking sensations; digestive disorders; changes in hearing, vision, smell, or touch; and so forth. The major body areas in which complaints are most frequently reported are the head and neck and the chest and abdomen.

Hypochondriacs are also quite susceptible to suggestions of illness. They may, for example, see an advertisement on television for a pain remedy and develop a severe headache or a multitude of aches and pains. They may also be unusually attentive to medical information in the media, which they interpret as having direct implications for themselves.

People suffering from hypochondriasis inevitably experience some degree of disability in the conduct of their everyday lives. This may range from relatively limited interference with their social life or their work to extreme instances in which a patient becomes a social recluse or a chronic invalid and may even be permanently bedridden. Generally, however, the disorder follows a fluctuating course over a long period, the problem becoming worse at times and seeming to get better at others. Ultimately, many patients recover completely.

Clinicians distinguish two types of hypochondriasis.

Hypochondria

From 40 to 60% show no evidence of other concurrent disease; they are classified as having *primary* hypochondriasis. The remaining patients have other, associated organic or psychiatric illness—*secondary* hypochondriasis. The general pattern of symptoms is quite similar in both the primary and secondary types, but there is some evidence that primary cases include more who focus on problems associated with skin care, physical appearance, and general muscular functioning.

Who is affected?

In 1941 the writer E.B. White described hypochondria as "the imaginary complaints of indestructible old ladies." Hypochondriasis, however, is equally prevalent in men and women. Moreover, it generally first appears between the ages of 20 and 30. Among males it is most prevalent in the 30–40-year-old group; among females, between ages 40 and 50. A majority of hypochondriacs come from middle and upper socioeconomic groups. This may reflect the fact that persons in lower socioeconomic groups have a higher frequency of *actual* minor and major bodily ailments and therefore proportionally fewer purely hypochondriacal complaints.

It is interesting that transient hypochondriasis often arises in persons engaged in the study of medicine or human biology. It has been estimated, for example, that more than 70% of medical students suffer from short-lived hypochondriacal concerns at some time during their medical training—often developing the symptoms of the disease or disorder that they are currently learning about.

Are symptoms "real" or imagined?

Conscious experience can be fully appreciated only by the person who has the experience. An outside observer cannot directly check the validity of a statement that somebody else is experiencing a specific symptom or a specified degree of pain or discomfort. Controlled studies can be conducted of the assessments that people make of the unpleasantness caused by the application of uncomfortable stimuli. However, these studies do not really explain the nature of hypochondriacal complaints, and they do not provide a straightforward answer to the question: Are symptoms real or imagined?

Some patients may develop symptoms of hypochondria on the basis of a process termed *somatic amplification*—*i.e.,* the process whereby the patient experiences bodily discomforts as more distressing than other people do. Their experience of pain may be physically based—in other words, due to a greater actual intensity in the activity of the nervous system, leading to a genuinely greater sensation of pain or discomfort. Alternatively, the greater degree of pain that the hypochondriac experiences may be due to greater attention that he or she pays to bodily discomfort. Normally, a diminution of discomfort follows when an individual's attention is drawn away from a painful sensation. This does not occur with the hypochondriac, who, in focusing attention on bodily sensations more intensely and continuously than others, is less susceptible to the diminution that distraction normally brings.

There is some experimental and clinical evidence that certain individuals have a lower than normal tolerance for pain and that this occurs along with certain personality variables. In addition, it has been demonstrated experimentally that anything that directs a person's attention to his or her body will increase the perceived intensity of painful symptoms. To a certain extent then, hypochondriacs' symptoms may be "in the mind," and to a certain extent they may be "in the body." This, of course, presents a dilemma for the clinician who is trying to interpret the "symptoms."

Medical students are especially prone to developing hypochondriasis at some time during the course of their intensive study of disease processes and symptomatology.

Differentiation from other disorders

The diagnosis of hypochondriasis should be made only after other disorders with which it might be confused have been ruled out. Thorough medical examination is necessary to exclude the presence of an identifiable physical pathology. Even in the absence of obvious pathology, however, there are other distinct disorders in which the patient complains of bodily distress but for which the physician can find no physical basis. Therefore, the following alternative diagnoses should be considered.

Somatization disorder. This is a diagnosis that is applied to persons with a history of many bodily complaints that have no demonstrable physical basis. The condition differs from hypochondriasis in that the age of onset of somatization disorder is earlier (usually in the teens or, rarely, as late as the twenties). Furthermore, the diagnosis is seldom applied to males, whereas hypochondria affects males and females alike. The symptoms of somatization disorder include sensory and muscular impairment such as apparent blindness, deafness, and paralysis, and the personal life of the individual tends to be disordered and chaotic in many other ways.

Somatoform pain disorder. This disorder is one in which the patient is preoccupied with pain in the absence of any physical problems that are sufficient to explain the pain. It can be seriously incapacitating, and medication may be required for controlling the pain.

Delusional disorder. Persons with hypochondria acknowledge the possibility that their beliefs about their own symptoms might be mistaken. On the other hand, if the belief that one has one or many physical ills is held with an unshakable conviction, and the individual absolutely rejects the possibility that there may be no disease, the diagnosis of hypochondriasis may be abandoned in favor of the diagnosis of delusional disorder.

Mutual exasperation

When medical examination by a physician fails to find any evidence of actual disease, the patient is quite likely to go to another physician and begin the whole process over. This pattern of "doctor-shopping" (referred to 200 years ago in *Encyclopædia Britannica*) is generally accompanied by the increasing frustration and annoyance of the patients, who then conclude that the doctors are not taking their complaints seriously and that they are not receiving adequate medical attention.

It is true that hypochondriacs often encounter physicians in general medical practice who regard them as insufficiently medically interesting to warrant serious investigation. Nevertheless, such patients generally reject the suggestion that their complaints have a psychological basis and refuse to consult mental health professionals for help. Not surprisingly, physicians, too, become annoyed. They see these patients as wasting their time by their unreasonable refusal to accept the fact that they are not physically ill. In fact, certain derogatory terms (*e.g., crock, familiar face*) are sometimes used by exasperated doctors to describe hypochondriacal patients.

Origins of hypochondria

The origins of hypochondria as a psychological disorder vary widely with individual patients. The following are some of the potential origins that clinicians today consider important.

Experience with medical illness in childhood. Some hypochondriacal patients have had the early experience of living with a family member who suffered from a serious medical illness. These patients develop a fear that they, too, will suffer from the same disease; they are sometimes referred to as "disease phobic" because their hypochondria takes the form of a fear that they have a specific disease. There are, for example, many reported cases of hypochondria in which individuals have an intense fear that they have or will develop cancer; as children they became quite familiar with the pain and symptoms of a family member who suffered from cancer.

Another early childhood experience that may lead to hypochondriasis in later life is having a parent who is overprotective in matters of health. The parent exhibits obsessive concern with every minor change in the child's bodily functioning; the child thus learns to focus on any abnormality, ache, or pain, no matter how trivial. Although parents may pass on to their children their own tendency to be ultrasensitive to signs of disease, there is no known genetic basis for the occurrence of hypochondria.

Personality factors. Patients with hypochondria are often described as obsessive and compulsive as well as prone to anxiety and depression. It is difficult to be sure whether these characteristics are independent factors that predispose the individual to hypochondria or are integral aspects of the hypochondria disorder itself. Many common hypochondriacal symptoms are the same as the bodily accompaniments of anxiety—notably headaches, sleeplessness, muscular fatigue, and digestive upset—which often send the patient to the physician.

Obsessive-compulsive individuals exhibit extreme caution in any matter where a danger to health might exist. Their concerns may lead them to repeated handwashing or the refusal to shake hands with others for fear of contamination. Hence, it is not surprising that such individuals may be prone to exaggerated fears about the medical significance of minor bodily disturbances and may in fact become hypochondriacs.

Sensory and perceptual sensitivity. Some clinicians have speculated that hypochondriacal patients misinterpret their normal bodily sensations; they misattribute trivial sensations arising from normal bodily functions, including emotional arousal, to a serious disease process, whereas normal persons attribute such somatic symptoms not to disease but to such things as overexertion, situational stress, diet, normal processes of aging, and so on. Once the individual has made such a misattribution, it persists because normal somatic experiences continue to be interpreted within this erroneous perceptual framework.

Hypochondria as a coping strategy. It has been suggested that hypochondria enables some people to avoid stressful situations. The status of "patient" is one that brings with it certain benefits, among them, the fact that the individual is generally excused from major responsibilities, receives sympathy and attention (at least at first), and may be protected from criticism and rejection. For such persons, the refusal of the physician to offer a medical diagnosis is particularly frustrating, as it constitutes an obstacle to the successful assumption of the role of sick person.

Cultural differences. Persons from different cultures may have different perceptions of the significance of physical symptoms and quite different views about the appropriate way to respond to them. Investigators have compared the responses of people from different ethnic groups, including those who have recently immigrated to the U.S. In one such study, Jewish immigrants worried the most about the possible medical significance of painful symptoms. Those of Italian cultural background were more disturbed by the experience of the pain itself rather than its possible significance for an underlying medical problem. Those from a New England "Yankee" background were more likely to be stoic in their reactions, not seeking medical attention for painful symptoms until the discomfort became intense. The "Yankee" statesman, scientist, and philosopher Benjamin Franklin wrote in his *Poor Richard's Almanac* (1760), "Nothing is more fatal to *Health,* than an *over Care* of it." Another Yankee, Thomas Jefferson, wrote in a letter to his eldest daughter, Martha (1787), "Idleness begets ennui, ennui the hypochondriac, and that a diseased body. No laborious person was ever yet hysterical."

The cultural differences in reactions to symptoms just described have been ascribed to patterns of child-rearing—and particularly to the attitudes of the mother. Typically, Jewish mothers are anxiously protective of their children's health; Italian mothers tend to be protective but in a more sympathetic, less anxious, manner; while the more stoical "Yankee" mothers emphasize the need to take pain "like a man" and not complain about it.

Diagnostic caveats

The diagnosis of hypochondriasis requires the observance of certain cautions. Above all, it is important that the physician consider the possibility of true organic disease before concluding that a patient is suffering from hypochondriasis alone.

Diagnostic error. As noted previously, the diagnosis of hypochondriasis rests primarily on a failure to find any positive evidence of physical disease to account for the patient's specific complaints. While modern methods available to test for the presence of physical disease are very sophisticated, they are not perfect. Even with the use of procedures that employ the highest levels of technology, some diseases may go undetected. For example, the early stages of certain neurological disorders (*e.g.,* multiple sclerosis), endocrine disorders (*e.g.,* thyroid disease), and autoimmune disorders (*e.g.,* systemic lupus erythematosus) may not be recognized by the physician. When this happens, the physician may have little choice but to conclude that the patient is indeed hypochondriacal. One study of patients who had been given such a diagnosis found that 15% had genuine physical disease that had not been detected.

Concurrent disease. Even if organic disease such as multiple sclerosis or thyroid disease is diagnosed, there may also be coexisting hypochondriasis. Hypochondria is also quite common in conjunction with certain psychiatric disorders, particularly depression. Clinical investigators have reported that more than 80% of depressed patients have accompanying symptoms of hypochondriasis. Other psychiatric disorders that may be present in conjunction with hypochondriasis in a significant number of patients are schizophrenia, generalized anxiety disorder, and panic disorder. Hence, while the diagnosis of hypochondria-

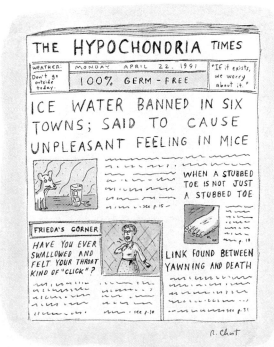

Drawing by Roz Chast

sis may not indicate diagnostic error, it is also necessary to consider the possibility that it is accompanied by another psychiatric disorder.

Treatment principles

In 1927 the U.S. physician William J. Mayo said to colleagues at the Mayo Clinic in Rochester, Minn., "If we are unable to find physical disease we say that a patient needs no medical attention, although he may be urgently in need of reassurance and mental comfort." Indeed, it is unfortunate that many patients are rejected by the doctors to whom they have turned for help.

For the reasons already stated, hypochondriacal patients rarely seek psychiatric help and typically refuse it when it is offered. Hence, there are no adequate controlled studies of the effects of treatment on the disorder and no solid basis for prescribing which kinds of psychological treatment might be useful. Nonetheless, several general principles have been suggested for the treatment of these patients.

A first principle is that patients should be convinced that their complaints are being taken seriously. The patient first receives a thorough medical examination, and a careful medical history is taken. When no significant pathology has been found, the clinician should reassure the patient that his or her health is good and suggest that in the long run the current distressing symptoms will clear up.

A second step involves providing the patient with accurate information about the insignificance of many common bodily symptoms. Additionally, the clinician should explain the role of selective attention to bodily processes and how this leads to an exaggerated concern about the possibility of disease. Because this information is likely to be misconstrued by the patient, it is important that it be repeated as often as necessary.

Physical exercise is known to have the effect of increasing psychological well-being. Hypochondriacal patients are reported to engage in exercise only rarely, a fact that has suggested the possible therapeutic value of exercise in the treatment of this disorder. Some clinical investigators have reported a reduction in hypochondriacal symptoms in patients who have undertaken a regular exercise program. Patients may also benefit from practicing a technique of relaxation and from thinking of some other topic whenever preoccupation with bodily processes occurs.

Finally, drug treatment of hypochondriasis has produced disappointing effects, although it is sometimes useful in the treatment of coexisting anxiety or depression. In any case, when pharmacological treatment is deemed appropriate, the specific medication used is determined by the nature of the accompanying psychological disorder.

Complications

Because patients may go from doctor to doctor in search of treatment, problems can arise from the effects of repeated medical procedures, such as exploratory surgery, that may be used in order to determine a problem. Untoward physical consequences associated with these procedures often arise and serve only to exacerbate the patient's hypochondriacal concerns.

One of the outcomes of the typical unsatisfactory relationships that develop between hypochondriacs and doctors is that the patient, having failed to persuade a physician to prescribe a specific drug or treatment, treats himself or herself with a wide range of nonprescription medications. Continued self-medication can result in quite a number of physical complications.

The British writer Laurence Sterne (1713–68) said that hypochondriacs ("people who are always taking care of their health") are "like misers . . . hoarding a treasure which they have never spirit enough to enjoy." Another "complication" of hypochondriasis is that these individuals become so self-centered, seclusive, and even monomaniacal in the attention they give to their perceived bodily ills that others soon become exasperated and ultimately rejecting. Initially hypochondriacs may receive sympathetic attention from family and friends, if not from doctors. But as their complaints mount and their "symptoms" enlarge, not surprisingly they become social outcasts.

A "real" disorder

Considerable time and resources for medical care are spent on the hypochondriacal patient, with a consequent burden on the cost of health insurance and on the patient's own finances. At a time when the costs of health care are out of bounds and need to be contained, it is imperative that available resources be directed toward those who have serious medical problems and that other kinds of support be provided for those who do not have major illnesses. This will require a better understanding than medical professionals presently have of the processes that cause hypochondria. Such understanding is needed not only because hypochondria is a costly problem but also because it is a serious one that causes considerable discomfort and distress to many patients.

Wisdom Teeth
by L. Anne Hirschel, D.D.S.

In spite of the promise their name implies, wisdom teeth are rarely regarded with enthusiasm. In fact, not only do they fail to impart special sagacity, these four teeth—which dentists usually refer to as third molars—often cause a mouthful of health problems. In the United States such problems are so common and the teeth are removed so frequently that, according to federal government statistics, the estimated annual cost of third molar surgical extractions amounts to $425 million. Figures compiled by Blue Shield of Pennsylvania show that expenditure for third molar extractions is greater than the expenditure for any other single surgical procedure. Whether all of these wisdom teeth really need to be removed is still somewhat controversial.

The overcrowded mouth

The wisdom teeth, generally one on each side in the back of the upper and lower jaws, develop behind the permanent second molars. The time of eruption (emergence through the gums) is variable, but it usually occurs long after all other permanent teeth are in place, usually between the ages of 15 and 18. By this time, however, there may be insufficient space left for these teeth to erupt straight enough to function usefully—or, in some cases, to erupt at all—and that is the crux of the problem.

Several theories have been put forward to explain why the modern human jaw is often too small to accommodate all 32 permanent teeth. Anthropologists point out that during the course of evolution the human braincase, or cranium, enlarged at the expense of the jaw. Further, humans no longer have a need for a powerful masticatory apparatus to chew rough food. Consequently, jaws are getting smaller, and the number of teeth is decreasing. From this evolutionary viewpoint, third molars can be considered vestigial organs for which there is no longer any use. This would explain why many people are congenitally missing one or even all of these teeth—evolution tends to eliminate organs that are no longer functional. In addition, there may be a disproportion between jaw size transmitted genetically from one side of an individual's family and tooth size transmitted from ancestors on the other side. Individual factors such as premature loss of primary (baby) teeth may also contribute to eventual crowding of permanent teeth.

Ironically, while dental health generally is improving in developed countries as tooth decay and even gum disease are brought under better control, the problem of impacted wisdom teeth is growing. More people reaching adulthood now have a full complement of permanent teeth. With almost no teeth being lost as a result of dental disease, there are more teeth sharing the available space in the jaw. Consequently, the wisdom teeth, which are the last to develop, are caught short of space.

To extract or not?

When emerging wisdom teeth become trapped in the bone of the jaw or under the gum or get caught behind the backs of the adjoining second molars, they are said to be impacted. Impaction may be partial—that is, part of the crown of the tooth protrudes through the gum—or the tooth may be totally buried, or completely impacted. An impacted third molar may tip forward, lean sideways, lie horizontally, or, more rarely, face backward or even develop upside down. (*See* diagrams, page 434.) Occasionally the tooth migrates into a bizarre position in the bone. X-rays, possibly including a panoramic film (view of the entire mouth), are essential so that the exact anatomy and position of the tooth and its relationship to other oral structures and neighboring teeth can be revealed.

In spite of their reputation as troublemakers, some third molars develop normally and function efficiently throughout life. Sometimes there may be impaction on one side of the mouth, yet the wisdom teeth on the other side are aligned acceptably. Furthermore, according to some recent studies, even when they are impacted, third molars do not necessarily give rise to as many complications as was once believed. At times they may even be an advantage. Should

432

a second molar be lost, the third molar may move (naturally) or be moved forward to take its place. Wisdom teeth have also been transplanted within an individual's mouth (autogenic transplantation), usually to replace a missing first molar. Alternatively, wisdom teeth can provide support for fixed bridges or removable dentures, and when other teeth have been lost, they may help maintain the correct vertical dimension of the lower part of the face.

Nevertheless, the impaction of wisdom teeth can cause diverse oral health problems, including infections, periodontal (gum) disease, tooth decay, resorption (breakdown of hard tooth tissues), cysts, and, in rare cases, tumors. Investigations continue into how often these problems arise and how they can be predicted accurately. Because of the debate over the appropriate management of wisdom teeth, the National Institute of Dental Research (NIDR) sponsored a consensus conference on this topic in 1979. Several studies have since been conducted to gain further insights, but in many cases the question of whether to extract an asymptomatic third molar or leave it alone remains controversial. As a general rule, if symptoms occur, wisdom teeth should be extracted.

Impaction: common problems

The most common complaint involving impacted wisdom teeth in the lower jaw is pericoronitis, an often painful infection of the soft tissues surrounding the crown of a partially erupted tooth. The condition may be aggravated when an upper third molar impinges on the swollen, inflamed tissues overlying the opposing, partially erupted lower tooth. Although sometimes mild, pericoronitis may develop into a serious local or systemic infection and can spread into the face and neck. It can also cause swallowing difficulties and trismus (muscle spasm that prevents opening of the mouth). The infection tends to recur, especially during times of lowered resistance or stress. Although mild pericoronitis can occasionally be treated successfully by surgical exposure of the partially erupted tooth, extraction is usually recommended if the condition is recurrent.

Related periodontal problems are also common. After repeated episodes of pericoronitis, the destruction of gum tissue behind the adjacent second molar may result in deep pocketing of the gum in this area, creating a space where food particles and bacteria may collect. Such defects are almost impossible to correct even after the wisdom tooth is removed. Thus, the best course is to extract the tooth without undue delay.

Partially erupted or malposed (improperly positioned) third molars, because of their location far back in the oral cavity, may be difficult to keep clean, especially if the teeth are nonfunctioning. (Nonfunctioning teeth are deprived of the cleansing action that accompanies normal chewing.) Such teeth act as food traps,

and the constantly accumulating debris and plaque put the individual at even greater risk of developing or aggravating gum disease.

Because they are difficult to brush and floss adequately, wisdom teeth are also susceptible to decay. When impacted or malposed, such teeth are often difficult or impossible for the dentist to fill successfully and must be removed. If debris becomes trapped between the wisdom tooth and the neighboring second molar, the posterior (back) surface of the latter may also decay. When an impacted wisdom tooth makes contact with a second molar and presses on it, the second molar may develop a hollow area from resorption at the point of contact.

The development of cysts, known as dentigerous cysts, in the tissues surrounding the crown of the impacted tooth is a further health hazard associated with wisdom teeth. If a cyst is diagnosed, it should be removed and the tooth extracted. Because it is generally impossible to differentiate a cyst from a benign or malignant tumor on an X-ray, all such lesions must be removed and the excised tissue examined under a microscope. Some dentigerous cysts grow for long periods of time without causing any discomfort and may be discovered only when dental X-rays are taken as part of a routine examination. They may thus grow and enlarge undetected, damaging adjacent teeth, bone, or nerve tissues. In some cases the mouth or face may be affected by sudden pain and swelling.

Completely impacted wisdom teeth sometimes cause pain even in the absence of any of the above described pathological conditions. Headaches, including migraines, and pain in the ear, eye, neck, opposing jaw, or temporomandibular joint (joint between the lower jaw and head) have all occasionally been attributed to impacted wisdom teeth. They have also been implicated in causing dimmed vision, blindness, ear inflammation, and ringing and buzzing in the ears, although no clear cause-and-effect relationship is understood. Occasionally, however, wisdom teeth may be extracted in an attempt to correct such problems, although usually only as a last resort after all other possible causes have been ruled out. Another problem sometimes attributed to the presence of an impacted third molar is fracture of the jaw as a result of trauma to the side of the face. Some authorities therefore suggest that athletes in contact sports have their wisdom teeth removed as a precautionary measure.

Indications for extraction

All wisdom teeth should be evaluated when the individual is between 16 and 18 years old. If there is any pain—or other symptoms—at that time, extraction is generally recommended. The same usually applies to a normally erupted third molar that opposes one scheduled for extraction. The former should not be left in place; it will be nonfunctional and is likely to

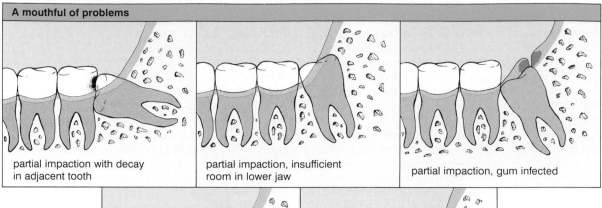

A mouthful of problems

partial impaction with decay in adjacent tooth

partial impaction, insufficient room in lower jaw

partial impaction, gum infected

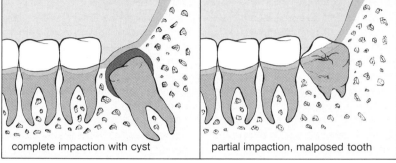

complete impaction with cyst

partial impaction, malposed tooth

elongate, only to become a potential food trap and focus of periodontal infection after its opposing partner is extracted. Deciding when to leave an asymptomatic malposed wisdom tooth alone, in the hope that it will cause no future problems, is more difficult. Nevertheless, this determination should be made promptly, because the timing of these extractions is important.

Operative and postoperative complications are less frequent or are minimized in healthy patients in their teens or early twenties. This is due in part to the fact that at this age the roots of one's third molars are usually only one-half to two-thirds formed and the jawbone is not yet very dense. Later in life the bone becomes more dense, and molar roots may fuse with it. In the elderly the bone tends to become brittle and may fracture during the extraction procedure.

Further, surgical risk increases as patients get older. While only 3.9% of patients under 24 have systemic health problems, this figure rises to 32.7% for patients over 35. For medically compromised patients as well as those over 35, the potential harm from surgery may outweigh the potential benefits gained by extraction. The most prudent course may be to leave the wisdom teeth of these higher risk individuals in place but keep them under close observation with regular X-rays, especially as some studies show that problems associated with impacted wisdom teeth do not commonly develop later in life.

Cancer patients scheduled for radiation therapy of the jaw or surrounding area are a special case. Because bone heals poorly after irradiation, it is important that they have all potential dental and periodontal problems, including impacted wisdom teeth, attended to before such therapy is started.

Impacted wisdom teeth are sometimes discovered on an X-ray in edentulous (toothless) persons. Generally, if such teeth lie beneath pressure-bearing areas of a proposed denture, they are best removed. Leaving them in place could result in pain and ulceration of the gum. Should the tooth subsequently become partially exposed, a pathway for infection would be created between the tooth and the mouth. Extraction of such impacted teeth is therefore indicated unless their removal would result in enough bone loss to compromise the stability of the denture.

According to the conclusions reached at the above-mentioned NIDR conference, there is no rationale for extracting third molars in the anticipation that this will relieve crowding of the anterior (front) teeth. Nor is there any justification for removing third molar tooth buds in children as young as seven to nine in order to prevent impaction problems later, as was advocated by some authorities in the past. Predicting which third molars are likely to become impacted is too difficult in those so young.

The surgery

Many third molar extractions, especially if complex, are referred to an oral surgeon. The degree of complexity depends on the position of the tooth; the amount of bone covering it; the stage of development, shape, and number of its roots; the presence of infection; the ease of access to the tooth; and the physical and emotional status of the patient. Surgery may be per-

434

formed in the oral surgeon's office or in the hospital on an outpatient basis. Less commonly, the patient is admitted to the hospital overnight. As a general rule, the costs of third molar extractions are covered by dental (but not all medical) insurance plans. In cases where hospital admission is necessary, benefits may sometimes be coordinated between the medical and dental plans.

Patients should prepare for the procedure by carefully following all of the dentist's preoperative instructions. These may include the following:

● restrictions on eating and drinking for several hours before surgery

● use of prescribed anxiety-relieving medications, possibly to be started the night before the extraction is to take place

● use of prescribed prophylactic antibiotics for patients with certain heart conditions and those with artificial joints

For some medically compromised patients—for example, those who are taking immunosuppressive drugs or who have chronic diseases—there may be additional special instructions. These are usually worked out in a preoperative consultation between the individual's physician and dentist. Finally, most dentists and oral surgeons recommend that patients have someone drive or otherwise accompany them home following the extraction procedure.

Essentially, the steps involved in removing an impacted wisdom tooth are incision of the soft tissues to reflect a gum flap; turning back of the flap to expose the jawbone; removal of as much overlying bone as is necessary to gain adequate access; removal of the whole tooth or, in some cases, sectioning the tooth to allow its removal in segments, thus minimizing trauma to the surrounding tissues; and repositioning and su-

turing of the gum flaps. An antibiotic dressing may be placed in the tooth socket before suturing.

One, several, or all four wisdom teeth may be extracted at a single appointment. The decision depends on the surgeon's judgment and the preferences of the patient. Although multiple extractions increase the level of postoperative pain, they spare the patient the necessity of facing several surgeries. Also, for patients having general anesthesia or so-called conscious sedation—a state of pleasant relaxation induced by drugs—extracting all teeth at one time reduces the expense and inherent risks, however small, that always accompany anesthesia.

Depending on the complexity and the number of teeth involved, extraction may take anywhere from less than 10 minutes to an hour. The choice of drugs to control pain and anxiety—and there are many safe and effective drug combinations from which to choose—is determined by several factors, including the surgeon's preferences, the degree of difficulty of the extraction, and the medical status and emotional needs of the patient. In addition to injecting a local anesthetic, the dentist may administer nitrous oxide (laughing gas), which is inhaled, or intravenous sedatives to allay anxiety. Conscious sedation has the advantage that the patient retains no clear memory of the procedure.

As noted above, oral sedatives or antianxiety agents are sometimes prescribed to be taken several hours prior to surgery. When a great deal of postoperative pain is anticipated, relatively new long-acting local anesthetics may be used. These keep the operative area numb for many hours, eliminating the need for strong painkillers in the six to eight hours—or sometimes more—following surgery. It is during this period that postoperative pain is otherwise most severe.

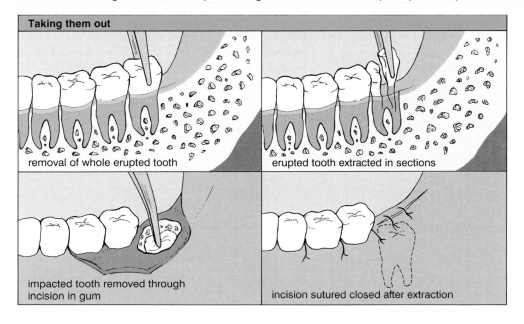

Taking them out

removal of whole erupted tooth

erupted tooth extracted in sections

impacted tooth removed through incision in gum

incision sutured closed after extraction

Besides numbing the operative area, local anesthetics also help control bleeding. Occasionally, general anesthesia is the correct choice, perhaps because of allergy or infection or because the patient is medically compromised or emotionally unable to tolerate the procedure any other way.

Complications

Complications encountered during surgery may include hemorrhage; very close proximity of a nerve, which may make some nerve damage inevitable; fracture of a tooth root or of the jawbone itself; perforation of the sinus cavity or dislodgement of all or part of a tooth into the sinus; or damage to an adjacent tooth. Postoperative problems may be the result of either the surgery or the anesthetic and may include excessive pain or swelling; hemorrhage; trismus; infection; development of a painful "dry socket" (described below); development of abnormal sensation such as burning, prickling, or numbness in the surrounding facial area; formation of a hematoma (a mass of clotted blood); or ecchymosis (a leakage of blood into the tissues, causing blue, red, or yellow discoloration of part of the face and neck). Several of these complications are relatively rare, but a certain amount of bleeding, pain, and swelling is inevitable. Oozing of blood from the incision site is common during the first 24 hours after surgery. Excessive bleeding or bleeding that starts after the first day, however, may have to be treated by the dentist.

Postoperative pain

Just how much postoperative pain a patient experiences depends on the length of the procedure and the degree to which the tissues are traumatized. To some extent, pain also appears to be part of a self-fulfilling expectation—*i.e.,* the more anxious patients, who anticipate more pain, tend to experience more pain. The perception of pain is highly individual—what is excruciating to one person may seem quite tolerable to another. Aspirin or acetaminophen (Tylenol), often in conjunction with more potent medications such as codeine, is commonly prescribed to control the postoperative pain. In recent years the use of nonsteroidal anti-inflammatory drugs such as ibuprofen (Motrin, Advil) and, more recently, flurbiprofen (Ansaid) has become common. When started before surgery, they assure the patient of a minimum of postoperative pain and also act to reduce swelling.

In the normal healing process, a blood clot forms in the tooth socket. One fairly common cause of postoperative pain is a so-called dry socket—*i.e.,* one that is either partially or totally devoid of the blood clot. Pain due to a dry socket usually starts two to seven days after the extraction and may last from a few days to several weeks; it can be severe and occasionally requires repeated follow-up visits. The following have been implicated in contributing to the development of a dry socket: birth control pills, advanced age, pre-existing infection, and smoking. Inappropriate rinsing also may lead to loss of the blood clot, and failure to comply with the dentist's recommendations regarding when and how much to rinse is a factor that may contribute to the development of a dry socket.

Sometimes, because of close proximity of the tooth to a nerve, nerve injury is unavoidable. The resulting numbness or altered sensation in the lower lip, chin, or tongue may remain for several weeks. Occasionally such numbness is permanent.

Until sometime in the distant future when humans may be born without any third molars, there is little one can do about these potentially troublesome teeth except to have them carefully evaluated and, when necessary, removed. However, there is no reason to suffer needlessly. Patients can reduce undue discomfort by complying with their dentist's postoperative instructions regarding the application of pressure to control bleeding, the use of medications and ice packs to reduce pain and swelling, appropriate brushing and rinsing, and avoidance of hard or chewy foods. Any untoward symptoms—excessive bleeding, persistent swelling, fever, drug reactions—should be promptly reported. A follow-up visit is usually scheduled about a week after surgery to remove sutures and to confirm that healing is progressing normally.

Aching All Over: The Fibromyalgia Syndrome

by Don L. Goldenberg, M.D.

Many people have had days when they ached all over, felt exhausted, and were too tired to work yet unable to sleep soundly; a bout of the flu or a stressful event may bring on such an episode. However, some individuals feel this way virtually every day. During the past 10 years, medical scientists have come to recognize such chronic and persistent symptoms as characteristic of a discrete but poorly understood medical illness, termed fibromyalgia syndrome.

Fibromyalgia was described by French and English physicians in the early 1800s. During the past two centuries, many different names have been given to the disorder, including fibrositis, myofibrositis, and muscular rheumatism. *Fibromyalgia* is now the generally accepted term, as it describes the two most important aspects of the condition: *fibro* refers to the fibrous connective tissues such as tendons and ligaments, which typically are tender; *myalgia* means "muscle pain"—stiffness and achiness of the muscles being the most prominent symptom. Fibromyalgia falls into the broad category of soft-tissue rheumatic disorders. Thus, pain and dysfunction may involve muscles, tendons, ligaments, and bursa (tiny sacs that act as cushions at points of friction between tendons and bones) but not the joints or bones themselves.

Fibromyalgia is a very common condition. Recent estimates are that three million to six million Americans may suffer from it, although not all of these have been diagnosed or even have sought medical attention. As many as 5% of all patients who consult a general physician (family practitioner, internist) for any reason meet current diagnostic criteria for fibromyalgia. The syndrome has been reported in virtually every part of the world, but it is not known if any racial or ethnic factors influence the risk of developing it. What is clear is that there is a striking predominance of female patients over males—a ratio of about 10:1. The general age of onset is from 30 to 50 years, although the condition is known to occur in persons of all ages.

Symptoms

Fibromyalgia patients generally report that they hurt "all over," although initially the pain is often more localized. Certain muscle-tendon junctions—*e.g.,* at the top of the scapula (shoulder blade), outside of the elbow, inner side of the knee—are found upon examination to be painful to the touch. These "tender points" (*see* diagram, page 438) are the key physical finding in fibromyalgia, and most patients have tenderness at a number of characteristic anatomic locations, usually on both sides of the body. Despite their general soreness and stiffness, people with fibromyalgia are often unaware that these particular sites are tender until they are palpated by the physician, who must know precisely where to look for the tender points and how firmly to press. In the process of physical examination, the physician generally discovers that the muscles are not only tender but also taut, or in spasm. In addition to deep muscle pain, the patient may report sensations of numbness, burning, swelling, and coldness in the involved muscles or in an extremity. Patients may complain of muscle weakness or joints that are painful and swollen. However, careful medical examination generally reveals no significant evidence of arthritic changes in the joints or inflammation of the muscles. Even biopsy (surgical sampling) of affected muscle tissue shows no evidence of pathology. This absence of identifiable physical abnormalities is typical of soft-tissue rheumatic conditions.

In addition to chronic muscle pain, persistent fatigue is the other most predominant symptom of fibromyalgia. Fatigue can be broadly classified into different subcategories: (1) muscular fatigue due to strenuous exercise; (2) exhaustion such as one experiences after a poor night's sleep; and (3) tiredness and lack of energy associated with feelings of de-

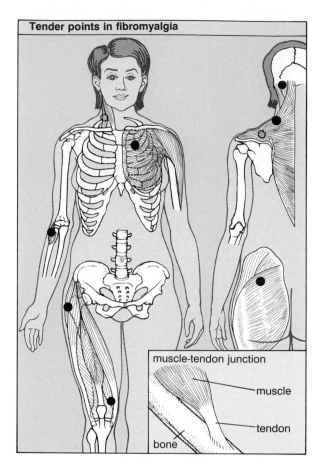

Tender points in fibromyalgia

muscle-tendon junction

muscle

tendon

bone

pression. Patients with fibromyalgia report elements of each of these types of fatigue and specifically note that they began to sleep poorly around the time that their painful symptoms first developed. The sleep disturbance typical of fibromyalgia is characterized by frequent awakenings during the night and a feeling of being unrefreshed in the morning. Many patients also complain of depression and heightened anxiety, but they usually attribute these to their physical symptoms. Other common symptoms include muscular, or tension, headaches, recurrent diarrhea or constipation often associated with abdominal discomfort, increased overall sensitivity to cold, and an unusual sensitivity of the skin to cold and heat as well as touch.

Diagnosis

It is only in the past decade that the medical profession has widely recognized fibromyalgia as a discrete entity. This recognition followed a number of clinical studies that evaluated a large number of patients with fibromyalgia and compared their symptoms with those of patients with other rheumatic complaints. A large, multiclinic, North American study completed in 1990 demonstrated that a set of simple criteria can be used to make a definitive diagnosis. These criteria include generalized muscular pain or stiffness of greater than

three months' duration and pain in at least 11 of 18 characteristic locations, or tender points, on each side of the body.

Often symptoms have persisted for years; patients may have undergone numerous blood tests and X-rays and seen many different specialists before the appropriate diagnosis was made. Although some blood tests, such as for anemia and abnormal thyroid function, should be performed in the initial evaluation of an individual suspected of having fibromyalgia, more sophisticated tests generally are not warranted and usually are performed only because physicians fail to recognize this common condition. Thus, it is especially important that someone with possible fibromyalgia see a physician who is familiar with the disorder. Such a physician will usually be able to make the diagnosis on the basis of a careful medical history and thorough physical examination, with few additional tests.

Speculation about causes

The cause of fibromyalgia is not known. Many patients identify a specific event as having triggered their symptoms, most notably physical trauma (such as a motor vehicle accident, fall, sports injury, or work-related strain), emotional stress (*e.g.,* divorce, loss of job, or death in the family), or a viral or other medical illness. However, at least 50% of patients do not recognize any single event as having precipitated the onset of the condition. Furthermore, it is not clear how a physical or emotional trauma can actually cause chronic pain and fatigue long after both the physical damage and emotional scars would have been expected to heal. Similarly, the role of a viral or other illness in causing an ongoing chronic condition such as fibromyalgia would require evidence that the virus or another pathogen persists in the body.

The possible role of a chronic viral infection in fibromyalgia is especially interesting in view of the recent medical research into the etiology of chronic fatigue syndrome (CFS). Only a few years ago, CFS was thought to be caused by the Epstein-Barr virus, the organism that causes chronic infectious mononucleosis. However, recent studies have not confirmed this association, nor has any other virus been conclusively linked with CFS. Nevertheless, most investigators continue to believe that CFS begins with a viral illness. The symptoms of CFS are strikingly similar to those of fibromyalgia, including fatigue, muscle aches, headaches, and sleep disturbances. This author, along with colleagues at Tufts University School of Medicine, Medford, Mass., Boston University School of Medicine, and Harvard Medical School, recently found that almost 70% of patients with CFS do indeed meet the diagnostic criteria for fibromyalgia. Fibromyalgia and CFS seem, therefore, to be overlapping conditions. A virus or another infectious agent may be one of a number of triggering factors.

Whatever the trigger, a cycle or cascade of symptoms—chronic pain, fatigue, sleep disturbance, and mood disturbances—characterizes fibromyalgia. As mentioned above, physical examination and X-ray studies reveal no structural abnormalities or inflammation in the muscles, tendons, or other painful areas. Some researchers have found that the sore and tender muscles of people with fibromyalgia become hypoxic during exertion; *i.e.,* run out of oxygen too quickly. This leads to an accumulation of lactic acid and other harmful substances in the muscle tissue, which in turn causes further muscle pain and reflex muscle contraction. Patients then become physically "deconditioned" as they find it increasingly difficult to exercise. Inactivity progressively weakens their muscles; this negative effect further discourages them from exercising.

Because of the absence of major pathological changes in the muscles, tendons, and fibrous tissue in fibromyalgia, research has recently explored possible hormonal or central nervous system aspects of this syndrome. Neurological or neuroendocrine dysfunction could account for the absence of structural abnormalities in the musculoskeletal system and help to explain the relationship of the various symptoms. One such hypothesis postulates that the chronic symptoms in fibromyalgia are determined by a change in brain neurotransmitters such as serotonin or the natural pain-relieving substances called endorphins. A deficiency of these substances could result in an exaggeration of the pain produced by various stimuli. Neurotransmitters also help to maintain blood flow to muscles, and their deficiency would promote tissue hypoxia, lactic acid accumulation, and muscle pain and spasm. Any muscle could be affected, including the skeletal muscles, causing typical fibromyalgia pain as well as muscular headaches, or the muscles surrounding internal organs such as the bowel or bladder, leading to an irritable bowel or bladder condition.

Neurotransmitters are also important in sleep, especially in the promotion of deep sleep. Studies of patients with fibromyalgia have demonstrated frequent sleep abnormalities, especially interruptions of a specific stage of restorative sleep. Interruptions of this phase chronically cause early-morning awakening and a sense of muscular fatigue, as well as extreme tiredness and difficulty in concentrating. Neurotransmitters such as serotonin are also important in mood disturbances, especially in endogenous depression (arising internally rather than as a reaction to an outside event). Research has shown that at least one-half of the patients with fibromyalgia and CFS have a history of major depression; they are also more likely to have a family history of mood, or affective, disorders. Although some feelings of depression may be attributed to the patient's chronic pain and inability to function, as well as to worry about the condition itself, these studies indicate that there are possible biochemical and genetic links between fibromyalgia and mood disturbances.

Treatment

By far the most important aspect of treatment is patient education. Most persons with fibromyalgia have seen many physicians without getting satisfactory answers as to either diagnosis or treatment and have become increasingly frustrated and angry. Many have been told that all their tests are normal and, therefore, there is nothing wrong with them but that they are simply "stressed out." They are advised to see a mental health professional, which may make them feel guilty or angry, and often the counselor or therapist can find no psychiatric basis for their symptoms. Therefore, the cornerstone of treatment is for the physician to explain what fibromyalgia is and also what it is not. Patients need to understand that the absence of a specific cause or pathology to explain the symptoms does not negate their presence. Patients should not be made to feel that they have to prove that their symptoms are "real," not imagined. At the same time, patients should be reassured that fibromyalgia does not cause joint or muscular deterioration, does not produce nerve damage, causes no disfigurement, and is never fatal.

Treatment then is aimed at the factors thus far identified as promoting the chronic pain and fatigue. Since a number of research studies have demonstrated the role of muscle hypoxia and muscle spasm in fibromyalgia, treatment should include exercises to improve both of these problems. Hypoxia of the muscles can be alleviated by aerobic exercises, begun gently, then gradually increased in intensity. The goal is to slowly improve the patient's aerobic capacity but to stick to low-impact activities that do not strain muscles. Fast walking, indoor or outdoor biking, and swimming and aquatic exercises are among the most effective ways to achieve better cardiovascular fitness with the least muscle resistance. The workout should also include appropriate exercises to stretch tight, contracted muscles and to maintain the range of motion of the joints. The exercise program must, however, be tailored to the individual's fitness level, age, and body type and should be carefully monitored. Some patients, particularly those who have previously exercised regularly or participated in athletics, will be able to set up their own program or can go to a local "Y" or health club. However, patients who are physically unfit, elderly, or in severe pain will require a sophisticated exercise program with careful instruction and monitoring, usually working with a physical therapist. Such programs can be found at hospitals or rehabilitation facilities and generally should be supervised by a medical professional. It is important for patients to know that they may feel somewhat achier and more fatigued when they initially embark on a new exercise program and that it may take several months before they feel any overall improvement.

Physical therapy, massage, heat or cold applications, ultrasound and electrical stimulation, whirlpool baths, saunas, chiropractic or osteopathic treatments, and acupuncture have all been used to treat the muscle pain and spasm of fibromyalgia, as well as related types of soft-tissue rheumatism. In some patients one of these modalities may be very helpful, whereas others may not benefit. Therefore, the patient has to be an informed health consumer—willing to try those treatments that make sense, are the least costly, and are not likely to have significant adverse effects.

Medications that have been most helpful in treating fibromyalgia include those commonly used to treat depression, such as the tricyclic antidepressants (amitriptyline, nortriptyline, imipramine, and others). However, these medications have usually been given in doses that are much lower than those used to treat depression. Their effectiveness in fibromyalgia may relate primarily to their alleviation of sleep disturbances, but they also act on the central and peripheral nervous systems to decrease pain. Certain muscle relaxants, most notably cyclobenzaprine (Flexeril), have also been helpful in relieving pain and sleep disturbances; the chemical structure and action of cyclobenzaprine are similar to those of the tricyclic antidepressants. Fluoxetine (Prozac), which has been available in the U.S. only since 1988, has not been adequately evaluated in therapeutic trials. Some patients do feel better on low doses of this relatively new antidepressant, but sleep disturbances may worsen with fluoxetine, necessitating the addition of other medications to counter the sleep problem.

The above-mentioned medications are thought to work by restoring to normal levels chemical neurotransmitters, most specifically serotonin. Because these neurotransmitters influence pain sensation, sleep, and muscle oxygenation, as well as mood, medications that enhance the quantity or quality of substances such as serotonin could have beneficial effects in fibromyalgia. In fact, studies show that approximately one-third of fibromyalgia patients placed on these medications feel much better and are able to tolerate the minor side effects of dry mouth, constipation, and increased appetite without much difficulty. Another one-third have modest improvement and often try other medications, and one-third experience no improvement or find the side effects too unpleasant. It is often necessary to try a number of different drugs at various dosages. Pain-relieving medications, including simple analgesics such as acetaminophen (Tylenol, Panadol) and anti-inflammatory medications such as aspirin or ibuprofen (Advil, Motrin, Nuprin), are helpful for diminishing pain but should be used only when necessary. Narcotic and other potentially habit-forming or toxic drugs should not be used.

A team approach to the treatment of fibromyalgia is helpful when patients do not respond adequately to therapy. Such a team would include a psychiatrist or a psychologist to assess and treat any accompanying depression or anxiety and a rehabilitation team (including a physiatrist and a physical therapist) to evaluate the patient's physical condition and to create and supervise an appropriate exercise program. At the core of this team should be a caring and knowledgeable physician who is willing to spend the necessary time and give the encouragement needed during the treatment of this frustrating disorder. It is important for patients to understand that stress is likely to exacerbate their symptoms—just as it may elevate blood pressure, worsen migraine headaches, or precipitate gastric ulcers. Therefore, it is essential that an overall focus be kept on the patient's emotional and physical well-being. Relaxation techniques (e.g., biofeedback, meditation, guided imagery) and programs that emphasize coping skills and promote wellness are very helpful.

Getting appropriate help

Fibromyalgia and other perplexing syndromes that cause chronic pain, fatigue, and mood disturbances are of considerable current interest to researchers in many different branches of medical science, including rheumatology, psychiatry, physiatrics, neurology, and infectious diseases. These illnesses are model conditions for the study of the complicated mind-body interactions that are now known to be an important aspect of most chronic illness. However, until there are more public interest, more research, and a better understanding of fibromyalgia, it will probably continue to be a common but frustrating disorder.

Although the medical interest in and knowledge of fibromyalgia have expanded during the past decade, there are still many physicians who do not make the diagnosis when they should or who believe that all patients with this condition are either depressed, highly stressed, or seeking an excuse to qualify for disability payments. As specialty practitioners, rheumatologists have been the most interested in fibromyalgia and have done much of the recent research; therefore, a rheumatologist, a rheumatology department at a medical center, the Arthritis Foundation (1314 Spring Street NW, Atlanta, GA 30309), or a local Arthritis Foundation chapter would be an appropriate source for information and referrals. Another source of information is the Fibromyalgia Network, 7001 School House Lane, Bakersfield, CA 93309, which publishes a newsletter and can help patients find support groups.

The Only Child
by Stephen P. Bank, Ph.D.

To have only one child offers parents and children the chance to have a high-quality relationship, undiluted by the demands of other children. For today's busy, dual-career couples, it also offers greater financial and vocational freedom. Yet some parents worry about whether an only child might in some way be socially handicapped without a brother or sister; the very idea of having "only one" also brings to the fore feelings about the meaning of the word *family*. Some couples never even consider having just one child, assuming that such a choice would mean losing the rich, emotionally charged connections and opportunities that abound in larger families.

Changing views of family

Two hundred years ago, when America was being settled, families were large, consisting of five, six, or more children. Children were not wanted just for their own sake; they were needed for practical economic reasons. Rural farming life required many hands; children were needed to help with the sowing and harvesting and all the daily chores. They were also needed to help care for other children. The biblical injunction "Go forth and multiply" and God's promise to make Abraham's descendants "as numerous as the stars in the sky" were taken seriously by a society that demanded large numbers of people to develop the frontier. If a family had just a single child, it was not by choice but the result of the deaths of other children or of infertility. A family with an only child was considered unfortunate.

Families have changed, and so have parents' reasons for having children. Today's children are conceived to enhance family intimacy, companionship, and enjoyment. Advances in preventive medicine make it possible for most families to bear only one child confidently, whereas previous generations conceived many children in order to ensure the survival of a few. With effective contraception readily available to millions of families, Americans believe that couples can and should control their lives. The average number of births per woman in the U.S. is now less than 2; in some European countries and in Japan it is around 1.5, while in China the fertility rate has hit an all-time low of 2.5.

Although today more families are "stopping at one" than did 20 years ago (in the U.S. 15% in 1988 versus 11% in 1972, according to the Bureau of the Census), the two-child family is still the most popular choice. In a Gallup Poll (1986) a majority of Americans said that ideally they preferred a two-child family, while only 5% preferred having a single child. When times are economically tough, the only-child option becomes more popular: at the height of the Great Depression, there were nearly twice as many families (20–23%) that had only one child than during the "boom" that came afterward.

In most areas of the world, if the first child is a girl, parents are likely to "try for a second." In fact, in the United States if a girl is conceived first, there is a shorter time between that birth and the birth of a second child than if the first child is a boy. Yet while the perpetuation of the family name through a male child still appears important to some parents, modern girls who are "onlys" appear to be loved and valued just as much as boys, perhaps because modern parents see the potential for girls to develop in spheres that were once thought to be the special province of males. The tendency to devalue a baby girl appears strongest in some Third World countries. In ancient China firstborn girls were often killed; this practice is still reported from time to time in remote sections of present-day China.

Shrinking resources and the one-child family. Single-child families are strongly promoted by those who believe that the survival of the Earth depends on limiting population. In the United States, the world's biggest consumer of energy, it is estimated that by age 75 each person will have produced 52 tons of garbage, used more than 3,000 bbl of oil, and required enormous quantities of precious water resources. To some

441

Big families were not only desired but necessary on the American frontier. Rural farming life required many hands; as soon as children were old enough, they worked in the fields, helped prepare meals, and cared for their younger siblings.

the single-child family offers the best hope for a world worth living in.

The Chinese try to put the view into practice; the government has declared a "single-child rule," on which rest the country's hopes of raising the desperately low standard of living of its 1.1 billion people. Couples are asked to sign a one-child contract, which carries financial penalties if a second child is conceived. Although the Chinese have accepted the one-child policy ambivalently, the latest available figures show a dramatic rise in one-child families.

Some social scientists believe that because costs of raising children are skyrocketing, single-child families could become more attractive as the 21st century nears. U.S. government estimates suggest that the basic costs of raising a child born today to age 18 will amount to more than $150,000. This figure does not include lost income from parents' staying home to raise a child, nor does it include financing of such things as music lessons, orthodontics, or summer camp! Prospective parents swallow hard when they compute added costs for college education.

More than economics. Child rearing, however, takes more than money. It takes enormous amounts of emotional and physical energy. Before a child's 18th birthday, he or she will have created nearly 10,000 hours of extra housework for the parents. But even beyond their concerns about money and energy, today's

China, which has the world's largest population, offers economic incentives to parents for having just one child. Increasingly, couples are complying with the policy, considering one child "enough" and believing that they can lead a better life by limiting the size of their families.

parents are concerned about the emotional needs of offspring. Psychological research on the potential influence of parents on their child's well-being has been avidly absorbed by couples who are contemplating family life. Childhood is now viewed as a complex series of stages and opportunities—all requiring the sensitive guidance of parents. Parents of the 1990s are more involved participants in all their child's activities than were parents of previous generations. They are consciously and even anxiously concerned about being better parents to fewer children, and often both of them must balance the demands of their jobs with the needs of their child.

Studies of " onlys"

Prejudices and stereotypes have given only children an undeservedly bad reputation. The very term *only child* seems to imply the parents' misfortune—a *mere* one child. Psychologists at the beginning of this century had hardly anything favorable to say about only children. The influential American psychologist G. Stanley Hall, whose thinking was accepted by other psychologists for decades, described the situation of being an only child as "a disease." "Because of the undue attention he demands and usually receives," wrote Hall, "we commonly find the only child selfish, egotistical, dependent, aggressive, domineering, or quarrelsome." In the past, parents who opted for having but one child were disparaged as selfish, materialistic, and uninterested in parenthood.

The single child has been the subject of hundreds of research studies. Both proponents and opponents of single-child families can cite findings in their favor. Overall, however, the most reliable of these studies have found that being an only child has many ad-

vantages. Among the findings: having a sibling is *not* a basic necessity for normal development. Compared with children from two-child families, only children develop and function just as well; moreover, only children often cope and function *better* than children from large families. These findings are important; a major reason for conceiving more than one child springs from parents' conviction that giving the first child a sibling is essential for their offspring's happiness, self-esteem, and social development.

Surveys of parents of only children portray them as quite satisfied with their relationship with their child. Parents of one child describe their relationship with their children as affectionate and rewarding more often than do parents with many offspring. They cherish this single, undiluted relationship. Studies have found that the single child often receives much attention, is read to more than the child with siblings, and never experiences the well-documented regression that accompanies the birth of a second baby. The absence of favoritism is important; recent studies show that favoritism can be felt by a "less desired" sibling throughout life and can cause lasting psychological damage.

From their earliest years, only children are likely to participate in adult conversation; they do not have to struggle with other children to make their voices heard. Given a chance to try on adult roles at an early age, only children generally have acquired social graces and are more cultured and mature by the time they are adolescents.

Studies show that only children not only read more than children from large families but tend to seek intellectual work when they become adults. They are motivated to achieve and excel, get high grades, obtain good test scores, attend college, and marry

New parents delight in their four-week-old son. Couples who delay childbearing and choose to have just one child are usually extremely satisfied with their decision; they feel they can offer many more advantages than if they had several children.

Elizabeth Crews—Stock, Boston

people who are well educated. Only children routinely appear in the ranks of eminent individuals: astronauts, scientists, artists, politicians, and famed sports figures. Leonardo da Vinci, Franklin D. Roosevelt, Hans Christian Andersen, Indira Gandhi, William Randolph Hearst, Elvis Presley, Kareem Abdul-Jabbar, James Audubon, Robert Penn Warren, Queen Victoria, and Ingrid Bergman, to name a few, all were only children.

Many assumptions have been made about emotional difficulties of only children—that they are selfish, egocentric, and spoiled; that they are lonely; that they cannot stand up for themselves; that they are hypochondriacs; and so forth. However, studies do not bear out such assumptions. Rather, only children appear to be as well adjusted as children with siblings. They have no greater incidence of severe emotional problems; in tests of self-esteem administered by psychologists, only children score no lower, and in some instances score higher, than children from large families. Only children are more resilient when their parents divorce—probably because their single-parent mothers are less taxed by responsibility than are mothers of two or more children. Moreover, their own marriages end in divorce no more frequently than do others'.

What about their ability to make friends, cooperate, and communicate? Nearly every only child has wished for a brother or sister at one time or another. In elementary-school years only children become sharply aware that other children have brothers and sisters to play with. They feel envious and curious, even though most acknowledge that they enjoy their privacy and the exclusive attention of their parents.

Studies show that only children tend not to join team activities or participate in sports such as football and basketball in the same numbers as do children with a sibling. They have a less extensive social life— e.g., fewer dates in high school. Yet, significantly, having no siblings does not mean that only children find themselves in a shell of lonely isolation; rather, they learn instead to make use of the many hours they have to themselves. Not only do they read a great deal but they become stamp collectors, musicians, and photographers, while their peers more often prefer team activities and sports.

The only child is not viewed by his or her peers as antisocial or friendless. Only children themselves, however, tend to describe themselves as slightly less sociable than other children. Being alone can make only children realize that "you have only you," which may account for their self-sufficiency and their sense of independence. Only children are more likely to recognize that friends will not come to them unless they make an effort. Though they may have fewer friends, their friendships have importance and intensity, probably because they lack a sibling to fall back on.

Special problems

No childhood is perfect, and only children do have problems that are unique to their situation.

Too close for comfort. Parents of an only child may invest so much in that one child's life that the child seems to be living not for himself or herself but for the parents. The parents' hopes, dreams, and satisfactions may rest entirely on their one offspring. This situation, in which the emotional connection between parents and child prevents the child's individuation, is what psychologists term *enmeshment.*

The problem of enmeshment can be compounded if the parents are emotionally troubled or if there are conflicts in the marriage. The only child, lacking a sibling who may understand what it is like to live in

The world is full of famous and highly accomplished only children. Queen Victoria, who was the mother of nine children, was an only child. Kareem Abdul-Jabbar, who surpassed the all-time high-scoring record during his stellar professional basketball career, was also an "only."

Only children tend to be resourceful, self-disciplined, and independent. They often devote considerable time to hobbies, at which they excel and from which they derive great pleasure.

the same turbulent home, can feel responsible for the conflict or may feel that it is his or her role to be the sole source of solace to upset parents. It is a good idea for such only children to be exposed to relatives and other adults so that the child can benefit from the benevolent influence of other people.

While many parents today choose to have just one child, this was not always so. But even today, a significant portion of single-child families are not by choice; they are the result of divorce, infertility, or the death of another child. If parents wished for a second child with special characteristics that the first does not have—physical appearance, charm, talents, or being "the right sex"—their feelings of unhappiness and disappointment may be carried into parenting, and they may place unreasonable demands and expectations

on their child. These parents need to come to terms with and resolve their sad or angry feelings so that they are able to truly appreciate their one child's uniqueness.

In having children, parents like to perpetuate those parts of their own childhood that were most satisfying. In general, if one was an only child and if that experience was a happy one, a parent can cheerfully have just one child and feel completely fulfilled. Other parents may feel that their childhood was empty because they lacked a brother or a sister; for them, having a family with many children and a home filled with activity makes up for strong, unmet desires. Similarly, if a parent's childhood was marred by having too many brothers and sisters—e.g., too many mouths to feed, not enough attention from parents—a sense of having

"According to this, everything we've done up to now is right."

been deprived of a childhood can engender strong feelings of commitment to having only one child.

Parents of one child get just one chance. It is true that they may overreact or become overly alarmed when their child has problems—*e.g.,* encounters difficulty with schoolwork, gets rejected by a friend, becomes ill, or simply is in a "bad mood." It is a good idea for parents of only children to have contact with other parents in order to gain perspective on—and even add levity to—the trials and tribulations of child rearing.

Making friends. Peer relationships are important in any childhood. Parents who have a single child should consider settling in a neighborhood where there are other children who can be playmates. The single child may not require as many companions as other children, but friendships take on a greater importance. Recognizing this, parents should encourage their child to cultivate friends, which may mean arranging transportation to other children's homes and extending invitations for other children to visit their home. If a child's friendship is suddenly lost, parents need to provide sympathy and support. Only children often enjoy becoming friends with other only children. Bonds of understanding and gratitude about being alike often occur when "onlys" pair up.

Parents can expect to hear their child periodically demand: "When are you going to give me a sister or brother?" This should not be taken literally. The expression of a wish for a sibling usually does not reflect real unhappiness on the part of the only child but the normal desire to be like the majority. Parents should listen with understanding, helping the child to form good relationships; nurturing an only child's relationship with a cousin is often a good investment.

Having grown up without the normal fighting and shouting that goes with having a sibling, only children are sometimes shocked and upset when other children are boisterous. They sometimes take literally the verbal barbs that children with siblings so naturally hurl at one another. Situations such as having a friend over or having to share a room for the first time—at camp or in college—can make them feel uncomfortable. Only children are often tidy and used to maintaining an orderly personal environment. A parent can help them recognize that not everyone shares their sense of order and of personal privacy. Parents of only children can also be helpful in pointing out that there are two sides to any argument; learning to compromise is an important early lesson for "onlys."

When only children are adults and become parents themselves, they may react anxiously when fighting breaks out among their children. Only children as parents require feedback—from other parents, the family pediatrician, relatives, teachers, school counselors—about what is and is not normal rivalry.

Older and only

Perhaps the enriched life of an only child carries costs that are felt most sharply when he or she reaches middle age and must shoulder the emotional, physical, and financial responsibility for the care of elderly and debilitated parents. The fact that an inheritance will not have to be shared hardly compensates for this often overwhelming responsibility. Ideally, only children will have developed strong relationships with relatives and will have spouses and their own children to support them in the care-giving role.

Thornton Wilder, in his play *Our Town,* asked, "What's left when memory's gone?" Memories are fundamental to meaningful existence. *Shared* memories are all the more enriching. The only child who has no sibling with whom to reminisce about the mirth and heartaches of childhood—no one who knew exactly what it was like to grow up in the same house and the same neighborhood, to have the same parents, and to experience the same special occasions and the same tragedies—is acutely aware of this disadvantage. There is an emptiness to remembering one's childhood alone. Moreover, when the parents die, the only child is truly alone.

If an only child marries another only child, there will be no uncles or aunts and no cousins for *their* children to form relationships with and to share in such family occasions as birthdays, confirmations, bar mitzvahs, graduations, and weddings. When only children themselves grow old or infirm, they have no siblings to look after them, whereas elderly siblings often form relationships that are loyal, congenial, and intimate, looking out for one another's welfare, tending to one another when sickness strikes or spouses die. Indeed, sibling relationships tend to gain in importance as individuals age. Elderly only children must rely on other relationships.

Trade-offs

Only children may miss some of the rich variety, support, and companionship that come with having a lifelong sibling connection. Furthermore, they carry throughout life an awareness of being somehow "different." Yet only children appear to flourish and bask in the undiluted attention of their parents, who are generally quite satisfied with having one child. Far from being social misfits, they generally make significant achievements in life and have valued, lasting, and intimate relationships.

Like most of life's most important decisions, opting to have a single child involves trade-offs; parents must weigh these for themselves. Their child will have many special advantages but will have a few unique disadvantages as well. The latter, however, should not necessarily discourage the choice to have only one.

Food Cravings
by Myron Winick, M.D.

Appetite is a longing or an intense desire to satisfy a need (from the Latin *appetere,* meaning "to strive after, desire"). The desire for food is one of the basic drives of humans and other animals. A series of complex, interacting physiological, psychological, and cultural factors influence both what people eat and how much they eat. One aspect of appetite that is currently receiving considerable attention is cravings for certain foods. Before examining what is known about food cravings, it is important to distinguish several appetite-associated phenomena.

Hunger and satiety, cravings and aversions

Since human survival depends on food, *hunger* for any kind of food becomes the overwhelming concern of those who are faced with extreme food deprivation. Studies of hunger among the Jewish victims of Nazi brutality within the Warsaw Ghetto (performed by Jewish physicians, themselves starving) demonstrated how powerful a drive hunger can be. The physicians noted among the early effects of starvation "dryness in the mouth, rapid weight loss, and a constant craving for food." According to the reports that emerged from these studies, when the starving ghetto inhabitants were presented with bread, meat, or sweets, they would "become very aggressive"; they would "grab the food, and devour it at once," even though they risked being beaten by Nazi authorities.

Thus, when a person is starving, both the subconscious and conscious mind fix on food, and almost all endeavors concentrate on the acquisition of food of any kind. Specific food preferences are buried beneath the all-consuming desire for any kind of nourishment, and even the strongest food aversions are no longer operative. People under extreme conditions have been known to consume things that they would never consciously eat in normal circumstances—even turning to cannibalism. Hunger induced by the absence of food is the strongest physiological stimulus for eating. It is present in all animal species, and it suppresses all other stimuli for eating or avoiding specific foods.

Nevertheless, very little is actually known about the mechanisms that govern hunger. Clearly, the absence of sufficient food triggers both peripheral (throughout the body) and central (within the brain) events, which lead to the feeling of hunger. Levels of nutrients in the blood, the body's secretion of certain hormones, and the release by the brain of certain neurotransmitters (chemicals that transmit nerve impulses) all are involved in the process, but their precise roles remain a mystery.

Medical scientists know much more about *satiety,* those factors involved in turning off eating behavior. As a meal distends the stomach, a number of hormones are released locally. Cholecystokinin (CCK) stimulates the vagus nerve (a nerve that is connected to the brain stem and supplies the nerves of the viscera, including the stomach), which in turn transmits impulses through a series of relays to a special area in the brain (the lateral hypothalamus). Within this area is the satiety center, which, when stimulated, causes the cessation of eating. Thus, satiety is a response to a single meal. It may occur even when a person is undergoing chronic food deprivation and hunger if a single, substantial meal is consumed. If hunger is great enough, however, it will override the satiety mechanism, and a person will gorge excessive quantities of food. There is evidence to suggest that some cases of severe bulimia—an eating disorder involving binge eating of large amounts of food, followed by purging—are accompanied by an inadequate CCK response. Presently, CCK and other satiety hormones are being intensively investigated as medications for the treatment of bulimia and obesity.

Cravings and *aversions* are different from hunger and satiety in that they involve a single food, or a single class of foods, whereas the latter pertain to all food. Hunger and satiety are common to all people regardless of their genetic background, cultural or religious heritage, and physiological or psychological makeup. Cravings or aversions vary widely among individuals, and genetics, culture, physiology, and psychology all influence their occurrence.

Origins of cravings

It is not known when during life particular food cravings begin. To the extent that certain cravings appear to be related to taste preferences, they may have their origins very early in life. Newborn infants clearly prefer sweet solutions. Some people apparently maintain a "sweet tooth" throughout their lives.

447

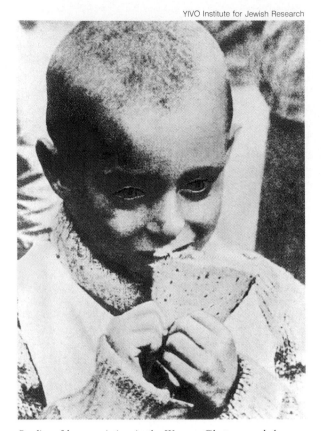

Studies of hunger victims in the Warsaw Ghetto revealed many profound physiological effects, including constant craving for food; the starving Jews did not crave specific foods but had an overwhelming desire for nourishment of any sort.

By contrast, other taste preferences, *e.g.,* for salty foods, are learned. The preference for highly salty foods—learned early in life and reinforced by consumption of such popular foods as potato chips, pretzels, "fast foods," and salt-cured meats (bologna, frankfurters, bacon, sausages, etc.)—is at least partly responsible for the high incidence of hypertension (high blood pressure) in the United States. Both animal experiments and studies of humans strongly suggest that the response of the body to consumption of relatively large amounts of salt is under genetic control— *i.e.,* only people with a particular genetic predisposition will develop high blood pressure from eating salty foods. This may explain the higher incidence of hypertension among black Americans.

The tendency for Americans and people from other cultures—for example, Asians—to have cravings for salty foods and to consume relatively large amounts of them is a learned response, with environmental and cultural inducements. It is not based on any physiological need for salt. However, under certain conditions, actual salt craving based on need can occur. In extremely hot, dry climates, physical exertion accompanied by profuse sweating may lead to salt

deprivation. Similarly, diseased and poorly functioning adrenal glands that are unable to produce sufficient adrenocortical hormones (which enable the body to retain essential amounts of salt) can result in severe salt depletion. In both these circumstances, the body somehow translates its acute need into an intense desire for salt.

There is no evidence, however, that most cravings have any physiological significance or that they represent the filling of a need for some deficient nutrient. The foods that are sought usually are easily obtainable and common within the culture of the individual harboring the powerful desire.

Cravings in pregnancy

Perhaps the most dramatic evidence of widespread food cravings and aversions is their occurrence in women during pregnancy. Some studies indicate that 90% of pregnant women show specific food cravings or aversions. In one study 50% of pregnant women craved chocolate or ice cream and 40% craved citrus fruit, milk, and sweet starchy foods. Other foods craved with some frequency during pregnancy include fruits, vegetables, and cola drinks. The craving for pickles is probably more alleged than real.

The aversions to specific foods that occur during pregnancy are much less frequent. Fried foods head the list—affecting about 20% of pregnant women. About 15% of respondents to surveys of food habits during pregnancy claim that they have aversions to certain meats, spicy Italian foods, coffee, and fish. Interestingly, several of the foods craved by some are avoided by others. Fried foods, ice cream, milk, citrus fruits, and vegetables all fall into this category.

Food cravings that occur during pregnancy often persist well into the postpartum period and are unaffected by whether the mother breast-feeds. Aversions generally tend to disappear within a month after delivery.

Investigations into the causes of pregnancy-related cravings and aversions have turned up very little. There seems to be no relation to the overall nutritional status of the woman, to the amount of weight gained during pregnancy, to her intake of vitamins and minerals, or to any other dietary practices. Nonetheless, expectant mothers can be reassured that their food cravings and aversions are not likely to imperil their pregnancy in any way. Their particular desires for foods are rarely the cause of too much or too little weight gain nor, in most cases, do they prevent the mother from getting the nutrients she needs.

Cravings for nonfoods

While specific cravings, whether for pickles, prunes, or pancakes, may be common in pregnancy, they are also benign. Another kind of pregnancy-related craving, however, can be quite dangerous. Some

448

The preference for salty food is learned early in life and usually is reinforced through consumption of highly processed foods and by the addition of large quantities of salt to food.

pregnant women, as well as some young children, develop a bizarre craving for nonnutritional, inedible substances; the condition is known as pica. Probably the most common type of pica during pregnancy is the consumption of cornstarch. This practice has been most widely observed among poor black women in the southern United States. Eating paint chips also occurs during pregnancy, but it is more common in young children. This habit, as well as that of chewing batteries, can lead to excessive ingestion of lead and, in many cases, to lead poisoning. Other distorted cravings that are often seen with pica are for chalk, dirt, hair, and gravel.

The cause of pica is unknown. Some data suggest that in young children certain forms of pica may be related to iron deficiency and that the pica represents an "iron-seeking" behavior. In some cases iron supplementation has resulted in cessation of the pica, but in others it has not. There is no evidence that pica in pregnant women is related to iron deficiency.

Hormonal influence

Women also exhibit cravings and sometimes aversions at certain times during their menstrual cycles. The foods they crave are varied and are similar to those craved during pregnancy. One theory, discussed below, associates particular cravings for carbohydrates with so-called premenstrual syndrome (PMS). However, most studies show that cravings related to menstruation have no apparent relation to the duration or severity of other menstrual symptoms, such as cramps and headaches. Some studies have shown that food cravings just before menstruation are more common among black women.

Their association with pregnancy and the menstrual cycle and their more common occurrence in women than in men suggest that food cravings may be related to the female hormones estrogen and progesterone.

However, just how the levels of either or both of these hormones are associated with specific food cravings is not known. Moreover, food cravings unrelated to menstruation also occur in women and men of all ages and in children of both sexes.

Teenagers: junk-food "junkies"

Surveys of adolescents' food preferences and eating habits have shown that cravings for so-called junk foods are prevalent. It is difficult to know whether the craving for certain foods during adolescence is based on internal (hormonal) changes that lead to a desire for certain foods or to powerful peer pressure and cultural inducements to consume these foods. Probably it is the latter. Such a conclusion, however, in no way minimizes the importance of these cravings. Un-

Although it is probably a myth that pregnant women have a passion for pickles, their cravings for ice cream, chocolate, and other sweets are apparently quite common.

Food cravings

fortunately, teenage indulgence in junk foods may be partly responsible for some of the poor eating habits that are known to contribute to chronic and life-threatening diseases in adulthood—notably, heart disease, diabetes, obesity, and certain cancers.

Geriatric sweet tooth

A condition that has been called geriatric sweet tooth has been described in older persons being treated for depression. Clinical depression has been estimated to afflict at least one million elderly people in the United States and is the most common psychiatric disorder of advanced age. The primary chemical treatment for depression in this population is a class of drugs known as tricyclic antidepressants. These commonly used medications (*e.g.,* amitriptyline, imipramine, desipramine) have many potential side effects; one that is mentioned infrequently in the medical literature but has been reported in nearly 50% of tricyclic-treated elderly patients is "an insatiable desire to eat, especially sweet foods." The number of people who develop such cravings and the severity of the cravings themselves are directly proportional to the dose of the drug taken. Excessive weight gain is often the result. Such weight gain is often associated with complications, especially in older persons who have other medical conditions such as diabetes or hypertension.

There are at least two lessons to be learned from the studies that have demonstrated these drug-induced cravings for sweets in the geriatric population. First, drugs frequently may be an overlooked cause of food cravings and excessive eating in older persons. Second, the fact that antidepressants are primarily targeted in the brain suggests that certain food cravings may be wholly physiological in nature—initiated by chemical activity within the brain.

Carbohydrate cravings: a tempting theory

If cravings amount to powerful passions for consuming certain foods, the question inevitably arises: Do cravings lead to obesity? There is currently in vogue a theory that certain cravings can be induced. Specifically, a diet that is high in protein will stimulate cravings for calorie-dense, sweet, carbohydrate foods, which are consumed primarily in the late afternoon and evening hours. Those who are subject to these cravings may eat normally at mealtimes, but during the later part of the day, they will consume an excess 800 or more calories, leading to weight gain. This condition is called carbohydrate-craving obesity.

The scientific explanation for such cravings is that a high-protein diet creates an excess of certain amino acids—most notably tryptophan—circulating in the bloodstream. Amino acids are nutrients that are present in most foods and constitute the main "building blocks" of protein. Amino acids are carried into the brain (*i.e.,* across the blood-brain barrier) by an active transport system that has room for just so many molecules before it becomes saturated. One might compare this transport system to a train with just so many seats; a number of amino acids must compete for the available seats. Because protein contains proportionally more of the amino acids tyrosine, leucine, and valine, they get the seats and tryptophan is excluded.

Tryptophan is a precursor of the brain neurotransmitter serotonin and is directly used in serotonin's synthesis. Serotonin is important in controlling mood,

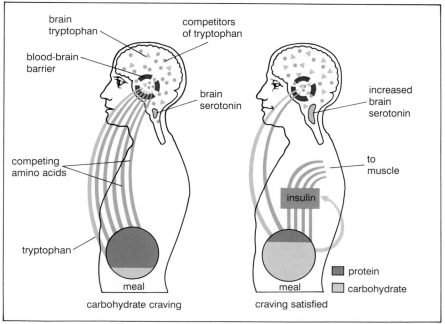

Some researchers theorize that a high-protein diet can induce carbohydrate craving by reducing levels of the neurotransmitter serotonin in the brain. A high-protein meal lowers brain levels of tryptophan, an amino acid used to make serotonin, because other amino acids from the meal are present in the bloodstream to compete with tryptophan for access across the blood-brain barrier to the brain (right). Eating carbohydrates stimulates the body to release insulin, which diverts many of the competitors of tryptophan from the bloodstream into muscle (far right). Thus, tryptophan enters the brain in increased amounts, more serotonin is made, and the craving disappears.

sleep, and appetite. According to the proposed theory, without tryptophan, serotonin levels within the brain are reduced and carbohydrate craving occurs. When carbohydrates are consumed, a number of things happen. One is that the body releases insulin. The increased insulin diverts the other amino acids named above to the muscles, thus making room in the brain for tryptophan. As tryptophan enters the brain in increased amounts, serotonin is synthesized and the craving disappears. According to researchers, carbohydrate cravers report that their consumption of caloric snack foods has a calming effect and also improves their mood.

The theory in question thus holds that cravings for carbohydrates occur because the brain needs to restore adequate levels of serotonin. Proponents contend that carbohydrate craving leads to obesity because the foods selected are primarily fat-sugar complexes that are very high in calories (cakes, cookies, pies, etc.). What they fail to explain adequately is why the preferences are for fattening snack items and why the cravings occur only in the late afternoon and evening. One must ask why complex carbohydrates such as pasta, rice, and potatoes, which are even more potent serotonin releasers, are not craved. The latter foods presumably would achieve the desired effect even more efficiently and without the resulting weight gain.

If the observations of those who propose carbohydrate craving as a major cause of obesity are correct, there seems to be a piece of the puzzle missing. Low brain serotonin levels may dictate a need for consumption of carbohydrates, but in the late afternoon and evenings, for some unexplained reason, the brain somehow interprets the message as a need for sweet-tasting, fattening snack foods to be consumed. Clearly much more evidence is necessary before this interesting theory can be accepted as fact. And, even if the theory is correct, it raises many more questions than it answers in regard to the involvement of the brain in food cravings.

Recently the proponents of the carbohydrate-craving hypothesis have suggested that the same mechanism is operant in two other disorders: PMS and seasonal affective disorder (SAD). Those affected by PMS suffer from monthly mood disorders of depression, lethargy, irritability, confusion, sleep disturbances, and increased appetite (notably cravings for carbohydrates), which occur during the last one or two weeks before the female menses. In the fall and winter months, SAD sufferers experience episodic bouts of depression combined with hypersomnia (excessive sleep), difficulty in concentrating, extreme fatigue, social withdrawal, and excess appetite for carbohydrates with resultant weight gain.

It is claimed that both afflictions may be due to reduced brain levels of serotonin induced by an inadequate carbohydrate intake. These conclusions are based on studies showing a greater reduction of symptoms after a carbohydrate meal than after a protein meal. While one possible explanation could be that serotonin levels are central in these disorders, other explanations are equally plausible. A simple one is that if a person showing the above symptoms also has a craving for carbohydrates, then relief of one frustration by supplying carbohydrates could easily relieve some of the other symptoms. Serotonin might not be involved in any of this.

The notion that carbohydrate cravings are induced by low brain serotonin levels is of considerable scientific interest, and it may open new avenues of research in the areas of nutrition and behavior in general and food cravings in particular. At present, however, the evidence is not strong enough to explain most obesity, PMS, or SAD.

Prader-Willi syndrome: uncontrollable hunger

The genetic condition known as Prader-Willi syndrome, which is estimated to affect one of every 10,000 people, is one disorder in which distinctly abnormal desires for food inevitably lead to severe obesity. Among the many characteristics that develop in childhood are a voracious appetite and a constant search for food. Several recent reports have suggested that the syndrome may be caused by an abnormality in chromosome 15, which is thought to affect the appetite-control center of the hypothalamus.

Much more to learn

Medical scientists are just beginning to learn about food cravings. Like hunger and satiety, cravings (and aversions) undoubtedly begin with both peripheral (body) and central (brain) cues. However, these cues must be further refined by the brain on the basis of a host of stored experiences. These experiences, in turn, involve the individual's environment, culture, religion, and a number of other factors.

Until the exact causes of food cravings are unraveled, it is important to try to understand their effects. Most are harmless, particularly if they are infrequent. Sometimes, though infrequently, food cravings suggest an underlying medical condition, such as a craving for salt caused by adrenal insufficiency. Some cravings may be beneficial, such as under conditions of severe body stress or disease; others may be detrimental, particularly if associated with excess caloric intake. A particular danger is the craving for nonfood substances, some of which are extremely toxic.

As with any area where myths mingle with science, more research must be done before facts can be totally separated from fiction. In the meantime, food cravings will remain an interesting but not-well-understood phenomenon.

Graves' Disease
by Manfred Blum, M.D.

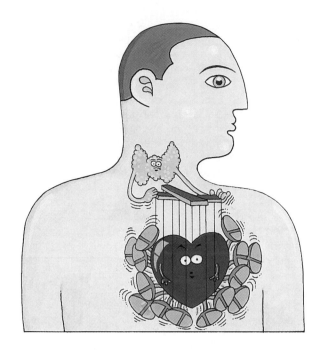

Graves' disease is a condition that affects many parts of the body and is usually associated with overactivity of the thyroid gland (hyperthyroidism). Descriptions of people with the typical manifestations of this disorder were recorded in antiquity. However, the modern awareness of its clinical characteristics comes from three almost simultaneous descriptions in the medical literature of the first half of the 19th century: by British physicians Caleb Parry and Robert Graves and the German physician Karl von Basedow. In English-speaking countries Graves is given primary credit for identifying the condition, while much of Europe continues to honor Basedow, calling it Basedow's disease.

It has been estimated that 4 of every 1,000 people have Graves' disease—more than one million in North America alone. Women are four to five times more likely to be afflicted than men. The disease occurs most commonly in young adults, but newborns, children, and older people may also be affected.

Clinical manifestations

Typical symptoms include bulging of the eyes, anxiety, irritability, intolerance of heat, excessive sweating, sleeplessness, fatigue, palpitations (rapid heartbeat) with a rapid or irregular pulse, shortness of breath, weight loss in spite of a good appetite, frequent loose bowel movements, tremor, muscle weakness, and clumsiness. Swelling of the neck may occur, but it is usually painless. Some patients develop a patchy loss of skin pigmentation (vitiligo). A rare complaint is swelling of the shin (pretibial myxedema).

In young people a shortened attention span, academic difficulties, and behavioral problems are sometimes the initial manifestations of Graves' disease. In female patients menstrual irregularity and a decreased frequency and duration of periods may be the symptoms that prompt them to seek medical attention. Older persons especially may experience severe muscle weakness or weight loss. An already existing medical condition can be magnified when Graves' disease develops. For instance, people with heart disease may experience angina (chest pain), irregular heartbeat, or congestive heart failure. An underlying psychiatric disorder also may be exacerbated.

Friends and family members may notice that the affected person's eyes seem to stare fixedly, move unusually, or protrude. The eye symptoms of Graves' disease can be mostly an annoyance—excessive tear-ing or a gritty, irritated sensation—but there may be disfigurement if the bulging of the eyes becomes pronounced. Functional impairment such as double vision is less common; in rare cases there may even be loss of vision. For as yet unknown reasons, the eye problems of Graves' disease may occur before, after, or concurrently with the symptoms of thyroid overactivity. Likewise, the eye problems may be either more or less severe than the hyperthyroidism.

The course of the thyroid manifestations is highly variable. Some people experience a single spurt of hyperthyroidism with no recurrence. Others have repeated cycles of thyroid overactivity that may be precipitated by emotional factors, physical trauma, or infections. Hyperthyroidism may alternate with periods of hypothyroidism (deficient thyroid activity).

Normal thyroid function

The thyroid gland is a fleshy structure located in the front of the neck just below the larynx. It consists of two lobes connected by the isthmus, a small piece of tissue that arches over the trachea.

The thyroid gland converts dietary iodide into a hormone that regulates many of the body's metabolic functions. (Iodides, substances containing iodine, are found naturally in seafood and are added to table salt as a dietary supplement.) The hormone is carried in the bloodstream by a binding protein; the bound hormone is not active. When required by the body, a minute proportion of the bound hormone is "unloaded" from the carrier protein. This unbound hormone can enter cells to regulate the production of proteins. The thyroid gland actively produces thyroxine, or T_4 (which contains four iodine atoms); T_4 is converted outside of the thyroid gland to triiodothyronine, or T_3 (containing three iodine atoms). T_3 is responsible for most of the function of thyroid hormone at the cellular level.

The pituitary gland regulates production of thyroid hormone by manufacturing thyrotropin, or thyroid-stimulating hormone (TSH), which enhances production of thyroid hormone in the thyroid gland. Increased amounts of circulating thyroid hormone reduce the production of TSH; a deficiency in thyroid hormone causes increased TSH production. The entire system is regulated by a part of the brain called the hypothalamus. This structure sends a chemical signal to the pituitary in the form of thyrotropin-releasing hormone (TRH), which also regulates TSH production.

Abnormal function

Usually too small to be noticeable, the thyroid may become obvious when it enlarges, a condition called goiter. Conditions that may cause enlargement of the thyroid gland include hyperthyroidism, hypothyroidism, development of uniform (smooth) or nodular goiters, inflammation of the thyroid (thyroiditis), and development of benign or malignant tumors. Another cause of abnormal swelling of the thyroid is iodine deficiency. Swelling can also occur normally in adolescents and pregnant women.

Thyrotoxicosis is a general name for any condition caused by an excess of thyroid hormone. Hyperthyroidism is the form of thyrotoxicosis in which the excessive thyroid hormone is actively produced by the thyroid gland. Thyrotoxicosis without hyperthyroidism may be caused by the ingestion of thyroid hormone or by thyroid inflammation, which causes the release of abnormally high levels of hormone. Hyperthyroidism is usually caused by abnormal regulation of the thyroid gland, and its most common cause is Graves' disease.

There are other causes of thyrotoxicosis. Spotty, nonregulated thyroid function (toxic nodular goiter) is a common reason for hyperthyroidism especially in older people. An uncommon cause is a benign thyroid tumor (an autonomous, or "hot," nodule). Excess of the normal regulator, TSH, caused by pituitary or hypothalamic abnormalities is very rare. Malignancies as a cause of hyperthyroidism are yet more rare. In some forms of hyperthyroidism, excessive intake of iodine may aggravate the condition; in others, iodine-containing medication may ameliorate it.

What causes Graves' disease?

The triggering mechanism of Graves' disease is not yet known. However, medical science does know that Graves' disease runs in families—yet it should be emphasized that it is not a contagious or infectious illness. Relatives of patients with the disease have an increased frequency of other autoimmune disorders—among them, thyroid goiter, hypothyroidism, rheumatoid arthritis, and pernicious anemia.

In autoimmune diseases the immune system mistakenly identifies the body's own tissues as "foreign" and attacks them. In the case of Graves' disease, it is thyroid tissue that is targeted. As a result of abnormal interactions between thyroid tissue and the immune system, cells of the immune system known as T-lymphocytes do not recognize the thyroid gland as normal body tissue, and they produce substances that destroy or alter it. T-lymphocytes direct another immune system component, the B-lymphocytes, to produce a variety of antibodies, called immunoglobulins, that have various effects on the thyroid. In Graves' disease one of these immunoglobulins, thyroid-stimulating immunoglobulin, or TSI, reacts with a chemical receptor that is normally activated by TSH. The receptor is stimulated by TSI to enhance thyroid function and to produce thyroid hormone. The elevated levels of T_4 and T_3 are then sensed by the pituitary gland, causing TSH to be suppressed.

Other antibody systems are also found in patients with autoimmune thyroid disease. Antibodies that occur in both hyperthyroid and hypothyroid conditions serve as useful markers in diagnosing such disorders. One of these, antithyroglobulin antibody, is directed against a protein (thyroglobulin) that serves as a reservoir for thyroid hormone. Another, antithyroid microsomal antibody, is directed against an enzyme that is necessary for the production of thyroid hormone. Some antibodies block rather than stimulate the TSH receptor, resulting in hypothyroidism.

Actually, enlargement of the thyroid gland due to an immunologic injury is more common than Graves' disease. This condition is called Hashimoto's disease and may be associated with normal thyroid function or hypothyroidism.

Insights into immune function help to explain the clustering of hyperthyroidism and hypothyroidism and other related disorders in families and the occurrence in the same person of hyperthyroidism at one time and hypothyroidism at another time. However, the specific factors that misdirect the immune system remain to be determined.

In addition to helping to explain epidemiological factors, knowledge of immune function is helpful in making a diagnosis. In evaluating a patient for suspected autoimmune thyroid disease, the physician may order a measurement of antithyroid antibodies. In some circumstances, when Graves' disease is suspected, a test for the presence of TSI may be done. Because this immunoglobulin crosses the placenta from a pregnant woman to her fetus, it is useful to measure the concentration of the material in a pregnant patient with Graves' disease in order to assess the risk of neonatal Graves' disease. Armed with this information, the obstetrician and the pediatrician are forewarned about the possibility of complications in the newborn.

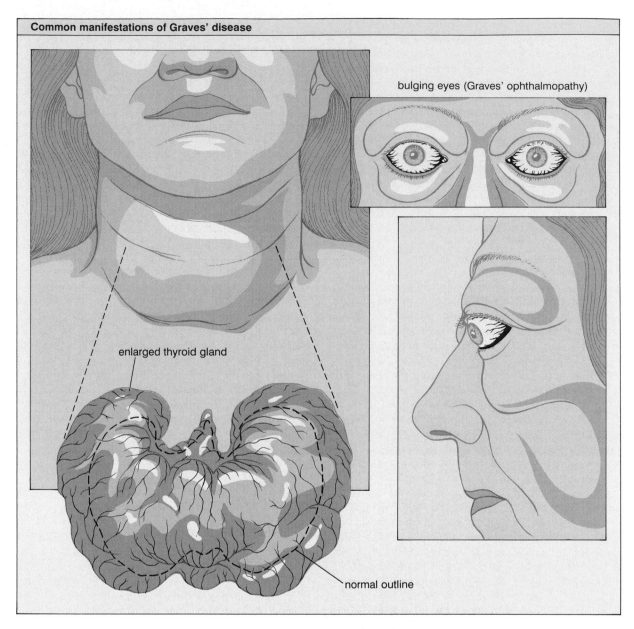

Common manifestations of Graves' disease

bulging eyes (Graves' ophthalmopathy)

enlarged thyroid gland

normal outline

Diagnosing Graves' disease

Tests are performed to assess thyroid function and to identify the various types of abnormalities. The amount of T_4, T_3, or both circulating in the blood is elevated in patients who suffer from hyperthyroidism due to Graves' disease. Because of cost and technical considerations, it is generally easier to measure the total level of bound rather than free thyroid hormone. However, when binding is excessive or deficient, this measurement can be elevated and yet not accurately reflect the level of active free hormone.

Genetic factors, disease, and medications can alter the binding of thyroid hormones. Binding will be high in conditions where there is excessive estrogen, such as pregnancy, when estrogen-containing medication

is used, or in the presence of liver disease. Binding will be reduced if there is inadequate production of binding protein or when, because of kidney disease, binding protein is lost in the urine.

An indirect assessment of binding called the T_3 resin test, in combination with the measurement of total T_4 and total T_3, allows calculation of the free-T_4 or free-T_3 index, which correlates reasonably well with the concentrations of the free hormones in the bloodstream. At times, the concentration of free hormone in the blood must be measured directly, which is more complicated and expensive. Even when there are binding abnormalities, however, the levels of free T_4 and T_3 are normal in people with proper thyroid function and elevated in those with hyperthyroidism.

Sometimes additional blood tests are required for understanding the meaning of elevated levels of T_4 and T_3. The most useful of these examinations employs the inverse relationship between the amounts of thyroid hormones and TSH circulating in the bloodstream. The blood level of TSH will be very low—or undetectable—when there is thyrotoxicosis unless there is a problem with the pituitary gland or hypothalamus (both exceedingly rare conditions). Measurement of TSH is especially useful in assessing thyroid function in older people who may have very few symptoms of the condition (so-called apathetic, or masked, hyperthyroidism) and in those with heart disease. A very sensitive assay, which became available in 1990, allows differentiation of normal levels at the low end of the spectrum and the suppressed TSH of thyrotoxic patients. When the diagnosis is in doubt, the physician may need to employ another test, the TRH test. This involves the injection of the hypothalamic hormone TRH; TSH is measured before and at intervals after the injection. Patients with hyperthyroidism typically have no TSH response to TRH, whereas there is a rise in TSH in people with normal thyroid function.

Thyroid tissue has an ability to accumulate, or concentrate, iodide. The thyroid gland needs iodide in order to produce T_3 and T_4. Measuring the accumulation of iodide can be useful in determining the cause of hyperthyroidism. It is accomplished by introducing into the body a small amount of radioactive iodine (RAI) and measuring its uptake by the thyroid gland, a process called the RAI uptake test. Since the test employs a very small amount of radioactive material, it is not done during pregnancy. RAI uptake is elevated in patients who have hyperthyroidism and is reduced when excessive iodide has been ingested, when thyroid medication has been taken, or in certain kinds of inflammation of the thyroid. One type of inflammation, silent thyroiditis, can be differentiated from actual hyperthyroidism only by the RAI uptake test.

Elevated RAI uptake does not necessarily indicate hyperthyroidism; the uptake may be high when there is a deficiency of iodide in the diet or an abnormality in the production of thyroid hormone. In the RAI uptake test, the distribution of radioactive iodine within the thyroid gland is measured by a scanning technique. Typically in Graves' disease, the distribution is uniform.

Eye problems

Like Graves' disease itself, the associated eye condition, also called Graves' orbitopathy or Graves' ophthalmopathy (or sometimes infiltrative ophthalmopathy), is thought to be caused by an autoimmune reaction. It is characterized by the infiltration of T lymphocytes into the extraocular muscles, which control normal movement of the eyeball. The time of onset is variable and, as noted above, the condition may appear before, with, or after the hyperthyroidism. The eye changes have been known to worsen after treatment of the thyroid dysfunction, but usually they improve once thyroid function has returned to normal.

The human eye sits in the front of a bony conical box, called the orbit, which contains the eye muscles and fat. The optic nerve runs through the center of the orbit, passing to the brain through a narrow canal at the apex of the cone. In Graves' disease inflammation and an accumulation of fluid (edema) within the orbit and behind the eye create increased pressure, thus pushing the eye forward. The protrusion may be sufficient to prevent proper covering by the eyelids. The resulting drying of the eye and its mucous membranes causes additional inflammation. In an attempt to improve the situation, the tear glands increase the flow of tears. However, damage to the mucous membranes of the eyelids and the sclera (outer covering of the eye) may occur, especially during sleep, when the lids fail to cover the eyes completely. The pressure may also squeeze the optic nerve, causing visual impairment. Inflammation injures the extraocular muscles by causing imbalance in their function, which may lead to double vision and occasionally to inability to move the eyes (paralysis of gaze).

Treatment

Treatment of Graves' disease must be tailored to the individual, taking into account the patient's age, sex, reproductive plans, life-style, and any concomitant medical problems. It is important that patients fully understand the risks and benefits of alternative therapies.

Medication. The first step is usually to relieve the most troublesome symptoms. This is best done by addressing those symptoms of thyroid hormone excess that mimic the effect of excessive adrenaline—most notably, the palpitations. Drugs such as propranolol (Inderal), which belong to a group of medicines called beta adrenergic blockers, are prescribed for this purpose. These medications slow the pulse and make the patient feel better, but they do not reduce the level of thyroid hormone, nor do they address the cause of the disease in any other way.

The hyperthyroidism itself is treated by reducing the level of thyroid hormone. One method of accomplishing this is with medication to reduce the production of thyroid hormone. Antithyroid drugs such as propylthiouracil (available only as a generic) and methimazole (Tapazole) inhibit the conversion of iodide to thyroxine within the thyroid gland and thus block production of thyroid hormone. Drug therapy must be continued for months or years. The patient must be monitored closely, with periodic examinations and testing. The dose can then be adjusted so that the level of circulating thyroid hormone is kept in the normal range. The medication must be taken regularly to maintain adequate regulation. Another drug regimen that has been advocated intermittently over the years

Graves' disease

and that is again under consideration involves the long-term use of a large amount of an antithyroid drug, along with another medication, L-thyroxine, which prevents the patient from becoming hypothyroid. Although these medications do not profoundly influence Graves' disease, large doses are believed to have a beneficial effect on the immune abnormality of the disease. Recurrence is common after drug therapy is stopped.

Patients taking propylthiouracil or methimazole must be monitored because of the possibility of serious side effects. The untoward effects are rare, but they require prompt notification of the physician and usually discontinuation of the drug. The most serious adverse effect is agranulocytosis—a reduction in the white blood cell count that can result in fever, sore throat, and severe infections. A decrease in platelets, components of the blood necessary for normal clotting, can result in bruising and a bleeding tendency. Itching, rash, and hives may also occur. Less common side effects include abnormalities of the liver, swelling of the joints, and swelling of the lymph nodes.

Especially in young people with Graves' disease, the immunologic stimulation of the thyroid gland abates over a period of months or years; when such remission occurs, antithyroid medication may be discontinued. When this is the case—or if antithyroid drugs cannot be used owing to intolerance or because the thyroid gland is too large—a portion of the thyroid gland must be removed or destroyed either surgically or with radioactive iodine. Large amounts of nonradioactive iodides can reduce the level of thyroxine temporarily, and these medications are sometimes used as ancillary agents in management of Graves' disease.

Surgery. Surgical removal of part of the thyroid gland (subtotal thyroidectomy) was the mainstay of treatment prior to the 1940s, but it is seldom done today. Before surgery can be performed, however, it is necessary either to interfere with the effect of thyroxine (using a beta-blocking drug) or to reduce thyroid hormone levels (with antithyroid drugs). This precaution is essential to the prevention of a complication of thyroid surgery, called thyroid storm, which may be fatal. Furthermore, iodides are administered for one to two weeks prior to the surgery to make the thyroid gland less bloody.

Thyroid surgery entails certain unavoidable risks. Among them is injury to the parathyroid glands, four small organs located adjacent to, or embedded in, the thyroid. If these glands are damaged or removed, the body's ability to metabolize calcium is compromised. The recurrent laryngeal nerves, which control the vocal cords and lie very close to the thyroid gland, can also be injured, resulting in hoarseness. Bleeding may occur and cause pressure on the trachea, interfering with breathing. Surgery also entails anesthesia, which always carries with it certain risks.

It is often difficult for the surgeon to assess how much thyroid tissue must be removed. Occasionally, hyperthyroidism persists even after the surgery; in some cases the patient may become hypothyroid and thereafter need to take thyroid medication.

Radioactive iodine therapy. Most mature adults with Graves' disease are treated with radioactive iodine, the least expensive and simplest form of treatment currently available. Radioactive iodine concentrates in the thyroid gland just as nonradioactive iodide does. However, one form of radioactive iodine, the isotope I-131, emits energy that destroys tissue in immediate contact with it. Since other tissues do not concentrate iodine to the extent that the thyroid does, only the thyroid gland is subject to a significant portion of the destructive effects of the radiation.

The benefits from treating hyperthyroidism with radioactive iodine far outweigh potential risks. It is considered to be a safe procedure for most adults and may be used in some children. As in diagnosis, radioactive iodine is not employed in treatment when there is a possibility that the patient may be pregnant. No untoward side effects have been reported except that most patients who take radioactive iodine eventually become hypothyroid and require lifelong thyroid medication; anyone who has received radioactive iodine therapy must be monitored for life. There is no evidence that it causes an increased incidence of cancer in the thyroid or elsewhere.

Therapy in pregnancy. Pregnant women with Graves' disease may require treatment with propylthiouracil to control their hyperthyroidism. Since the drug crosses the placenta, the dose must be minimized to reduce the risk of goiter or hypothyroidism developing in the fetus. It is best for women to avoid nursing when they are taking this drug. Iodides are not used in management of hyperthyroidism during pregnancy or in nursing mothers. Occasionally, surgical removal of the thyroid may be required; the second trimester seems to be the best time.

Therapy for the eye. The treatment of the eye problems in Graves' disease must address the patient's particular complaints. If the eye changes are minimal, no specific treatment is needed. Mild symptoms can be treated by elevating the head at night and placing pads over the lids to cover the eyes. Eye drops that reduce the evaporation of tears are also helpful. Double vision can sometimes be managed with prism eyeglasses. In severe cases the inflammation may be reduced with anti-inflammatory agents such as cortisone, but such drugs can have untoward side effects when used on a long-term basis. Sometimes radiation therapy to the region behind the eyes is employed. In some cases, ophthalmologic surgery may be required for managing the muscle problems or enlarging the orbit, allowing the swollen tissue room to expand.

Lip Sores

by Robert M. Ossoff,
D.M.D., M.D., and
Michael J. Koriwchak, M.D.

Sores on the lip are a common complaint. They range from self-healing sores caused by drug reactions or minor infections to lesions that represent early cancer of the lip. Some lip sores may be due to local trauma; others are signs of systemic disease. Most are not serious and may heal spontaneously. However, a sore on the lip that does not go away within three weeks of its discovery may be an early cancer; it should be brought to the attention of a physician immediately.

Aphthous ulcers (canker sores, cold sores)

Aphthous ulcers, also called aphthous stomatitis, are among the most common lip sores as well as the most uncomfortable—the word *aphthous* is derived from a Greek word meaning "to set on fire."

Aphthous ulcers may occur singly or in clusters. The sore typically has a depressed, craterlike white center surrounded by a red rim. The ulcer is usually several millimeters across but not more than one centimeter (0.39 in) in diameter. However, large, or major, aphthous ulcers may grow to two or three centimeters in diameter.

The cause of aphthous ulcers in unknown. They may be due to bacteria or viruses. Other theories cite nutritional deficiencies (iron, folic acid, or vitamin B_{12}) or problems with the individual's immune system as factors in the development of aphthous ulcers. They may also be precipitated by physical trauma (such as a burn or accidental bite), emotional stress, allergies, or exposure to irritating foods such as tomatoes, hot peppers, spicy foods, and alcohol. Some people seem to be particularly predisposed to developing them, although no one knows why.

Aphthous ulcers usually heal spontaneously within two weeks, but some cases require a physician's attention. Treatment consists of a pain-relieving preparation applied directly to the sore or used as an oral rinse, usually before meals. Examples include lidocaine and diphenhydramine (Benadryl) in viscous form. Some authorities believe that steroid preparations such as triamcinolone acetonide (Kenalog in Orabase) applied to the ulcer accelerate healing. Others recommend a tetracycline antibiotic in liquid form that is held in the mouth and then swallowed. *Lactobacillus acidophilus,* a harmless bacterium commonly found in dairy products, taken in capsule form may reduce the frequency and severity of recurrent aphthous ulcers. Occasionally, aphthous ulcers are so severe that the pain interferes with eating and drinking. Severe cases may be treated with steroids taken by mouth. None of these treatments has actually been proved to accelerate healing or prevent recurrence. However, they do maximize the comfort of the patient, allowing adequate food and fluid intake until the ulcers heal.

Herpes labialis (fever blisters)

Herpes labialis (from the Latin *labium,* "lip") is also very common. The herpes simplex viruses are among the best known members of the family that also includes the viruses that cause chickenpox and shingles. There are two forms of the herpesvirus: herpes simplex type 1, or HSV-1, which is most commonly found in the oral cavity and on the lips, and herpes simplex type 2, or HSV-2, which is more commonly associated with genital herpes. However, either HSV-1 or HSV-2 may be found in the mouth or on the genitalia.

The first infection with HSV-1 usually occurs early in childhood. Often, however, the first infection produces no symptoms and passes unnoticed. In some cases a distinct illness develops after an individual's first exposure to the virus, characterized by multiple scattered sores on the lips and mouth and accompanied by fever, sore throat, and enlarged lymph nodes (swollen glands) in the neck. Headache and other flulike symptoms such as muscle aches may also be present.

The sores of herpes labialis follow a distinct evolution in appearance. First, very small reddened areas develop. These give rise to vesicles, or tiny, tender blisters. The vesicles rupture, producing a cluster of ulcers. Those ulcers around the outer edges of the lips near the skin of the face may develop a crust. The ulcers heal spontaneously within 10 to 14 days. Virus capable of causing infection is shed from the mouth and lips throughout this process until the ulcers are nearly healed. Oral herpes is therefore quite contagious during the time that vesicles and ulcers are visible. In order to prevent spread of the virus to other parts of the body, patients are cautioned not to touch the sores with their fingers. Herpes infection of the eye may be very serious. Kissing and other direct skin contact should be avoided. The sharing of eating utensils, lipsticks, and the like should be discouraged.

After the primary infection, oral herpes can recur for the rest of the infected individual's life at intervals varying from a few weeks to several years. The virus migrates upward into the nerves that supply sensation to the mouth and lips. Subsequent episodes of oral herpes take place when the virus migrates back down the nerve endings. This migration may be triggered by fever (hence the name fever blisters), stress, the menstrual period, trauma, or sun exposure. Shortly before the sores appear, a burning or tingling sensation develops at the site. The sores follow the same pattern of development as in the primary infection. They also shed herpesvirus and are therefore contagious. Sores of recurrent infections resolve somewhat faster than those of the primary infection.

As in the case of aphthous ulcers, treatment of oral herpes is aimed primarily at maximizing patient comfort through use of the drugs mentioned above. The antiviral medication acyclovir, which slows the rate of virus reproduction, may help the ulcers heal faster. However, once the herpesvirus has entered the body, no treatment can eliminate it. People who have recurrent herpes labialis when exposed to the sun should either avoid exposure or apply a maximal-protection sun block to the lips.

The sores of herpes labialis and aphthous ulcers are very similar, but there are ways to tell them apart. The aphthous ulcer never takes a blisterlike form. Therefore, any vesicles observed on the lips are more likely to be herpes than aphthous ulcers. The two types of ulcers vary in location as well. Aphthous ulcers tend to occur on the inside of the lip rather than around the edges. The ulcers of herpes are more common on the outside of the lip, near the border of the lip and the skin of the face. Still, these two kinds of lesions are often confused, and they may even be misdiagnosed by physicians. Complicating the problem further are ulcers of unknown cause called herpetiform ulcers, which are virtually identical in appearance to herpes labialis.

Other lip sores

A variety of lip sores may be caused by trauma (from lip biting, badly misaligned teeth, or poorly fitting dentures), burns, infections, allergies, and drug reactions. Those that recur frequently or do not heal should receive medical attention to correct the underlying problem.

Among the worst of lip sores from drug reactions is erythema multiforme. It is characterized by the rapid development of extensive vesicles or ulcerative sores or both. These individual lesions fuse and then are covered by a pseudomembrane, or thin coating, which peels off easily to reveal the raw, ulcerated surface of the lip. This disorder may be triggered by a rare reaction to sulfa-type antibiotics or by certain infections. It is sometimes also caused by recurrent oral herpes infection, which may make the diagnosis more difficult. Suspected cases should be evaluated by a physician.

Angular cheilitis is a yeast infection of the corners of the mouth, characterized by angular cracks, or fissures. It is common in elderly individuals who have lost their teeth and either do not have dentures or do not wear them. It is caused by a lack of support inside the mouth, which teeth or dentures normally provide. Treatment may include antifungal, antibiotic, and anti-inflammatory drugs.

A mucocoele appears as a smooth, round nodule, usually on the lower lip, that may fluctuate in size. It is common among those who bite their lips. Fibrolipomas also occur frequently in lip biters.

The ulcer, or chancre, that is characteristic of primary syphilis appears as a single hard lesion on the lip, accompanied by swollen glands in the neck. The chancre itself, which is painless, becomes evident approximately three weeks after the individual contracts the syphilis bacterium.

Lip cancer

Cancer of the lip may appear very similar to any of the benign lip sores described above. It occurs most frequently in elderly men; the lesion usually appears near the center of the lower lip. In women, however, the upper lip is more commonly involved. When discovered and treated in the early stages, lip cancer has a cure rate of greater than 90%. However, more advanced cancers require extensive, potentially disfiguring surgery, and even after such an operation, as many as 50% recur. For this reason, doctors emphasize the importance of seeking an expert opinion about any sore of the lip that does not heal within at least three weeks of its discovery.

Port-Wine Stains
by Elliot Lach, M.D.

Birthmarks associated with abnormal blood vessels in the skin are the most common congenital deformity in humans. Because there is no standardized terminology to describe these abnormalities, definitions can be quite confusing. In general, birthmarks follow one of two main developmental courses, which allow them to be differentiated and classified as either hemangiomas or vascular malformations.

Hemangiomas, sometimes called strawberry hemangiomas, are raised reddish or purplish growths. They enlarge very rapidly during the first 12 months of life but usually disappear spontaneously, either partially or completely, by the childhood years. While a hemangioma is growing, however, it may cause pain, infection, or troublesome bleeding. Permanent deformities can result, especially if there is incomplete regression of a hemangioma on the face. On the other hand, vascular malformations—the most common of which are called port-wine stains—usually continue to grow larger as the individual gets older; they do not disappear. Growth may be accelerated by hormonal stimulus, trauma, or certain infections. Often, however, there are no accompanying medical complications. Furthermore, a vascular malformation is always present at birth to some degree, although it is not always obvious, whereas a hemangioma may not appear for several days or weeks.

A port-wine stain is also known medically as a nevus flammeus and should not be confused with the temporary pink staining that is seen over the nape of the neck or on the forehead of many newborns; the latter (nevus flammeus neonatorum) is a harmless lesion often called a "stork bite," "angel's kiss," or "salmon patch." There is frequently a familial history of nevus flammeus neonatorum, and parents should be reassured that it is both benign and transitory.

Incidence and location
Port-wine stains occur in approximately 3 out of every 1,000 people. They are found in persons of all races, although they are most visible in individuals of Caucasian and Asian ancestry. The medical literature does document some instances of families in which port-wine stains have been passed from generation to generation, but for the most part hereditary predisposition is not believed to be a factor in their development. The incidence among males and females is identical (in contrast to hemangiomas, which affect females three times as often).

All vascular malformations of the skin consist of overgrown and improperly formed blood vessels. Any one vessel or several—capillary, artery, vein, or lymphatic vessel—can be involved. The lesion may occur virtually anywhere on the body, although typically a single area is affected. Port-wine stains occur most commonly on the head and neck, and nearly half of these are located on areas of facial skin supplied with sensation by the trigeminal nerve. They may be as small as a pinhead or cover an entire limb or even an entire side of the body. Although the stain is most often limited to one side, some individuals have staining on both, with one typically being less extensive. The lips, tongue, and mucous membranes of the mouth can also be stained.

Development and changes with aging
Scientists are not yet certain how or when vascular malformations of the skin originate. It is known that the capillaries of the skin develop quite early, somewhere between 3½ and 4 months of gestation. It is probably during this period that the permanent changes resulting in a port-wine stain occur. The exact defect involves convoluted capillaries in the skin that are dilated (overstretched) and abnormally thin walled.

At birth the stain is flat, and its texture is the same as that of the surrounding skin. The character and color of the birthmark change as the individual ages. In a young child the lesion may be light pink, deepening to bright red with crying, emotional outbursts, or exposure to cold. During adolescence and adulthood the color darkens, turning finally to a deep purple as the blood within the capillaries diffuses throughout the layers of the skin as it thickens with age.

459

As the lesion matures, the skin in the area will thicken sometimes to the point of causing severe deformities, especially when the port-wine stain is located on or adjacent to the lip, cheek, or eyelid. The lesion gradually takes on a characteristic bumpy appearance described as "cobblestoning." Small tumors in the skin, known as pyogenic granulomas, are typically seen in the port-wine stains of adult patients. These tumors probably arise from minor trauma; some appear spontaneously. Although they are not malignant, pyogenic granulomas are frequently a source of irritating bleeding and further disfigurement. Surgical removal is usually the best option. In addition to the visible changes seen on the surface of the skin, many people with port-wine stains at some stage experience some degree of pain from them.

Associated physical problems

In certain cases there may be a more complex and extensive vascular malformation located deep within the skin lesion. This in turn may result in disabling and disfiguring overgrowth of structures beneath the stain, including bone, muscle, or nerves. Glaucoma of one eye can be another serious complication. It develops in nearly half of those who have a facial port-wine stain that involves the sensory distribution of the upper two branches of the trigeminal nerve. It is not yet known whether the development of glaucoma, which leads to blindness, can be prevented or reversed with removal of the port-wine stain itself.

A port-wine stain may also be a sign of an underlying, sometimes extremely serious condition. For example, the features of Sturge-Weber syndrome can include a port-wine stain as well as many pathological structural changes on the face and body. In the congenital neural tube defect known as meningomyelocele, there is often a characteristic port-wine stain on the affected individual's back.

Psychological consequences

In many cases a port-wine stain is limited to the skin and has no secondary or underlying manifestations aside from the progressive thickening of the skin. The psychological impact of a highly visible birthmark can be devastating, however, even when no physical disability is involved. Because of its obviousness, a port-wine birthmark on the face may cause significant problems. The individual may suffer from embarrassment, self-consciousness, shyness, or low self-esteem, and in some cases the disfigurement may affect the person's ability to make friends and function socially. Even in ancient times such birthmarks were considered a social problem. In the Talmud, the ancient compendium of Jewish law, it was written that "red skin"—presumably a reference to port-wine stains—was a blemish that could disqualify a man from the priesthood, probably because it would be a focus of

attention that would detract from his performance of ritual duties.

Children with port-wine stains are often asked if they have spilled grape juice on their skin or need to have their faces washed. Sometimes the stains are a source of cruel teasing, provoking nicknames such as "pinkface," "cherry-cheek," or "acidface." When families are supportive, however, and work to reinforce the child's self-esteem, they can provide invaluable help in coping with the cosmetic aspects of these birthmarks. The vast majority of affected individuals have adjusted well to their situations.

Superstitions about birthmarks

Many misguided theories have been put forth over the centuries to explain the occurrence of birthmarks, whether of vascular or of other origin. In many cultures people believed that certain rituals performed in association with conception could influence either or both parents in a way that would be reflected in the physical characteristics of the offspring. Probably the earliest example of this notion of parental impression is found in the Bible (Genesis, chapter 30), where it is written that Jacob increased the numbers of rare spotted goats and sheep in his herds by standing tree branches, with the bark partly removed so that they too appeared spotted, in the water troughs of the breeding animals. In a similar manner, mimetic rituals were believed to influence the course of human development.

The Chaldeans of ancient Babylonia regarded birthmarks and other birth defects as divine omens. In their writings specific congenital disorders were linked to certain predictable outcomes in a dependable "if, then" formulation. If, for example, a woman gives birth to an infant who has "branches of flesh" on its head (probably a reference to hemangiomas), "there will be ill-will" and the family will perish.

The concept of maternal or paternal impression remains the most popular folk explanation for port-wine stains, hemangiomas, and indeed most other birth defects. The 16th-century French surgeon Ambroise Paré wrote that some of his contemporaries thought that beyond the 42nd day after conception it was not possible to affect the appearance of a child through the "mother's imagination," as the infant was already fully formed. Paré himself believed that for safety's sake women should be protected throughout pregnancy from the sight of any deformities.

In the 19th century, exposure of a prospective mother to "objects of desire or aversion" was cited by the Philadelphia physician Thomas Bateman as a popular albeit illogical explanation for birthmarks. It was supposed that a woman who was overcome by a craving for strawberries during pregnancy would give birth to a child with a birthmark resembling the fruit. Similarly, if a pregnant woman was frightened by the sight of her husband with a bloody wound on his face, the baby was certain to be born with a red birthmark on its face.

Still another theory regarded vascular birthmarks as a sign of divine preference or blessing; hence the term "angel's kiss." While the explanations of different cultures vary widely, all grew out of the same need: families, and the affected persons themselves, had to have a way to account for the occurrence of something that marked them so distinctively.

Traditional modes of treatment

Because of both physical and psychosocial concerns, each individual must decide how he or she will live with a port-wine stain and whether to seek medical intervention. One way of concealing a port-wine stain of the face is with an opaque makeup. Applying it, however, can be a time-consuming process; further, although the lesion can be totally camouflaged, cosmetics cannot halt its progressive enlargement or the gradual thickening of the skin. Thus, many people have preferred to opt for removal. Many methods of removing a port-wine stain have been tried over the years.

Irradiation. Shortly after X-rays were first introduced in 1895, extended exposure to high-energy irradiation was used to cause superficial blistering and burning of the skin in persons with port-wine stains. It was hoped that the lesion could be obliterated and that the resultant scar would be preferable in appearance to the birthmark. Gamma rays, similar to X-rays, continued to be employed for this purpose into the 20th century, but the risk of developing a malignancy precluded their widespread use. Effective treatment without further disfiguration could not be achieved reliably with radiation.

Burning, freezing, cauterization. Various chemical scarification agents, including carbolic acid, mercurial plasters, and others, were also used in the past, again the replacement of the birthmark with scar tissue

being regarded as the lesser of two evils. Extensive electrical cauterization has had similar results. Other less-than-satisfactory methods have included freezing by exposure to liquid nitrogen or carbon dioxide snow (dry ice).

Tattooing. The attempt to mask port-wine stains with pigments introduced into the skin via tattooing has gone into and out of vogue for over 150 years. With this process a skin lesion may initially be completely impregnated with pigment and thus hidden, but the dynamic nature of a port-wine stain causes the tattoo, sometimes in as little as a few months, to be completely obliterated by the development of new blood vessels at the site of the original stain. Sometimes a yellow, green, or brown discoloration may persist. Tattooing also can lead to further disfigurement and grotesque skin alterations.

Surgery. Until very recently the only guaranteed method for removing a port-wine stain was surgical excision. This involves an operation in which all of the layers of the skin in the area of the lesion are removed. If the lesion is extensive, a skin graft must be applied to close the surgical wound. The port-wine stain is removed once and for all, and the skin is replaced with "normal" skin harvested from other sites on the patient's body. Surgery has been used for both small and large stains with some success.

In addition to all of the risks posed by any major surgical procedure—including those associated with general anesthesia—and the pain of undergoing an extensive operation, there are other drawbacks. One is that the grafted skin does not match the surrounding skin, having a different color and texture. It will also lack the sensibility of natural skin. Furthermore, if an extensive lesion is removed, there will be a need for a large amount of replacement skin and, possibly, for blood transfusions. Nonetheless, some patients considered these to be acceptable risks, and for them the surgery was preferable to living with a disfiguring birthmark.

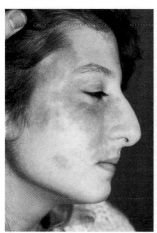 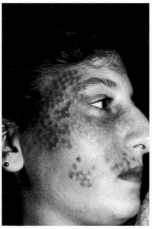 

Now that successful laser treatment is available, surgery is no longer the only effective method for removing a port-wine stain. These photographs, taken over a 10-month period, show a patient with an extensive port-wine stain (left), immediately following one of seven treatments with the tunable dye laser (center), and after the completion of the process (right).

Elliot Lach, M.D., University of Massachusetts Medical Center

Lasers: new light on the problem

Enthusiasm for the medical applications of laser technology has grown steadily since the first laser was developed in 1960. Lasers produce narrow beams of intense light that can be very precisely focused. Laser light is monochromatic—that is, the light waves are derived from a narrow band of wavelengths (in contrast to conventional light, which is composed of a broad spectrum of wavelengths). The beam is preferentially, or selectively, absorbed by materials with a similar wavelength-absorption profile, which means that specific biological substances (such as pigments) can be targeted by different kinds of lasers. After laser light is absorbed by the molecules of the targeted material, part of the light energy is converted to heat. This heat is so profound as to cause living tissues to boil, coagulate, or be vaporized.

Argon lasers, which were developed in the early 1970s, have been used in the treatment of vascular lesions, including port-wine stains, for many years. The argon laser emits a blue-green light that has both a 488-nanometer (nm; a billionth of a meter) and a 514-nm wavelength. The treatment is based on the principal that hemoglobin, the pigment that gives blood its red color, is absorbent of these wavelengths. As the light energy is absorbed and concentrated in the vessel walls of the port-wine stain, the blood-filled capillaries coagulate and are permanently obliterated.

While many people have been treated successfully with the argon laser, the procedure is not without problems. Melanin, a skin pigment that is also absorbent at these wavelengths, competes with hemoglobin for the laser energy and decreases the efficiency of treatment. Moreover, the result of laser light interaction with both hemoglobin and melanin is the production of heat, which, in turn, causes pain. Anesthesia is therefore necessary. Healing following argon laser treatment is usually similar to healing following a second-degree burn. A certain percentage of patients—especially children—have unacceptable scarring following argon laser treatment. Automated scanning devices are now used to reduce the total exposure time of the skin to the argon laser light, but they have not completely eliminated complications from scarring or the need for anesthesia.

Because hemoglobin actually absorbs light better in the 530–580-nm spectrum of wavelengths than at 488 or 514 nm, further research was undertaken to develop a laser beam that could be fine-tuned to the appropriate wavelength. A wavelength was chosen that was sufficiently far away from melanin's absorption to spare surrounding tissue but close enough to that of hemoglobin to damage abnormal capillaries. Further refinements of the process by researchers at Harvard Medical School in the mid-1980s produced a so-called flashlamp pumped pulsed tunable dye laser, which emits a laser light with many useful characteristics.

First, because a flashlamp is used to generate, or pump, the laser, energy is released in instantaneous pulses—as opposed to the continuous beam of the argon laser. This greatly reduces the amount of heat that is generated. Second, the color of the light is closely controlled, or tuned, by being passed through a dye-containing liquid (hence the term *tunable dye laser*). The light is tuned to a yellowish wavelength of 585 nm, which is extremely selective in targeting hemoglobin. Only dilated capillaries close to the skin's surface absorb the laser beam and are injured in the process. Normal blood vessels, which would not be unusually dilated and are located in deeper layers of the skin, do not become coagulated, and hair follicles and sweat glands are selectively spared. Other abnormal vessels in the skin, such as so-called spider veins, can also be targeted.

Because of the reduction in the amount of heat generated, the pain is much less severe than with argon laser treatment. Each pulse lasts just 450 millionths of a second. The process might be compared to the action of rapidly passing an unprotected finger through a candle flame and experiencing neither pain nor a burn. If the finger were to remain in the flame for even one second, of course, a deep and painful burn could result. Most patients receiving the new treatment do not require anesthesia; they feel only a stinging sensation like the snap of a rubber band against the skin.

Another important consideration is the usefulness of this treatment for children's port-wine stains. Because of the risk of unsatisfactory scarring, most physicians have tried to avoid treating children with the argon laser. It is this group, however, that is perhaps the most traumatized by having a highly visible birthmark. By the time a youngster is old enough to safely undergo argon laser treatment, permanent emotional scarring may already have taken its toll. In addition, any overgrowth of skin in the lesion—which can be avoided by early treatment—will have become well established.

With the tunable dye laser, treatment of children as young as two days old has thus far proved to be safe, and those who practice the technique expect the healing process to be virtually without significant complications. In fact, preliminary experience indicates that the earliest possible treatment may be the most effective, as the immature blood vessels of the newborn respond well to the process.

Because the laser light is highly selective, it is not always possible to eliminate the troublesome vessels in a single session; thus, repeat treatments are often necessary, especially for a port-wine stain that is well established in mature skin. The size of the area treated in a single session ranges from relatively small (the size of, say, a dime) to relatively large (dollar-bill-size), depending on the physician's judgment. A

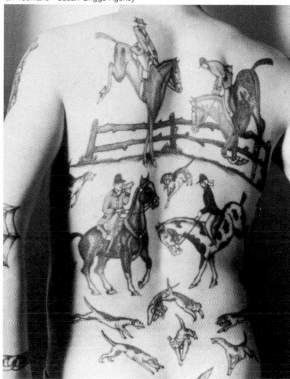

The desire for a tattoo may pass but, as many people unhappily discover, the tattoo itself is all too permanent. Now a new laser technology makes possible the removal of these once-ineradicable pigmented marks.

single session may take anywhere from 5 minutes for a small lesion to 20 minutes for a large one. Immediately afterward the treated skin will turn a grayish blue color. This discoloration, which lasts from 3 to 12 days, is due to the presence of coagulated blood in the capillaries of the port-wine stain. The redness of the original lesion will then return but will clear over the course of the next three to four weeks. There is a localized feeling of warmth following treatment, a result of low-level inflammation at the treatment site.

Following treatment, the patient is advised to avoid aspirin or aspirin-containing products because these may promote bleeding in the skin. On occasion there may be slight blistering in the treated area, or a scab-like crust may form. Sunscreen should be applied before exposure to sunlight and ultraviolet sources (including fluorescent light) for several months after treatment, as there may be a tendency toward increased tanning of the treated skin. This precaution is especially important if the lesion requires more than one treatment—the increased deposition of melanin that occurs with tanning can keep laser light from reaching the abnormal vessels. Makeup should not be applied to the treated area until the bluish discoloration disappears.

Following the initial treatment session, the lesion will lighten either slightly or appreciably. Treated skin is then usually reexamined at six- to eight-week intervals. From one to six sessions are needed to determine if maximal clearing has taken place and to decide if further treatments are necessary. If the blood vessels of the port-wine stain are particularly large and deep or if the lesion is located on the legs, the tunable dye laser may not completely obliterate the stain. The incidence of scarring from this new procedure has been extremely low or insignificant when treatment is administered by a qualified physician. Specialists trained in plastic surgery and dermatology are administering laser treatment at many major medical centers throughout the United States. The technique is also widely available in Japan and Australia, and treatment centers are currently being established in Europe as well. Compared with the cost of cosmetic surgery procedures or any major surgery, the cost of pulsed tunable dye laser treatment is low.

Unwanted tattoos

A similar pulsed laser technology is now being used to treat other pigmented targets in the skin, including tattoos and the brown spots commonly called "age spots" or "liver spots." The laser used in this process is a Q-switched ruby laser. The Q-switch is an electronic device that permits the laser energy to be intensified and released in bursts lasting only billionths of a second (as opposed to millionths with the tunable dye laser). The thermal energy released is so instantaneous that the skin is not appreciably injured, and the risk of scarring is thus minimized. Light released from the ruby is in the red spectrum at 694 nm, a wavelength that causes tattoo pigments, especially those containing carbon, to fragment and vaporize. Dark-colored tattoos containing black, brown, and blue pigments, in which carbon is a major ingredient, are more absorbent at this wavelength and respond better to laser treatment than do other colors such as yellow, green, or red. It is possible, though, that other colors will be found to respond well, as they may be made from formulas that contain susceptible pigments.

FOR FURTHER INFORMATION:
Sources of information on locating a board-certified physician who treats vascular birthmarks are:
American Society of Plastic and Reconstructive Surgeons
444 East Algonquin Road
Arlington Heights, IL 60005

American Society for Laser Medicine and Surgery
2404 Stewart Square
Wausau, WI 54401

Flatfeet

by John Robinson

Low-arched feet—a clinical condition known as pes planus but more commonly called flatfeet—have typically been considered undesirable. This prejudice is based on both aesthetic considerations and a belief that flatfeet may increase the risk of injury to the lower extremities. In the United States for years—until 1990, in fact—men with flatfeet were routinely barred from military service because of their presumed higher risk of injury. In addition, coaches traditionally believed that runners and other athletes with flatfeet were at a disadvantage because high-arched feet were considered more rigid, providing an appropriate lever for sprinting.

The bias against flatfeet is not a strictly modern development, however. Early Arab writings indicate that a high arch, pes cavus, was considered a trait of feminine beauty; the feet of comely women were described as "so arched that little streams can run beneath." Flatfeet have also been identified with awkwardness and clumsiness. Although scientific research seldom changes the cultural perception of grace and beauty, recent studies indicate that the association of pes planus and foot injury is not what had been supposed.

Arch structure

The 26 bones of the foot form three arches—the medial longitudinal arch, the lateral longitudinal arch, and the transverse arch (*see* diagram, page 466). The calcaneus (heel bone), talus (ankle bone), navicular bone, cuneiform bones, the first three metatarsals, and the sesamoid bones make up the medial longitudinal arch. The posterior (rear) base of this arch is formed by the tuber calcanei, two prominent points also called the medial and lateral processes of the calcaneus. The first three metatarsals form the anterior (front) foundation.

The lateral longitudinal arch often cannot be seen when the foot is bearing the body's weight. It is formed by the calcaneus, the cuboid bone, and the fourth and fifth metatarsals. The tuber calcanei is the posterior base of support; the distal heads of the fourth and fifth metatarsals form the anterior foundation.

The transverse arch is perpendicular to and an integral part of both longitudinal arches. Formed by the cuneiforms, cuboid, and metatarsals, it is difficult to observe because of surrounding soft tissue.

Infants' and children's feet. Even though the arches are formed early in the development of the foot, there is a common misconception that babies' feet are flat. In one study, for example, 97% of the 18-month-olds

examined were characterized as having flatfeet, compared with only 4% of the 10-year-olds. The fact is that infants have large subcutaneous fat pads in the soles of their feet; fat thus fills in the arches, giving feet the appearance of being flat. These fat deposits can persist for up to two years before they gradually disappear. Parents who are worried because their child has flatfeet should consider this natural course of development before resorting to corrective measures.

Male versus female. Although human sexual dimorphism (the differences in body size and shape of men and women) has been studied extensively, relatively little is known about differences in foot structure. One recent study reported significant differences in arch height between men and women. In this study two measurements—dorsum height and navicular height—were used. Dorsum height is the distance between the floor and the highest point on the top, or instep, of the foot at 50% of foot length. Navicular height is the distance between a specific point on the underside of the navicular bone and the floor. Differences in arch height between men and women were apparent only when comparisons were made with respect to foot length. For example, men and women were found to have a similar average total dorsum height index (dorsum height per foot length) of 0.26, but for a given foot length, the men had greater dorsum height index values—*i.e.*, higher arches—than women. The high-heeled shoes often worn by women have not been shown to detrimentally affect arch structure. They do cause other foot problems, however.

Natural arch support

Three factors combine to maintain the integrity of the arches—bone structure, ligamentous connections, and muscle activity. To use an architectural analogy, if the bones of the foot are akin to stones in an arch, then the talus, the cuboid bone, and the intermediate cuneiform bone function as keystones; the talus provides support for the medial longitudinal arch, the cuboid bone for the lateral longitudinal arch, and the intermediate cuneiform bone for the transverse arch. The shape counteracts the tendency of the structure to collapse into the center. The articulated surface of the bones also provides support.

Although skeletal structure is important, without ligaments and muscles the arches would collapse. Plantar ligaments tie the inferior (lower) edges of the bones together, thus aiding arch support. The most important ligament in the maintenance of the medial longitudinal arch is the plantar calcaneonavicular, or spring, ligament. Because it attaches to (or "inserts" on) the calcaneus and the navicular bone, this ligament acts like a tie beam and supports the talus. The long and short plantar ligaments provide the main support for the lateral longitudinal arch. The deep transverse ligaments support the transverse arch.

The plantar aponeurosis, a sheet of tissue that extends from the calcaneus to the plantar pads of the metatarsophalangeal joint, provides arch support and is part of a mechanism to increase arch height. Extension of the toes causes the plantar aponeurosis to wrap around the heads of the metatarsal bones, shortening its effective length and increasing arch height. This mechanism of action is analogous to that of a windlass; the metatarsal head functions as the drum of the windlass and the plantar aponeurosis as the cable that is wound onto the drum.

The foot has both intrinsic muscles, originating in and inserting on the foot itself, and extrinsic mus-

After examining the arch structure of 300 army recruits, researchers concluded that, contrary to a long-held theory, low-arched feet are not prone to injury. Rather, flatfeet actually were associated with a decreased risk of training-related injury.

The New York Times, 1953

cles, originating in the leg and inserting on the foot. Several of the intrinsic muscles—*i.e.,* the abductor hallucis, flexor hallucis brevis, flexor digitorum brevis, and abductor digiti minimi—are positioned to support the longitudinal arch. Some of the extrinsic muscles (flexor hallucis longus, tibialis anterior, tibialis posterior, peroneus longus, and peroneus brevis) also help to stabilize the arches.

A study to determine the role of muscle activity in arch support found that men standing on one foot could support loads of 45–90 kg (100–200 lb) without any electromyographic evidence of muscle activity. (Electromyography is a method of recording the electrical currents in an active muscle.) Some muscles became active with loads of 180 kg (400 lb). This finding suggests that the primary nonskeletal mechanism of arch support is ligamentous and that muscle activity provides support only when loads become excessive. However, the muscles do become active during locomotion.

Some researchers believe that standing for long periods of time causes the arches to flatten. They suggest that in the absence of support from the relatively inactive intrinsic muscles, the arch-supporting ligaments stretch during standing, when the foot is loaded. These researchers believe that because the intrinsic muscles are active during locomotion, exercise may help to strengthen them and thus enhance their contribution to arch support. There is no conclusive evidence in favor of this theory, however.

Measuring arch height

Foot type is often characterized by arch height. Because both the lateral longitudinal arch and the transverse arch are difficult to distinguish when the foot is bearing weight, characteristics of the medial longitudinal arch dominate foot-type classification. The term *fallen arches* thus usually refers to the collapse of the medial longitudinal arches.

There are two ways to measure arch height, direct methods and indirect methods. Indirect methods use measurements of length, width, and surface area obtained either from footprints or from other methods of assessing the extent of the plantar area (the sole of the foot) when it is in contact with the ground. Some investigators dispute the use of footprint data as an indicator of arch height. They argue that these techniques are based on invalid assumptions concerning foot-structure relationships. For example, to compare footprint data from individuals with different-sized feet, the clinician must assume that there is proportionate dimensional similarity of arch length, width, and height. However, a recent study of the foot measurements of close to 900 subjects undertaken by this author found significant differences of proportion in arch measures when comparing different foot lengths. Another common assumption is that the pattern of contact of the plantar area of the foot is representative of bone structure. This disregards the effect of soft tissue on the dimensions of the contact area. For example, the fatty tissue of the heel pad spreads when bearing weight, thereby distributing the load applied by the calcaneus over a larger surface area than when not bearing weight. The footprint therefore represents more than bone structure.

In a study of the reliability of indirect methods for evaluating arch height, clinicians were asked to categorize participants' feet as high, low, or normal arched. Their responses indicated wide disagreement, which was especially evident in the evaluations of high and low arches. This study points out the need for an objective method for measuring arch height.

Direct methods for measuring arch height use an index based on the distance between a point on the plantar surface of the foot and a representative point on the arch. The two most commonly used measurements, described above, are the dorsum and navicular height indexes. One device for collecting such data consists of a clear acrylic platform with mirrors attached to it, on which the subject stands. The foot is then photographed. The mirrors allow anterior, posterior, medial, and plantar views of the foot to be recorded in a single photographic slide. Points on the slide image are plotted on a graph, and the resulting data are used to calculate measurements of linear dimensions, surface area, and curvatures.

Studies of these direct measures of arch height indicate that the distribution of high, normal, and low arches in the general population can be displayed on a bell-shaped curve. This pattern suggests that there are about as many people with "low" arches (15%)

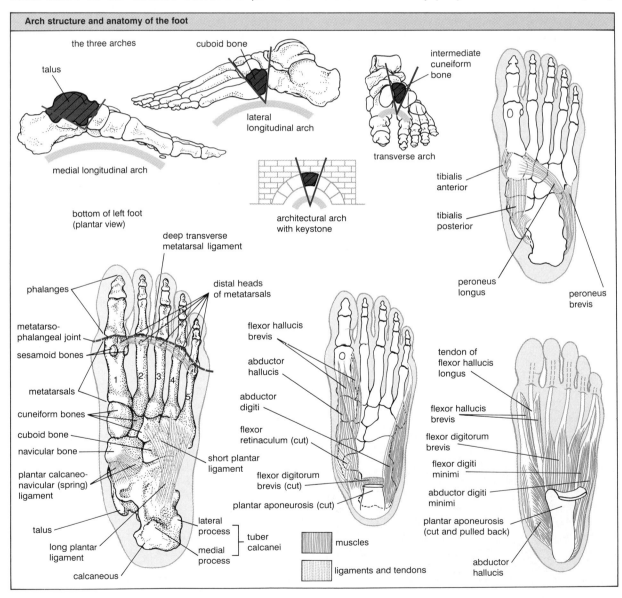

Arch structure and anatomy of the foot

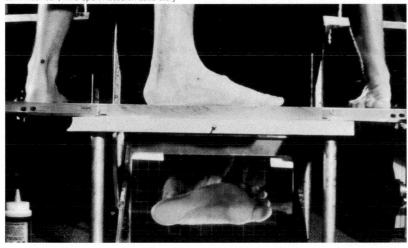

One device for directly measuring arch height consists of a mirrored platform that allows four views of the foot to be photographically recorded at once. Points on the photo are then plotted on a graph, and the resulting data are used to calculate and compare arch heights.

as "high" arches (15%); about 70% of the population have arches that are considered to be in a normal range.

Arch functions

The arches of the foot support the body when a person is standing still and during locomotion. The magnitude of this task is apparent when the ground reaction forces (GRFs) that are measured as athletes perform such maneuvers as jumping and running are considered. In studies of athletes the largest-peak vertical GRFs—over 14 times body weight—were seen in professional basketball players as they landed from a maximal jump. These athletes weighed an average of about 90 kg, indicating that in some instances the arches of human feet support 1,270 kg (2,800 lb). Peak vertical GRFs measured in runners (at 8 minutes per 1.6 km [one mile]) average about 2.5 times body weight. At this pace approximately 550 to 600 steps are taken over a distance of a mile. Thus, for a 68-kg (150-lb) athlete running a one-mile distance, the cumulative peak load supported by the arches is 97,800 kg (215,625 lb).

The arches also allow the body to be supported without compression of the soft tissues of the feet, thus enabling proper function of the muscles, blood vessels, and nerves. Normally, the highest plantar pressures during standing or locomotion are located under the foundations of the longitudinal arches, on the tuber calcanei and the distal heads of the metatarsals. Muscle groups on the plantar surface of the foot are generally situated so that the contractile tissue is between these areas of high pressure. This allows muscular function while the foot is supporting large forces during running and jumping. The medial and lateral plantar blood vessels and nerves, which supply the plantar surface, originate deep in the flexor retinaculum and then pass beneath the foot anterior to the tuber calcanei. Again, the arches serve to

prevent undue pressure on these delicate tissues.

Research has shown that the arches flatten when bearing a load, then recoil as the load is removed. During locomotion this springlike action reduces muscular work and also provides protection from rapid deceleration at impact. Ligaments, tendons, and muscles that support the arches stretch under tension and shorten as the tension is released. Tests indicate that tendons recover at a rate of about 93% after stretching. Similar scores have been reported for the stretching of rubber. Although tendinous tissue breaks when it is stretched by about 8% (whereas rubber can stretch 200% before breaking), it has a large capacity to store energy. This capacity is evident when one considers that about 78% of the energy used to flatten the foot is returned at recoil. The energy returned reduces muscle action.

Joints of the longitudinal arches allow the rotating motions of the foot called pronation and supination. Pronation can be demonstrated by turning the sole of the foot so that it faces laterally, away from the midline of the body; supination is demonstrated when the sole of the foot is turned so that it faces medially, toward the midline of the body. At heel strike during running, the foot is in a supinated position. After initial heel strike the foot pronates, and the arch flattens as a spring does when it is compressed. This motion is believed to cushion the body from impact with the ground.

Injuries and other problems

Some people have a low opinion of flatfeet because of a basic misconception about arch function. If arches serve important functions, they reason, then higher arches must be preferable. This viewpoint has some merit. In the individual whose arches are too low to support the body adequately during standing or locomotion, for example, compression of soft tissue on the plantar surface of the foot can hinder muscle

467

action, reduce blood flow, and impair nerve function. Because of these potential problems, patients—or the parents of children with an apparent problem—often become concerned about low arches and seek corrective measures. Treatment may not be necessary, however. Clinical research has shown in most instances that flatfeet are asymptomatic and, in some instances, are actually beneficial.

A 1989 study of army recruits at Fort Benning, Georgia, examined the risk factors associated with training-related injuries of the ankles and feet. The research was done by investigators from the U.S. Army Research Institute of Environmental Medicine in Natick, Mass., in collaboration with scientists at the NIKE Sport Research Laboratory in Beaverton, Ore. Direct measurements of arch height were collected from the new recruits before basic training. Frequency and type of training-related injury were recorded during training. Before analyzing the injury data, researchers divided the recruits into groups according to their measured arch heights. They found that there was an increase in injury with increased arch height. This finding suggests that recruits with low arches have not the highest but the *lowest* risk of training-related lower-extremity injury. One explanation has to do with stability; given similar bases of support, higher platforms are less stable than lower ones. If arches are considered to be platforms, high arches would be associated with decreased stability and increased risk of injury. Another explanation is reduced ability of the arch to provide proper cushioning. In some cases high-arched feet are very rigid and allow only limited natural pronation during locomotion. In runners, for example, this lack of a cushioning mechanism, which is normally afforded by adequate pronation, can result in injury from the repeated impacts with the ground.

In some cases, however, low arches are an indication of problems, such as stretched ligaments and hypermobile, or overly flexible, feet. More motion is not always better. Although pronation is a protective mechanism, it may sometimes be associated with chronic foot, knee, hip, and back injuries. An excessive rate or angle of pronation during running is believed to stress muscles, tendons, and ligaments. When repeated over time, this stress leads to inflammation and a condition commonly called runners' knee. Diagnosis of this problem in a dynamic situation is difficult because pronation occurs rapidly during running. There are several different techniques and devices to track this motion during running; however, cost, time, and lack of specialists with the necessary technical expertise prohibit their widespread use. Many clinicians examine foot flexibility in a non-weight-bearing situation and then determine effects during locomotion on the basis of extrapolations. This type of judgment is extremely subjective, and the practitioner needs to be highly experienced to make a correct diagnosis.

Some authorities believe that flatfeet contribute to the development of plantar fasciitis, inflammation of the plantar aponeurosis (or plantar fascia), the tissue that connects the calcaneus with the metatarsophalangeal joint. The primary symptom of this condition is pain in the arch near the heel, which is intensified by walking, prolonged standing, and other weight-bearing activities. Tight calf muscles, weak foot muscles, and insufficient flexibility of the foot are believed to play a part in plantar fasciitis. Therapeutic measures include exercises to stretch the calf muscles, Achilles tendon, and intrinsic muscles of the foot and exercises designed to strengthen the foot muscles.

Shoes for problem arches

Several athletic footwear companies produce so-called stability shoes specifically designed for those with an excessive pronation problem. These shoes have several structural components that support the calcaneus and reduce pronation. One of these is a heel counter, consisting of a rigid material in the shoe upper that surrounds the back, sides, and bottom of the heel. Some stability shoes also have increased counter rigidity to prevent the calcaneus from moving excessively. Midsoles are made of material that cushions the body against impact with the ground during locomotion. The medial portion of the midsole is often made of a higher density material, providing support to correct excessive pronation. Specially shaped and positioned wedges in some stability shoes place the foot in a supinated position. In instances where an orthopedic surgeon or podiatrist indicates the need for treatment to correct foot structure, orthopedic shoes, which contain components similar to those in athletic stability shoes, may be prescribed.

Another approach involves the use of orthotics, devices made of cork, leather, or plastic that can be put into the shoes to provide support for weak joints or bones. In most cases the orthotic conforms to the plantar surface of the individual's foot. These inserts restrict the motion of the foot and help to overcome the diagnosed structural foot problem.

To treat or not?

Although there is disagreement, most orthopedic surgeons and podiatrists believe that flatfeet should be "corrected" only when there is pain, hypermobility, or abnormal stiffness. Those who disagree suggest that treatment at an early age can prevent pain and dysfunction in later years. No clear-cut evidence is available to substantiate this latter hypothesis, however.

In cases of rare but extreme hypermobility accompanied by pain, the clinician may recommend surgery. Arthrodesis is a sometimes effective surgical procedure that immobilizes a joint, allowing the bones to grow together.

Following Your Doctor's Orders?

by Marshall H. Becker, Ph.D., M.P.H.

How do people go about deciding whether to undertake or continue behaviors recommended by health professionals? Despite decades of warnings about cigarette smoking, the largest single preventable cause of illness and premature death in the United States, about 30% of adults still are regular smokers. A lack of adherence to prescribed treatments is also evident in the fact that, on average, about 50% of patients do not take prescribed medications in accordance with instructions, and scheduled appointments for treatment are missed 20–50% of the time. Such noncompliance disrupts or neutralizes the benefits of preventive or curative services offered and often involves the patient in additional and unnecessary diagnostic and treatment procedures. Moreover, a recent study found that in the U.S. and England in a single year, more than 230 million prescriptions were not taken at all, and the U.S. National Council on Patient Information and Education estimates that each year tens of thousands of Americans die needlessly as a result of not taking prescription medications properly. Indeed, the difficulty of enlisting patient cooperation is well documented, and some authorities consider it the most serious problem facing medical practice today.

Health care providers are often surprised to learn of these high levels of noncompliance. Physicians generally overestimate the degree of patient compliance in their own practices and have no better than an even chance of predicting the likelihood of an individual patient's adherence to therapy. They tend to blame noncompliance on the patient's personality and express little desire to understand or sympathize with the uncooperative patient (although when they themselves are ill and under another doctor's care, their own compliance-related attitudes and performance are similar to those of their patients).

Why bother complying?

Often overlooked are all the instances where compliance did not achieve the desired outcome or where noncompliance did not result in poor health. For example, it is not uncommon, despite the patient's faithful adherence to a prescribed regimen, for the treatment not to work. This may occur because the diagnosis was incorrect, the prescribed therapy was incorrect (or inadequate), the patient did not respond to a particular treatment, the patient misunderstood the instructions and was therefore following the wrong regimen, the illness was chronic and thus the regimen was not curative (so that symptoms continued despite adherence), or the preventive measure was not sufficient (as with the person who avoids risky behaviors—does not smoke, sticks to a low-fat, low-cholesterol diet, exercises, etc.—and still has a heart attack). An entirely understandable response to such events is: Why bother following the doctor's advice?

Similarly, there are instances where, despite poor compliance, the patient nonetheless recovers (or does not become ill). This might occur because the diagnosis was incorrect, because the patient's natural defenses proved to be sufficient (much acute illness disappears without treatment, and symptoms of chronic disease can abate for long periods of time even in the absence of medical intervention), or because most high-risk behaviors (such as cigarette smoking, overeating, eating foods high in saturated fats, or exercising too little) do not result in readily observable illness in the short run and in many cases do not ever cause the risk taker to become ill. Here again the likely attitude of the patient is: Why bother complying?

The tendency for patients to have doubts about the merits of complying with treatments proposed by health professionals is further exacerbated by the mass media's regular reporting of controversies, contradictions, and reversals with regard to public health and medical care recommendations (*e.g.,* the ongoing debates about whether getting influenza immunizations, achieving "ideal" body weight, and eating oat bran to help lower cholesterol are worthwhile preventive measures). It is therefore not surprising that persons untrained in health matters decide for themselves how much and what kind of advice to follow.

Many studies have been directed at identifying determinants of patient noncompliance, and much practical knowledge has emerged. There are now some promising approaches to increasing patient cooperation that clients and health care providers can implement.

Provision of information

An important contributor to poor compliance is often the patient's inadequate understanding of, or knowledge about, various aspects of the regimen. A recent study found that at least half of the patients attending a clinic did not know what dose of their medication to take or how long to take it, and 25% did not know the purpose of the medications they were taking. One problem is poor recall; studies have shown that patients remember the diagnosis better than they do the prescribed therapy. In fact, five minutes after speaking with their physician, patients usually have forgotten about half of the treatment instructions. Moreover, provision of general information about the nature of illness or the action of the medication does not usually increase adherence. Such findings suggest that it is best for medical practitioners to speak briefly and selectively, emphasizing and then repeating information that is crucial for compliance, and to provide simple, individualized, written instructions to which the patient may later refer (a combination of oral and written instructions results in the highest levels of information retention).

The flow of information from patient to provider is also critical. The accuracy of a diagnosis depends heavily on the patient's description of the problem, which is often limited by various factors; *e.g.,* time constraints of a busy clinical practice, the patient's tendency to be reticent about "embarrassing" symptoms, reluctant to discuss certain areas of the body, or concerned about possibly being labeled a hypochondriac. Patients should be as complete and candid as possible, and practitioners should always encourage openness (for example, by asking if there are any other symptoms or problems).

Making the regimen easy

One of the most effective ways to achieve an improved level of compliance is to make the regimen easy to follow—by minimizing its complexity, duration, requirements of changes in life-style, inconvenience, and cost. Reductions in complexity can be achieved through avoidance of the *routine* prescription of noncritical medications (such as vitamins and tranquilizers) and emphasis on the necessity of adhering to particularly critical aspects of the treatment plan ("prioritizing the regimen")—*e.g.,* taking the prescribed daily dosage of the drug isoniazid for treatment of active tuberculosis.

Medical jargon can often add to the regimen's complexity. Various surveys have revealed the following examples of patients' misunderstanding of medical terms commonly used by practitioners. *Incubation period* was interpreted as "how long the patient should stay in bed"; it actually refers to the time between contracting an infection and the manifestation of the illness (with symptoms). *PRN* was assumed to mean that the medicine should be taken regularly; PRN is from the Latin *pro re nata,* meaning "as needed." *Lumbar puncture* (spinal tap) was interpreted as "draining the lungs." *Workup* was construed as "making someone angry." A patient thought that pills prescribed "as needed for water retention" would cause (rather than relieve) fluid buildup. And medication to be taken every six hours was taken three rather than four times a day (since the patient slept at night). Either avoidance or full explanation of such medical terms is therefore strongly encouraged.

If alterations of critical behaviors (such as smoking, diet, or exercise) are needed, the practitioner should request that these changes be made gradually over the course of many visits, starting with an area chosen by the patient (thus capitalizing on the patient's motivation). Setting short-term goals that are achievable is followed by reinforcing whatever compliance is achieved, and only then is the next objective added. Thus, a complex treatment plan is broken into simpler stages that can be implemented sequentially ("graduated regimen implementation").

Investigations have shown improvement in compliance with medication schedules by linking the regimen

It pays to comply

condition	results with good compliance	results with poor compliance
high blood cholesterol	39% drop in risk of heart disease; 19% drop in blood cholesterol	11% drop in risk of heart disease; 4.4% drop in blood cholesterol
depression	90% of patients who took 90% of doses improved	none of patients who took less than 80% of doses improved
epilepsy	25% of seizures occurred among high compliers	60% of seizures occurred among poor compliers; partially compliant patients had effective drug action only 30 to 80% of the time
contraception	rate of conception would be 0.1% with full compliance	rates of conception with imperfect compliance range from 3 to 16%
high blood pressure	mean decrease in diastolic blood pressure (DBP) of 18 mm Hg	mean decrease in DBP of 8 mm Hg; number of hospital readmissions related to number of "lack of drug" days; risk of death increased by 53%

Source: National Council on Patient Information and Education, Washington, D.C.

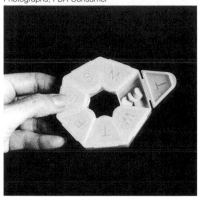
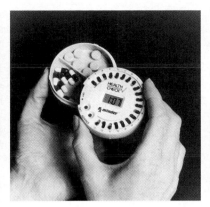
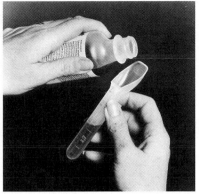

Special containers help patients comply with medication regimens. Pills can be measured out into compartments for each day of the week (left); the center container has an alarm that can be set for specific intervals or times of day; and a spoon with dosage calibrations (right) ensures that the right amount of liquid medication is taken.

to the patient's regular daily activities, thus increasing convenience and making it more difficult to forget to take pills or other medicines on time ("tailoring the regimen"). The practitioner should also seek other ways to make drug-taking compliance easier, such as dispensing a supply of the medication directly from the clinic so that the patient can avoid a lengthy wait at the hospital pharmacy or a special trip to a drugstore. (Studies have shown that a large number of prescrip-

A poster emphasizes the importance of taking antihypertensive medications. Even if patients with high blood pressure have no symptoms at all, they are at risk for damage to the heart, brain, and kidneys.

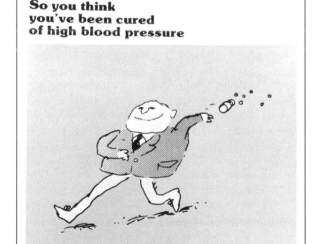

So you think you've been cured of high blood pressure

You feel OK . . . your blood pressure reading is normal again. Can you stop taking the high blood pressure pills? No! Most high blood pressure can be *controlled* but not *cured*. If you stop the pills, your blood pressure will go up again. Take your medication. Keep your blood pressure down and under control.

High Blood Pressure... Treat it for Life

tions never get filled at all.) Special pill containers that help patients remember to take the right dose at the right time are also available, and certain medications, such as birth control pills, estrogen-replacement pills and patches, ulcer drugs, methotrexate for psoriasis, and dexamethasone and methylprednisolone for allergic and inflammatory disorders, are available in convenient "dosepaks" or "calendar packs" that make it easy for the patient to keep track of pills taken. In addition, many therapeutic drugs are now being manufactured in once-daily dosages or sustained-release formulations—also aimed at improving patient compliance.

Several studies have demonstrated that compliance rates are highest when the prescribed medication needs to be taken only once a day. One study monitored patients with epilepsy who were divided into groups that took an antiepileptic drug either once, twice, three times, or four times daily. Special pill bottles electronically recorded the number of times the bottles were opened. Those on the once-a-day regimen had an 87% compliance rate; compliance for the twice-daily pill takers was 81%, and the rates were 77% and 39%, respectively, for those on three- and four-times-daily schedules. Another study, of patients taking antihypertensive drugs, found that compliance improved from 59% with a three-times-a day regimen to 83% when patients were given medication that could be taken just once a day.

Another effective approach is to reduce the regimen's duration when possible. The practitioner thus should employ the most aggressive (but safe) treatment in order to bring the condition under control as early as possible. Follow-up visits should be scheduled soon after the initial visit so that progress can be demonstrated to the patient; this way the patient is able to appreciate the treatment's importance. Follow-up telephone calls can also foster compliance. A few days after the initial visit, someone from the doctor's

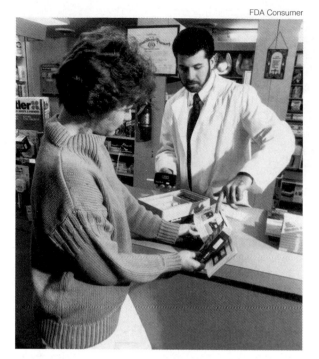

By providing clear and understandable instructions, both orally and in writing, pharmacists dispense a critical service as well as a drug. Studies show that such client counseling fosters proper and safe use of prescribed medications.

office or clinic telephones the patient to inquire about how things are going with the regimen. Besides allowing the health professional to identify potential compliance problems and possibly adjust the regimen, the call provides between-visit contact that enables the patient to feel there is shared responsibility for dealing with the illness. Also, many studies have shown that mail and telephone reminders increase the likelihood that patients will follow a prescribed regimen and keep follow-up appointments.

The physician may be able to reduce the cost of the treatment by prescribing generic drugs, avoiding unnecessary prescribing, checking to see whether the patient's health insurance covers medication costs, and encouraging the patient to compare prescription rates at different pharmacies (generally large chain stores offer lower prices than smaller independent pharmacies).

The power of patients' beliefs

Much research has shown that patients' beliefs about their health, and about particular illnesses and treatments, have a strong influence on the likelihood of compliance with preventive and curative recommendations. These beliefs have to do with the "health motivation" of the patient—his or her degree of interest in, and concern about, health matters in general; the patient's estimation of the severity of an illness and of the probable seriousness of the consequences,

both physical and social, of leaving it untreated; and the patient's estimation of benefits versus costs—*i.e.,* perceptions of how effective the advocated health behavior might be in preventing or treating the condition, weighed against certain perceived obstacles that might be encountered or hardships involved in undertaking the recommended action (*e.g.,* expense, physical or emotional discomfort, possible adverse side effects, inconvenience). Social approval—the patient's beliefs about whether others think positively or negatively about the recommended behavior, and the degree to which that matters to the patient—is also an important factor in compliance behavior.

To the surprise of many practitioners, the factor that probably affects compliance the most is the patient's acceptance of the diagnosis. Why, clinicians wonder, would a person seek out and undergo expert examination and consultation (often costly and uncomfortable), only to subsequently reject that professional's conclusions? Yet patients often have firm personal perceptions of their susceptibility or vulnerability to a particular illness, and those beliefs strongly affect whether they accept the practitioner's assessment of their condition.

At least three kinds of situations can undermine belief in diagnosis. First, incidents may occur during the medical history taking or physical examination that are interpreted by the patient in such a manner as to weaken confidence in the diagnosis. An example of such a circumstance is: "I came in complaining of a sore throat, but the doctor spent a lot of time checking my ears and decided I have an ear infection."

Second, patients may reject an unanticipated diagnosis that is psychologically painful, especially if there are no outward symptoms (as is often the case with high blood pressure—appropriately dubbed the "silent killer"). They often react initially to a life-threatening illness by denying that they have it (a similar denial process leads to delay in seeking diagnosis of symptoms related to serious diseases). One study showed that people accord to others a greater risk of contracting illnesses than they are willing to estimate for themselves.

Third, and probably most significant, individuals often possess powerful and well-defined but scientifically erroneous health beliefs that conflict with the physician's assessment of the problem. "I can't have diabetes; everyone knows that's hereditary, and there's none in my family." "I can't have high blood pressure because I'm not the nervous type." "My child can't have arthritis; that's a disease of old people." These are all examples of erroneous beliefs. Such beliefs can have multiple origins—they may be embedded in the thinking of cultural subgroups, or they may come from parents' beliefs, prior experiences with an illness, misinterpretation of factual information, or false information conveyed by nonmedical sources.

A recent study of health beliefs and compliance with prescribed medication for hypertension among black women, aged 45–70, in New Orleans, La., found that a significant number of these patients possessed strong folk beliefs about their condition. They viewed their disease variously as "pressure trouble," "high blood," or "high-pertention"—a disease "of the nerves." The causes they ascribed to their illness ranged from "hot," "rich," or "thick" blood that rose within the body to having a lot of worries to hot weather. Some of these women thought their illness could be treated by avoidance of spicy food or "grease"; some thought garlic water or vinegar would cool, or thin, the blood and cause it to "drop back." Compliance with taking prescribed antihypertensive drugs was markedly poorer among the women who held such beliefs than among women in the study who accepted a biomedical model of hypertension. The study also found that the physicians treating these patients were generally unaware of their patients' beliefs about their condition.

The results suggested that if physicians elicited their patients' beliefs about their illness before selecting a therapeutic regimen, higher rates of compliance could be achieved and unnecessary mortality in such high-risk populations could be reduced.

By learning which beliefs affect individual patients and are likely to inhibit their compliance, the practitioner can tailor an intervention to suit each client's unique needs. Thus, along with a medical diagnosis, an "educational diagnosis" should routinely be made to determine: Is the patient excessively or minimally concerned about health? Does he or she agree with the diagnosis? perceive the condition as very serious or not at all serious? feel the recommended action will work? fear possible side effects? or feel the regimen will be too hard to follow?

Improving the likelihood of compliance

Of course, knowing what beliefs are problematic does not dictate any particular strategy for change. Some-

Patient Medication Contract

For the next _____ days, I, _____ , agree to take the following steps to help my medicines work safely and effectively:

1. I will take my   *(medicine name)*   _____ times a day at: _____ .

2. I will continue to take my   *(medicine name)*   for   *(time period)*

3. I will avoid the following foods, beverages or other medicines that could interfere with my medicine:

   _____

4. I will report any of the following side effects to my health care provider: _____

   _____

   _____

5. If I receive any new medicines, I will tell my doctor or pharmacist about *(medicine name)* and about all the other prescription and over-the-counter medicines I take.

6. I will tell my health care providers about my progress in following treatment and ask their help in solving any problems that occur.

7. I will also follow these special instructions: _____

   _____

8. I will read the written information my doctor or pharmacist gives me about the medicine.

I am taking these steps because I expect the following benefits to my health: _____

_____

To help me follow treatment, my health care provider has agreed to: _____

_____

When I successfully complete this contract, I will reward myself by: _____

_____

Signed_____

Patient's Name _____ Date _____

Provider's Name _____ Date _____

When patients and their health care providers spell out the goals of a treatment plan in a formal contract like the one at left, patients are more likely to make therapeutic behavior changes and stick with them. Such contracts emphasize the benefits to be gained by the patient from following the prescribed regimen.

National Council on Patient Information and Education, Washington, D.C.

times merely providing corrective factual information will prove sufficient. In other cases, motivational appeals are necessary (such as focusing on patient-desired short-term goals or appealing to the patient's sense of pride or responsibility). Practitioners' oral exhortations to patients to persevere in their efforts to change behavior or to continue taking a medication, even if the effects are not readily apparent, can help patients overcome stumbling blocks. Sometimes a "second opinion" is necessary to ensure compliance—recommendations from other sources of information that have greater credibility for the patient (perhaps another patient for whom the same treatment was successful).

Ultimately, compliance will depend on an individual's so-called self-efficacy expectations—the degree of self-confidence the patient has in his or her own ability to follow a recommended treatment plan successfully. Perhaps the key to continued compliance is the prevention of relapses, which involves anticipating and coping with lapses in appropriate behavior. A person's failure in attempting to modify a particular behavior in a high-risk situation (*e.g.,* an individual on a strict low-calorie diet who cannot refuse a proffered ice cream sundae at a party) often induces lowered perceptions of self-efficacy. Combined with the initial gratification that a return to old habits provides, such a lapse often leads to guilt and perceived loss of control, thus lessening the probability of continued compliance.

The practitioner-patient relationship

The literature on patient compliance documents numerous aspects of the practitioner's behavior that have a direct effect on patient behavior. Noncompliance is more common when the physician is formal, rejecting, or controlling or interviews the patient at length without allowing a dialogue. Noncompliance also tends to be high when the patient's expectations are left unmet and when an explanation of the diagnosis is not provided. By contrast, adherence is considerably more likely when the patient is satisfied with the visit, does not perceive the appointment as an inconvenience, and is not kept waiting for an excessive time before and during the appointment. The compliance situation clearly benefits when the care provider asks about and respects all the patient's concerns and provides responsive information about the patient's condition and progress, when sincere concern and sympathy are shown, and when the practitioner and client agree substantially about the specifics of the regimen.

The orientation of the care provider toward the patient and his or her demonstrated desire to influence compliance are also important factors. For example, a study of hypertensive patients found that those who received medical care oriented toward considering them as active participants in the treatment process

("active patient orientation") were significantly more likely than other patients to have their blood pressure under control and to display more favorable behavioral responses to the management of their illnesses. Dietitians in this study tended to involve hypertension patients in counseling sessions to a greater extent than did other care providers, and a high level of patient compliance resulted.

In fact, it has been shown that when health professionals other than physicians are brought into the compliance picture, they often provide additional assessment, instruction, clarification, and reinforcement. It has been suggested that nurses, by virtue of their numbers and amount of contact with patients, have great potential for influencing compliance-related behaviors, including diagnosing and monitoring of adherence levels, implementing health education and attitude-change strategies, enlisting the support of the patient's family or others, and so forth.

A number of recent investigations have provided strong evidence for the value of involving pharmacists in trying to increase patient cooperation with prescribed drug therapies. Pharmacists can play a critical role in ensuring safe and effective use of medications—particularly when a patient is taking several drugs that may interact in unexpected ways. Many pharmacies now have computerized record-keeping systems that enable the druggist to keep track of all the medications a patient is taking (often prescribed by several different physicians). The computer alerts them if untoward interactions of drugs are likely. Also, some pharmacists automatically send patients reminders when it is time to have their prescription refilled. In 1990 the National Association of Chain Drug Stores began a training program for pharmacists to teach them appropriate counseling skills, called PHO-CUST—Pharmacists' Opportunities in Compliance Using Skills Training. Pharmacists have been called the "final checkpoint in the health care system," and increasingly they are realizing their responsibility to dispense a service as well as a product.

Putting it in writing

A relatively recent approach aimed at improving compliance attempts to capitalize on and improve the provider-patient relationship through a formal "contract," wherein both parties set forth on paper an attainable treatment goal, the specific obligations of each party in attempting to achieve that goal, and a time limit for its achievement. Agreed-upon rewards create incentives for achieving the compliance goals. This is just one of many innovative strategies for encouraging patients to be more fully involved in their own health care so that they will gain the full benefit from available medical therapies.

X-Rays and the Pregnant Woman
by Eric Hall, D.Sc.

It has never been possible to show directly and unequivocally that the low doses of medical X-rays used for diagnostic purposes on pregnant women cause congenital malformations in their babies. In the natural course of events, the number of babies born with a defect of some sort is already too high (about 1 in 10) for any small increase due to the low doses of X-rays used in medicine to be detected. There have been claims that X-raying the mother of an unborn child can cause cancer and leukemia in that child. Surveys performed in the British National Health Service, for example, indicate that children who died of cancer or leukemia before 10 years of age were more likely to have been X-rayed *In utero* than those who did not die with a malignancy. Some have claimed that these data show that very small doses of radiation from two or three X-ray films received by pregnant women result in cancer and leukemia in the offspring. The data are controversial, however. It has not been proved that the X-rays caused the cancers; indeed, the weight of the evidence suggests that the women who were X-rayed while pregnant represent a selected group who may well have had various medical problems, which was why they had been seen by a doctor and were X-rayed in the first place!

The National Research Council of the National Academy of Sciences regularly convenes panels to assess new information on the effects of ionizing radiations. Their principal concern is with carcinogenesis and the genetic effects of radiation, but they also consider effects on the unborn child. The most recent report of the Biological Effects of Ionizing Radiation (BEIR) Committee appeared in 1990. Many of the committee's conclusions are summarized in the discussion that follows.

Effects of high doses

It is known with certainty that large doses of X-rays during pregnancy cause deleterious effects on the offspring. The evidence comes from two sources.

Animal studies. Laboratory studies of rats and mice are one source of evidence. In these investigations the effects observed depend on the X-ray dosage and on the stage of pregnancy at which the radiation is delivered. In rodents and in humans, the time from conception to birth can be divided into three major periods.

After conception the fertilized egg undergoes rapid division until it becomes firmly embedded in the wall of the uterus; this period is known as preimplantation and lasts from five to six days in rats and mice and about nine days in humans. A sizable dose of radiation delivered during this period may kill the newly formed embryo, which at this stage consists of only a limited number of cells, but does not appear to produce other effects such as reduction in growth or gross abnormalities. In other words, radiation appears to have an all-or-nothing effect at this stage of development. The death of so early an embryo, which also occurs frequently from natural causes, would probably go unnoticed in most cases.

The period of development after the fertilized egg has implanted in the wall of the uterus is known as organogenesis, because it is then that cells begin to form the specialized organs and parts of the body—the eyes, the brain, the arms, the legs, and so forth. While organs and limbs are being formed, the embryo is most vulnerable to disease, to drugs, and also to radiation. In humans this period lasts from the ninth day to the sixth week after conception. When the drug thalidomide, introduced in West Germany in 1958 and given to pregnant women in Europe, Australia, New Zealand, and Canada to suppress "morning sickness," was taken during this organogenesis period, babies were born with severe malformations such as stunted and flipperlike arms and legs. Also during the organogenesis period, an attack of rubella (German measles), normally not a serious illness, can produce gross abnormalities in the fetus.

Modest amounts of radiation can also have catastrophic consequences on the developing embryo in animals during this time. A spectrum of defects can occur, including cleft palate, stunting of the limbs, an abnormally developed brain, and quite a few others. The organs and limbs that are developing do so in a strict sequence; the radiation will affect those that happen to be developing at the moment of exposure.

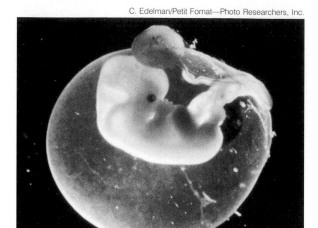

The child in the womb is highly vulnerable when cells are beginning to form specialized organs. The human embryo above, at about five to six weeks after conception, is at risk for malformations if the mother is exposed to high-dose X-rays.

The last period of gestation—from the sixth week to term—is known as the fetal period. Little information is available from animal studies regarding the effects of irradiation at this time, except that large doses produce permanent growth retardation—*i.e.,* the offspring are smaller than usual at birth and remain below average in size throughout life.

Atom bomb survivors. The second source of information on the effects of radiation comes from humans who have received high doses of irradiation—principally, the survivors of the atom bomb attacks on Hiroshima and Nagasaki, Japan. About 1,200 individuals who were irradiated in the womb have been followed from birth to maturity. Some have a reduced head diameter, and some suffer from severe mental retardation. The most sensitive period appears to have been 8 to 15 weeks postconception. The wide range of other malformations seen in experimental animals at birth were not noted in the Japanese children. In the Japanese survivors who were irradiated *in utero,* the incidence of mental retardation increased as the dose of radiation got larger, reaching 40% by a dose of 100 rads. The data are limited but are consistent with a threshold of about 20 rads; *i.e.,* doses below this level did not produce observable mental retardation.

No one disputes that *large* doses of X-rays given during sensitive periods of pregnancy can produce catastrophic effects. (Large doses of radiation can also lead to sterilization of both men and women, affecting ovulation in women and sperm counts in men.) The important question is whether *low* doses can also produce deleterious effects, because a large number of women would thus be at risk.

Pregnancy dilemma: to X-ray or not to X-ray?

Because of the sensitivity to radiation of the embryo and fetus, it is clearly best to avoid X-rays during pregnancy. Women of reproductive age who could possibly be pregnant should always check before agreeing to be X-rayed. Pregnancy tests are quick, inexpensive, and readily available.

Sometimes, however, the health or life of an individual may be at stake, and X-ray procedures may be indicated even if the patient is pregnant. Examples might include suspected cancer of the bladder, stomach, or colon. Then the risk must be weighed against the benefit. With modern films and equipment, it is unlikely that any *single* X-ray procedure would result in a radiation dose that would have deleterious effects on the unborn child, but an accumulation of many procedures could.

There is limited scope for protecting the unborn child during X-rays of parts of the body remote from

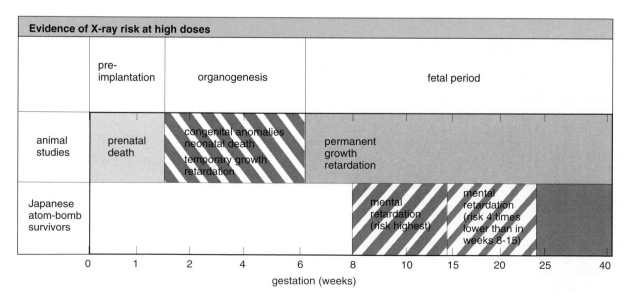

Evidence of X-ray risk at high doses

	pre-implantation	organogenesis	fetal period		
animal studies	prenatal death	congenital anomalies neonatal death temporary growth retardation	permanent growth retardation		
Japanese atom-bomb survivors			mental retardation (risk highest)	mental retardation (risk 4 times lower than in weeks 8-15)	

gestation (weeks): 0 1 2 4 6 8 10 15 20 25 40

Radiation and the unborn child		
category	radiation dose per examination	procedures
a	less than 0.01 rad	chest X-rays dental X-rays skull cervical spine extremities shoulder thoracic spine, ribs mammography CT of the head and chest
b	0.01 to 0.25 rad	upper GI cholecystography/ cholangiography hip and femur pelvis CT outside the abdominal region
c	0.25 to 1 rad	lumbar/lumbosacral spine urography, intravenous or retrograde pyelogram urethrocystography abdomen (kidney, ureter, bladder) pelvimetry hysterosalpingography
d	1 to 5 rads	fluoroscopy in the abdominal region, CT in the abdominal region

Compiled by M. Rosenstein, M.D., Center for Devices and Radiological Health

the pelvis. For example, a lead rubber apron should always be used to cover the body while dental films are being taken. In fact, however, lead rubber aprons are of little use otherwise since most of the dose to the fetus comes from scatter inside the body when remote areas—the chest, for example—are X-rayed.

The table above lists common radiological procedures, which are divided into four categories according to the amount of radiation that reaches the unborn child. These are representative values; doses may vary widely with different machines. Procedures in categories a and b, including dental X-rays, X-rays of the extremities, and even computed tomography (CT) scans outside the abdominal region, pose no problem. Not surprisingly, the highest doses (category d) are recorded for fluoroscopy and CT scans of the abdominal region. X-ray pictures of the pelvis or abdomen and specialized procedures to aid the urologist or obstetrician are not far behind (category c). This table supports the claim of the American College of Radiology that no *single* radiology examination poses a serious threat to the unborn child.

No single procedure involves a dose comparable to the threshold of about 20 rads that the Japanese data suggest might result in mental retardation if delivered at a sensitive time. It is not difficult to imagine a situation, however, where multiple procedures in categories c and d could be performed, or procedures repeated on the same patient, which may be prescribed by several doctors separately, such that the accumulated dose could reach levels that would be dangerous to an unborn child, though not to the mother.

How, then, to answer the question, To X-ray or not to X-ray? A single procedure, administered with great care, may be recommended even in a woman known to be pregnant, especially if her life or health—or that of the fetus—is threatened.

Therapeutic abortion

Despite the best-laid plans, it happens occasionally that a woman discovers that she is pregnant *after* a whole series of X-ray procedures has been performed. The question then is, What should be done? The first step is to enlist the services of a medical physicist to estimate carefully the radiation dose to the embryo or fetus. The age of the embryo or fetus postconception is the other vital factor. A small dose delivered early postconception during preimplantation, or late during fetal life, is unlikely to cause a problem.

However, if a "large" dose was received during a sensitive period, then a therapeutic abortion may be indicated. But what is "large"? A figure of 10 rads is frequently quoted, but this may be revised upward or downward depending on other factors, including social and religious views. For example, if the mother is young, with many potential childbearing years ahead, or if she already has several children, she may not wish to run the risk of delivering an abnormal child and may choose to have a therapeutic abortion even if she has had a relatively low radiation dose. On the other hand, an older woman who has been trying to have a child for years may be reluctant to terminate the pregnancy, being willing to take the chance that the child may be abnormal—a chance that is already much greater in an older woman. Members of religious groups that oppose abortion may refuse a therapeutic abortion after any radiation dose, arguing that having a baby is a very risky business in the first place, to which radiation adds an extra but small risk.

It should always be remembered that if the child subsequently born is abnormal in some way, it will never be possible to say with any certainty whether the radiation was the cause, since naturally occurring and radiation-induced malformations are indistinguishable. What radiation can do is to increase the chance that a malformation will occur.

Dose limits: medical and occupational

There are no regulations—international, national, or local—to govern or limit the amount of radiation that may be given for medical reasons to anyone, and that includes a pregnant woman. There is the general guideline "as low as reasonably achievable" (ALARA), but no dose limit is specified; it is tacitly assumed that medical X-rays always confer more benefits than risks.

There are, however, strict regulations for the amount of "man-made" radiation that can be received other than for medical purposes. Individuals who are exposed to radiation in the course of their jobs are limited to an annual dose equivalent of 0.05 sievert (Sv). A member of the general public who is not occupationally exposed may receive up to 0.005 Sv annually. For a woman exposed to radiation in the course of her work—as a radiologist, a nurse, or a dental technician, for example—and who is or becomes pregnant, regulations dictate that the child she is carrying may not receive more than 0.005 Sv during the entire nine months of gestation. The reasoning is that, while the mother is a radiation worker and may receive 0.05 Sv per year, the unborn child must be considered a member of the general population for whom the limit is 0.005 Sv! This regulation may restrict the jobs that women can perform in the nuclear industry after a pregnancy is declared.

International dose limits are recommended by the International Commission on Radiological Protection and in the United States by the National Council on Radiation Protection and Measurements, an independent body chartered by Congress. Enforcement of these recommendations is the job of various agencies, including the Department of Energy, the Nuclear Regulatory Commission, the Food and Drug Administration, and the Environmental Protection Agency.

Nuclear medicine

In nuclear medicine, unsealed radioactive materials (radionuclides) that are administered orally or by injection are taken up by various tissues or organs. A radioactive isotope, *e.g.,* radioiodine, can be easily detected with modern instrumentation and localized and quantified within the body. Nuclear medicine techniques are used to image specific organs, including the thyroid, liver, spleen, cardiac chambers, adrenal glands, bones, and joints, or to scan the total body. The doses of radiation the patient is exposed to with such diagnostic procedures are significantly lower than with other X-ray techniques.

The therapeutic use of radioactive materials is a special case and is usually avoided at all costs during pregnancy. The same general considerations apply as in the use of X-rays. The unborn child is particularly sensitive to radiation during organogenesis, and the use of radioactive materials in treatment quantities could cause serious damage at this stage. For example, the thyroid of the unborn child can be obliterated by a dose of radioactive iodine used to treat thyroid disease in the mother. While the amounts of radioactivity used for diagnosis as opposed to therapy are

much smaller, precautions should always be taken to ensure that a woman is not pregnant before radioactive materials are administered for medical purposes.

Nonionizing radiation: more questions than answers

X-rays used in medicine, as well as cosmic rays that come from space and alpha particles from naturally occurring radon gas in homes, are known as *ionizing* radiations. Radiation is said to be ionizing if it is able to disrupt the atoms of the material in which it is absorbed, by knocking an electron out of orbit. This leads to the breaking of chemical bonds and so to a biological effect.

Besides X-rays there are many other types of man-made radiations to which humans are exposed in the course of everyday life. Sources include microwave ovens, electric power transmission lines, electric blankets, video display terminals, and ultrasound and magnetic resonance devices used for imaging in medicine. These are termed *nonionizing* radiations because they do not ionize atoms by knocking an electron from orbit.

All these sources of nonionizing radiation have been suspected of causing undesirable effects in the human. In no instance, however, has it been proved convincingly that they are dangerous at the low levels at which they are used, nor has a mechanism for deleterious effects of these radiations been proposed or demonstrated in the laboratory. Nonetheless, the possibility cannot be ruled out. There is more than 90 years' experience in the use of ionizing radiation, including excessive use in the early days of X-rays and the experience of Japanese survivors of Hiroshima and Nagasaki. Medical science does not have comparable experience with nonionizing radiations. It remains an open question as to whether the various forms to which people are exposed cause deleterious effects in the unborn baby of a pregnant woman—or, for that matter, in anyone else.

Too many X-rays?

The potential problem always exists that the proliferation of diagnostic X-ray machines, particularly complex and expensive devices such as CT scanners, leads to their overuse. It has been estimated that one-third of all X-ray procedures are not based on the medical need of the patient; rather, they are ordered to generate income, or they represent the practice of defensive medicine. It is difficult to know how widespread this problem is and even more difficult to solve it in a country such as the United States, which is devoted to free enterprise in medicine as in other walks of life.

Fungal Diseases
by Alan D. Tice, M.D.

Fungi are ubiquitous organisms that often produce mild skin disease in humans and occasionally invade the body to produce serious, and sometimes even fatal, diseases. By definition, members of the kingdom of fungi have a true nucleus enclosed by a nuclear membrane, a cytoplasmic membrane, and a cell wall composed of the horny substance called chitin. They are distinct from the plant kingdom in that they do not contain chlorophyll. More than 100,000 species of fungi have been described. These include the group known collectively as the dermatophytes, which commonly produce skin diseases such as ringworm and athlete's foot; the yeasts, which cause such conditions as thrush and diaper rash; the molds, such as bread mold; and the multicelled structures that form mushrooms.

Fungal diseases have been known for centuries. Descriptions of what was probably thrush—a yeast infection of the mouth and throat—can be found in the works of Hippocrates and Galen. It was not until 1839, however—several years before bacteria were discovered to cause disease—that a causal relationship was identified between fungi and human infection. Since then more than 150 species of fungi have been recognized as capable of causing disease in animals (zoophilic), and an additional 50 have been recognized as causing infection in humans (anthropophilic). Most species live in the soil, where they have adapted to virtually every climate and environment, and most are worldwide in distribution. In general, fungi flourish in warm, wet regions where there is abundant organic matter in the soil. Some, however, grow only in certain geographic areas that are specifically suited to supporting them. *Coccidioides immitis,* for example, the cause of valley fever, is found only in the region of the San Joaquin Valley of California.

Fungi that cause human disease are classified as either molds or yeasts on the basis of the physical characteristics of the colonies they form. Molds have a fluffy cotton-wool appearance, sometimes including a powderlike aerial growth; colonies of yeasts appear opaque and creamy or pasty. The microscopic appearance of these organisms can be used to further distinguish them. Yeasts are typically round or oval in shape and reproduce by budding. Molds develop by branching and extension of tubular structures known as hyphae. Some fungi, such as *Candida* species, have the ability to form both buds and hyphae, de-

pending on the growth media and surrounding environment. None of the fungi is motile, but they are easily able to spread by means of spores that are carried through the air. When spores alight in a suitable environment, they start new colonies. Spores may live for a year, waiting for the right conditions for growth.

Who is susceptible?

Even though fungi were the first organisms to be recognized as a cause of human infection, bacteria quickly assumed the limelight in medicine because of the more sudden and severe diseases they produce. Bacteria are also easier than fungi to grow in the laboratory, a fact that contributed to the development of effective antibacterial agents. In recent years, however, there has been a resurgence of interest in fungi, in part because of the growing number of individuals who, because their immune systems are compromised, are especially vulnerable. Fungal infections are a serious problem for persons infected with the human immunodeficiency virus (HIV, the virus that causes AIDS) and are an increasing problem for patients receiving immunosuppressive medication. The development of increasingly potent antibacterial agents has also contributed to an increase in fungal infections by eliminating the layer of normal, protective bacteria that live on the skin and mucous membranes. This creates a fertile field for fungal growth in susceptible persons.

An individual's susceptibility to fungal infections depends on many things. Some people seem immune but, given the right circumstance, most are susceptible. One such circumstance is exposure to a heavy concentration of organisms. These concentrations can be found in a variety of situations and environments—

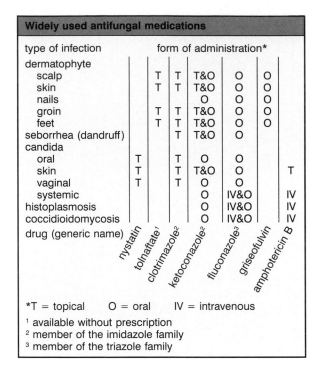

on the floor of a health club shower stall, in the air of a cave that is covered with bat droppings, on the skin of a pet, or on the thorns of a rose bush. One fungus, *Candida albicans,* is a normal inhabitant of the human body but can cause disease when the individual's immunity is depressed because of medical conditions such as diabetes or other factors, such as poor nutrition or long-term use of antibiotic or corticosteroid drugs. Persons with indwelling catheters or artificial heart valves and those receiving parenteral nutrition are also at increased risk of developing fungal infections.

Skin, hair, and nail infections

Fungal infections of the skin, hair, and nails can be caused by either molds or yeasts. Although they are some of the most common human infections, they are fortunately seldom more than an annoyance or a cosmetic problem. Most are caused by the dermatophytes. The spores of these organisms may live in a free state for many months waiting for the opportunity to attach to keratin-producing cells such as are found in the outermost layer of the skin, the nails, or the hair.

Ringworm. Dermatophyte infections of the skin usually appear as round, dry, scaly patches with a raised border and central clearing. They are commonly referred to as ringworm because of their ringlike appearance. In medical terminology they are called tinea infections, and the type of tinea is designated according to its location. Thus, tinea capitis is an infection of the scalp, usually caused by *Trichophyton tonsurans* or *Microsporum canis.* For unknown reasons, black people have a higher incidence of *T. tonsurans* and tend to carry the organism more than whites. *M. canis* is often associated with dogs or cats, which can carry this zoophilic organism.

Tinea corporis and pityriasis (tinea) versicolor are fungal infections of the skin on the central part of the body. Like tinea infections on the head, they commonly produce irregular ringlike lesions with a scaly surface, a raised border, and a center that clears as the lesions enlarge. Some itch, and some do not. Tinea corporis is usually due to *T. rubrum;* pityriasis versicolor is most often due to *Pityrosporum ovale,* a dimorphic fungus (one that can assume both mold and yeast forms), which is technically not a dermatophyte.

Ringworm is commonly spread from one infected person or animal to another and may also be transmitted to humans via animals. In the days before antifungal drugs, it was common to shave the scalp of a person with tinea capitis and apply antiseptic solutions. A number of topical antifungal drugs, such as the imidazoles, are now available and are so effective that shaving is no longer necessary. The imidazole family of compounds (ketoconazole, econazole, clotrimazole, and others) act by preventing the synthesis of a component of the cytoplasmic membrane, which causes the cells to rupture. Other topical preparations include halprogin (Halotex), ciclopirox (Loprox), naftifine (Naftin), and tolnaftate (Tinactin), some of which are available without prescription. Although these lotions and creams are quite effective in eradicating infection, they do not prevent recurrence. An alternative drug, griseofulvin (Fulvicin, Grifulvin, Grisactin), an oral medication that acts on the nucleus of the organism, is effective in prevention, but it must be taken for weeks to be incorporated into the cells of the skin. It thereby prevents growth of the fungus in new cells as old ones are shed. The imidazole ketoconazole (Nizoral) and the newer triazole drug, fluconazole (Diflucan), also come in oral form and can be used for widespread or severe dermatophyte infections.

Athlete's foot and "jock itch." Tinea pedis, commonly called athlete's foot, and tinea cruris (jock itch) are other common forms of dermatophyte infection. Both are frequently due to *T. rubrum* or *T. mentagrophytes.* These organisms are less likely to produce the ring-shaped lesions commonly seen in tinea capitis and tinea corporis. *T. rubrum* causes dry, scaly patches on the feet in a moccasin-like pattern of distribution. A common source of infection is locker-room floors— hence the condition's name. *T. mentagrophytes* is more likely to cause infections in the spaces between the toes and may cause vesicular (blisterlike) eruptions on the instep of the plantar surface (sole) of the foot. It may well penetrate the skin deeply enough to cause a serious secondary bacterial infection.

Although athlete's foot responds well to the newer topical or systemic antifungal agents, there is a strong

The youngsters in this 1951 photograph have tinea capitis, or ringworm infection of the scalp. In the days before the development of antifungal drugs, shaving the head and applying a topical antiseptic was the standard remedy. Outbreaks of ringworm were once fairly common in U.S. schoolchildren; those who were infected were allowed to return to the classroom if they kept their heads covered.

tendency for the infection to recur—particularly with repeated exposure. It is thus important to consider preventive measures. Thorough cleaning and drying of the feet is crucial. Avoiding contact with the floors of locker rooms and public showers by using bath clogs or shower sandals also helps. Footwear that prevents accumulation of moisture—*e.g.,* absorbent socks of cotton or other natural fibers—is also recommended, as is regular use of talcum powder or cornstarch to keep the spaces between the toes dry. A number of over-the-counter remedies—powders, creams, and sprays—are also available to treat tinea pedis infections. The active ingredients vary from undecylenic acid (Desenex) to tolnaftate and the imidazole miconazole (Micatin). Prescription medications are similar to those used for tinea corporis and consist largely of imidazoles. In situations where exposure cannot be entirely avoided, periodic application of these remedies may prevent infection. Tinea cruris can be treated with most of the same nonprescription preparations as tinea pedis, although the trade names of the products may vary. There are also prescription medications for both tinea pedis and tinea cruris that combine an imidazole with a steroid. In topical form these preparations speed clearing. Oral ketoconazole, miconazole, and griseofulvin are useful in treating widespread or particularly recalcitrant infections.

Jock itch usually starts in the folds between the scrotum and inner thighs, but it may extend to the perineal area, buttocks, and sometimes even the lower abdomen. Skin in the affected area appears red and scaly and often itches. The condition is more common in hot humid weather and is often associated with the use of athletic supporters, hence its name. Preventive measures include frequent bathing, careful drying of the groin area, avoidance of tight clothing that chafes or irritates the area, and use of either medicated or nonmedicated powders.

Seborrhea (dandruff). Seborrheic dermatitis, which has only recently been clearly attributed to the yeast-like organism *P. ovale,* is one of the most frequent infections of humans. It classically causes a hyperproliferative state of the skin (*i.e.,* abnormal increase in cell production) and most frequently affects the scalp. The typical manifestation is excessive scaling, flaking, and shedding of the skin. Although dandruff seldom presents more than a social embarrassment—white flakes that fall on the neck and shoulders of one's clothes—it can spread beyond the scalp to the face and even over the torso in persons who are immunosuppressed—particularly those with HIV infection. A variety of over-the-counter shampoos are available for treatment and prevention of ordinary dandruff. Those that contain selenium are particularly effective. Systemic antifungal drugs such as ketoconazole are sometimes used to control or treat the infection, especially if it is more widespread.

Infections of fingernails and toenails. Fungal infection of the nails (onychomycosis) is also commonly due to dermatophytes such as *T. rubrum* and *T. mentagrophytes,* which may burrow under the nail and cause it to become discolored or thickened. Because of the warm, moist environment provided by shoes and socks, the toenails are more commonly affected than the fingernails. Again, such infection is rarely serious and seldom causes more than a cosmetic

481

problem. Since the organism lives and reproduces beneath the nail, it cannot be reached with topical medication such as creams or ointments. Effective treatment usually requires an oral antifungal such as griseofulvin or ketoconazole, which may need to be taken for months to eradicate the infection. Unfortunately, these infections, too, often return after therapy. A fungal infection may also affect the tissue along the sides of the nail (paronychia). These infections are usually easier to treat than those under the nail because they can be more easily reached with topical medications. Gentle treatment of the cuticles and careful cutting to avoid ingrown nails are particularly helpful preventive measures.

Candidiasis

Candida organisms can be found almost anywhere in the environment but are most frequently found as a normal inhabitant of the skin, mouth, and intestinal tract of mammals. Of the 150 species recognized, only about 10 are associated with disease in humans. *C. albicans* is the most common of these. Serious or deep (invasive) disease due to candida was very rare prior to the advent of antibiotics in the 1940s. With antibiotics, however, it is possible to destroy most of the normal bacteria in the body—which also serve to keep fungal growth in check. As antibiotics have become more potent, the health problems associated with candida infection have mounted; today tissue infections due to candida may involve the brain, the heart, and the abdominal cavity. The increase in serious infections has also been promoted by the use of corticosteroid drugs, which enhance fungal growth, and by surgery, which breaks the protective barrier of the skin. The immune suppression that occurs in diabetes and AIDS seems particularly to increase the risk of candida infections. Candidiasis is now one of the most common hospital-acquired infections.

Thrush, the most common manifestation of candida, involves the mucous membranes of the mouth and throat. It appears as raised, white plaques on the gums, pharynx, and insides of the cheeks. Thrush is a very common "opportunistic" infection (*i.e.,* one that takes advantage of depressed immunity) in people with AIDS. It also frequently occurs in persons receiving antibacterial therapy. Vaginal yeast infections, characterized by a whitish curdlike discharge and itching, are common in women who take antibiotics for prolonged periods, because normal vaginal bacteria are destroyed by these drugs. Other candida infections of the skin such as diaper rash and intertrigo may occur when the environment is suitable—such as within damp skin folds or on skin covered by a warm, wet garment such as a diaper. Candidiasis may also affect the nails.

While skin infections with candida may clear up with careful cleaning and drying, the use of antifungal creams containing nystatin or an imidazole is sometimes necessary. Thrush and vaginal candidiasis often resolve once a course of antibacterial treatment has been completed. Otherwise, thrush should be treated with a course of nystatin in solution or with clotrimazole lozenges (Mycelex). Vaginal candidiasis can be treated topically with creams or suppositories containing nystatin, clotrimazole, or miconazole; the latter two became available in 1990 for use without prescription. For severe thrush or vaginitis, oral ketoconazole and fluconazole are also available.

Systemic candida infections, which occur in severely immunosuppressed individuals, are usually life-threatening. Candida has also been postulated to be responsible for a host of minor human ills from headaches to fatigue and joint pains. While some theories about so-called disseminated candidiasis have gained interest in the lay press, there is no scientific basis for them and no controlled study that demonstrates the value of special diets or nystatin, the remedies that are usually advocated.

Histoplasmosis

Histoplasma capsulatum is another dimorphic fungus, taking either mold or yeast form depending on the environment. In its native habitat, the soil, the mycelium (mold form) produces tiny spores that easily become airborne and can be inhaled into the lungs. Once they reach the small airways, the spores are recognized by the immune system as foreign and are engulfed by infection-fighting cells called macrophages. Unfortunately, after being taken into the macrophages, they multiply as the yeast form instead of being destroyed. With growth, they cause the macrophages to rupture, and they then spread to multiple sites throughout the body before an effective immune response can be mounted. They may also exist within the body in a living but dormant state for many years and may produce serious infection again years after the original exposure.

Histoplasma are found throughout the world, but the largest recognized endemic areas are along the Ohio and Mississippi river valleys, where as many as 80% of the population in some areas have evidence of prior infection. Outbreaks are often traced to areas where birds or bats roost. Their droppings cause the soil to become a particularly fertile medium for growth of the fungus.

The symptoms associated with inhaling the spores of histoplasma are usually no more than those of a cold or bout of flu—cough, chills, headache—and malaise that may occur a week or two after exposure. In most cases the infection is easily contained by the body, but in some people it can progress to a lung disease that appears similar to tuberculosis. In HIV-infected individuals the disease may disseminate rapidly throughout the body. Evidence of prior infection with histoplasmosis can be obtained by a test, the delayed hypersensitivity test, which involves injecting a small amount of killed yeast extract under the skin and waiting to see if the body reacts by producing a local inflammatory reaction (slight redness and swelling at the injection site) within the next two to three days. Blood testing for antibodies to the fungus may also be helpful in determining prior infection and may provide a clue as to whether the disease is active.

Amphotericin-B (Fungizone) is the usual treatment for histoplasmosis. Unfortunately, it is a relatively toxic drug and must be given intravenously. Some of the newer oral antifungal agents such as ketoconazole and fluconazole, however, may prove useful in treating or suppressing this disease.

Coccidioidomycosis (valley fever)

Coccidioides immitis is another fungus that commonly affects persons living in the United States. This organism is similar to histoplasma in that its natural habitat is the soil, where it grows in the mycelial phase, producing spores that are carried through the air. The spores may settle in other areas where the soil and environment are suitable for reproduction, or they may be inhaled. The semiarid climate of the Lower Sonoran Life Zone, which stretches across the southwestern United States from Texas through California, provides an ideal environment for its growth and spread.

Humans and a variety of domestic animals become infected through inhalation of spores. The most common initial symptoms are lower respiratory tract infection with cough, chest pain, malaise, and fever. The infection is usually self-limited, but a form of progressive disease may develop, in which masses of inflamed tissue (granulomas) form in the lungs and leave thin-walled cavities that can still be seen on X-rays for years. Treatment of coccidioides is with intravenous amphotericin B, although oral ketoconazole and fluconazole may also be effective.

In the San Joaquin Valley of California, coccidioides infections are commonly called valley fever. Skin and blood tests indicate that more than a million people in this area have been infected; there are more than 100,000 new cases each year. The number of infections is likely to increase with the rapid population growth in the southwestern states. As with histoplasmosis, there is no risk of transmission of coccidioides from one infected person to another. Coccidioides, however, does pose a real threat in the laboratory. If it is present on culture plates, it may grow rapidly; when the lids of the plates are opened for inspection, the spores may be inhaled by the unwary lab worker. Therefore, if coccidioides is suspected in a laboratory specimen that is being cultured, the culture plates should be sealed and sent to a lab that is specially prepared to prevent the airborne spread of the fungus.

Other deep-tissue infections

Other fungi can cause human disease, although they do so only infrequently. Aspergillus, a mold of worldwide distribution, is one such organism. It is associated with decaying vegetation and manure and stored grain, but it has been recovered from hospitals and even from operating rooms, particularly where there has been recent construction. It has been associated with hospital outbreaks, particularly in patients taking immunosuppressive drugs, and has recently been reported as a late complication of AIDS.

Sporothrix schenckii is a dimorphic fungus most often found in the soil or on living plants. It may cause disease in humans after inoculation via a puncture from a thorny plant—classically, a rose or sphagnum moss. Farm workers and horticulturists are at greatest risk of sporotrichosis. After being introduced beneath the skin, the organism produces a series of granulomas that extend up the lymphatic system of the involved extremity. The infection responds to amphotericin B, but it may also be treated with potassium iodide saturated solution and possibly some of the newer imidazole compounds as well.

A variety of other fungi may occasionally cause human disease—*Cryptococcus neoformans* (cryptococcosis), *Pseudallescheria boydii* (pseudallescheriasis), and *Paracoccidioides brasiliensis* (paracoccidiomycosis), just to name a few. These organisms seem content to live off the organic matter in the soil and do not take an invasive role unless the environment is disturbed (e.g., by construction projects) or they come into contact with people who are severely immunosuppressed. With advances in medicine that, on one hand, create new means of immunosuppression and, on the other, provide increasing ability to control bacterial and the usual fungal infections, the potential for human disease due to even more unusual opportunistic fungi will probably increase.

The best means of preventing fungal infections are eating a balanced diet and paying careful attention to any underlying medical condition—general principles of good health. In addition to avoiding exposure to known high-risk situations or geographic areas, one can best guard against fungal infections of the skin by frequent bathing to eliminate buildup of organic material such as dead skin and dirt. Keeping susceptible areas—such as skin folds and the spaces between the toes—clean and dry is also advisable.

Contributors to the World of Medicine

Gerard F. Anderson, Ph.D.
Health Care Financing
Director, Johns Hopkins Center for Hospital Finance and Management, Johns Hopkins University, Baltimore, Md.

Shmuel Banai, M.D.
Heart and Blood Vessels (coauthor)
Visiting Associate from Israel, Cardiology Branch, National Heart, Lung, and Blood Institute, National Institutes of Health, Bethesda, Md.

M. Flint Beal, M.D.
Neurology (coauthor)
Associate Professor of Neurology, Harvard Medical School; Associate in Neurology, Massachusetts General Hospital, Boston

Michael Bigby, M.D.
Skin and Hair Disorders (coauthor)
Assistant Professor of Dermatology, Harvard Medical School; Associate Dermatologist, Beth Israel Hospital, Boston

Patrick E. Brookhouser, M.D.
Hearing Disorders
Director, Boys Town National Research Hospital; Father Flanagan Professor and Chairman, Department of Otolaryngology and Human Communication, Creighton University School of Medicine, Omaha, Neb.

Edward P. Cohen, M.D.
Cancer
Professor, Department of Microbiology and Immunology, University of Illinois College of Medicine, Chicago

Elizabeth B. Connell, M.D.
Sexual and Reproductive Health
Professor, Department of Gynecology and Obstetrics, Emory University School of Medicine, Atlanta, Ga.

Karen J. Connell, M.S.
Special Report Arthritis: The Aerobics Advantage
President, Institute for Inquiry in Education, Inc.; Director, Education Component, Northwestern University Multipurpose Arthritis Center, Northwestern University Medical School, Chicago

Serge A. Coopman, M.D., M.Sc.
Skin and Hair Disorders (coauthor)
Clinical Fellow, Department of Dermatology, Harvard Medical School, Boston; Department of Dermatology, University of Louvain, Belgium

Harvey J. Dworken, M.D.
Gastrointestinal Disorders
Professor Emeritus, Case Western Reserve University School of Medicine; Attending Physician, University Hospitals, Cleveland, Ohio

Stephen E. Epstein, M.D.
Heart and Blood Vessels (coauthor)
Chief, Cardiology Branch, National Heart, Lung, and Blood Institute, National Institutes of Health, Bethesda, Md.

Donald P. Forster, M.B. B.S., M.Sc.
Special Report Examining Health in Eastern Europe
Senior Lecturer in Epidemiology, Division of Epidemiology and Public Health, The Medical School, University of Newcastle-upon-Tyne, England

Arthur L. Frank, M.D., Ph.D.
Occupational Health
Professor and Chairman, Department of Preventive Medicine and Environmental Health, University of Kentucky College of Medicine, Lexington

Jean A. Hamilton, M.D.
Special Report Medical Research: The Forgotten 51%
Associate Professor of Psychiatry, University of Texas Southwestern Medical School/Veterans Administration Medical Center; Adjunct Professor of Psychology, Southern Methodist University, Dallas

Bradley T. Hyman, M.D., Ph.D.
Neurology (coauthor)
Assistant Professor of Neurology, Harvard Medical School; Neurology Service, Massachusetts General Hospital, Boston

Sherry Jacobson
AIDS
Medical Correspondent, Gannett News Service, Arlington, Va.

Louis A. LaMarca, M.A.
Pharmaceuticals
Capitol Hill News Editor, *F-D-C Reports: "The Pink Sheet,"* and Senior Editor, *Weekly Pharmacy Reports: "The Green Sheet,"* F-D-C Reports, Inc., Chevy Chase, Md.

Morton Lippmann, Ph.D.
Environmental Health
Professor, Institute of Environmental Medicine, Anthony J. Lanza Research Laboratories, New York University Medical Center, Tuxedo, N.Y.

Wendy K. Mariner, J.D., LL.M., M.P.H.
Health Care Law
Associate Professor of Health Law, Boston University School of Medicine/School of Public Health

Andrea Marks, M.D.
Adolescent Medicine
Clinical Associate Professor of Pediatrics, Cornell University Medical College; Private Practice, Adolescent-Young Adult Medicine, New York City

Melvin H. Marx, M.A., Ph.D.
Psychology
Professor of Psychology, Florida Institute of Technology, Melbourne

Gail McBride, M.S.
Special Report Interventional Neuroradiology: Brave New Specialty
Free-Lance Medical Journalist, Chicago

W. Joseph McCune, M.D.
Systemic Lupus Erythematosus
Associate Professor of Medicine, University of Michigan Medical School, Ann Arbor

Charles-Gene McDaniel, M.S.J.
Special Report *The Serious Business of Child's Play*
Special Report *Joint Replacements: Great Strides*
Professor of Journalism, Roosevelt University, Chicago

Robert Keene McLellan, M.D., M.P.H.
Special Report *A Thoroughly Modern Malady*
Associate Medical Director, Center for Occupational Health, Exeter Hospital, Exeter, N.H.; Assistant Clinical Professor, Occupational Medicine Program, Yale University School of Medicine, New Haven, Conn.

Beverly Merz
Genetics
National Editor, Science and Technology, *American Medical News,* American Medical Association, Chicago

Diane H. Morris, Ph.D., R.D.
Diet and Nutrition (coauthor)
Assistant Professor, Department of Foods and Nutrition, College of Human Ecololgy, University of Manitoba, Winnipeg

Thomas H. Murray, Ph.D.
Death and Dying
Professor and Director, Center for Biomedical Ethics, Case Western Reserve University School of Medicine, Cleveland, Ohio

Eddie Joe Reddick, M.D.
Surgery
Director, Laparoscopic Laser Center, Baptist Hospital, Nashville, Tenn.

Robert Reinhold, M.S.
Special Report *Southern California Clears The Air*
Chief, Los Angeles Bureau, *New York Times*

Arnold D. Richards, M.D.
Special Report *Burgeoning and Beleaguered: Psychoanalysis in the '90s*
Assistant Professor of Psychiatry, New York University School of Medicine; Training and Supervisory Analyst, Psychoanalytic Institute, New York City

James M. Rippe, M.D.
Diet and Nutrition (coauthor)
Associate Professor of Medicine and Director, Exercise Physiology and Nutrition Laboratory, University of Massachusetts Medical School, Worcester

Clay B. Siegall, Ph.D.
Heart and Blood Vessels (coauthor)
Research Investigator, Bristol-Myers Squibb Pharmaceutical Research Institute, Wallingford, Conn.

Jack Thomas Stapleton, M.D.
Hepatitis
Associate Professor of Medicine, University of Iowa College of Medicine; Research Associate, Veterans Administration Medical Center, Iowa City

Peter E. Tanguay, M.D.
Special Report *The World Within: Understanding Autism*
Professor and Acting Director, Division of Child and Adolescent Psychiatry, University of California at Los Angeles

Rudolph E. Tanzi, Ph.D.
Neurology (coauthor)
Assistant in Genetics, Massachusetts General Hospital; Instructor in Neurology, Harvard Medical School, Boston

Carl E. Taylor, M.D., Dr.P.H.
Child Health
Professor Emeritus of International Health, Institute for International Programs, Johns Hopkins University School of Hygiene and Public Health, Baltimore, Md.; Senior Consultant, UNICEF

David E. Trentham, M.D.
Back Care
Chief, Division of Rheumatology, Beth Israel Hospital; Associate Professor of Medicine, Harvard Medical School, Boston

Kenneth E. Warner, Ph.D.
Smoking
Professor, School of Public Health, University of Michigan, Ann Arbor

Gertrude M. Webb, Ed.D.
Special Report *Collegiates Conquer Dyslexia*
Dean, Graduate School, and Director, Program for Advancement of Learning, Curry College, Milton, Mass.

Contributors to the Health Information Update

Stephen P. Bank, Ph.D.
The Only Child
Adjunct Associate Professor of Psychology, Wesleyan University; Private Practice, Family and Child Psychotherapy, Middletown, Conn.

Marshall H. Becker, Ph.D., M.P.H.
Following Your Doctor's Orders?
Professor and Associate Dean, University of Michigan School of Public Health, Ann Arbor

Manfred Blum, M.D.
Graves' Disease
Professor of Clinical Medicine and Radiology, New York University School of Medicine; Director, Nuclear Endocrine Laboratory, New York University Medical Center; Chief, Endocrine Clinic, Bellevue Hospital, New York City

Marc K. Effron, M.D.
Women and Coronary Disease
Cardiologist, Scripps Memorial Hospital; Clinical Instructor, University of California at San Diego School of Medicine, La Jolla

Don L. Goldenberg, M.D.
Aching All Over: The Fibromyalgia Syndrome
Chief of Rheumatology, Newton-Wellesley Hospital, Newton, Mass.; Professor of Medicine, Tufts University School of Medicine, Boston

Eric J. Hall, Sc.D.
X-Rays and the Pregnant Woman
Professor of Radiation Oncology and Radiology and Director, Center for Radiological Research, Columbia University College of Physicians and Surgeons, New York City

L. Anne Hirschel, D.D.S.
Wisdom Teeth
Free-Lance Medical Writer, Southfield, Mich.

Michael J. Koriwchak, M.D.
Lip Sores (coauthor)
Resident in Otolaryngology—Head and Neck Surgery, Vanderbilt University School of Medicine, Nashville, Tenn.

Elliot Lach, M.D.
Port-Wine Stains
Assistant Professor, Department of Surgery, Pediatrics, and Cell Biology, University of Massachusetts Medical School; Attending Plastic Surgeon, Division of Plastic Surgery, University of Massachusetts Medical Center, Worcester

Brendan A. Maher, Ph.D.
Hypochondria
Dean, Graduate School of Arts and Sciences, and Edward C. Henderson Professor of the Psychology of Personality, Harvard University, Cambridge, Mass.

Diane H. Morris, Ph.D., R.D.
"Where's the Beef?"
Assistant Professor, Department of Foods and Nutrition, College of Human Ecology, University of Manitoba, Winnipeg

Robert H. Ossoff, D.M.D., M.D.
Lip Sores (coauthor)
Guy M. Maness Professor and Chairman, Department of Otolaryngology, Vanderbilt University School of Medicine, Nashville, Tenn.

John Robinson
Flatfeet
Director of Research, Nike Sport Research Laboratory, Beaverton, Ore.

Alan D. Tice, M.D.
Fungal Diseases
Private Practice, Infectious Diseases; Clinical Assistant Professor, University of Washington, Tacoma

Myron Winick, M.D.
Food Cravings
President and Distinguished Professor of Pediatrics and Nutrition, University of Health Sciences/The Chicago Medical School, North Chicago, Ill.

Title cartoons by Skip Williamson

Index

This is a three-year cumulative index. Index entries to World of Medicine articles in this and previous editions of the *Medical and Health Annual* are set in boldface type; e.g., **AIDS.** Entries to other subjects are set in lightface type; e.g., aspirin. Additional information on any of these subjects is identified with a subheading and indented under the entry heading. The numbers following headings and subheadings indicate the year (boldface) of the edition and the page number (lightface) on which the information appears. The abbreviation *il.* indicates an illustration.

AIDS, *or* acquired immune deficiency syndrome **92**–245; **91**–241; **90**–253
　　blood-bank testing **90**–389
　　cesarean delivery **91**–358
　　diagnosis for women (special report) **92**–318
　　drug-testing regulations **92**–364; **91**–274
　　lymphoma **92**–263
air
　　disease transmission **92**–107
　　lead poisoning in children (special report) **91**–288

All entry headings are alphabetized word by word. Hyphenated words and words separated by dashes or slashes are treated as two words. When one word differs from another only by the presence of additional characters at the end, the shorter precedes the longer. In inverted names, the words following the comma are considered only after the preceding part of the name has been alphabetized. Examples:

　　　Lake
　　　Lake, Simon
　　　Lake Charles
　　　Lakeland

Names beginning with "Mc" and "Mac" are alphabetized as "Mac"; "St." is alphabetized as "Saint."

arthrodesis
 flatfeet **92**–468
artificial joint **92**–272; **90**–357
artificial light
 depression treatment **92**–93
artificial tear
 Sjögren's syndrome **91**–461
ARV: *see* human immunodeficiency virus
asbestos **90**–476
 drinking water contamination (special report) **91**–295
 removal **92**–290, *il.* 291
ascorbic acid: *see* vitamin C
Asendin: *see* amoxapine
Ashford, Bailey **90**–34
Asia **92**–21
Asian (racial group)
 melanin production **91**–431
Asian flu
 influenza pandemics **91**–418
Asian sudden death syndrome: *see* sudden unexplained death syndrome
asparaginase
 cancer chemotherapy **91**–93
aspartame
 gestational diabetes **91**–425
aspergillus
 fungal diseases **92**–483
aspiration, fine needle: *see* fine needle aspiration
aspirin, *or* acetylsalicylic acid
 drug abuse **90**–432
 heart attack treatment **91**–325; **90**–339
 heart disease and women **92**–426
 influenza and children **91**–421
aspirin-induced asthma **91**–254
ASPRS: *see* American Society of Plastic and Reconstructive Surgeons, Inc.
assassin bug **90**–125
assembly line
 meatpacking industry (special report) **90**–311
"Assisted Death" (report)
 right to die issue **92**–279
assisted suicide
 right-to-die issue **92**–276
Association of Official Analytical Chemists, *or* AOAC (U.S.)
 food-energy analysis **90**–451
Association of Pathology Chairmen (U.S.)
 autopsy rate **90**–392
Association of Pet Behavior Consultants (U.K.)
 behavioral consultants **91**–122
associative learning
 Aplysia **92**–129
Asthma, *or* reversible airway disease **91**–253; **90**–259
 camps for children with chronic diseases **91**–455
astronaut
 ocean survival **91**–157
AT-1 Computerized Ataxiameter
 balance disturbance treatment **91**–149
atenolol **91**–334
atherosclerosis
 coronary heart disease **92**–332; **91**–325; **90**–339
 exercise **90**–51, 361
 stress **92**–31
 women **92**–423
atherosclerotic plaque
 heart disease **92**–333
 laser use **91**–151
athlete **90**–407
 arches **92**–467
 ethics of erythropoietin use (special report) **91**–312
 life expectancy **92**–137
athlete's foot, *or* tinea pedis
 fungal diseases **92**–480
Ativan: *see* lorazepam
Atkinson, Robert
 "Today's Teenagers—Not So Mixed-Up After All" **90**–178
atmosphere
 greenhouse effect **90**–120
atom bomb
 radiation effects on fetus **92**–476
atom smasher: *see* cyclotron
atopic asthma **91**–253
atopic dermatitis, *or* atopic eczema
 skin and hair disorders **92**–385
atrial fibrillation
 nerve-cell death **92**–351
atrial natriuretic peptide, *or* auriculin, *or* atriopeptin
 hormone research **91**–50
atrioventricular node
 electrophysiological study **91**–326
attention deficit disorder, *or* attention deficit disorder with hyperactivity, *or* attention deficit hyperactivity: *see* hyperactivity
Atwater, Wilbur O. **90**–449
atypical mole: *see* dysplastic nevus
audit
 scientific fraud (special report) **90**–375

augmentation mammoplasty
 patient dissatisfaction (special report) **91**–403
aura
 migraine headaches **91**–320
auriculin: *see* atrial natriuretic peptide
Australia **90**–183, *il.*
autism
 description and treatment (special report) **92**–337
autoantibody
 Sjögren's syndrome **91**–462
autocrine activity
 hormones **91**–44
autogenic training
 stress therapy **92**–38
autoimmune disorder **90**–284
 Graves' disease **92**–453
 Sjögren's syndrome **91**–459
autologous bone marrow transplant
 insurance coverage **92**–310
autologous transfusion
 blood-bank storage **90**–389
automated portable test system
 chronobiology research (special report) **91**–397
automation **91**–275
AutoMicrobic System
 bacterial contamination detection **91**–150
automobile
 accidents and safety **91**–230; **90**–247
autopsy, *or* postmortem examination
 pathology and laboratory medicine **90**–386
average wholesale price
 prescription drug costs **91**–278
aversion
 food cravings **92**–447
aversive conditioning **90**–141
Avicenna **92**–12
AVM: *see* arteriovenous malformation
"Awakenings" (film)
 encephalitis lethargica **92**–202
Awards and Prizes 90–269
awareness
 anniversary reactions prevention (special report) **91**–350
"Awash in Hormones: The New Endocrinology" (Christy) **91**–41
Axid: *see* nizatidine
axillary lymph node
 breast cancer detection **91**–77
axon, *or* nerve fiber **90**–32
 mechanisms of memory *il.* **92**–129
Ayers examining table *il.* **90**–109
azathioprine
 systemic lupus erythematosus **92**–115
azidothymidine, *or* AZT: *see* zidovudine

b

B lymphocyte, *or* B cell, *or* bone-marrow-derived lymphocyte
 childhood cancer **91**–94
 systemic lupus erythematosus **92**–409
babbling
 infants (special report) **92**–300
baby-farming industry
 Hart's crusade **92**–192, *il.*
Back Care 92–257
backache **92**–257
 herniated disk **90**–427
bacteremia
 epidemiological investigations **92**–100
bacteria
 artificial-joint infection **90**–358
 ethics of genetics research (special report) **91**–309
 fungal diseases **92**–479
 gene transfer experiment **90**–332
 gum disease **90**–445
bacterial infection **91**–421
bacterial meningitis **90**–294
Bahnson, Henry T. **90**–37
Bailey, Pearl **92**–274
BAL, *or* British anti-lewisite, *or* dimercaprol
 lead poisoning treatment (special report) **91**–291
balance
 falls among the elderly **91**–237, *il.*
 medical uses of space technology **91**–149
balanced billing
 physician payment plan **92**–310
"Ballad of Reading Gaol, The" (Wilde)
 Wilde's prison experience **90**–197
balloon angioplasty: *see* percutaneous transluminal coronary angioplasty
balloon atrial septostomy **90**–470
balloon flotation catheter **90**–469
balloon valvuloplasty **90**–470
Baltimore, David
 Jackson Laboratory association (special report) **91**–313
 research-fraud controversy **92**–200, *il.*; **90**–373, *il.*

Bangladesh
 adolescent survey **90**–184
 flooding disasters **90**–291
 global-warming effect **90**–129
bangungut: *see* sudden unexplained death syndrome
Bankhead, Tallulah *il.* **90**–114
Banting, Frederick **91**–42, *il.*
Barnard, Christiaan N.
 heart transplantation (special report) **90**–342
"Barnets århundrade" (Key): *see* "Century of the Child, The"
Barr, Martin **92**–339
Barrett, D. S. **92**–184
basal-cell carcinoma *il.* **90**–130
 sunbathing risk **90**–440
basal ganglia
 obsessive compulsive disorder **90**–143
basal layer
 epidermis **91**–431
basal metabolic rate, *or* BMR
 middle-age spread **91**–471
baseball, Little League: *see* Little League baseball
Basedow's disease: *see* Graves' disease
basement membrane
 angiogenesis **90**–341
basophil **90**–262
Bateman, Roy, Jr. **90**–276
Baulieu, Etienne-Emile *il.* **91**–48
Bayes theorem
 medical decision aid use (special report) **91**–367
Bayview Research Campus (Baltimore, Md., U.S.)
 medical research **90**–42
Bazelon, David L. **90**–264
BCH 189
 AIDS treatment research **92**–250
Beard, George Miller **92**–353
Beaufort, Sir Francis **92**–48
Becker muscular dystrophy **92**–351
Bedlam, *or* Bethlehem Royal Hospital, *or* Hospital of St. Mary of Bethlehem (London, U.K.)
 eponyms **90**–116
bedsore: *see* pressure sore
beef **92**–417
Beef Trust
 meatpacking industry (special report) **90**–312
Beerbohm, Max *il.* **90**–197
behavior, human
 compulsions and obsessions **90**–136
behavior therapy, *or* behavior modification
 liquid very low-calorie diets **91**–353
 mental illness treatment **91**–339
 obsessive compulsive disorder **90**–141
 urinary incontinence treatment **91**–237
behavioral conditioning
 multiple chemical sensitivity **92**–356
behavioral consultant
 unusual therapies for pets **91**–122
behavioral genetics
 Jackson Laboratory research (special report) **91**–315
behavioral psychology **92**–377
Behçet's syndrome **90**–322
BEIR Committee: *see* Biological Effects of Ionizing Radiation Committee
Beirut (Leb.) *il.* **90**–88
Bell, Charles II. **90**–110
"Bell Ringers' Bruises and Broken Bones: Capers and Crises in Campanology" (paper)
 medical journals **92**–186
Belladenal, *or* Bellergal: *see* phenobarbital
belt, safety: *see* safety belt
Belzer, Folkert O. **91**–411
Benacerraf, Baruj **91**–316
Benson, Herbert **92**–32
benzene
 Perrier contamination (special report) **91**–294
benzodiazepine
 insomnia treatment **91**–391
 relaxation aid **92**–42
benztropine mesylate, *or* Cogentin (drug) **91**–235
Bergalis, Kimberly **92**–247, *il.*
Berkowitz, Deborah **90**–315
beryllium
 occupational hazard **90**–361
Best, Charles **91**–42, *il.*
Best Foods (Am. co.)
 food labeling **92**–285
beta blocker, *or* beta-adrenergic blocking agent
 athletes' use **90**–412
 drug-induced asthmas **91**–254
 treatment
  Graves' disease **92**–455
  heart disease and women **92**–426
  hypertension **91**–334
  migraine **91**–320
beta carotene
 tanning pill **90**–444

beta cell
 diabetes **90**–284
beta$_2$-adrenergic agonist
 asthma treatment **91**–257
Bethlehem Royal Hospital (London, U.K.): *see* Bedlam
Bettelheim, Bruno *il.* **90**–177
 "Letting Children Be Children . . . While They Can" **90**–166
Bevan, Aneurin **91**–69
Beyle, Marie-Henri: *see* Stendhal
Bible
 guinea worm disease **92**–10
bicycle: *see* cycling
bifocal lens
 contact lens innovation **90**–319
bikini condom **90**–273
bilateral pulmonary fibrosis
 lung transplant cause **91**–410
bile acid
 gallstones **92**–294; **90**–323
bile duct
 primary sclerosing cholangitis **90**–325
biliary atresia
 liver transplant cause **91**–408
bilirubin
 gestational diabetes **91**–424
 hepatitis **92**–342
Billings, John Shaw **90**–27, *il.* 26
binge eating
 bulimia nervosa **91**–281
biochemistry
 alcoholism **92**–161
 memory **92**–131
bioequivalence study
 generic drug testing **91**–279
bioethics: *see* Medical Ethics
biofeedback
 constipation treatment **90**–323
 incontinence treatment **91**–236
 stress therapy **92**–34, *il.*
biologic contaminant
 indoor pollution **90**–476
Biological Effects of Ionizing Radiation Committee, *or* BEIR Committee
 X rays during pregnancy **92**–475
biological response modifier
 metastatic tumors **90**–406
biological rhythm
 chronobiology (special report) **91**–394
 melatonin's role **91**–55
biological therapy
 cancer treatment **92**–262
biology
 depression basis **92**–85
 schizophrenia role **91**–340
biomedical patent **91**–248
"Biomedical Patents: Profits and Pitfalls" (Andrews) **91**–248
biophysical profile, *or* BPP
 pregnancy and older women **91**–480
biopsy
 cancer diagnosis **91**–101
  breast **91**–76
  cervix **91**–465
  prostate gland **91**–412
 heart-transplant recipient (special report) **90**–344
 Sjögren's syndrome **91**–461
biotechnology
 biomedical patents (special report) **91**–251
 FDA regulation **91**–276
 property rights of body parts **90**–208
biotinidase deficiency
 neonatal screening **90**–394
bipolar disorder **92**–79, *il.* 80
birth: *see* Obstetrics and Gynecology
birth center
 childbirth alternatives **91**–358, *il.* 359
Birth Control 90–270
 Eastern European policies (special report) **92**–372
 sexual and reproductive health **92**–383
birth control pill: *see* oral contraceptive
birth defect, *or* congenital disorder
 cardiac catheterization **90**–470
 gestational diabetes **91**–424
 heart murmurs **91**–450
 maternal drug use **90**–303
 nutrition during pregnancy **91**–447
 pregnancy and older women **91**–479
 retinoid use **90**–403
 sexual and reproductive health **92**–380
 syphilis **90**–356
birth weight
 cesarean delivery link **91**–356
 infant mortality role **91**–445
 pregnancy and older women **91**–480
 premature infants **90**–395
birthmark **92**–459
birthrate
 long-term care effects **91**–164
bisphosphonate, *or* diphosphonate
 osteoporosis **91**–364
bitter (taste)
 taste disorders **90**–461
Bittner, John **91**–316

tranquilizer
delusions treatment **91**–440
Stendhal syndrome treatment **91**–183
transcendental meditation, *or* TM **92**–36, *il.*
transcendentalism: *see* mysticism
transcortical motor aphasia
savant (special report) **92**–339
transcutaneous electrical nerve stimulator, *or* TENS
back pain therapy **92**–259, *il.*
interstitial cystitis treatment **91**–415
transforming growth factor α, *or* TGFα
coronary restenosis **92**–336
transforming growth factor beta, *or* TGF-β, *or* polyergin
angiogenesis research **90**–341
bone-remodeling role **91**–362
transfusion
Jehovah's Witnesses **92**–314
laboratory medicine **90**–389
sickle-cell disease treatment **91**–387
transgenic animal
development controversy **90**–413
Jackson Laboratory research (special report) **91**–317
transient global amnesia **92**–120
transmission electron microscopy, *or* TEM
asbestos measurement **92**–291
Transplantation 91–408
fetal brain tissue **91**–236; **90**–379
gene therapy **91**–306
hair **92**–389
heart and lung **91**–324; **90**–342
Jackson Laboratory research (special report) **91**–316
medical ethics **90**–366
pancreas **90**–287
scientific fraud (special report) **90**–371
see also specific organs by name
transportation
earthquake hazards (special report) **90**–298
Transportation, Department of, *or* DOT (U.S.)
passive restraint controversy **91**–230
transverse arch
foot structure **92**–464
trauma
fibromyalgia cause **92**–438
head injury **91**–322
memory loss **92**–120
trauma center **91**–399
travel
Stendhal syndrome **91**–176
treadmill **91**–381
stress testing *il.* **92**–319
"Treatments of Psychiatric Disorders" (American Psychiatric Assoc.)
mental health publications **91**–338
Treatwell (nutritional program) **92**–281
trench mouth: *see* acute necrotizing ulcerative gingivitis
tretinoin: *see* retinoic acid
Treves, Sir Frederick **91**–63
TRH: *see* thyrotropin-releasing hormone
trial of labor
obstetrics **91**–357
trichinosis
eosinophilia **90**–34
Trichophyton mentagrophytes
fungal diseases **92**–480
Trichophyton rubrum
fungal diseases **92**–480
Trichophyton tonsurans
fungal diseases **92**–480
trichotillomania **90**–145, *il.*
tricuspid valve
heart murmurs **91**–452
tricyclic antidepressant **92**–87
geriatric sweet tooth **92**–450
triflupromazine **91**–440
trigeminal neuralgia
headache **91**–323
trigger finger
meatpacking workers (special report) **90**–311
trihalomethane
safe drinking water (special report) **91**–293
trihexyphenidyl (drug) **91**–235
triiodothyronine, *or* T₃
Graves' disease **92**–453
trimethoprim-sulfamethoxazole
pneumocystis pneumonitis **91**–95
triplets **92**–56, *il.* 62
trisodium phosphate
lead exposure **90**–479
trisomy
pregnancy and older women **91**–480
trisomy 21: *see* Down syndrome
tropical oil **90**–10
tropical spastic paraparesis
HTLV-I infection **90**–357
Trotter, Wilfred **91**–66
Trypanosoma
global-warming effect **90**–125
trypanosomiasis, *or* sleeping sickness
global-warming effect **90**–125

tryptase
mast cells **90**–260
tryptophan
food cravings **92**–450, *il.*
Tsai, Fong **92**–288
tsetse fly
trypanosomiasis **90**–125
TSH: *see* thyrotropin
TSI: *see* thyroid-stimulating immunoglobin
TTS: *see* temporary threshold shift
tuberculosis, *or* TB
AIDS association **90**–354
body weight association **91**–351
refugees **91**–141
tuberosities, ischial: *see* ischial tuberosities
Tucker, Maurice a'Court **90**–199
Tufts University (Boston, Mass., U.S.)
body fat research **91**–473
Tufts University School of Veterinary Medicine (Medford, Mass., U.S.)
racehorse research **90**–414
tumor
angiogenesis research **90**–341
cancer **92**–261; **90**–273
breast **91**–76
childhood **91**–90
hot flashes **90**–457
interventional neuroradiology (special report) **92**–287
intracranial pressure **91**–322
molecular pathology **90**–387
see also types of tumors, *e.g.*, melanoma
tumor-infiltrating lymphocyte therapy, *or* TIL therapy
melanoma treatment **92**–262, 303; **90**–406
tumor necrosis factor, *or* TNF
cancer treatment **92**–262
tumor suppressor gene
cancer **92**–264
Turkey
adolescent survey **90**–186
Turnbull, Derek *il.* **92**–144
Turner, Reginald **90**–201, *il.* 205
Turner's syndrome
chromosomal abnormalities **91**–46
"Turning Kids On to Fitness" (Freedson, Rippe, and Ward) **90**–44
TV: *see* television
20th-century disease: *see* multiple chemical sensitivity
twins
alcoholism **92**–159
autism (special report) **92**–340
dyslexia (special report) **92**–325
multiple births **92**–62
see also identical twins
Twitchell, Ginger and David *il.* **92**–313
two-point shoulder belt **91**–232
TXG
medicine and space technology **91**–157
type I diabetes: *see* insulin-dependent diabetes mellitus
Type I Gaucher disease
drugs **92**–365
type II diabetes: *see* non-insulin-dependent diabetes mellitus
type V hybrid (flotation device)
cold-water immersion protection **91**–469
type A(H3N2)
influenza strains **91**–419

u

UCLA (U.S.): *see* California at Los Angeles, University of
Uffizi Gallery (museum, Florence, It.)
Stendhal syndrome **91**–180, *il.* 184
ulcer
acupuncture treatment **91**–110
laparoscopy **92**–408
ulcer, gastrointestinal: *see* peptic ulcer
ulcer, stomach: *see* gastric ulcer
ulcerative colitis
kidney stone causation **91**–430
ultrasonic humidifier
indoor air pollution **90**–476
ultrasonography
coronary artery disease **92**–333
fetal scanning *il.* **92**–66
gestational diabetes **91**–426
intravascular imaging *il.* **92**–333
medicine and space technology **91**–151
pregnancy and older women **91**–480
prenatal surgery potential **91**–401
prostate cancer detection **91**–412
ultraviolet A rays, *or* UVA rays
psoriasis treatment **90**–403
tanning risk **90**–441
ultraviolet B rays, *or* UVB rays
ozone depletion and health risks **90**–122, 441
psoriasis treatment **92**–386; **90**–403
ultraviolet radiation, *or* ultraviolet light, *or* UV radiation
eye damage **90**–319

medicine and space technology **91**–157
skin problems of blacks **91**–431
unconjugated estriol
prenatal screening **90**–330
"Understanding Compulsive Gambling" (Lesieur) **90**–135
UNDP: *see* United Nations Development Program
UNICEF: *see* United Nations Children's Fund
union, trade: *see* trade union
Union of Soviet Socialist Republics, *or* U.S.S.R.
abortions **91**–360
alcoholism **92**–166
aneurysm treatment (special report) **92**–287
cigarette smoking **92**–397
guinea worm disease **92**–18
United Kingdom, *or* Great Britain
abortion laws **91**–360
breast cancer studies **90**–271
death and dying **92**–279
insanity defense (special report) **90**–263
medical decision aids (special report) **91**–369
multiple births **92**–62
neural tube defects research **91**–372
Salmonella controversy **90**–17
United Kingdom Study of Triplets and Higher Order Births, *or* the National Study **92**–63, *il.* 70
United Nations
children's health *il.* **92**–268
refugee assistance **91**–126
United Nations Children's Fund, *or* UNICEF
child health **92**–267
guinea worm disease **92**–21
United Nations Development Program, *or* UNDP
guinea worm disease **92**–25
United Network for Organ Sharing, *or* UNOS (U.S.)
heart transplantation (special report) **90**–344
United States
accidents and safety **91**–230
adolescent survey **90**–186
AIDS occurrence **92**–246; **91**–241
alcohol consumption **92**–163; **90**–15
asthma **91**–253
child health **92**–271
cigarette consumption **90**–60
diabetes **90**–283
drug abuse **90**–301
health care costs **92**–307
hypertension research **91**–335
infectious diseases **90**–354
influenza vaccination **91**–422
insanity defense (special report) **90**–263
long-term care financing **91**–175
meat consumption **92**–418
medical aids (special report) **91**–369
medical education and practice **90**–25
nursing profession **90**–381
obesity **91**–353
physical fitness **91**–376; **90**–44
pregnancy and older women **91**–477
safe drinking water (special report) **91**–292
single-child family **92**–441
smoking **92**–395
steroid use **90**–407
United States National Senior Olympics **92**–144
University of . . . : *see under* substantive word, *e.g.*, Pittsburgh, University of
University of Wisconsin solution
organ preservation **91**–411
UNOS (U.S.): *see* United Network for Organ Sharing
"Unraveling DNA: Knotty Issues" (Murray) **91**–308
unresolved mourning
anniversary reactions (special report) **91**–347
unsaturated fat
meat consumption **92**–419
"Unscrupulous Researchers: Science's Bad Apples" (Rennie) **90**–371
Upjohn Co. (U.S.) **91**–276
upper-body fat: *see* abdominal fat
upper-body strength
children and fitness **90**–58
Uptown (cigarette)
advertising campaign **92**–399
Urban, Jerome **91**–82
urea **90**–340
urease **90**–325
urge incontinence **91**–236
uric acid
kidney stone role **91**–428
urinary bladder
interstitial cystitis diagnosis **91**–415
urinary incontinence
aging **91**–236
home health care **90**–349
medicine and space technology **91**–152

pressure sore risk **90**–455
prostate cancer surgery **91**–413
urine
kidney stones **91**–427
Urology 91–412
laparoscopy **92**–409
uroscopist
caricature **91**–29
ursodeoxycholic acid, *or* ursodiol, *or* Actigall
gastrointestinal treatments **90**–323
urticaria: *see* hives
U.S. Agency for International Development, *or* USAID
guinea worm disease **92**–23
U.S. Army
therapeutic drug use **92**–376
U.S. Coast Guard
cold-water immersion protection **91**–469
U.S. Court of Appeals for the Federal Circuit
biomedical patents (special report) **91**–248
U.S. National Center for Health Statistics
physical fitness survey **91**–376
U.S. Public Health Service
physical fitness objectives **91**–376
USAID: *see* U.S. Agency for International Development
USDA: *see* Agriculture, U.S. Department of
U.S.S.R.: *see* Union of Soviet Socialist Republics
Utah (state, U.S.)
epidemiological studies **91**–193
uterine cervix: *see* cervix
uteroplacental insufficiency
multiple births **92**–66
uterus
electromagnetic fields (special report) **91**–301
nutrition during pregnancy **91**–446
obesity's role **91**–351
utilization review
health care costs **92**–310
UV radiation: *see* ultraviolet radiation
UVA rays: *see* ultraviolet A rays
UVB rays: *see* ultraviolet B rays
uveitis, *or* intraocular inflammatory disease
treatments **90**–321

v

vaccination: *see* immunization
vaccine
FDA approvals **92**–368
infectious diseases
AIDS research **92**–246; **91**–244; **90**–256
hepatitis B virus **92**–345
measles **90**–396
pertussis **91**–374
vaccine-associated polio **91**–16
vaginal yeast infection **92**–482
valley fever: *see* coccidioidomycosis
valproate, *or* Depakene (drug)
children's treatment **91**–371
Valsalva maneuver **90**–110
Van Horn, Linda **90**–418
Vancouver Group: *see* International Committee of Medical Journal Editors
Vantage Excel cigarette **90**–73
varicella: *see* chickenpox
variocele
infertility role **91**–477
vascular malformation
birthmarks **92**–459
vasculitis
Sjögren's syndrome **91**–460
vasoactive intestinal polypeptide
asthma role **91**–256
vasoconstriction
hypertension role **91**–333
vasodilator
migraine treatment **91**–320
vasoocclusive crisis
sickle-cell disease **91**–385
vasopressin, *or* antidiuretic hormone, *or* ADH
cancer link **91**–53
VD: *see* sexually-transmitted disease
VDT: *see* video display terminal
veal **92**–417
vegetable **92**–282
vegetable oil **92**–285
vegetative state **90**–368
vein **90**–340
Velschius, G.H.
guinea worm disease **92**–13
venereal disease: *see* sexually-transmitted disease
venereologist **91**–65
venous leak
impotence diagnosis **91**–415
ventilation system
indoor air pollution **90**–476
ventilator
bronchopulmonary dysplasia **90**–394